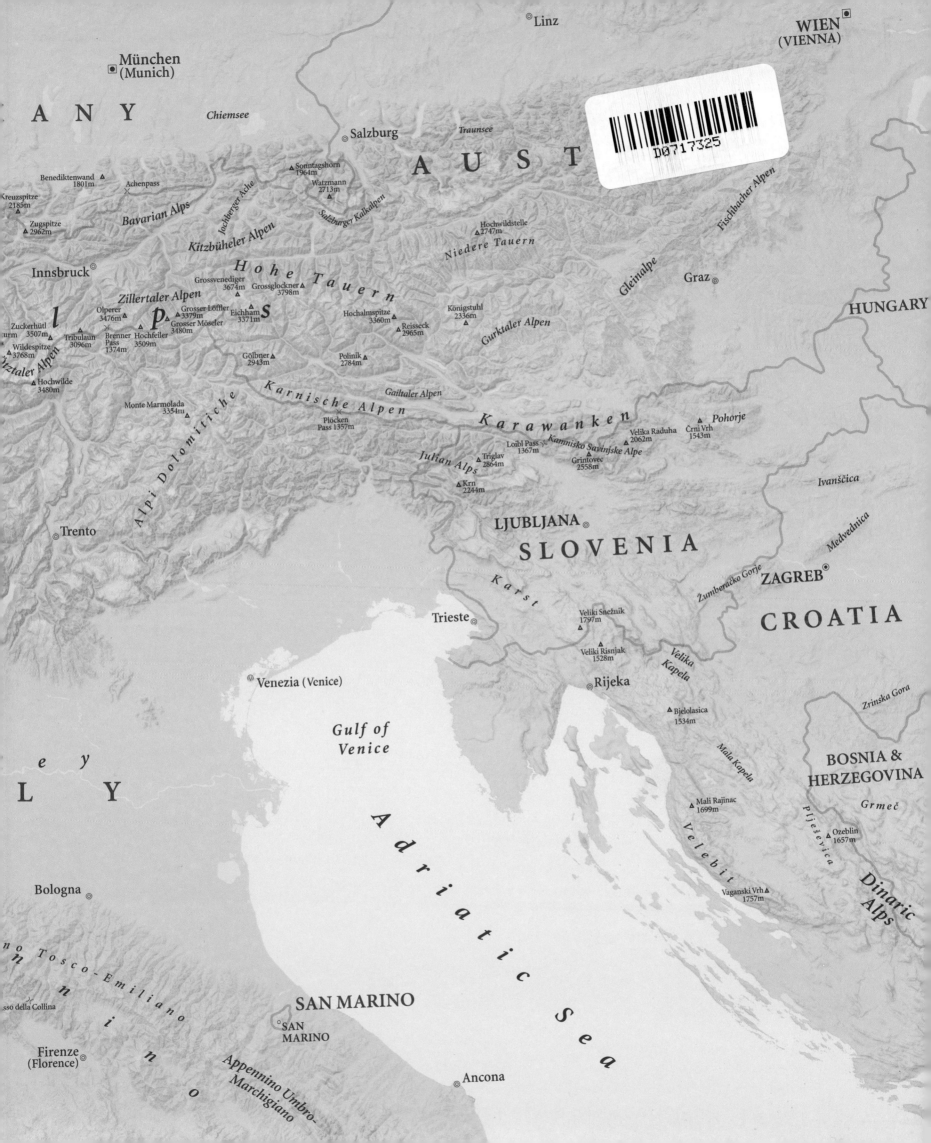

München
(Munich)

Linz

WIEN
(VIENNA)

Chiemsee

Salzburg

Traunsee

AUST

ANY

Benediktenwand △
1801m

Achenpass

Sonntagshorn
1964m

Watzmann
2713m

Bavarian Alps

Jochberger Ache

Salzburger Kalkalpen

Hochwildstelle △
2747m

Fischbacher Alpen

Kreuzspitze △
2185m

△ Zugspitze
2962m

Kitzbüheler Alpen

Niedere Tauern

Gleinalpe

Graz

HUNGARY

Innsbruck

Hohe   Tauern

Zillertaler Alpen

Grossvenediger
3674m

Grossglockner
3798m

Königstuhl
2336m

Zuckerhütl
3507m

Olperer
3476m

Grosser Löffler
3379m

Eichham
3371m

Hochalmspitze
3360m

Reisseck
2965m

Gurktaler Alpen

l   P   s

△ Wildespitze
3768m

Tribulaun
3096m

Brenner
Pass
1374m

Grosser Möseler
Hochfeiler
3509m   3480m

ztaler Alpen

Hochwilde △
3480m

Gölbner △
2943m

Polinik △
2784m

Karnische   Alpen

Gailtaler Alpen

K a r a w a n k e n

Velika Raduha
2062m

Črni Vrh
1543m

△ Pohorje

Monte Marmolada
3354m

Alpi Dolomitiche

Plöcken
Pass 1357m

Julian Alps

Triglav △
2864m

Loibl Pass
1367m

Kamnisko Savinjske Alpe

Grintovec
2558m

Ivanščica

Krn △
2244m

Medvednica

Trento

LJUBLJANA

SLOVENIA

Karst

Žumberačko Gorje

ZAGREB

CROATIA

Trieste

Veliki Snežnik △
1797m

Veliki Risnjak
1528m

*Velika
Kapela*

Zrinska Gora

e y

Venezia (Venice)

Rijeka

△ Bjelolasica
1534m

BOSNIA &
HERZEGOVINA

L Y

*Gulf of
Venice*

Mala Kapela

Grmeč

A
d
r
i
a
t
i
c

Mali Rajinac △
1699m

Plješevica

Ozeblin △
1657m

Velebit

Bologna

*Dinaric
Alps*

no *Tosco-Emiliano*

Vaganski Vrh △
1757m

sso della Collina

n   i   n   o

SAN MARINO

S e a

SAN
MARINO

Firenze
(Florence)

n   i   n   o

*Appennino Umbro-
Marchigiano*

Ancona

MOUNTAINEERS

THE ALPINE CLUB

MOUNTAINEERS

GREAT TALES OF BRAVERY AND CONQUEST

ROYAL GEOGRAPHICAL SOCIETY

LONDON, NEW YORK,
MUNICH, MELBOURNE, DELHI

Senior Editor Bob Bridle
Senior Art Editor Sharon Spencer
Jacket Designer Silke Spingies
Production Editor Tony Phipps
Production Controller Erika Pepe
Managing Editor Stephanie Farrow
Managing Art Editor Lee Griffiths

Produced for Dorling Kindersley by
TALL TREE LTD

Managing Editor David John
Senior Editor Rob Colson
Senior Designer Ben Ruocco
Editor Debra Wolter
Designers Peter Laws, Malcolm Parchment
Picture Researcher Louise Thomas

Written by Ed Douglas
Additional writing Richard Gilbert,
Philip Parker, Alasdair Macleod

Published by Dorling Kindersley Ltd in association
with the Royal Geographical Society (with IBG)
and The Alpine Club

First published in Great Britain in 2011
by Dorling Kindersley Limited
80 Strand, London WC2R 0RL

Penguin Group (UK)
2 4 6 8 10 9 7 5 3 1
001 – 179532 – Oct/2011

A CIP catalogue record for this book is
available from the British Library.

ISBN 978-1-4053-6559-8

Colour reproduction by
Media Development Printing Ltd, UK
Printed and bound by
Star Standard, Singapore

Discover more at
www.dk.com

CONTENTS

INTRODUCTION

Climbing mountains serves no obvious purpose. The risk of life and limb to summit a great peak is often for no better reason than "because it is there", as George Mallory famously put it. Yet in pursuit of such unformulated goals mountaineers have pushed themselves to the very limits of the physical – to achieve ever higher, more difficult, or simply more beautiful climbs. It is not surprising, therefore, that their exploits have captivated a wide audience.

For millennia the world's mountain ranges were largely devoid of people. Homes to gods and monsters, mountains were seen as dangerous, inhospitable, and mysterious, avoided by all but a few traders or religious sects in search of solitude. In Europe, popular fear of the mountains was beginning to change by the Renaissance, with climbers such as

Swiss naturalist Conrad Gesner defying local superstitions to ascend Mount Pilatus. The accounts of Gesner and others of their experiences, and of the delight they found in the mountains themselves, inspired others to follow their lead, and by the middle of the 19th century, alpinism was enjoying its "Golden Age". Gentlemen climbers, particularly from Britain, raced to claim the first ascents of the highest peaks in the Alps, and the modern sport of mountaineering was born. In the freedom of the mountains, women also began climbing, feeling less restricted by the constraints of society.

The sport's first disaster was not long in coming, as Edward Whymper's first ascent of the Matterhorn in 1865 turned to tragedy when four of his party died on the descent. Thus began a debate that continues today.

Do the risks justify the rewards? The following pages abound with accounts of climbers whose lives were cut short by the mountains, or who survived catastrophe through endurance, team-work, or sheer luck.

By the 20th century, attention had turned to the highest peaks in the world, the Great Ranges of Asia. Large expeditions laid siege to the "8,000ers" – the 14 highest mountains in the Himalaya and the Karakoram – and their conquest became a matter of national pride. By now, mountaineering was no longer the pastime of the upper classes. New generations of committed, skilful, and often professional climbers were emerging, and new equipment began revolutionizing the sport. And as technology was raising standards, attention turned more and more to the style of the climbs. Challenging routes, particularly up precipitous north faces, were actively sought out. Purists favoured fast, lightweight "alpine-style" ascents from which the climbers left the mountain just as they had found it. With almost every mountain of note climbed, the definition of "possible" still constantly needed redefining, no more so than when the legendary Reinhold Messner stunned the world in 1980 by climbing Everest solo and without bottled oxygen.

This book tells the story of mountaineering, from its first pioneers to the greats of today. While the reasons for climbing may be difficult to express, the images and stories gathered here leave little doubt as to the immense rewards mountaineering can offer. And as to the dangers, British alpinist Mick Fowler put it simply. "We enjoyed ourselves and lived to climb another day. These are important things."

THE EARLY MOUNTAINEERS

THE EARLY MOUNTAINEERS

3000BCE	300BCE	300CE	700CE

3000BCE
A Neolithic man, known to scientists as Ötzi, dies while crossing the Ötztal Alps. He was dressed for the mountains with a grass cloak and stuffed boots (see pp.16–19).

◀ **1450BCE**
Egyptian pharaoh Thutmose III leads his army in single file through the mountain pass of Aruna to surprise his enemies and crush their revolt at the Battle of Megiddo in Israel.

1200BCE
The **ancient Pueblo** people first emerge in southwestern regions of North America; they build communities around so-called Great Houses (see pp.32–33).

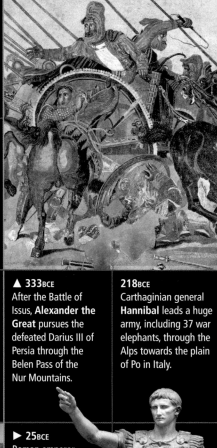

▲ **333BCE**
After the Battle of Issus, **Alexander the Great** pursues the defeated Darius III of Persia through the Belen Pass of the Nur Mountains.

218BCE
Carthaginian general **Hannibal** leads a huge army, including 37 war elephants, through the Alps towards the plain of Po in Italy.

▼ 399
Fa Xian the Monk sets off from China across the Karakoram Range to India in search of Buddhist holy texts to translate (see pp.24–25).

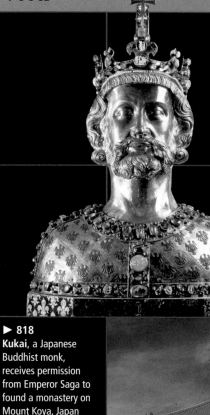

*c.***550**
St Catherine's Monastery is founded at the foot of Mount Sinai in Egypt, where Moses is believed to have received the ten commandments from God.

◀ **773**
Frankish king **Charlemagne** leads his army across the Alps to aid the papacy against invaders; in 778 he crosses the western Pyrenees to aid local Moorish rulers against the emir of Córdoba.

▶ **818**
Kukai, a Japanese Buddhist monk, receives permission from Emperor Saga to found a monastery on Mount Koya, Japan (see pp.28–29).

▶ **25BCE**
Roman emperor **Augustus** begins a series of campaigns to pacify the mountain tribes of Cisalpine Gaul, ending in 16BCE (see p.20).

629
Xuanzang, a Chinese Buddhist monk, sets off on an epic journey across the Hindu Kush, visiting the colossal statues of Bamiyan en route to India (see p.25).

▲ **430BCE**
Greek philosopher **Empedocles** is said, in some accounts, to have climbed Mount Etna in Sicily, and thrown himself into the fires in a bid to deify himself.

◀ **79CE**
Mount Vesuvius erupts, burying the Roman cities of Pompeii and Herculaneum in lava and ash.

632
The **First Potala palace** is built in Llasa, Tibet, rising 300m (1,000ft) above the valley floor.

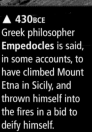

◀ **962**
St Bernard of Menthon founds a hospice at the highest point of an ancient Alpine pass that connects the Swiss canton of Valais with Aosta, Italy.

◀ PP 10–11 Carthaginian general Hannibal emerges from an Alpine pass at the head of his army and points the way to Italy.

Although people have always lived in the shadow of mountains, the difficulties of travelling at high altitude prevented their extensive early colonization. Mountains were only to be crossed at times of dire necessity. Cultures in Europe, Asia, and the Americas regarded high peaks with religious awe, as places where the gods (or God) dwelt and which needed to be approached with care. This same sense that they were special led eventually to the foundation of monasteries and the coming of pilgrims. Finally, as the hold of Christianity on Europe's intellectual life weakened during the 15th century, curiosity about mountains themselves, and a desire to travel in them and set down observations, came to replace the sense of horror and danger that had predominated in earlier writings.

1000CE

1500

▶ **c.1100**
Tibetan yogi **Milarepa** wins a legendary duel with a religious rival to reach the summit of Mount Kailash, ensuring the peak's holiness; it has never been climbed.

▶ **1532**
The invasion of the **Inca empire** by conquistador Francisco Pizarro sends Incas into hiding places in the mountain valleys of Vilcabamba (right) and Machu Picchu.

1188
Canterbury monk John de Bremble describes the suffering of pilgrims crossing the Alpine Mont Cenis Pass in winter, in which whole parties are buried in avalanches.

◀ **1255**
The Cathars, a persecuted gnostic Christian sect, are besieged in their final mountain stronghold of Quéribus, southeast France; many slip away to avoid massacre.

1544
Swiss writer **Johannes Stumpf** sets off on a journey through the Valais and begins the *Schwytzer Chronica*, a monumental work describing the topography of the Alps (see p.40).

1257
Mongols destroy the mountain **fortress** of **Alamut** in Persia, stronghold of the Assassins, a Muslim sect that posed a strong military threat to the Persian Sunni authorities.

▶ **1336**
Tuscan poet **Petrach** climbs Mont Ventoux in Provence, France, purely for poetic inspiration, possibly the first recorded climb for pleasure (see pp.36–37).

◀ **1551**
Josias Simmler, a Swiss theologian, writes *De Alpibus Commentarius*, the first work devoted solely to the Alps and advising the Alpine traveller (see pp.40–41).

1555
Swiss naturalist **Conrad Gesner** scales Mount Pilatus; in the preface to a work of 1541, he extols the joy of climbing mountains, not only for science, but for exercise (see pp.44–45).

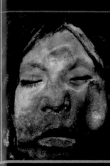

◀ **1450**
The Inca sacrifice child **"La Doncella"** on LLullaillaco in the Andes (see pp.74–75).

1492
Antoine de Ville is ordered by King Charles VIII of France to scale Mont Aiguille in Vercors, France, which he does using medieval siege equipment (see pp.38–39).

1572
Machu Picchu is abandoned by the **Inca** and remains a ruin known only to local mountain people until its scientific discovery in 1911.

1646
English horticulturalist **John Evelyn** describes his misadventures crossing the Simplon Pass in the Italian Alps after spending four years in Italy (see pp.46–47).

CLIMBING FOR SURVIVAL

Historically, mountains have often been seen as dangerous places, notorious for bandits and evil spirits. Yet humans have been thriving at altitude for millennia, solving the same problems of survival that tax modern climbers – and reaping the rewards.

MOUNTAIN STRONGHOLD
The fortress of Khertvisi was first built in the 2nd century BCE to protect the tribes in the mountainous region of southern Georgia. The current walls date back to 1354.

You don't have to be a mountaineer to know that the weather is worse in the mountains. For a start, it's colder – for every 300m (1,000ft) you ascend, the temperature drops by roughly 1°C (2°F). It's windier too, as air currents are intercepted by the huge bulk a mountain presents. When air hits a mountain it has nowhere to go but up, so the higher you climb, the stronger the wind. As air rises, it also cools, resulting in precipitation, falling as rain or snow.

HEIGHT GAINS

Extreme weather makes mountains harder places to survive. In the era before down insulation and rainproof jackets, why did anyone bother climbing them? However, mountains offer distinct advantages for those who are prepared to endure their hardships or innovate solutions to the challenges they present. Even today, mountain communities hunt and take advantage of high pastures to fatten livestock for winter.

Dairy products such as cheese are a regular staple of mountain communities. Early Alpine climbers describe tucking into a fondue with their guides at their bivouac the night before a big climb. The Swiss climber Erhard

PREHISTORIC PROTECTION
More than 5,000 years ago, the cultures of the Copper Age were equipped for mountain places. This is a replica of a woollen cap worn by Ötzi the Iceman.

Loretan (see pp.334–35) became one of the world's best high-altitude climbers on a diet of cheese.

Pastoralism in the mountains often requires mobility. Tenzing Norgay (see pp.266–67), one of the first two men to climb Everest, was probably born in a tent next to his parents' grazing yaks far from their home village of Moyey, Tibet. Yak-hair tents are cleverly constructed – they are loosely woven to let the smoke from a yak-dung fire escape, but oily enough to stop rain coming in.

Mountains are often good places to find resources that are prized and in short supply in the lowlands. The lapis lazuli used to make the death mask of King Tutankhamun, for example, came from the mines of Badakshan in modern Afghanistan, thousands of miles from Egypt.

AVOIDING PERSECUTION

Mountains are also places of refuge used by displaced peoples trying to make a new start. Several ethnic groups in Nepal, such as the Sherpas (see pp.262–63) who live near Everest, and the Khas people of Nepal's western middle hills, who retreated in the face of Mughal invaders in the 15th century, were migrants from elsewhere.

Security, both spiritual and political, is a common theme in mountain

> Although mountains are often perceived as places of danger and suspicion, not fit for habitation, humans have frequently adapted to living and travelling at altitude – for material benefit, security, or out of sheer geographical necessity.

ranges around the world. Tibetan Buddhism has a tradition of *beyul* – valleys hidden in the mountains that offer sanctuary for spiritual practice in times of crisis. Imam Shamil, the "Lion of Islam", kept the might of the Russian empire at bay from his stronghold in the Caucasus Mountains in the 19th century. The Tellem people, who inhabited the Bandigara escarpment in modern Mali until the 14th century, lived on cliff faces, as did the ancient Pueblo people in North America (see pp.32–33).

ADAPTING TO HARDSHIP

Lessons learned from Ötzi, the 5,000-year-old corpse preserved in the snows of the Ötztal Alps in Austria (see pp.16–19), show that we have an ancient relationship with high mountains. The earliest pioneers endured the same problems that climbers face today, although the latter are protected by the latest technology. Moving across snow without suffering frostbite or slipping, insulating against the cold, navigating complex terrain – mountaineers both ancient and modern have faced the same challenges. Mountain travellers in Ötzi's day lacked modern textiles to protect themselves, but their ingenuity was staggering. Modern polar adventurers such as Fridtjof Nansen used the same kind of grass to insulate their boots. Ötzi also carried a basket on his back with a strap over his head in a fashion commonly used in the

DRESSED TO LIVE
A Tibetan boy from Xining in China wears a traditional *chuba*, a sheepskin coat with long sleeves that is often worn off the right arm for freedom of movement and heat regulation.

YAK ESSENTIALS
The staple of high-altitude travel in the Himalaya, yaks are used by Tibetan nomads for everything from transport and food to clothing, fuel, and shelter.

SETTING THE SCENE

- The long human story of living and travelling in the high mountains is intimately bound up with the **ability to understand and adapt to an extreme environment**: harsher winters, stronger winds, and often higher precipitation.

- Mountain regions offer **opportunities to prosper** for those proficient in survival – from pasturage and hunting to mining minerals and precious stones. Humans **evolve to compensate for reduced air density** on the high Tibetan plateau and in the Andes.

- Mountains are nature's political boundaries, **offering refuge to displaced peoples** that are easily defended. They are also bound up with our **spiritual understanding** of the world, offering sanctuary to those wishing to practise religious freedom.

- The discovery of Ötzi the Iceman in 1991 near the Tisenjoch in the Ötztal Alps **radically expands our understanding of prehistoric mountain travel**. Just as polar travellers such as Fridtjof Nansen drew on millennia of experience from the Inuit in Greenland, so **early mountaineers benefited from local experience and technology**.

Himalaya today. Nansen learned how to kayak from Inuit he met at Godthaab after crossing Greenland in 1888, using a technology that is at least 4,000 years old. Many of the technologies mountaineers use – such as ropes, crampons, skis, and axes – also have their roots in antiquity.

The physiological problems associated with high altitude have been known for centuries, even if the medical reasons for them were little understood. In the Andes, chewing coca leaves or drinking *mate de coca* – a coca herbal tea – is commonly practised to alleviate the symptoms of ascending to a higher altitude. In some parts of the world, mountain people have lived so long at altitude that their bodies have evolved to cope. Tibetans have specific genetic adaptations to deal with the reduced oxygen of high altitude, particularly when it comes to the physiological problems of childbirth in low-oxygen environments.

HIDDEN INCA TRAILS
The Inca ruins of Winaywayna, high above the Urubamba Gorge at 2,700m (8,860ft), lie close to the Inca trackway that leads to Machu Picchu. These "roads" reached to 5,000m (16,400ft).

WE THOUGHT IT WAS A MOUNTAIN CLIMBER OR A SKIER WHO'D HAD AN ACCIDENT PERHAPS 10 YEARS PREVIOUSLY

HELMUT SIMON AFTER FINDING 5,000-YEAR-OLD ÖTZI

ÖTZI THE ICEMAN

THE WORLD'S FIRST KNOWN ALPINIST

SOUTHERN EUROPE

C.3000BCE

THE DISCOVERY IN 1991 of a 5,000-year-old corpse buried in the ice of an Alpine pass between Austria and Italy provided the very earliest evidence of man's penetration into mountain regions. It also revolutionized our understanding of Neolithic life in Europe. The corpse – soon dubbed "Ötzi the Iceman" after the Ötztal area of the Alps where it was found – had been incredibly well preserved by the ice in which it had lain and soon became an archaeological sensation. The reasons for Ötzi's Alpine journey are unclear, but he can be regarded as the first known mountaineer.

On 19 September 1991, two German hikers, Erika and Helmut Simon, who had just climbed the 3,516-m (11,535-ft) Fineilspitze on the Italian–Austrian border, were on their way down along the Tisenjoch Pass to the nearby Similaun mountain refuge when they veered slightly from the main path. They came across a low wall of rock that formed an enclosure around a long gully. Protruding from the ice that filled the gully was what appeared to be a pile of rubbish.

Looking closer, though, they were horrified to see a human head and torso emerging from a layer of ice, which the unusually warm summer had partially melted. Rushing back to the refuge, the Simons reported their find to the guardian. Nothing at this stage indicated that the body in the ice was anything other than the remains of one of the hikers who from time to time go missing in the mountains.

The iceman's body was found at a height of 3,210m (10,530ft) at the edge of the Niederjochferner Glacier, which had retreated in the 70 years since the border between Italy and Austria had been demarcated at the end of World War I. The change in the topography led to some initial uncertainty over which side of the border the body had been found. Initially, however, the Austrians took the lead and, on 20 September, a government mountain rescue helicopter flew in to assess it. Already the corpse had emerged a further 10cm (4in) from the ice, but even with the aid of a pneumatic chisel the rescue team could not dislodge it. They departed, taking with them an axe blade that they'd found on a nearby ledge, which they would look at to determine whether the corpse was that of a hiker who had perished in recent times or of a more ancient mountaineer.

A UNIQUE FIND

The following day, the Italian mountaineer Reinhold Messner (see pp.308–11) and his companion Hans Kammerlander, who happened to be in the area, reached the scene, and discovered further artefacts, including a container made of birch bark, a shoe, and a bow. On 23 September, a second government rescue team finally broke the body loose from the ice and sent it, with various parts of its clothing and other artefacts, in a hearse to Innsbruck in Austria for a regular autopsy.

Messner had thought the body might be several hundred years old, but it was only when archaeologist Konrad Spindler looked at the body the day after the

(see pp.308–11)

MURDER IN THE MOUNTAINS
Archaeologists have used forensic methods to piece together the story of Ötzi's death in the Ötztal Alps (pictured). The evidence reveals that his last days were exhausting and violent. He travelled from sub-alpine regions to the valley floors and then up again to the Tisenjoch, where he died from his injuries.

COPPER-BLADED STATUS SYMBOL
In Ötzi's time, axes were symbols of rank, prompting some historians to speculate that he might have been a tribal leader. He may have used his axe to cut ice.

FROZEN IN TIME
Ötzi's body is seen here shortly after it was discovered. It had been buried by snow, then by ice, which prevented its decomposition. Even the body's eyeballs were intact.

autopsy that the stunning truth became apparent: the corpse was 5,000 years old. It was the most complete body ever found from that era and it still had its clothes and tools, the everyday possessions of a Neolithic man.

SECRETS OF THE ICEMAN

A proper archaeological examination of the site in early October yielded further artefacts, including the remains of a grass cloak that the iceman had worn as an overgarment. By now, responsibility for Ötzi had been transferred to the Italian authorities' base in Bolzano, as a

detailed survey of the area revealed that his body had lain just inside the Italian border. A further investigation of the site the following July uncovered even more of the iceman's possessions, together with small pieces of muscle and hair, and even one of his fingernails.

By this time, medical examination had begun to reveal the first real information about the iceman, although it was more about his physical condition than who he was and how he had come to die on an isolated Alpine pass.

Apart from the damage to his left hip caused by the initial attempt to move him, Ötzi was almost intact. After he died, he had been covered with a layer of snow, which was permeable to the air. This allowed a slow process of freeze-drying to take place, leaving his body flexible and able to be moved without falling apart, even after 5,000 years. He was an adult male, about 1.59m (5ft 2in) tall,

weighed about 50kg (110lbs) and, although all of it had come away from his head, had dark brown or black hair and probably wore a beard. His teeth were free from decay, although worn down by eating grain that contained small particles of stone from the grinding process. He also had a completely healed break on his ribs on the left-hand side, and an unhealed break on the right, which may have happened shortly before his death.

The raw data from the corpse, and its incredible age, were surprising enough, but it was the detailed examination of the artefacts found with it, and the even more detailed analysis of the body that, over the next decade, brought something of Ötzi's story to life.

DRESSED FOR HIGH ALTITUDE

Whoever Ötzi was, his clothing showed that he had not gone into the mountains completely unprepared. Most previously discovered Neolithic clothing – which actually amounted to very small fragments – had been woven, but the iceman's garments were mainly made of leather or fur – far more appropriate for the freezing conditions high up in the Alps.

He wore a cap of bear fur, held on by two leather straps, an upper garment made of long rectangular strips of goatskin sewn together,

RECOVERY FROM THE ICE
Using ski poles and ice axes, the team freed Ötzi from the glacier after four days. No archaeologists were present, so the process was recorded on film.

which reached to his knees, and goatskin leggings. Underneath, he sported a leather loincloth and on top of his other clothes he wore a cloak of twined grass that may have provided protection from wind and rain, as well as doubling up as a rudimentary ground sheet or blanket when he slept.

Ötzi had climbed with a full set of weapons. His axe, its copper head indicating that he lived in an age when knowledge of metalworking was already spreading across Europe, was the first fully preserved prehistoric axe ever found complete with its haft.

He also carried a flint dagger with a triangular blade, together with a retoucheur, a specialist implement for intricate finishing work on flint tools. The remains of a net that could be used to catch rabbits showed that he had gone prepared for hunting. But there were also signs that he'd left home in a hurry. His bow, fashioned from a 1.8-m (6-ft) length of yew, was unfinished, an indication, perhaps, that he had been forced to craft it himself while on the move. In the quiver there were just two finished flint-tipped arrows and a dozen unsmoothed and untipped shafts.

NATIVE OF THE ALPS

On his final journey, Ötzi carried a type of backpack or pannier made of larch and hazel, two birch bark containers, one of which was used for carrying embers to help keep him warm and some fragments of birch fungus, which may have been for tinder.

There were also some objects whose purpose is less clear, including a small tassel and a pair of ibex horns. His last meal, determined from the contents of his stomach, had been a stew of meat and vegetables mixed with einkorn – an early type of wheat. From all this, it seems that Ötzi was probably not unfamiliar with the mountains, and a later

analysis of hornbeam pollen found on his body showed that he had stopped to drink water at Katherinaberg, a 12-hour journey south from where he died.

Whether this was his home village at the time is not known. Analysis of the isotopes in his teeth determined that as a child he had lived in the upper Eisack or lower Pusack valleys in Italy's Bolzano province.

A VIOLENT END

Initially, scientists thought that Ötzi died around September. The way in which his possessions were arrayed – the axe placed on one ledge and the quiver on another – indicated his death had been an accident. It was speculated that he had been in the mountains either through choice, as a trader or shepherd, or because he had been forced to flee his home, and, having found shelter in the gully, had died of hypothermia.

The time of year of Ötzi's demise was then revised because of the presence of the hornbeam pollen, which showed he had in fact died in late spring or early summer, but at a time when there might still have been snow along his route.

Then, in 2001, the previous speculation about the manner of his death was dramatically overturned by new X-ray findings. These showed a flint arrowhead embedded in his left shoulder. It had penetrated to just above his lung, severing a major blood vessel, which would have caused massive bleeding and probably death within a few minutes.

Scientists also found abrasions to his hands consistent with a hand-to-hand struggle and a major trauma to the back of his skull, caused by a violent blow or a fall. From this wealth of new information, it has been possible to determine that the iceman did not die through

a fall that killed him outright or one that rendered him unable to get off the mountain – as has happened to so many of the mountaineers who followed him. It is clear that he was murdered. He may have been fleeing his home, possibly pursued by violent intruders, taking refuge in a landscape that, while forbidding in itself, was not – as his equipment indicates – totally alien to him. Whether he had come this way before is impossible to determine, but it was men, and not the mountains, who killed him.

THE ICEMAN LIVES AGAIN
This naturalistic reconstruction of Ötzi, complete with matted hair, weather-beaten face, a hardy, sinewy build and animal-skin garments, was completed by two Dutch forensic artists in 2011.

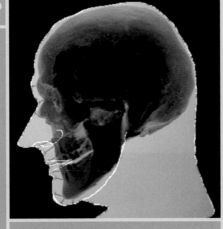

PRESERVING ÖTZI

Today, Ötzi's mummified body, and the artefacts found with it, are preserved in the South Tyrol Museum of Archaeology in Bolzano in Italy, where they are the subject of ongoing research. The mummy is stored in a sophisticated refrigeration chamber, which is kept at a constant temperature of -6°C (21°F) and with a relative humidity of 98 per cent, artificially recreating the conditions of the glacier ice in which it was found. Visitors to the museum can look at the mummy through a small viewing window. Recently, to mark the 20-year anniversary of Ötzi's discovery, experts in reconstructive interpretation produced a new model of the ice man based on CAT scans, 3D images of his skull, infrared and tomographic images, and other evidence. The amazingly life-like result, unveiled in 2011, reveals a man who looks much older than 45 – the age scientists believe Ötzi was when he died.

A PROJECTED SHAPE FOR ÖTZI'S FACE IS SUPERIMPOSED OVER THE IMAGE OF HIS SKULL

HANNIBAL

GENERAL WHO LED AN ARMY THROUGH THE ALPS

CARTHAGE   248–183BCE

HANNIBAL BARCA CAME FROM A powerful family in the North African city of Carthage, and rose to become the Carthaginian leader in the Second Punic War against Rome (218–202BCE). Late in the war's first year he led a huge army (including elephants) through the Alps, the earliest crossing by a large military force. It was a daring move that surprised the Romans, who then suffered a series of defeats at Hannibal's hands. Although Hannibal finally lost the war, his march remains one of the most famous feats of Alpine endurance.

ROME IN THE ALPS

After its defeat of Hannibal, Rome gradually conquered the Gaulish lands south of the Alps, but it was only a series of campaigns under Augustus from 25–16BCE that brought a Roman presence into the mountains themselves. The defeat of the tribes was commemorated by a great "trophy" (a three-story tower) some 50m (160ft) high at La Turbie. The Romans did not build roads into the mountains, but generally stuck to previously known passes.

LA TURBIE, THE TROPHY OF AUGUSTUS, ADORNS THE FOOTHILLS OF THE ALPES MARITÍMES, NEAR MONACO

That the Romans were not prepared for the direction of Hannibal's attack was not surprising. Romans and Greeks alike had tended to ignore the mountains, seeing them as *inacessi* (inaccessible), *gelidae et nubiferae* (icy and cloudy), or downright *inhospitales* (inhospitable). Reflections on mountain scenery played little part in Roman poetry, and later on, Julius Caesar, when crossing the Alps to Gaul in the 50s BCE, is said to have composed two books on analogy rather than on anything inspired by the mountains. Similarly, there are almost no accounts of mountain climbs for scientific or pleasurable

WAR ELEPHANTS
Hannibal was not the first to use war elephants. Alexander the Great, depicted here on an Egyptian coin, adopted them into his army after seeing them in action at the battle of Gaugamela (331BCE).

pursuits. For the purposes of trade, too, sea routes were preferred rather than land for their speed in transporting cargoes, and mountains were to be avoided at all costs. A land route existed from about 300bce that skirted the southern Alps to bring goods into Italy from Massilia (Marseille) but at the time of Hannibal a century later, the Alpine routes were thoroughly unfamiliar both to Romans and Carthaginians.

A BOLD STRIKE

Hannibal, who had been a child during the First Punic War (264–241BCE), was determined to avoid the mistakes that led to Carthage's defeat in that conflict. He decided on a bold move – rather than trying to defeat Rome at sea, or invading through Sicily and southern Italy as his predecessors had done, he would strike north from Spain, cut across southern Gaul (France) and approach Rome from the north.

So, once war had broken out with the Romans early in 218BCE, Hannibal assembled a huge army at Cartagena in southern Spain. The army consisted of 90,000 infantry, 12,000 cavalry, and a force of African war elephants, and climbing July pushed north across the River Ebro in Spain towards the Pyrenees. The one major

A LIFE'S WORK

- Is the son of Hamilcar Barca, the **leading Carthaginian general** in the First Punic War

- Succeeds his brother-in-law Hasdrubal as **Carthaginian commander** in Spain in 221BCE

- **After taking his army across the Alps**, inflicts the **worst series of defeats** the Romans have ever suffered, at Trebia (218BCE), Trasimene (217BCE), and Cannae (216BCE)

- Fails to move against Rome itself and becomes **bogged down in attritional warfare**

- **Returns home after 15 years**, but after Carthage's defeat in 202BCE, is exiled by the Romans in 195BCE, and commits suicide in 183BCE

flaw in Hannibal's strategy was its requirement for the crossing of the Alps by a large military formation, without any reliable allies among the mountain tribes and late in the year, when the weather would be unpredictable. However, the far less daunting prospect of traversing the Pyrenees had led to 3,000 men mutinying and, once Hannibal had dispensed with units he thought unreliable, his army was reduced to a much more manageable 50,000 infantry, 9,000 cavalry, and 37 elephants.

THE TROUBLES START

The Carthaginians crossed southern Gaul largely unmolested. Only after he crossed the Rhône near Fourques and marched 140km (85 miles) along the river to the foothills of the Alps did Hannibal's troubles begin. The Allobroges, a Gaulish tribe, harried the Carthaginians incessantly from strongpoints along the heights of the river valley, inflicting heavy losses. Already, at the end of the first day of what would turn out to be a 15-day crossing, Hannibal found himself in serious difficulty. He only broke through when his scouts revealed that the Gauls abandoned their mountain-top positions at night and he sent elite units of his

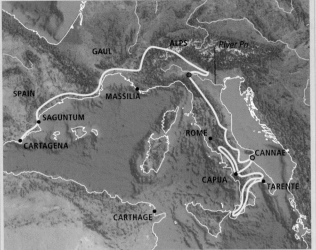

ACROSS EUROPE

SECOND PUNIC WAR 218–202BCE

— **Hannibal's route**
Starting from Spain, Hannibal passes through Gaul and over the Alps to attack Rome from the north.

⊙ **21 December 218BCE –**
Battle of the Trebia
Hannibal wins first battle of the war.

⊙ **2 August 216BCE –**
Battle of Cannae
Hannibal inflicts a heavy defeat on the Romans; despite this victory, he is eventually driven from Italy.

army to occupy them under cover of darkness, forcing the Allobroges to retire. After Hannibal captured a nearby town, whose existence was testament to the surprisingly populous nature of the Alpine valleys, his way was largely unopposed through the Bassin de Gap. On the seventh day, after a difficult crossing of the flooded River Durance, the local tribesmen came into the Carthaginian camp with symbols of friendship – olive branches and wreaths –

giving Hannibal hostages and offering their services as guides. Although suspicious, the Carthaginians accepted the Gauls' offer, but the next day a trap was sprung. When the army had entered a narrow gorge, probably at the valley of Queyras, Gaulish warriors stationed on the cliffs above sent rocks tumbling down, smashing anything in their path. Fortunately, Hannibal had placed most of his heavy infantry in the rear as a precaution and they escaped largely unscathed.

On the ninth day, the army reached the high pass through the Alps. Centuries of scrutiny by scholars of Livy and Polybius, the main historical sources for the campaign, have not identified this with any certainty, but a very likely candidate is at the Col de la Traversette. Having rested two days, Hannibal forced his tired army to press on. The way was narrow, and alarmingly steep, much of it covered by light snowfalls on top of a frozen icy layer that caused footsoldiers to slip to their deaths and in which the hooves of the pack animals became stuck fast. At one point the Carthaginians had to use fire, vinegar, and crowbars to crack open a huge rock that barred the path. The death toll was high and Hannibal tried to raise morale by taking some of his troops to the top of a peak from which the plain of the Po, their distant objective in Italy, could be seen.

Hannibal finally reached that plain on the 15th day. Only 20,000 infantry and 6,000 cavalry had survived the march but, amazingly, all 37 elephants made it. Of the graves and bones of the more than 30,000 who perished nothing has ever been found. Their memorial is the series of victories Hannibal won against Rome, and the epic tale of the Alpine crossing itself.

OUT OF THEIR ENVIRONMENT
The turrets mounted on the elephants as depicted here are probably fanciful. The animals themselves were of the African forest elephant species, now extinct.

WHAT MOUNTAINS MEAN

MOUNTAINS ARE NOT JUST PHYSICAL ENTITIES – THEY HAVE REPRESENTED A WIDE SPECTRUM OF IDEAS, NEEDS, AND FEARS FOR VARIOUS PEOPLES AT DIFFERENT TIMES IN HISTORY. IN SEVERAL CULTURES, THEY WERE REGARDED WITH AWE AS THE PLACES WHERE THE GODS RESIDED.

OL DOINYO LENGAI
The "Mountain of God" is an active volcano in Tanzania, Africa. It is sacred to the Maasai tribe who, when suffering sickness or loss of livestock, climb it to pray and make a sacrifice.

In India, the ancient works of Hindu mythology called the Puranas feature a passage that extols the appeal of the Himalaya: "In the space of a hundred ages of the gods, I could not describe to you the glories of Himachal … As the dew is dried up by the morning sun, so are the sins of mankind by the sight of Himachal."

North of the Himalaya, in Tibet, ancient cultures worshipped the mountains as manifestations of warrior gods. According to Tibetans, their first ruler was a god who descended from the sky on a magic rope of light, landing on Yarlha Sampo, a sacred peak in the Yarlung Valley. When Guru Rinpoche brought Buddhism to Tibet in the 8th century, he "subjugated" these gods, making them protectors of sacred landscapes.

The idea of mountains as refuges is very strong in Hinduism and Buddhism, too. In the ancient Indian epic *Mahabharata*, Prince Arjuna treks to the Himalaya to seek Lord Shiva's help.

When he comes to leave, he says, "Mountain thou art always the refuge of the good, who practice the law of righteousness, the hermits of holy deeds, who seek out the road to heaven."

When Muslims arrived in South Asia in the 12th century, the Himalaya became a refuge in another way, as Hindus fled to the remote valleys. The Kalash in Chitral, northern Pakistan, are a surviving remnant of the peoples who lived in the Hindu Kush in antiquity.

GODS' HOMES

The ancient Greek gods, whose home was Mount Olympus, were vengeful and capricious, but Olympus itself seems originally to have been a myth, an idealized mountain that only later came to be associated with a specific peak – the snowcapped 2,917-m (9,570-ft) mountain that straddles the border between Thessaly in Greece and Macedonia.

Mountains feature strongly in other ancient European cultures too, often as places where demons or evil spirits resided – a belief that grew more prevalent after the arrival of Christianity, when the more positive aspects of older, pagan attitudes towards nature became proscribed.

In Scandinavia, mountains were the homes of trolls, who would lure people to their high-altitude lairs. The Swedish word *bergtagning*, or "taking to the mountains", is meant to suggest abduction, even possession, by spirits. In northern Germany, which shares many cultural links with Scandinavia, the Harz mountains have a long association with witches, who were said to meet on the

DEVILS TOWER
This peculiar flat-topped rock formation in Wyoming, US, is possibly an ancient volcanic neck and rises 386m (1,267ft) above its base. Sacred to American Indian Plains tribes since Neolithic times, it was known to them as Grizzly Bear Lodge. Ceremonies are held at its foot in June each year.

SACRED SHIVLING
The name of this twin-summited peak in India's Garhwal Himalaya literally means "the phallus of Shiva", a reflection of its status as a sacred symbol of the Hindu god Shiva.

BROCKEN SPECTRE
In the 19th century, travellers in the Harz mountains, Germany, saw what they thought was a haloed spirit beckoning them. They named it Brocken after the highest summit.

SETTING THE SCENE

- The **largest features** in natural landscapes, with their own, often dramatic weather systems, **mountains evoke feelings of dread and awe** for much of human history. For early cultures, their floods, avalanches and rockfall, complex geography, and high winds make them the obvious **location for deities**.

- As well as being seen as the physical embodiment of capricious gods, mountains also offer a **glimpse of the sacred**. As the American scholar and mountaineer Edwin Bernbaum put it, "Floating above the clouds, materializing out of the mist, mountains appear to belong to a **world utterly different** from the one we know, inspiring in us the experience of the sacred as the wholly other."

- **Those who dare**, and have the ingenuity to protect themselves from the exigencies of high-altitude travel, exploit mountains for **security, hunting, and trade.**

Brocken, the range's highest summit, to hold revels with their demons, as witnessed in the legend of Faust in which the eponymous hero joins the devil on top of the peak. The Brocken is mist shrouded and cloud-wrapped for about 300 days in the year, a factor that has given rise to its many legends.

> Not until the 18th century were mountains viewed with anything like scientific objectivity. For the first four millennia of recorded history, they were shrouded in superstition and myth, and feared as places of danger and evil.

GHOSTLY APPARITIONS

The mountain also gave its name to the Brocken Spectre, an optical illusion created when low sun shines behind someone looking down into fog from a ridge or mountain top. The atmospheric conditions throw the person's shadow forward, creating a seemingly huge, ghostly figure, the head of which is often surrounded by halos of coloured light – caused by light diffraction – known as a "glory". In German culture, these phenomena were considered sinister. In China, however, Buddhist monks on Mount Emei in Sichuan saw them as positive, the halo being a sign of holiness.

In the Alps, Celtic tribes held sway before the arrival of the Romans. According to the Roman historian Livy they worshipped a sky god, whom the Romans called Poeninus, from *pen*, the Celtic word for summit. A temple to Poeninus has been excavated on the Great St Bernard Pass in Switzerland. The Romans themselves had little appreciation for the Alps, viewing them as hateful and largely ignoring them. But they grasped their political relevance, especially after the invasion by the Carthaginian general Hannibal (see pp.20–21).

The Celtic gods in France and Switzerland were eradicated with the arrival of Christianity, but their association with mountains endured longer in Britain, where pagan attitudes to nature were co-opted to spread the faith.

In Ireland, the tradition of mountain pilgrimages is similar to the Tibetan people's reverence for the landscape and their custom of walking in the hills.

HEAD OF THE SUMMIT
In Greek mythology, the 12 Olympians – the foremost deities of the Greek pantheon, including king of the gods, Zeus (left) – were believed to reside on the summit of Mount Olympus.

FA XIAN THE MONK

BUDDHIST MONK WHO CROSSED THE GREAT RANGES

CHINA
C.350–C.422CE

ALTHOUGH BUDDHISM REACHED CHINA in the 3rd century BCE, it only really established a firm foothold there in the 2nd century CE. The lack of adequate translations of Buddhist scriptures then began to pose a serious hindrance for Chinese converts. A monk, Fa Xian, sought to solve this problem by travelling to India, the homeland of the Buddha, in 399CE. His hazardous journey took him through Central Asia and across the vastnesses of the Hindu Kush, the Karakoram, and the Himalaya before he returned 15 years later bearing a treasure trove of the sacred Buddhist texts.

THE BUDDHA ON THE MOUNTAIN
A Chinese silk banner shows the Buddha preaching on Vulture Peak, a mountain sacred to Buddhism in India. Fa Xian climbed it, and found the cavern where the Buddha had meditated.

High mountains play an important role in Buddhist cosmology. The mythical Sumeru is conceived of as a central world-mountain that soars to a vast height and descends deep into the oceans. For Buddhists, the impossible ascent up such a fabulous peak, or the arduous scaling of real mountains, can be compared symbolically to the ascent of the soul to higher grades of being as it nears the perfect spiritual state of nirvana.

Various real mountains were singled out by early Buddhists as especially sacred and became the objects of pilgrimage. In Japan, the holiest mountain was Mount Fuji; in Tibet, it was Mount Kailas, known as the "Mountain of Precious Snow". In China, four mountains were especially revered by Buddhists – Wutai Shan (Shanxi province), Emei Shan (Sichuan), Jiuhua Shan (Anhui), and Putuo Shan (Zhejiang). Over the centuries, clusters of temples sprang up on these holy peaks through the centuries to service the throngs of pilgrims who flocked to them.

Yet China's great distance from the original founts of Buddhism in northern India meant that no amount of sacred sites could make up for the lack of original scriptures available to early Chinese devotees. Fa Xian, who had been placed in a monastery at the age of three, felt this need especially profoundly. In order to obtain texts to translate into Chinese, he resolved to travel to India himself in order to collect them. At the end of the 4th century, such a journey was far from easy. China itself, under the disabled Eastern Jin emperor Andi (382–419), was weak and prone to revolts, and its control over the critical Central Asian routes that might facilitate travel to India was tenuous.

FAR FRONTIERS OF THE EMPIRE
It took Fa Xian and his companions more than a year to reach Dunhuang on the edge of the Gobi Desert, the furthermost effective reach of Jin power. Instead of heading westwards into unfriendly territory, the monastic caravan struck south, straight through the desert. As Fa Xian later recorded in his *Record of Buddhist Kingdoms*, the desert was a place of evil spirits and hot winds, either of which could cause a man to perish. As for finding a trail, "No guidance is to be obtained, save from the rotting bones of dead men, which point the way."

After 17 days' travel, the monks were released from the perils of the Gobi, and reached the Buddhist kingdoms on the edge of the great

A BUDDHIST MARVEL IN THE HINDU KUSH
As he travelled along the Silk Road, Fa Xian came to Bamiyan (in present-day Afghanistan), where two giant statues of the Buddha had been carved into a cliff. This photograph was taken before 2001, when the statues were destroyed by the Taliban.

A LIFE'S WORK

- **Dedicated to a Buddhist monastery** at the age of three, he decides at the age of ten to continue a monastic life

- Following ordination, and a period of study, he **embarks on a 15-year odyssey** across the top of Central Asia, and through India, Sri Lanka, and Java **in search of Buddhist teachings** not then available in China

- The journey takes him across China's **Kunlun, and Tian Shan** ranges, then over the **Pamirs and Karakoram** of Central Asia

- During the return voyage, his ship is caught in a severe storm and the passengers are ordered to throw their belongings overboard; he **holds on to the precious Buddhist texts** that he has so painstakingly collected

- Writes an **extensive account of his travels**, but only *Record of Buddhist Kingdoms* survives

OF THOSE WHO ENCOUNTER THESE DANGERS, NOT ONE IN TEN THOUSAND ESCAPES "

FA XIAN'S *RECORD OF BUDDHIST KINGDOMS,* ON CROSSING THE PAMIR MOUNTAINS

mountain chains of the Himalaya and Hindu Kush. Travelling through the lands of the Tartars and Kashmir, Fa Xian's group found Buddhist monasteries wherever they went, and in Kashgar joined in an assembly of monks over which the king of the region was presiding.

HIGH-MOUNTAIN CROSSING

Yet Fa Xian's true objective lay over the Great Ranges and the monastic party had to cross them in order to reach the plain of the River Ganges and the Buddhist centres that held the original scriptures they so ardently sought. First they crossed the Bolor-Tagh range in the eastern Pamirs of Central Asia. As Fa Xian discovered, "on these mountains there is snow in winter and summer alike," although his assertion that there were also venomous dragons which, if provoked, would spit out poisonous winds, rain, snow, and even stones was a fanciful description of the all-too-real dangers inherent in such a crossing.

The monks had a brief respite at a monastery but then they had to take to the mountain path again, travelling for 15 days over a vertiginous section where the mountainside seemed like a stone wall 3,000m (8,800ft) high: "on nearing the edge, the eye becomes confused … the foot finds no resting place". Previous travellers had carved 700 steps in the sheer rock and placed ladders and rickety rope suspension bridges across which the monks made careful progress.

Finally entering northwestern India, Fa Xian was free of the mountains, and proceeded to spend a number of years enthusiastically visiting the most important seat of Buddhist learning and seeking out the scriptures for whose collection he had risked so much.

Perhaps deterred from retracing his steps by the rigours of his overland journey, Fa Xian chose to return to China by sea, although the long, storm-tossed voyage turned out to be almost as perilous. He arrived back in 414,

XUANZANG

CHINA   C.602–C.664

In 629, the Buddhist monk Xuanzang set out for India without imperial permission, and a warrant was issued for his arrest.

Like Fa Xian before him, Xuanzang was seeking new Buddhist texts – he was determined to reconcile what he thought were puzzling discrepancies in those that had made it into China. He travelled via Turfan in China's northwest, where the local ruler, dazzled by his intellect, tried to detain him. But the monk escaped, and struck out again across the harsh terrain of the Taklamakan Desert. He then travelled through Tashkent, Samarkand, and Bactria in Central Asia before crossing the high peaks of the Hindu Kush, where he braved deep snow drifts. Finally reaching India in 633, he remained there for 12 years before returning with a rich hoard of Buddhist texts.

15 years after setting out, and retired to a monastery, where he spent the rest of his life translating the scriptures for whose sake he had become the first Chinese Buddhist to traverse the symbolic and real barrier of the mountains.

MOUNTAIN PORTRAIT

KILIMANJARO

RISING UP FROM THE PLAINS OF NORTHERN TANZANIA to more than 3 miles (5km) in height, Kilimanjaro is the highest mountain in Africa, and is often described as the largest freestanding peak in the world. In fact, this vast, lozenge-shaped massif was formed by three separate volcanoes. Its very existence arises from its proximity to the Rift Valley, where *Homo sapiens* first evolved, making our relationship with Kilimanjaro among the oldest with any mountain.

Nobody knows for sure where the name "Kilimanjaro" came from, but it may mean "the little hill of the Njaro people". According to the German explorer Johannes Rebmann, who became the first European to see the peak in 1848, the Chagga people who lived in the area described the two obvious summit masses, Kibo and Kimawenzi – now abbreviated to Mawenzi – but had no word for the whole massif.

What is certain is that Kilimanjaro is sacred to the people who live near it, and that in Western culture, thanks in part to the work of Ernest Hemingway, the

mountain is the apotheosis of an African adventure. Early explorers did not believe that a mountain so close to the equator could have ice on it; they wondered if the white on its summit was silver.

Climate scientists predict that what ice there is will be gone by 2050, and the routes described here will be steep slopes of rubble. There are six trekking routes to the summit, renamed Uhuru Peak on Tanzania's independence, on Kibo, but for mountaineers, the most dramatic routes are on the hanging glacier of the Southwest Flank, created by an ancient landslip.

IN PROFILE

Name: Kilimanjaro. During German colonial rule, the summit was named Kaiser Wilhelm Spitze; on independence from Britain, it was renamed Uhuru Peak.

Location: Tanzania

Height: 5,895m (19,341ft)

Prominence: 5,100m (16,732ft)

Notable features: Kilimanjaro is an inactive stratovolcano with five stratified ecological zones at progressively higher altitudes: the lower slopes, montane forest, heath and moorland, alpine desert, and the summit zone.

First recorded ascent: Ludwig Purtscheller, Hans Meyer, 1889

First ascent of Mawenzi: Edward Oehler, Fritz Klute, 1912

First female ascent: Sheila MacDonald, 1927

Fastest ascent: 8hr 27min round trip to and from Mweka Gate, by local guide and ultrarunner Simon Mtuy in 2004.

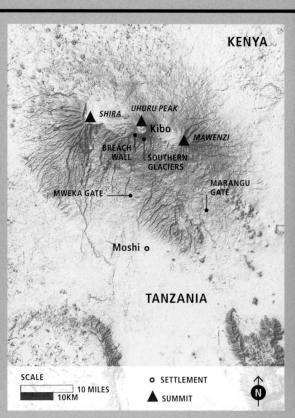

KENYA

SHIRA · UHURU PEAK · Kibo · MAWENZI
BREACH WALL · SOUTHERN GLACIERS
MWEKA GATE · MARANGU GATE

Moshi

TANZANIA

SCALE
10 MILES
10KM

○ SETTLEMENT
▲ SUMMIT

N

CLIMBING ROUTES

❷

Kilimanjaro's disappearing ice is not just a modern phenomenon – climbers have long been aware of how fickle climbing conditions can be on the south side of Kibo, which holds the mountain's glaciers. The most difficult routes are on the Breach Wall. Apart from the Messner route featured here, notable climbs were made by John Temple and Tony Charlton in 1974, and by Temple and Dave Cheesemond in 1975.

BREACH WALL
— WESTERN BREACH
(E Oehler, F Klute, 1912) Also known as the Arrow Glacier Route, climbs rocks to the right of the Little Breach Glacier. Although little more than easy scrambling, it is not suitable for trekkers.

❶ **The Breach Wall** is a massive rock face emerging from Kibo's southwestern rim. Kilimanjaro's hardest climbs are focused here.

BREACH WALL DIRECT
(R Messner, K Renzler, 1978) A serious route that requires moisture from the Diamond Glacier to form an 80-m (260-ft) icicle linking the Baletto and Diamond glaciers. Prone to rockfall.

❷ **Glaciers have been formed** on Kilimanjaro's northwestern flank too, such as the Penck, and these have been climbed. But they are retreating even more quickly than on the southern side.

SOUTHERN GLACIERS
— HEIM GLACIER
(A Nelson, H J Cooke, D N Goodall, 1957) This classic climb takes a gully to the right of the Window Buttress that separates the Breach Wall from the Heim Glacier.

KERSTEN GLACIER ORIGINAL
(W Welsch, L Herncarek, 1962) Takes the left side of the glacier with few technical difficulties.

KERSTEN GLACIER DIRECT
(I Allan, W O'Connor, J Cleare, 1975) This difficult direct line straight up from the lowest ice climbs a vertical icicle and several serac bands.

— DECKEN GLACIER ORIGINAL
(E Eisenmann, T Schnackig, 1938) This easier route is getting harder as the glacier melts and steeper icefalls form. Up to 65-degree ice.

❸ **The Mweka trekking route** ascends to the southeast flank of Kibo from the Barafu Hut 3km (2 miles) east of the Decken Glacier.

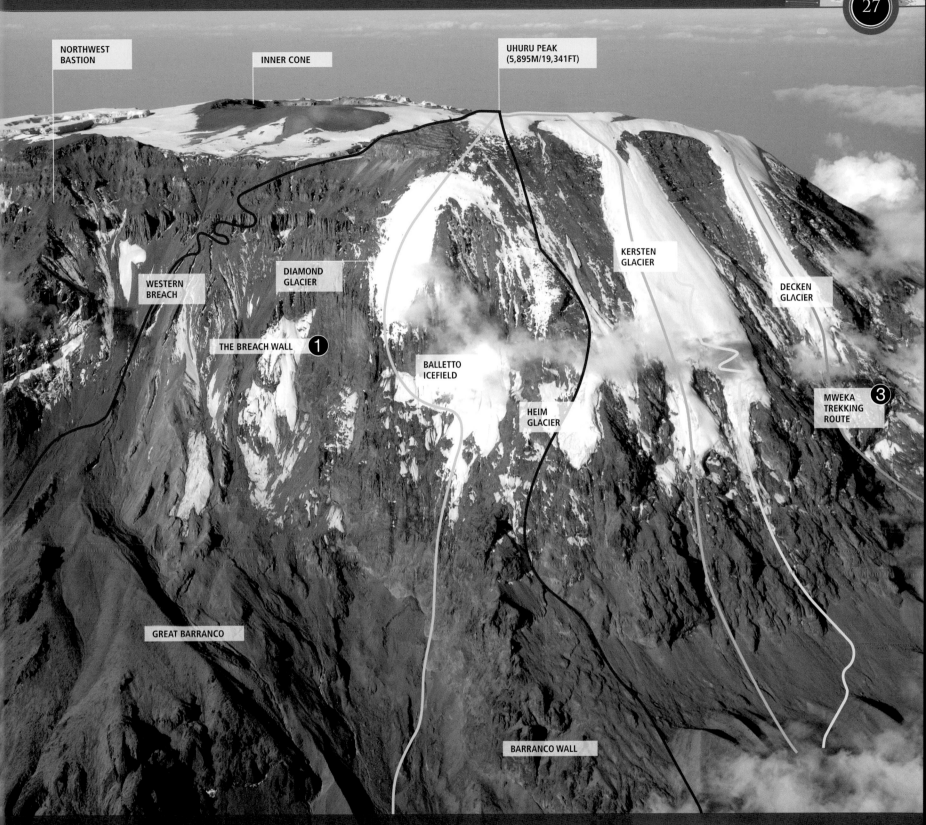

NORTHWEST
BASTION

INNER CONE

UHURU PEAK
(5,895M/19,341FT)

WESTERN
BREACH

DIAMOND
GLACIER

KERSTEN
GLACIER

DECKEN
GLACIER

THE BREACH WALL ❶

BALLETTO
ICEFIELD

MWEKA
TREKKING
ROUTE ❸

HEIM
GLACIER

GREAT BARRANCO

BARRANCO WALL

MOUNTAIN FEATURES

Ⓐ **Lying just three degrees** south of the equator, Kilimanjaro looms above the clouds that cover the surrounding savannah of Tanzania.

Ⓑ **Climbers camp** near an ice wall in Kibo's outer crater. The most recent volcanic activity was 200 years ago.

Ⓒ **Porters carry** trekkers' equipment and supplies. Working conditions vary widely between different agencies. There are three large hut complexes on the trekking routes

Ⓐ

Ⓑ

Ⓒ

KUKAI

BUDDHIST FOUNDER OF A MOUNTAIN MONASTERY

JAPAN   774–835

THE BUDDHIST MONK Kukai, also known as Kobo Daishi, founded the school of Esoteric Buddhism known as Shingon, which would become hugely influential in Japan. His search for a location for the new sect's headquarters led him to found a monastery on a forested plain on the slopes of Mount Koya, south of Osaka, in 819. It was the start of an era in which mountains – long regarded as sacred in Japan's traditional religion, Shinto – came to be the location for a growing number of Buddhist monasteries and temples.

A LIFE'S WORK

- Leaves his studies to become a **Buddhist monk, living as a hermit in the Japanese mountains**
- Writes the *Indications*, a **synthesis of Taoist, Confucianist, and Buddhist thought**
- Accompanies an imperial expedition to China to **learn more about Buddhist sutras**
- Spends two years in China studying Indian Buddhism, Hindu teachings, Sanskrit, and calligraphy and **founds the Shingon ("True Words") form of Buddhism**
- Receives permission from Japan's emperor to **found a monastic retreat on Mount Koya;** funding takes many years and the project is not fully realized until after his death
- Writes *The Transmission of the Shingon Dharma* **to summarize his teachings**
- Becomes one of Japan's best known and **most beloved Buddhist saints**

Kukai's parents were aristocrats whose clan had produced many administrators and scholars. When he was born, his parents gave him the birth name Totomono or, according to one source, Mao ("true fish"), but he was known throughout most of his life as Kukai. Following his death, he has come to be known as Kobo Daishi, which means "Great Teacher".

DISCOVERING BUDDHISM

Kukai, who from childhood had been regarded as highly gifted, was sent to the capital, Nara, at the age of 14 to study under his maternal uncle, the tutor to the crown prince. At 17, he entered university to study the Chinese

Classics and Confucianism. While he was studying, the alleged involvement of his clan chief in the assassination of a rival led to Kukai's family being eclipsed in imperial circles, which deprived the young man of potential patrons. With a position in government now less likely, Kukai's interests veered from Confucianism (useful for a career in the bureaucracy) towards Buddhism and he abandoned university for the life of an itinerant Buddhist monk.

It was during these years as a hermit that Kukai first turned to the mountains. As an aid to meditation he climbed Tairyu in southern Japan, recounting that "the valley reverberated to the sound of my voice as I recited, and the

planet Venus appeared in the sky". In ancient Japan, mountains were believed to be one of the main places that the Shinto *kami*, or deities, resided and numerous temples were sited on their slopes. Yet mountains had been comparatively neglected in Japanese Buddhist practice, and no major monasteries were built on them before Kukai's time.

MISSION TO CHINA

As he lived the life of a hermit, Kukai began the first of his many religious writings, and in 797 produced the *Indications of the Goals of the Three Teachings,* in which he created a synthesis of Buddhism, Confucianism, and Taoism – a testament to his acceptance of other spiritual traditions. Yet he also found access to the core Buddhist scriptures awkwardly limited, as some had not yet been translated into Japanese and so, in 804, he jumped at the opportunity to participate in an expedition being despatched by Japan's emperor to Chang'an in China.

During the journey, one of the Japanese flotilla's four ships sank in a storm and a second turned back home, but two succeeded in landing in China's Fujian province, one carrying Kukai himself, the other bearing Saicho, another distinguished Buddhist monk.

CULTURAL EXCHANGE
The Japanese delegation sets out on its arduous journey to the then Chinese capital, Chang'an. At the time, China had the most cosmopolitan culture in the world and Kukai's studies there made him one of Japan's most influential figures.

NOVICES OF MOUNT KOYA
The monastery's novice monks trudge through deep snow to the temple on Mount Koya – just as Kukai did more than 1,000 years before them.

> # MEDITATION SHOULD BE PRACTISED ON A FLAT AREA DEEP INTO THE MOUNTAINS
>
> **KUKAI**, TO THE EMPEROR SAGA, 816

In his two years in China, studying under the Esoteric master Hui-kuo, Kukai developed the teachings of the Shingon school, in which an understanding of the Buddha can be gained through a series of mantras (chants) and mandalas (mystical diagrams).

On his return to Japan in 806, Kukai discovered that a new emperor, Heizei, had come to the throne and he was not as well disposed towards Buddhism as his predecessor. Although he was summoned to take up residence at the Takaosan temple at Kyoto in 809, and in 810 received a further promotion to the role of administrative chief of the great Todaiji temple in Nara, Kukai still felt the Shingon school lacked a focal point.

MOUNTAIN HEADQUARTERS
In 816, he wrote to Heizei's successor, Saga, asking to be allowed to establish a monastic retreat on a small plain on top of Mount Koya,

a 1,000-m (3,300-ft) high peak in the Yamato region south of Osaka. Kukai told the emperor that it was a place "where the mountains are high, the clouds let fall much rain, thus nourishing vegetation and that where drops of water accumulate fishes and dragons breed and multiply." The mountain was an appropriate site to build a place adapted for peaceful meditation he argued, since "High peaks surround it on all four directions; no human tracks, still less trails, are to be seen there."

The emperor granted permission for the monastery, and although Kukai's duties at the imperial court were increasingly demanding, he climbed the mountain in 818 to develop a scheme for the adaptation of the landscape to the doctrines of Shingon Buddhism.

Although Kukai visited Mount Koya whenever he could, he found the visits arduous, noting that "the mountain is high, the snow is deep, and walking is painful". Equally difficult

was the raising of the vast funds necessary to complete the work in such a remote location. Just months before he died, Kukai appealed for more money, saying, "even a penny or a grain of rice will be welcome". More welcome was his retirement to Mount Koya, which the emperor had finally permitted in 832. At his death in 835, his body was interred in a shrine on the eastern peak of the mountain.

Kukai's work and influence did not fade away. It was continued by a succession of disciples, notably Rigen Daishi (832–909), who founded the Shugendo fraternity that formed part of the monastic movement of the Yama-bushi ("those who sleep on mountains").

The Shugendo particularly frequented the wilder mountain peaks of Japan, such as Mount Omine, near Nara, and helped ensure that Kukai's regard for the mountains as a necessary aid for meditation would remain a permanent part of Shingon Buddhism.

MOUNT FUJI

A beautifully coned stratovolcano that last erupted in 1707, Mount Fuji is one of Japan's three holy mountains, along with Mount Tate and Mount Haku. Although climbed regularly by pilgrims since the first recorded ascent in 663, its sacred summit was forbidden to women until the late 19th century. The first foreigner to climb it was Sir Rutherford Alcock, the British consul-general to Japan, in 1860. Today, more than 100,000 people make the summit each year. The climb takes eight to ten hours.

MOUNTAIN LIVES

PUEBLO PEOPLE

THE ANCIENT PUEBLO PEOPLE of North America built a series of cliff-top towns – or *pueblos*, from the Spanish for "villages" – in the southwest of the present-day US from the 9th century. Rising up to five storeys high and sometimes containing hundreds of rooms, the largest of their buildings required hundreds of thousands of man-hours to build. They are the monuments of a people extraordinarily well-adapted to life in high places.

The ancestors of the Pueblo people lived in a harsh environment – the desert plateaus and canyons received barely enough water to support agriculture. In about 800CE, the "Basketmaker" people began to build structures on the cliff-tops at the edge of the *mesas* – plateaus – that ran through the region. Protected by the high cliffs of the canyon walls, these pueblos were defensible positions that could shelter up to 1,000 people.

The structures, built of stone and adobe – a type of mud-brick – were well-adapted to the environment. As the Pueblo people prospered, larger buildings called "Great Houses" were built. They reached their most complex in about 1050CE with structures like Pueblo Bonito, which has 700 rooms.

The Pueblo people traded widely for goods that the desert could not provide. The growth of the settlements demanded the importation of large quantities of timber after 750CE, while luxury items included marine and fossil shells, as well as turquoise from as far away as Mexico.

A series of droughts devastated the Pueblo people, and many migrated away. They built new homes cut into the rock-faces of the canyons – such as the "Cliff Palace" in Mesa Verde – when forced to cluster together in even more defensible settlements. These are the most spectacular Pueblo settlements, but are the last remnants of the culture – the people succumbed to further droughts between 1225 and 1290.

LIVING IN THE DESERT
In their heyday, the Pueblo people grew beans, squash, and corn on the fertile mesa-top above their canyon dwellings. They stored water in cisterns and cut irrigation channels for their crops. They also kept turkeys and hunted for game.

❶ Structures varied in their usage – smaller rooms, such as these adobe-walled spaces in Grand Gulch, Utah, were used for storage. ❷ The Pueblo people left a variety of petroglyphs (rock engravings) and art on the canyon walls, such as these hand prints at Grand Gulch. ❸ Decorated pottery, such as these examples from Mesa Verde, was used for both ceremonial and everyday purposes.

CARVING OUT A WAY OF LIFE
The Pueblo people used a range of building materials: adobe, stone masonry, and timber were used in Chaco Canyon for smaller houses. Stronger buildings were built with parallel walls in-filled with rubble and finished off with dressed stone.

❶ Pueblo Bonito in Chaco Canyon, located in modern-day New Mexico, contained individual dwellings, communal plazas, and *kivas* – ritual sites. ❷ This artist's impression depicts ritual activity at a *kiva* at Mesa Verde. ❸ The inhabitants of Mesa Verde lived in the area from about 550CE, and began to build pueblos beneath the overhanging cliffs in about 1190.

THE PUEBLO COMMUNITY OF CHACO CANYON FLOURISHED BETWEEN 800 AND 1100CE, DESPITE ITS LONG WINTERS, SHORT GROWING SEASON, AND ELEVATION OF 1,800M (6,000FT), HIGH UP IN THE DESERT OF NEW MEXICO.

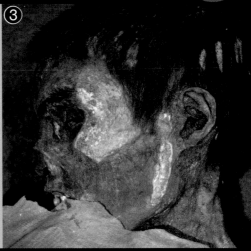

② SETTLING THE CANYONS

③

The elaborate cliff- and canyon-dwellings of the Pueblo people were the culmination of more than 1,000 years of settlement in the area. In about 500ᴄᴇ the inhabitants switched from hunter-gathering to farming, and over time the settlements grew in size.

❶ The ancestors of the Pueblo people were hunter-gatherers in areas such as Mesa Verde, Colorado. ❷ While Pueblo Bonito in Chaco Canyon contained at least 700 rooms, most Pueblo dwellings had 10 rooms or fewer. ❸ The early Basketmaker culture made use of the dry conditions to mummify their dead.

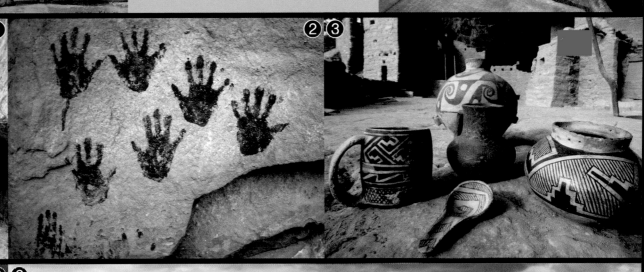

MOUNTAINS AND CHRISTIANITY

MOUNTAINS HAVE LONG PLAYED AN IMPORTANT SYMBOLIC ROLE IN CHRISTIANITY. THEIR HARSH TERRAIN AND THE DIFFICULTIES AND GRAVE DANGERS INVOLVED IN REACHING THEIR SUMMITS BECAME A METAPHOR FOR THE SOUL'S STRIVING TO REACH SALVATION IN HEAVEN.

MOUNTAIN PILGRIMS
Peaks, valleys, and rugged roads, representing the soul's passage through life – the "pilgrim's progress" for these nuns – have long been part of Christian iconography.

As Christianity emerged in the 1st century ce, it revealed its Old Testament antecedents in many ways, among them the importance it attached to the imagery of mountains. One of Christ's most important sermons was the Sermon on the Mount – which may have been a promontory near Capernaum on the Sea of Galilee – while at the end of his life he spent the final night before his betrayal by Judas on the Mount of Olives and was crucified on the hill of Golgotha just outside Jerusalem.

HOLY MOUNTAINS

Pre-Christian religions had viewed mountains as places where the gods physically resided. Once Christianity became established as the state religion of the Roman empire, its leaders sought to co-opt or destroy the sacred sites of the old religions, many of which were located on mountains. In places such as the Harz mountains in Germany and the Great St Bernard Pass in Switzerland, pagan temples were destroyed – as they were in the towns and forests of the plains.

Elsewhere, though, the idea that the divine resided in the mountains proved too strong, and it is no accident that St Catherine's Monastery was sited at the foot of Mount Sinai in Egypt in the mid-6th century CE. Mountain-top monastic complexes in Greece, such as Mount Athos, and the monastic houses atop the soaring pinnacles

ST PATRICK'S MOUNTAIN
Croagh Patrick, the peak where St Patrick (left) began his ministry, had been venerated since pagan times. Today, almost one million people climb it in an annual pilgrimage.

of the Metéora, acted as refuges equally as remote as the hermitages of the Egyptian desert.

Mountains often feature as the locations of the triumphs of Christian saints over adversaries. In Ireland, St Patrick is said to have climbed a peak in County Mayo in 441CE and fasted there for 40 days, in imitation of Jesus's fasting in the desert, before banishing demonic forces from the country.

A more theologically nuanced view of mountains came from St Augustine of Hippo, the early 5th-century North African theologian who wrote, "There are men who go to admire the high places of mountains, the great waves of the sea, the wide currents of rivers, the circuit of the ocean and the orbits of the store – and who neglect themselves." In other words, he believed that too high a regard for the physical world can lead to moral doom.

Pilgrimages to mountains eventually became a feature of Christian spirituality. Aside from monasteries, among the peaks to attract

such attention was Rochemelon above Susa in Piedmont, Italy, where, in the early 14th century, a knight named Bonifacio Rotario of Asti hauled up a heavy brass triptych containing an image of the Virgin Mary. The faithful climbed the mountain each year to look at it, but so many fell to their deaths that it was eventually taken down to the town.

FROM FEAR TO UNDERSTANDING

Crossing mountain ranges themselves was strictly an act borne of necessity, however fervently the travellers might call on God's protection. In Europe, only as the Middle Ages blossomed into the Renaissance did the fear and religious awe of mountains begin to transform into something like familiarity. In his long narrative poem *The Divine Comedy* (c.1308–21), the great Italian poet Dante Alighieri uses the image of a hill that the author cannot climb as a metaphor for the soul's ascent from Hell through the steep and winding path of Purgatory to the summit where the Earthly Paradise lies. The language Dante uses to describe the mountains suggests that he was familiar with them, and in the 200 years that followed, scholars, writers, and thinkers would build on his work and begin to provide a more complex picture in which mountains became no mere theological metaphor but real objects to be described, endured, and even categorized.

> Christianity emerged from older religious traditions in which certain mountains were regarded as sacred. The new faith continued to treat mountains with reverence, seeing them as places close to God, where special revelations might be found.

COMMUNING WITH GOD
According to Jewish and Christian traditions, it was on Mount Sinai that Moses received the Ten Commandments from the hands of God.

NO ORDINARY HILL
In the Celtic world, Neolithic ritual and the later Christian faith sometimes merged on high places, such as Glastonbury Tor in England, sacred long before the Christian era.

GREETING THE DAWN ON JEBEL MUSA
The assumed identification of Jebel Musa (Mountain of Moses) in Egypt's Sinai peninsula as the Biblical Mount Sinai has made the peak a powerful magnet for hermits and pilgrims since the early days of Christianity.

SETTING THE SCENE

- In the religious traditions that influence early Christianity, **reverence for high places and the gods of mountains** plays a significant role. The Greeks believe that their gods have a home on Mount Olympus in central Greece, from where they can watch the doings of mankind.

- Many ancient Near Eastern peoples place altars or temples in high places. At Petra in present-day Jordan, the Nabataeans set up a **"high place of sacrifice"** to their mountain god Dushara. From around 2000BCE, the Sumerians and Babylonians build ziggurats, huge step pyramid temples, whose soaring profiles emphasize that **in order to worship the gods better, it is necessary to do so from the greatest height possible.**

- In the **Old Testament**, when God punishes mankind for its sins, but saves Noah and his family, the ark – the boat that Noah built – finally **comes to rest on a high mountain**, Mount Ararat, in present-day Turkey.

- Many other **Old Testament events take place on mountains** – for example, Abraham is set to sacrifice his son Isaac on top of a peak at God's request until an angel intervenes.

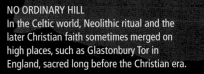

PETRARCH

FIRST TO CLIMB FOR RECREATION

TUSCANY   1304–74

FRANCESCO PETRARCA – known in the English-speaking world as Petrarch – spent most of his life in minor clerical positions, but achieved prominence as one of Italy's greatest poets. In 1336, he became the first person known for certain to have climbed a mountain simply "for the view". A man of great passion, torn by his love for "Laura", the unobtainable woman who was the subject of most of his poems, and his tussles with Christian theology, he used his climb to reflect on these shaping forces in his life.

In the 14th century, Europe's mountains had not been wholly abandoned since Hannibal's feats in the 3rd century BCE (see pp.20–21), but most mountain journeys remained strictly those forced by the exigencies of travel. The passes across the Alps into Italy were particularly busy, their routes dotted with French and German pilgrims en route to the holy places in Rome.

A clutch of royal or imperial travellers completed the scene, including Holy Roman Emperor Henry IV, who crossed over Mont Cenis, a French Alpine pass, in 1076 in his bid to patch up a quarrel with Pope Gregory VII.

A hospice had existed at Mont Cenis since 859 for the convenience and protection of the many travellers who passed that way, and about a century later, it was re-established by St Bernard of Menthon, an illustrious Benedictine monk.

CLIMBING FOR PLEASURE

Apart from an alleged attempt by King Pedro III of Aragon (r.1236–85) to climb Pic Canigou in the Catalan Pyrenees because he had been told it was the abode of a dragon, Petrarch seems to have been the first to climb a peak for the sake of it, rather than because it lay on a travel route.

The young poet had spent two years in the orbit of the papal court, which at that time was in exile from Rome at Avignon in southern France. From his window he could see the massive bulk of Mont Ventoux, which lay some 50km (30 miles) to the northeast, and the "wish to see what so great an elevation had to offer" stayed in his mind for years. Well-versed in Classical literature, the idea of an expedition to the mountain took hold after he read about the ascent of Mount Hemus (in Bulgaria), which Philip II of Macedon (Alexander the Great's father) had undertaken in c.340BCE.

A LIFE'S WORK

- Born in Arezzo, Italy, he lives his first few years there before the **family move to Avignon in France**

- Abandons his law studies for his true interests, **literature and the religious life**

- Sees Laura at a church in Bologna; she becomes **the inspiration for much of his poetry**

- Travels around northwestern Europe in the company of his younger brother

- Makes the **first recorded ascent** of a mountain – Mont Ventoux in Provence, France

- Is crowned with a laurel wreath in a public ceremony in Rome in recognition of his achievement as a poet, **making him the first "poet laureate"**

Casting about for a companion to join him on his adventure, Petrarch rejected several candidates before deciding on his younger brother, Gherardo. Not too impetuous, utterly reliable, and strong, he would be the perfect foil for Petrarch's more artistic temperament during the assault on Mont Ventoux.

SPIRITUAL HEIGHTS

Petrarch's account of the ascent includes no details about the preparation or planning for the expedition, but on 24 April 1336 the brothers set out, staying with two servants at Malaucène, a small village sited at the foot of the 1,912-m (6,273-ft) mountain.

Two days later, Petrarch and Gherardo, accompanied by the servants, began their climb. Passing a ruined monastery, they encountered an aged shepherd, who told them that 50 years previously he himself had reached the summit, that the way ahead was difficult, and the reward – scratches and hard labour – not worth the effort. Depositing their excess baggage with him, the party headed upwards.

The letter Petrarch wrote after the ascent to his spiritual guide Father Dionigi da Borgo San Sepolcro is laced with metaphysical interpretations of the event. To the poet, the expedition symbolized man's striving from the material to the spiritual, and to reach the mountain's summit was to leave sin behind and, purged, to approach God himself.

There were, however, much more mundane obstacles to be overcome. Petrarch was keen to reach the top but, his stamina being less than that of his brother, kept switching back and forth along the slopes. Gherardo, in contrast, ploughed straight up the ridges, taking the steepest, but the shortest course. Time and time again, Petrarch reached a point, only to find his brother enjoying a rest.

Finally, the party reached the summit, from where they were rewarded with a view as far as Marseilles on France's southeast coast, although the Pyrenees were concealed from them by haze.

Overcome by emotions, by thoughts of the Greek gods' lofty home on Olympus, and of his own unrequited passion for the ever-present and unapproachable muse of his poetry, Laura, Petrarch pulled a book from his pocket, the *Confessions* of the 5th-century theologian St Augustine. Not the most obvious choice for a mountaintop read, but then Petrarch was not the most obvious of mountaineers.

Gherardo and Petrarch then began the descent. Night had fallen by the time they reached the inn at Malaucène and, by his own account, Petrarch uttered not a single word all that long way down, so caught up was he in the mood of introspection inspired by the peak. He then set himself to write it all down, penning a letter to Father Dionigi in an effort to capture his feelings before they faded into memory.

Although he spent ten of the next 17 years in places within easy reach of Mont Ventoux, Petrarch seems never to have climbed that mountain again, or contemplated the ascent of any other. For him, to have reached such spiritual heights just once was enough, and it was sufficient to earn him the reputation of the world's first genuine mountaineer.

ACT OF LOVE
Petrarch's climb up Mont Ventoux, which he described as a "voyage of the soul", was also an act of devotion to Laura, the idealized subject of most of his sonnets (left).

ALLEGORICAL MOUNTAIN
Petrach's *Triumphs*, a series of poems, tells of the six victories of Love, Chastity, Death, Fame, Time, and Faith and inspired many artists. In this 1450 painting, a mountain forms a scenic backdrop.

ANTOINE DE VILLE

MEDIEVAL LORD WHO BESIEGED A MOUNTAIN

FRANCE   D.1504

Amid the ranks of holy men and natural philosophers who populate the annals of early mountaineering, the provincial squire and military man Antoine de Ville stands out. Thanks to a king's will and a military machine, de Ville was the first man to scale a peak of any technical difficulty. His 1492 expedition to conquer Mont Aiguille, a precipitous mountain in the Vercors near Grenoble encircled by sheer limestone cliffs, used techniques that were far ahead of their time. As such it is justly recognized as the first truly "Alpine" climb.

Little is known of the life of Antoine de Ville, the man ordered by Charles VIII of France to climb Mont Aiguille. His title "Seigneur de Dompjulien et de Beaupré" tells us the towns in the Lorraine region of eastern France over which he was lord, and his likely place of birth. As a local squire, de Ville would have pledged his allegiance to the king, and indeed, his only appearances in the historical record – aside from his high-altitude exploits – relate to his years of military service.

THE INACCESSIBLE MOUNTAIN

De Ville's place in history is inextricably tied to the mountain that captured the whim of his sovereign, Charles VIII. Dubbed *Mons Inascensibilis* ("unscalable mountain" in Latin) by the papal chronicler Gervase of Tilbury in 1211, by which time it was already counted as one of the "Seven Wonders" of the Dauphiné region, Mont Aiguille is located some 57km (37 miles) south of Grenoble. A vast monolith of solid limestone oriented northeast to southwest, its parallel Northwest and Southeast Faces form a formidable barrier of sheer, 300-m (1,000-ft) high cliffs, rising to a 2,085-m (6,841-ft) summit

FOOL KING
Charles VIII was considered a foolish youth, unsuited to kingship. His mother ruled as regent until 1491, when Charles turned 21; a year later, he ordered de Ville up Mont Aiguille, possibly on a whim.

at its northeastern terminus. When viewed in profile, the reason for its name becomes clear – *aiguille* is French for needle.

The topographical quirk that made Mont Aiguille so beguiling is the tabletop plateau that surmounts its vertiginous limestone cliffs. Just visible from the valley floor, this tantalizing domain is said to have prompted Charles to order that the cliffs be scaled, since a place as yet unvisited could not be considered truly within his realm. Whether this story is true cannot be verified, but the king, who was known for his ill-conceived ventures both at home and abroad, may well have yielded to such a passing whim.

THE FIRST TRUE ALPINISTS

Whatever the reason, the royal decree went out in June 1492, and de Ville set about assembling a task force that would be equal to the job. Reputedly a master of sieges – although his 1494 command of 220 crossbow-men in the king's Romagna campaign suggests his expertise may have lain as much in the marshalling of men and the application of his wits to any task – de Ville's first team member was a man named Reynaud, an *escallor* ("ladder man") and officer

in charge of the Charles's siege engines – machines used to break down city walls. Cathelin Servet, chief stonemason of the Church of the Holy Cross in Montélimar and Pierre Arnaud, master carpenter of Montélimar, provided technical knowledge, while churchmen Sébastien de Caret and François de Bosco oversaw the spiritual side of the expedition. Guillaume Sauvage, described as a "lackey", and Jean Lobret, an experienced montagnard (mountain-dweller) from the nearby town of Die, rounded off the party.

The expedition set off on 26 June 1492 with an array of military siege equipment, including large quantities of rope, rings, grappling hooks, and ladders. After identifying the Northwest Face as the least perilous route by which to assail the mountain they set about fixing ropes and ladders to the lower half of the wall. As night fell, de Ville and the troop retreated to the base of the cliffs to spend the night at a bivouac.

A MOST HORRIBLE PASSAGE

On the morning of the second day of the expedition, de Ville contemplated "the most horrible and terrifying passage that I or my company have ever seen". Nevertheless, ropes and ladders were fixed up the remaining half of the wall, and all bar Sauvage, who stayed at the bottom to act as messenger, were soon standing on the summit plateau. De Ville immediately sent word to the Grenoble parliament requesting verification of the climb, describing the

THE MOUNTAIN WHICH WAS SAID TO BE INACCESSIBLE, I, BY SUBTLE MEANS AND ENGINES, HAVE FOUND THE MEANS OF CLIMBING

ANTOINE DE VILLE

Eden-like landscape as "the most beautiful place [we] had ever visited … a beautiful meadow that would require 40 men to mow … and a beautiful herd of chamois, which will never be able to get away." De Bosco wrote of three different types of sparrow, a red-footed chough, and a large variety of flowers, especially lilies.

After remaining on the summit for three days, the party made its descent, and de Ville went back into the service of the king. Whether for his climb or his subsequent valour in the Romagna campaign two years later is unclear, but de Ville was rewarded by Charles VIII with the title Duke of St Angelo, a post in which he "behaved himself with a great deal of honour and reputation", according to the court chronicler Philippe de Commines. To put de Ville's mountaineering achievement into context, Mont Aiguille was not successfully climbed again until 1834.

ALPINE EQUIPMENT?

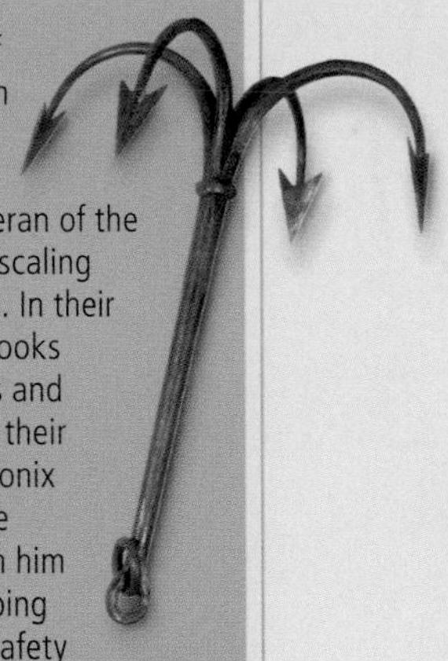

De Ville's use of rope in his ascent of a large rock wall anticipated alpinism by more than four centuries, although it must have seemed a natural technique to a seasoned veteran of the medieval siege, which could involve scaling city walls more than 10m (30ft) high. In their way, de Ville's rings and grappling hooks may have prefigured later karabiners and pitons. His use of ladders prefigured their use in the early ascents of the Chamonix Aiguilles. Only de Ville's need to take churchmen along with him to ensure the climbing party's spiritual safety is seriously at odds with modern requirements.

SIEGE ROPES (LEFT) WERE ATTACHED TO GRAPPLING HOOKS (ABOVE) AND THROWN OVER BATTLEMENTS TO SCALE MEDIEVAL CASTLE WALLS

THE TABLE TOP OF MONT AIGUILLE
The ascent of Mont Aiguille was the first recorded climb of any technical difficulty. At the time, Charles VIII was investing heavily in siege engines and it is possible that he ordered the mountain to be scaled to test the skill of a siege commander.

JOSIAS SIMMLER

THE FIRST MOUNTAINEERING AUTHOR

SWITZERLAND   1530–76

THE THEOLOGIAN AND CLASSICIST Josias Simmler spent most of his career in the safe academic confines of Zurich University, where his output consisted largely of biblical commentaries and tracts against Catholics and heretics. Yet his love for the history of his native country, combined with his fascination with Classical accounts of its mountains, led to *De Alpibus Commentarius*, the first work devoted exclusively to the Alps and the strategies necessary to survive their crossing.

EARLY ALPINE KIT
Simmler described the use of wooden hoops laced with twine to prevent sinking into the snow – the first recorded mention of snow shoes in the Alps.

Josias Simmler's theological career was typical of an educated churchman in Switzerland in the period just after the Protestant Reformation. His father was the Protestant pastor of the small town of Kappel and Josias looked likely to follow in his footsteps. Yet he had powerful patronage in the form of Heinrich Bullinger, a prominent Protestant theologian and leader of the Reformed Church living in Zurich.

Simmler went to the city to study under Bullinger, and after completing his education in Basel and Strasbourg, returned to gain some experience as a pastor in the villages around it. In 1552, he became professor of New Testament studies at Zurich University and, in 1560, was promoted to professor of theology, obliging with a succession of works in which he castigated a variety of heretical sects.

PROMOTING THE ALPS

It is hard to find a 16th-century university academic who was not steeped in the Classics, and Simmler was no exception. Propelled by his interest in the mountains of Switzerland he produced an edition of the *Antonine Itineraries* (although it was only published towards the end of his life, in 1576).

This 2nd-century description of a series of "itineraries" (or routes) throughout the Roman Empire also included mention of a number of the Alpine passes by which trade and travellers journeyed to and from Rome.

Simmler's interest in Classical knowledge, and his growing awareness of the historical importance of the mountains, also linked him to another early Swiss pioneer of Alpine studies, Conrad Gesner (see pp.44–45), who happened

STUMPF'S CHRONICLE

German-born Johannes Stumpf (1500–57) was a pastor at Bubikon in the Swiss canton of Zurich. Inspired by his father-in-law, Heinrich Brennwald, who had written a history of Switzerland, Stumpf set off in 1544 on a journey that took him through the Valais, Lausanne, and Bern regions of the country. He used his notes from this trip to compile a monumental account of the history and topography of the region, which became known as the *Schwytzer Chronica* ("Swiss Chronicle"). The book became a standard until the 18th century, and was one of the inspirations for Simmler's own work on the Alps.

STUMPF'S ACCOUNT CONTAINS BEAUTIFUL HISTORICAL MAPS, SOME DRAWN BY THE AUTHOR

to be a contemporary of Simmler's as a professor at Zurich. In 1555, Simmler compiled a new edition of Gesner's *Bibliotheca Universalis*, a compendium of all the authors who had written in Latin, Greek, or Hebrew, and in 1566 he completed the first biography of Gesner, just a year after his colleague's death.

It was perhaps Gesner who sparked in Simmler a desire to apply the same level of scholarship to an examination of Switzerland and the Alps as he had previously devoted to the Bible. Simmler conceived an ambitious project and began it in 1551, but just two fragments of it were finished by the time he died. The first, the *Descriptio Vallesiae*, published in 1574, is a detailed account of the canton of Valais in southwest Switzerland.

SIMMLER'S TIPS AND TRICKS

It is a chapter at the end of this volume called *De Alpibus Commentarius* ("Concerning the Difficulties of Alpine Travel and the Means by which they may be Overcome"), that really secures Simmler his place as an Alpine pioneer. Although he assiduously avoids any sense of personal recollection, his depth of knowledge about conditions at altitude clearly indicates that he was familiar with them at first hand. Simmler knew many of the tools and tricks of the Alpine traveller. He relates how merchants travelling in opposite directions across a pass would agree to meet at the top at a prearranged time so that they could pass each other and not get blocked in a narrow place. He was also familiar with primitive alpenstocks and crampons, noting that "to counteract the slipperiness of the ice, they firmly attach to their feet shoes resembling those of horses, with three sharp spikes in them, so that they may be able to stand firmly. In some places they use sticks tipped with iron, by leaning upon which they can climb steep slopes."

Simmler was acutely aware of the dangers of crevasses, saying that "the old ice which sometimes has to be traversed has crevices in it, three or four feet wide … into which, if a man fall, he must indubitably perish," and warns of the dangers of fresh snow covering them over. He also recommends the use of ropes tied round the waist as a safety device while crossing such treacherous terrain. As for avalanches, he warns that these may be set off by the most trivial of things, from the flight of a bird to the voice of a traveller, and gives advice in case the worst

HOW TO CROSS THE ALPS
De Alpibus Commentarius has the earliest known advice for merchants and pilgrims passing through high Alpine passes.

should happen: "If a man is able to move his hands about, and clear a little space around him before the snow has hardened, he acquires a certain power of breathing, and may keep alive for two or even three days."

When travelling in the mountains, Simmler advised that the eyes should be protected from the glare of the snow by "glass spectacles", and that the rest of the body "should be well fortified against the cold by skins and thick garments." His final piece of advice is perhaps the most practical of all: "The most useful thing of all, however, is to keep continually moving."

Although the other completed part of Simmler's grand project, the *De Republica Helvetiorum*, dealing with the history of the Swiss Republic, brought him greater fame during his lifetime, his reputation among alpinists grew in the 19th century. It is fitting, therefore, that the first modern translation of the *De Alpibus Commentarius* was undertaken by the American scholar W A B Coolidge (see p.145), a respected mountaineer and, just as Simmler had been, an eminent theologian.

THE VALAIS
Simmler's *Descriptio Vallesiae* is a detailed geographical survey of the Valais – a wild and little-known place that would later become famous for its iconic peak, the Matterhorn.

MOUNTAINEERING INNOVATIONS

ROPE

A FUNDAMENTAL PART OF THE MOUNTAINEERING EXPERIENCE, there is no piece of equipment more emblematic of the sport than the rope – proficiency in its use is a basic requirement of climbing expertise. Even without karabiners and modern protection devices, a skilled alpinist can make great use of a rope's versatility. The Germans even have a word for the link that the rope makes between climbers – *Seilschaft*. It's hardly surprising, then, that the first internationally recognized climbing-equipment standard, introduced in the 1860s, guaranteed the quality of climbing ropes.

NATURAL FIBRES

Rope is one of the oldest technologies known to mankind. Using rope made from a wide variety of natural fibres for practical tasks, such as climbing trees or cliffs, has been common to different cultures for much of human history.

The appearance of synthetic fibres in the 20th century transformed climbing. Before synthetic ropes were developed during World War II, climbing ropes were made first of hemp, and then of manila, expensive cotton, or even more expensive silk. Damp hemp especially is prone to rot, and while appearing in good condition on the outside, it can fail unexpectedly under load. Thus sailors – "Jack Tars" – tarred their ropes.

Another crucial shortcoming of hemp, apart from its comparatively low breaking strain, was lack of elasticity. A sudden loading, such as that caused by a fall by the lead climber, would all too frequently snap the rope. The consequent philosophy – that the leader must never fall – lasted until the advent of nylon

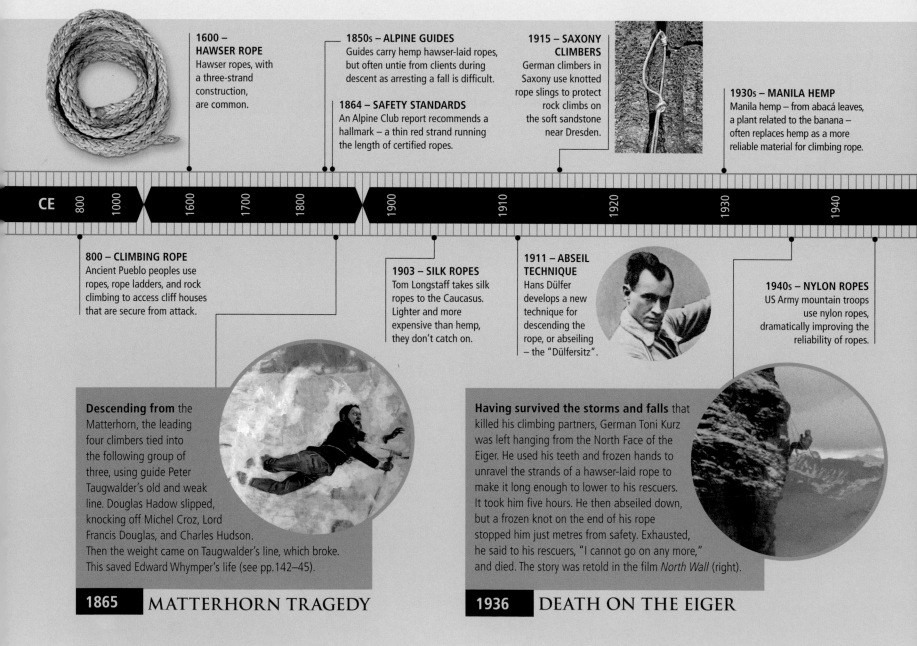

1600 – HAWSER ROPE
Hawser ropes, with a three-strand construction, are common.

1850s – ALPINE GUIDES
Guides carry hemp hawser-laid ropes, but often untie from clients during descent as arresting a fall is difficult.

1864 – SAFETY STANDARDS
An Alpine Club report recommends a hallmark – a thin red strand running the length of certified ropes.

1915 – SAXONY CLIMBERS
German climbers in Saxony use knotted rope slings to protect rock climbs on the soft sandstone near Dresden.

1930s – MANILA HEMP
Manila hemp – from abacá leaves, a plant related to the banana – often replaces hemp as a more reliable material for climbing rope.

CE | 800 | 1000 | 1600 | 1700 | 1800 | 1900 | 1910 | 1920 | 1930 | 1940

800 – CLIMBING ROPE
Ancient Pueblo peoples use ropes, rope ladders, and rock climbing to access cliff houses that are secure from attack.

1903 – SILK ROPES
Tom Longstaff takes silk ropes to the Caucasus. Lighter and more expensive than hemp, they don't catch on.

1911 – ABSEIL TECHNIQUE
Hans Dülfer develops a new technique for descending the rope, or abseiling – the "Dülfersitz".

1940s – NYLON ROPES
US Army mountain troops use nylon ropes, dramatically improving the reliability of ropes.

Descending from the Matterhorn, the leading four climbers tied into the following group of three, using guide Peter Taugwalder's old and weak line. Douglas Hadow slipped, knocking off Michel Croz, Lord Francis Douglas, and Charles Hudson. Then the weight came on Taugwalder's line, which broke. This saved Edward Whymper's life (see pp.142–45).

1865 MATTERHORN TRAGEDY

Having survived the storms and falls that killed his climbing partners, German Toni Kurz was left hanging from the North Face of the Eiger. He used his teeth and frozen hands to unravel the strands of a hawser-laid rope to make it long enough to lower to his rescuers. It took him five hours. He then abseiled down, but a frozen knot on the end of his rope stopped him just metres from safety. Exhausted, he said to his rescuers, "I cannot go on any more," and died. The story was retold in the film *North Wall* (right).

1936 DEATH ON THE EIGER

ropes and modern protection devices. It also explains why early climbers were more prepared than seems sensible to climb solo.

Nonetheless, ropes were still useful for protecting or aiding the second climber from above, for abseiling, glacier safety, and other utilitarian purposes where there would be little or no shock loading. Even so – as the 1865 Matterhorn tragedy (see pp.136–37) showed – if the rope was old or sub-standard, or there was slack between the climbers, it was vulnerable to breakage. The fatal rope from 1865, resembling window-sash cord, is on display in the Zermatt museum in Switzerland.

MATERIAL DEVELOPMENTS

In 1864, the Alpine Club investigated the manufacture and safety standard of climbing equipment. The subsequent recommendation that any rope meeting the required standard should carry a thin red thread along its length lasted until the 1950s. Climbing ropes were hawser-laid, meaning that they comprised three

MIND THE GAP

Mountaineers frequently cross snow-covered glaciers and climb icefalls where concealed crevasses are a constant danger. In such places, it is essential that climbers move roped together and remain alert. Spare rope is carried coiled around the shoulder and used to help extricate a partner who has fallen through a snow bridge. Crevasses and gaps between rock pinnacles can be crossed using a rope technique known as a Tyrolean Traverse.

CROSSING A CREVASSE USING THE TYROLEAN TRAVERSE TECHNIQUE

strands twisted together. Alternatives to hemp began to appear in the 20th century – cotton and silk ropes had some elasticity, and were much lighter than manila ropes, but were expensive. The development in Germany of

Kernmantel ropes, meaning "core and sheath", allowed for a looser construction that absorbed more energy and was less prone to kinks and freezing. A braided sheath also protected the core from wear.

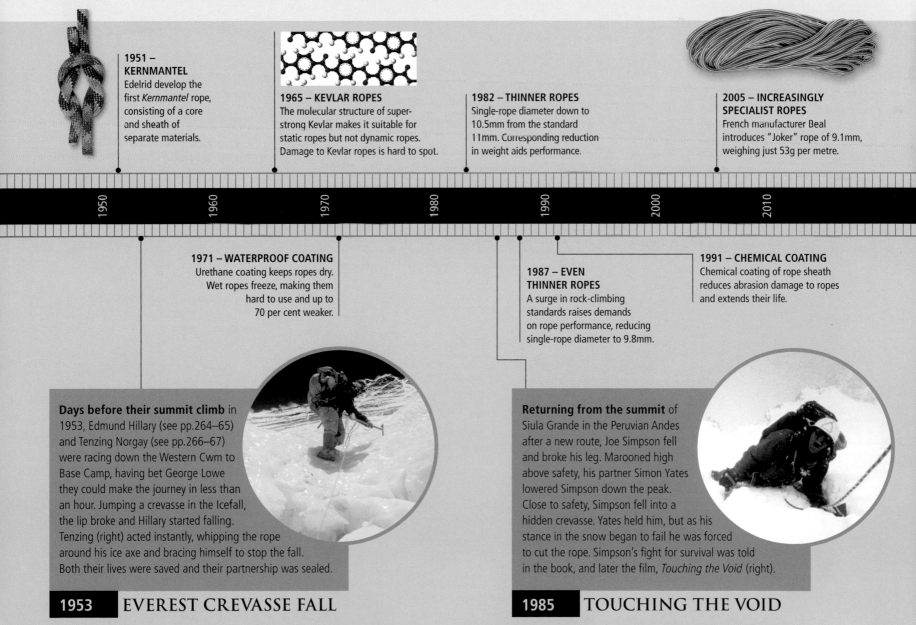

1951 – KERNMANTEL
Edelrid develop the first *Kernmantel* rope, consisting of a core and sheath of separate materials.

1965 – KEVLAR ROPES
The molecular structure of super-strong Kevlar makes it suitable for static ropes but not dynamic ropes. Damage to Kevlar ropes is hard to spot.

1982 – THINNER ROPES
Single-rope diameter down to 10.5mm from the standard 11mm. Corresponding reduction in weight aids performance.

2005 – INCREASINGLY SPECIALIST ROPES
French manufacturer Beal introduces "Joker" rope of 9.1mm, weighing just 53g per metre.

1950   1960   1970   1980   1990   2000   2010

1971 – WATERPROOF COATING
Urethane coating keeps ropes dry. Wet ropes freeze, making them hard to use and up to 70 per cent weaker.

1987 – EVEN THINNER ROPES
A surge in rock-climbing standards raises demands on rope performance, reducing single-rope diameter to 9.8mm.

1991 – CHEMICAL COATING
Chemical coating of rope sheath reduces abrasion damage to ropes and extends their life.

Days before their summit climb in 1953, Edmund Hillary (see pp.264–65) and Tenzing Norgay (see pp.266–67) were racing down the Western Cwm to Base Camp, having bet George Lowe they could make the journey in less than an hour. Jumping a crevasse in the Icefall, the lip broke and Hillary started falling. Tenzing (right) acted instantly, whipping the rope around his ice axe and bracing himself to stop the fall. Both their lives were saved and their partnership was sealed.

1953 EVEREST CREVASSE FALL

Returning from the summit of Siula Grande in the Peruvian Andes after a new route, Joe Simpson fell and broke his leg. Marooned high above safety, his partner Simon Yates lowered Simpson down the peak. Close to safety, Simpson fell into a hidden crevasse. Yates held him, but as his stance in the snow began to fail he was forced to cut the rope. Simpson's fight for survival was told in the book, and later the film, *Touching the Void* (right).

1985 TOUCHING THE VOID

CONRAD GESNER

MOUNTAIN-LOVING BOTANIST AND STORYTELLER

SWITZERLAND   1516–65

A MAN OF WIDE-RANGING TALENTS, the naturalist and bibliographer Conrad Gesner rose from a humble background to become one of the most respected scholars of his day. His love of botany led him to make frequent explorations of the Swiss countryside, and in particular the Alps. His writings were the first to instil a positive delight in the mountains and a joy in the scenery for its own sake, and his description of his ascent of Mount Pilatus in 1555 is one of the early classics of mountain literature.

Conrad Gesner's father was a furrier whose modest means left him unable to provide a proper education for his children. It fell to Gesner's great-uncle, Hans Frick, to fund his basic schooling in Latin and Greek, and it was only through the goodwill of a series of patrons – including the German religious reformer Wolfgang Fabricius Capito – that he was able to take his studies further, including stints at the University of Bruges and the Sorbonne in Paris. Throughout his peripatetic academic career, Gesner continued to study the botany of whichever locality he found himself in, laying the foundations of his future work and fame.

After serving as professor of Greek at Lausanne for three years from 1537, Gesner finally completed his medical studies at Basel in 1541. He took up the chair of natural philosophy at Zurich, a post he occupied for the rest of his life. This comparative stability allowed him to begin the preparation of his greatest work, the *Historiae Animalium* ("Animal Histories"), which was issued in four volumes between 1551 and 1558, with a fifth volume on snakes appearing in 1587, after Gesner's death.

LOVER OF MOUNTAINS

In 1541, Gesner wrote a letter to his friend Jakob Vogel of Glaurus in the form of a dedicatory preface to a work on milk, the *Libellus de lacte et operibus lactariis*, which was published in 1543. In it, his love of mountains for their own sake comes through strongly. He declares that he has "resolved for the future, so long as God suffers me to live, to climb mountains, or at all events to climb one mountain ever year", although as a botanist he held that this must be "at the season the vegetation is best".

Gesner extolled mountaineering as the "proper exercise of the body". Yet he believed that there was more to be gained from the mountains than mere exercise or the gathering of botanical specimens – he viewed the high slopes as virtually another world, spiritually

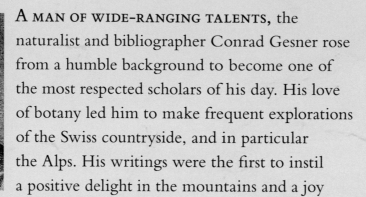

ARRESTING ALPENHORN
Gesner described the alpenhorn, which he first saw on Mount Pilatus, as a *lituum alpinum*, after the curved war-trumpets used by the Romans.

uplifting in themselves, and where the normal rules of nature do not apply. "There the snow is everlasting," he notes, "and this softest of substances that melts between our fingers cares nothing for the fierceness of the sun and its burning rays."

It is unfortunate that a record survives of only one of Gesner's Alpine expeditions. He set it down in the *Descriptio Montis Fracti Juxta Lucernam*, which was published in 1555. Yet few of his trips can have been more compelling than this one. His purpose was to climb to the summit of Mount Pilatus, a 2,128-m (6,982-ft) high mountain to the southwest of Lucerne. For centuries the peak had been considered cursed, and haunted by the spirit of the Biblical figure Pontius Pilate.

Travelling via Eichental, Gesner's party reached Lucerne, where they were obliged to hire a guide. No one was permitted to approach the mountain without one, in case they acted in such a manner as to provoke the irascible spectre of Pilate. Ever the naturalist, Gesner observed that in one stream large trout were to be found and that they were "the only fish that are found in its higher reaches; further down … crayfish are also found."

FACTS AND FABLES

For his *Historiae Animalium*, Gesner mixed fact with a compendium of Classical writings about animals. Although he sought to separate truth from fiction, he still felt unable to omit stories such as that about the bouquetin (steinbock), telling how this Alpine goat would hook its horns around the summit of a high mountain when nearing the end of its life. The dying goat was then believed to twirl itself around at ever-greater speed until the horn wore through or snapped, and it was sent hurtling down to its death.

A MOUNTAIN GOAT DEPICTED IN *HISTORIAE ANIMALIUM*

He also remarked on the presence of chamois, steinbock, and Alpine mice, as well as pheasants and ptarmigans.

PROVOKING PILATE

Gesner relished the approach to Mount Pilatus, commenting during a stop to eat bread and drink water from a cool spring that he doubted "… whether the human senses are capable of any greater and more epicurean pleasure." Everything about the trip delighted him, especially the "marvellous and unaccustomed spectacle of mountains, ridges, rocks, woods, valleys, streams, springs, and meadows." To gaze up at the peak provoked in him the sense of "dwelling among the clouds".

The way was not easy; the guides took them up a difficult slope on which there was no proper path, and Gesner and his companions were equipped with alpenstocks – long, iron-tipped staffs to assist with balance over tricky terrain. But before too long they did reach the summit, and there caught sight of the rock upon which Pilate was believed to sit and stir up storms. A multitude of names and family crests had been carved there by previous climbers. Nearby was a level area of ground, bare except for a small patch of grass. Here, Gesner's guides claimed, had stood the druid who cast Pilate into his watery grave in the hilltop lake.

HEROIC HORNBLAST

Gesner had sounded an alpenhorn at the final cowherd's hut before completing his ascent of Pilatus, but if he feared Pilate's retribution for his trespass, none came. Not that he had ever really believed that the spirit of the Roman procurator would smite him dead. He commented acidly: "For my own part, I am inclined to believe that Pilate has never been here at all."

Gesner returned down the slope to continue with his botanical studies and to further, undocumented mountain travels. Yet he must always have cherished the thought that he expressed in his account of the Pilatus ascent: "The highest pleasures and the keenest delights of all the senses are derived from walking tours in the mountains, undertaken with friends."

THE LEGEND OF PILATE

According to legend, the Emperor Tiberius, angry that Pilate had allowed Jesus Christ to be crucified, condemned him to death by the most shameful means that could be devised. Pilate committed suicide to avoid the penalty and his body was flung into the River Tiber, where his angry spirit caused continual storms. The Romans took the corpse to Vienne in southern France, where it provoked equally terrifying tempests. The body was finally thrown into a marsh on Mount Pilatus, and Pilate's wife was cast into a nearby lake for good measure.

The presence of Pilate's body on Mount Pilatus was said to cause great storms, particularly if rocks were hurled into its lake. When six priests tried to climb the peak in 1387, they were imprisoned for risking Pilate's wrath. In 1518, a group of Swiss scholars including Vadianus – whose brief account maintains that the legend must be true – ascended to the summit. It took a 1585 ascent by Pastor Johann Müller of Lucerne for the myth to be exposed. On reaching the summit he threw stones into the lake, defying Pilate to strike him. But no ghost stirred, and the mountaintop lost its menace.

MOUNT PILATUS
Rising above the shores of Lake Lucerne, Mount Pilatus is the most prominent peak in the area. Despite the legend, its name is thought to originate from the Latin word *pila*, meaning "pillar".

JOHN EVELYN

ACERBIC DIARIST OF AN ALPINE MISADVENTURE

ENGLAND

1620–1706

THE 17TH-CENTURY WRITER and noted gardener John Evelyn was one of the first generation of Grand Tourists, visiting France and Italy in search of culturally improving sights. His return journey to England in 1646 took him through the Alps, a crossing he regarded with a mixture of fascination and horror. Evelyn's account of the adventure remained lost until his diaries were discovered in 1817. His principal influence for the century after his death was as the author of *Sylva*, a major work on trees.

A LIFE'S WORK

- His travels in Europe between 1643 and 1647 take him **across the Simplon Pass** from Italy to Switzerland

- In 1652, he publishes the *Elysium Britannicum*, the earliest definitive history of British gardens and gardening

- In 1661, he publishes *Fumifugium*, the first English work to deal specifically with **pollution**

- His greatest work, *Sylva*, **on the cultivation of trees**, is published in 1664

- After the restoration of the English monarchy in 1660, he holds a number of government posts, culminating in 1664–67 in the position of **Commissioner for the Sick** during the Anglo-Dutch Wars

- In 1697 he publishes *Numismata*, which deals with **the history of coins and medals**

Evelyn set off for continental Europe in late 1643, escaping the increasingly difficult situation for Royalists in England, where King Charles I's armies were losing ground to the supporters of Parliament in the civil war. Evelyn's travels through France to Italy were unexceptional, although his reputation as an acute if jaundiced observer is affirmed by his description of Geneva, where he noted that "the houses are not despicable". For the next three years, Evelyn journeyed through Italy before a combination of travel-weariness, his need to attend to his family estates, and his impending marriage prompted a return home.

INTO THE MOUNTAINS

In May 1646, Evelyn and his travelling companion, a Captain Wray, set off from Milan in something of a hurry after the Scots mercenary colonel who had been their host died suddenly. Up until then, Wray and Evelyn had lived in comparative luxury, but, at Marguzzo in the foothills of the Alps, the discomforts of the road began – a factor that would feature large in Evelyn's account of the journey. He had to endure a bed stuffed with beech leaves that "did so prick [his] skin" he could not sleep. The next day they reached Domodossola (close to the present-day Swiss–Italian border), where they exchanged their asses for mules and began the real mountain ascent over the Simplon Pass.

Evelyn was soon struck with wonder at the bleakness of the landscape, writing that they passed "through strange, horrid and firefull Craggs and tracts, abounding in Pine trees, and onely inhabited with Beares, Wolves, and Wild Goates," where they could not "see above a pistole shoote before us, the horizon being terminated with rocks, and mountaines, whose

TREE EXPERT
Evelyn's fame as an author on trees was established long before the lost account of his Alpine adventures was discovered.

tops cover'd with Snow, seem'd to touch the Skies." The most dangerous stretches involved the crossing of ravines, over which huge fir trees had been felled to create a primitive bridge, and edging along narrow paths cut in the rock above precipitous drops. Evelyn took time out from his description of the alternate dangers of "freezing in the sun, and anon frying by the reverberation of the Sun against the Cliffs" to comment on the goitres that afflicted many of the inhabitants of the mountain valleys who had "monstrous Gullets or Wenns of flesh growing to their throats, some of which I have seene as big as an hundred pounds bag of silver hanging under their Chinns." He ascribed their condition to the drinking of too much melt water.

SOME OF THESE VAST MOUNTAINES WERE BUT ONE INTIRE STONE, 'TWIXT WHOSE CLEFTS NOW AND THEN PRECIPITATED GREATE CATARACTS OF MELTED SNOW

JOHN EVELYN, *DIARIES*, 1646

Evelyn initally thought the people "very honest and trusty", but he had cause to revise his opinion after Wray's dog, a water spaniel (which Evelyn thought "a huge filthy cur") chased a herd of goats, causing one to fall to its death. As they set off from their inn the following day, they were set upon by a crowd which pulled them from their mounts, disarmed them and locked them in a nearby house. They were taken before a magistrate and fined "one pistole" for killing the goat and ten times that much for trying to escape without reporting the incident. Threatened with a long detention before the next formal judicial sitting, Evelyn and Wray paid up and hurried on their way.

The road ahead was hard. Evelyn commented that he thought it had been covered with snow "since the Creation" and that frequent fresh snowfalls made it easy to lose the path. Further misfortune followed as Wray's horse slid down a precipice "more than thrice the height of St Paul's" and it took the party more than 3km (2 miles) of trudging through the snow to reach the beast which, amazingly, survived the fall. The main part of the ordeal was over, however, and Evelyn and Wray passed into Brig in the Valais before dispensing with their guide and heading towards Lake Geneva.

UNWELCOME GIFT

At Saint-Maurice near Lake Geneva, Evelyn's tiredness overcame him and he brusquely insisted that the keeper of the local inn turf his daughter out of her own bedroom so that the English traveller might rest. As a result, Evelyn contracted smallpox – the girl had been recovering from the disease – an affliction that was commonly fatal at the time and from

which it took him 16 days to recover. Not until October the following year did Evelyn finally reach England, having married his young wife Mary in Paris. The pair lived quietly in London until the Restoration of the monarchy in 1660, after which Evelyn's career took off in a small way as a government official and more importantly as a writer on gardening. It seems he'd had his fill of mountains, however, for he never returned to the Alps.

Smallpox had been just one more unwelcome gift of the road for Evelyn, whose attitude to the mountains remained very much that of other 17th-century travellers, for whom the Alps were to be endured, not enjoyed. His descriptions of his adventures however, were more than the simple pious renderings of the Alps as a sign of God's wrath – a view that had characterized medieval accounts. Although they could not influence subsequent writers until their publication more than a century later, his diaries were a sign that, in viewing the mountains, observation was overcoming awe.

THOMAS BURNET
ENGLAND   1635–1715

A leading natural philosopher of his day, Burnet taught at Cambridge University in the 1660s and 1670s.

However, he was absent for extensive periods as he travelled on the continent, acting as the tutor to Lord Wiltshire on his Grand Tour of Europe. He became master of London's Charterhouse School in 1685, and while there published his *Telluris theoria sacra* ("Sacred Theory of the Earth"), in which he speculated that the Earth was egg-shaped and hollow and that it had been full of water until the Flood at the time of Noah, when this water had escaped to form the oceans. The mountains, too, according to Burnet, had been formed by this disaster. He also theorized that the world would in future be purged again, but this time by fire, rather than water, and that after the day of judgment it would be transformed into a star, like the Sun.

CLIMBING FOR
SCIENCE AND ART

CLIMBING FOR SCIENCE AND ART

| 1600 | 1700 | | | 1780 |

▼ 1600
Using the genealogies of the Bible, Archbishop **James Ussher of Ulster** calculates that the Earth was created on 24 October 4004BCE.

◄ 1725
Swiss scholar **Johann Jakob Scheuchzer** finds a fossilized skeleton he believes is a victim of the Biblical Flood; his Swiss studies add much to mountain knowledge (see pp.54–55).

► 1761
Genevan philosopher **Jean-Jacques Rousseau** publishes *La Nouvelle Héloïse*, a novel that extols the beauty of the natural landscape.

► 1741
William Windham and **Richard Pococke** (right) set off from Geneva to explore the Chamonix Valley (see pp.92–93).

► 1781
Swiss Benedictine monk **Placidus à Spescha** moves to the Lukmanier hospice high in the Swiss Alps, sparking an interest in climbing that lasts a lifetime (see pp.106–07).

◄ 1785
Scottish geologist **James Hutton** circulates among friends and scholars his theory of the formation of rocks and the age of the Earth (see pp.56–57).

1773
English author **Dr Samuel Johnson** tours the highlands of Scotland with fellow writer James Boswell, writing an account that popularizes travel in the mountains.

▼ 1777
German poet **Johann von Goethe** travels to the Harz mountains, and writes of his emotional response to the wild beauty of nature.

1786
Mont Blanc is climbed for the first time, by **Michel-Gabriel Paccard** and **Jacques Balmat**; they reach the summit on 8 August 1786; Balmat claims de Saussure's reward (see pp.94–97).

▼ 1787
Swiss physicist **Horace-Bénédict de Saussure** reaches the summit of Mont Blanc after several failed attempts, he is assisted by an entourage of guides and porters (see pp.60–63).

1669
Danish geologist **Nicholas Steno** formulates theories of stratigraphy after finding fossils within samples of rock, developing the understanding of how mountains are formed.

1696
English theologian **William Whiston** attempts to prove that the Biblical Flood, caused by a comet, was responsible for creating rock strata and mountains.

► 1778
Swiss painter **Caspar Wolf** produces a series of 200 Alpine paintings that challenges the pejorative perceptions of mountains (see pp.78–79).

1799
English poet **William Wordsworth** publishes *Prelude*, a poem that uses mountains and landscape as a metaphor for the poet's development.

BEFORE CLIMBING MOUNTAINS was seen as a rewarding activity in its own right, the early Alpine adventurers required a reason to venture up the peaks that so beguiled them. Amid the culture of enquiry unleashed on the minds of Europe during the 18th-century's Age of Enlightenment, mountains became a hunting ground for scientific discovery, and it was chiefly in pursuit of knowledge that these pioneers climbed higher than ever before. As the human body was proven capable of withstanding the rigours of altitude, so the clientele of the mountains grew to include artists, poets, clerics, tourists – including women – as well as the scientists. By the early 19th century, a few lone mountain lovers were treading a path that led to the future – the pursuit of mountaineering for its own sake.

1800

◄ 1802
Prussian polymath **Alexander von Humboldt** climbs Chimborazo in the Andes (see pp.70–71).

► 1807
German painter **Caspar David Friedrich** completes *The Cross in the Mountains*, one of the first Romantic depictions of religion and nature.

1808
French maid **Maria Paradis** makes the first female ascent of Mont Blanc, cajoled by Jacques Balmat to reach the summit (see pp.100–01).

◄ 1812
Gottlieb Meyer climbs the Jungfrau, crowning the mountaineering exploits of his father, uncle, and grandfather (see pp.102–03).

► 1816
English poets **Percy Shelley** and **Lord Byron** (right), visiting Switzerland at the same time, draw on the majesty of the Alps as inspiration for their Romantic writings.

1820

◄ 1819
English painter **J M W Turner** travels to Italy, having first seen the Alpine landscapes in 1802; his paintings bring the mountains to the masses (see pp.82–83).

1836
Austrian cleric **Peter Carl Thurwieser**, dubbed the "first real mountaineer", records his first ascent of the Fernerkogel in the Eastern Alps (see pp.108–09).

► 1838
French aristocrat **Henriette d'Angeville** climbs Mont Blanc, the first woman to do so under her own volition (see pp.100–01).

1840
Louis Agassiz tours Scotland, crossing the Strahlegg in the Swiss Alps later the same year (see pp.72–73).

1827
Swiss scientist **Franz Joseph Hugi** sets off to study the Unteraar Glacier in Switzerland in an attempt to fathom the movement of the giant sheets of ice (see pp.64–65).

▼ 1842
James David Forbes makes a scientific study of the Mer de Glace (see pp.66–67).

1850

► 1851
English impresario **Albert Smith** ascends Mont Blanc, writing a book of his experience that he later adapts for the stage, popularizing mountaineering for a new audience (see pp.110–11).

1858
Von Humboldt's scientific masterwork *Kosmos* is virtually complete – the fourth volume is published a year before his death in 1859.

▼ 1861
English mountain lover **John Ruskin** lives and paints in Switzerland, while continuing – in his guise as an art critic – to push a naturalistic style of painting (see pp.86–89).

1863
Swiss mountaineer **Gottlieb Studer** forms the Swiss Alpine Club, only the second such organization in the world (see pp.104–05).

A NEW FRONTIER

UNTIL ABOUT 1700, MOST EUROPEANS BELIEVED THAT THE EARTH WAS LESS THAN 6,000 YEARS OLD AND THAT ITS FEATURES HAD BEEN CREATED DURING THE BIBLICAL FLOOD. AS THE CENTURY PROGRESSED, NEW SCIENTIFIC DISCIPLINES LED TO THEORIES THAT OVERTURNED THIS VIEW.

CHARLES LYELL
As an advocate of uniformitarianism – the idea that present-day geological processes can explain the history of the Earth – Lyell anticipated some of Darwin's breakthroughs.

"Creationists" such as the Irish Anglican Archbishop James Ussher (1581–1656) believed that God had created the Earth much as we see it and that any modifications were attributable to the Flood. However, such rigid views always came face to face with anomalies such as how gemstones and other minerals were formed – the German philosopher Albertus Magnus (c.1206–80) thought that a heavenly radiation acting on the Earth's surface was responsible.

FOSSILS IN THE ALPS
Similar intellectual contortions were needed to explain the presence of ancient fossils in rock formations. Some believed that God had placed them there at the time of the Creation, others that they were natural products of the rock itself.

Gradually these views changed, as scholars such as the French naturalist Antoine de Jussiue (1686–1758) found that some fossils in the Alps were of a type found only in distant places, such as India, and had to have been carried there by the actions of an ancient ocean.

MOUNTAIN MEASUREMENTS
Scientists such as Louis Agassiz carried scientific instruments on glacier field trips, though ink and thermometers often froze.

By the 19th century, under the influence of men such as Scottish geologist Charles Lyell and French zoologist Georges Cuvier (1769–1832), the idea was taking hold that fossils were the remains of ancient creatures. Cuvier put forward a theory that there had been several catastrophic events in which most living creatures had been destroyed and replaced by new kinds of life.

THEORIES OF MOUNTAINS
The notion that the Earth was not an immutable divine creation began to shape views of how its mountains had been formed. Danish geologist Nicolaus Steno (1638–86) had already observed the presence of geological strata (levels) in mountains and had concluded that mountains had been pushed up or torn apart by the actions of earthquakes and volcanoes.

These ideas were developed by the Venetian Abbé Anton Lazzaro Moro (1687–1740), who noted that some mountains had no strata (he called these "Primary Mountains") and that "Secondary Mountains", in contrast, had a succession of strata, and by the Italian geologist Giovanni Arduino (1714–95), who concluded that no single catastrophic event had caused the raising up of mountains, but that they had been formed by a series of smaller upliftings.

German mineralogist Abraham Werner (1749–1817) proposed that the minerals of the Earth's crust had originally been held in

In the 18th and early 19th centuries, scientists and mountaineers engaged in the new disciplines of geology and glaciology, and formed revolutionary ideas about the age of the Earth and how its mountains and glaciers had been formed.

suspension by a primitive ocean, and that as these waters subsided, successive geological strata were laid down. This "Neptunian" theory was undermined by the work of men such as the German geologist Leopold von Buch, Alexander von Humboldt (see pp.70–71), and James Hutton (see pp.56–57), whose alternative theory – dubbed "Plutonist" – held that rock strata had been shaped not by water, but by volcanic action from the interior of the Earth.

STUDYING THE ICE
In the specialized field of glaciology, and specifically how glaciers had helped form the mountains, the early mountaineers were at the forefront of developing scientific theories. Horace-Bénédict de Saussure (see pp.60–63) reasoned that the heat of the Earth caused the bases of glaciers to melt and that they then slid downhill under their own pressure, while Franz Josef Hugi (see pp.64–65) considered that the motion of glaciers derived from internal forces, rather than simply their own weight. Louis Agassiz (see pp.72–73) was the first to realize that, during a relatively recent ice age, the Alps had been covered by a vast ice sheet, from which glaciers were later spawned.

This new alpine science was very far removed from the theory that mountains had been formed by Noah's Flood, but for all that, it was no less strange and wonderful.

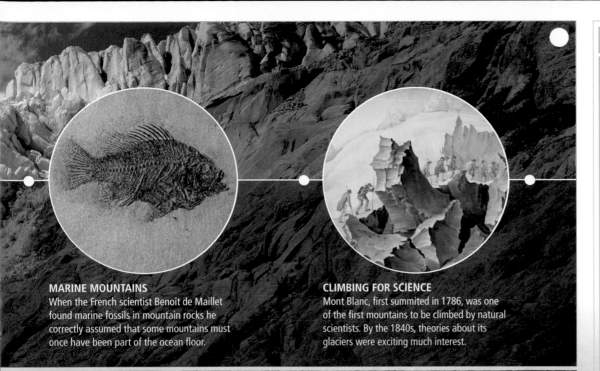

MARINE MOUNTAINS
When the French scientist Benoît de Maillet found marine fossils in mountain rocks he correctly assumed that some mountains must once have been part of the ocean floor.

CLIMBING FOR SCIENCE
Mont Blanc, first summited in 1786, was one of the first mountains to be climbed by natural scientists. By the 1840s, theories about its glaciers were exciting much interest.

SETTING THE SCENE

- The 6th-century BCE Greek philosopher and mathematician **Pythagoras** describes the **birth of a mountain** near Troezen in Greece's Peloponnese; he believes that **winds** trapped in the ground **pushed it upwards**, as though inflating the bladder of a goat.

- Most Christian writers in the **Middle Ages** believe that the Biblical Flood **shaped the surface of the Earth.** In the 11th century, the **Muslim writer Avicenna** holds that **mountain** landscapes were formed by earthquakes and **the erosive effects of wind and water** – a surprisingly modern view.

- In the 13th century, the **Italian writer** Ristorro d'Arezzo observes that **fossilized fish** are **found on mountain tops,** and in sand that he believes originally came from rivers. He thinks that mountains were once located **beneath the sea**.

- Georgius Agricola (1494–1555), the German **"Father of Mineralogy"**, concludes that **mountains were formed** through a **variety of agents**, including water erosion, the accumulation of sand by winds, and by earthquakes and volcanoes, but he thinks that **water was the main cause**.

ALPINE LABORATORY
Artist and alpinist Gabriel Loppé painted this view of the Grandes Jorasses from near the summit of Mont Blanc in 1869. The Talèfre Glacier can be seen in the top left. By the 1840s and 50s, the area had inspired some radical new ideas in geology.

JOHANN JAKOB SCHEUCHZER

PIONEER ALPINE SCIENTIST AND DRAGON-CHASER

SWITZERLAND   1672–1733

FANTASTICAL DESCRIPTIONS and gaudy illustrations of mythical creatures aside, Johann Jakob Scheuchzer's scientific observations and Swiss travelogues were an important contribution to the 18th-century understanding of mountains. While his work was very much of its time, revolving around theories that struggled against the tide of new discoveries being made about the natural world, his writings on mountains, and particularly glaciers, helped to inform and define the alpine sciences.

A LIFE'S WORK

- Is an early proponent of **the idea that fossils are the remains of former organisms**; he believes that the best way to explain the presence of fossils is to invoke the Flood

- Makes 11 journeys through his Swiss homeland and collects his observations and theories in the **first scientific publications** to be written **about the alpine environment**

- Publishes a topographic map of Switzerland in 1712, the eastern portion of which is based on his own observations and is by far **the most accurate representation of the area** to date

- Leaves a total of more than **260 folio volumes to the library** in Zurich

- **Achieves his ambition** of chair of physics and senior town physician shortly before his death

Scheuchzer was born into a wealthy and influential Zurich family. He studied medicine at the Altdorf academy near Nuremberg in Germany before receiving his doctorate from the University of Utrecht in the Netherlands. After further mathematical study at Altdorf, he was made junior town physician of Zurich in 1696.

FOSSIL EXPERT

A diligent and proficient man with a broad interest in the natural sciences, Scheuchzer's initial specialism was fossils. He began collecting specimens as early as 1690, and soon built up a collection that brought him to prominence in European scholarly circles. Several honorary academic positions were conferred upon him, bringing him a recognition that was only partly undermined by his later research into species of "alpine dragon" he believed prowled the remote Swiss valleys.

In common with many thinkers of his day, Scheuchzer's fascination with the natural world was an extension of his Christian faith. A contemporary and friend, the English naturalist John Woodward, had theorized that the Biblical Flood had re-formed rocks and the remains of animals and plants into "one common confused Mass", an explanation for the existence of fossils to which Scheuchzer also

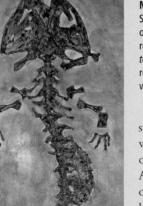

MISTAKEN IDENTITY
Scheuchzer used his discovery of what he thought were human remains, the so-called *Homo diluvii testis* (left), in an attempt to reconcile the Biblical Flood story with modern geology.

subscribed and around which he slotted his observations and theories. And there was no shortage of observations. Such was his scholarly fascination that Scheuchzer made important contributions in a range of disciplines, virtually defining the group that came to be known as the alpine sciences: botany, geology, geophysics, glaciology, mineralogy, palaeontology, meteorology, and cartography, to name but a few.

SURVEYING SWITZERLAND

Assisted by a grant from the authorities in Zurich, Scheuchzer set out in 1702 to make a comprehensive survey of the Swiss Alps. Unsurprisingly, given the nature of his entry onto the academic scene, collecting fossils was his primary aim. He had initially believed that his fossilized findings were "figured stones, as sports or jests of Nature", reflecting a common view that fossils were no more than unusually shaped rocks. He changed his tune after translating Woodward's *Natural History of the Earth* into Latin, adopting the view that fossils were relics of the Flood.

But Scheuchzer's wanderings were not solely directed towards fossil hunting. He also wrote a series of travelogues that described the natural

ON GLACIERS

In 1699, Scheuchzer compiled a pamphlet of 186 questions on subjects including alpine frost, the form of snowflakes, and the height of mountains. In his travels through the Alps, he circulated the pamphlet among a range of people, including "inhabitants of the Alps, farmers, diggers, root-cutters". He published an account of his travels, *Itinera alpina*, in 1708, and a year later published a detailed description of the Swiss glaciers based on the information gathered from his questionnaire.

SCHEUCHZER'S PORTRAIT ADORNS AN
ILLUSTRATED ACCOUNT OF HIS ALPINE TRAVELS

history and ethnology of Switzerland. They were published weekly between 1705 and 1707. Such was the quality of his work that a special edition, *Travels in the Alpine regions of Switzerland*, was produced by the Royal Society in London in 1708, with a frontispiece paid for by its president, Sir Isaac Newton. Scheuchzer's writings were accompanied by his own detailed illustrations of the plants, watercourses, walkways, and mineralogy of the region.

STUDYING MOUNTAINS

Scheuchzer's prodigious output soon built up into an important body of work on the nature of the mountain environment. His were the first significant descriptions of the rivers, lakes, mineral springs, avalanches, and glaciers of the Alps and he was also one of the first scientists to use mathematical instruments in fieldwork.

One of his major contributions, which would lead to much future exploration of mountain regions, was his work on glaciology. After observing the Rhône Glacier in south-central Switzerland in 1705, he theorized that glacial motion derived from water collected within

THIS REGION IS SO RUGGED WITH SO MANY CAVES THAT IT WOULD BE STRANGE NOT TO FIND DRAGONS

JOHANN JAKOB SCHEUCHZER *PROOF OF THE EXISTENCE OF DRAGONS*

cracks in the ice, forcing the glacier downhill through the natural expansion of water as it froze. Although this "Dilation Theory of Flow" was inaccurate – gravitation was recognized as the driving force some 50 years later – it was nevertheless the first real attempt to explain the physics of glacial motion.

Towards the end of Scheuchzer's life, though, an incident occurred that later led many to question his scientific judgment. In 1725, he examined a fossilized skeleton that had

been recovered from a quarry. He named it *Homo diluvii testis* in the belief that it was "the bony skeleton of one of those infamous men whose sins brought upon the world the dire misfortune of the deluge."

His claim that the skeleton was human went largely unchallenged until 1811, when the bones were re-examined and identified as those of a prehistoric giant salamander. Despite this mark on his reputation, Scheuchzer's extensive writings provided many vital contributions to the field of alpine science.

ALPINE DRAGONS
As part of his survey of the region, Scheuchzer collected reports of the "alpine dragons" sighted by locals in remote valleys of the Swiss Alps. His findings were published in *Proof of the Existence of Dragons*, with his own engravings (left). He also describes several subspecies of this elusive creature.

JAMES HUTTON

FOUNDING FATHER OF MODERN GEOLOGY

SCOTLAND   1726–97

PHYSICIAN, CHEMIST, AGRICULTURALIST, and pioneering geologist, James Hutton was the first to consider the age of the Earth scientifically. In doing so, he encouraged future scientists to scour for evidence among the rock layers of mountains and the striations of glaciers. A product of the Scottish Enlightenment and a leading light of the Royal Society of Edinburgh, Hutton's major contribution was his theory of "Deep Time" – that the Earth was very much older than the estimates given by biblical scholars.

HERETICAL THINKER
Hutton, seen here with his geologist's hammer, overturned ancient beliefs about how and when the world was formed. His ideas were considered heresy by religious thinkers.

In 1749, Hutton was awarded his Doctor of Medicine, but he had doubts about committing his future to a medical career. Instead, after corresponding with an Edinburgh friend, James Davie, with whom he had previously conducted scientific experiments, the pair arrived at a scheme to put their chemistry expertise to profit. In 1750, Davie and Hutton went into partnership in the production of "sal ammoniac", or ammonium chloride – a salt used in the dyeing process, when working brass and tin, and as an ingredient of smelling salts. The chemical plant was a commercial success, but Hutton soon changed direction once again, perhaps a reflection of his inquisitive nature.

A LIFE'S WORK

- Establishes the **principles of geology as a science** in its own right

- Originates **one of the fundamental principles of geology** – Uniformitarianism

- **Is the first to propose** that the Earth's surface has evolved over an immense period of time

- **Clashes with the Church**, which declares that the Earth is only about 6,000 years old, and also with eminent scientists of the day

- Finds evidence to support his theory of the Earth's age in **layers of rock and sandstone in the Scottish Highlands**. His theory is later confirmed as accurate

FERTILE GROUND

Although not a farming family, the Huttons owned two farmsteads in the Scottish borders: one in the uplands and the other at a lower elevation. At the age of 24, Hutton resolved to become an agriculturalist. In 1752, he visited Norfolk to further his understanding of farming, and in 1754, he even ventured to Holland, Flanders, and Picardy to learn about animal husbandry.

Hutton took to the simplicity and hardships of rural life, and this newfound outlet for his interest in the natural world evidently stimulated his scientific mind. He made several journeys on foot to learn from other farmers, observing the natural phenomena that he passed en route. In a letter written in 1753, he revealed that he had "become very fond of studying the surface of the earth … looking with anxious curiosity, into every pit, or ditch, or bed of a river, that fell in [the] way."

Returning to the family farms in 1754, Hutton introduced agricultural improvements, including drainage ditches and fences, and more productive methods of ploughing, crop rotation, and plant and animal husbandry.

SHAKING THE FOUNDATIONS

It was during the groundwork on his farms that Hutton began to formulate his ideas on how rocks were formed. "Neptunism", the prevailing theory of the day, held that sediment from the Biblical flood had been compressed into rocks, and that fossils were the remains of plants and

animals that had perished in this catastrophic event. Hutton realized that this process had to be much longer and more ancient than was thought – the Earth's creation had been dated to 4004BCE, based on Biblical analysis – and began to investigate beyond the borders of his farms. In 1764, with his agricultural and chemical interests inseparable, Hutton took a geological tour of the north of Scotland with agriculturalist George Clerk-Maxwell.

An involvement in the construction of the Forth and Clyde canal from 1767 added to Hutton's geological understanding, but it wasn't until he conducted concerted fieldwork that his theories began to gather momentum. His quest for greater understanding drew him to the highlands and mountains of Scotland. In 1785, for example, he noticed granite – an igneous rock formed by volcanic activity – penetrating layers of schist – an older metamorphic rock – at Glen Tilt in the Scottish Highlands. Then, in 1787, he studied angular unconformities – layers of sedimentary rock laid at an angle on top of older, tilted, eroded rock – on the Isle of Arran, concluding that the phenomenon, which came to be known as the "Hutton Unconformity", was proof of separate phases of deposition. With further notable unconformities seen in Scotland – at Jedburgh and Siccar Point – the weight of geological evidence proved to Hutton that, far from emanating from a single event, the rocks of the Earth were evidence of "Deep Time", a continual process of geological compaction, erosion, and volcanic and tectonic activity.

THE RESULT … OF OUR PRESENT ENQUIRY IS, THAT WE FIND NO VESTIGE OF A BEGINNING, NO PROSPECT OF AN END "

JAMES HUTTON, FROM HIS *THEORY OF THE EARTH*

He wrote that "the result, therefore, of this physical enquiry, is that we find no vestige of a beginning, no prospect of an end." Crucially, he theorized that the fundamental force behind this never-ending process was the Earth's subterranean heat. Just as importantly, in his "Theory of Uniformitarianism", Hutton realized that these processes occur at constant rates, making it possible to estimate the age of actual formations of rock.

The legacy of Hutton's theories, which were dubbed "Plutonism" at the time, was to challenge the established "Neptunist" theory of the age and origins of the Earth, and even of the origin of species: he applied Uniformitariansim to the evolution of animals as well as geological processes. The Victorian geologist Sir Charles Lyell adopted and built upon Hutton's work, while his thoughts on natural selection were also read with keen interest by Charles Darwin.

THE SEARCH FOR PROOF
Hutton visited Arran, Scotland (below) in 1787 to make the first geological investigation of the island. He returned to Edinburgh satisfied that he had found the first critical field evidence he needed to support his Theory of the Earth.

THEORY OF THE EARTH

Based on his studies of rock formations in the highlands and mountains of Scotland, Hutton's *Theory of the Earth*, published in 1788, proposed that much of the land had once been sea bed, and that layers of rock had been distorted and pushed upwards over time. He suggested that this process had probably happened many times, meaning that the Earth was much older than Biblical scholars had previously thought. Hutton's concept of repeating cycles gradually won acceptance in the decades following his death.

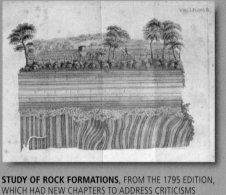

STUDY OF ROCK FORMATIONS, FROM THE 1795 EDITION, WHICH HAD NEW CHAPTERS TO ADDRESS CRITICISMS

MOUNTAINEERING INNOVATIONS

ICE AXE

THE FIRST ICE AXE WAS A COMBINATION OF TWO TOOLS. The alpenstock – a long wooden pole tipped with an iron spike that was used by shepherds to travel across snow and glaciers for centuries before mountaineering began – was combined with a smaller woodcutter's axe. Jacques Balmat, the Chamonix hunter who acted as a guide in the first ascent of Mont Blanc in 1786, was known to carry these separate tools, with the axe tucked into his waistband. Merged into a single tool in the early 1860s, the axe blade was rotated to become an adze, forming the first modern ice axe.

FORGING AN ICE TOOL

The first manufacturers of ice axes were alpine blacksmiths, such as the Simond family in Chamonix, who were exclusively making mountaineering products by 1861. The Grivels, on the other side of Mont Blanc in Italy, had been making climbing equipment since 1818. With the modern shape of a pick and an adze established, the metal pick – originally the same length as the adze – grew to become twice as long by the end of the 19th century. The shaft was a standard length of about 130cm (4ft 3in).

Other innovations, however, came to nothing. In 1864, a new type of ice pick that was curved in relation to the swinging arc of the arm was illustrated in the *Alpine Journal*. This made the pick more secure in ice, but was also awkward to remove – an inconvenience for mountain guides cutting steps for their clients. Since it was the guides who were either manufacturing or commissioning ice axes, there was little impetus to change their design. Because of their length, these ice axes were only

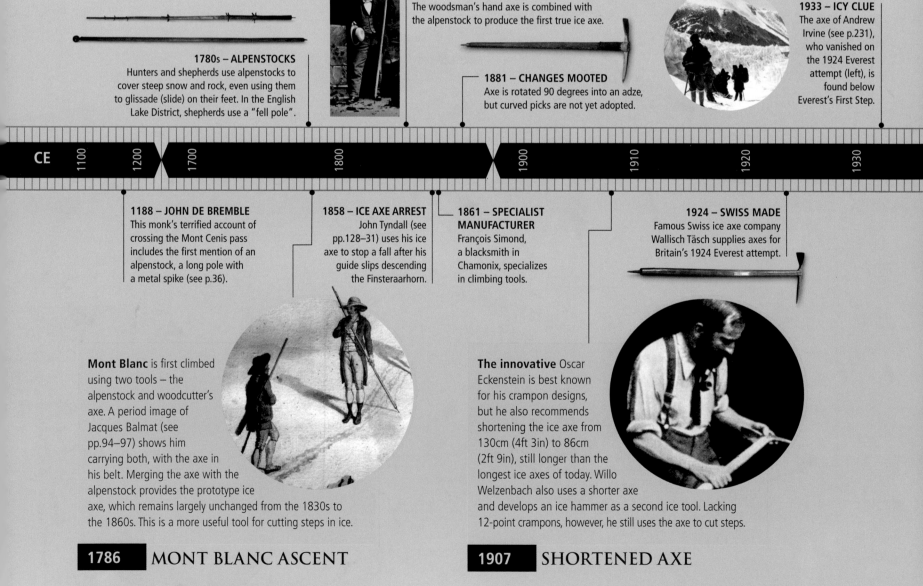

1840s – FIRST ICE AXES
The woodsman's hand axe is combined with the alpenstock to produce the first true ice axe.

1780s – ALPENSTOCKS
Hunters and shepherds use alpenstocks to cover steep snow and rock, even using them to glissade (slide) on their feet. In the English Lake District, shepherds use a "fell pole".

1881 – CHANGES MOOTED
Axe is rotated 90 degrees into an adze, but curved picks are not yet adopted.

1933 – ICY CLUE
The axe of Andrew Irvine (see p.231), who vanished on the 1924 Everest attempt (left), is found below Everest's First Step.

CE 1100 1200 1700 1800 1900 1910 1920 1930

1188 – JOHN DE BREMBLE
This monk's terrified account of crossing the Mont Cenis pass includes the first mention of an alpenstock, a long pole with a metal spike (see p.36).

1858 – ICE AXE ARREST
John Tyndall (see pp.128–31) uses his ice axe to stop a fall after his guide slips descending the Finsteraarhorn.

1861 – SPECIALIST MANUFACTURER
François Simond, a blacksmith in Chamonix, specializes in climbing tools.

1924 – SWISS MADE
Famous Swiss ice axe company Wallisch Täsch supplies axes for Britain's 1924 Everest attempt.

Mont Blanc is first climbed using two tools – the alpenstock and woodcutter's axe. A period image of Jacques Balmat (see pp.94–97) shows him carrying both, with the axe in his belt. Merging the axe with the alpenstock provides the prototype ice axe, which remains largely unchanged from the 1830s to the 1860s. This is a more useful tool for cutting steps in ice.

The innovative Oscar Eckenstein is best known for his crampon designs, but he also recommends shortening the ice axe from 130cm (4ft 3in) to 86cm (2ft 9in), still longer than the longest ice axes of today. Willo Welzenbach also uses a shorter axe and develops an ice hammer as a second ice tool. Lacking 12-point crampons, however, he still uses the axe to cut steps.

1786 MONT BLANC ASCENT

1907 SHORTENED AXE

of use as walking sticks and for cutting steps. In response, Oscar Eckenstein (see pp.196–97) designed a shorter ice axe measuring 86cm (33in), but this met with opposition from conservative British climbers. Although Willo Welzenbach (see pp.236–37) used shorter axes to great effect, and alpine axes did shrink as Eckenstein recommended, their design remained largely unchanged until the 1960s.

AGGRESSIVE AXES

In the mid-1960s, blacksmith and leading climber Yvon Chouinard (see pp.302–03) redesigned ice axes and developed a 55-cm (21-in) tool with a curved pick and sharp "teeth". Similar to the idea first proposed in 1864, he stated that "a curve compatible with the arc of the axe's swing would allow the pick to stay put better in the ice. I had noticed that a standard pick would often pop out when I placed my weight on it." Chouinard's "Zero" axes would prove popular, and 55cm (21in) is still considered an optimum length for a general-purpose alpine axe. At the

ICE CLIMBING TECHNIQUES

With crampons widely used by the 1950s, two common techniques were adopted: French style, where all the crampon points were applied to a slope with a flexed ankle, or the German and Austrian technique of front-pointing. With the arrival of short axes with curved or dropped picks in the late 1960s, front-pointing became ubiquitous. Modern ice protection – reliable and easier to place than earlier incarnations – has transformed climbers' confidence.

STEEP ICE EQUIPMENT EVOLUTION HAS ENABLED VERTICAL ICE WALLS TO BE SCALED

same time, in Scotland, climbers experimenting with front-pointing on crampons began to reheat the heads of their axes, angling the pick steeply before re-tempering them. Hamish MacInnes produced a model called the

"Terrordactyl", with a short shaft and a steeply angled pick ideal for climbing steep ice. With two of these tools, one in each hand, and front-point technique for the feet, step-cutting became obsolete, and climbing standards surged.

1940 – TROTSKY ASSASSINATED
Joseph Stalin's arch enemy, Leon Trotsky, is murdered with an ice axe by NKVD agent Ramón Mercador in Mexico.

1974 – SCOTTISH GENIUS
Hamish MacInnes designs and produces a dropped-pick ice axe, the Terrordactyl, with a metal shaft.

1990s – MODULAR SYSTEM DESIGNS
Replacing a single, steel axe-head, modular systems are developed that allow picks to be changed for different types of climbing.

2000s – LEASHLESS CLIMBING
Anatomical hand-grips allow climbers to dispense with wrist loops, making axe use more convenient.

1940   1950   1960   1970   1980   1990   2000

1950s – ICE DAGGER
Swiss guide Erich Friedli uses an ice dagger to make fast ascents of Willo Welzenbach's ice climbs. He also develops the tubular ice screw.

1978 – END OF WOOD
Safety standards are set for ice axes, ending the widespread use of wooden shafts.

1986 – CURVED SHAFTS
Curved shafts prevent the knuckles from bruising on ice and improve the arc of the swing.

From the mid 1960s, climbers in the US and Scotland experiment with ice axe design. Yvon Chouinard (right) and Tom Frost develop a curved pick with jagged teeth that improves security after placement. Hamish MacInnes, one of the leading lights of post-war Scottish climbing, produces the "Message", the first unbreakable all-metal ice axe. The introduction of wrist loops spreads the strain of hanging from an axe through the whole arm.

Shafts become curved or shaped to give the hand greater clearance and protection, enabling a more efficient swing radius for the axe. Materials such as carbon fibre and Kevlar reduce weight, and anatomically shaped grips remove the need for a leash. Modular systems allow climbers to use different axe heads for different styles of climbing. Thinner picks reduce the risk of ice "dinner-plating" (fracturing in large sheets).

1960s   ICE AXE REVOLUTION

2000s   RAPID DEVELOPMENT

HORACE-BÉNÉDICT DE SAUSSURE

PHYSICIST AND EARLY MOUNTAIN EXPLORER

SWITZERLAND   1740–99

A DISTINGUISHED SCIENTIST and an inveterate traveller, Horace-Bénédict de Saussure was the founder of "scientific alpinism". His years of journeying in the Alps, and his insatiable thirst for the tiniest details, formed the basis of his monumental, four-volume work *Voyages in the Alps*, and his theories on glaciation were far in advance of those of most of his contemporaries. Although he failed in his lifelong ambition to be the first to climb Mont Blanc, he made the second successful ascent of the mountain.

A LIFE'S WORK

- Visits Chamonix and **resolves to climb Mont Blanc**. He offers a prize to any man who can find a route to the summit; the money is claimed 26 years later by Jacques Balmat (see pp.94–97), one of the first two men to ascend the peak

- **Devotes his life to the study of the Western Alps**. His geological and other scientific observations there form the basis of his *Voyages in the Alps*, a book that **paves the way for glacial theory** and our understanding of how mountains form

- His life and work help **transform Europe's perception of the Alps**. Once feared and avoided, the mountains become respected for their **scientific and aesthetic appeal**

- **Leads two attempts on Mont Blanc** to conduct scientific experiments; on the second try he realizes his dream of reaching the summit

- **Spends 14 days making observations** on the crest of the Col du Géant with his son

- Becomes aware of the ability of glass to trap the Sun's heat and **creates the Western world's first solar energy collector**

De Saussure was 20 years old when he visited Chamonix, in the shadow of Mont Blanc, for the first time in 1760. From a privileged and cultured background, and just two years shy of a precocious appointment as professor of natural philosophy at the Geneva Academy, the one unconventional and disquieting aspect of his personality was his obsession with the Alps.

This early trip was strictly exploratory, spent in the lower foothills and glaciers of the great mountain, but so taken was de Saussure with the notion of reaching the summit, something no one had yet achieved, that he offered a reward to whoever should get there first.

He then returned to Geneva to pursue his university career, his yearning for the heights rather stifled by the disapproval of his wife, whom he chided: "you would rather see me as fat as a canon and asleep all day in the chimney corner than making the most sublime discoveries at the cost of a few ounces of weight and several weeks' absence from you."

NAVIGATIONAL AID
De Saussure took a keen interest in scientific instruments. Among the apparatus he carried up Mont Blanc in 1787 was this silver pocket compass and sundial.

Nonetheless, he made seven trips to the Alps between 1774 and 1784, exploring the area south to Piedmont and eastwards to the Bernese Oberland of Switzerland. As well as sheer curiosity about the nature of the terrain (at a time when Alpine maps were few and mostly misleading), he was driven by a desire to understand the formation of the mountains, and in particular the great glaciers that filled so many valleys with impenetrable sheets of ice.

GLACIAL THINKING

At first unable to break away wholly from Biblical notions of the Flood, de Saussure observed the stratification of rock layers in the Alps and finally concluded that these had been formed, not by a deluge in the time of Noah, but by a process of compression of one new layer onto the next. As to how glaciers moved, he reasoned that the heat of the Earth caused their bases to melt and that they then literally slid downhill under the pressure of their own weight; the knowledge that they are actually viscous and "flow", just like water, proved beyond him.

Typical of de Saussure's Alpine journeys was the one he undertook around Mont Blanc in 1778 in the company of two other scientists. His companions were tasked with taking

readings from a barometer and a magnetometer they had hauled into the mountains, while de Saussure's role was to make geological observations. To get the best possible results, the trio ascended Mont Buet, whose summit – at 3,099m (10,167ft) – gave them a perfect vantage point to measure the height of Mont Blanc using a sextant, and to conduct experiments on the adverse effects of high altitude on breathing.

I DID NOT BELIEVE MY EYES, IT SEEMED TO ME THAT IT WAS A DREAM, WHEN I SAW UNDER MY FEET THESE MAJESTIC SUMMITS, THESE FRIGHTENING NEEDLES "

HORACE-BÉNÉDICT DE SAUSSURE, ON REACHING THE SUMMIT OF MONT BLANC

A GENTLEMAN'S EXPEDITION
For his successful ascent of Mont Blanc in 1787, depicted here by Chrétien de Mechel, de Saussure was accompanied by 18 guides carrying not only scientific equipment, but also a bed complete with a mattress and a curtain. On the summit, he tested the boiling point of water, the temperature of the snow, and the pulses of his guides.

TRIUMPHANT PARTY DESCENDS
The 1787 party's descent of Mont Blanc was fast. They stopped for one night to camp at a point 500m (1,600ft) above the Grands Mulets, which de Saussure called "The rock of the happy return".

towards Mont Blanc, which, with its bright, brilliant snow, seemed almost alive. The rather ponderous party set off far too late the next morning, as the Bourrits sluggishly refused to stir before 6.15am. They pressed on upwards for five hours, until further progress was halted by a layer of soft snow. The group's chief guide, Pierre Balmat, went ahead to scout out conditions higher up the slopes, and returned with the news that the fresh snowfall made the way to the summit too treacherous to proceed.

TRYING AGAIN

Thwarted, de Saussure was forced to retreat back to the Aiguille, where he made further scientific observations before returning to Geneva. His disappointment was made more acute by the news the following August that Mont Blanc's summit had finally been achieved by Paccard and Jacques Balmat (see pp.94–97). Just five days after climbing Mont Blanc, Balmat arrived in Geneva to claim the prize that de Saussure had promised a quarter of a century before. There was clearly

De Saussure's other Alpine trips similarly combined science and exploration, such as the one in 1783 that took him past the Swiss lakes of Thun and Interlaken, where he paused to measure the depth and temperature of the water.

The eclectic breadth of his interests allowed him to make observations equally on the magnificent thunderstorms he observed, the very particular German dialects of the Val Formazza, and on the monks of the St Gotthard hospice, who regarded his geologist's mania for collecting interesting rock specimens as a type of strange mental disorder.

COMPULSION TO CLIMB

There remained one Alpine achievement for which de Saussure yearned, and that was the conquest of Mont Blanc. Already, however, there were others on the scent of the summit.

Marc Théodore Bourrit, the precentor of Geneva cathedral, and a rather fawning, self-seeking, admirer of de Saussure's, had tried and failed in 1783 with a young doctor, Michel-Gabriel Paccard (see pp.94–97). Bourrit and Paccard also mounted separate attempts the following year. Finally, in 1785, de Saussure was ready to tackle the mountain himself.

He felt compelled to invite Bourrit to join him, as his rival's 1784 expedition had opened up a route from the village of Bionassay that looked like a promising approach to the summit itself. Completing the party were Bourrit's 21-year-old son, Isaac, and four guides.

Making Base Camp near the Aiguille du Goûter rocks, de Saussure found that the thermometer he had brought along to test how boiling points varied according to altitude had failed. He consoled himself by looking up

MARC T BOURRIT

FRANCE   1739–1819

Bourrit occupies an ambivalent position in the history of alpine exploration.

Vain and self-promoting, his jealousy of other Alpinists' achievements often clouded his judgment and marred his relations with them. A self-appointed "Historian of the Alps", his efforts to scale the heights were hampered by his aversion to the cold and rain and constant attacks of vertigo, none of which endeared him to his climbing companions. Yet he was undeniably knowledgeable about the Alps, and, in 1783, he tried to climb Mont Blanc in the company of Paccard. He was deterred from continuing by the icy conditions, and an attempt the following year was said by Paccard to have been aborted because Bourrit had a headache brought on by the cold. His reputation today rests on his widely read and admired histories of the mountains.

> MY OBJECT WAS NOT ONLY TO REACH THE HIGHEST POINT, I WAS BOUND TO MAKE THE SCIENTIFIC OBSERVATIONS ... WHICH ALONE GAVE VALUE TO MY VENTURE

HORACE-BÉNÉDICT DE SAUSSURE, *VOYAGES IN THE ALPS*

SCIENTIFIC TOOLS
De Saussure's high-altitude meteorological studies were thwarted on his first Mont Blanc attempt by the failure of his thermometer.

not too much hard feeling between the two men, however as, in July 1787, de Saussure set off to make his second attempt on the mountain in the company of none other than Balmat.

Accompanying the pair into the Alps was de Saussure's wife, who made several short climbs and professed to have thoroughly enjoyed them. Marc Théodore Bourrit, who was doggedly following de Saussure's progress, begged to be allowed to join the attempt on the summit, but this time was brusquely rebuffed.

The party's departure was delayed for a week by heavy rain, but finally, on 1 August, the clouds broke and the expedition set out. Madame de Saussure stayed behind to follow the climbers' progress through a telescope.

HIGH-LEVEL RESEARCH

De Saussure rode for the first two hours on a mule, and then proceeded on foot between the Bossons and Taconnaz glaciers. After a climb of nearly seven hours, the group pitched camp at the top of the Montagne de la Côte. On the second day, their progress was hampered by the crossing of an icefall riven with crevasses, where one of the guides nearly fell to his death. The party finally made camp on the Grand Plateau, some of them now beginning to suffer altitude sickness. They passed a thoroughly uncomfortable night there, freezing cold and plagued by thirst.

They set off again the next morning at around 7am and covered the first 500m (1,600ft) fairly easily until a wide crevasse caused a delay, after which a rapidly weakening de Saussure was forced to call for ever more frequent halts.

The last 300m (1,000ft) to the top took two hours and so dispirited was de Saussure at the arduous nature of the ascent that, far from savouring the triumph, his initial feelings were "of anger, rather than of pleasure." He then settled down to enjoy the glorious panorama, even spying through his telescope a flag Madame de Saussure had unfurled to signify that she had seen her husband safely reach the summit. De Saussure spent the next four hours making scientific observations, until the gathering clouds forced the party back down the mountain.

A FAMILY EXPEDITION

The outbreak of enthusiasm that greeted de Saussure on his return to Geneva fuelled his appetite for further Alpine exploration. In 1788, he ventured onto the recently opened

Col du Géant, which leads past Mont Blanc to Courmayeur, intent on a lengthy stay to conduct a range of scientific experiments. It was a bold move, for few people had spent even one night at such high altitude, let alone a fortnight as de Saussure planned to do. He set out on 2 July, again accompanied by Jacques Balmat, but this time also taking along his son Théodore.

The approach to the Col du Géant was reasonably trouble-free, although the only suitable place for the camp proved to be a narrow ledge just 2m (7ft) wide with a stone shelter at the end, barely enough for de Saussure and Théodore's beds to lie side by side. Father and son undertook a scientific relay, the elder

conducting experiments until midnight, while the younger rose at 4am to commence a morning shift. Battered by thunderstorms and high winds, and with the cold sometimes freezing the water in their glasses, the pair remained in their high-altitude hovel for 14 days. Finally, the patience of Balmat and his fellow guides wore thin at the constant trips they were forced to make up and down to the Col bearing supplies and letters. The guides simply stopped bringing food and so, with their provisions almost totally exhausted, on 20 July the de Saussures made their way back down to Courmayeur.

De Saussure's Alpine days were not totally over. In 1789, he visited Zermatt and climbed one of the lower summits of Monte Rosa, pausing to stare with awe at the Matterhorn. Yet his many Alpine expeditions had damaged his health and he retired soon afterwards to Geneva. Towards the end of his life he completed the last volumes of his *Voyages in the Alps*, securing his reputation as a pioneer of alpine science.

THE CLIMBING SCIENTIST
De Saussure's mountaineering augmented his studies. From the top of Mont Blanc he noted that "a single glance dissipated doubts which years of work had not been able to clarify."

FRANZ JOSEF HUGI

MAVERICK GLACIOLOGIST AND CLIMBER

SWITZERLAND   1791–1855

GEOLOGIST, BOTANIST, TEACHER, AND CLERGYMAN, Franz Josef Hugi was one of the first alpine thinkers actively to study the movement of glaciers. From his base on the Unteraar Glacier in Switzerland's Bernese Alps, Hugi measured the progress of the ice over a period of three years, as well as undertaking climbing sorties on the surrounding peaks. Although some of his glacial theory was off the mark, Hugi's pioneering – if rather crude – fieldwork and mountaineering accomplishments are what set him apart.

A LIFE'S WORK

- Undertakes **research on Switzerland's Unteraar Glacier**, which supports the theory held by some scholars that **glaciers are not static**, and can advance and retreat huge distances

- As head teacher at a school for orphans, he **pioneers a new approach to teaching**, involving showing students real-life samples

- Excluding scientific equipment, his **expedition kit includes**: travel pharmacies, eye balm, Eau de Cologne, boot dubbing made from fish oil and grease, and wine "of excellent quality"

- Makes the **first genuine Alpine winter climb**, crossing the Strahlegg pass to observe the state of the glacier in winter conditions

- While studying the rocks of the Rottal area on the southwestern slopes of the **Jungfrau**, he makes a **failed attempt** on the mountain

- In 1828, is a member of the first party to **climb the Finsteraarhorn**, the highest peak of the Bernese Alps

Hugi was born the son of a miller in the village of Grenchen at the foot of the Jura mountains. After basic schooling, he went on to study theology in Bavaria in southeast Germany and the natural sciences in Vienna, Austria, before returning to Solothurn in Switzerland in 1819 to be ordained as a Roman Catholic priest.

As a priest, Hugi was appointed head teacher of the orphans' school in Solothurn, a post that enabled him to devote his time to teaching and studying the natural sciences. He applied himself with great enthusiasm, but not

everyone appreciated his methods. His approach to teaching, which included using plants, animals, and fossils in the classroom, was criticized as not befitting a classical education, while his interest in star-gazing, especially as a clergyman, was decried as "impious". Nevertheless, Hugi continued his own studies and activities and co-founded the Solothurn Natural History Society in 1823 as a forum for the reporting and debating of theories and findings. He also applied himself to gathering botanical and geological samples.

The nearby Jura mountains proved a rich source of materials and Hugi took to roaming their cliffs and crags in search of fossils.

LIVING ON ICE

Hugi's most significant contribution came in the field of glaciology. An area of study that was attracting growing attention, thanks largely to the 18th-century work of Johann Jacob Scheuchzer (see pp.54–55) and Horace-Bénédict de Saussure (see pp.60–63), empirical data on the actual behaviour of glaciers was nevertheless scarce. Evidence of the movement of glaciers came in the form of "glacial erratics", boulders that were conspicuously positioned in locations that would have been impossible had some external agent not moved them there, so Hugi set out to gather information on how such glacial motion could occur.

Switzerland's Unteraar Glacier was chosen as the site for Hugi's investigations, and in the summer of 1827 he set off to commence a season of glacial study. Travelling in an entourage that at times numbered up to a dozen people – including mountain guides, artists, botanists, and natural history enthusiasts – Hugi had a crude stone shelter built to act as the "expedition" headquarters. From this base on the surface of the glacier, he went about

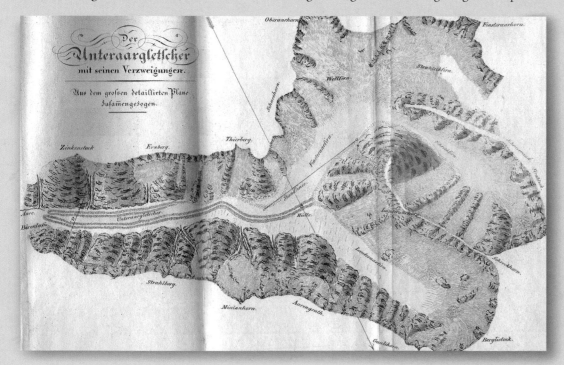

ALPINE ADVENTURE
Hugi's map of the Unteraar Glacier was reproduced in his *Naturhistorische Alpenreise*. In the same volume he illustrated the boulders used to mark glacial progress.

implementing the methods to prove his belief that the glacier was not static, but in motion. In a move that was primitive but effective, Hugi drove a series of stakes into the ice of the glacier and chiselled marks on the adjacent rocks, which he hoped would allow him to measure movement.

MOUNTAIN DISTRACTION

Glaciers not being known for their rapid pace of movement, Hugi and his party engaged in a variety of activities to pass the time. As well as conducting geological studies, the attraction of the surrounding peaks proved impossible to ignore. Hugi returned to the Unteraar Glacier every summer between 1827 and 1830, but in early August 1828 he resolved to climb the Jungfrau, a 4,158-m (13,642-ft) peak nearby, via the Inner Rottal Ridge on the Southwest flank of the mountain. He did not make it to the summit, but the experience whetted his appetite for high-altitude exploration.

Hugi travelled on to the Finsteraarhorn – at 4,274m (14,022ft) the highest peak in the Bernese Alps, and the highest outside the main chain of the Alps – attempting an ascent from the western side with four companions on 19 August. Met by bad weather during the climb, the party was forced to retreat after coming within 200m (600ft) of the summit – Hugi later wrote that they had been in mortal danger. Undeterred, he tried again a year

later, and on 10 August 1829, the guides Jakob Leuthold and Johann Währen reached the summit (Hugi himself was injured and unable to cross a steep ice slope beneath the summit).

After concluding his fieldwork in 1830, Hugi was appointed professor of natural sciences at Solothurn University in 1833. He published his glacier findings in several volumes, concluding, somewhat controversially, that glacial motion derived from internal movement, as well as from the mechanical operation of the sheer weight of ice. He also theorized that glacial erratics were deposited by separate ice floes, rather than by the main

glacier itself. These beliefs brought him into opposition with other glaciologists, notably Louis Agassiz (see pp.72–73), whose more precise work gradually superseded Hugi's. Nevertheless, Hugi's fieldwork was an important stepping-stone in understanding how the great glaciers worked, and his mountaineering achievements made him a pioneer of his day.

SLIPPERY SLOPES
Hugi and his team were among the first to attempt the Jungfrau from the southwest. Inadequate planning hindered their progress up the mountain, and as they crossed the Rottal Glacier (below), mishap lurked at every crevasse.

SCIENTIFIC MIND

For Hugi, an interest in the mountains and glaciers of his native Switzerland was just one component of a desire to build a greater understanding of how the natural world worked. He was also keen to enthuse others with this thirst for learning, donating his sizeable collection of fossil and mineral specimens to the city of Solothurn, and designing a botanical garden for the school that included a range of exotic plants, such as Chinese hemp, maize, sugarcane, and ginger.

HUGI AND COLLEAGUES, IN THE BOTANICAL GARDEN OF SOLOTHURN UNIVERSITY

JAMES DAVID FORBES

PIONEER OF BRITISH MOUNTAINEERING

SCOTLAND   1809–68

A GIFTED SCIENTIST and a capable high-altitude explorer, James David Forbes was one of the first Britons to be considered a true Alpine mountaineer. Drawn to the Alps in search of scientific discovery, Forbes found a landscape of beauty and inspiration that satisfied both his thirst for mountain exploration and his urge to push back the boundaries of understanding. He is largely remembered today for a long-running dispute on the motion of glaciers with rival scientists Louis Agassiz and John Tyndall.

MAPPING THE MOUNTAINS
In 1873, Forbes's biographers published this map of the Mer de Glace to illustrate his work. The red marks show where he set up his trigonometrical stations. No one had measured from such a height before and the results were more accurate.

Born into a noble Scottish family in Edinburgh, Forbes's early life was marked by tragedy and illness – his mother died when he was just 18 months old – and as a result he was educated at home, a factor that may have contributed to his single-minded, and rather aloof, nature. Although his father favoured a career in law for his son, Forbes's true calling began to emerge when he was 17. In 1826, during a tour of Europe with his family, he showed a particular interest in Italy's Mount Vesuvius. Not content just to admire the smouldering volcano from afar, Forbes conducted detailed investigations into the geological nature of the area.

On returning to his studies at Edinburgh University, Forbes was evidently spurred by his experience of scientific fieldwork. He showed a particular aptitude for physics, but his achievements came not only in the classroom. Writing anonymously, he submitted two papers on his Italian investigations to the *Edinburgh Journal of Science*, and then wrote an eight-part series entitled *Physical Notices of the Bay of Naples* when his initial submissions were accepted.

PRECOCIOUS SCIENTIST

Forbes's scientific writings were remarkably accomplished for a man of just 19, particularly since his scientific training was in its infancy. His work brought him to the attention of the wider scientific community, including the pioneering geologist Sir Charles Lyell. He soon abandoned the idea of practising law.

After furthering his scientific career in Cambridge and London – including a spell canvassing for the establishment of the British Association for the Advancement of Science, which would later lead to an important introduction – Forbes returned to Europe

in 1832, travelling up the River Rhine to Switzerland in order to make further scientific contacts. He became professor of natural sciences at Edinburgh University a year later, an appointment that led him to undertake scientific research across western Europe.

ICY INVESTIGATIONS

Forbes had long been an admirer of the natural world and exploratory forays became a feature of his travels at home and abroad. While conducting fieldwork in Scotland's western highlands and islands in 1836, he made an ascent of Sgurr Alasdair, at 993m (3,258ft) the highest mountain on the Isle of Skye.

In 1840, he made a connection that gave him access to the highest scientific hunting grounds of all – at a British Association meeting in Glasgow, he was invited by Louis Agassiz (see pp.72–73) to visit Switzerland's Unteraar Glacier. The following year, Forbes travelled to the icy laboratory where the Swiss scientist conducted his fieldwork, and became hooked on glaciology himself. In 1842, he began to conduct his own fieldwork on the Mer de Glace above the Chamonix valley, measuring the velocity of the

MOUNTAINEERING SCIENTIST
As part of his scientific research, Forbes made numerous minor ascents in the Alps and in Norway, including the first British ascent of the 3,000-m (10,000-ft) Wandfluhhorn (the peak in the foreground on the far right) in 1841.

A LIFE'S WORK

- Is recommended for **fellowship of the Royal Society of Edinburgh** at the **age of 20**, but has to wait until he reaches the minimum age of 21 before taking up the honour

- During a lecture tour, he demonstrates his **theory of glacial motion** with the aid of a home-made glacier consisting of glue mixed with plaster of Paris creeping slowly down an inclined trough

- Publishes *Travels Through the Alps of Savoy*, the first book describing the mountains and glaciers of the Alps to be written by a Briton; it becomes **a landmark study**, invaluable both geologically and for early mountaineers

- Introduces his long-time guide Auguste Balmat to the young Alfred Wills (see pp.118–19), **bridging the gap** between the age of **scientific exploration** and the coming **Golden Age** of alpinism

HAPPY THE MOUNTAIN TRAVELLER WHO... STARTS ON HIS ... DAY'S WALK AMONG THE ALPS ... BRUSHING THE DEW BEFORE HIM AND, ARMED WITH HIS STAFF, MAKES FOR THE HILL-TOP

JAMES DAVID FORBES

ice on the surface of the glacier and at different depths, at different times of day, and in different seasons. He realized that the veined, ribboned structure of the ice was created by stresses within the glacier, which led to the theory of plasticity – that the ice moved not as a brittle, rigid mass, but like a viscous liquid.

UNDER THE SPELL OF THE ALPS

High-mountain travel was an integral component of Forbes's studies, and an aspect of his work that he evidently relished. He described it as "a satisfaction and freedom from restraint", which would "dispel anxiety and invite to sustained exertion." In 1841, he accompanied Agassiz on the fourth ascent of the 4,158-m (13,642-ft) Jungfrau, becoming the first non-Swiss to climb the peak. In 1850, he spent time exploring the Chamonix area, making a first crossing of the 3,264-m (10,709-ft) Fenêtre de Saleinaz near Mont Blanc.

Forbes had a mountaineering tick-list that matched his scientific credentials, but he did not achieve the same success in his relationships with his peers. He fell out with Agassiz over who had come up with the theory of plasticity, and became embroiled in a dispute with physicist John Tyndall (see pp.128–31), who claimed not only that Forbes's theories were incorrect, but had been stolen from an earlier amateur glaciologist. Nevertheless, Forbes published more than 100 scientific papers on glaciers and geology, produced an important study on the boiling point of water at different altitudes, and wrote several books about his travels in the Alps.

ALFRED WEGENER
GERMANY   1880–1930

Half a century after the death of Forbes, Alfred Wegener was another scientist who struggled to convince the scientific community of the validity of his theories.

Born in Berlin, Wegener studied physics, astronomy, and the developing field of meteorology before gaining a PhD in 1905. Today, he is best known as the originator of the theory of continental drift. Comparing the coastline of the world's continents on a map, he realized that various landmasses – such as the Atlantic coasts of Africa and South America – fit together like a jigsaw. Investigation of the geology and fossil record lent support to his theory, which explained how mountain chains, such as the Himalaya, were pushed up over millions of years as landmasses collided.

MOUNTAIN PORTRAIT

MONT BLANC

STRADDLING THE BORDER BETWEEN ITALY AND FRANCE, Mont Blanc – Monte Bianco in Italy – is the highest mountain in Western Europe at 4,808m (15,771ft). Taller than its closest rival by 163m (568ft), Mont Blanc's scale feels suitably grand, and its various satellites make up the finest group of glaciated peaks in the Alps. The range's excellent granite has attracted generations of alpinists, making Mont Blanc mountaineering's most popular testing-ground.

Mont Blanc is a peak with a split personality. Seen from the northern, French side, rearing over Chamonix and the Arve Valley, the mountain is less impressive – a distant, snowy hump overlooking a vast spread of easy-angled glaciers. This aspect was the first to be climbed, in the wave of 18th-century exploratory zeal begun by Horace-Bénédict de Saussure (see pp.60–63).

On the southern, Italian side, towering above the Aosta Valley, Mont Blanc's character is far more impressive. Steep, mixed faces of rock and snow are bounded by the dramatic Brouillard, Innominata, and

Peuterey ridges. The remote Brouillard Face is orientated to the southeast, its Hypercouloir a classic route from the 1980s. On the other side of the Innominata is the Frêney Glacier, bounded to the north by the Peuterey Ridge. Stretching north beyond this, and facing east, is the Brenva Face, and the shadowy north-facing Grand Pilier d'Angle. This aspect of the mountain has seen a succession of exciting new routes, from the bold Brenva Spur in 1865 to the magnificent Divine Providence in 1983 – still one of most ambitious climbs yet attempted in the Alps.

IN PROFILE

Name: Mont Blanc

Location: Haute-Savoie, France/Italy

Height: 4,808m (15,771ft)

Range: Mont Blanc massif, Alps

Notable features: Glaciated northern aspect, steep granite southern aspect

First ascent: Michel-Gabriel Paccard, Jacques Balmat, 1786

First female ascent: Maria Paradis, 1808

First ascent via the Goûter Ridge route: M Anderegg, J J Bennen, P Perren, L Stephen, F Tuckett, 1861

First winter ascent: Isabella Straton, J Charlet, S Couttet, 1876

First ascent of the Brenva Face: J and M Anderegg, A W Moore, F and H Walker, G Mathews, 1865

Fastest ascent: 5hr 10min 14sec for a round trip to and from Chamonix, by Swiss Pierre-André Gobet in 1990

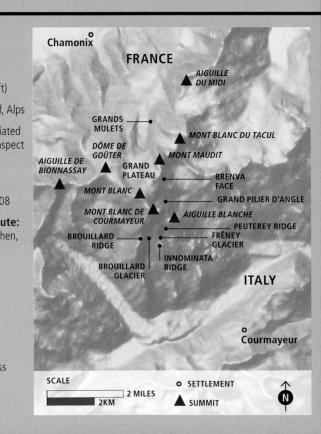

Chamonix

FRANCE

AIGUILLE DU MIDI

GRANDS MULETS

DÔME DE GOÛTER

MONT BLANC DU TACUL

AIGUILLE DE BIONNASSAY

GRAND PLATEAU

MONT MAUDIT

BRENVA FACE

MONT BLANC

GRAND PILIER D'ANGLE

MONT BLANC DE COURMAYEUR

AIGUILLE BLANCHE

PEUTEREY RIDGE

BROUILLARD RIDGE

FRÊNEY GLACIER

INNOMINATA RIDGE

BROUILLARD GLACIER

ITALY

Courmayeur

SCALE

2 MILES

2KM

○ SETTLEMENT

▲ SUMMIT

N

CLIMBING ROUTES

The Grand Pilier d'Angle and Brenva Face, seen here, are home to about 25 long and often serious routes, which end close to the summit of Mont Blanc de Courmayeur and Mont Blanc itself. This face is more accessible and safer to approach than the Frêney and Brouillard. While the Brenva was once a testing-ground for would-be stars, the harder routes of the Grand Pilier d'Angle are now in fashion.

GRAND PILIER D'ANGLE
— **DIVINE PROVIDENCE**
(P Gabbarou, F Marsigny, 1984) Now climbed free, this 900-m (2,950-ft) route combines remoteness and technicality.

BONATTI GOBBI
(W Bonatti, T Gobbi, 1957) 900m (3,000ft) in length up loose rock and then icy mixed ground.

❶ **Peuterey Ridge** Climbers completing routes on the Grand Pilier d'Angle face another six hours to reach the summit via this ridge before descending.

— **CECCHINEL-NOMINÉ ROUTE**
(W Cecchinel, C Nominé, 1971) The best mixed climb on the face and probably the safest line.

PEUTEREY RIDGE
— **DAMES ANGLAISES RIDGE**
(J Eccles, M Payot, A Payot, 1877) Geologist James Eccles first climbed the upper section of the Peuterey Ridge in 1877. The longer, now standard route climbs up from the Frêney Ridge.

❷ **The upper section** of the Frêney Face and its soaring pillars, including Central Pillar, which was first climbed in 1961.

❸ **The upper section** of the Brouillard Ridge was climbed by the influential British climber Geoffrey Winthrop Young.

BRENVA FACE
— **THE PEAR BUTTRESS ROUTE**
(T G Brown, A Graven, A Aufdenblatten, 1933) A difficult and dangerous line, 1,300m (4,265ft) long.

— **ROUTE MAJOR**
(T G Brown, F Smythe, 1928) The best route on the Brenva Face, safer than its neighbours, but with strenuous climbing at 4,400m (14,435ft).

RED SENTINEL ROUTE
(T G Brown, F Smythe, 1928) A masterpiece of route-finding but with many potential dangers.

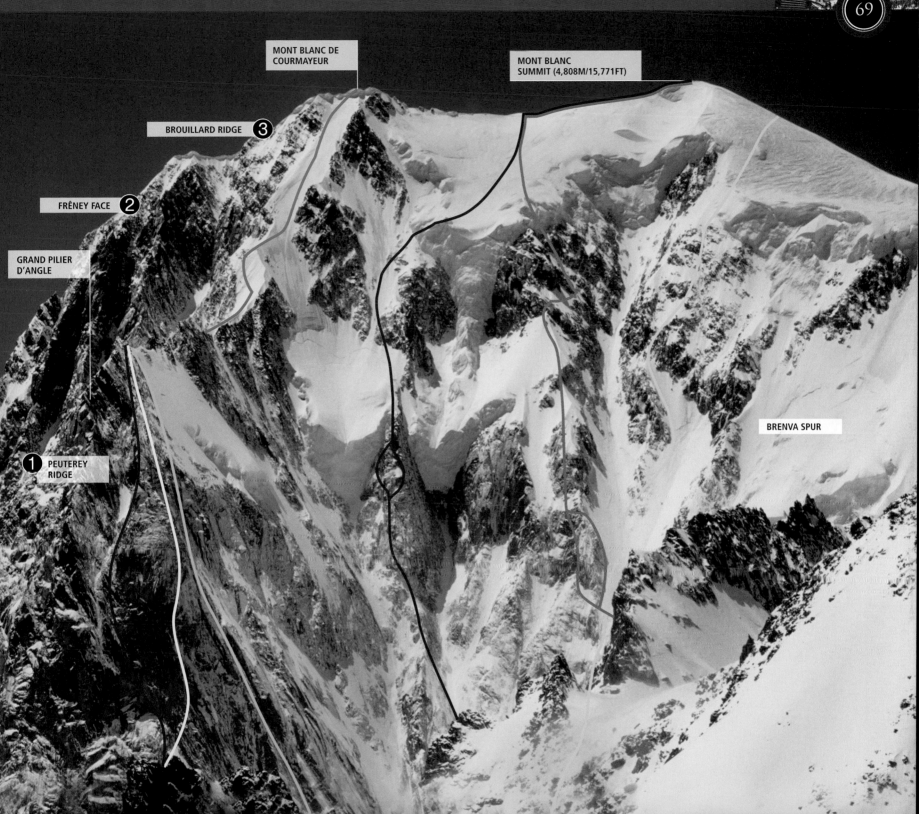

MONT BLANC DE
COURMAYEUR

MONT BLANC
SUMMIT (4,808M/15,771FT)

BROUILLARD RIDGE ③

FRÊNEY FACE ②

GRAND PILIER
D'ANGLE

BRENVA SPUR

① PEUTEREY
RIDGE

MOUNTAIN FEATURES

Ⓐ **East side** This aerial shot was taken over the summit of one of Mont Blanc's satellites, the Aiguille Verte. In front is the east side of Mont Blanc.

Ⓑ **Snowy summit** A week of acclimatization is required before attempting the summit, which is nearly 5km (3 miles) above sea level. Any less time risks altitude sickness.

Ⓒ **Mer de Glace** This famous glacier starts to the east of Mont Blanc. It moves at about 1cm (½in) per hour.

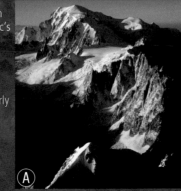

Ⓐ

Ⓑ

Ⓒ

ALEXANDER VON HUMBOLDT

EXPLORER, VOLCANOLOGIST, AND ICON OF SCIENCE

PRUSSIA   1769–1859

A PIONEERING EXPLORER and natural scientist whose meticulous approach laid the foundations for an evidence-based scientific method, von Humboldt's travels also took him to a series of mountain environments. Regarded as the founding father of the modern field of geography, his multi-disciplinary approach included contributions to the fields of geology, volcanology, and glaciology. On a five-year trip to South America, he broke the world altitude record in an attempted ascent of Chimborazo in Ecuador.

A LIFE'S WORK

- **Scales several South American volcanoes**, unaware of the dangers of high-altitude climbing. On Chimborazo he notes the presence of "enormous heaps of ice … covered with sand, and, in the same manner as at the Peak, far below the inferior limit of the perpetual snows"
- **On Chimborazo**, he reaches a height of 5,878m (19,286ft) before turning back
- Makes an **important contribution to cartography** by using shading to depict relief on his map of New Spain
- **Publishes the findings of his South American expeditions** in 30 volumes over a period of 29 years
- **Is the first to propose** that South America was once joined to Africa
- Leaves a legacy that comes to be known as **"Humboldtian science"** – the holistic view that the whole of nature can be investigated and explained through the collection of data

In common with many of the great polymaths of his day, Alexander von Humboldt was born into a life of privilege. Such was his childhood interest in collecting specimens that he was nicknamed "the little apothecary", but it was not until he studied at the prestigious Göttingen University at the age of 20 that he received any formal scientific education.

SAILING FOR THE NEW WORLD
In 1792, he took a job in Berlin as assessor of mines in order to cement his scientific knowledge, performing his duties with such rigour and efficacy that he was soon promoted. Four years later, following the death of his mother, he inherited a substantial income and used it to pursue his ambition of applying his talent as a naturalist to the field of exploration.

Scientific expeditions were not new to von Humboldt: he had toured the Rhine valley in 1789, conducted geological and botanical surveys in Switzerland and Italy in 1795, and undertaken fieldwork as part of his job as mines assessor. Following his inheritance, he was invited on an Antarctic circumnavigation under Frenchman Nicolas Baudin, but when this expedition failed to get off the ground, he travelled to Marseille in France in the hope of joining a Swedish party bound for Egypt.

His plans were foiled again, but he soon obtained an audience with the Spanish king, Carlos II, in Madrid and convinced him that scientific opportunities lay in the New World. He was duly granted passage on a Spanish ship bound for the country's dominions in South America and sailed from Cadiz in June 1799.

VOLCANO FLOWERS
Von Humboldt found the slopes of Chimborazo covered in a blue haze of forget-me-nots. He discovered 60,000 new plants on his South American travels.

While mountaineering was never an objective in its own right for von Humboldt, he wasn't shy of taking on the challenge in the name of scientific enquiry.

HIGH-ALTITUDE HIATUS
It was during a stop-over at Tenerife during the voyage to the New World that he climbed Mount Teide, a volcano 3,718m (12,198ft) in height that had last been active in 1798. Although von Humboldt was modest about the climb, claiming "we see almost nothing but what has been already seen and described by former travellers", his account of the ascent is peppered with botanical, geological, and meteorological observations.

Setting out on 21 June 1799, his party climbed halfway up the volcano before spending the night sleeping in the open "on a heap of burnt rocks". Rising at 3am, von Humboldt ascended the upper slopes of the volcano, passing a "cavern of ice" of which he wrote, "the ice is preserved in it on account of its mass … not, like the true glaciers of the Alps, fed by the snow waters that flow from the summits of the mountains." The final approach to the summit

OUR HANDS AND FACES WERE FROZEN, WHILE OUR BOOTS WERE BURNT BY THE SOIL ON WHICH WE WALKED

ALEXANDER VON HUMBOLDT ON MOUNT TEIDE, TENERIFE

was made with difficulty: "We ascended the Piton by grasping these half decomposed scoriæ [volcanic rocks], the sharp edges of which remained often in our hands. We employed nearly half an hour to scale a hill, the perpendicular height of which is scarcely ninety toises [175m/575ft]".

REACHING NEW HEIGHTS

Von Humboldt's five years in the New World included expeditions in Venezuela, Cuba, Colombia, Ecuador, Peru, and the United States. His primary interest was to study and catalogue the flora, fauna, ethnography, and geology of the previously undocumented lands, and he found his curiosity taking him to the rocky mountains of the Andes.

While von Humboldt's primary interest was the natural history of the lands he passed through – he could not resist experimenting on electric eels – rather than the climbs he undertook, his expedition reports offer glimpses of the methods employed in the conquering of summits. Exploring near the River Orinoco, he "climbed with difficulty, and not without danger of falling to a great depth below, a steep and perfectly bare granite precipice. It would be

GRAND OLD MAN

After returning to Europe from his travels, von Humboldt devoted the rest of his life to writing up his findings. His five-volume masterwork *Kosmos* was still in progress when he died in 1859. His greatest contribution to the mountain sciences came in the fields of geology and volcanology. He regarded the study of glaciers as "the duty of those natural philosophers who visit the Alps of Switzerland". In the wider geological field, his studies of igneous rocks provided further evidence against Neptunism.

VON HUMBOLDT IN HIS STUDY, AGED 86, FROM A PAINTING BY EDUARD HILDEBRANDT, 1855

hardly possible to keep one's footing on the smooth surface, if it were not for large crystals of feldspar, which, resisting 'weathering', project as much as an inch from the face of the rock."

Travelling overland from Colombia to Ecuador in 1801, von Humboldt crossed the Cordillera Real. In 1802, he explored a number of volcanoes in the region, including Pichincha (4,784m/15,696ft), Cotopaxi (5,896m/19,344ft), and Chimborazo

(6,268m/20,565ft). It was during his attempt on the last, which was thought at the time to be the world's highest mountain, that he set the modern altitude record. Although he didn't reach the summit, turning back due to altitude sickness, his party climbed to 5,878m (19,286ft), the highest documented altitude of any traveller at the time.

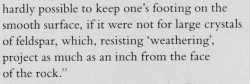

VOLCANOLOGIST IN THE FIELD
In South America, von Humboldt (below, with Cotopaxi in the background) correctly surmised that volcanos form in linear groups that correspond to subterranean fissures in the Earth's crust.

LOUIS AGASSIZ

CHAMPION OF THE "ICE AGE" THEORY

SWITZERLAND   1807–73

ONE OF THE BEST-KNOWN NATURAL SCIENTISTS of the mid-19th century, glaciologist, zoologist, and palaeontologist Louis Agassiz contributed to the new scientific theory that a recent "Ice Age" had once gripped the Earth. However, unlike his contemporaries, he argued – in persuasive and dramatic prose – that this glaciation had taken the form of a vast sheet of ice. Building on the earlier work of his compatriot Franz Josef Hugi, Agassiz undertook landmark fieldwork on Switzerland's Unteraar Glacier to support his theories.

A LIFE'S WORK

- Accepts his first professional position as a professor of natural history at Neuchâtel in Switzerland; his first project, a five-volume work on fish fossils, **helps forge his reputation as a naturalist**

- Takes up the study of glaciers as something of a sideline to his other work, but his intense research **revolutionizes geology** and **establishes the foundations of glaciology**

- Lives on the Unteraar Glacier in order **to investigate the structure and movement of the ice**; the conclusions of his experiments there support the **Ice Age theory**, which proposes that past glacial movement is responsible for modern geological configurations

- His **methods for measuring** glacial movement are soon carried out on other glaciers in the Alps

- **Moves to the US to teach zoology and geology** at Harvard University, becoming renowned for his innovative teaching methods, and for instituting new learning facilities

Louis Agassiz was born in the village of Môtiers in the French-speaking part of Switzerland, the son of a Lutheran pastor. After his schooling at Lausanne he studied medicine and natural sciences at Zurich, Heidelberg, and Munich, achieving doctorates in philosophy in 1829 and medicine in 1830. He made his first scholarly mark by compiling a report on a collection of Brazilian freshwater fish, and became interested in the fossilized fish of Lake Neuchâtel, having been encouraged into palaeontology by Alexander von Humboldt (see pp.70–71).

FROM FISH TO ICE

Agassiz was appointed professor of natural history at the University of Neuchâtel in 1832, and began to dabble in the nascent field of glaciology. While he was first and foremost a natural scientist, his position of influence meant that his scientific views received considerable attention. As president of the Swiss Natural

History Society, he was ideally placed to pick up the theories of the day, while his contacts with overseas scientists, particularly members of the Geological Society and Royal Society in London, ensured a ready audience for his views.

It was in conjunction with the German naturalist Karl Schimper and the Swiss geologist Jean de Charpentiers that the idea of a recent "Ice Age" was first mooted. Although credit for the term probably lies with Schimper, who published a paper, *Ueber Die Eiszeit* ("About the Ice Age"), in 1837, the idea that such features as glacial erratics, moraines, and scored rocks indicated the extent of the ice was not new. Agassiz's most significant contribution – and the theory to which his contemporaries, particularly Charpentiers, objected most strongly – was the notion that extensive ice sheets had covered the Alps and much of the higher latitudes.

MODERN SCIENTIST
On his research expeditions to the Unteraar Glacier, Agassiz took with him the most modern scientific equipment of the day, including a brass microscope similar to this one.

In an 1837 address, Agassiz correctly likened this ice sheet to the glacial ice of Greenland, a theory he reiterated in his 1840 *Études sur les glaciers* ("Studies on the Glaciers"). While this work was being prepared for publication, Agassiz gave lectures in Britain to an enthralled Victorian public. His work reportedly turned "geologists glacier-mad". Most significantly, he visited sites in Scotland with his friend William

SINCE I SAW THE GLACIERS, I AM QUITE OF A SNOWY HUMOUR, AND WILL HAVE THE WHOLE SURFACE OF THE EARTH QUITE COVERED WITH ICE

LOUIS AGASSIZ

ILLUSTRATING THE ICE AGE
Agassiz came to the attention of European and US geologists with his illustrated *Studies on the Glaciers* (right), which showed that, in the relatively recent past, Switzerland had been covered by a vast ice cap whose meltwaters carried great tracts of sand and gravel.

Buckland, an English geologist, and saw further evidence of glaciation, adding more proof to his theory.

GLACIER STUDIES AND MOUNTAIN FORAYS

Though he claimed to work "as an amateur, devoting my summer vacations, with friends desirous of sharing my leisure, to excursions in the Alps, for the sake of relaxation" Agassiz's fieldwork reached a level of detail and precision that surpassed any previous investigations.

In August 1838, he visited the glaciers of Mont Blanc in France, in 1839 the Matterhorn on the Swiss-Italian border and Monte Rosa in Switzerland, and in 1840 began fieldwork on the Unteraar Glacier in Switzerland's Bernese Alps, formerly the theatre of operations of Franz Josef Hugi (see pp.64–65).

Agassiz and his companions took up residence on the glacier, building a shelter under a large rock, which they reinforced with dry-stone walling. From this base, which soon came to be known as the "Hôtel des Neuchâtelois", Agassiz and his team deployed a range of instruments, from barometers, thermometers, and equipment for measuring humidity, to microscopes and a boring apparatus. They set about surveying the annual location of 18 prominent rocks and through this were able to calculate the rate of motion of different parts of the glacier.

Agassiz took full advantage of his summer seasons in the Alps, climbing a number of prominent peaks around the Unteraar Glacier.

With the experience of Jakob Leuthold and Johann Währen – the guides who had led Hugi up the Finsteraarhorn in 1828 and 1829 – at his disposal, Agassiz and his party crossed the 3,315-m (10,876-ft) Strahlegg Pass in late August 1840.

On the small summit plateau, Agassiz took measurements and made observations. The following year, he and a party including Scottish geologist James David Forbes (see pp.66–67) reached the precipitous, mist-shrouded summit of the Jungfrau (4,158m/13,642ft) with the assistance of ladders, ropes, "a little bread and wine, in case of exhaustion", and step-cutting and trail-breaking from Jakob Leuthold.

Alongside his glaciological work, Agassiz continued to press on with his zoological studies. In 1846, this took him from the ice of Europe to the United States, where he took up a professorship at Harvard University and revolutionized the study of natural history in his adopted homeland.

However, his later career and scientific judgment were not wholly without blemish. In 1865, for example, he travelled to Brazil, where he was convinced he saw glacial landforms. In fact, there have never been large glaciers in Brazil during any of the recent Ice Ages.

SCIENTIFIC RACISM

Today, the biggest stain on Agassiz's reputation was his lifelong opposition to Darwin's theory of evolution and his belief in "polygenism", the theory that different racial groups have unequal attributes and separate origins, which he developed during his time in the United States. At the core of Agassiz's "scientific racism" was the assertion that the white race was superior to all other races, and he found a willing audience for his lectures in the southern slave-owning states of the US. This theory was countered by Darwin, who considered racial differences to be superficial and argued that all races had a common origin, and also by many Christians, who believed that it was a denial of the biblical story of creation. In recent years, his name has been removed from many landmarks and institutions that once bore it as a consequence of his racist views.

Despite these issues, Agassiz had been an Alpine protagonist in the truest sense, conducting fieldwork and scaling mountains with as much gusto as any before or since.

PROBING THE ICE

Agassiz made use of the latest scientific apparatus to pore over the ice of the Unteraar Glacier. An iron auger – a drill-like boring apparatus – mounted on a winch was driven into the ice to a depth of 50m (165ft), allowing him to study the variations in the composition, temperature, and humidity of the glacier throughout its depth. This new technique, along with the duration and systematic methodology of his glacier study, allowed Agassiz to reach a fuller understanding of glaciology than anyone before him. Measurements of the movement and temperature of the ice at different times of day, and in different seasons of the year, revealed a more complete picture of the behaviour of the ice.

HARVARD PROFESSOR AGASSIZ USED THE LATEST SCIENTIFIC METHODS IN HIS TEACHING OF GEOLOGY

MOUNTAIN LIVES

ICE MUMMIES

WHILE SEARCHING THE SUMMITS OF THE ANDES for remnants of the Inca, US anthropologist and mountaineer Johan Reinhard made a series of startling discoveries that challenged perceptions of the capabilities of ancient peoples. He uncovered a number of Inca ritual sites at an elevation of more than 6,700m (22,000ft), the most chilling of which included the mummified remains of infants, seemingly left to die as sacrifices to the Inca gods.

The Inca empire in South America – which spanned thousands of kilometres of mountainous terrain across parts of present-day Colombia, Ecuador, Peru, Bolivia, Chile, and Argentina – was an advanced civilization truly at home at altitude. Even its capital city, Cuzco, lay at an elevation of 3,310m (10,860ft), while the mountaintop ruins of Machu Picchu attest to the aptitude of the Inca to build sophisticated cities in vertiginous surroundings.

But the true extent of the Inca's relationship with the mountains was cast in a new light by Johan Reinhard's discoveries. One of only a few people able to apply archaeological techniques at altitude thanks to his skills as an experienced mountaineer,

he investigated the Inca practice of human sacrifice in the Andes. Mountains were venerated by the Inca as a source of water and as the realm of the gods. Reinhard's work began to yield results in 1995 when he uncovered the mummified remains of an Inca child near the summit of Mount Ampato in Peru.

Over the next five years he found another 14 mountaintop sacrifice sites, culminating in 1999 with the excavation of three perfectly preserved mummies on Llullaillaco, on the Chile-Argentina border. These richly adorned, high-status children were left to the mercy of the elements as a sacrifice – evidence of how far the Inca were prepared to go to appease their gods.

THESE INCA REMAINS WERE FOUND INTERRED NEAR THE VILLAGE OF COQUESA IN SOUTHERN BOLIVIA. AT AN ALTITUDE OF 3,673M (12,050FT) IN THE ANDES, THE MUMMIES REMAIN PRESERVED BY THE COLD, THIN AIR.

PERFECT PRESERVATION

The remarkable condition of the mummies is due to the cold, dry environment in which they lay. Dating from the 15th and 16th centuries, they were frozen at high altitude, which preserved their skin, organs, hair, and clothing despite being exposed to the thin air.

1 This mummy is known as "Juanita", an Inca girl between the ages of 11 and 15 sacrificed on Mount Ampato. Her braided hair and headdress denote her as a child of the ruling elite. **2** The remains of 15-year-old *La Doncella* – "the Maiden" – were scorched by a lightning strike on Llullaillaco.

RECOVERING THE MUMMIES

Reinhard's surprise discovery of his first mummy in 1995 led to the hurried strapping of the 40kg (90lb) corpse to his backpack and impromptu storage in a freezer. Subsequent investigations were more methodical – the 1999 Llullaillaco excavation was conducted over three weeks.

1 The archaeologists carefully uncovered the remains of the mummified children. **2** The three Llullaillaco mummies were packed and wrapped in foam. **3** The precious cargo required a slow descent to Base Camp at 4,900m (16,100ft). **4** On his 1995 trip to Mount Ampato, Reinhard had to contend not only with altitude, but also the eruption of Sabancaya, a nearby volcano.

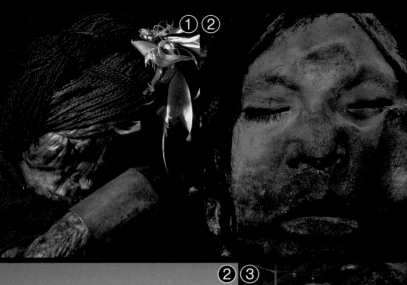

JOHAN REINHARD
UNITED STATES   B.1943

A globetrotting, real-life Indiana Jones, Reinhard has the climbing credentials to back up his status as a high-altitude archaeologist.

He conducted research in Tibet, Nepal, Bhutan, and India during a decade spent living in the Himalaya. No stranger to hardship, his Andean work included underwater archaeology in Lake Titicaca, and excavations on Llullaillaco – the highest archaeological site in the world.

SITES OF SACRIFICE

Inca beliefs held that in the mountains, humans could approach the realm of the gods, so high-altitude sites were selected for occasional child sacrifices. The chosen few were given coca leaves to chew as they climbed, to counteract the effects of altitude sickness.

❶ The children left to die on 6,741-m (22,116-ft) Llullaillaco were housed in a stone hut. ❷ Mummified Inca remains were first discovered here at 5,100m (16,730ft) on Cerro del Plomo, Chile, in 1954. ❸ The "Ploma" mummy was a boy aged eight or nine from a wealthy family, as attested by his portly physique. ❹ Child sacrifices were usually accompanied by grave goods for the afterlife, such as food, and figurines like this one.

THE CULTURAL HEIGHTS

T HE ALPS BEGAN TO ATTRACT A MORE ARTISTIC FOLLOWING IN THE LATE 18TH CENTURY. THE ROMANTIC MOVEMENT ENCOURAGED AN APPRECIATION OF THE SIMPLE, AESTHETIC APPEAL OF THE HEIGHTS, AND OF THE SENSE OF THE SUBLIME THAT THEY PROVOKED IN THE VIEWER.

ROMANTIC INSPIRATION
Artists and poets of the Romantic era – including Percy Bysshe Shelley, seen here in Joseph Severn's *Baths of Caracalla* – travelled through the Alps to Italy in search of inspiration.

The increasing accessibility of the Alps from the early 18th century, and the influx into Switzerland of foreigners conducting "Grand Tours", coincided with a shift in artistic sensibility that provided new avenues for the appreciation of the mountains. While mountains in literature and art continued to be – with a few exceptions – places of foreboding and terror, the growth of the Romantic movement in the late 18th century led some to actively embrace the terror and wildness of the high mountains.

THE MOUNTAIN AESTHETIC

In his *Philosophical Enquiry into the Origins of Our Ideas of the Sublime and the Beautiful* (1757), the Anglo-Irish philosopher Edmund Burke sought to explain why passions were excited in the human mind by "terrible objects", such as a precipice. Soon after, Dr Samuel Johnson's journey to western Scotland in 1773 produced some of the finest accounts of mountain scenery that had yet been produced. However, a fuller appreciation of the mountain aesthetic was first developed by European thinkers, including the German writer Johann von Goethe,

MAN AND NATURE
As a young man, Goethe reacted against the scientific rationalism of the 18th century, and gave free rein to his subjective feelings. He found inspiration in the natural world.

whose *Sturm und Drang* ("Storm and Stress") period early in his career had rejected the rationalism of the Enlightenment in favour of an emotional response to landscape. In 1777, he travelled in the Harz mountains in northern Germany, writing, "I go out of the door and there lies the Brocken in the sublime, splendid moonlight above the pine trees. Today I was up there, and I offered the most heartfelt thanks to God upon the witches' altar."

The French philosopher Jean-Jacques Rousseau took delight in the beauty and precariousness of the mountains. Saint-Preux, the hero of his *La Nouvelle Héloïse* (1761) remarks on the "astonishing mixture of wild and cultivated Nature" in the Valais, Switzerland. Rousseau himself enjoyed travelling along the road from Lyons to Chambéry, which had a wall along its side that he could "look down and experience vertigo just as I pleased … I enjoy this giddiness greatly, provided that I am safely placed."

NATURE AS POETRY

The English Romantic poets refined the artistic appreciation of the mountains to a new level. For William Wordsworth, the hills of the Lake District seemed almost to have a personality of their own. He wrote in his *Prelude* of 1799: "a huge peak, lack and huge/As if with voluntary power

Unlike their predecessors, who had recorded their impressions of the mountains as a by-product of travel in the Alps, 18th- and early 19th-century artists and writers increasingly went to the mountains purely in search of inspiration.

instinct … Towered between me and the stars, and still, for so it seemed, with purpose of its own."

Two other English Romantic writers actually visited the mountains of Switzerland in search of inspiration. Percy Bysshe Shelley went to the Villa Diodati at Cologny on Lake Geneva in 1816, by coincidence at the same time as his fellow poet Lord Byron. Shelley was overcome by the mountains and "the immensity of the aerial summits," which "excited when they suddenly burst upon my sight, a sentiment of ecstatic wonder not unallied to madness."

Shelley's stay yielded the narrative work *History of a Six Weeks' Tour*, which ended with his *Mont Blanc* (1817). In poetic verse he described the mighty mountain as a place where "Frost and the Sun in scorn of mortal power have piled: dome, pyramid, and pinnacle, a city of death, distinct with many a tower". Byron's visit was equally as productive in artistic terms, providing the basis for many of his most famous poems, including *Childe Harold's Pilgrimage* and *Manfred* (1812–18).

Even before the advent of the Romantic movement, artists had drawn inspiration from the Alps. One of the early pioneers, the Swiss Caspar Wolf (see pp.78–79), transcended his early interest in religious works to produce powerful paintings of the Alps that prefigured the works of later Romantics, such as those of

AMERICAN ROMANCE
In the United States, the Romantic movement was led by artists inspired by the wilderness. Among them was Albert Bierstadt, who painted this view of the Yosemite Valley in 1868.

GRAND TOURISTS
The 18th-century fashion for wealthy young men to take a "Grand Tour" through the Alps to Italy and beyond began a trend for glacier tourism and Alpine exploration.

SETTING THE SCENE

- Swiss artist Konrad Witz's 1444 altarpiece *La pêche miraculeuse*, showing Christ walking on water, contains the **first known serious attempt to depict the topography of the Mont Blanc range**.

- Throughout the Renaissance, many artists **use mountains as the settings for their works**, including Brueghel, Titian, and Mantegna.

- After **he visits the Alps**, Leonardo da Vinci paints two works entitled *The Madonna of the Rocks* (1483–86 and *c.*1508), which feature **delicately imagined mountain imagery**.

- In Dante's poem *The Divine Comedy*, the Earthly Paradise is conceptualized **as the top of a tall mountain**, to which the author must ascend from the depths of the Inferno.

- German artist and printmaker Albrecht Dürer (1471–1528) makes a **remarkable series of paintings and drawings of the Alps and Italian mountains**, most notably the watercolour *Alpine Landscapes*.

- English artists such as J M W Turner seek to **re-evaluate the natural world**, depicting nature as a "divine creation" in contrast to "human artifice".

the German artist Caspar David Friedrich. The travels of the English landscape painter J M W Turner (see pp.82–83) in Switzerland, which he visited several times between 1802 and 1842, resulted in more than 400 sketches. These initial brush strokes, painted from life in the heart of the mountains, were eventually among his most memorable paintings.

It was one of Turner's admirers, the English art critic and mountain lover John Ruskin (see pp.86–89), who would formalize the aesthetic of the mountains in his book *Modern Painters* in 1856. The mountains now had not only their very own artistic and literary genre, but also a critical theory to encapsulate it.

CAPTIVATING WILDERNESS
In his 1818 work *Wanderer Above the Sea of Fog*, German Romantic painter Caspar David Friedrich uses a figure staring from a rocky precipice as a metaphor for self-reflection and an unknown future.

CASPAR WOLF

FIRST PAINTER OF THE HIGH PEAKS

SWITZERLAND   1735–83

INSPIRED BY THE MOUNTAINS around his home in northern Switzerland, Caspar Wolf was an early pioneer of mountain painting, capturing the grandeur and drama of the Alps with scientific accuracy. Before him, the majesty of the higher peaks had served merely as a scenic or allegorical backdrop in Alpine art, but Wolf ventured high into the mountains himself, observing their topography and then producing landscapes from sketches often made in situ. His work anticipated that of the landscape artists of the 19th-century European Romantic movement.

A LIFE'S WORK

- Following his artistic training in Switzerland and southern Germany, he creates his main works – **200 oil paintings of the Swiss Alps** – for the publisher Abraham Wagner in Bern

- From 1769–71, he studies in Paris under **Philippe-Jacques de Loutherbourg**, who has a major influence on his development

- Accompanies scientific expeditions into the Alps and sketches the features and landscapes there at close range, bringing new values and **a fresh approach to Alpine art**

- Despite his artistic reputation, **financial success eludes him**; on his death he is buried in a pauper's grave

- **Modern scientists use his paintings** to help date periods of **glacier extension and retreat** in the Bernese Oberland

Caspar Wolf was born in Muri in northern Switzerland, the son of a cabinet-maker. As a young boy, he had admired the precision with which his father worked and this led him to train as an artist-draughtsman.

Following an apprenticeship with the court painter Johann Jakob Anton von Lenz at Konstanz in southern Germany, the 18-year-old Wolf travelled widely through Bavaria, working as a jobbing artist and taking commissions where he could.

EXPEDITION ARTIST

In addition to undertaking decorative work in churches and private chapels, Wolf began to make personal sketches of the southern German landscape. His technical ability was matched by a passionate appreciation of the mountains and rock formations he saw on a daily basis, and by the time he returned to Muri in 1760, his paintings and sketches of the natural world had become more important to him than commissions from wealthy patrons for wallpaper and panel designs.

Unlike later Alpine artists, Wolf was not content with just recording his own visual interpretation of the landscape. He began to work alongside geographers, geologists, botanists, and glaciologists, almost as an "artist in residence" during

frequent fieldwork expeditions. During the 1770s, he made regular trips to the mountains with Swiss researchers Abraham Wagner, a publisher, and Jakob Samuel Wyttenbach, a pastor and geologist, to record rock formations, waterfalls, glaciers, and other Alpine features in sketches. The two men were to be influential in the long-term scientific impact of Wolf's work.

In 1777, Wyttenbach published his short pocket handbook *Instruction for trips to see the Glaciers and the Alps of the Canton of Bern*. This concise early mountaineering guide to the

Swiss Alps provided adventurous young men with basic guidance on supplies (drinking chocolate being recommended as a substitute for the lack of quality bread) and the essential need for a local guide to act as a translator of rarified Alpine dialects. More importantly, Wyttenbach provided a selection of first-hand, tried and tested Alpine routes, many of which he had explored for the first time with Wolf. The handbook included paintings made from sketches drawn by Wolf in situ in the mountains. To cope with the extreme weather conditions at

MIGHTY MOUNTAINS
For his series of pictures in *Remarkable Views of Swiss Mountains*, Wolf was tasked with depicting the "glaciers, ice fortresses, waterfalls, and mountain crests in their total ruggedness". This painting shows the Upper and Lower Grindelwald glaciers.

INTERIOR OF THE "BEAR'S CAVE"
It was probably Wolf's curiosity about the sources of mountain water that led him to carry his artist's tools deep inside the cave systems of Germany and Switzerland.

series of prints from 1776–77. These in turn were followed by a French edition with coloured aquatints: the market for Alpine art was booming.

CAVE MAN

For many, Wolf's work provided their first window on the dramatic beauty of the higher Swiss peaks, but his intention was to create a scientific degree of accuracy.

Unlike the artists of the later Romantic period, Wolf was not satisfied with allowing his imagination to "enhance" his visual observations of the Alpine landscape. Climbing high up in the mountains with his compatriots, Wolf often returned to the location of a sketch or view to check his work for topographical accuracy. And, in order to provide a heightened sense of scale and dimension, he often included scientists at work in his paintings, sometimes adding his own figure, too.

As an artist, Wolf was particularly attracted to rock formations and the movement of water. He also developed a great passion for caves, creating numerous depictions of them and earning himself the nickname "Cave Wolf".

altitude, Wolf had developed a special pigment that contained sufficient oil to prevent paints from freezing at sub-zero temperatures.

It was Wagner – as publisher of Wyttenbach's guide – who suggested to Wolf that his representations of the Alpine landscape could appeal to a much wider audience. Wagner commissioned from Wolf a series of 200 paintings entitled "Remarkable Views of the Swiss Mountains", which were produced as a

ALPINE ARTIST

Wolf produced finished paintings in his studio in Bern from the colour sketches he had made on the mountains. After finishing a painting, he would often return to the exact spot the original sketch had been made to check its topographical accuracy. The result was a body of work that provided climbers with a reliable record of the Swiss Alps. "He penetrated more deeply into the ice and snow of the Alps than any artist before him," said critic Karl Gottlob Küttner.

BREITHORN GLACIER, ONE OF 200 ALPINE PICTURES COMMISSIONED BY BERN PUBLISHER ABRAHAM WAGNER

His most famous cave painting depicts the "Barenhöhle" ("Bear's Cave") near Solothurn. The fine detail and accuracy in Wolf's work has left a lasting legacy for science as well as art. Today, his paintings are a valuable source of information for geologists and historians studying changes to the Alpine environment.

GABRIEL AND MATHIAS LORY

MASTERS OF ALPINE PRINTMAKING

SWITZERLAND   1763–1840; 1784–1846

THE SWISS CITY OF BERN PRODUCED TWO GENERATIONS of exceptional printmakers in the late 18th and early 19th centuries. Though not a man to take to the mountains himself, Gabriel Ludwig Lory tapped into a burgeoning tradition of depicting the landscape – a subject-matter to which Bernese artists had just begun to turn – to create the first great series of accurately observed engravings of the Alps. His son, Mathias-Gabriel, whom he trained, took his father's work a stage further, engraving some of the most hauntingly enduring of all Alpine landscapes.

As the main city of Switzerland's largest republic, 18th-century Bern was at the forefront of the country's artistic developments. It was the home of leading architects, such as Erasmus Ritter and Nicholas Sprüngli, and boasted the construction of great new buildings, including the Church of the Holy Ghost (constructed 1726–29) and the Corn House (1711–16). Bern was also the centre of a thriving artistic community, featuring figures such as Johann Rudolf Humber, Emmanuel Handmann, and Johann Ludwig Aberli (see opposite).

A LIFE'S WORK

- Gabriel Ludwig publishes **Recueil de paysages suisses** in 1797, while his son Mathias-Gabriel begins to work for him

- In 1798, the Lorys move to Hérisau in northeastern Switzerland to work on an **audacious set of engravings for Tsar Paul I of Russia**

- The Lorys move to Neuchâtel in 1805 for a commission to commemorate **Napoleon's ambitious trans-Alpine highway**

- Gabriel Ludwig founds **the Society of Bernese Artists** in 1812

- The Lorys publish a collection of pictorial folios that contains **nearly 500 individual prints**

- Mathias-Gabriel publishes his magnum opus, *Souvenirs de la Suisse*, in 1829, **comprising a total of 37 aquatints**

It was in Alberli's studio that Gabriel Ludwig Lory made the first steps in his illustrious career. He had been forced to start work at a very young age to provide support for his widowed mother (his father had died when he was seven), who was prone to bouts of religious hysteria. The freshness and simplicity of his watercolour work soon brought him attention, including a commission to colour a series of views of the area around Mont Blanc based on paintings by Caspar Wolf (see pp.78–79). He coloured a set of engravings of Chamonix for the artist Bacler d'Albe, before moving to St Gall in northeastern Switzerland to commence working for the print-seller Bartholomé Fehr, whose daughter Wilborada he married.

Lory's own artistic production in these early years concentrated on landscapes, such as the *Glacier inférieur de Grindelwald* (1788) and *Vue des environs de Thoune* (1794), but reached its culmination in his 1797 collection *Recueil de paysages suisses*. For this landmark publication, Lory himself engraved nine of the 13 plates, while watercolourist Daniel Lafond – his main collaborator – produced three.

KINDRED COLLABORATIONS

Shortly after the publication of the *Recueil*, Lory was called to Hérisau by the businessman Jean Walser to work on a series of views of Russia commissioned by Tsar Paul I. Although lucrative, the work was disrupted by the advance of the French Revolutionary armies on Switzerland in 1798–99, and then brought to an abrupt end by the assassination of the tsar in 1800. Gabriel Ludwig had re-located with his 14-year-old son, Mathias-Gabriel – who, like his father, had begun his artistic career precociously early – as well as his nephew, Friedrich-Wilhelm Moritz. He collaborated extensively with both of his young protegés, the most notable result being the *Voyage pittoresque de Genève á Milan par le Simplon*, which the Neuchâtel publisher d'Ostervald had commissioned to document a new route that had opened up through the Simplon Pass.

Mathias-Gabriel had previously worked mainly on conventional subjects, which formed the bulk of his first public exhibition in Bern in 1820. But the *Voyage pittoresque* set him on a new course. His travels with his lifelong friend, the artist Maximilien de Meuron, to Paris in 1808 and then to Italy in 1809–11 exposed him to Classical landscapes and wider artistic influences – such as his meeting with the landscape artist Johann-Christian Reinhard – that dictated the course of his later career.

Born in Winthertur in northeastern Switzerland, Aberli went to Bern aged 19 to study as a pupil of Johann Grimm.

Aberli showed early talent as a portraitist, but turned to watercolours of the Bernese countryside after visiting the Oberland in 1759. After 1772, his frequent journeys with Sigmund Greenberg (1745–1801) yielded a number of fine engravings, particularly of the inhabitants of the mountains. He pioneered the technique of hand-painted line engravings in which only the outline was initially engraved, allowing copies to be printed that could later be hand-coloured. It was to perform this task that artists such as Heinrich Rieter, J J Biedermann, and Gabriel Ludwig Lory worked in his studio.

DESCRIPTIVE DETAIL
This print, entitled *Vue du Lac de Chede*, typifies the precise, naturalistic style of the Lorys. The Alps are always the towering backdrop to simple scenes of working life.

His travels also took him to the UK, spreading his reputation outside the comparatively narrow confines of Bern.

FROM FATHER TO SON

In the 1810s and 20s Mathias-Gabriel created a series of Swiss views that established him as one of the finest landscape engravers the world had ever seen. His work largely made use of the new technique of aquatint, by which the copper plates were exposed repeatedly to a solution of aqua–nitric acid, which ate away at those areas not coated with a special varnish. This had the effect of adding areas of shade directly to the copper plate, rather than being applied by the artist performing the hand-colouring. In 1815, Mathias-Gabriel, in collaboration with his father, produced the *Voyage pittoresque aux glaciers de Chamouni*. This work was illustrated with seven aquatints of the Chamonix valley. Seven years later, Mathias-Gabriel documented the Bernese Oberland in the 30 aquatints of the *Voyage pittoresque de l'Oberland bernois*.

The fine line-work and immediacy of Mathias-Gabriel's engravings created a growing appetite for his work, and in 1824 he collaborated with his cousin Moritz on *Costumes suisses*, which portrayed the people and traditional costumes of the country rather than its landscape. He returned to views of the mountains in 1829 with his *Souvenirs de la Suisse*, the first large-format illustrated book produced in Switzerland. His reputation firmly established, in 1832 Mathias-Gabriel left Neuchâtel to return to his home town of Bern. He purchased l'Oranienbourg, an elegant Louis XVI-style villa, where he received clients. International recognition

MOUNTAIN SPLENDOUR
The Lorys' Alpine views, such as this 1811 coloured aquatint of Monte Rosa and the Simplon Pass, brought the high mountains into the fashionable drawing rooms of Europe.

followed with the granting of a professorship at the Academy of Fine Arts in Berlin, where he taught from 1834 to 1836.

Although they were neither intrepid explorers nor pioneering mountaineers, the topographic exactness of the Lorys' Alpine engravings further fuelled the growing interest in travel through the Alps. The evocative illustrations of their series of *Voyage pittoresque* helped to bring the mountains into people's homes.

J M W TURNER

ARTISTIC "PRINCE OF ROCKS"

ENGLAND   1775–1851

BORN IN LONDON'S COVENT GARDEN, a stone's throw from the River Thames, Joseph Mallord William Turner, the son of a barber, demonstrated a precocious artistic talent that would develop into genius. Although he did not climb the mountains he saw on his travels, he was in the vanguard of English painters returning to Europe after the French Revolution. His paintings of the European mountain landscape, which embraced the ideals of the Romantic Movement, would inform and encourage generations of later travellers.

Nicknamed "Prince of Rocks" during early scrambles along the River Avon as a young man, Turner's first true experience of the grandeur and wilderness of mountains came between 1797 and 1799 in the north of England. It was while travelling in the Lake District, where he carried leather-bound sketchbooks and paint stored in animal bladders, that he began to re-create the effects of light and water on the mountainside, a skill for which he soon became well known.

Inspired by his sojourns around England, Turner made frequent journeys to mainland Europe, first in 1802 when, for the first time

in 22 years, there was a brief respite from the hostilities between France and Britain thanks to the Peace of Amiens. It is likely that he was influenced by the philosopher Edmund Burke, who, in his 1756 *Philosophical Enquiry into the Origins of Our Ideas of the Sublime and Beautiful*, saw the mountain landscape as beyond human understanding, inspiring awe and adding the thrill of danger when viewed from a distance.

CHANGING PERCEPTIONS

Turner's Alpine works had the effect of encouraging closer examination of the mountains, turning spectator into participant. The Alps had been viewed with distaste by earlier generations of well-heeled British "Grand Tourists". Crossed by necessity en route to the civilized pleasures of Italy, the mountains were often described as ugly or threatening: it was common practice for carriage blinds to be lowered for the Alpine portion of a journey.

In 1739, the English poet Thomas Gray and politician Horace Walpole travelled over the Swiss Alps. Gray described "Magnificent rudeness and steep precipices … You here meet with all the beauties so savage and horrid a place can present you with … all concur to form one of the most poetical scenes imaginable." Walpole in turn wrote about the Alps to his friend the Irish politician Richard West – "Such uncouth rocks, and such uncomely inhabitants! My dear West, I hope I shall never see them again!" Turner's eloquent visual representations did much to alter this perception. His journey of

1802 took him through Switzerland's western cantons into the Valle d'Aosta and then onwards to Schaffhausen and Basel. Returning to Paris, he met a compatriot by the name of Farington to whom he described "much fatigue from walking". Despite complaints of inferior accommodation and a poor diet, Turner still reported enthusiastically that he had witnessed

Alpine scene led him to return repeatedly in the 1830s and 40s. He regularly revisited favourite locales, such as Chamonix and the St Gotthard Pass, where he would re-work earlier compositions.

FELLOW MOUNTAIN PAINTERS

Turner's greatest supporter and admirer was also a mountain lover. English poet and artist John Ruskin (see pp.86–89) was 21 when he first met the 65-year-old Turner in 1840. Ruskin remarked: "Introduced today to the man who beyond all doubts is the greatest of the age; greatest in every faculty of the imagination, in every branch of scenic knowledge, at once the painter and poet of the day."

In 1841, on his first return to the Alps since 1802, Turner created the basis for a new series of ten watercolour sets. But the commercial response to the work was muted, with sales limited to a close-knit circle of admirers, among them Ruskin himself, who astutely predicted that the drawings would "… be recognized in a few years more, as the noblest landscapes ever yet conceived by human intellect."

On Turner's Swiss sketches of 1842, Ruskin commented, "the warm colour given to the rocks is exactly right" – in fact, the poet returned to London with rock samples to convince viewers

ICE SKETCHING
Turner was not afraid to get his feet cold when searching for subjects to paint. This 1812 etching of the Mer de Glace in the Chamonix valley was done from sketches made in situ.

of the accuracy of his friend's work. Ruskin records how Turner would alter the visual facts in order to communicate his impression of a site, going so far as to instruct the felling of trees to suggest a higher elevation. At all times he acknowledged Turner's "deeper mental vision", by which he combined impressions from a single day in the Alps to create his often-idealized studio work, inviting the viewing public to consider Turner's drawing as being "a perfect example of the operation of invention of the highest order".

The four sets of watercolours that resulted from Turner's Alpine trips are today considered to be among the artist's greatest creations.

PACKED PAINTBOX
Turner was a master of the subtle use of colour – his paintbox contained a range of hues for depicting the movement of light and shade across the landscape.

"very fine thunderstorms amongst the Mountains" and that the "precipices [were] very romantic and strikingly grand". His marvel at the mountain landscape generated a series of some 400 sketches. Turner also created diagrammatic sketches, marking distances and the location of landmarks that would aid him in his London studio. His fascination with the

EXPERIENCING THE MOUNTAINS

POETRY

In October 1799, two young poets, William Wordsworth and Samuel Taylor Coleridge, went on a walking tour of the English Lake District. This was already a popular destination for wealthy tourists who came for a "picturesque tour". The poets weren't at all rich, however, and, avoiding the crowds around the frequently visited sights, they set out across the mist-shrouded fells. Their romantic and spiritual impressions of the area were in keeping with a new reverence for wild landscapes in the imaginations of leading poets across Europe.

The year before, Wordsworth and Coleridge had published their *Lyrical Ballads*. Now Wordsworth was showing his younger friend the hills of his youth. Coleridge was already familiar with the landscapes of his own youth, England's Quantock Hills and Germany's Harz mountains, which had so inspired Johann Wolfgang von Goethe in his poem *Harzreise im Winter*.

The Lakes became a similar source of inspiration for Coleridge, who undertook a second tour in August 1802, this time alone, which was recorded in his *Notebooks* and his letters to Sara Hutchinson, with whom he was infatuated. Coleridge was attracted to whatever stretched his imagination, be it opium or danger, and at this moment in his life found himself excited by the same visceral thrill that some climbers will recognize – an addiction to a "sort of gambling" where the wager is his life, and to which he is "much indebted". In a letter to Hutchinson, he described how, having reached the top of England's second-highest

peak on a muggy summer's day, he almost carelessly became committed to climbing down Broad Stand, even now a dangerous scramble and the scene of many accidents. Having lowered himself onto a narrow grassy ledge, Coleridge found himself trapped, unable to continue or retrace his steps – with a storm brewing. He lay down on his back and laughed at himself, before succumbing to a state "of almost prophetic Trance and Delight."

Risk-taking as self-realization became a calling card for the Romantic poets. Percy Bysshe Shelley's 1816 work *Mont Blanc* captured the transformation such experiences could bestow: "Thou hast a voice, great Mountain, to repeal/Large codes of fraud and woe ..." Shelley boasted of his own addiction to risk, describing how "dangers which sport upon the brinks of precipices have been my playmate." Even if he was exaggerating, the psychological drama that mountains afforded was fixed in the public's romantic imagination.

Ⓐ PERCY BYSSHE SHELLEY
Shelley's 1817 poem *Mont Blanc* was inspired by his visit to Chamonix. It compares the power of the mountain with that of the human imagination.

Ⓑ NATURE AND POLITICS
This is Shelley's original manuscript for his poem *Ode to the West Wind*. The Romantic poets' relationships with wild landscapes and the forces of nature underpinned a political awakening in Europe.

Ⓒ SAMUEL TAYLOR COLERIDGE
In this manuscript for *Hymn Before Sunrise in the Vale of Chamouni*, Coleridge addresses Mont Blanc as "thou dread ambassador from Earth to Heaven."

Ⓓ ALBRECHT VON HALLER
Anatomist, mathematician, and doctor, even among polymaths von Haller (1708–77) was exceptional. His poem *Die Alpen* marked the start of a cultural awakening of interest in mountain landscapes.

THE WIND OF MOUNT FUJI I'VE BROUGHT ON MY FAN! A GIFT FROM EDO

MATSUO BASHO (1644–94)

E SCAFELL PIKE
William Wordsworth introduced Coleridge to England's Lake District in 1799. Coleridge is often credited with the first English rock climb, a descent of Broad Stand on Scafell.

F WILLIAM WORDSWORTH
In his principal work, *The Prelude*, Wordsworth often uses his journeys among mountains as a metaphor for the poet's development.

G ALFRED LORD TENNYSON
Tennyson succeeded Wordsworth as England's poet laureate. He shared Wordsworth's romantic sensibility and included wild landscapes in his poetry as a metaphor for emotional freedom.

H MATSUO BASHO
A century before the Romantic poets made the Alps fashionable, the Edo-era poet Basho found inspiration travelling in the Japanese wilderness.

I GOETHE'S VISION
Goethe, a leading light of the German Romantic movement, drew on his experience in the Harz mountains, and his ascent in 1777 of the atmospheric Brocken, to write his play *Faust*.

THEY SEEM TO HAVE BEEN BUILT FOR THE HUMAN RACE, AS AT ONCE THEIR SCHOOLS AND THEIR CATHEDRALS

JOHN RUSKIN ON MOUNTAINS

DOCUMENTING THE ALPS
At the age of seven, Ruskin illustrated his first volume of poetry with what he described as "my first effort at mountain drawing". Later, during his many visits to the Alps, he produced sketches, watercolours, and oils of the scenery, including this view of Lyskamm (inset, and above) near Zermatt in the Swiss Alps. His art was not just a holiday pastime – it was his way of investigating the Alps.

A LIFE'S WORK

- First encounters the Alps at the age of 14, on a family visit to Switzerland. Bewitched, he **draws sketches** of them and **writes poems** and prose passages

- **Mont Blanc** and the then small village of **Chamonix become central to his life**. He witnesses many events in the history of mountaineering there and observes the changing character of the village

- His **interest in mountains** stems from a desire to know and understand them from an **artistic, scientific, and spiritual** point of view, rather than a sporting one

- Becomes **the preeminent art critic and tastemaker** of the 19th century. His masterwork, *Modern Painters*, is published in five volumes over a 17-year period. In an early volume he proclaims **J M W Turner's** superiority to all earlier landscape painters, championing the **"truthful" depictions of nature** in his work

JOHN RUSKIN

CRITIC AND PASSIONATE MOUNTAIN LOVER

ENGLAND   1819–1900

ART CRITIC, ARTIST, ESSAYIST, and social thinker, John Ruskin combined a breathtaking range of interests with a lifelong love of Switzerland. His writings were a counterbalance to the mid-19th century's increasing emphasis on exploration and the conquest of Alpine summits. Although he travelled extensively in the Alps, his writings, in particular *Modern Painters*, emphasize the aesthetic and the sublime nature of mountains, whose beauty in themselves should be enough to inspire, without the need to trample all over them.

In the early 19th century, Switzerland was seeing an increasing number of visitors, facilitated by novelties such as steam ships on Lake Geneva after 1823 and the appearance of the first railway between Baden and Zurich in 1847. The trip that John James Ruskin, an importer of Spanish wines, made to Switzerland in 1832 was a part of this movement. With him were his family, including his 14-year-old son John, upon whom the country and its mountain scenery would make a strong impression.

MOUNTAIN EPIPHANY

The previous year John had been given a copy of *Italy* by Henry Telford, a book that had been illustrated by J M W Turner (see pp.82–83). The naturalism of Turner's work fascinated Ruskin and he became a lifelong defender of the artist. He was equally captivated by the Swiss Alps, writing in his "Account of a Tour of the Continent" that "There is not another scene like Chamouni [Chamonix] in the whole of Switzerland." (Like many British visitors, Ruskin had mistakenly located French Chamonix in Switzerland.)

Ruskin's father was a devout evangelical Christian and a deeply controlling personality. On the Ruskin family's trips to the Alpine countries, which became an almost annual event over the next 15 years, he constantly sought

to temper his son's enthusiasm. During a visit to Chamonix in 1844, John James engaged the local captain of the guides, Joseph-Marie Couttet, to show his son the mountains, but warned him to avoid any dangerous routes or over-exertion. On what was to be Ruskin's highest mountain expedition, Couttet took him to the relatively modest peak of Le Buet, but a change in the weather caused it to be smothered in cloud, so the pair confined themselves to less challenging climbs for the rest of their tour.

Although this visit failed to turn Ruskin into a mountaineer, it irrevocably infused in him the spirit of the mountains. He visited the Alpine village of Macugnaga for a month in 1845 and spent time at Zermatt in 1854, but didn't contemplate climbing any more mountains. He would later write that "the Alps were, on the whole, best seen from below."

ARTIST AND ART CRITIC

Yet despite this, and in spite of his evangelical background, Ruskin developed an increasingly complex approach to the mountains. In 1844, on the Simplon Pass, he met the naturalist James David Forbes (see pp.66–67), who took him up a nearby ridge and

PORTABLE PAINTS
By the mid-19th century, Ruskin would have made use of the new portable metal paint boxes for painting in the field.

COMBINING FACTS AND ART
As a painter and critic, Ruskin believed art should observe the inner "truth" of nature. He spent hours making studies of clouds, ice, rock formations, and vegetation before picking up his brush to create watercolours such as these, depicting Uri Rostock and Lake Lucerne (right), the Mer de Glace (top), and Lake Geneva (above).

rekindled in him the interest in geology that had led his father to comment, "from boyhood my son has been an artist, but he has been a geologist since infancy". Ruskin's artistic observations of the mountains led him to conceive of their fundamental shape not as the jagged, linear form that the untutored eye conceives, but as a curve, like a wave. By the time of the publication of the fourth volume of his masterwork, *Modern Painters*, in 1856, he had developed the idea that mountains actually moved.

Ruskin's intentions in his early Alpine trips continued to veer towards the scientific; in Chamonix in 1842 he recalled, "I did not draw much – the things I now saw were beyond drawing – but took to careful botany." However, his early interest in Turner drew him back to more artistic endeavours and he made a number of early watercolours and drawings of the mountains, such as his 1845 sketches of the Pass of St Faido on the St Gotthard.

It was, though, as an art critic that Ruskin would make his name. In the works he produced in this capacity his response to landscape in general, and to mountain scenery in particular, would strike a distinctive and sometimes controversial chord. At the age of 24, and still feeling the need to conceal his true identity under the pseudonym "An Oxford Graduate", he published the first volume of

Modern Painters. Although it didn't deal with mountain scenery as much as a later volume would, the work stressed the importance of the experience of a landscape over its ownership. "All high or noble emotion or thought," he wrote, "is rendered physically impossible, while the mind exults in what is very likely a strictly sensual experience."

MOUNTAIN GLOOM AND GLORY

It was the fourth volume of *Modern Painters*, however, which appeared in 1856 and whose final chapters are entitled "The Mountain Gloom" and "The Mountain Glory", that would encapsulate Ruskin's more mature approach to the mountains. The book contains the seeds of later controversies he provoked among the burgeoning mountaineering fraternity.

The first part of Ruskin's extended treatment of the thoughts inspired in him by the Alps begins on a rather negative note with "The Mountain Gloom". He asserts that, although the scenery may be sublime, the inhabitants do not appreciate it and one need only "enter the streets of one of those villages, and you will find it foul with that gloomy foulness that is suffered only by torpor, or by the anguish of the soul." It is his self-appointed mission to arouse "the attention of the Swiss and Italian peasantry to an intelligent administration of the natural treasures of their woods and streams."

Having sketched such an unhappy picture, Ruskin moves on, in "The Mountain Glory", to more uplifting themes, creating a hymn to the beauty of the mountains. True to his devout religious upbringing, he highlights the sense of sacred respect that mountains have inspired, from the Greeks' placing of the shrine of Apollo at the cliffs of Delphi to "the peculiar awe with which mountains were regarded in the Middle Ages, as bearing continual witness against the frivolity of the world".

As an artist, he praises their "general gift of exciting the poetical and inventive faculties". Finally, as a geologist, he pauses to nod in the direction of de Saussure (see pp.60–63), whom he praises as "the only writer whose help I did not refuse in the course of these inquiries".

CLIMBING CRITIC

Although his tone in "The Mountain Gloom" might have been regarded as slightly sour, his praise of the hills in "The Mountain Glory" was, if effusive, not particularly controversial. It was elsewhere that Ruskin's ambivalence towards the climbing of mountains came out in full force. Already, in *Modern Painters*, he had remarked that, "To get back to awe for hills, we must begin by divesting ourselves as far as may be of our modern experimental and exploring activity, and habit of regarding mountains chiefly as places for gymnastic exercise."

ALPINE CONSERVATION

Ruskin's fears about the effects of tourism on fragile mountain ecosystems were well-founded. With the coming of the railways to the Alps, visitor numbers increased exponentially, and in many areas, tourism soon replaced agriculture as the main industry. Today, winter sports have become a cause of significant erosion. Steep mountain slopes are vulnerable to soil erosion, and the subsequent loss of vegetation affects all aspects of the ecosystem, polluting streams and reducing biodiversity. Careful planning is needed to conserve the Alpine splendour that Ruskin celebrated.

THE ZMUTT GLACIER (RIGHT) IS RETREATING DUE TO GLOBAL WARMING, A GROWING THREAT TO ALPINE ECOSYSTEMS

GO TO NATURE ... REJECTING NOTHING, SELECTING NOTHING AND SCORNING NOTHING

JOHN RUSKIN, ADVICE TO ARTISTS IN *MODERN PAINTERS*

he was a member of the club from 1869 to 1882 and in "Sesame and Lilies" wrote of it that "Whatever the Alpine Club have done, or may yet accomplish, in a sincere thirst for mountain knowledge and in happy sense of youthful strength and play of animal spirit, they have done, and will do, wisely and well", although he added the caution: "but whatever they are urged to by mere sting of competition and itch of praise, they will do, as all vain things must be done for ever, foolishly and ill."

In return, the Alpine Club was generous towards its sometime critic and sometime muse, with

Leslie Stephen (see pp.134–35) commenting that "the fourth volume of *Modern Painters* infected me and other early members of the Alpine Club with an enthusiasm for which, I hope we are still grateful. Our prophet indeed ridiculed his disciples for treating Mont Blanc as a greased pole. We might well forgive our satirist, for he had revealed a new pleasure which we might mix with ingredients which he did not fully appreciate."

In his promotion of mountains – and the Alps in particular – as landscapes to be admired and valued for the sensations they provoke in the beholder, rather than conquered or merely feared, Ruskin carved out a unique and highly respected niche in the annals of mountaineering.

GENTLEMAN SCHOLAR
Ruskin is pictured here in about 1855. His very broad range of interests made him a polymath in the tradition of the Enlightenment.

This was a clear dig at those mountain climbers who, in his view, prized peak-bagging over feelings for the sublime.

Ruskin had always been rather protective of his mountains, seeing them as a place of purity that human footfalls could so easily defile. Of the Zmutt Glacier, he wrote, "it looks like a world from which not only the human, but also the spiritual, presence have perished and the last of its archangels, building the great mountains for their monument, had laid themselves down in the sunlight to an eternal rest, each in his white shroud."

In his lecture "Sesame and Lilies", delivered in 1864, Ruskin was even more caustic. In it, he accused mountaineers of wanting to "get as fast as possible from place to place, and secondly at every place they arrive to get the kind of accommodation and amusement to which they have been accustomed in Paris." In a more serious criticism given his championing of the aesthetic appreciation of mountains, he added, "The Alps themselves, which your own poets used to love so reverently, you look upon as soaped poles in a bear-garden which you set yourself to cling and slide down again with 'shrieks of delight'."

ALPINE CLUB APPROVAL

Yet, paradoxically, Ruskin's relations with the mountaineering community, and with the Alpine Club in particular, were cordial. Despite his lack of climbing experience,

THE FIRST SUMMITEERS

S CIENCE AND LITERATURE TRANSFORMED THE THE ALPS IN THE PUBLIC EYE – FROM A DANGEROUS BACKWATER INTO AN ENTICING LANDSCAPE WHERE AMBITIONS COULD BE REALIZED. YET SOME WEREN'T CONTENT TO LOOK AT MOUNTAINS – THEY WANTED THE SUMMITS THEMSELVES.

JEAN-MICHEL CACHAT
A legend in Chamonix, Cachat (1755–1840) was an Alpine explorer, hunter, and storyteller who participated in the second, third, and fourth ascents of Mont Blanc.

The question every mountaineer has to face is, "Why?" Climbing a mountain might be dangerous, and will certainly involve privations, so what possible motivation can there be?

By the late 18th century and early 19th century, people had long been walking in the hills and mountains, sometimes even climbing to their summits. But the sudden scientific and cultural interest in the Alps that developed during this period – and the transport revolution it precipitated – produced a small band of individuals who felt drawn to climb not just for scientific knowledge or spiritual enlightenment, but for its own reward.

The motivations of these early mountaineers were as diverse as they are among today's alpinists. Some climbed for fame, others out of curiosity, or for the pleasure experienced in the exertion of the ascent and the reward of an unparalleled view from the summit.

CURIOUS CLIMBERS

Mountaineering is sometimes described as a British invention, but, by the early 19th century, there were many Europeans who were part of the growing fashion for climbing Alpine peaks. They were scientists and cartographers, priests, hunters, and gentlemen of leisure. Many of the earliest ascents were made by local men, and even a few women. While not quite rivalling Gottlieb Studer's

appetite for climbing (see pp.104–05), Johann Jakob Weilenmann (1819–96) of St Gallen in Switzerland reputedly scaled 320 mountains, including the second ascent of the Dufourspitze.

UNCHARTED TERRITORY

For those pioneers experiencing the urge to mountaineer, the Alps must have been an irresistible prospect. A few wealthy tourists were starting to trickle into the Swiss village of Zermatt, where they could marvel at a cirque of imposing summits – all of them pristine and untouched – dominated by the slender, asymmetrical pyramid of the Matterhorn.

Italy's Dolomites were terra incognita, and France's Dauphiné Alps completely unknown. The English poet William Wordsworth (see p.84–85) had written of "feasting on the morning landscape" during his tour of the Alps, but mountaineers would soon consume the mountains' very summits. These early alpinists, however, faced challenges similar to those in the Himalaya a century later. In his early 18th-century work *Die Alpen* (*The Alps*), the Swiss biologist Albrecht von Haller had extolled the region's peasant life, rather than its natural beauty. By contrast, *Murray's Handbook*, the first true guidebook to the Alps, which was published in 1838,

> The cultural and scientific awakening of the 18th-century Enlightenment opened the way to the mountains. They were a new frontier to be measured and explored, where the hardy and the daring could win fame with a summit.

MEASURING ON THE MOUNTAINS
A hygrometer, for measuring humidity, was one of the scientific instruments carried up Mont Blanc by Genevan scientist Horace-Bénédict de Saussure in 1787 (see pp.60–63).

commented on the region's splendid scenery, but reported that the locals were mired in poverty.

BOOSTING THE ALPS

In the high Alpine passes, little had been done to improve the passage for travellers since Roman times, apart from the introduction of hospices during the Middle Ages. Carriage roads were opened across the Simplon Pass in 1805 and the St Gotthard Pass in 1830, but using them was a hair-raising experience. It was only with the arrival of the railways in the late 19th century that access to the Alps became available to all who could afford it.

At first, there was little accommodation for visitors in Alpine villages. The exception was Chamonix, at the foot of Mont Blanc, where the Hôtel de Londres was established in 1743 to welcome visitors on the European "Grand Tour", an itinerary popular with wealthy young British men. One of the earliest to explore Chamonix for pleasure was a young Englishman named William Windham (see pp.92–93), who, in 1741, hired local guides and walked up Montenvers. But it was two locals, Jacques Balmat and Michel-Gabriel Paccard (see pp.94–97), who really put the Alps on the map, by beating their rivals to the top of Mont Blanc.

SETTING THE SCENE

- Balmat and Paccard's **ascent of Mont Blanc** in 1786 marks the transformation of the Alps from somewhere to avoid – a "place of torment" – into a **magnet for Earth scientists, and cultural titans** such as the poet William Wordsworth (see pp.84–85) and the artist J M W Turner (see pp.82–83).

- **Slow transport** links and **political upheaval** during Napoleon's reign mean that 25 years after the first ascent, only nine more parties reach the summit of Mont Blanc. At the end of the Napoleonic Wars in 1815, there is a **huge influx of wealthy tourists** to the Alps, but until the railways arrive, getting there is expensive and time-consuming.

- Scores of important **peaks are climbed** before alpinism's Golden Age by **local climbers**, several of them priests – including Father Horasch of Döllach, who climbs the Grossglockner in 1800.

HUNTER MOUNTAINEERS
Hunters seeking chamois took advantage of the animal's habit of looking for danger from below. The higher the hunter could climb, the better the chances of surprising the animal.

SEA OF ICE
On seeing a glacier northeast of Mont Blanc that resembled "a sea, stirred by a strong breeze, then suddenly frozen to ice", William Windham named it the Mer de Glace.

THE HEIGHTS OF FASHION
This mid-19th century impression of climbers on Mont Blanc reflected a lingering public perception of mountains as impossibly alien and exotic. By the 1860s, however, a climbing season in the Alps had become the height of fashion.

WILLIAM WINDHAM

GRAND TOURIST OF THE MONT BLANC GLACIERS

ENGLAND   1717–61

AN IMPETUOUS ARISTOCRAT with a penchant for pushing the boundaries, William Windham blazed the tourist trail to the glaciers of Mont Blanc. In a colourful 18th-century outing that included firearms and a team of servants, Windham had the audacity to go where only hardened montagnards had trod before in search of chamois and quartzite. His rocky climb to the Chamonix Glacier – later named Mer de Glace (Sea of Ice) thanks to his evocative description of it – marked the beginning of glacier tourism.

RICHARD POCOCKE
ENGLAND   1704–65

Born in Southampton in 1704, Pococke studied at Oxford before following the path trodden by his father and father-in-law by entering the priesthood.

However, an insatiable appetite for the exotic meant that Pococke was to spend much of his life away from his ecclesiastical duties. He toured Europe from 1733 and the Middle East from 1737, visiting Egypt, Jerusalem, Palestine, and Greece. By the time he arrived in Geneva in 1741, Pococke boasted a baggage train that included a mummy from Saqqara, a stone statue of Isis, and a set of Egyptian robes complete with turban, slippers, and curved dagger. Although Pococke's verve for exploration was music to Windham's ears, he does not seem to have been particularly impressed by the Mer de Glace – he failed to mention it at all in his extensive travel writings.

The latest in the long line of Windhams, a family of minor nobility stretching back to the 15th century, the young William was packed off on a Grand Tour at the age of 20 by his exasperated father. After three years roving the fashionable spots of Europe, in 1740 Windham took up with a mixed bag of young English and Scottish aristocrats in Geneva.

COMMON ROOM CAPERS

The collection of Britons soon caused a stir in the puritan, Calvinist city, meeting daily for after-dinner frivolities in a group they later called "our Common Room in Geneva".

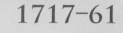

VEÜE DE LA VALLÉE DE CHAMOUNY ET DES GLACIÈRES. du Costé Meridional depuis L'Eglise de Chamouny. pris sur les Lieux. l'an 1741.

GENTLEMAN'S "GLACIÈRES"
Windham published his private correspondence as *An Account of the Glacieres or Ice Alps of Savoy, in two letters*, which won him admittance to the Royal Society.

Windham in particular was described as having "an utter abhorrence of restraint", and was a central figure in a series of plays and pantomimes that were performed in public.

Windham's horizons were not restricted to the stage. He longed to explore the distant white peaks visible from Geneva, but failed to rouse the enthusiasm of his cohorts. His chance came in 1741 with the arrival of Richard Pococke, an experienced traveller en route to England after a four-year study-tour of the Near East, which, Windham wrote, "he had visited with great exactness". After minor sorties into the valleys around Geneva, Windham and Pococke were emboldened to aim for a loftier objective: the icy, mountain realm around Chamonix.

INTO THE MOUNTAINS

A party of 13, consisting of eight "gentlemen", including Windham's long-suffering tutor, and five servants, set off from Geneva on horseback

on 19 June 1741, equipped with firearms to protect themselves against the brigands (armed thieves) who were reputed to roam the 80-km (50-mile) route into the mountains. After three days of travel, the party reached Chamonix, which sits in the deep valley below the looming hulk of the then unnamed Mont Blanc, whereupon Windham hired three local hunters to act as guides.

He had planned to conduct scientific experiments on the expedition, but when the most skilled mathematician of the group, John Williamson, elected to stay behind, the scientific instruments – including thermometers, barometers, and a quadrant – stayed with him. The primary aim of the trip became the exploration of the glacier, so when the locals reluctantly directed them only to the broken ice falls that tumble down into the Chamonix valley, they reacted with dismay: "we had come too far to be content with so small a matter". Demanding a more impressive spectacle, Windham was led higher up the mountain.

A LIFE'S WORK

- Encourages his Common Room collaborators to adopt a **natural style of acting** that later becomes fashionable in London's theatres

- **Is elected to the Royal Society** in 1744 after publication of the Windham-Martel letters detailing his ascent to the Mer de Glace

- Is dubbed **"Boxing Windham"** after an episode in which he and his "bruizers" defend his friend David Garrick, the celebrated actor, from rivals who were trying to boo him off stage

- **Inherits the family estate** in 1749, then sits as MP for Aldeburgh, Suffolk, from 1754

HE HAD AN UTTER ABHORRENCE OF RESTRAINT

ALDWORTH NEVILLE ON WILLIAM WINDHAM

The party agreed upon a regimen that included walking in strict single file at a slow pace and stopping at every spring for a refreshing draught of water mixed with wine. It was a physically demanding, occasionally dangerous climb that took nearly five hours past avalanche debris and "several pieces of ice, which we took at first for rocks, being as big as a house". Eventually they reached a large flat area above the glacier now known as Montenvers, where they were met by a view that rendered the usually effusive Windham almost speechless: "I am extremely at a loss how to give a right idea of it, as I know no one thing which I have ever seen before that has the least resemblance to it," he wrote later.

PISTOL SALUTE

Descending onto the ice, Windham found the frozen surface to be much easier to walk on than the rocky moraine the group had just climbed down, despite describing the glacier as a "lake put in agitation by a strong wind, and frozen all at once". Lacking instrumentation for any scientific measurements, the intrepid adventurers instead drank a toast and fired a pistol-salute to naval hero Admiral Vernon. After noting their guides' opinion that the ice moved and inspecting the crevasses running across the glacier, they set off on the return journey, reaching Chamonix by sunset.

Although Windham had reached a height of only 1,900m (6,200ft), the impact of his climb was immeasurable. He wrote of the expedition to an artist friend in Geneva after returning to London in 1742, an account that was later published, with additions, by Pierre Martel, a Genevan engineer who followed his route and conducted scientific experiments a year later. Windham's feat spurred the residents of Chamonix and Geneva – including Horace-Bénédict de Saussure (see pp.60–63), who held a copy of Windham's account in his personal library – to recognize the wonders on their doorstep, while his description of the "terrible havock" of the ice encouraged countless tourists from across Europe to flock to the mountains and glaciers of the Alps.

FOUR TIMES THE SNOW BRIDGES ... GAVE WAY BENEATH OUR FEET, AND WE SAW THE ABYSS BELOW US

MICHEL-GABRIEL PACCARD ON THE SUCCESSFUL ASCENT OF MONT BLANC

A LIFE'S WORK

- After several significant explorations by Paccard and one by Bouritt, Paccard and Balmat team up to **make the first successful ascent of Mont Blanc**

- Despite obtaining Balmat's signature on a statement that the **route and leadership of the climb were entirely Paccard's**, the doctor's own version of events is **not universally accepted until over a century later**

- Paccard **continues recreational climbing** in the mountains around Chamonix

- Balmat makes **seven more ascents of Mont Blanc** as a guide

PACCARD AND BALMAT

FIRST TO REACH THE SUMMIT OF MONT BLANC

DUCHY OF SAVOY 1757–1827; 1762–1834

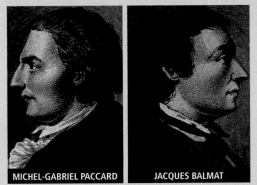

MICHEL-GABRIEL PACCARD

JACQUES BALMAT

IN 1786, TWO MEN with very different temperaments joined forces to take on the might of the as-yet-unscaled Mont Blanc. Michel-Gabriel Paccard, a doctor noted for his modesty and sympathetic character, and Jacques Balmat, an opportunistic crystal gatherer chasing glory, made history with a stupendous feat of mountaineering, climbing an untested route without ropes or ice axes to the summit of the highest mountain in Europe.

Michel-Gabriel Paccard was born in Chamonix, and became the town physician by the age of 26. Like many other educated men in the region, he was interested in botany, the natural sciences, and the mountain that loomed high above his home – Mont Blanc. As others in the valley began to make forays onto the peak – spurred on by the reward that had been offered in 1760 by Horace-Bénédict de Saussure (see pp.60–63) to the first person to find a route to the top – Paccard followed suit, recording and commenting on the efforts by the various parties in sparse but precise detail in his notebook.

The junior of the duo by five years, chamois hunter Jacques Balmat was also a native of Chamonix. He first appeared on the climbing scene just months before making his successful ascent with Paccard, and although physically strong and a capable climber, he was notorious for his cunning and was generally disliked by the other mountain guides.

and glaciers in search of plant specimens. It was one of the earliest and most thorough expeditions into the heart of the Mont Blanc massif, but it would be another eight years before Paccard made a serious attempt on the mountain's summit, in which time only two other parties had tried – and failed.

In 1783, Paccard was approached by the influential Genevan Marc Théodore Bourrit (see p.62), who was obsessed with the idea of climbing Mont Blanc himself, but also wanted to associate himself with anyone else likely to make the first ascent. He persuaded Paccard to lead him up the mountain, but his ego proved to be stronger than his nerve: after an overnight bivouac, they were forced to retreat. Paccard wrote in his notebook, "Monsieur Bourrit did not dare go on the ice." Although the men had failed to get anywhere near the top of Mont Blanc, Bourrit's penchant for exaggeration ensured that the climb sent ripples through the small circle of would-be Mont Blanc-baggers.

EXPEDITION LEADER

While Balmat was still a youth, Paccard was making his first trips into the mountains around his valley home. In 1775, Paccard escorted a visiting Scottish naturalist, Thomas Blaikie, on a roving five-day tour of the nearby mountains

CLIMBING OBSERVATIONS
Paccard recorded scathing insights in his notebook (left), revealing that Bourrit climbed by leaning on the shoulder of one guide while being pulled by the collar by another.

RIVERS OF ICE
Balmat and Paccard negotiating the glaciers on Mont Blanc with simple, iron-tipped alpenstocks: "We escaped catastrophe by throwing ourselves flat on our batons laid horizontally on the snow … we slid along them until we were across the crevasse," Paccard later told de Saussure.

In 1784, Paccard explored several potential routes on Mont Blanc, finding no way past the Géant Glacier on the northeast slopes of the mountain, but having more luck via the Bionnassay Glacier to the west. He reached as far as the Tête Rousse, a rocky outcrop at 3,167m (10,391ft), and, convinced it had potential as a route to the top, wrote to de Saussure.

Somehow, Bourrit got wind of the route and attempted to trump his former ally, setting off on 16 September. True to form, he fell ill after reaching Paccard's high point, but two of his guides pushed on to the snowy summit of the Dôme de Goûter, at 4,304m (14,120ft) – the highest point yet attained on Mont Blanc.

ENTER THE HUNTER

Paccard's Bionnassay route spelt disaster for the village of Chamonix, which had begun to draw a small profit from the trickle of tourists coming to marvel at Mont Blanc. The most direct approach to the Bionnassay Glacier was from the village of St Gervais, some 25km (15 miles) to the west, meaning that the inn and guiding trade was in danger of being lost should the summit be conquered from that direction.

In the summer of 1786, a group of Chamoniard guides gathered to prove that the Dôme de Goûter – the preferred access point to the upper slopes of Mont Blanc – could be reached from Chamonix in less time than it took to climb via the Bionnassay Glacier.

One party would sleep above the Bionnassay Glacier while another would sleep at the top of the Montagne de la Côte, with both groups racing for the Dôme de Goûter at first light. All was proceeding to plan when, unexpectedly, Jacques Balmat entered the fray. Against the wishes of the other guides, he was permitted to join the latter group so long as he brought his own food and water.

PUBLICIZING THE ALPS
In addition to de Saussure's reward, Bourrit's books and illustrations covering the Mont Blanc region, from 1773 onwards, stimulated interest in the valley and the mountain, turning Chamonix into a fashionable resort.

Chamonix's future was secured when Balmat's group won the race by as much as three hours, but the onward route to the summit was investigated and deemed impossible. Rather than descend, Balmat stayed to search for quartzite and became separated from his companions, who left him to fend for himself. After a night in the open he awoke shivering with cold, his clothes rimed with hoar frost, but elated to be alive – at the time it was believed impossible to survive a night at such an altitude. Balmat later claimed he had stayed on the mountain to investigate an entirely new route – one of many fabrications.

UNLIKELY CLIMBING TEAM

On his return to Chamonix, Balmat went straight to the town physician, Paccard, for treatment of his sunburn. The doctor grilled the hunter on the details of the climb, and must have been impressed by his ability to spend a night in the open. The germ of an idea for an unlikely alliance was born, though exactly whose idea it was would be contested for years to come. On 7 August 1786, they set out to

UNFORGETTABLE NIGHT OUT
On his 1786 attempt on Mont Blanc, Balmat was forced to spend a night perched high on the mountain. He later claimed that it was then that he spotted a route right up to the summit.

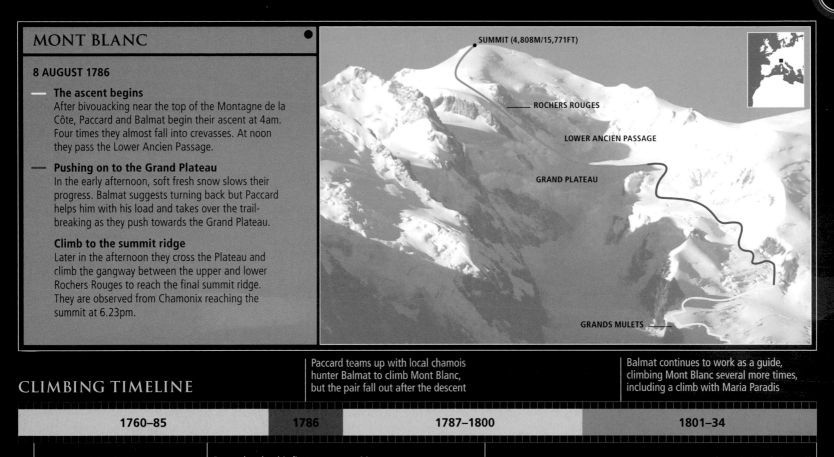

MONT BLANC

8 AUGUST 1786

— The ascent begins
After bivouacking near the top of the Montagne de la Côte, Paccard and Balmat begin their ascent at 4am. Four times they almost fall into crevasses. At noon they pass the Lower Ancien Passage.

— Pushing on to the Grand Plateau
In the early afternoon, soft fresh snow slows their progress. Balmat suggests turning back but Paccard helps him with his load and takes over the trail-breaking as they push towards the Grand Plateau.

Climb to the summit ridge
Later in the afternoon they cross the Plateau and climb the gangway between the upper and lower Rochers Rouges to reach the final summit ridge. They are observed from Chamonix reaching the summit at 6.23pm.

SUMMIT (4,808M/15,771FT)

ROCHERS ROUGES

LOWER ANCIEN PASSAGE

GRAND PLATEAU

GRANDS MULETS

CLIMBING TIMELINE

Paccard teams up with local chamois hunter Balmat to climb Mont Blanc, but the pair fall out after the descent

Balmat continues to work as a guide, climbing Mont Blanc several more times, including a climb with Maria Paradis

1760–85	1786	1787–1800	1801–34

Horace-Bénédict de Saussure offers a prize to the first person to climb Mont Blanc

Paccard makes his first attempt on Mont Blanc with Marc Théodore Bourrit, but they turn back after an overnight bivouac

Despite the duo's continued bickering, Paccard marries Balmat's sister Marie in 1796

Balmat dies by falling off a cliff while prospecting for gold in the Sixt Valley

---

climb Mont Blanc. That evening, the men bivouacked near the top of the Montagne de la Côte. Rising at 4am, they negotiated the ice and crevasses of the Taconnaz Glacier with difficulty, finding the going tough. Paccard wrote later, "Four times the snow bridges, by which we tried to cross the crevasses, gave way beneath our feet, and we saw the abyss below us". By noon they had only reached the Grands Mulets rocks, at 3,051m (10,009ft) still more than 1.5km (1 mile) vertically below the summit. Paccard became sure that a bivouac high on the mountain would be necessary.

Sharing the laborious trail-breaking through soft, fresh snow, the duo eventually approached the steep ramp between the lower and upper Rochers Rouges. At about 4,550m (14,930ft), this section of the climb was the steepest and most exposed of the route. Without ropes or ice axes, and burdened with heavy scientific equipment, the men proceeded carefully, using the iron spikes of their batons to pick

out steps. Once this final obstacle was cleared, they climbed the straightforward summit slope and reached the top together.

Paccard spent some time trying to take measurements with a barometer and thermometer, but found that his ink had frozen. Meanwhile, Balmat signalled to the watching villagers of Chamonix with a handkerchief tied to his baton, and the two men set off to inform de Saussure.

DISUNITED IN VICTORY

Suffering from snowblindness, exhaustion, and frostbite, the duo started their descent, reaching the previous night's bivouac shortly before midnight. At dawn they continued to Chamonix. Remarkably, the doctor and the hunter had triumphed where all before had failed. Although others had greater resources, Paccard's years of studying the mountain and Balmat's daring paid off in a collaboration between scientific endeavour and hardy spirit.

CRYSTAL HUNTER
Early Chamonix guides such as Balmat were peasants who lived by a combination of farming, chamois hunting, and, above all, quartzite prospecting.

LATER ASCENTS

Mont Blanc is today considered a relatively easy ascent, and 20,000 people climb it every year. However, storms and rockfall still regularly claim victims, even among experienced climbers. The first woman to reach the summit was Maria Paradis (see pp.100–01) in 1808, with Balmat as her guide. Notable figures who have climbed the peak since include US President Theodore Roosevelt and Pope Pius XI.

THE LAST ASCENT OF MONT BLANC,
PRINT BY J D H BROWNE IN 1853

Sadly, the summit of Mont Blanc was the last place that Paccard and Balmat were truly united. Bourrit published an account of the climb that cast Paccard as a buffoon who would have been left helpless on the mountain were it not for Balmat. The hunter lost no time in claiming de Saussure's reward and built a guiding career on his pioneering feat. The pair wrangled for years over who should have the glory for conquering the mountain.

MOUNTAINEERING INNOVATIONS

CRAMPONS

WALKING ON SNOW AND ICE IS AN OLD PROBLEM. Neolithic Europeans wore footwear designed for travelling across snow, and traditional solutions still in use by the Arctic Sámi people today are millennia old. Roman friezes show men wearing spiked shoes, while the first documented use of crampons or "grappettes" dates from the late 16th century. Used by woodsmen and hunters in the Alps, grappettes were normally fitted with four spikes and were fixed under the heel of shoes to avoid slipping on ice. This pattern continued in various forms until the late 19th century.

GENTLEMAN'S CHOICE

Although grapettes were in use for centuries before the advent of mountaineering, they weren't practical on steep snow and ice, and British climbers preferred their more familiar nailed boots – another style of footwear dating back to the Romans. Guides would use their axes laboriously to hack a line of steps up steep slopes of snow for their employers to follow, a tedious and time-consuming process at which they became incredibly adept. Later, when crampons were developed, British alpinists continued using the footwear they trusted.

Crampons made for the express purpose of climbing and which covered the whole of the boot appeared in 1876, particularly in the Tyrol, where they soon became widespread. Ten-point crampons that were articulated between the heel and front of the foot appeared in Austria in 1884. These innovations were embraced by the new wave of European alpinists, but not by the British, who eschewed crampons for several more decades. Luminaries from successive

3300BCE – NEOLITHIC SNOW BOOTS
Ötzi the Iceman perishes in the Alps wearing boots suitable for hiking in snow (see pp.16–19).

315CE – SPY'S SHOES
A sandal with spikes, for use by Roman spies, is depicted on the Arch of Constantine in Rome.

1510 SIMPLE SPIKES
A simple wood-and-rope attachment is used for walking on firm snow. A similar version is made from bamboo.

1876 – FIRST COMPLETE CRAMPON
A six-point crampon is developed by Pastori de Brescia, while an Austrian ten-point model appears in 1884. Their use becomes widespread in the Tyrol.

1910 – BOOTS FOR ANTARCTICA
British explorer Robert Falcon Scott uses boots with nails hammered through the soles for traction in Antarctica.

| BCE | 4000 | 3000 | CE | 300 | 500 | 1500 | 1600 | 1700 | 1800 | 1900 | 1910 | 1920 | 1930 |

1574 – THREE SPIKES
Josias Simmler (see pp.40–41) writes of 16th-century glacier travel: "To counteract the slipperiness of the ice, they firmly attach to their feet shoes … with three sharp spikes in them."

1588 – GRAPETTES
A signore de Villemont describes the use of "grapettes" – four spikes fixed under shoes – by woodsmen and hunters to avoid slipping.

1908 – ECKENSTEIN
Designs for 10-point crampons are published by Eckenstein. He organizes crampon competitions in 1912 to demonstrate their effectiveness.

1929 – FRONT POINTS
Laurent Grivel adds front points to crampons, allowing climbers to kick the toe into the slope, rather than place the sole of the foot flat on ice. Front points also emerge in the Eastern Alps in the early 1930s.

The origins of skiing probably lie among the forebears of the Sámi of Arctic Europe (right), but there is little evidence of skiing in the Alps until the 17th century. Ötzi the Iceman, who lived about the time the earliest remains of skis have been found in Sweden, used snowshoes. The earliest known iron spikes for walking on snow and ice are Roman.

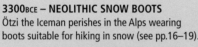

Blacksmiths in the Tyrol develop an articulated crampon that straps onto the whole boot rather than just the heel. Eckenstein's later design is far more effective, allowing climbers to ascend without cutting steps. This becomes known as the "French technique", which guide Armand Charlet (see p.125) turns into an art form. For steep angles step-cutting is still necessary, and Willo Welzenbach (see pp.236–37) climbs 75-degree ice in the 1920s in this way.

3300BCE EARLY SNOWSHOES

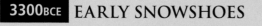

1884 10-POINT CRAMPON

generations, including Clinton Dent (see pp.164–65) and Harold Raeburn, condemned their use as unsporting, and even dangerous.

POINTED REVOLUTIONARY

It took an iconoclast like Oscar Eckenstein (see right and pp.196–97) to refine the rudimentary designs into the standard from which modern crampons derive. In 1929, Laurent Grivel – whose father Henry was the blacksmith who turned Eckenstein's plans into reality – had the idea of adding a pair of "front points" and the ten-point crampon became the 12-point, revolutionizing the way climbers moved on ice. Four years later, his younger brother Amato produced the first chrome–molybdenum steel crampons, vastly improving their durability.

In the 1960s, Austrian manufacturer Stubai moved the secondary points closer to the two front points, improving stability. In 1967, Yvon Chouinard (see pp.302–03) and Tom Frost invented rigid crampons that required less of a kick to force the points in, and worked well

A SPIKY CHARACTER

When British railway engineer Eckenstein took his plans for a new design for a ten-point crampon to Henry Grivel of Courmayeur, the blacksmith was initially doubtful, but saw that his client was serious and willing to pay. The crampons were fashioned – appropriately – from old railway ties, and Eckenstein and his friend Arthur Andrews published articles explaining how they removed the need for step-cutting. Eckenstein was instrumental as much for his advocacy of crampons as his technical innovation.

TO DEMONSTRATE HIS INVENTION, ECKENSTEIN (RIGHT) HELD CRAMPON RACES

with the shorter ice axes that were becoming popular. Subsequent innovations included single front-points for vertical ice, and heel spurs for overhanging climbs. Crampons are now anatomically shaped, and often feature a rubber

plate to prevent snow collecting beneath the sole – the cause of many falls in the past. Bindings are also crucial: fiddling with straps used to put climbers at risk of frostbite, but was resolved with the development of snap-in bindings.

1938 – ANDERL HECKMAIR
Twelve-point crampons are used by Heckmair (see pp.290–91) on the first ascent of the Eiger's North Face. He recognizes that the ascent will include many pitches of steep ice.

1975 – RIGID CRAMPONS
Yvon Chouinard develops a rigid crampon that is more stable and needs less force to place in ice.

1979 – ANTI-BALLING
Crampons can cause a ball of ice to form under the sole, which can lead to slipping and tripping. A rubber plate is developed to prevent snow accumulating.

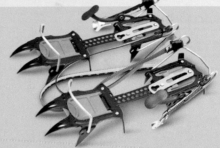

1940   1950   1960   1970   1980   1990   2000   2010

1937 – VIBRAM SOLES
Vitale Bramani develops a new type of rubber boot sole that makes boots much warmer and more secure on rock.

1960 – NEW INNOVATIONS
Manufacturer Stubai moves the front horizontal points forwards and inclines them, adding extra purchase. Salewa develops adjustable crampons that don't require fitting in a workshop.

1986 – MONOPOINTS
Grivel and Charlet develop a single front-point, or "mono-point" crampon for vertical ice. Vertical rather than horizontal blades on the front points also help penetration.

The combination of short ice axes, front points, and rigid crampons – developed from the mid-1960s by Yvon Chouinard and Tom Frost – revolutionizes ice climbing. In 1972, Mike Lowe develops the "footfang", a rigid crampon with prominent front points and a ski binding for easy fitting. In general use by the late 1970s, Lowe's design – along with plastic mountaineering boots with rigid soles – heralds an era of increasing specialization in climbing equipment.

Plastic boots and rigid crampons are ubiquitous during the 1980s, but towards the end of the century designs are lighter and more ergonomic, with rigid and semi-rigid crampons appearing that imitate the outline of the foot. Performance advantages include a more natural and less tiring climbing style, with the crampons acting as an extension of the foot. Single front-points for climbing vertical ice and heel spurs for overhangs also appear.

1979   **FOOTFANGS**

2000s   **MODERN DESIGNS**

PARADIS AND D'ANGEVILLE

COURAGEOUS WOMEN OF CLIMBING'S EARLY DAYS

DUCHY OF SAVOY
FRANCE

1778–1839
1794–1871

MARIA PARADIS   HENRIETTE D'ANGEVILLE

THE FIRST WOMEN TO STAND ON Mont Blanc, Maria Paradis and Henriette d'Angeville were separated by 30 years and had very different motivations. For Paradis, a Chamonix stallholder and maidservant, the ascent was a publicity stunt cooked up by the wily Jacques Balmat to enliven her trade. For d'Angeville, an aristocratic lady with a love for the mountains, it was a combination of personal pleasure and gender-equality statement.

A TRAMP ABROAD
Mark Twain's travel classic *A Tramp Abroad* (1880) unfairly suggests that Balmat was Paradis's lover. Twain collected such stories and trivia during his journey through the Alps.

Other than the year of her birth, little is known of the early life of Maria Paradis. A peasant born in the Chamonix valley, she owes her place in the story of mountaineering to Jacques Balmat (see pp.94–97). D'Angeville, by contrast, was born during the French Revolution to an aristocratic family who were dispossessed of their land. After they relocated to Bugey, east of Lyon, d'Angeville developed a love for walking, doubtless inspired by the Alps, which were just visible from her home.

RELUCTANT MOUNTAINEER
In 1808, following in the wake of gentleman-scientists and local hunters, Paradis became the first woman to climb Mont Blanc. It seems that she didn't go on the mountain entirely of her own volition, however. According to Balmat, who had taken part in the first ascent of the mountain 22 years earlier, her presence on the summit was due to his persuasive words: "I am an old wolf of the mountains … all I ask of you is to be courageous". Paradis gave a far more pragmatic reason for the climb: "[The guides told me] you are a pretty girl and you need to earn money. Travellers will ask to see you, and they will tip you well."

Paradis set off with Balmat and two other guides on 13 July, climbing to the Grands Mulets, where the group spent the night.

The next day she found the going arduous, begging Balmat to "throw me in a crevasse and go where you want" on the Grand Plateau. Instead, the two guides grasped her by the arms and hauled her to the top – Paradis was too valuable for Balmat's reputation as a guide to leave languishing below the summit.

On her return to Chamonix, Paradis was quizzed on her experience, but was so chastened that she could give no detail, merely stating that the mountain was available for all interested parties should they wish to look for themselves. She later said of her ascent: "I climbed, I could not breathe, I nearly died, they dragged me, carried me, I saw black and white, and then I came down again." Paradis's feat had the desired effect commercially, though – she became one of Chamonix's most famous residents, adopting the name "Maria de Mont-Blanc", and opening a profitable tearoom at her home in Les Pèlerins.

CLIMBING FOR WOMEN
The story of Paradis's woes on Mont Blanc served to reinforce the view that the highest mountain in Europe was no place for a woman. When d'Angeville started to consider making an ascent in the 1830s, such was the strength of opinion against the idea that she

was forced to stop receiving guests at her Geneva lodgings. Disregarding the well-meaning advice of, among others, her doctor and her priest, she set about planning an expedition for 1838. After making training sorties to the Talèfre Glacier (2,600m/8,530ft) and Mont Joly (2,525m/8,284ft), d'Angeville set off from Chamonix on 4 September with a team of six guides and six porters, politely declining the advice to team up with other male-led parties on the mountain. She had been very careful to make sure that provisions for her entourage were adequate and the party were laden down with 18 bottles of wine and an impressively large array of luxury foodstuffs.

Climbing fully under her own steam – declining yet another offer, this time for a mule to carry her up the lower slopes – she proved adept at the Rochers Rouges, the most technical part of the climb, but nearly succumbed to altitude sickness on the summit slopes. She recovered in time for her guides to hoist her onto their shoulders in celebration, elevating her to the position of highest person in Europe. She later wrote, "As soon as I was on the top, the resurrection was immediate. I recovered all my strength at once … and all my intellectual power, which enabled me to enjoy that magnificent scene in all its grandeur!"

The pioneering climb was not a one-off for d'Angeville – she went on to make another 29 climbs, including a repeat ascent of Mont Blanc. Her final climb was the 3,125-m (10,250-ft) Oldenhorn in 1865, when she was 69, after which she hung up her climbing gear with the words "it is wise at my age to drop the alpenstock before the alpenstock drops me".

In their different ways, Paradis and d'Angeville had blazed a trail for women climbers – proving that they were physically capable, and then by showing they could climb competently without assistance from men.

MY BREATH BECAME SHORT ... I FELT A DESIRE TO CLIMB, SO ARDENT THAT IT GAVE MOVEMENT TO MY FEET

HENRIETTE D'ANGEVILLE ON HER ASCENT OF MONT BLANC

ON TOP OF THE WORLD
D'Angeville had given public notice of her attempt on Mont Blanc and crowds of well-wishers saw her off; on reaching the top, she released a carrier pigeon to announce her success.

THE MEYER FAMILY

A MOUNTAINEERING DYNASTY IN THE BERNESE ALPS

SWITZERLAND ACTIVE 1787–1812

JOHANN RUDOLF MEYER

LONG BEFORE THE MIGHTY Unteraar Glacier attracted droves of scientists bearing instruments to measure the movement of the ice, three generations of a single family – the Meyers of Aarau – were making great strides among the towering peaks of the surrounding Bernese Alps. Coming first for the purpose of a cartographical survey, then climbing for climbing's sake, Johann Rudolf Meyer and his sons and grandsons made a number of notable ascents, including the first ascent of the Jungfrau.

A LIFE'S WORK

- One of Johann Rudolf's topographical models, at a scale of 1:60,000 and measuring 1.5 × 4.5m (5 × 15ft) – is so detailed that it is **confiscated by Napoleon's war ministry** while on display in an exhibition in Paris

- Johann Rudolf junior makes the **first crossing of the Tschingel Pass** (2,820m/9,252ft) in 1790 at the age of 22

- Gottlieb encounters a wide bergschrund during the first ascent of the Jungfrau in 1812 and crosses it with the poles that had been **intended for flying a flag from the summit**

- During their 1812 climbing attempts, Rudolf and Gottlieb **cross three previously unexplored high-mountain passes**: the Strahlegg Pass, the Grünhornlücke, and the Oberaarjoch, all higher than 3,000m (10,000ft)

- Rudolf surprises the shepherds pasturing their sheep on the meadows above the lower Grindelwald Glacier in 1812, since **no one has descended from the Strahlegg Pass** before

- After studying medicine, Rudolf Meyer later becomes professor of natural sciences in Aarau, publishing *The Spirits of Nature* in 1820

The first in the line of the Meyer dynasty was Johann Rudolf, born in 1739 in the town of Aarau in northern Switzerland. Despite a limited education, he made his fortune as a merchant by selling cloth and, from 1783, by running a silk ribbon factory, becoming a wealthy and prominent citizen of the town. His first documented forays into the mountains came in 1787, during the conception of an

ambitious atlas of Switzerland, the *Atlas Suisse*, and these exploits must have made an impression on his teenage sons, Johann Rudolf junior and Hieronymous.

Meyer put his wealth from the flourishing international trade in silk ribbon to several good uses, including extensive underground works to improve Aarau's water supply and the construction of a state school for the town. But as well as being a civic-minded individual, Meyer had a fascination with the Alps. In the summer of 1787 he climbed the Titlis, a mountain in central Switzerland of 3,238m (10,623ft) in height, with Johann Weiss and Joachim Muller, a geometrist and a carpenter, who would play a crucial role in realizing his dream of mapping the mountains.

MAPPING THE ALPS

Inspired by contemporary advances in surveying in Britain and France, Meyer commissioned, at his own expense, a survey that would eventually lead to the publication of the 16-sheet *Atlas Suisse* between 1796 and 1802. Weiss was the

mathematical brain behind the endeavour, overseeing the triangulation required to survey the complex maze of mountains and valleys, while Muller was the skilled craftsman who constructed detailed scale models of the mountain landscape. The resulting map of Switzerland was the first based on accurate scientific survey and astonishingly detailed.

FOR CLIMBING'S SAKE

Johann Rudolf's two sons shared his interest in mountains, although their approach to them was rather different from his own. Johann Rudolf junior and Hieronymous boldly took to climbing for no better reason than the thrill of the activity itself. They didn't trouble to dress their adventures with grand scientific purpose, as others felt compelled to do at the time – they climbed without any scientific ambitions or instruments, because they believed "these merely hampered a daring climber".

The peak most closely associated with the Meyers is the Jungfrau, at 4,158m (13,642ft), the third-highest mountain in the Bernese Alps. The highest point of a formidable wall 10km (6 miles) in length that rears some 3,000m (10,000ft) above the valley floor, the Jungfrau sits alongside the Mönch (4,105m/13,468ft) and the Eiger (3,970m/13,025ft), the North Face of which is still considered to be the most daunting in the Alps.

MEYER FAMILY HOME
Johann Rudolf Meyer senior was born in this merchant's house in Aarau. By the time he was working in the Alps on his atlas, the town was a hotbed of political radicalism, with many supporting the revolutionary ideas spreading over the mountains from neighbouring France.

The Meyer brothers attempted to climb the Jungfrau in August 1811, approaching the mountain from the Grimsel Pass on a 30-km (18-mile) long, two-day march, during which they endured bad weather. Setting up a base camp on the Aletsch Glacier, the two brothers then ascended the gentler, southern side of the mountain with two guides on 3 August to reach what they took to be the summit, but was in fact a lower, secondary summit at 4,089m (13,415ft).

PROVING THE POINT

Although the brothers had planted a black flag on a pole to prove their claim to the summit, witnesses had failed to spot it from the valley below, so a third generation of Meyers stepped in to salvage the family honour. The sons of Johann Rudolf junior, Rudolf and Gottlieb, spent the summer of 1812 exploring the area around the Jungfrau and Finsteraarhorn. Rudolf, the elder at 21, attempted but failed to summit the Finsteraarhorn (4,274m/14,022ft)

via the steep East Face in August, while 19-year-old Gottlieb succeeded in reaching the true, higher 4,158-m (13,641-ft) peak of the Jungfrau on 3 September. On the same day, Rudolf made the first authentic passage of the 3,315-m (10,876-ft) Strahlegg Pass, a feat that was repeated by his uncle Hieronymous the next day.

Following their bumper climbing season of 1812, nothing more is heard of the Meyer family in the annals of mountaineering. Nevertheless, their daring, lengthy expeditions

to the high mountain passes of the Bernese Alps made them early pioneers of climbing. In addition, Johann Rudolf senior's detailed topographical maps were a vital contribution to the later exploration of the Swiss Alps, enabling others to venture into previously unknown regions. His atlas was unsurpassed until Henri Dufour's surveys of the 1850s (see p.214), while the mountaineering exploits of his sons and grandsons marked the start of the age of conquest of the high mountains of the Swiss Alps.

SCIENTIFIC INSTRUMENTS MERELY HAMPERED A DARING CLIMBER

JOHANN RUDOLF MEYER JUNIOR

MIGHTY JUNGFRAU
Together with the Eiger, the Mönch (left) and the Jungfrau (right) form a huge wall overlooking the Bernese Oberland. The summit of the Jungfrau was first reached in 1812 by brothers Rudolf and Gottlieb Meyer.

GOTTLIEB STUDER

PROLIFIC CLIMBER AND TOPOGRAPHER ●

SWITZERLAND   1804–90

EXPLORER AND DRAUGHTSMAN of the mountains of Switzerland, Gottlieb Studer explored the lesser known high-altitude areas of his country over a period of more than 60 years. Although he made several first ascents, Studer was not a trailblazer of high-profile Alpine peaks, preferring instead to explore and document the mountain environment through a series of panoramic vistas that became his trademark. In 1863, he co-founded the Swiss Alpine Club, at that time only the second mountaineering society in the world.

ALPINE ATLAS
Studer published *Topographical Newsletter from the Alps* in 1843 (right). It contained a series of his coloured "folding" panoramas (below).

Gottlieb Studer was born near Langnau in central Switzerland, but moved with his family to his mother's hometown of Bern after the death of his father. Following his education and training as a legal clerk, he worked for the Bern state authorities as secretary to the judiciary until 1847, then as a governor from 1850. His public-service career enabled him to devote himself to his first love – the Swiss Alps.

A PANORAMIC VISION

Like his father, who had painted watercolours of the Alps in his spare time from his job as a clerk, Studer possessed an artistic talent for accurately sketching the natural landscape. It was this topographical skill that drove him into the remoter reaches of the Swiss mountains – he largely shunned the showpiece peaks of the day, such as the Matterhorn.

Studer's first serious climb came in 1825 when he attempted to scale the 3,210-m (10,531-ft) Diablerets in the Bernese Alps. The climb was evidently too difficult for the 21-year-old aspiring alpinist. Returning only in 1850, with a full 25 years of mountaineering to his name, the route to the summit was described as "somewhat dangerous for the steepness of the ice-slope that has to be surmounted … The expedition is one that requires thorough training, good guides, and the use of the rope and ice-axe."

Despite this early setback, Studer continued to make regular excursions into the high peaks of Switzerland. He made the first ascent of the Sustenhorn in 1841, a 3,503-m (11,493-ft) high mountain in the eastern Bernese Alps, and a year later made the fifth ascent of the Jungfrau. He claimed another first ascent in 1843, climbing the 3,248-m (10,656-ft) high Wildhorn, a satellite peak of the Finsteraarhorn, partly for the view it afforded of the nearby Pennine Alps: " … the view … from this peak [is] the finest and most complete attainable from any point on the north side of that great range."

Studer was a keen mountaineer who saw no need to combine his desire to climb with scientific study. However, his explorations were not carried out merely for the sake of enjoyment. He sketched the panoramas of peaks that spread out before him from

PANORAMA ARTIST
Studer was a master of the topographically accurate mountain panorama, a commercial art form that grew rapidly as the Alps opened up to tourists and mountaineers during the late 18th and early 19th centuries.

his mountain perches – such as that on the Wildhorn – then turned his preliminary drawings into detailed topographical engravings on his return to Bern. His first work appeared in 1849 in the form of a map of half of the southern valleys of the Valais region of Switzerland, which incorporated vistas from many of the

peaks he had climbed in the Bernese Alps and neighbouring Pennine Alps. This was to be the first of more than 700 such works.

BORN IN THE BAHNHOFBUFFET

Studer's steady progress across the Swiss Alps brought him to the attention of the wider mountaineering community. In 1859, he became the first foreign honorary member of the Alpine Club, the world's first mountaineering society, which had been founded two years earlier in London. Inspired by the actions of his British counterparts, Studer resolved to take similar steps to encourage his countrymen to take to the hills.

On 19 April 1863, the Bahnhofbuffet – railway-station restaurant – in the northern Swiss town of Olten hosted a low-key meeting that would have lasting implications for mountaineering in Switzerland. In conjunction with geologist Theodor Simler and theologian Melchior Ulrich, Studer founded the Swiss

STUDERHORN
The peak named in honour of Studer rises 3,638-m (11,936-ft) near Ulrichen, Switzerland. Nearby is the Finsteraar Glacier.

Alpine Club, only the second such organization in the world. Grouped into regional sections – Studer himself was president of the Bern section – and focused on building mountain huts to enable ready access to Switzerland's peaks, the Swiss Alpine Club grew into a more open organization than the Alpine Club, which operated as a gentlemen's club.

Studer retired from his job for the Bern state authorities in 1866, increasingly devoting himself to the Swiss Alpine Club. His four-part masterwork, *Over Ice and Snow*, an illustrated guide to the history of mountaineering in Switzerland, was published between 1869 and 1873, at which point he was made honorary

president of the Swiss Alpine Club. He continued to climb well into his retirement, scaling Mont Blanc at the age of 68, the 2,998-m (9,836-ft) Pic d'Arzinol at 79, and finally the 1,950-m (6,398-ft) Niederhorn at 81. With more than 600 ascents to his name, a back catalogue of panoramic illustrations, and as co-founder of a pioneering club for alpinists, Studer was truly one of the founding fathers of Swiss mountaineering.

[HIS] DESCRIPTIONS OF THE LESS KNOWN PARTS OF THE ALPINE CHAINS, OF WHICH HE WAS ONE OF THE FIRST EXPLORERS, ARE APPRECIATED BY ALL ALPINE TRAVELLERS "

JOHN BALL, FIRST PRESIDENT OF THE ALPINE CLUB, ON GOTTLIEB STUDER

PLACIDUS À SPESCHA

MOUNTAINEERING MONK

SWITZERLAND   1752–1833

IMPRISONED AS A SUSPECTED SPY by an invading Austrian army and ostracized by his fellow Benedictine monks for his scientific pursuits, Placidus à Spescha paid a high price for his love of the mountains. He was the first to investigate and document the geologically uncharted region around his monastery in eastern Switzerland – making more than 30 first ascents along the way. Sadly, most of his work was lost when his monastery was burned down by the French army during the Revolutionary Wars.

MAPPING BY HAND

In keeping with à Spescha's self-taught approach to climbing, his map-making efforts were self-penned affairs that loosely depicted the location of neighbouring peaks, valleys, and rivers rather than accurately charting their positions. Since he was untrained in surveying and lacking the necessary equipment, his maps possess a simplistic quality that reflects his first-hand knowledge of the areas he explored, such as the Urserental Valley (below), a former holding of the abbey at Disentis. Despite their lack of precision, his maps were still used against him when he was arrested by the French.

À SPESCHA DREW SIMPLE MAPS, SUCH AS THIS EXAMPLE OF URSERENTAL, SOME 40KM (25 MILES) WEST OF DISENTIS

Born in Trun, a small village in a long and wide, steep-sided valley in eastern Switzerland, Placidus à Spescha showed an interest in the natural world from an early age, reportedly scrambling among the rocks around his home. He was educated at Chur, a town 50km (35 miles) downriver that also lay on the valley floor, and began his novitiate into the town's Benedictine order of monks in 1774, attracted to the monastic life as a means to further his studies of nature.

However, it was seven years before à Spescha's interest in mountaineering was sparked, during a posting to the Benedictine

hospice at the Lukmanier pass in the Swiss Alps. The 29-year-old monk was able to leave the confines of the valley for the first time in his life, climbing to his new home at an elevation of some 1,920m (6,300ft). Surrounded by peaks that reached up to 3,000m (9,000ft), the hospice was a spectacular setting in which to fall in love with the high mountains.

HIGH INSPIRATION

À Spescha began avidly reading the works of the Swiss naturalists of the period, particularly those of Horace-Bénédict de Saussure (see pp.60–63), and was inspired to climb the peaks in search of quartzite samples.

After his final year of monastic training, in 1782 à Spescha left the hospice to return to his home valley as a full member of the Abbey of Disentis. Despite his relocation to a less elevated landscape, he resolved to explore and document the uncharted, pristine mountains there, just as de Saussure had done in the Western Alps.

In the 1780s, mountaineering had yet to reach eastern Switzerland so à Spescha taught himself the basic skills. He learned how to draw mountain panoramas and rudimentary maps and developed a crude scheme for calculating the progression of glaciers. He schooled himself the best he could in climbing

CRYSTAL HUNTING

Many of the earliest alpinists climbed in search of chamois or crystals, and it was the prospect of finding quartzite (left) that first lured à Spescha to the Alps.

ways, from predicting mountain storms to the necessity for hobnailed boots. Despite this, he appears to have been reluctant to cross glaciers, and his fear of the ice may have prevented him from tackling the very highest peaks.

BEGINNING TO CLIMB

He spent the next 20 years combining his monastic duties with mountaineering. As the area's high point at 3,614m (11,857ft), the Tödi was his focal point, and his earliest recorded first ascents were made around the mountain.

In 1788, he climbed the Stoc Grond, an outlying summit of the Tödi at 3,422m (11,214ft). The following year, he turned his attention to the south of the region, climbing the Rheinwaldhorn, a peak of 3,402m (11,149ft) in the vicinity of the Lukmanier hospice. The nearest high mountain to his abbey, the 3,328-m (10,926-ft) Oberalpstock followed in 1792, while in 1793 he climbed Piz Urlaun, another summit in the Tödi group, at 3,359m (11,020ft).

A LIFE'S WORK

- Climbs mostly **without guides**, but hires local hunters for some of his expeditions. Since the **region is unexplored**, he has to cajole them to go far beyond their usual range

- As well as first ascents, he makes a number of **important journeys in mountain areas**, although he largely avoids travel on glaciers

- His **resting point** on the Tödi during his fifth and final attempt on the mountain comes to be known as **Porta da Spescha** (3,352m/10,997ft)

- Suggests the formation of a **Swiss Alpine club**, a recommendation that is later taken up by Gottlieb Studer (see pp.104–05)

IN THE CHOICE OF COMPANION FOR A MOUNTAIN EXPEDITION, ONE CANNOT BE TOO PARTICULAR

PLACIDUS À SPESCHA

GATHERING CLOUDS

Although à Spescha performed his monastic duties in a manner that won him respect and influence, he also drew criticism from monks who felt that mountaineering was an inappropriate pastime for a man of the cloth. Ironically, the very same attributes that led à Spescha into the mountains – a liberal outlook and an interest in the outside world – came to be highly prized by his fellow monks. In 1799, Napoleon's army occupied the area, and à Spescha was sent to mediate French demands for tribute. He was successful in his task, but at a price – he was forced to hand over a large portion of his scientific collection.

Further misfortune came when two decades of work was burned in a fire while à Spescha was away from the abbey, only for him to be charged with spying for the French by Austrian forces on his return – his hand-drawn maps were cited as evidence. He was deported to Innsbruck in Austria, where he was imprisoned in a convent.

UNDIMMED PASSION

It appears that à Spescha passed his time in Innsbruck agreeably, but on his release he was out of favour with the Abbey of Disentis. As a result, he spent much of his later life working as a chaplain in neighbouring parishes. His unrelenting thirst for the mountains may also have been a factor in this choice: he went on to expand his list of first ascents by climbing the 3,124-m (10,250-ft) Piz Aul in 1801, the 3,151-m (10,338-ft) Piz Terri in 1802, and the Guferhorn (3,383m/11,099ft) in 1806.

The jewel in the crown – the Tödi – came in 1824, although à Spescha was not able to claim the prize for himself. Realizing he would not be able to reach the top, the 72-year-old urged his guides on up to the summit. In à Spescha's own words, "the old barrack collapsed". When he died a few years later, it marked the end of 50 years of mountaineering. While he may have lacked the scientific clout of some of his contemporaries – he published only a tiny portion of his work – his self-taught exploits made him a true pioneer of alpinism in the eastern Swiss Alps.

MONK ON THE RHEINWALDHORN
À Spescha preferred to be led by older hunters on his ascents. "Young men are not very suitable," he advised in a piece on selecting a guide, "because they dare too much, and in an emergency they cannot give advice."

PETER CARL THURWIESER

PIONEER IN THE AUSTRIAN ALPS

AUSTRIA   1789–1865

CLERIC, PROFESSOR, and amateur meteorologist, Peter Carl Thurwieser was also a prolific mountaineer who clambered over the peaks of the Austrian Alps, despite limited material resources. He made more than 70 climbs between 1820 and 1847 and, along with the Meyer family, was among the first alpinists to do so purely for the pleasure of the climb itself. He made several major first ascents, as well as repeats of two of the highest peaks in the Eastern Alps – the Grossglockner and the Ortler.

Born in the village of Kramsach in the Austrian Tyrol, Thurwieser was slight in stature and suffered poor health as a child, in common with a surprising number of would-be mountaineers. He studied theology at Salzburg at the age of 21 and was ordained in 1812, serving as an assistant priest until his appointment as professor of oriental languages at the University of Salzburg in 1820.

WANDERING THE HILLS
Despite his childhood ailments, Thurwieser had always seized every chance available to venture outdoors. As he reached adulthood, he developed a rare strength and an endurance to add to his gaunt physique – characteristics that came in particularly useful when exploring the limestone mountains that overlooked the city

of Salzburg. But Thurwieser was no city-dwelling weekend hiker. From 1820 onwards, he increasingly took to exploring the high mountains of the Austrian Alps, becoming a familiar sight to the shepherds and peasants who worked in the hills. Although he carried a barometer for measuring the altitude of the summits he reached, as well as a botanical box for collecting interesting plant specimens, these were not his primary motivations – he later described the joy of revelling in the natural beauty of the mountains, combined with the thrill of overcoming dangerous and difficult terrains.

Thurwieser's first recorded ascent was the Watzmann in 1820, a mountain 2,713m (8,900ft) in height with three distinct summits, some 25km (15 miles) south of Salzburg. In

POSTHUMOUS FAME
An illustrated, popular volume of Thurwieser's selected writings was published after his death.

1822, he turned his attention to the Ankogel, a mountain of 3,246m (10,649ft) that had first been climbed in 1762 by a local peasant, while in 1824 he scaled the Grossglockner, at 3,798m (12,460ft) the highest mountain in Austria. On this occasion, Thurwieser was accompanied by Simon Stampfer, a university colleague, and carried a unique array of instruments and pseudo-scientific equipment to the summit. Upon reaching the top, the pair let off fireworks and rockets for supposedly scientific purposes. Thurwieser reported that "the inhabitants of the neighbouring mountains believed to see blazing dragons, and they prophesied the most evil results from this supernatural appearance."

BREAKING FRESH GROUND
From 1824, Thurwieser began to venture into mountain regions where few had trodden before him. His first objective was the Gross Wiesbachhorn, a 3,564-m (11,693-ft) peak that had been climbed by two farmers during the previous century, but had not been repeated. It has a Southeast Face that rears 2,418m (7,933ft) from valley floor to summit, but Thurwieser avoided this to take an easier route to the top. In 1833 he made a first ascent of the 3,295-m

THE FIRST MAN WHO CLIMBED FOR THE SAKE OF CLIMBING ... THE FIRST REAL "MOUNTAINEER"

W A B COOLIDGE ON PETER CARL THURWIESER, 1908

(10,810-ft) Strahlkogel, a mountain in the Stubai Alps of western Austria. The Dachstein and south summit of the Watzmann followed in 1834, while the Habicht and Fernerkogel were taken in 1836.

But Thurwieser was not solely motivated by the prestige of first ascents. Mixed in with his new climbs were repeat ascents of other major peaks, such as the Ortler (3,905m/12,812ft) in 1834. He recorded his climbs in precise detail, describing the features and attractions of his routes, and took advantage of his academic position to publicize some of his first ascents. In 1840 he published *The Ascent and Measuring of the Fernerkogel and Habicht in 1836*, while *The Ahornspitze in the Zillertal* was in the bookshops soon after.

MAN OF THE MOUNTAINS

Thurwieser's final recorded first ascents came as he neared the age of 60, when he was still in peak condition from years of exercise at altitude. In 1846, he climbed the 3,285m (10,777ft) of the Gross Mörchner and

in 1847 the Schrammacher at 3,411m (11,190ft), both situated in the Zillertal Alps of western Austria.

By this time, his incongruous appearance in the mountains was well known – he was described as "… a small, even puny, man with thick glasses and flowing hair, who wore the garb of a lay priest (knee-breeches and a blue coat) and a well-worn mountaineer's hat bearing a tuft of edelweiss."

After the many dangerous climbs he had made in the rock and ice of remote altitudes, Thurwieser's life, as with those of many mountaineers, ended in a relatively trivial accident.

MOUNTAIN STUDY
Thurwieser's book on the Ahornspitze in the Zillertal Alps, illustrated by the engraver Josef Riedl, shows the mountain's routes and topography.

He died in 1865 of injuries sustained in a fall from the roof of his house, where he had ventured to capture straying chickens.

Undoubtedly his country's first true lover of the mountains, Thurwieser had showed that mountaineering could be pursued as an activity in its own right – and in so doing, he racked up an impressive list of first ascents over a half-century of active climbing.

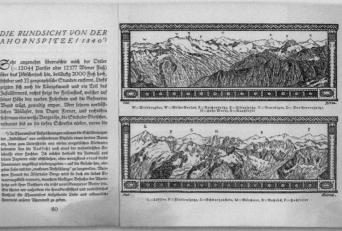

ALBERT SMITH

THE FIRST MOUNTAINEERING CELEBRITY

ENGLAND   1816–60

A FLAMBOYANT SHOWMAN, Albert Smith's stage production of his ascent of Mont Blanc at the Egyptian Hall in Piccadilly, London, excited huge public interest. Before Smith, mountaineering had been an obscure pastime but his showmanship made it a craze, even though the only mountain he ever climbed was Mont Blanc. His lectures on this single outing ran for more than six years, and made him, in today's terms, a millionaire. He became a star, but earned the contempt of some contemporaries.

The son of a surgeon who studied medicine in London and Paris, Albert Smith's journalistic accounts of his experiences as a young doctor in France set him on a career as a writer and humourist. Affable and never far from insolvency, he was an early contributor to the satirical magazine *Punch*, and in 1842 published his first and most successful novel, *The Adventures of Mr Ledbury*. By the end of the 1840s, after publishing several more novels, plays, and stage adaptations – and his own magazine, *The Man in the Moon* – Smith left London for a tour of Istanbul in Turkey.

As a young man, Smith had been thrilled by stories of the early climbing pioneers, and had entertained his sister with a show and tell, featuring panoramas of Mont Blanc, which he'd constructed and painted himself. When he returned from Istanbul, after writing a book about the trip, he did something similar, producing an entertainment that was staged at Willis's Rooms in London. It wasn't long before he had an inspired idea: that his own ascent of Mont Blanc would give him the material to do something altogether more extraordinary, so he sank his earnings from this first show into his long-dreamed-of expedition to the mountain.

A LAVISH ASCENT

There was nothing new about Smith's climb, made in August 1851. It was about the 40th ascent, and remarkable only for the vast quantity of supplies his 36 guides and porters took with them. These included 60 bottles of *vin ordinaire*, six bottles of Bordeaux, 15 bottles of St George, three bottles of cognac, 35 small fowls, and 20 loaves of bread. Altogether, the climb cost Smith and his three companions £240, a staggering sum in 1851. There was little drama in their ascent. Smith contemplated turning back at a place called the Mur de la Côte, since he was

A LIFE'S WORK

- As an impoverished medical student, **visits Chamonix** and decides to climb Mont Blanc when he has the funds

- His **first and best novel**, *The Adventures of Mr Ledbury*, is published in 1842

- Spends a decade writing novels and plays before **taking a journey to Istanbul**, which becomes his first "adventure entertainment"

- Climbs Mont Blanc in 1851 in a lavish party with **36 porters and guides** and huge quantities of alcohol

- Becomes enormously wealthy entertaining the public with his show "The Ascent of Mont Blanc"; he becomes a celebrity and for a brief period makes **mountaineering part of popular culture**

TALL TALES OF HIGH PEAKS
Here, Smith thrills a rapt Victorian audience at the Egyptian Hall in London with his tales of derring-do on Mont Blanc. More than willing to play to the gallery, he mixed fact with a liberal splashing of fiction in his shows.

A BORN ENTREPRENEUR

Smith may have been the first to spot the potential for lucrative spin-offs from a popular hit. No sooner had he described his experiences in another book, *The Story of Mont Blanc*, than he was marketing everything from plates decorated with his own portrait to ladies' fans as souvenirs of his show. He was probably the first mountaineer to see climbing a mountain as a route to riches.

NEW GAME OF THE ASCENT OF MONT BLANC,
A BOARD GAME DEVISED BY SMITH IN 1856.

stumbling and desperate for a nap – not surprising, perhaps, given the sheer quantity of alcohol he'd brought with him. But, Smith reckoned, what are guides for, if not to support you to the summit, literally if necessary? As he descended, cannons were fired in the village to celebrate his achievement. This annoyed John Ruskin (see pp.86–89), who happened to be staying in Chamonix at the time. What Smith did next would be judged even more crass, if not by the paying public.

TALENTED IMPRESARIO

Hiring the Egyptian Hall in Piccadilly, London, Smith commissioned an extravagant set as a backdrop, including a mock-up of a Swiss chalet with a pool in front of it surrounded by real Alpine plants. In full evening dress, he performed a show of anecdotes, literary description, impersonations, and "patter songs". There were even authentic Swiss dairy maids.

The show was a massive hit. "The Ascent of Mont Blanc" was wildly popular with the public, and in the first two seasons alone more than 200,000 people saw it, earning Smith £17,000 – equivalent to over £1.2m ($1.8m) today. He gave performances every evening,

WINE ON THE SUMMIT
John MacGregor's ascent of Mont Blanc two years after Smith's is depicted in this print by George Baxter. Like Smith, he will have saved a good vintage to celebrate at the top.

and matinees three times a week. Ultimately, he gave 2,000 performances, netting £30,000. He even performed for Queen Victoria at Osborne House, alarming her with his St Bernard dogs.

Smith also understood the value of merchandising. He published a popular book about the ascent in 1853 and offered all sorts of souvenirs: engravings and stereoscopic pictures, magic lantern slides, even a Mont Blanc board game. When the show grew stale, he travelled to Hong Kong, and pepped it up with tales of his experiences in China.

Smith had some useful advice, even for his peers. As a young man he had become friends with American circus impresario Phineas Barnum, and when Barnum was in London, Smith invited him along to the Egyptian Hall. Barnum got quite a shock: several of the stories he had told Smith over the years had been appropriated and written into the Mont Blanc show.

Afterwards, during dinner at the Garrick Club, Smith introduced Barnum to his friends as his mentor in show business, and acknowledged his debt to the American. "Of course, as a showman," Smith told him, "you know very well that to win popular success, we have to appropriate and adapt to our uses everything of the sort that we can get hold of."

ALPINE CLUB DISDAIN

Smith's success with the public didn't cut much ice with his contemporaries, though. Douglas Jerrold, a more successful colleague on *Punch* and a campaigner against poverty, thought Smith's entertainment ghastly and crass. "His initials," Jerrold mocked, "are only two thirds of the truth." And although he was one of the founding members of the Alpine Club, younger climbers thought Smith and his hyperbole vulgar and laughable.

What rankled them most was Smith becoming a commercial and popular success without going through the stress and work of being a "proper" climber. Despite this, Smith inspired a new generation of young climbers, just as the railways arrived. And Smith was always welcome in Chamonix, which saw a boost in business. He did not live long to enjoy his wealth, however, dying of bronchitis the day before his 44th birthday.

SMITH POLKA
Such was Smith's celebrity that this "Chamouni Polka" dance was dedicated to him, and played in drawing rooms across Europe.

THE GOLDEN AGE
OF ALPINISM

OF ALPINISM

▶ 1854
British lawyer **Alfred Wills** climbs the Wetterhorn from Grindelwald, traditionally seen as the starting point for the Golden Age (see pp.118–19).

▶ 1861
British physicist **John Tyndall** (see pp.128–31) makes the first ascent of the Weisshorn. His rival, Edward Whymper, switches his interest to the Matterhorn as a consequence.

▼ 1861
British academic **Leslie Stephen** climbs the Goûter Ridge of Mont Blanc in its entirety; he goes on to write *The Playground of Europe*, one of the sport's classic memoirs (see pp.134–35).

▶ 1870
Meta Brevoort brings her nephew **W A B Coolidge** to the Alps, where they begin climbing (see pp.152–53); their dog Tschingel accompanies them to many summits.

▶ 1871
Lucy Walker beats Meta Brevoort to the first female ascent of the Matterhorn (see pp.140–41).

▲ 1857
The Alpine Club is formed at Ashley's Hotel in London; here, members are pictured at a meet in England's Lake District (1882).

1862
Christian Almer, the greatest of the early guides (see pp.122–23), leads a group including Leslie Stephen and Adolphus Moore on the first crossing of the Jungfraujoch.

1863
The **Swiss Alpine Club** is formed, part of a rapid spread of organization in the Alps that leads to the construction of a network of mountain huts.

◀ 1859
Peaks, Passes, and Glaciers is published, a forerunner of the *Alpine Journal* – **the world's first mountaineering periodical**.

▶ 1865
The first ascent of the **Matterhorn** by Edward Whymper, Charles Hudson, and their party is swiftly followed by tragedy as four of the team fall to their deaths (see pp.142–45).

▶ 1859
Lucy Walker meets Melchior Anderegg (see pp.152–53), beginning their long friendship; Walker goes on to become the most successful of the early female alpinists.

1865
The day after the Matterhorn tragedy, **Adolphus Moore** (see pp.162–63) climbs the Brenva Spur on Mont Blanc (see pp.68–69), a major first ascent that opens the next phase of alpinism.

▲ 1874
Alpine guides (see pp.124–25) from Grindelwald pose for a photograph. Melchior Anderegg (see pp.126–27) is seated in the centre sporting his famous beard.

1876
Mont Blanc is first climbed in winter by the British alpinist Isabella Straton and her future husband, the guide Jean Charlet.

Mountaineering reached a tipping-point in the mid-19th century. Some major summits had been climbed, the numbers of tourists and climbers had steadily increased, and a cadre of mountaineers was starting to share information, building momentum behind an entirely new sport. Europe-wide revolutions in 1848 changed the political scene in the Alps, notably in Switzerland, where a new constitution was signed. This was the political platform that allowed the construction of an impressive railway network, providing easier and cheaper access throughout the Alps. The stage was set for mountaineering to become more widely practised. Between 1854 and 1865 – the "Golden Age" – 36 summits higher than 4,000m (13,000ft) were first climbed, 31 of them by British parties with their guides.

1880	1890	1900

► 1880
British alpinist **A F Mummery** (see pp.168–71) attempts the Dent du Géant, but declares the climb "impossible by fair means" (Dent du Géant, right).

▼ 1881
Zermatt Pocket Book is the first climbing guidebook, by **Martin Conway** (see pp.184–85); *The Tourist's Handbook to Switzerland* by Robert Allbut (below) follows in 1884.

1884
Ludwig Purtscheller and the **Zsigmondy brothers**, **Otto** and (below) **Emil** (see pp.172–73) make the first guideless traverse of the Matterhorn.

1885
Katherine Richardson makes the first female ascent of the Grand Pic of La Meije, days after the first ascent of the Aiguille de Bionassay's South Ridge.

1892
A F Mummery, Geoffrey Hastings, Norman Collie, and Charles Pasteur make the **first traverse of the Grépon**, in the Chamonix Aiguilles.

1893
Led by guides **Christian Klucker** and **Emile Rey**, German geologist **Paul Güssfeldt** makes the first ascent of the Peuterey Ridge in a four-day effort.

1895
German skier **Wilhelm Paulcke** makes the first solo ascent of the Matterhorn via the Hörnli Ridge.

1889
Italian cleric **Achille Ratti**, later **Pope Pius XI**, climbs the Matterhorn and Monte Rosa.

► 1907
British adventurer **Elizabeth Le Blond** (see pp.156–57) becomes the first president of the **Ladies' Alpine Club.**

◄ 1908
New Zealand climber **Freda du Faur** makes the first female ascent of Mount Cook with guide Peter Graham; she later makes the first traverse, too (see pp.158–59).

▼ 1912
German alpinist **Paul Preuss** resolves to climb solo after witnessing the deaths of climbers tied by rope on the Mont Rouge de Peuterey (see pp.176–77).

▲ 1898
Railway construction in Switzerland reaches new heights with the first section of the **Jungfrau line** (above: the Kalpetran bridge on the line from Visp to Zermatt).

CANTABO NON LENTO
WEDNESDAY
11 DECEMBER 1912
LADIES'
ALPINE CLUB

A FASHION FOR CLIMBING

B Y THE 1850s, THE FASCINATION WITH MOUNTAINS BORN FROM ROMANTICISM AND SCIENCE WAS GIVING WAY TO A NEW, ECCENTRIC FASHION FOR CLIMBING FOR ADVENTURE. BRITISH MOUNTAINEERS LED THE WAY FOR A DECADE, BEFORE OTHER EUROPEANS CAME TO THE FORE.

PLAYGROUND OF EUROPE
With the arrival of the railways in the second half of the 19th century, Swiss villages such as Grindelwald attracted Alpine tourists, drawn to the fashionable spa resorts and hotels.

In the autumn of 1857, a small group of English mountaineering friends met at the home of one William Mathews. The discussion revolved around the triumphs of the previous summer, particularly the first British ascent of the Finsteraarhorn, in the Swiss Alps, made in August by Mathews and others present that evening, including Edward Shirley Kennedy. But they had another agenda, too: to discuss the notion of forming a mountaineering club, a convivial association where climbers could share their experiences over dinner. This quickly developed into something grander – a focus for the growing interest in climbing mountains for sport.

A list of possible members was drawn up, and Kennedy approached them, either personally or by letter. Those who responded favourably met at Ashley's Hotel in London on 22 December, and so the Alpine Club was born. In March 1858, John Ball (see pp.120–21) was elected its first president. There were 12 original members and by 1865, the numbers had increased tenfold.

The most common members' occupation was barrister, followed

CLIMBING CATALOGUE
By 1900, the famous English Burberry brand was catering to tourists heading for the Alps, offering a range of elegant outfits in its catalogue.

by clergyman, landowner, and don. This was not a sport for the aristocracy, but the professional elite, and the hallmark of most members was their immense energy; they not only led busy working lives, but public ones too, in the spirit of Victorian philanthropy. If the early issues of the *Alpine Journal* were politeness itself, the Alpine Club's archive of private papers reveals a group happy to have escaped the pressures of a conformist society.

The Alpine Club was one of many sporting bodies founded in the mid-19th century, but from the start its aim was not mass participation but elitism. Its members had strong ideas about what constituted a mountaineer. Although Albert Smith (see pp.110–11) was a founding member, his type of popularization was not typical of the Alpine Club, and the climber wondered aloud if the bar for membership had been raised too high. The club was, however, deeply literary, and from the start put a premium on publishing useful and entertaining material.

SETTING A TREND
In Europe, several nations soon established their own alpine clubs, reflecting the growing popularity of climbing in Europe. In 1862, the

> The formation of the world's first mountaineering club in the mid-19th century presented a view of climbing as an activity free from rules and regulations, an activity for all mountain lovers, and one that was as cultural as it was sporting.

Austrian Alpine Club was formed, and a year later a similar body in Switzerland elected geologist Rudolf Simler as its first president. That same year, Italian alpinists founded the Club Alpino Torino, which three years later became the Club Alpino Italiano under the direction of politician Quintino Sella. The German Alpine Club was launched in 1869, merging with its Austrian neighbour in 1874.

If the Alpine Club was elitist – the preserve of dedicated mountaineers obliged to reach a standard – its European equivalents had no such limitation and consequently grew much faster. The Swiss Alpine Club had as many members by the end of its first year as the Alpine Club had at the end of the Golden Age (see pp.114–15). By 1887, the Alpine Club still only had 475 members, while the German and Austrian Alpine Club had more than 18,000.

Continental clubs started a programme of hut-building high in the mountains to offer shelter to alpinists and hikers. And while British alpinists had to limit their ascents to the summer holidays, those living in Munich, Turin, or Geneva could climb at weekends. As mountaineering grew in popularity, it began to attract participants from a broader social spectrum, including working-class climbers from Alpine countries unburdened by the high costs faced by their British counterparts.

EARLY MOUNTAIN GUIDES
As long-time residents of the mountains, local guides such as J Maquignaz (above), soon won a reputation among their illustrious clients, and could command high fees for their services.

"BAGGING A PEAK"
Climbers are seen crossing crevasses with ladders in this photograph taken in Switzerland in 1886. From the first days of Alpine climbing, professional studios recorded scenes like this.

SETTING THE SCENE

- English climber Alfred Wills's ascent of the Wetterhorn in 1854 (see pp.118–19) is traditionally seen as the **start of mountaineering's "Golden Age"** in the Alps. Although not in itself important, the event is a signpost of **a growing interest in mountaineering** in the mid 1850s. In Britain, books by Wills, and lectures by English alpinist Albert Smith raise the sport's profile.

- **The arrival of the railways** in Europe coincides with Smith's ascent of Mont Blanc, **bringing the Alps within reach** for those professional classes with ample time and money to afford long holidays there, and the expense of hiring guides. Political changes in Switzerland after 1848, and the federal government's appropriation of land, lead to a **rapid expansion of Alpine railways**.

- The **growing membership of European Alpine clubs** leads to a transformation of the infrastructure at the base of mountains, and on the peaks themselves. By 1890, the Swiss Alpine Club has built 38 mountain huts and the French Alpine Club 33. Climbers no longer need to carry tents. **Fixed ropes and other equipment** make some mountains safer for guides and their clients, boosting trade.

CLIMBING ELITE c.1890
Here, a well-heeled English party is about to embark on a guided ascent. Although literary and elitist, the Alpine Club was no rambler's organization. A circular issued soon after its inauguration made it clear that it sought members "who have explored high mountainous ranges."

ALFRED WILLS

POPULARIZER OF MOUNTAINEERING AS A SPORT

ENGLAND   1828–1912

REMEMBERED AS THE CHIEF JUSTICE who passed sentence on the Irish writer Oscar Wilde, Alfred Wills was an austere figure whose judgment encapsulated the 19th-century establishment's intolerance. But he was also a dedicated mountain lover whose passion for the Alps lasted a lifetime. His ascent of the Wetterhorn, although not the first, was long regarded as the starting gun for alpinism's Golden Age, and his role in the establishment of the Alpine Club in 1857 gave the new sport of mountaineering long-term impetus.

In 1892, three years before the Wilde trial, Wills commented: "I belong to a generation of mountain lovers already past, and have been rather a pioneer than one of the good soldiers by whom the triumphs of mountaineering have been won." By then, he had been visiting the Alps for almost half a century.

As a young man, Wills experienced the region at the tail end of the Romantic period – before the arrival of the railways – when only a few ascents had been made. He witnessed the dramatic retreat of glaciers

A LIFE'S WORK

- Visits the Alps aged 18, **before the railways make travel easy**

- Forms **a close friendship** with the French guide Auguste Balmat

- His 1854 **ascent of the Wetterhorn** marks the beginning of a sustained period of mountain climbing in the Alps and helps make the idea of **mountaineering as a sport** fashionable

- **Publishes an influential and trend-setting account** of his climbs, *Wanderings Among the High Alps*

- Is a **founder member of the Alpine Club** and intervenes after the Matterhorn disaster to protect mountaineering's reputation

- Builds a summer chalet, the "Eagle's Nest", in Sixt, France, and every year **plays host to a select group** of British climbers there

in the late 19th century, the impact of tourism and subsequent loss of biodiversity, and the rapid development of a sport that had barely existed when he began.

Born in Birmingham, England, Wills was the son of a solicitor. After school, he studied at University College in London, was called to the Bar in 1851, and by 1884 had been appointed a High Court judge.

His first trip to the Alps was in 1846, when still a student in London. The journey took a week, with tiring, dusty days punctuated by nights at inns of questionable repute. At the time, Alpine travel was still largely undertaken by scientists with something to prove – men such as the Scottish physicist James David Forbes (see pp.66–67), whose 1843 book *Travels Through the Alps of Savoy* had made an impression on the young Wills. His own first journey to the Alps, however, instilled in him a deep love for the pristine wilderness he found there. Among his early adventures was an ascent of the Schynige Platte above the Lauterbrunnen valley, Switzerland, then isolated and remote, but by the end of his life the site of a hotel thronging with tourists who arrived by a new cog railway. He also visited Zermatt, then an obscure little village with its own share of the poverty that blighted the Alps before tourism.

ADVENTUROUS INSTINCTS

In 1852, Wills became bolder, crossing high mountain passes such as the Monte Moro that took him into the Saas valley and its beautiful

THE "ZERMATT CLUB ROOM"
This 1864 engraving by Edward Whymper shows members of the Alpine Club and their guides outside the Monte Rosa Hotel in Zermatt. Alfred Wills is in the foreground in white. Lucy Walker, the only female climber included, is at the back, right.

forests. That same year he met the priest Johann Joseph Imseng at Saas, who, Wills wrote, could still walk for 24 hours without rest even in his 60s. Imseng guided Wills on a crossing of the Allalin pass, the first from Sass to Täsch. Wills spent nine weeks travelling, at a cost of less than £40, having "stinted ourselves in nothing". Back in England, Forbes introduced Wills to his guide in Chamonix, Auguste Balmat. That summer, crossing passes in Chamonix and Saas, guide and client formed a close friendship, the first climbing partnership of a kind that would soon become common. With Wills's help, Balmat would later reform the restrictive practices employed by Chamonix guides. Balmat secured building permission for Wills's chalet at Sixt, the "Eagle's Nest", where the guide lived during his final years.

In 1854, Wills married Lucy Martineau and they spent a honeymoon in the Alps. He took her to the Jardin de Talèfre, then a lush patch of flowers set among the seracs of the Talèfre Glacier above Montenvers. From Chamonix, in September, they continued to the Bernese Oberland in Switzerland.

ATOP THE WETTERHORN

Wills had yet to reach the summit of a peak, and towards the end of his honeymoon, he took a fancy to the Jungfrau. The chief local guide, Ulrich Lauener, thought it too late in the season to climb it, so Wills suggested the Wetterhorn, a spectacular sight from Grindelwald. Lauener readily agreed, implying either that the Wetterhorn was still unclimbed – not the first time a wealthy client had the wool pulled over his eyes – or simply that it was unclimbed from that side. The sudden appearance of two local shepherds, one of whom was Christian Almer (see pp.122–23), preparing to grab the summit ahead of Wills suggests the latter. After some discussions, the two groups joined forces and Wills finally reached his summit, "a few yards of glittering ice at our feet, and then, nothing between us and the green slopes of Grindelwald, nine thousand feet beneath."

Wills published his book *Wanderings Among the High Alps* in 1856, and, like his ascent of the Wetterhorn, it set a trend. The following year he was invited to become one of 12 founding members of the Alpine Club. As its third president, he asked Edward Whymper (see pp.142–45) to break his silence after the Matterhorn disaster of 1865: "Give your own account, let it be truthful, manly and unflinching … To some extent also the Club is on its trial. People are daily writing to abuse us and our doings." He also showed compassion, opening a subscription for the family of guide Michel Croz, who had died in the accident.

THE ALPINE CLUB

Founded as a London gentlemen's club in 1857 by 29 friends, the Alpine Club was the world's first mountaineering association. The initially elitist organization has historically been more concerned with exploratory mountaineering than technical climbing, and was once disparagingly dismissed as a club for "walking steeply uphill". Today, membership is open to all suitably qualified mountaineers, and the club has shed its earlier reputation as an organization for amateurs. The club's annual *Alpine Journal*, first published in 1863, features reports from the year's expeditions, and its back catalogue constitutes a comprehensive history of British mountaineering. The club now boasts 1,200 members, all of whom are accomplished climbers who have met its strict entry requirements.

ALFRED WILLS, PHOTOGRAPHED ON THE STEPS OF HIS FRENCH CHALET, WAS PRESIDENT OF THE ALPINE CLUB FROM 1864–65

JOHN BALL

BOTANIST, CLIMBER, AND GUIDEBOOK PIONEER

IRELAND   1818–89

JOHN BALL WAS AN INDEFATIGABLE Alpine traveller who explored every corner of the Alps before and after the arrival of the railways. He also wrote definitive guidebooks to the region. As the first president of Britain's Alpine Club, Ball guided its influential early publications. He was also a distinguished naturalist whose scientific papers on botany and glaciology influenced Charles Darwin. Elected to parliament in 1852, Ball used his political influence in support of natural science.

A LIFE'S WORK

- **Crosses the main Alpine chain** 48 times by 32 different passes, and another 100 passes on lateral ridges the length of the range
- Makes the first **ascent of Monte Pelmo**
- Becomes the **first president** of the Alpine Club
- **Contributes hugely to the topographical knowledge** of the Alps, especially the eastern ranges and the Dolomites
- His **encyclopedic knowledge** is evident in his famous series of Alpine guides

PEAK JOURNAL
In *Peaks, Passes and Glaciers*, published in 1859, Ball brought the delights of the Alps to an avid Victorian readership.

Born in Dublin, Ball was the son of a lawyer and Liberal politician, and indeed went on to become those things himself, but succeeded in organizing his life so as to pursue his passion for the natural world. He first saw the Alps at the age of nine while travelling with his family over the Col de la Faucille in the Jura above Geneva. He later said that no other incident would have so great an influence on the pattern of his life.

Almost the only Catholic among the early British mountaineers, Ball was educated at Cambridge University in England, before being called to the Irish Bar in 1845. That was also the year he visited Zermatt, Switzerland, studying the flora of the St Nicholas valley and making glaciological observations. From a young age, he had been passionate about the natural world and found the perfect way to combine his love of the Alps and science in his extensive exploration.

UNRIVALLED KNOWLEDGE

Ball visited the Alps almost every year from the mid 1840s until his death, building up an unprecedented knowledge of their natural history and geography. Although climbing for its own sake wasn't often his principal motivation, he relished the adventure it entailed. In the summer of 1845, in Zermatt, he crossed the 3,731-m (12,238-ft) Schwartztor pass, despite being lumbered with a guide who panicked while climbing through the seracs of the Schwarz Glacier.

More than anyone, Ball personified the complex attractions of early mountaineering. He felt spiritually refreshed wandering the Alps, even as he worked at researching the scientific questions that interested him. With his trusty umbrella – "often scoffed at" – in his rucksack in case of rain, or more likely, hot sun, he strode

MONTE PELMO

EAST FACE, 19 SEPTEMBER 1857

— **Along a secret ledge**
Ball hires a hunter who shows him a secret ledge just 1m (3ft) wide that traverses the peak at the foot of the face; Ball describes it as "somewhat sensational".

— **Ball continues alone**
A final difficult section leads to a bowl that is a steep walk to the peak's upper section. Ball continues upwards while his guide waits for him here, not seeing the point of climbing for the sake of it.

— **Up to the summit ridge**
A traverse left above a band of cliffs leads to a col and the summit ridge beyond. The climb takes Ball about five hours.

SUMMIT
(3,168M/10,393FT)

PASSO DEL GATTO

across the entire range, always carrying his own gear. Weighed down with thermometers, a pocket clinometer, a Kater's compass, a tin box for plant specimens, and a geological hammer, he was a walking laboratory.

Ball's scientific leanings and passion for Alpine travel meant that his list of first ascents was much shorter than some of his contemporaries in the Alpine Club. Yet he was often the first to visit a new area. In 1857 he made the first ascent of Monte Pelmo, near Cortina, Italy – the first significant Dolomite peak to be climbed – and of Cima Tosa, the highest peak in the Brenta Dolomites, in 1865.

Through the 1850s, Ball spent his summers in the Alps while pursuing his political career at home. He was made under-secretary of state for the colonies in 1855, but his political star faded when he lost his seat at the general election of 1857 and he chose not to stand again.

POPULARIZING THE ALPS

There were greater mountaineers than Ball in the mid-19th century, but his experience of politics, his wealth, and his deep knowledge of the Alps made him the ideal first president of the Alpine Club when it formed in 1857.

Steeped in academic journals, Ball was a Fellow of the Royal Society and could see obvious advantages in collating and disseminating mountaineering knowledge. In 1858, he wrote to the publisher William Longman, saying, "What would you say to bringing out an *annual volume*, made up of contributions of travellers? If carefully selected, I should say that such a volume would be generally interesting, and secure a large sale." By travellers, Ball meant people like him – Alpine Club men – and being a scientist by inclination, he saw science as a subject fit for inclusion. The annual was called *Peaks, Passes and Glaciers* and was first published in 1859, under Ball's editorship. This would become the *Alpine Journal*.

Yet it was as a guidebook writer that Ball had the most influence, publishing what became the famous *Ball's Alpine Guides*, in three volumes covering the Western, Central, and Eastern Alps. Scores of correspondents were recruited to check and contribute information. The guides' arrival coincided with and even prompted a new surge of interest in the Alps and were mountaineering's sacred works until they were updated and rewritten at the end of the 19th century.

MOUNTAIN BOTANIST

Ball has enjoyed an enduring reputation as a botanist, "his favourite science" according to his Royal Society obituary, and in his guidebooks offered valuable advice on the best locations to find rare plants in the Alps. He contributed several papers on Alpine plants to scientific journals, and in 1879, he gave a lecture at the Royal Geographical Society "On the Origins of the Flora of the European Alps". This drew on the two decades he spent tabulating species and charting their distribution across the range. Ball's theories intrigued Charles Darwin, and Ball corresponded with many of the leading botanists of his day.

ALPINE CATCHFLY, ONE OF MANY HARDY ALPINE SPECIES CATALOGUED BY BALL

PARADE OF PEAKS
The Dolomite peaks of the Croda da Lago massif near Cortina are seen here from the northwest. From this angle, the Cima di Lago (2,709m/8,888ft) appears to be the highest summit, but the Cima d'Ambrizzola at the far end tops it by 6m (20ft).

CHRISTIAN ALMER

LEGENDARY GUIDE FROM GRINDELWALD

SWITZERLAND   1826–98

WITH ONLY MELCHIOR ANDEREGG as a genuine rival, Christian Almer was the greatest of the early Alpine guides. As a young man in Grindelwald he famously tried to beat Alfred Wills to the Wetterhorn and thereafter climbed with many of the Victorian stars. Tough and nimble-footed, with a calm temperament, he was widely admired by his clients. His many first ascents included the Mönch and the Eiger in the Bernese Oberland, and the Aiguille Verte in the Mont Blanc range.

A LIFE'S WORK

- Makes his mark **attempting to beat Alfred Wills** to the first ascent of the Wetterhorn from Grindelwald

- **First crossing of the Jungfraujoch** with Adolphus Moore, Leslie Stephen, and others

- Between 1857 and 1884 **makes numerous first ascents**, including the Mönch, Eiger, Gross Fiescherhorn, Barre des Écrins, Aiguille Verte, Grand Cornier, Nesthorn, and Ailefroide

- In the Dauphiné with Moore and Whymper, **he works with Michel Croz**, greatest of the Chamonix guides

- First season with W A B Coolidge in 1868, who calls him **"unsurpassed and unsurpassable"**

Born in Grindelwald, Christian Almer spent the early part of his life as a shepherd and cheese-maker on the Zasenberg Alp. He married at 20, and fought in the short-lived Sonderbund campaign, the Swiss civil war that pitched Catholic cantons against Protestant in 1847.

Beyond guiding travellers across passes, he had little to do with mountaineering before the mid 1850s. One writer who visited the Eiger Glacier described the shepherd of Zasenberg coming down "from the heights with the speed and sureness of a chamois". Yet it was more Almer's character – his blend of cordial simplicity and probity – that won him admirers.

A WILFUL INDEPENDENCE

Some early guides had a creative attitude to recording their clients' ascents – not surprising, perhaps, since the grander an achievement, the bigger the bonus for the guide. Almer, however, wouldn't countenance such a thing. When the Romanian-born feminist Princess Helena Kolzow-Massalasky, known by her pen name of Dora d'Istria, made an attempt on the Mönch in 1853, Almer refused to sign a certificate confirming her "ascent", pointing out that she

CROSSING THE JUNGFRAUJOCH
Almer led the historic winter crossing of the Jungfraujoch with English climbers Adolphus Moore and Leslie Stephen.

hadn't got anywhere near the summit. But it was another act of independence that brought him recognition.

In 1854, Almer heard that the English climber Alfred Wills (see pp.118–19) was planning to make an ascent of the Wetterhorn. Together with his brother-in-law, Ulrich Kaufmann, Almer resolved to beat Wills to it and claim the feat for Switzerland. Wills and his guides were infuriated to see two local shepherds ahead of them on the snow slopes leading to the summit. Things were settled amicably, however. The two parties joined forces, and Wills's guide, Auguste Balmat, offered them chocolate cake, calling them, in a rather patronising way, *bons enfants*. Almer's audacity was the talk of Grindelwald, winning him many admirers.

In the spring of 1856, he qualified as an official guide and was given his *Führerbuch* ("leader book"). Numbered 78, it became the most famous such book in the history of the Swiss guides. Soon Almer was making important first ascents, such as the Mönch, which he climbed in August 1857 with his client, Dr Sigismund Porges. Porges wrote in Almer's book: "During this ascent, which was by far the most dangerous I have ever undertaken, this man confirmed the excellent opinion I had formed of his extraordinary qualities." The following year Almer guided Irishman Charles Barrington on the first ascent of the Eiger.

THIS MAN CONFIRMED THE ... OPINION I HAD FORMED OF HIS EXTRAORDINARY QUALITIES

DR SIGISMUND PORGES ON CHRISTIAN ALMER

ALMER IN HIS FINAL YEARS
With an edelweiss in his hat and a piercing gaze, Almer seemed as rugged and immutable as the mountains themselves. Around the time this photo was taken, he and his wife climbed the Wetterhorn on their golden wedding anniversary.

In 1861, he was in Chamonix, guiding Hereford George – the *Alpine Journal*'s first editor – up Mont Blanc in record time. Almer had never climbed it before. George was impressed, and shared his views in London.

FAME AND LATER YEARS

Almer may have been a guide, but he was also ambitious for first ascents. In 1862, Adolphus Moore (see pp.162–63) and George Macdonald asked him what was the most "desirable thing remaining to be accomplished" in the Oberland. Almer suggested the Fiescherhorn, and led them to the summit. In 1864 and 1865, when Moore and Whymper (see pp.142–45) enjoyed the greatest seasons of their lives, it was usually Almer leading them.

In later years, Almer's most regular clients were Meta Brevoort (see pp.152–53) and her nephew W A B Coolidge (see p.145), the great chronicler of alpinism. Almer befriended Coolidge with a gift of his dog Tschingel, whose climbing skills were extraordinary. The dog accompanied aunt, nephew, and their guide on many of their climbs.

On a winter ascent of the Wetterhorn in 1885, Almer and his clients were caught in a storm. His feet froze and he lost all his toes. Despite this, he continued to work into his 70s and became a great mentor for future generations of guides, including his sons.

MOUNTAIN LIVES

ALPINE GUIDES

THERE HAD BEEN GUIDES FOR CENTURIES in the Alps, men who were willing to show travellers across remote snowbound passes, help them over rocks, and judge the strange mountain weather for them. To begin with, as interest in climbing mountains first developed, Alpine guides were merely extending this role. But by the mid-19th century a small cadre of climbing experts had emerged – the forebears of an exceptional professional body.

Travel in the Alps was dangerous, especially in winter, which is why St Bernard founded a refuge in the 10th century on the pass that still bears his name. However, the first record of a climber hiring a guide dates to 1588, when a Seigneur de Villamont employed two men to help him up the 3,538-m (11,608-ft) Rochemelon in Piedmont, Italy.

Guiding was an alternative source of income for mountain men who hunted chamois or prospected for crystals. With Mont Blanc on its doorstep, Chamonix had enough regular guides to form La Compagnie des Guides de Chamonix, with Jacques Balmat (see pp.94–97) at the head of the list. The Bernese Oberland, another early centre of alpinism, followed suit in 1856. In the early days, climbers had to be

careful they weren't taken advantage of. Hotel owners weren't averse to adding superfluous men or overcharging. The ascent of Mont Blanc was notoriously over-priced, with each climber in the party required to hire four guides at 100 francs each – a month's wages for a farm labourer. But given the disparity in wealth between clients and guides, it was hardly surprising.

This new mountain trade was passed from father to son; in 1898 there were 38 Simonds among the Chamonix guides. Most guides preferred the novice end of the market, taking well-paying clients up familiar peaks. Even then, the risk of orphaning one's children was real enough. Yet the few stars who emerged from this tourist trade became the forerunners of the modern guiding profession.

MOUNTAIN HUTS SUCH AS THIS ONE SPRANG UP THROUGHOUT THE ALPS AS THE POPULARITY OF MOUNTAINEERING GREW, ALLOWING GUIDES TO LEAD THEIR CLIENTS TO A SUMMIT FROM PART-WAY UP A MOUNTAIN.

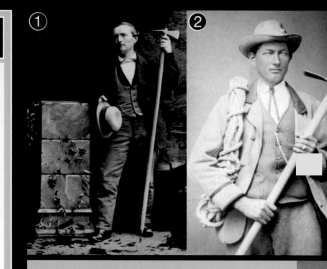

THE MODERN GREATS

As climbing grew in popularity between the wars, a new kind of guide emerged, epitomized by Armand Charlet (see box). Unlike earlier guides, these new stars climbed for fun, and saw guiding as a way to support their lives in the mountains.

❶ Gaston Rébuffat (1921–85), right, with Riccardo Cassin (see pp.292–93), was part of the golden age of French alpinism. ❷ René Desmaison (1930–2007) was mentored by Jean Couzy (see pp.276–77) and made a winter ascent of the Frêney Pillar on Mont Blanc. ❸ Jean-Christophe Lafaille (1965–2006) was a brilliant rock climber who became a guide in the 1990s.

GUIDES AT WORK

Few work places are as dangerous as the high mountains. Training to become a mountain guide takes a minimum of three years, assuming the student is already an expert climber on rock and ice, and an expert ski-mountaineer too.

❶ A working guide cuts out a platform in the snow on the summit of Titlis in Switzerland, while his clients wait behind. ❷ The guides of Zermatt pose with their ropes and ice axes for a group photograph in 1885. ❸ Zermatt guide Ulrich Inderbinen leading a climbing group in his 90s. He finally retired aged 95, and died in 2004 aged 103.

THE FIRST GUIDES

As tourists started to visit the Alps in the early 19th century, local men with expertise from hunting and prospecting found seasonal work as guides. A small elite emerged whose skills soon outstripped those of their clients.

① Johann-Joseph Bennen (1824–64) led John Tyndall up the Weisshorn (see pp.128–31). **②** Emile Rey (1846–95), from the Aosta valley, was one of the greatest guides of his day. **③** Jean-Joseph Maquignaz (1829–90) made the first ascent of Pointe Sella on the Dent du Géant. **④** Jakob Anderegg (1827–78) was bolder than his cousin Melchior (see pp.126–27) on Mont Blanc.

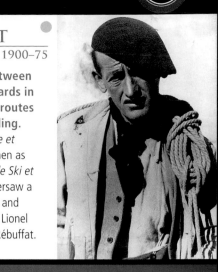

ARMAND CHARLET

FRANCE   1900–75

Arguably the greatest guide between the wars, Charlet pushed standards in climbing – he climbed five new routes on the Aiguille Verte – and guiding.

As a leading instructor in *Jeunesse et Montagne* during World War II and then as director of the new *École Nationale de Ski et d'Alpinisme* in Chamonix, Charlet oversaw a rise in professionalism among guides and acted as mentor to the generation of Lionel Terray (see pp.276–77) and Gaston Rébuffat.

MELCHIOR ANDEREGG

GENTLEMANLY GUIDE WHO WON FAME AND FORTUNE

SWITZERLAND   1828–1912

BORN IN THE HASLITAL NEAR MEIRINGEN, Melchior Anderegg was among the best of the early guides, and an interesting contrast to Christian Almer. A large, genial and intelligent man, his usual occupation was woodcarving, and he later exhibited his craft in London. His first ascents included the Rimpfischhorn, Mont Blanc by the Bosses Ridge, Monte della Disgrazia, the Zinal Rothorn, Mont Blanc by the Brenva Face, Dent d'Hérens, and Mont Mallet. He was one of the few early guides to become rich from his work.

In *Scrambles Amongst the Alps*, Edward Whymper (see pp.142–45) wrote, "Who is Melchior Anderegg? Those who ask the question cannot have been in Alpine Switzerland, where the name of Melchior is as well known as the name of Napoleon. Melchior, too, is an Emperor in his way, and a very Prince among guides. His empire is among the eternal snows – his sceptre is an ice-axe." It's revealing that Whymper, an innovator of climbing equipment, had his own ice axe made to the same specification as Anderegg's. This "prince" was born in the hamlet of Zaun, near Meiringen, where he excelled at the kinds of pursuits common to most early guides: chamois hunting – from which he gained early experience of rock and ice climbing – and woodcarving chief among them.

TALENT SPOTTED
Aged 20, Anderegg was working at the Grimsel Hotel in the upper Valais. His experience of the mountains soon led to guiding work, although Whymper said this was just for *Trinkgelt*, or tips.

After Christian Almer (see pp.122–23), Anderegg was among the early Grindelwald guides to be registered. Tragically, though, his first *Führerbuch* (guide's book) was stolen by an impersonator who traded on his name and robbed history of the early account of Anderegg's career.

The Grimsel Hotel was to provide another lucky break for Anderegg, for it was there in 1855 that he met Thomas Hinchliff, a writer and sometime president of the Alpine Club, and guided him across the Strahlegg to Grindelwald. They met again a

BROTHERS ANDEREGG
Anderegg's brother, Jakob, was also a distinguished guide. He is pictured back row, left. Lucy Walker is also in the back row, next to her beloved Melchior Anderegg, back right.

A LIFE'S WORK

- As a young man working at the Grimsel Hotel he is hired as a guide by Thomas Hinchliff and is later **introduced to Leslie Stephen**

- Makes **first ascents of Rimpfischhorn and Mont Blanc's Bosses Ridge** in 1859, which secure his reputation

- Enjoys **a brilliant season in 1864**, with first ascents of the Zinal Rothorn and the Brenva Face of Mont Blanc

- Becomes a **wrestling champion** by 1864

- Is **guest of honour** at the Alpine Club's London annual dinner in 1888

CLIENT'S COMMENDATION
The *Führerbuch* of Jakob Anderegg features this effusive entry by Adolphus Moore (see pp.162–63). Melchior's own *Führerbuch* has been lost to posterity.

year later at the Schwarenbach Inn, where Anderegg was working as a woodcarver, and renewed what became a close friendship.

Hinchliff praised Anderegg in his book *Summer Months in the Alps*, and introduced him to Leslie Stephen (see pp.134–35), who became one of his most important clients, immortalizing his character in his writings. They met during the first ascent of the Rimpfischhorn in 1859. That same summer, with Charles Hudson (see pp.138–39), Anderegg also climbed the Bosses Ridge on Mont Blanc. Hudson wrote afterwards, "For difficulties, the best guide I have ever met."

GENTLEMAN GIANT
Anderegg was also an enthusiastic wrestler, carrying with him the hopes of the Haslital region in competitions. In 1864, when Anderegg's reputation as a guide was assured, Stephen and friends found their departure from the Lauterbrunnen Valley delayed when their guide decided to chance his arm in a local contest. His opponent was larger and younger, but while Anderegg held his own, both men were injured. Stephen had to hire another guide.

DAUNTING PEAK
The Rimpfischhorn in the Pennine Alps of Switzerland rises to 4,199m (13,776ft). Anderegg made the first ascent with Leslie Stephen in September 1859.

By the mid 1860s, Anderegg was a celebrity who had travelled to London. Like many of the best guides, he was insatiably curious, and amazed his hosts Stephen and Hinchliff by "guiding" them back home from London Bridge station to Lincoln's Inn Fields having done the journey just once and in thick fog. Looking across the chimney-pots of London one day, Stephen commented that the view wasn't the same as from Mont Blanc. "Ah, sir," Anderegg replied, "it [the view of London] is far finer."

Despite his large size, Anderegg was gentle and courteous. English climber Charles Matthews said of him that he never used "an expression to which the gentlest woman might not have listened." His qualities drew the devotion of Lucy Walker (see pp.152–53), who climbed with him for 20 years, and would have married him had someone not beaten her to it.

Anderegg's hallmark was his caution in an age when alpinism was considerably more dangerous because of the limitations of equipment. This prudence was in evidence on the summit of the Dent Blanche in 1876, with Anderegg's clients, Davidson, Matthews, and Morshead, looking across at the then-unclimbed Zmutt Ridge and wondering if it would, in climber's parlance, "go". Anderegg offered his opinion: "It goes, but I'm not going."

Anderegg married Marguerite Metzener, and raised a family of 12. The eldest, also Melchior, became a woodcarver; his second son, Andreas, a highly respected guide. Melchior senior took a close interest in guiding standards, and was still working aged 69, guiding the 61-year-old Lucy Walker in the Eastern Alps.

CLIENT AND GUIDE
Anderegg (left), minus beard, is pictured here in about 1870 with his client and longtime friend, Leslie Stephen. Anderegg was by then about 42, and something of a celebrity.

JOHN TYNDALL

GLACIOLOGIST AND ALPINE PIONEER

IRELAND   1820–93

ONE OF THE OUTSTANDING SCIENTISTS of the Victorian era, John Tyndall is remembered today for proving that the Earth's atmosphere has a greenhouse effect. Resilient, charming, and forthright, he used his intellectual gifts to escape an impoverished childhood and became an avid popularizer of science. Visiting the Alps to further his interest in glaciology, he fell in love with mountains and mountaineering. His ascent of the Weisshorn in 1861, at the relatively advanced age of 36, was one of the landmarks of the Golden Age.

Towards the end of his long and distinguished career, Tyndall spoke about his life at a dinner held in his honour. "I have climbed some difficult mountains in my time," he said, but "the hardest climb by far that I have accomplished was from the banks of the Barrow to the banks of the Thames."

The River Barrow was in his native County Carlow, where his parents invested what little they had in their children's education. Tyndall excelled in algebra, trigonometry, and geometry, but was prevented from going to university through lack of funds. Instead, he joined the Ordnance Survey of Ireland as a draughtsman. In 1842, he was transferred

to Preston, in England, where he was later dismissed for protesting about poor working conditions. After lucrative spells as a surveyor in Manchester and Halifax during the railway mania of the mid 1840s, Tyndall found himself out of work again, and took a teaching job at Queenwood College in Hampshire, which had recently been founded by the Quaker educationalist George Edmondson. Dedicated to science, Queenwood was the first school in Britain to have a chemistry laboratory. Tyndall did not stay long. After saving sufficient funds, he went to the University of Marburg in Germany with another Queenwood teacher, the chemist Edward Frankland, and sprinted through the degree course, earning his doctorate in record time. He then worked with the German physicist Rudolf Kohlrausch on researching diamagnetism, recently discovered by English scientist Michael Faraday. Tyndall's research career had begun.

SCIENTIST AND GLACIOLOGIST

It was, however, his abilities as a lecturer that drew Tyndall into the scientific establishment. Faraday heard him speak at a British Association meeting in Ipswich in 1851, and Tyndall subsequently gave a dazzling lecture at the Royal Institution in early 1853. Soon after, he became professor of natural philosophy there, taking over from Faraday as superintendent in 1867. His scientific career was wide-ranging and significant, mixing the theoretical with the practical, and sometimes, according to his critics, erring on the side of over-enthusiasm.

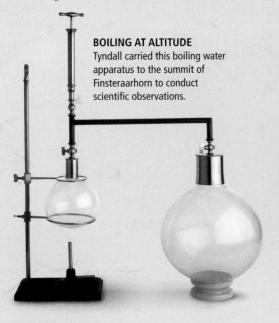

BOILING AT ALTITUDE
Tyndall carried this boiling water apparatus to the summit of Finsteraarhorn to conduct scientific observations.

A LIFE'S WORK

- Born into a humble Irish family, he becomes one of the **giants of Victorian science**

- Studies at Marburg University in Germany, where he **develops a fascination with the Alps**

- His research in glaciology prompts an **interest in mountaineering**

- His memoirs, *Glaciers of the Alps*, are a major landmark in the **"glacier wars"**

- Climbs Mont Blanc, the **highest Alpine Peak**, several times

- Is the **first to climb the Weisshorn**, and almost reaches the summit of the Matterhorn

- Retires in 1887, and later dies from an **accidental overdose** of chloral hydrate, used to treat his insomnia

PIC TYNDALL
A year before Edward Whymper's first attempt, Tyndall climbed within a few hundred metres of the summit of the Matterhorn. However, on reaching the peak that was later named in his honour – Pic Tyndall, pictured here to the left of the summit – he and his team could advance no further. The jagged ridge that separated them from the final summit was split by a deep, impassable cleft. "The summit was within almost a stone's throw of us," Tyndall wrote later, "and the thought of retreat was bitter in the extreme."

I HAD NEVER BEFORE WITNESSED A SCENE WHICH AFFECTED ME LIKE THIS

JOHN TYNDALL ON THE SUMMIT OF THE WEISSHORN

"

He explained the greenhouse effect by showing the capacities of various gases in the air to absorb radiant heat. But Tyndall was also a brilliant innovator of laboratory equipment, using the practical skills he had learned as a surveyor to illuminate his intellectual insights.

Science also brought him to the mountains. In 1849, after exams at Marburg, Tyndall had walked through Switzerland, crossing dangerous glaciers, sleeping rough, and living off bread and milk to eke out his limited funds. His command of German was good enough for him not to stand out as a tourist, and he traded quotations from German poet Friedrich Schiller with fellow travellers. Seven years later, and now a professor at the Royal Institution, Tyndall returned to the Alps with English biologist

Thomas Huxley for research purposes. It was then that his passion for the mountains really began. In later life he said, "glaciers and mountains have an interest for me beyond their scientific ones. They have been to me well-springs of life and joy." So began 15 years of mountaineering.

A PASSION FOR THE ALPS
In 1857, Tyndall climbed Mont Blanc with the English mathematician Thomas Hirst, a friend from his time in Halifax. It was his first major ascent, and Tyndall showed his characteristic grit, mixed with a kind of fearless disregard for the dangers he faced. The following year he transported his apparatus for boiling water, which he used for

CHARTING GLACIERS
Tyndall made detailed drawings of many glaciers, including these of the Mer de Glace on the northern slopes of the Mont Blanc massif in France.

READY TO CLIMB
Guide Johann-Joseph Bennen (right), poses with his alpenstock prior to an ascent. Tyndall formed a close working relationship with Bennen, with whom he climbed throughout his Alpine career.

experiments at altitude, and telescope to the summit of the Finsteraarhorn in order to make observations. Johann-Joseph Bennen, his Swiss guide, recommended they rope up for the descent, saying, "Now have no fear. No matter how you throw yourself, I will hold you." But it was Bennen who lost his footing, dragging his client down with him until Tyndall jammed in his ice axe to stop their fall.

In summer 1857, Tyndall climbed Monte Rosa twice in one week, the second time alone, not for any scientific purpose, but simply because "the unspeakable beauty of the morning" filled him "with a longing to see the world from the top of Monte Rosa". Ever the scientist, however, he observed his own mood and performance, describing how almost losing his ice axe had "made my flesh creep", since without it he could not descend safely.

The experimental work Tyndall did during these years was published in 1860 in his book *The Glaciers of the Alps*. He had assumed that, with the completion of his studies, his interest in the Alps would end, but he found himself drawn back. Like Huxley, Tyndall was a champion of agnosticism in the controversy that raged between science and the Church in the 19th century, yet he confessed a deep religious feeling when looking at the mountains he loved.

TYNDALL'S SANDWICH

Tyndall preferred to climb wearing only light clothing and carrying minimal provisions. For an ascent of Monte Rosa in 1858, he calculated that one ham sandwich contained enough energy to sustain him for the climb, so that was all the food he carried with him. He wrote, "I knew the immense amount of mechanical force represented by four ounces of bread and ham, and I therefore feared no failure from lack of nutrition."

SAVING THE PORTER

Edward Whymper made this dramatic engraving of Tyndall and Johann-Joseph Bennen rescuing their fallen porter from a Jungfrau crevasse in 1862.

CALL OF THE WEISSHORN

Tyndall made an abortive attempt on the Matterhorn in 1860, but in 1861 pulled off one of the great ascents of the mid-19th century. Many mountaineers consider the Weisshorn to be the finest peak in the Alps, thanks to its scale and shape, and, in contrast to the Matterhorn, its relative remoteness. After a failed attempt on the South Face the year before, by Charles Mathews and his guide Melchior Anderegg (see pp.126–27), the mountain had a daunting reputation.

Tyndall chose to climb the East Ridge, which, at 1,500m (4,900ft) long, was a huge undertaking. With his guides, Bennen and Ulrich Wenger, he set out from Randa in August, and bivouacked on a ledge at the foot of the ridge. Chastened by their close view of the peak, the small team set out during the night under a full moon, the ridge becoming narrower and the faces either side steeper, until Bennen reached a knife-edge of snow that seemed too fragile to climb. The guide tested his weight on it, and continued. After six hours of climbing, the summit still seemed far above them. But after food and drink, Bennen cast aside his doubts. Standing on the summit hours later, Tyndall was overwhelmed. "The delight and exultation experienced were not those of Reason or Knowledge, but of Being: I was part of it, and it of me and in the transcendent glory of Nature I entirely forgot myself as a man," he wrote later.

In 1862, Tyndall made a strong attempt on the Matterhorn, as Edward Whymper (see pp.142–45) awaited the outcome in Breuil, "filled with anguish" at the thought that Tyndall might succeed. His team, once more including Bennen, and Breuil's resident Matterhorn obsessive, Jean-Antoine Carrel (see pp.146–47), attempted the Italian Ridge and made good progress lower down, where the rocks were solid, but were disturbed by what Tyndall termed the "wondrous havoc" of frost-shattered rock above. They reached the shoulder of the ridge, 232m (761ft) short of the summit and planted a flag.

Work and ill health later took Tyndall away from mountaineering, but he built a chalet at Bel Alp in Switzerland, which, incongruously, resembled an English cottage.

HONOURED WITH A MOUNTAIN

Mount Tyndall (below), a 4,273-m (14,018-ft) peak in the Sierra Nevada, California, was named in honour of Tyndall, as was a glacier in Chile and a mountain in Tasmania.

WEISSHORN

EAST RIDGE, 9 AUGUST 1861

— Climb to the ridge
After a fondu for dinner, Tyndall and Bennen leave the bivouac at 3.30am, with Bennen cutting steps to the bergschrund. The team climbs the couloir and rocks on the right to reach the ridge.

— Endless rock towers
A succession of loose rock towers becomes interminable and Bennen suggests Wenger goes down. Tyndall struggles to concentrate in the heat, but champagne revives him.

— Reaching the summit
The last section of ridge begins as a narrow snow crest, then broadens and steepens. Ten hours after leaving the bivouac, they reach the summit.

SUMMIT (4,506M/14,782FT)

EAST RIDGE

CLIMBING TIMELINE

Travels to Germany, where he earns a degree and starts his career in scientific research

Makes first ascent of the Weisshorn, a target for many leading alpinists; later, he attempts the Matterhorn and reaches shoulder of Italian Ridge

1820–38	1839–46	1847–55	1856–60	1861–68	1869–93

Born in Co. Carlow, Ireland, Tyndall is educated locally and shows his intellectual brilliance from an early age

Leaves school to work as a surveyor, first in Ireland and later in England, where he campaigns for better working conditions

His work on glaciers takes him to the Alps, where he develops a passion for mountaineering

Becomes a famous science educator, travelling to the United States to lecture; also becomes a bitter opponent of Irish Home Rule

THE ALPINE PROFESSIONALS
Here, the Grindelwald guides pose with their equipment in 1896. Originally local men who found they could make seasonal income by leading tourists along mountain trails, by the 1850s they had become a unique cadre of professionals (see pp.124–25), with precise knowledge of routes, weather, glacier conditions, and rock climbing. The best among them could charge significant fees.

LESLIE STEPHEN

ACADEMIC TURNED MOUNTAINEER

ENGLAND   1832–1904

A SUCCESSFUL AUTHOR AND JOURNALIST, Leslie Stephen was also one of Britain's finest alpinists of the Golden Age, and a leading light of the Alpine Club, joining the year after its foundation in 1857. Originally destined for a career in the Church, Stephen lost his faith in God, but found spiritual renewal in the Alps, valuing mountaineering for its own sake, rather than as the means to a scientific end. He wrote one of the great classics of mountaineering literature, *The Playground of Europe*.

Born into the "intellectual aristocracy" of Victorian England, Stephen's father, Sir James Stephen, was a lawyer and colonial administrator and, in retirement, a professor of Modern History at Cambridge University. The fragile Leslie, and his elder brother James, were removed from the thuggish atmosphere of Eton College to grow up in London.

Tall, thin, and rather shy, Stephen blossomed at Cambridge, where he won a scholarship after his first year. He shone as a rowing coach and earned a reputation as a prodigious walker. He once walked from Cambridge to London in 12 hours – a distance of 80km (50 miles) – to attend an Alpine Club dinner, and led the "Sunday Tramps", which brought together some of the most distinguished thinkers of the age.

Stephen discovered the Alps in 1855, the same year he took holy orders. However, while he found his faith undermined by scientific discoveries, and felt compelled to give up his teaching post at Cambridge, the mountains left him enraptured, becoming to him "the elixir of life, a revelation, a religion". Between 1855 and 1894, he made more than 30 visits to the Alps.

A RESPECT FOR GUIDES

Stephen's record of first ascents was impressive. It included five peaks of more than 4,000m (13,000ft), and five significant peaks below that height. He made the first crossing of several important passes too, including the remote Col des Hirondelles below the Grandes Jorasses. Although he had been sickly as a child, as an adult he was a strong climber. Edward Whymper (see pp.142–45) recalled how, on a walk they shared up to the Eggishorn Hotel from Fiesch, Stephen disappeared ahead and arrived an hour ahead of him.

He was also a self-deprecating character who dressed for the Alps in grey flannels with a large purple patch sewn onto their seat. He confessed he would have got nowhere without his guides. "The true way to describe all my alpine ascents," he wrote, "is that Michel or Anderegg or Lauener succeeded in performing a feat requiring skill, strength and courage, the difficulty of which was much increased by taking with him his knapsack and his employer." Among Stephen's most significant first ascents were the Rimpfischhorn in 1859 and the

Shreckhorn – the "Mountain of Fear" – in 1861. He described his situation, clinging to this steep rocky peak, as being "like a beast of ill-repute nailed to a barn." It was a momentous ascent, and with it, one of the last strongholds of the Bernese Oberland had fallen, but Stephen's mood was a "lazy sense of calm repose".

In 1864, his best year, Stephen made the first traverse of Mont Blanc, along with ascents of the Eiger, Aletschhorn and Jungfrau, and Lyskamm. The highlight was the first ascent of the elegant Zinal Rothorn in the Valais Alps. Stephen was with his favourite guide, Melchior Anderegg (see pp.126–27), "his spirits rising in proportion to the difficulty", Melchior's cousin Jacob, and Stephen's friend Florence Crauford Grove.

Climbing the North Ridge in poor weather, Stephen found his hands numbed with cold as the team sheltered in the lee of an overhang, their narrow perch blasted by a strong wind. They had to overcome three rocky pinnacles, and Stephen found himself alternately wriggling like a caterpillar, and then straddling the ridge *à cheval*, "fumbling vaguely with my fingers at imaginary excrescences, my feet resting upon rotten projections of crumbling stone."

LITERARY LEGACY

In 1867, now in his mid 30s, Stephen overcame his diffidence with women to marry Harriet, the daughter of the novelist W M Thackeray. His trips to the Alps took on a less hair-raising character. In 1871, Stephen was made editor of *Cornhill Magazine*, and became more firmly

A LIFE'S WORK

- After poor health as a child, becomes **a strong athlete** at Cambridge, walking huge distances

- Is president of **the Alpine Club**, the world's first mountaineering club, for three years

- **Makes the first ascent of the Wildstrubel from the east** in 1855, marking the start of his successful mountaineering career

- **Climbs Mont Blanc** via both the Goûter Ridge and the Shreckhorn

- Climbs **the Zinal Rothorn** in 1864, his last major mountaineering first before marriage and a successful literary career

settled in his work, publishing his most important book, *The History of English Thought in the Eighteenth Century*, in 1875. When his wife died, he married Julia, the widow of publisher Herbert Duckworth, with whom he had four children, including the novelist Virginia Woolf and the artist Vanessa Bell.

The accounts of his climbs were collected in *The Playground of Europe*, published in 1871 to enduring acclaim. He could appear brusque, but underneath it Stephen was modest and warm-hearted, as well as intellectually brilliant. His great contribution was to acknowledge how much pleasure could be drawn from time in the mountains. "To the end of his days," Virginia Woolf wrote, "he would speak of great climbers and explorers with a peculiar mixture of admiration and envy."

ZINAL ROTHORN

NORTH RIDGE, 22 AUGUST 1864

— **Setting off at 1.50am**
Stephen, Grove, and the Andereggs leave Zinal. Four hours later, the weather is worsening. Melchior is pessimistic about the rock tower.

— **Along the ridge**
Progress is fast despite huge drops to either side and a freshening wind.

— **Final towers**
Melchior turns the first tower via an ice gully. The next two are climbed direct, the last by straddling it, to reach the summit.

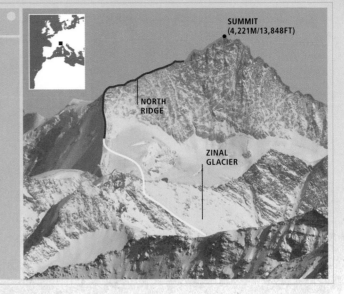

SUMMIT
(4,221M/13,848FT)

NORTH RIDGE

ZINAL GLACIER

I BELIEVE THAT THE ASCENT OF MOUNTAINS FORMS AN ESSENTIAL CHAPTER IN THE COMPLETE DUTY OF MAN

LESLIE STEPHEN

TRIO OF GREATS
Melchior Anderegg, Leslie Stephen, and Douglas Freshfield pose with their alpenstocks. Despite his tall, thin frame, Stephen was a strong climber.

THE PRICE OF ADVENTURE

O N JULY 14 1865, THE MATTERHORN WAS CLIMBED FOR THE FIRST TIME. BUT DURING THE DESCENT, FOUR OF THE SUCCESSFUL PARTY – LED BY ENGLISH CLIMBER EDWARD WHYMPER – FELL TO THEIR DEATHS. THE SURVIVORS MADE IT DOWN TO FACE INTENSE PUBLIC SCRUTINY.

ARTIST'S ACCOUNT
The Matterhorn tragedy inspired a host of artists and poets, attracted to the subject of the romantic mountaineer. Swiss artist Ferdinand Hodler painted this scene in 1894.

The colossal drama of that day's events would overshadow mountaineering for years to come. There had never been a triumph – or a tragedy – quite like it. With six more deaths in 1865, the year became a watershed in the early history of mountaineering. This was as many fatalities as had occurred in the entire history of the sport to that date. The alpinist and historian W A B Coolidge (see p.145) made his first climb three days after the Matterhorn disaster, and recalled "vividly the sort of palsy that fell upon the good cause after that frightful catastrophe". Nowhere were the aftershocks of the tragedy more keenly felt than in Britain.

The confidence engendered in the previous decade, with the rush of landmark ascents and the formation of alpine clubs around Europe, was deflated, momentarily at least. Certain vocal sections of British public opinion were enraged. "Why is the best blood of England to waste itself in scaling hitherto inaccessible peaks," complained a leader on the subject in *The Times*. "Is it life? Is it duty? Is it common sense? Is it allowable? Is it not wrong?"

In many ways, the Matterhorn disaster prefigured the response to mountaineering disasters in more recent years on Mount Everest and K2.

DANGER IN THE ALPS
This engraving from 1870 shows the falling body of a certain M Reynaud, after he had failed to jump over a bergschrund in the Dauphiné. Reynaud survived, but mountaineering was proving to be a highly dangerous new sport.

DAUNTING SUMMIT
The Matterhorn was the ultimate prize for Victorian adventurers in the Alps. Its allure lay in its awesome grandeur, and its reputation for being impossible to climb.

ROYAL CLIMBERS
Queen Victoria's son Arthur climbed in the Alps in 1865 (above); three years later, his mother visited. Her liking for the mountains and mountaineering had soured by the 1880s.

SETTING THE SCENE

- The **shock following the Matterhorn accident** is profound and without precedent in the history of mountaineering. The aftermath of the disaster is played out in the full glare of publicity. A board of enquiry is held, in secret, and **rumours of foul play persist for decades**.

- In the aftermath of the accident, expedition leader Edward Whymper's **behaviour is criticized** (see pp.142–45). After reaching Zermatt, he withdraws to his hotel, without at first offering an explanation for what happened. When he collects himself, he **assists in the recovery of the bodies of his companions**, including that of experienced climber Charles Hudson (see pp.138–39).

- Despite the accident, **the Matterhorn, and the Alps in general, become a huge draw for tourists**. By the time Whymper climbs the Matterhorn again, in 1874, there have been 75 ascents and a small hut has been built at 3,800m (12,500ft). **"Soon the biggest duffers will be able to get up,"** Whymper complains in his diary. He dwells on the accident for the rest of his life and does little difficult climbing after it.

There were intense inquiries into what went wrong and an attempt to find the cause of the accident and lay blame. Several books on this single accident have since been written by historians.

Most damaging to members of the Alpine Club, though, was the sense of moral outrage at the loss of life, suggesting that what happened was somehow sordid. The *Edinburgh Review* asked its readers: "Has a man the right to expose his life, and the lives of others, for an object of no earthly value, either to himself or his fellow creatures? If life is lost in the adventure, how little does the moral guilt differ from that of suicide or murder?"

> The 1865 Matterhorn tragedy, with an English aristocrat among the dead, provoked public outcry at the perceived folly of mountaineering, and led to calls for it to be banned, yet the disaster also increased interest in the new sport.

A BAN ON MOUNTAINEERING?

Although Queen Victoria enjoyed her visit to the Alps in 1868, she also regretted what she saw as a senseless loss of life that resulted from climbing mountains. Later in her reign, following further tragedies in 1882, she personally intervened to enquire if mountaineering could be banned. Her secretary, Sir Henry Ponsonby, asked the prime minster, William Gladstone, if she could say something "to mark her disapproval of the dangerous Alpine excursions which this year have occasioned so much loss of life."

True to his Liberal instincts, Gladstone advised that nothing could be done, and even offered two cheers of politely expressed support

for the mountaineering cause. "It may be questionable," he responded, "whether, upon the whole, mountain-climbing is more destructive than various other pursuits in the way of recreation which perhaps have no justification to plead so respectable as that which may be alleged on behalf of mountain expeditions." Gladstone offers no examples of "other pursuits", but the risks of horse-racing would have been an obvious comparison.

In fact, the Matterhorn accident, far from being a public relations disaster, may have accelerated the craze for mountaineering. Arnold Lunn, the skiing impresario, thought the Matterhorn disaster "did much to popularise the amusement," and that "a little hostile criticism" did climbing as a sport the power of good.

SHIFTING ATTITUDES

Public horror at the loss of life in the sport of mountaineering had come full circle by the time George Mallory and Andrew Irvine disappeared on Mount Everest in 1924 (see pp.228–31). Then, a leader in the *Morning Post* argued: "The spirit which animated the attacks on Everest is the same as that which … led to the formation of the Empire itself." In the aftermath of the Matterhorn tragedy,

the death toll among mountaineers was small – about three fatalities a year between 1868 and 1880. As the numbers of climbers in the Alps surged during the next two decades, the average death toll also rose, to around 15. *The Times* put the increase in numbers down to "foolhardy adventurousness, vanity, the spirit of emulation, want of experience, and even absentmindedness." Today, tens of thousands of climbers visit the Mont Blanc range every summer, and dozens are killed in this one area alone. Fifteen people still die on the Matterhorn every year, most of them on the descent. Many of the mountain's victims, including three from the first ascent disaster, are buried in Zermatt's cemetery.

MICHEL CROZ
French guide Michel Croz was in the lead on the descent from the Matterhorn. When the party's least experienced member slipped and fell into Croz, he lost his balance, and four men plunged to their deaths.

CHARLES HUDSON

STRONG AND SKILFUL CLIMBING CLERGYMAN

ENGLAND   1828–65

As a central figure in the Matterhorn tragedy, Charles Hudson's role proved particularly controversial. Regarded by some as the strongest climber of his generation, his decision to invite the novice Douglas Hadow on the demanding ascent was an error of judgment with horrifying consequences. Yet up to that point, Hudson had been a true pioneer, not just of new climbs, but of new approaches to mountaineering. A champion of guideless climbing, he was also interested in finding new routes on peaks already ascended.

MONTE ROSA

The imposing Monte Rosa massif on the Swiss–Italian border contains ten summits, the highest of which, the Dufourspitze, is the second-highest peak in the Alps. The massif is visible from far and wide on the Italian side, and Leonardo da Vinci is known to have explored the area extensively. The first serious attempt to ascend Monte Rosa was made in 1801 by Italian doctor Pietro Giordani, who reached one of the lower peaks now named Punto Giordani. In 1854, brothers Christopher, Edmund, and James Smyth climbed Ostspitze, convinced it was the highest peak. Christopher and James joined Hudson a year later to reach the massif's true high point.

MACUGNAGA, AN ITALIAN VILLAGE AT THE FOOT OF THE 2,600-M (8,500-FT) EAST FACE OF THE MONTE ROSA MASSIF

In the winter of 1864, Charles Hudson, an Anglican chaplain and mountaineer from Lincolnshire in the east of England, formulated a plan to attempt two of the most attractive unclimbed peaks in the Alps – the Aiguille Verte near Chamonix and the Matterhorn. He persuaded two old friends – the alpinists Thomas Kennedy and John Birkbeck – to join him, and had special equipment – a ladder and a wire rope – made to assist them.

At that time, most climbers assumed a successful ascent of the Matterhorn would come from the Italian side. But Hudson thought a way could be found from Switzerland, via the Hörnli Ridge. Kennedy had inspected this route and thought it viable, and the Parker brothers – Alfred, Charles, and Sandbach – had made

attempts from the Swiss side in 1860 and 1861. Yet even before he reached the mountains in June 1865, Hudson's plans began to go awry. News arrived of Edward Whymper's (see pp.142–45) ascent of the Aiguille Verte, and then Birkbeck became ill and had to return home. Yet Hudson persevered and, on 5 July, a fortnight before the Matterhorn climb, he made a new and more elegant route on the Verte via its South Ridge, with Kennedy and the guide Michel Croz.

A BORN MOUNTAINEER

The Verte climb was a departure for Hudson. Unlike all his other ascents, it was rocky. His previous routes had been on ice and snow, the sort of terrain where a steady nerve and a high level of fitness are essential – and Hudson had both. He was also known for his stamina, thinking nothing of walking 80km (50 miles) in a day and prepared to bivouac in winter.

In the eyes of his climbing contemporaries, he was seen as being "almost as great as a guide". "His long practice," Whymper wrote, "made him surefooted, and in that respect he was not greatly inferior to a born mountaineer." Ten years earlier, Hudson's party had made the first ascent of the Dufourspitze, the highest peak in

CLIMBING RECORD
Like the other gentleman climbers of the day, Hudson recorded his climbing experiences. In these pages he describes his ascent of Monte Blanc.

the Monte Rosa massif, and although standards had increased by 1865, the Matterhorn's Hörnli Ridge was well within his capabilities. His imprudence and lack of caution on the Matterhorn came from a different source.

GUIDELESS CLIMBING

In 1862, Hudson had published a report on a climbing accident involving his friend John Birkbeck. It reveals both Hudson's pragmatism and a kind of providential optimism that everything will work out for the best. The previous year, while looking for a new route on Mont Blanc, Hudson's party stopped on the Col de Miage for breakfast. Birkbeck walked a short distance to relieve himself. When he failed to return, Hudson followed his tracks to the edge of an almost vertical snow slope and saw that he had slipped down it some 460m (1,500ft). Remarkably, Birkbeck was still alive, but, having fallen that distance across hard ice with

A LIFE'S WORK

- In 1855, makes **the first ascent** of the highest peak in the Monte Rosa massif

- That same year, he becomes the first to make a **guideless ascent of Mont Blanc**, breaking the cartel operated by the guides in Chamonix

- Climbs the "Moine" Ridge of the Aiguille Verte before joining Edward Whymper to make the first ascent of the Matterhorn; he **reaches the summit, but dies on the descent**

DAUNTING SUMMIT
The Matterhorn was the ultimate prize for Victorian adventurers in the Alps. Its allure lay in its awesome grandeur, and its reputation for being impossible to climb.

ROYAL CLIMBERS
Queen Victoria's son Arthur climbed in the Alps in 1865 (above); three years later, his mother visited. Her liking for the mountains and mountaineering had soured by the 1880s.

SETTING THE SCENE

- The **shock following the Matterhorn accident** is profound and without precedent in the history of mountaineering. The aftermath of the disaster is played out in the full glare of publicity. A board of enquiry is held, in secret, and **rumours of foul play persist for decades**.

- In the aftermath of the accident, expedition leader Edward Whymper's **behaviour is criticized** (see pp.142–45). After reaching Zermatt, he withdraws to his hotel, without at first offering an explanation for what happened. When he collects himself, he **assists in the recovery of the bodies of his companions**, including that of experienced climber Charles Hudson (see pp.138–39).

- Despite the accident, **the Matterhorn, and the Alps in general, become a huge draw for tourists**. By the time Whymper climbs the Matterhorn again, in 1874, there have been 75 ascents and a small hut has been built at 3,800m (12,500ft). **"Soon the biggest duffers will be able to get up,"** Whymper complains in his diary. He dwells on the accident for the rest of his life and does little difficult climbing after it.

There were intense inquiries into what went wrong and an attempt to find the cause of the accident and lay blame. Several books on this single accident have since been written by historians.

Most damaging to members of the Alpine Club, though, was the sense of moral outrage at the loss of life, suggesting that what happened was somehow sordid. The *Edinburgh Review* asked its readers: "Has a man the right to expose his life, and the lives of others, for an object of no earthly value, either to himself or his fellow creatures? If life is lost in the adventure, how little does the moral guilt differ from that of suicide or murder?"

> The 1865 Matterhorn tragedy, with an English aristocrat among the dead, provoked public outcry at the perceived folly of mountaineering, and led to calls for it to be banned, yet the disaster also increased interest in the new sport.

A BAN ON MOUNTAINEERING?

Although Queen Victoria enjoyed her visit to the Alps in 1868, she also regretted what she saw as a senseless loss of life that resulted from climbing mountains. Later in her reign, following further tragedies in 1882, she personally intervened to enquire if mountaineering could be banned. Her secretary, Sir Henry Ponsonby, asked the prime minster, William Gladstone, if she could say something "to mark her disapproval of the dangerous Alpine excursions which this year have occasioned so much loss of life."

True to his Liberal instincts, Gladstone advised that nothing could be done, and even offered two cheers of politely expressed support for the mountaineering cause. "It may be questionable," he responded, "whether, upon the whole, mountain-climbing is more destructive than various other pursuits in the way of recreation which perhaps have no justification to plead so respectable as that which may be alleged on behalf of mountain expeditions." Gladstone offers no examples of "other pursuits", but the risks of horse-racing would have been an obvious comparison.

In fact, the Matterhorn accident, far from being a public relations disaster, may have accelerated the craze for mountaineering. Arnold Lunn, the skiing impresario, thought the Matterhorn disaster "did much to popularise the amusement," and that "a little hostile criticism" did climbing as a sport the power of good.

SHIFTING ATTITUDES

Public horror at the loss of life in the sport of mountaineering had come full circle by the time George Mallory and Andrew Irvine disappeared on Mount Everest in 1924 (see pp.228–31). Then, a leader in the *Morning Post* argued: "The spirit which animated the attacks on Everest is the same as that which … led to the formation of the Empire itself." In the aftermath of the Matterhorn tragedy,

the death toll among mountaineers was small – about three fatalities a year between 1868 and 1880. As the numbers of climbers in the Alps surged during the next two decades, the average death toll also rose, to around 15. *The Times* put the increase in numbers down to "foolhardy adventurousness, vanity, the spirit of emulation, want of experience, and even absentmindedness." Today, tens of thousands of climbers visit the Mont Blanc range every summer, and dozens are killed in this one area alone. Fifteen people still die on the Matterhorn every year, most of them on the descent. Many of the mountain's victims, including three from the first ascent disaster, are buried in Zermatt's cemetery.

MICHEL CROZ
French guide Michel Croz was in the lead on the descent from the Matterhorn. When the party's least experienced member slipped and fell into Croz, he lost his balance, and four men plunged to their deaths.

CHARLES HUDSON

STRONG AND SKILFUL CLIMBING CLERGYMAN

ENGLAND   1828–65

As a central figure in the Matterhorn tragedy, Charles Hudson's role proved particularly controversial. Regarded by some as the strongest climber of his generation, his decision to invite the novice Douglas Hadow on the demanding ascent was an error of judgment with horrifying consequences. Yet up to that point, Hudson had been a true pioneer, not just of new climbs, but of new approaches to mountaineering. A champion of guideless climbing, he was also interested in finding new routes on peaks already ascended.

MONTE ROSA

The imposing Monte Rosa massif on the Swiss–Italian border contains ten summits, the highest of which, the Dufourspitze, is the second-highest peak in the Alps. The massif is visible from far and wide on the Italian side, and Leonardo da Vinci is known to have explored the area extensively. The first serious attempt to ascend Monte Rosa was made in 1801 by Italian doctor Pietro Giordani, who reached one of the lower peaks now named Punto Giordani. In 1854, brothers Christopher, Edmund, and James Smyth climbed Ostspitze, convinced it was the highest peak. Christopher and James joined Hudson a year later to reach the massif's true high point.

MACUGNAGA, AN ITALIAN VILLAGE AT THE FOOT OF THE 2,600-M (8,500-FT) EAST FACE OF THE MONTE ROSA MASSIF

In the winter of 1864, Charles Hudson, an Anglican chaplain and mountaineer from Lincolnshire in the east of England, formulated a plan to attempt two of the most attractive unclimbed peaks in the Alps – the Aiguille Verte near Chamonix and the Matterhorn. He persuaded two old friends – the alpinists Thomas Kennedy and John Birkbeck – to join him, and had special equipment – a ladder and a wire rope – made to assist them.

At that time, most climbers assumed a successful ascent of the Matterhorn would come from the Italian side. But Hudson thought a way could be found from Switzerland, via the Hörnli Ridge. Kennedy had inspected this route and thought it viable, and the Parker brothers – Alfred, Charles, and Sandbach – had made

A LIFE'S WORK

- In 1855, makes **the first ascent** of the highest peak in the Monte Rosa massif

- That same year, he becomes the first to make a **guideless ascent of Mont Blanc**, breaking the cartel operated by the guides in Chamonix

- Climbs the "Moine" Ridge of the Aiguille Verte before joining Edward Whymper to make the first ascent of the Matterhorn; he **reaches the summit, but dies on the descent**

attempts from the Swiss side in 1860 and 1861. Yet even before he reached the mountains in June 1865, Hudson's plans began to go awry. News arrived of Edward Whymper's (see pp.142–45) ascent of the Aiguille Verte, and then Birkbeck became ill and had to return home. Yet Hudson persevered and, on 5 July, a fortnight before the Matterhorn climb, he made a new and more elegant route on the Verte via its South Ridge, with Kennedy and the guide Michel Croz.

A BORN MOUNTAINEER

The Verte climb was a departure for Hudson. Unlike all his other ascents, it was rocky. His previous routes had been on ice and snow, the sort of terrain where a steady nerve and a high level of fitness are essential – and Hudson had both. He was also known for his stamina, thinking nothing of walking 80km (50 miles) in a day and prepared to bivouac in winter.

In the eyes of his climbing contemporaries, he was seen as being "almost as great as a guide". "His long practice," Whymper wrote, "made him surefooted, and in that respect he was not greatly inferior to a born mountaineer." Ten years earlier, Hudson's party had made the first ascent of the Dufourspitze, the highest peak in

CLIMBING RECORD
Like the other gentleman climbers of the day, Hudson recorded his climbing experiences. In these pages he describes his ascent of Mont Blanc.

the Monte Rosa massif, and although standards had increased by 1865, the Matterhorn's Hörnli Ridge was well within his capabilities. His imprudence and lack of caution on the Matterhorn came from a different source.

GUIDELESS CLIMBING

In 1862, Hudson had published a report on a climbing accident involving his friend John Birkbeck. It reveals both Hudson's pragmatism and a kind of providential optimism that everything will work out for the best. The previous year, while looking for a new route on Mont Blanc, Hudson's party stopped on the Col de Miage for breakfast. Birkbeck walked a short distance to relieve himself. When he failed to return, Hudson followed his tracks to the edge of an almost vertical snow slope and saw that he had slipped down it some 460m (1,500ft). Remarkably, Birkbeck was still alive, but, having fallen that distance across hard ice with

THE DUFOURSPITZE

MONTE ROSA, 1 AUGUST 1855

— **Leaving the Riffelberg**
Hudson and his party start out at 1am, following the established route up the western flank of Monte Rosa.

— **New ground**
Hudson and Christopher Smyth strike up the steep slope direct for the highest summit.

— **Final push**
After another hour they reach the summit ridge, which Hudson wrote needs "a good head and sure foot in order to traverse".

SUMMIT (4,634M/15,203FT)

Hudson made just two other guideless climbs, though, leaving it to future generations to realize the potential of his experiment.

THE WEAKEST LINK

In late July 1865, Hudson was in Zermatt for his attempt on the Matterhorn. Kennedy had been forced to return home and Birkbeck had also gone, so he had teamed up with a 19-year-old Englishman, Douglas Hadow, whose only real mountaineering experience was a recent, fairly quick expedition on Mont Blanc, during which he had struggled on the descent.

Hudson originally planned to carry out a reconnaissance of the Hörnli Ridge before returning with a stronger partner. When his venture was joined with Whymper's, however, he was swept up in the ambitious plan for reaching the summit, assuring Whymper that Hadow had "done Mont Blanc in less time than most men". Less than two days later, Hudson, Hadow, Douglas, and Croz were all dead. "It was an incredible imprudence on the part of Hudson to let him come with us," Whymper wrote later.

his trousers round his ankles, he was horribly injured. An effective rescue was organized, thanks mainly to the large size of the group and the odd coincidence that they had brought with them a collapsible sledge, onto which Birkbeck was deposited. In recounting the incident, Hudson's tone is kindly, but phlegmatic: "To whom, then, is due praise for all these mercies," he said. "Surely to Him who guides and protects us day by day."

With such an outlook, it is hardly surprising that Hudson should have been an early advocate of guideless climbing – a concept that was strongly discouraged by the older alpinists of the day. When he made the first such ascent of Mont Blanc in 1855, opening up a new route to the summit, the local guides – most of them without a fraction of the ability of the greats such as Melchior Anderegg (see pp.126–27) – were charging each climber the-then colossal sum of £30. Many alpinists were starting to see Mont Blanc as an expensive tourist attraction, rather than a place for serious mountaineers.

CLIMBING PARTY, AUGUST 1855
Hudson (standing, left) praised the views from the summit of Monte Rosa, advising climbers to take "at least half a bottle of good wine, to be drunk just before the last 400 feet".

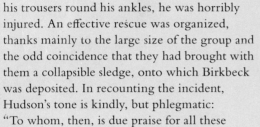

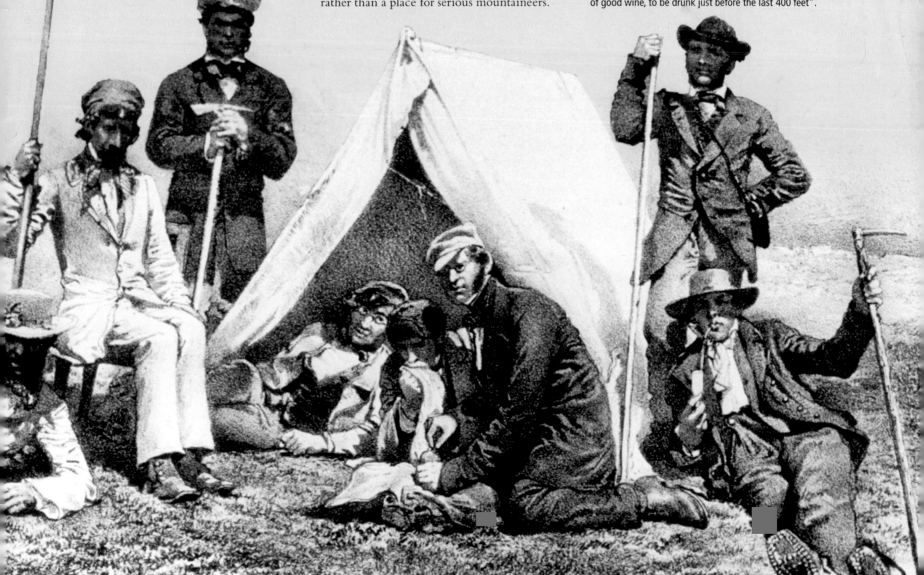

MOUNTAIN PORTRAIT

MATTERHORN

AN ASYMMETRICAL PYRAMID of precipitous proportions, the Matterhorn rears up some 1,400m (4,600ft) from base to peak at an elevation of 4,478m (14,692ft), soaring above the resort towns of Zermatt in Switzerland to the northeast, and Cervinia in Italy to the south. One of the last great Alpine peaks to be scaled, the Matterhorn was also the scene of one of the great tragedies of early alpinism on its first ascent in 1865.

The Matterhorn is one of the most iconic mountains anywhere in the world. Its stark, steeply angled flanks have inspired everything from chocolate bars to theme-park attractions, but it is for its myriad routes – spread across four equally challenging ridges and faces – that it is best known to mountaineers.

Iconic status comes at a price, however. The Matterhorn is one of the busiest mountains in the Alps, and the more accessible routes are crowded with hundreds of would-be ascenders each day during the summer season. The variable nature of the

rock is partly to blame for the overcrowding, since the crumbling and friable conditions, not to mention the threat of stonefall, lead most climbers to stick to the comparative safety of the ridges.

The North Face is one of the three great north-facing walls of the Alps. The South Face is prone to stonefall, while the East and West Faces suffer poor rock condition. The first ascent was made by a party led by English climber Edward Whymper (see pp.142–45) via the Hörnli Ridge, but triumph turned to tragedy when four of his group died on the descent.

IN PROFILE

Name: Matterhorn, from German *Matte* (meadow) and *Horn* (peak). Known as Il Cervino in Italy

Location: Border between Switzerland and Italy

Range: Pennine Alps

Height: 4,478m (14,692ft)

Notable features: Prone to rapid weather changes. Steep faces and isolation generate frequent banner clouds. There are two distinct summits on a 100-m (300-ft) long rocky ridge: the Swiss summit on the east is 1m (3ft) higher than the Italian summit on the west

First ascent: Via Hörnli route on 13 July 1865: Taugwalder and son, Whymper; Croz, Hadow, Hudson, Douglas died on descent

First female ascent: Lucy Walker, 1871

First solo ascent: Wilhelm Paulcke, 1898

First ascent of the North Face: Franz and Toni Schmid, 1931

Fastest ascent: 1hr 56 mins by Ueli Steck, 2009

ZINAL ROTHORN ▲

DENT BLANCHE ▲

OBER GABELHORN ▲

Zermatt ○

SWITZERLAND

Zmutt ○

HÖRNLI RIDGE

MATTERHORN ▲

DENT D'HÉRENS ▲

LION RIDGE

FURGGEN RIDGE

ITALY

○ Cervinia

SCALE

2 MILES
2KM

○ SETTLEMENT

▲ SUMMIT

N ↑

CLIMBING ROUTES

Although there are more than 30 routes on the Matterhorn, the ridge routes are by far the most frequently climbed. The North Face is best climbed in low temperatures and with good snow and ice cover, and boasts the headline routes on the mountain: Bonatti Direct and Zmutt Nose Direttissima. The South Face is the most complex on the mountain, with predominately rock routes.

NORTH FACE

— **BONATTI DIRECT**
(W Bonatti, 1965) Outstanding mixed route, first climbed solo in winter by Italian pioneer Walter Bonatti.

❶ Avalanche risk Includes steep, exposed climbing on the headwall with risk of snowfall and small avalanches.

— **ZMUTT NOSE DIRETTISSIMA**
(Piola, Steiner, 1981) Steep climbing on good-quality rock.

EAST FACE

— **HÖRNLI RIDGE**
(M Croz, F Douglas, D Hadow, C Hudson, P Taugwalder and son, E Whymper, 1865) A long and serious route, much of it on rock.

❷ Solvay Hut For emergency use only, this 10-person hut is located 475m (1,560ft) below the summit and was built in 1915.

— **FURGGEN RIDGE DIRECT**
(L Carrel, G Chiara, A Perino, 1941) Rock route, the most technical of the ridge climbs.

❸ Direct finish Furggen Ridge Direct follows the harder, final stretch of the Southeast Ridge to the summit.

SOUTH FACE

— **ZMUTT RIDGE**
(A Burgener, A Gentinetta, A F Mummery, J Petrus, 1879) One of the greatest mixed routes in the Alps.

❹ Zmutt Nose Zmutt Ridge avoids the overhanging Zmutt Nose by climbing out onto the West Face.

ITALIAN/LION RIDGE
(J-J and J P Maquignaz, 1867) High-quality rock climb on good rock, can be climbed free or using fixed ropes. **(not shown)**

SSE PILLAR OF PICCO MUZIO
(Calcagno, Cerruti, di Pietro, Machetto, 1970) One of the finest rock routes on the mountain. **(not shown)**

(Dashed line means route hidden from view)

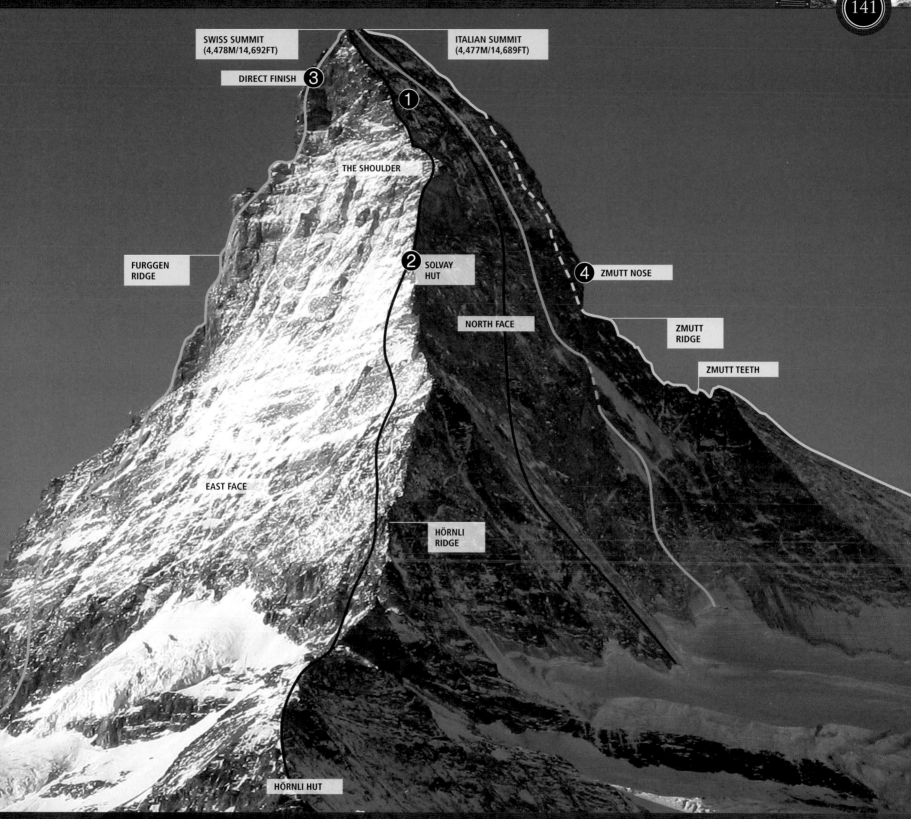

SWISS SUMMIT
(4,478M/14,692FT)

ITALIAN SUMMIT
(4,477M/14,689FT)

DIRECT FINISH ❸

❶

THE SHOULDER

FURGGEN
RIDGE

❷ SOLVAY
HUT

❹ ZMUTT NOSE

NORTH FACE

ZMUTT
RIDGE

ZMUTT TEETH

EAST FACE

HÖRNLI
RIDGE

HÖRNLI HUT

MOUNTAIN FEATURES

(A) **Banner clouds** These stationary clouds form in a lee eddy, which raises air downwind of a tall peak to condensation level.

(B) **Second summit** The Italian summit, marked by a large metal cross, lies at the western end of the Matterhorn's summit ridge.

(C) **South Face** The Matterhorn's South Face forms a 1,200-m (3,900-ft) rock wall dominated by Pic Tyndall, seen here on the left.

(A)

(B)

(C)

EDWARD WHYMPER

FIRST TO ASCEND THE MATTERHORN

ENGLAND   1840–1911

ONE OF MOUNTAINEERING'S most famous names, Edward Whymper is best known for his obsession with being the first to conquer the Matterhorn, perhaps the greatest prize of the Golden Age. He admitted that he was driven by his ego, and that he was most interested in making his mark. His success, so swiftly followed by a disastrous fall that killed four of his companions, defined his life and changed the course of mountaineering. His memoir, *Scrambles Amongst the Alps*, is regarded as one of the classics of climbing history.

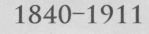

A LIFE'S WORK

- Aged 20, first visits the Alps for publisher William Longman to make a series of **engravings for travel guides**

- Targets first ascents and **climbs Mont Pelvoux in the Dauphiné mountains**, mistakenly thinking that it is a first ascent

- Tragedy follows triumph as **four of his companions die** on their return from the first ascent of the Matterhorn in 1865

- He **publishes** *Scrambles Amongst the Alps* **in 1871** and then switches his attention to exploring the Arctic

- In 1867, makes an **exploratory journey to Greenland**, proving that the interior could be explored with suitable sledges

- In 1880, makes ascents of the **Chimborazo and Cotopaxi volcanoes in Ecuador**, in the company of Jean-Antoine Carrel, to gather data for the study of altitude sickness

- In the early 1900s, he makes a **series of climbs in the Canadian Rockies**, promoting the region on behalf of the Canadian Pacific Railway

---

Born in London, the second of 11 children, Whymper trained as a wood-engraver, like his father before him. He felt himself an outsider, and it was work, rather than youthful romanticism, that drew him to the mountains. His biographer, F S Smythe (see p.247), was struck by the boy's world-weariness, saying, "To read this diary of the boy of fifteen, then to turn the next minute to the diary of the man of sixty is to bridge no gap, except in time."

In 1860, Whymper's skill as an engraver won him a commission from the publisher William Longman, a member of the Alpine Club, to visit the Alps and make a series of sketches for his publications. Before then, Whymper had little interest in mountaineering, although in 1858 he had attended Albert Smith's famous Mont Blanc extravaganza (see pp.110–11), then in its final year, and had been inspired. Like Smith, Whymper would eventually make his living as a lecturer, writer, and illustrator.

He did little climbing in 1860, seeing alpinism primarily as a stepping-stone to his childhood dream of exploring the Arctic. He did, however, walk huge distances, meet several of the leading climbers of the day, including Leslie Stephen (see pp.134–35), and see many of the great peaks, including the Weisshorn, which he described as "the noblest in Switzerland".

MAKING HIS MARK

Dreams of fame and a less constricted way of life led Whymper to concentrate from the start on first ascents rather than repeating the climbs of others. In 1861, he returned to the Alps with Reginald Macdonald, making what he believed, incorrectly, to be the first ascent of Mont Pelvoux in the Dauphiné mountains. Then he looked around for the kind of challenge that would get him noticed. The highest unclimbed peaks were the Weisshorn and the Matterhorn. On hearing that John Tyndall (see pp.128–31), a much more experienced climber, had succeeded on the Weisshorn on 19 August, Whymper chose to concentrate on the Matterhorn instead.

There had already been a few attempts on the peak. Tyndall and Vaughan Hawkins had climbed up the Italian Ridge as far as the Great Tower in 1860, and there had been earlier attempts by local climbers determined to make the ascent for the glory of Italy. Chief among these was Jean-Antoine Carrel (see pp.146–47), whom Whymper met for the first time that summer. It was the start of a tense friendship that saw them both co-operating and competing for the Matterhorn.

Whymper got nowhere on his attempt in 1861, but vowed to return "to lay siege to the mountain until one or the other was vanquished." The following year he brought with him new equipment, including a tent of his own design, along with grapnels and iron rings for abseiling. In the years that followed, Whymper was prepared to use whatever it took to achieve his ascents, even bringing ladders to overcome impassable sections. Over three weeks in July 1862, he made five attempts on the Matterhorn, climbing with Reginald Macdonald or Carrel, and even alone, returning bloodied but unbowed from a solo effort on 19 July when he fell

PHOTO TALENT
Whymper became a talented photographer. He took this image on the summit of Mont Blanc in 1893.

FROM THE MOMENT THE ROPE BROKE IT WAS IMPOSSIBLE TO HELP THEM. SO PERISHED OUR COMRADES!

EDWARD WHYMPER

SHORT-LIVED TRIUMPH

The first ascent of the Matterhorn, and the accident that followed, are recounted in Whymper's memoir, *Scrambles Amongst the Alps*. The climb is illustrated here by Gustave Doré. Whymper spent the rest of his life trying to make sense of the obsession that almost killed him. More than 500 people have since died climbing the mountain.

60m (200ft) "in seven or eight bounds". Badly injured, he struggled down the mountain and lay in bed, alone and uncared for. Dragging himself out for another go on 23 July, he took Carrel and "little" Luc Meynet, the so-called hunchback of Breuil. He tried again on 25 July, this time just with Meynet. Each time he went onto the mountain, Whymper got a little further.

He could almost taste success. Then John Tyndall arrived for another try. He and Whymper tried to agree terms for a joint attempt but the younger man seemed too brash. He had to wait as Tyndall, with Carrel in his party, reached the shoulder on the Italian Ridge that was later named after him, just 232m (761ft) from the summit, before finally turning back.

In 1863, Whymper made a circuit of the mountain and witnessed a violent electrical storm while camping on the Italian Ridge during his only attempt. The following year he did a number of first ascents elsewhere in the Alps, including the Barre des Écrins and the Aiguille d'Argentière, but, on arriving in Zermatt to renew his campaign, he found an urgent message calling him home.

The next year, 1865, would be Whymper's greatest – and last – serious Alpine season. He climbed five peaks, four of them first ascents, including the

west summit of the Grandes Jorasses, and the first ascent of the Aiguille Verte. In just five years, mostly due to his tenacious and ambitious nature, he had become a formidable alpinist. Yet it was the Matterhorn that obsessed him. In June, before these climbs, he had tried the peak's East Face. In the party was the guide Christian Almer (see pp.122–23), who bluntly asked him: "Why don't you try a mountain that *can* be ascended?" Instead, Whymper moved his base to Italy and sought Carrel's help again, which was initially offered. However, the newly founded Italian Alpine Club, and Italy's finance minister, wanted Carrel to guide an Italian group to the summit first. Knowing nothing of this, Whymper awoke on 11 July to the news that Carrel had left for the Matterhorn.

RACE TO THE SUMMIT

Feeling betrayed, Whymper was desperate to beat Carrel to the prize. Luckily for him, a young English climber had arrived in Breuil – Lord Francis Douglas, who was just 18 and making a name for himself. With him was the Zermatt guide Joseph Taugwalder. Taugwalder's father, Peter, believed there was another way to the summit – via the Hörnli Ridge from Switzerland – so they joined forces with

BLOW BY BLOW PAINTINGS
A series of paintings by Swiss artist Ferdinand Hodler depicting heroic Alpine ascents was inspired by the exploits of early pioneers such as Whymper.

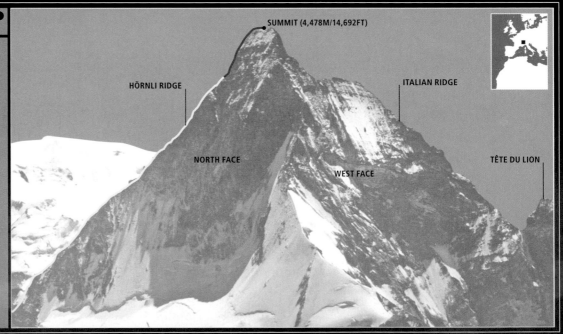

MATTERHORN

HÖRNLI RIDGE, 14 JULY 1865

— **Climb to the shoulder**
Party bivouacs on the East Face at 3,818m (12,526ft). The ridge to the shoulder proves far easier than anticipated, up moderately-angled rocks, without using rope.

— **From the shoulder to the summit**
Above the shoulder, Michel Croz goes into the lead, climbing rightwards onto the North Face to turn a difficult section. Rocks are covered with ice in places. Above this section, the going is easier, and they reach the summit at 1.40pm.

SUMMIT (4,478M/14,692FT)

HÖRNLI RIDGE

ITALIAN RIDGE

NORTH FACE

WEST FACE

TÊTE DU LION

Attends one of Albert Smith's final lectures, which he finds inspiring; is then commissioned by Longman's to travel to the Alps for material

His Alpine career reaches its climax, with new climbs in the Mont Blanc range, including the Aiguille Verte, before the tragic first ascent of the Matterhorn

Climbs the Matterhorn again in 1874

CLIMBING TIMELINE

1840–53	1854–57	1858–60	1861–63	1864–65	1866–71	1872–93

Born in London in 1840, the second

Is apprenticed to his father's studio where he soon shines, for his maturity and

Climbs Mont Pelvoux in the Dauphiné then turns his attention to the Matterhorn

Haunted by the accident, does little serious climbing; engages in research work in Greenland and writes

Whymper and left for Zermatt, where Taugwalder senior agreed to an attempt.

Also in Zermatt was Charles Hudson (see pp.138–39), perhaps the finest alpinist of his generation. He was with the guide Michel Croz, whom Whymper had employed earlier that year, and a young, inexperienced partner, Douglas Hadow. They too had their sights set on the Matterhorn. A deal was quickly worked out so the two teams could join forces. But having two young climbers was an obvious concern. Anxious about Hadow's inexperience, Whymper asked Hudson for reassurance. "He is a sufficiently good man to go with us," was the response. It was to prove a fatal error of judgment.

The team left early on 13 July in stunning weather and made good progress, camping at noon on the ridge. Checking the route ahead, the guides reported few difficulties. They could have gone to the summit that day, they claimed.

DISASTROUS DESCENT
An engraving by Gustave Doré captures the moment the rope broke. Rumours abounded that Whymper had cut it to save himself.

Starting at first light the next morning, they made fast progress on the left side of the ridge, on the East Face, but at the shoulder were forced to move onto the North Face to reach the summit snow ridge. Croz and Whymper untied from the rope and sprinted for the top, reaching it in a dead heat at 1.40pm. Traversing from the Swiss summit to the Italian, just 2m (7ft) lower and 100m (330ft) distant, they were certain they had beaten Carrel's group. When they looked down the ridge, however, the Italians could be seen 400m (1,300ft) below. Whymper threw stones down to attract their attention. Carrel, seeing Whymper's distinctive white trousers, knew exactly who had beaten him. Italians in Breuil, however, seeing a flag on the summit, believed Carrel had succeeded and started to celebrate.

Elated, and perhaps distracted, Whymper and Hudson decided on the order of descent. Croz would go first, then Hadow, followed by Hudson, Lord Douglas, Taugwalder senior, Whymper, and Taugwalder junior. This was a waste of Croz's expertise, and the decision seems bizarre. He would have been better placed above Hadow. The second mistake was using a weak rope to join Douglas and Taugwalder. Just below the summit, Hadow slipped, knocking over Croz, who was in front of him, and pulling those behind off their footing. As they fell, the rope to Taugwalder snapped. Four men – Croz, Hadow, Hudson, and Douglas – plunged down the North Face to their deaths.

W A B COOLIDGE

UNITED STATES   1850–1926

In the summer of 1865, soon after the Matterhorn disaster, a 15-year-old American boy sent his mother a letter from Zermatt with a diagram illustrating where the climbers had fallen: "A terrible distance," he concluded.

The boy was William Augustus Brevoort Coolidge, the son of a Boston merchant and a Dutch mother, raised near New York and in the Alps with his aunt Meta Brevoort (see pp.152–53) for the sake of his health. The cure worked. This physically weak, rather pampered, but intelligent young man would become the greatest – and most contentious – Alpine historian the sport had known, as well as a capable mountaineer himself. English mountaineer Percy Farrar said it would be as ridiculous to speak of Alpine matters without mentioning his name "as it would be to discuss the Bible without mentioning God".

Coolidge dominated Alpine matters, first as editor of *The Alpine Journal*, and later with Martin Conway, as editor of the first comprehensive series of climbing guidebooks. He applied to the subject the same rigour he brought to his work as a Cambridge history don, using an encyclopaedic knowledge gained by climbing some 1,700 routes throughout the Alps. He was a merciless critic, condemning one book because it missed an accent, and when asked to review one of his own books – on the basis that no one knew remotely as much – took himself to task for his errors. The mature Coolidge never passed up the chance of an argument, most famously with Whymper over his engraving "Almer's Leap" (see pp.122–23).

VOLCANOES OF ECUADOR
Whymper's serious mountaineering career ended with the Matterhorn disaster, but he nevertheless notched up a series of first ascents in South America, notably of the volcano Chimborazo and half a dozen other Andean peaks. He spent a night on the summit of Cotopaxi (shown here) as part of his studies into altitude sickness and aneroid barometers.

Produces his own series of guidebooks, revisiting old haunts in the Alps

Makes a series of trips to the Rockies, sponsored by the Canadian Pacific Railway, but his heavy drinking means little climbing is accomplished

1894–99	1900–05	1905–11

Makes a second trip to Greenland and, in 1880, a research expedition to Ecuador

Marries in 1899, but his wife dies suddenly a year later while he is away in the US

Remarries; they have a daughter but the marriage ends badly; makes final trip to Rockies, and then the Alps, where he dies

JEAN-ANTOINE CARREL

A PROUD ITALIAN PIONEER

ITALY   1829–90

A KEY PLAYER IN THE DRAMA of the Matterhorn's first ascent in 1865, Jean-Antoine Carrel regarded conquering the mountain – known in Italy as Il Cervino – as a matter of national pride and personal prestige. A stonemason by trade who had fought for Italian independence, Carrel became as obsessed with reaching this formidable peak as his English rival and erstwhile companion, Edward Whymper. Although disappointed by his narrow failure to be first to the top, Carrel remained friends with Whymper.

PEAK NATIONALISM

Carrel's determination that the Matterhorn should be climbed for Italy was a more overt expression of nationalism than had hitherto been seen in mountaineering in the 19th century, but it was hardly surprising. Italy's fight for independence was not yet complete in 1865, and climbing the peak was a symbol of Italy's self-esteem as a new nation. The link between nationalism and mountain climbing would reach its zenith just before and after World War II. The Italian fascists and the Nazi Party understood its propaganda value, but it also represented a positive way in which Italy, Germany, and France could recover from the trials of war.

THE FLAG OF FASCIST ITALY: AS IN GERMANY, ITALIAN MOUNTAINEERING BECAME A STATE-SPONSORED SPORT

Jean-Antoine Carrel grew up in the shadow of the Matterhorn in an era before the mountain's distinct shape became the archetype for mountains everywhere. In 1861, when the 21-year-old Edward Whymper (see pp.142–45) first saw Carrel walking up to Breuil, he described the Italian as "a well-made, resolute-looking fellow, with a certain defiant air, which was rather taking." Stocky, keen-eyed, and sporting the fashionable imperial beard, Carrel had what one historian called "a hell-for-leather countenance."

By then, Carrel was in his early 30s and a war veteran. He had first attempted the Matterhorn in 1857, inspired by his cousin, Jean-Jacques Carrel. Taking along a young theological student named Amé Gorret, the cousins climbed to the Col Tournanche, and,

for laughs, trundled boulders down onto the Tiefenmatten Glacier on the Swiss side of the mountain. Continuing along the ridge, they made the first ascent of Tête du Lion, a huge chunk of the rock gneiss on the frontier between Italy and Switzerland. Below them was the Col du Lion, an obvious starting point for what became known as both the Italian and Lion Ridge. This would be the scene for Carrel's long campaign for the Matterhorn. In 1858, the Carrel cousins returned, and reached a high point of 3,800m (12,500ft)

Carrel was far too proud to settle for being a simple guide. When Whymper arrived in Breuil, Italian guiding was still in its infancy. The terms Carrel offered to guide him were so unreasonable that the Englishman walked on.

BURNING AMBITION

At dusk on the day of his first attempt on the Matterhorn, Whymper saw two figures approaching his camp beneath the mountain, and recognized Carrel. "Oh ho," he called, "you have repented." But Carrel was there to make his own effort and had determined that the mountain should be his, not Whymper's.

The next day, Carrel, climbing again with his cousin, outstripped Whymper and his Swiss guide. At the highest point they reached before turning back, the Crête du Coq at 4,032m (13,228ft), he carved his initials in a rock. A year later, Whymper added his own next to them.

Carrel and Whymper were not alone in their efforts. English brothers Sandbach, Charles, and Alfred Parker made an unguided effort on the East Face. Another Englishman, Vaughan Hawkins, hired Jean-Jacques Carrel for his first attempt in 1860 with John Tyndall (see pp.128–31), who himself came close in 1862.

But the competition and co-operation between Whymper and Carrel is the most compelling part of the story of the Matterhorn's first ascent. "Carrel was not an easy man to manage," Whymper wrote. "He was perfectly aware that he was the cock of the Valtournanche, and he commanded the other men as by right. He was equally conscious that he was indispensable to me."

PRIEST MOUNTAINEER
The abbé Amé Gorret, seen here in nailed boots, accompanied Carrel on his first and second attempts at the Matterhorn.

A LIFE'S WORK

- Makes the **first reconnaissance of the Italian Ridge** with his cousin, Jean-Jacques

- **Narrowly loses out** to his rival, Edward Whymper, who beats him to the summit of the Matterhorn by just three days

- Joins Whymper on **an exploratory expedition** to the Andes in South America, where they research the effects of altitude on the body

Through the frenzied month of July 1862,
Carrel and Whymper climbed together and apart.
Tyndall reached the striking shoulder just below
the summit at 4,241m (13,914ft) that is now called
Pic Tyndall. From there, he could only watch as
his rivals closed in on the prize, and then sigh
with relief as they returned without it.

The dramatic events of 1865 revolved around
the complex relationship between Carrel and
Whymper. In 1863, a journalist and politician
called Giuseppe Torelli visited Carrel. Some
friends were setting up an Italian Alpine Club
and wanted to climb the Matterhorn first, for
Italy. For these Italian friends Carrel abandoned
the English Whymper in the summer of 1865.

When Whymper stood on the summit,
he thought of Carrel. "He was the man of all
those who first attempted the ascent of the
Matterhorn, who most deserved to be the first
upon the summit." Carrel did reach the summit,
three days after Whymper, making the first ascent
of the harder Italian Ridge with Jean-Baptiste
Bich. Carrel would climb the Matterhorn several
more times, including one ascent with Whymper.
He and his brother would also join forces with
Whymper in ascents in the Andes.

SCALING THE VOLCANO CHIMBORAZO
From 1879–80, Carrel and his brother Louis climbed
11 peaks in Ecuador with Whymper. They made seven first
ascents, including the country's highest peak, Chimborazo.

MATTERHORN

ITALIAN RIDGE

— 17 July 1867
Carrel had reached the notch in the Lion Ridge
with John Tyndall in 1862. On his ascent, he
avoided steep rocks at the top by traversing.
The direct finish to the top was climbed in
1867 by Joseph and Jean Pierre Maquignaz,
the route taken today and shown here.

SUMMIT (4,478M/14,692FT)
PIC TYNDALL
LION RIDGE

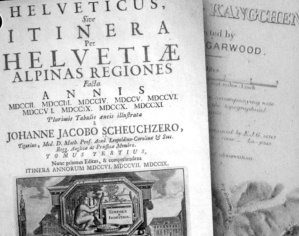

EXPERIENCING THE MOUNTAINS

SPREADING THE WORD

MOUNTAINS WERE A COMMON THEME in literature and science-writing in the early 19th century, but in Britain in the 1850s a new type of book appeared, describing the thrill of climbing in the Alps. With mountaineering taking place in environments exciting to the public, and the psychological demands of the sport so compelling to readers, mountain literature flourished, inspiring armchair adventurers and new adherents eager for information.

Mountaineering books proved to be the best way to spread the gospel of the high-altitude experience. At the same time, the sudden appearance of mountain literature demonstrated both a need and a desire for a mountaineering publishing industry to share information and describe achievements. The writing of James David Forbes (see pp.66–67), particularly his 1843 book *Travels through the Alps of Savoy*, inspired the small band of early Alpine travellers and mountaineers active at the time. Although illness prevented him from serious climbing, Forbes was the Alpine Club's first honorary member and inspired and supported the Irish artist and climber Anthony Adams-Reilly in publishing the first map of Mont Blanc.

Although accessible, Forbes' writing was deeply scientific. In the 1850s, a new kind of Alpine book appeared, describing the dramas and challenges of climbing for its own sake. *Wanderings Among the High Alps* by Alfred Wills (see pp.118–19) was published by Richard Bentley in 1856, and in the same year, William

Longman published *Where There's a Will There's a Way* by Charles Hudson (see pp.138–39) and Edward Shirley Kennedy. Despite first encountering alpinism through publishing in his mid-40s, Longman was so captivated that he later became president of the Alpine Club.

Longman also published the Alpine Club's proto-journal, *Peaks, Passes and Glaciers*, commissioning Edward Whymper (see pp.142–45) to make a series of drawings. In 1871, this surge of literary effort culminated in three classics – *Scrambles Amongst the Alps* by Whymper, *Hours of Exercise in the Alps* by John Tyndall (see pp.128–31), and *The Playground of Europe* by Leslie Stephen (see pp.134–35). The latter included an honest account of the author's ascent of the Rothorn: "My chief reliance was upon the rope; and with a graceful flounder I was presently landed in safety upon a comparatively sound ledge."

LOVE OF NATURE IS INTIMATELY CONNECTED WITH ALL THAT IS NOBLEST IN HUMAN[S]

LESLIE STEPHEN

A ALPINE ALMANAC
Johann Jakob Scheuchzer's 1723 *Itinera Alpina* was an early example of the scientific surge of interest in the Alps.

B VICTORIAN TRAVELOGUE
Published in 1843, *Travels through the Alps of Savoy* by James David Forbes was an inspirational but largely scientific work.

C AFRICAN ADVENTURE
Hans Meyer's 1890 account of his first ascent of Kilimanjaro was an exotic addition to the genre of mountaineering literature.

D AN ICY READ
Subtitled "Narratives of Daring and Disaster", this 1894 publication indulged the public's appetite for high-altitude danger.

E PUBLISHING THE HIGH PEAKS
As well as publishing books on the Alps, William Longman visited them himself in his mid-40s. A trip to the Aletsch Glacier involved being tied to his guide with a handkerchief.

JONSONG GLACIER
The Pyramid
Green Lake Glacier
ZEMU GLACIER
Simvu Glacier
TALUNG GLACIER

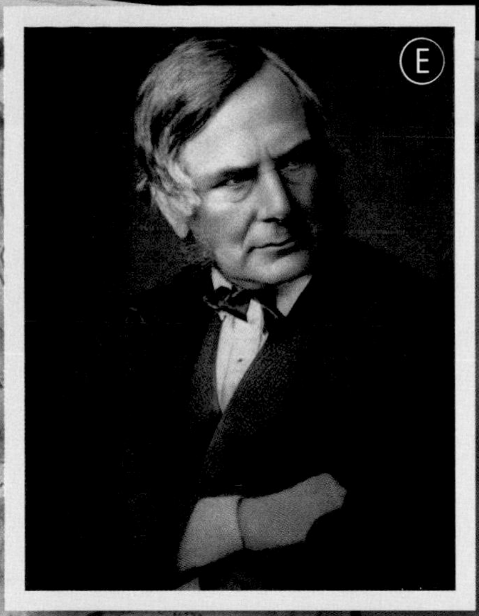

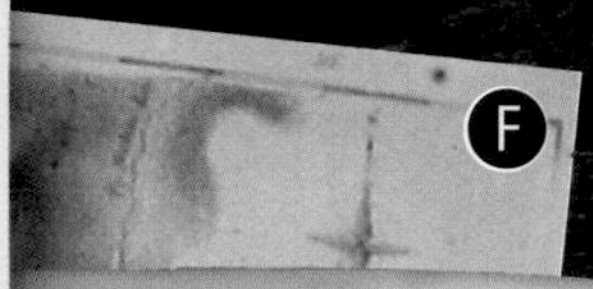

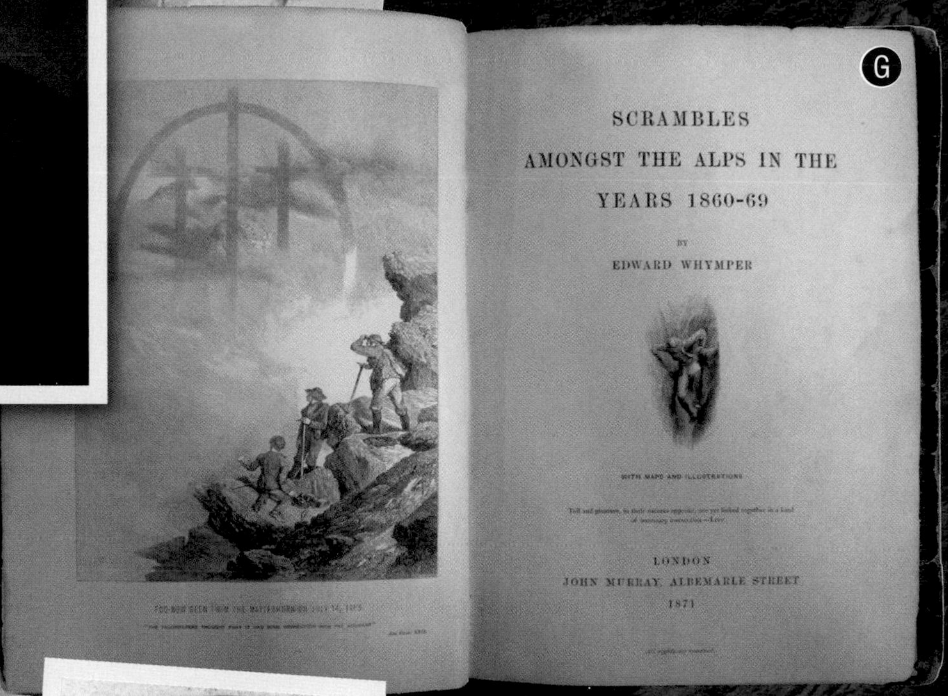

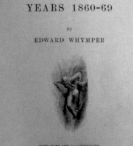

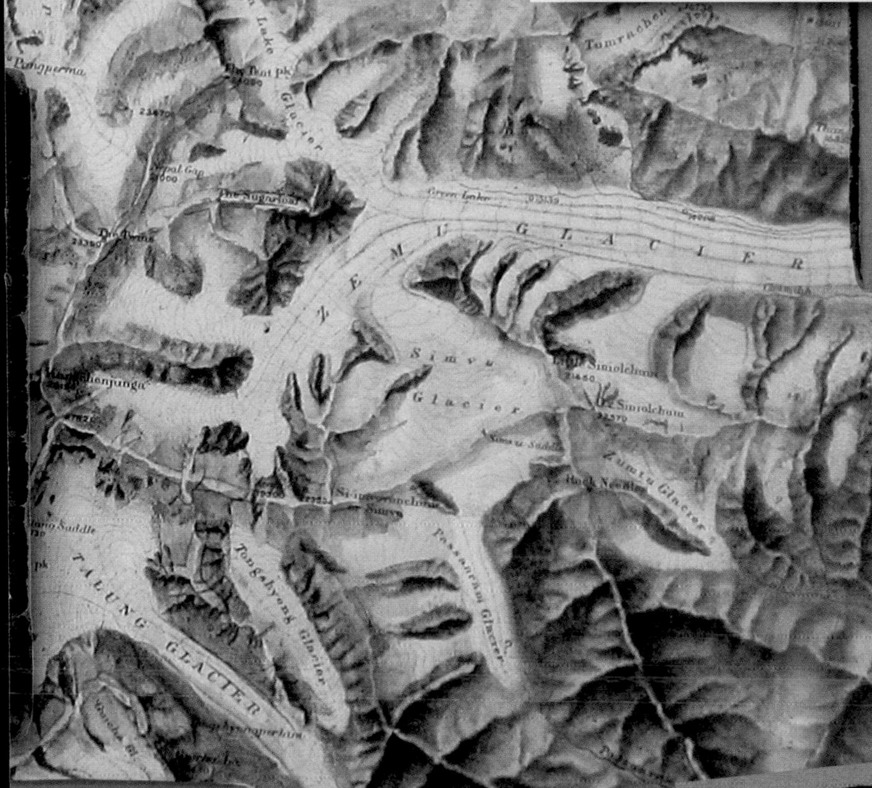

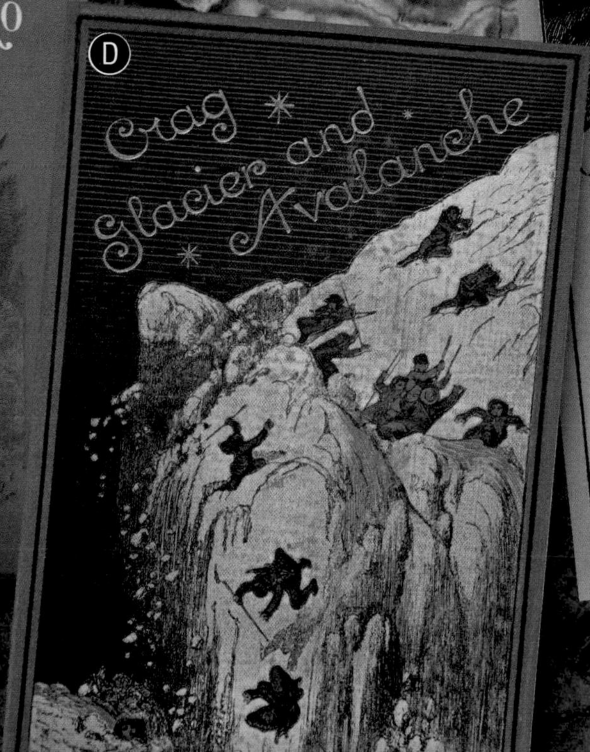

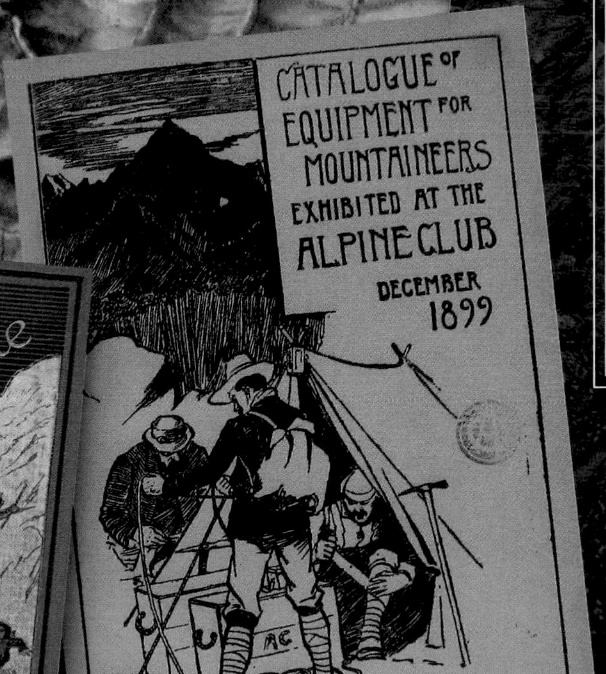

SCRAMBLES
AMONGST THE ALPS IN THE
YEARS 1860-69
BY
EDWARD WHYMPER
WITH MAPS AND ILLUSTRATIONS
LONDON
JOHN MURRAY, ALBEMARLE STREET
1871

ASCENT
MANJARO

Crag Glacier and Avalanche

CATALOGUE OF
EQUIPMENT FOR
MOUNTAINEERS
EXHIBITED AT THE
ALPINE CLUB
DECEMBER
1899

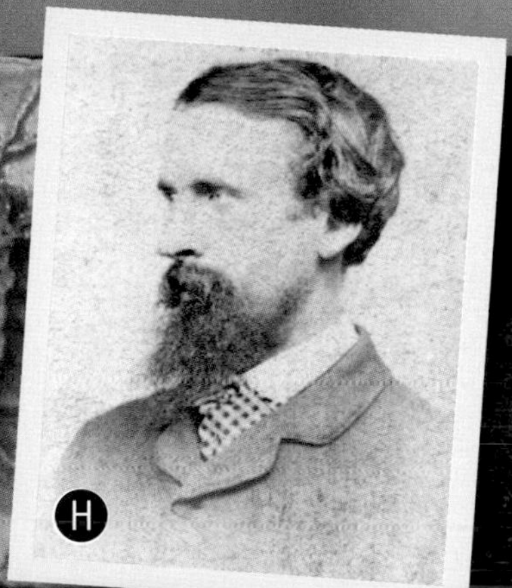

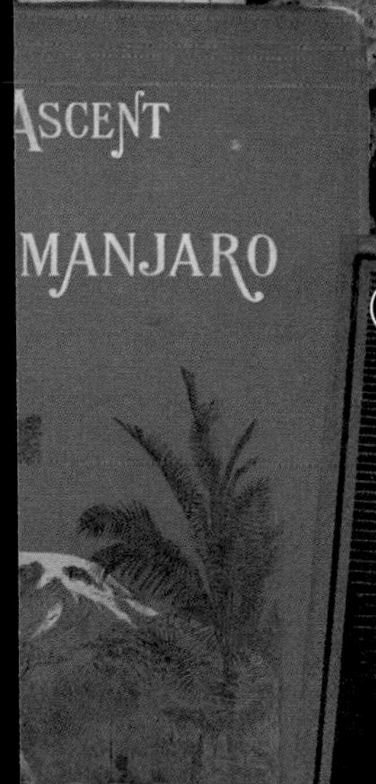

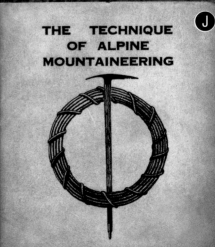

THE TECHNIQUE
OF ALPINE
MOUNTAINEERING
PUBLICATION OF THE UTO SECTION OF THE S.A.C.
ENGLISH EDITION ADAPTED BY MEMBERS OF THE
ASSOCIATION OF BRITISH MEMBERS OF THE S.A.C.

F MAP OF KANGCHENJUNGA, 1903
Alpine clubs across Europe acted as engines for disseminating useful information about routes to and up mountains all over the world.

G ICONIC CLIMBING CLASSIC
Published in 1865, Whymper's account of his Alpine climbing – and in particular, the first ascent of the Matterhorn – is regarded as one of the first classic mountaineering books, although it is somewhat marred by digressions on railway engineering.

H MOUNTAINEERING MEMOIR
British alpinist Leslie Stephen popularized the Alps with his best-selling 1871 climbing memoir *The Playground of Europe*.

I EQUIPMENT ADVICE
The glut of climbing publishing was often more pragmatic than inspirational, like this Alpine Club kit catalogue in an age before specialist retailers.

J HELPFUL HOW-TO GUIDE
Developments in climbing techniques and equipment meant there was a regular demand for updated instructional books. This one was published for British members of the Swiss Alpine Club.

"AN EASY DAY FOR A LADY"

I F CLIMBING MOUNTAINS WAS A MORALLY QUESTIONABLE ACTIVITY FOR MEN IN THE 19TH CENTURY, IT WAS EVEN MORE SO FOR WOMEN. YET A FEW FEMALE CLIMBERS FOUND SOCIAL FREEDOM IN THE MOUNTAINS AND PROVED THEMSELVES THE EQUAL OF THEIR MALE COUNTERPARTS.

LUCY WALKER AND PARTY
The demure Miss Walker (right) was in fact an indefatigable peak-bagger who made the first female ascent of the Matterhorn, beating her rival, Meta Brevoort, by a matter of days.

Mountaineering has often been characterized as a male, and even a macho activity, but women were active climbers from early in the sport's history. Maria Paradis (see pp.100–01) had stood on the summit of Mont Blanc in 1808 and, while she never climbed again, the feat was at least remarkable. The first woman to repeat it, Henriette d'Angeville (see pp.100–01), was an enthusiastic alpinist who reached the top unaided and carried on climbing until she was 69. In 1854, a Mrs Hamilton, climbing with her husband, became the first British woman on the summit of Mont Blanc. The first winter ascent of the peak, made as early as 1876, was by a team that included a woman – Isabella Straton.

During the 19th century, against a backdrop of limited personal freedom, women climbers made rapid progress in ability and achievement. Above the tree line, they found they could shed some of society's restrictions, along with some of the more restrictive clothing the era's mores demanded. They could also revel in physically demanding tasks, something that many women, especially those from the upper classes, were denied.

ROPE, CAMERA, ACTION!
in addition to her climbing gear, Elizabeth Le Blond hauled her camera to the summits, becoming a notable mountain photographer in the 1890s.

British climber Katherine Richardson was one woman who revelled in the freedom she found on the mountains. She made more than 100 major climbs, six of them first ascents, and a further 14 first female ascents. Her endurance was impressive. Despite being small and apparently fragile, she was formidably tough. In 1888, she climbed La Meije, in the Écrins, direct from La Bérarde in the valley below. She left her hotel at 9pm and returned the next day in time for tea at 5.30pm, barely stopping on her way to the summit. In the same year, with Emile Rey and J B Bich, she also made the first ascent of one of the most beautiful routes to the summit of Mont Blanc, via the Aiguille de Bionnassay and the West Ridge of the Dôme de Goûter.

HEIGHTS OF FREEDOM

There was also a subtext of sexual freedom, both in how women mountaineers were judged and in how they behaved. Isabella Straton married her guide from the Mont Blanc winter ascent, Jean Charlet, and Lucy Walker (see pp.152–53) held a lifelong passion for her guide, Melchior Anderegg (see pp.126–27), who, unfortunately for her, was already married.

In the 19th century, women from higher social classes led restricted lives, but many enjoyed the freedom and physical challenges of alpinism. However, it was not until the 1920s that climbing in trousers, rather than skirts, became socially acceptable.

A F Mummery (see pp.168–71) climbed with his wife, but also with the talented Lily Bristow. They succeeded on the Grépon, which prompted Mummery to quote – ironically – Leslie Stephen's observation (see pp.134–35) about climbs diminishing in difficulty until they are "an easy day for a lady". In a letter home about her ascent of the Dru with Mummery and others, Bristow wrote: "The climbing was pretty stiff, though not nearly so difficult as the Grépon, which is a real snorker." She remarked, too, on the stir Mummery's willingness to climb with a woman was making among the guests back at the hotel.

ON THE SUMMITS IN SKIRTS

Dress was undoubtedly a handicap for women mountaineers, who were culturally obliged to wear skirts. A Mrs Henry Warwick-Coleman, writing in 1859, complained: "A lady's dress is inconvenient for mountaineering even under the most careful management, and therefore every device which may render it less so should be adopted." She recommended sewing loops to the base of a skirt, which could then be gathered up when the climbing started.

A conspiracy of silence concealed much of what women climbers did and what they wore when doing it, a conspiracy shared by the men with whom they climbed. Subverting dress codes in this way carried social risks. Few had

SETTING THE SCENE

- Mountaineering is an unknown quantity in 19th-century society, so **most people have no idea what sort of freedoms are enjoyed by the women who pursue it.** For a handful of women, it becomes a form of social and physical emancipation.

- Lucy Walker and Meta Brevoort (see pp.152–53) are among the best known of the early women climbers. **Elizabeth Jackson makes 140 major climbs,** including a traverse of the Jungfrau. Beatrice Tomasson makes important firsts in the Dolomites.

- The Ladies' Alpine Club is founded in 1907 but is **regarded by some as junior to the men's club.** In 1921, **the Pinnacle Club** for female rock climbers is founded.

WOMEN'S SUFFRAGE
After World War I, the suffrage movement had begun to shift some of the attitudes that constrained women's lives. Even so, women were not permitted to join the Alpine Club.

CLOCHE HAT AND JODHPURS
By 1929, British climber Kate Gardiner (left) felt able to climb in jodhpurs without inviting scandal. Women's climbing achievements were yet to be fully recognized, however.

the courage to follow the lead of Mary Paillon, a climbing companion of Katherine Richardson, who adopted a logical solution – wearing men's clothing. Most early women climbers wore skirts, or breeches underneath their skirts, and removed the latter when they were out of sight of the last hotel.

ACHIEVEMENTS DISREGARDED

Then there was the propriety of sleeping out with men who weren't their husbands, and the ignominy of having their achievements disregarded by those who assumed that the men climbing with them had faced all the hardships. That wasn't an issue for the Pigeon sisters Anna and Ellen, who stunned the Alpine establishment by crossing the Seserjoch above Zermatt, Switzerland – a straightforward climb but a terrifying descent on the other side. Their guide, Jean Martin, lost his way and the ladies had to take over: "The powers of a mind sharpened by daily use in other matters will, we believe, be found to more than counterbalance the special knowledge of a Swiss peasant." The sisters later made the first female traverse of the Matterhorn from Breuil to Zermatt, bivouacking on the descent in bad conditions.

EDWARDIAN LADY STRIKES
Here, Madame Namur, a female mountaineer known for her masculine clothing, adopts a suitably assertive pose with her ice axe in 1908. Many female mountaineers of her day would hide their trousers under a skirt, which they removed when the serious climbing began.

WALKER AND BREVOORT

BLAZING A TRAIL FOR WOMEN IN THE ALPS

ENGLAND   1835–1916
UNITED STATES   1825–76

LUCY WALKER   **META BREVOORT**

IN THE 1860S AND EARLY 1870S, two women, one English and the other American, made most of the important female ascents in the Alps. In a curious repeat of the competition for the first ascent of the Matterhorn, in 1871 Walker and Brevoort became rivals in the race to claim the first female ascent of the mountain. Lucy Walker was younger, but she began climbing first and became the role model for future generations of women climbers.

A LIFE'S WORK

- Encouraged to visit the Alps for her health, Lucy Walker catches the climbing bug and becomes the **world's first great female mountaineer**

- Walker makes the **first female ascent** of Monte Rosa and the Finsteraarhorn, and later climbs the Rimpfischhorn

- Walker makes **98 expeditions**, many of them first female ascents

- With the aid of her favourite guide, Melchior Anderegg, **Walker beats Brevoort** to the first female ascent of the Matterhorn by a few days

- Back in London, Walker becomes a **champion of women climbers** as the second president of the Ladies' Alpine Club

- Brevoort **makes a number of major ascents**, but fails to achieve her main Alpine ambitions

- With her guide Nicholas Knubel, **Brevoort makes the first female ascents** of the Weisshorn, the Dent Blanche, and the Bietschhorn

- Under the name of her nephew, W A B Coolidge, Breevort **publishes an account of her achievements** for the *Alpine Journal*

Lucy Walker's father, Francis, was an early member of the Alpine Club. So was her brother Horace, who was a serious climber in his own right; he had made the first ascent of Pointe Walker, the highest peak of the Grandes Jorasses, a mountain in the Mont Blanc massif.

In 1858, Lucy's doctor recommended a walking cure for her rheumatism, so she joined her father and brother in the Alps. Her introduction was an ascent of the Théodule Pass, reaching a height of 3,301m

(10,830ft). Excited by the grandeur and isolation of the mountains, her passion for the Alps deepened. While Mrs Walker remained in the valley, the trio worked their way around the major peaks above Zermatt, Chamonix, Grindelwald, and in the Dauphiné mountains.

MEETING ANDEREGG
In 1859, at the Schwarenbach Inn below the Gemmi Pass in Switzerland, Walker met Melchior Anderegg (see pp.126–27), who became the family's favourite guide. In later

life, asked why she never married, she replied, "I love mountains and Melchior, and Melchior already has a wife."

Walker made 98 separate expeditions, all but three of them successful, and many of them first female ascents. She made the first ascent of the Balmhorn, and the fourth ascent of the Eiger, on the latter fuelled by champagne and sponge cake to beat her chronic altitude sickness. That she succeeded in the first female ascent of the Matterhorn was down to Anderegg, who tipped her off about Meta Brevoort's plans. Having made the first female ascent of the Weisshorn three days earlier, Walker dashed to Zermatt to be the first up to the summit.

In 1879, again following her doctor's advice, Walker gave up climbing but continued to visit the Alps. She did little exercise more strenuous than croquet; she entertained and embroidered, or else conformed to the Victorian model of doing socially useful work. None of the Walkers was interested in publicity, and there are few accounts of Lucy's climbing. She was, however, the only woman included in Edward Whymper's engraving "The Zermatt Club Room" (see pp.118–19). She later succeeded Elizabeth Le Blond (see pp.156–57) to become the second president of the Ladies' Alpine Club, where she was acclaimed as a pioneer of women's climbing.

LA MEIJE

PIC CENTRALE, 28 JUNE 1870

— **Setting out**
Coolidge and Brevoort set out with Christian and Ulrich Almer not knowing whether Grand Pic or Pic Centrale is the higher peak.

— **Easy progress**
The central section proves much easier than they had feared.

— **Stopping at Pic Centrale**
They see that Grand Pic is higher, but Almer considers the ridge leading to it impossible. It is climbed in 1885 by the Zsigmondy brothers.

PIC CENTRALE (3,973M/13,035FT)

GRAND PIC (3,984M/13,071FT)

FOUR-LEGGED MOUNTAINEER
Brevoort and Coolidge (second left) climbed for more than ten seasons; their canine companion Tschingel scaled an impressive 66 peaks.

INTREPID TRIO

Marguerite "Meta" Brevoort spent much of her youth in a Paris convent, later returning to Europe from the US as a companion for her nephew, W A B Coolidge (see p.145), whose doctors had recommended that he spend winters in the Mediterranean for his health.

In 1865, Brevoort and Coolidge travelled to Zermatt soon after the Matterhorn tragedy (see pp.136–37). Both became enraptured with the Alps. Brevoort dreamed of climbing the Matterhorn, and Coolidge recovered his health to become a resilient alpinist, spending 33 summers climbing there. He also went on to become the most important climbing historian of the 19th century.

While Lucy Walker was self-effacing and discreet, Brevoort was assertive and spoke her mind. When she witnessed mule-drivers beating their animals, she beat the mule-drivers. She was also determined to make her mark. "I am not quite sure what made us choose the Dauphiné as our battleground," Coolidge recalled, "but I believe it was ambition. There was a whole world for us to explore."

Brevoort and Coolidge made several first ascents in the Dauphiné Alps in southeast France, a range then largely unexplored, often in the company of Christian Almer (see pp.122–23), and taking with them the little dog, Tschingel, that Almer had given to Coolidge on their first expedition. The scarcity of tourists in the region meant poor accommodation facilities: "Fleas without end," Brevoort complained.

During their first season, in 1870, when Brevoort was 45, aunt and nephew made the first ascent of the Pic Centrale of La Meije and the second ascent of the Barre des Écrins. Despite climbing more than 70 major peaks, Brevoort's great ambition was to claim the first female ascent of the Matterhorn, and the first ascent of the Grand Pic of La Meije. In both she was thwarted, yet despite her disappointment she congratulated Lucy Walker on her ascent of the Matterhorn. Brevoort went on to make the first traverse by a woman and fourth overall.

After her traverse of the Matterhorn, on 5 September 1870, Brevoort went on a climbing spree. She climbed the Weisshorn by Kitson's route from the Bisjoch, the Dent Blanche via the South Ridge, and then traversed the Bietschhorn by the North and West Ridges. All were first female ascents. She wrote a famous account of her Bietschhorn climb for the *Alpine Journal*, but, being a woman, the article was published under her nephew's name. She died suddenly in 1876.

DRESSED FOR ACTION

The social norms of the 19th century meant that female mountaineers found themselves scaling mountains in clothes that were constricting and only really suitable for a Sunday walk in the park. Ankle-length skirts were awkward to climb in. The English climber Katharine Richardson was almost killed when her partner's skirt pulled away some rocks during one ascent. Yet Lucy Walker always climbed in skirts, usually a voluminous, white print dress. Elizabeth Le Blond solved the problem by wearing riding breeches under her skirt, which was whisked off once she had safely passed the last village on her ascent.

FLOUTING CONVENTION
A pair of female climbers defy social conventions by joining a climb. As one guidebook put it: "Touching the much vexed question as to whether ladies should climb, we do not hesitate to say, 'no'."

HIKING IN LONG SKIRTS *c.*1865
Here, guides lead a party of women tourists across the
Mer de Glace above Chamonix, France. Women have
been active mountaineers from early in the sport's history,
which they achieved against a background of prejudice and
limited freedom. Even in the 20th century, climbers such as
Freda du Faur (see pp.158–59) were criticized for
accompanying guides without taking chaperones.

ELIZABETH LE BLOND

EARLY MOUNTAIN PHOTOGRAPHER AND FILM-MAKER

ENGLAND   1860–1934

LIKE MANY OF THE WOMEN who made their mark in Victorian alpinism, Elizabeth (Lizzie) Le Blond found mountaineering socially liberating. In her autobiography she expressed "a supreme debt of gratitude to the mountains for knocking me from the shackles of conventionality." She made several first ascents and travelled widely, but her climbing in the Alps was curtailed following a tragic accident on Lyskamm. An accomplished photographer of mountain scenery, she also took some of the first moving images of winter sports.

ON TOP OF THINGS
Le Blond climbed the Alps in winter with the guide Christian Schnirtzler (left). For their ascent of Piz Morteratsch in 1898, they used the type of cumbersome snowshoe first used in Canada.

Born in London to an old Irish family and raised in County Wicklow in Ireland, Elizabeth Hawkins-Whitshed didn't grow up dreaming of mountains. Yet, in the opinion of one of the less progressive stalwarts of the Alpine Club, Colonel E L Strutt, she had the best mountain judgment of any climber he ever met, man or woman, amateur or professional.

Like a surprisingly large number of successful climbers, Le Blond suffered from poor health in her youth. After "coming out" in London society, she travelled to St Moritz with her first husband, the hugely famous adventurer, soldier, and balloonist Colonel Frederick G Burnaby, for the pure Alpine air. Walking up from Pontresina with a long alpenstock, Le Blond reached the Diavolezza Pass, where she was overwhelmed by the view, and resolved to take up climbing. The birth of her son Harry in 1880, and the death of her husband in battle in Sudan in 1885, didn't curtail her new passion. She hired the best guides, including Joseph Imboden and his son Roman when she was in Zermatt, and in Chamonix Emile Rey and Edouard Cupelin. She applied herself to learning as much as she could, and scaled the Matterhorn with Alexander Burgener (see pp.166–67).

WINTER ASCENTS
Many of Le Blond's greatest achievements took place in the early 1880s. In 1882, she climbed the Grandes Jorasses and the Dent du Géant on the Franco-Italian border. That winter, in January, she made the first crossing of several high Chamonix passes – the cols du Tacul, du Chardonnet, and d'Argentière. She also made the first winter ascent of the Aiguille du Midi. "It was always the new expeditions that gave me the greatest pleasure," she wrote.

A month later, she was climbing with the great Italian photographer Vittorio Sella (see p.199), attempting a winter ascent of Monte Rosa which ended at 4,200m (13,800ft) in bad weather. Le Blond took up photography herself, drawing praise from the English novelist E F Benson, who used her photographs to illustrate his book *Winter Sports in Switzerland*.

ROPE MATES
Le Blond bore disapproval and restrictions on her behaviour and dress with good humour. On one climb, having left her skirt trapped safely under a heavy rock so she could climb more freely in her riding breeches, she watched with alarm as an avalanche swept it away. Back in the village, she hid behind a clump of trees as Joseph Imboden, her guide, went back to the hotel with precise instructions on what to bring: "To my horror he appeared after a long interval with my best evening dress over his arm." Imboden was Le Blond's close climbing companion for more than 20 years. Together, and with his son Roman, they climbed most

In aid of the "ALPINE" MOTOR KITCHEN to be given by British Climbers for the use of the Chasseurs Alpins in the Vosges.

LANTERN LECTURE

"Mountaineering from a Woman's Point of View,"

AN ATTEMPT TO EXPLAIN TO NON-CLIMBERS THE CHARM OF MOUNTAINEERING.

WILL BE GIVEN BY

MRS. AUBREY LE BLOND

On Wednesday, May 12th, 1915, at 9 p.m.,
At the Grafton Galleries, W.

The Chair will be taken by Mrs. F. BULLOCK WORKMAN, F.R.G.S.

Tickets - 5s and 2/3 each.

PHOTOGRAPHIC LECTURE
A poster from 1915 advertises a "Lantern Lecture" given by Le Blond in London. Lantern lectures were talks that included a slide show.

A LIFE'S WORK

- Makes dozens of climbs in the Alps – becoming one of the **pioneer winter climbers** – and in the peaks and glaciers of Norway

- In the 1890s, her talent for photography leads to her also becoming **the world's first mountain film-maker**

- Chronicles her accomplishments in **eight books on mountain climbing**

- Largely through her efforts, the **Ladies' Alpine Club** comes into being

of the great peaks around Zermatt, famously climbing the Zinal Rothorn twice in one day. However, "one terrible day" in 1895, Roman Imboden was killed after falling through a cornice on Lyskamm while with another client. After that, neither Roman's father nor Le Blond felt the same way about the Alps: "I felt I could never again set out with his father in the light-hearted fashion in which we had so climbed heretofore."

Joseph Imboden and Le Blond visited Norway – then popular with British alpinists – for several years. One of Le Blond's books is dedicated to the Lyngen Alps, where she made a handful of first ascents. In the late 1890s she experimented with motion pictures of winter sports in the Engadine valley in Switzerland, becoming the first mountain film-maker.

In 1900, she married her third husband, Aubrey Le Blond, who joined her in Norway, and in 1907 she became the founding president of the Ladies' Alpine Club. Despite her new routes and pioneering of winter climbing, she saw herself as a cautious climber: "Adventures are seldom to the credit of a mountaineering party, of whom the proudest boast should be that no unnecessary risks were taken."

SCANDALIZING SOCIETY

Such was her privileged background, when Le Blond climbed Mont Blanc in 1882, she confessed to her companions that she had never put on her own boots before – her maid had always done it for her. When her last maid eloped, she discovered she was perfectly capable of doing such things for herself. Le Blond's climbing outraged the upper-class society in which she moved. Her great aunt, on seeing her sunburned face, wrote to her grandniece's mother with the command: "Stop her climbing mountains! She is scandalizing all London and looks like a Red Indian!"

BRAVING THE ALPINE SUN, LE BLOND MADE HERSELF A CLOTH MASK TO PROTECT HER FACE

ARCTIC PEAKS
In 1897, Le Blond started exploring the Lyngen Alps in the far north of Norway (shown here). After one ascent, she "ventured to call the little peak the Elizabethtind, finding no neighbouring glacier or valley after which to name it."

FREDA DU FAUR

FIRST WOMAN TO ASCEND MOUNT COOK

AUSTRALIA   1882–1935

No FEMALE MOUNTAINEER challenged the boundaries of sport and society quite as robustly as Freda Du Faur, and few were as articulate. After a sustained effort, she made the first female ascent of New Zealand's Mount Cook, in 1910, and was a leading light of the small New Zealand climbing scene before World War I. Later, she lived in London and worked for the suffragist cause, but became alienated from the world of mountaineering and never recovered from the premature death of her partner.

In January 1909, two climbers, Peter Graham, a New Zealand guide, and his client Freda Du Faur, found themselves blocked at the foot of Mount Cook. Roped together, they attempted to cross the bergschrund, or glacial crevasse. Graham tried to climb rocks off to one side, but realized that Du Faur, at just 51kg (112lb), would be unable to hold him if he fell. In the interests of safety, he retreated. Du Faur said it was "one of the bitterest moments I ever experienced". She felt that her own weakness had let her down, and it maddened her.

Freda Du Faur was born in Sydney and early family holidays to the Blue Mountains outside the city gave her a taste for wilder landscapes. At Ku-ring-gai Chase National Park, she experimented with rock climbing. Travelling in New Zealand with her father in 1906, she was intrigued by photographs she saw in an exhibition at Christchurch of the Southern Alps, including Mount Cook, and resolved to go there.

TAKE A CHAPERONE
At the Hermitage – the remote base camp for Mount Cook – Du Faur met Peter Graham, in his first year as chief guide, who taught her the basics of mountaineering. She became instantly hooked, both with the activity and with the mountains themselves: "The great peaks towering into the sky before me touched a chord that all the wonders of my own land had never set vibrating, and filled a blank of whose very existence I had been unconscious."

A LIFE'S WORK

- Becomes the **first woman to climb Mount Cook**, and publishes her account of the climb

- Makes the **first traverse of Cook's three summits**, one of the greatest achievements by a woman climber before World War I

- Is the **first person to summit the three highest peaks** in the Southern Alps (Cook, Tasman, and Dampier)

SEEKING EQUALITY

Du Faur and her partner Muriel Cadogan travelled to Europe in 1914, intending to tackle the Alps. The outbreak of World War I scuppered their plans but gave them the opportunity to stay and work in London. They were to remain in England until Cadogan's death in 1929. During the war, Du Faur campaigned for women's suffrage. A woman who had set new records in mountaineering for male or female climbers, she was dissatisfied with the subordinate status of the Ladies' Alpine Club, and sought full equality with male alpinists.

SUFFRAGETTES MARCH ALONG A CENTRAL LONDON STREET IN THIS PHOTOGRAPH TAKEN IN 1912

SPIRIT, IMAGINATION ... IT STEALS INTO THE HEART ON THE LONELY SILENT SUMMITS AND WILL NOT BE DENIED

FREDA DU FAUR

MOUNT COOK

GRAND TRAVERSE, 3 JANUARY 1913

Ascent to Low Peak
Du Faur, Graham, and Thomson leave their bivouac below West Ridge at 2am. Low Peak is reached at 7am.

Middle Peak
The descent from the first summit towards Middle Peak is "a jagged saddle of saw-like teeth".

High Peak
The party traverses the ridge of High Peak to reach the summit at 1.30pm. They spend more than an hour on there before descending.

SUMMIT (3,754M/12,316FT)

MIDDLE PEAK

HIGH PEAK

LOW PEAK

WEST FACE

SHEILA GLACIER

LOWER EMPRESS SHELF

Graham admired independent women, and considered guiding them to be "a privilege". When Du Faur returned in the summer of 1908–09, he so encouraged her natural ability that she decided to attempt the first female ascent of Mount Cook. However, compared with Europe, where female climbers were more numerous, a young woman in New Zealand climbing alone with a male guide attracted strong disapproval. The prospect of losing his clients was a sufficient deterrent for Graham not to become romantically involved, yet still there was gossip about their relationship. One woman begged Du Faur "not to spoil her life for so small a thing as climbing a mountain".

Although she had inherited a substantial sum from her aunt, Du Faur was furious at the limitations put on her independence. Only in the mountains did she feel fulfilled: "All the primitive emotions are ours – hunger, thirst, heat and cold, triumph and fear – as yard by yard we win our way to stand as conquerors and survey our realm ... Spirit, imagination, name it what you will, it steals into the heart on the lonely silent summits and will not be denied."

CLIMBING TEAM

Du Faur was guided by brothers Peter (right) and Alec Graham on her historic ascent of Mount Cook in 1910. In deference to Edwardian convention, she wore a skirt to just below the knee over knickerbockers and long puttees.

On her first climb, an ascent of Mount Sealy, she felt obliged to hire an extra porter as a kind of chaperone, and promptly saved his life with some deft ropework when he slipped.

MAKING HISTORY

When Du Faur returned to Sydney she adopted a rigorous training regime, and in doing so met a fitness instructor named Muriel Cadogan, who was later to became her lover. Thanks to Cadogan, Du Faur, now 28, returned to New Zealand in prime physical condition. Taking Graham's brother as a second guide, she completed the ascent of Mount Cook and was amazed at the flood of telegrams congratulating her. She was proud, too, of the political message her climb had conveyed. Du Faur continued to climb in the Southern Alps, making the difficult second ascent of Mount Tasman. But it was the first traverse of all three peaks of Mount Cook in 1913 that was her greatest achievement.

In 1914, she travelled to London with Cadogan, but was unimpressed with the Ladies' Alpine Club, not understanding why women couldn't assert their way into the male-only Alpine Club. Instead, she campaigned with the suffragettes. Du Faur remained in England with Cadogan for several years, but when her partner died after a mental illness, Du Faur returned to Australia, where she became withdrawn and lonely. She committed suicide in 1935.

BIRTH OF MODERN ALPINISM

AFTER THE TRIUMPHS OF THE GOLDEN AGE, MOUNTAINEERING TOOK ON A NEW FORM THAT WAS MORE CLOSELY ALLIED TO THE SPORT AS IT IS PRACTISED TODAY. HOW AND WHAT YOU CLIMBED, AND WHAT YOU TOOK WITH YOU, BECAME AS IMPORTANT AS GAINING A SUMMIT.

OPPONENT OF THE NEW FASHION
Guideless climbing was regarded as dangerous by senior members of the Alpine Club, such as Charles E Mathews (above), who had enjoyed strong personal relationships with their guides.

By 1870, most of the Alpine peaks – including those that had once been considered too treacherous and terrifying to climb – had been "conquered". English alpinist Clinton Dent (see pp.164–65) declared in 1876 that the older members of the Alpine Club had left the next generation of climbers with little to aspire to in the region. He was half joking, but he was serious about where mountaineers were looking as they sought to expand their skills. With the accessible snow and ice routes – often the easiest way to a summit – now claimed, the attention of the leading climbers turned to rock peaks, especially the various aiguilles (sharp, pointed pinnacles) that are a feature of the Alps. Dent himself would show the way with his determined siege of the Aiguille du Dru, the granite spire soaring high above Chamonix in the French Alps. Just as important, with the number of unclaimed Alpine peaks running low, was the idea that the route up a mountain should be as appealing as reaching the summit. Instead of being driven by the glory of a mountain's first ascent, there were new, more demanding, and more beautiful ways to reach the top. Standards were beginning to rise.

SNOW AND ICE GO OUT OF STYLE?
One-time president of the Alpine Club, Clinton Dent, urged climbers not to become too specialist, saying: "Rock climbing and rock peaks are much more in favour now … The snow mountains no longer attract as they did of yore. People talk of one form of mountaineering as a rock climb while they stigmatise the other as a snow grind."

THE LAST GREAT PRIZE
The Dent du Geánt, or "Giant's Tooth" has two summits, both of which were finally claimed in the summer of 1882, marking the end of alpinism's "Silver Age".

REACHING FOR LOFTIER PEAKS
After making several firsts in the Alps, German Paul Güssfeldt (centre) moved on to the Andes, where, in 1883, he attempted Aconcagua, the highest peak in the Western hemisphere.

SETTING THE SCENE

- In 1874, the German and Austrian Alpine Club merge and use their financial muscle to **build a system of huts throughout the Eastern Alps**, accelerating development in the region.

- **Climbing without guides** becomes more popular among elite mountaineers, but **a new, more ambitious type of guide also emerges**. The "prince of guides", the Italian Emile Rey, who climbs a new route on Mont Blanc with German alpinist Paul Güssfeldt, is more interested in adventure than pay.

- As the number of climbers and the pace of technical development increases, so does the the number of accidents. The Alpine Club **warns against solo climbing, but guided parties are equally at risk**. The brilliant Welsh rock climber O G Jones is killed on Switzerland's Dent Blanche when his guide falls.

- There are fears that a **love of risk for its own sake will undermine the new sport**. US scholar and climber W A B Coolidge (see p.145) writes: "If mountaineering is allowed to degenerate into a form of gambling … it will cease to be what it is now, the noblest form of recreation known to man."

This was also the era when ethical arguments came to the fore. If, by using "ironmongery" – artificial climbing aids – you could overcome any challenge, where was the adventure?

BY FAIR MEANS OR FOUL

Experienced climbers realized, though, that unlike exploration, where the means justified the ends, in mountaineering, the means were the ends. In 1880, the star of 19th-century British climbing, A F Mummery (see pp.168–171), attempted a first ascent of the Dent du Géant, one of the few remaining unclimbed peaks in the Alps. He failed and declared it to be inaccessible by "fair means". Two years later, the guide Jean-Joseph Maquignaz spent four days chipping out holds, nailing in pegs, and laying out some 150m (500ft) of fixed ropes, preparing the way for his clients to reach the coveted summit.

Another area of contention was the use of guides. From the very start of mountaineering, there had been a partnership between wealthy, often English, amateurs, and local men with experience of the terrain and geography. But as the expertise and knowledge of the amateurs grew, the role of the guide became less clear. A growing number of talented Austrian and German climbers in the Eastern Alps, and some British alpinists in the Western Alps, began to realize that climbing without guides put all the control, and all the rewards, into the hands of

> Between 1866 and 1882, the last of the Alpine peaks were overcome and alpinists began to explore the Caucasus, Pyrenees, Rockies, and Andes. In 1883, the first major expedition to the Greater Ranges of Asia was undertaken.

the climbers. In short, it was more fulfilling. And for the German and Austrian climbers, who were often penniless students living within touching distance of the mountains, not having to hire guides made economic sense, too.

RADICAL IDEAS

This was the era when alpinism really took hold in the Eastern Alps, and from this "school" of mountaineering would come many of its greatest practitioners. First among them was a teacher from Klagenfurt in southern Austria called Ludwig Purtscheller (see p.173), who climbed about 1,700 routes, mostly in the limestone peaks of his region.

Purtscheller was an early advocate of solo climbing, which would become almost an article of faith among some Austrian and German climbers. This extreme move alarmed the Alpine Club. Even Dent, who was a voice of progress, dismissed the idea of solo climbing as selfish. "Solitary expeditions," he wrote, "may be magnificent but they are not mountaineering." The subtext was that too many young climbers were reckless, and this was damaging the sport's reputation. This same fear of radicalism may explain why the Alpine Club blackballed Mummery's application for membership, because he believed

that the essence of the sport lay "not in ascending a peak, but in struggling and overcoming difficulties". Snobbery concerning Mummery's profession – he ran a tanning business – may also have been a factor in his blackballing, but he was finally elected in 1888.

Not all British climbers were reactionary, however. With the development of rock climbing in Britain, a cadre of technically capable innovators – including Norman Collie, Cecil Slingsby, and the Hopkinson brothers – emerged, and there were still capable traditional alpinists such as Geoffrey Winthrop Young.

However, the stalwarts of the Alpine Club now discovered what every subsequent generation of mountaineers has experienced since, that the game they thought they understood changes continually. The baton was passing from the Alpine Club to newer schools springing up in the heart of Europe.

NAILED CLIMBING BOOTS
High-lacing leather boots with a stiff, nailed sole – the patterns of which evolved over time – were the standard climbing footwear until the 1930s, when the first rubber-soled boots helped reduce the risk of frostbite.

ADOLPHUS MOORE

FIRST-CLASS EXPLORATORY MOUNTAINEER

ENGLAND   1841–87

THE DAY AFTER Edward Whymper reached the summit of the Matterhorn in 1865, a party including Adolphus Moore reached the summit of Mont Blanc via the treacherous Brenva Face. Their historic ascent paved the way for the next phase of mountaineering's development as a sport, and helped restore the Alpine Club's fortunes after the Matterhorn tragedy marked the end of the Golden Age. A brilliant administrator, Moore served as private secretary to the father of future British prime minster, Winston Churchill.

Moore was one of the greatest mountaineers of the Golden Age. According to the English alpinist and educationalist Geoffrey Winthrop Young, "in skill and daring he would seem to have been surpassed only by the Reverend Charles Hudson among his contemporaries." In terms of his mountaineering imagination, according to Young, he "overtopped them all". Like Whymper (see pp.142–45) and Leslie Stephen (see pp.134–35), Moore wrote a much admired account of his achievements – *The Alps in 1864* – which included the Brenva climb, but it was published privately and he never achieved the fame of his contemporaries.

Moore's father was a director of the East India Company in London, and Adolphus joined the firm after completing his education, spending much of his subsequent career in the India Office. He had to juggle these responsibilities with his passion for the mountains.

AN ALPINE EDUCATION

At 19, Moore was introduced to the Alps by the Reverend Hereford Brooke George, the first editor of the *Alpine Journal*. The pair covered a lot of ground, crossing passes and climbing minor peaks, and their exploits instilled in the young Moore a desire to explore fully the

A LIFE'S WORK

- Makes the **first ascent of Switzerland's Gross Fiescherhorn** and the first passage of significant passes such as the Jungfraujoch

- After success in the Dauphiné Alps with Whymper, including the first ascent of the Barre des Écrins, he **crosses the Moming Pass** near Zermatt, despite being warned it is impossible

- Most of the subsidiary peaks of the Mont Blanc range have been climbed, so he turns his attention to making a new route up the mountain – the eastern **Brenva Face**, one of the **most intimidating and demanding walls in the Alps**

- After a reconnaissance, he leads a team in **a successful attempt on the Brenva Face of Mont Blanc**; the route exceeds in difficulty any other route yet tried on the mountain

- Leaves the Alps to **explore and climb in the Caucasus** Mountains with fellow Englishmen Douglas Freshfield and Charles Comyns Tucker

- While recovering in Monte Carlo from overwork, he **dies prematurely of typhoid fever**

CAUCASUS CLIMBERS
Pictured holding the long alpenstocks that made their more daring ascents possible are (standing left to right): Moore, François Devouassoud, a guide from Chamonix, and Charles Comyns Tucker; seated at the front is Douglas Freshfield.

MONT BLANC

BRENVA FACE, 15 JULY 1865

— **Setting out at 2.45am**
Moore, G S Spencer, Frank and Horace Walker, and Jakob and Melchior Anderegg leave a bivouac below the Brenva Face.

— **Steep climb**
The bolder Jakob Anderegg takes the lead up the difficult ice arête.

— **Route to the summit**
Melchior Anderegg leads through the serac barrier, shouting back to the others that the route is possible. "That moment was worth living for," says Moore afterwards.

SUMMIT (4,808M/15,771FT)

ICE ARÊTE

mountain ranges he visited: "no one really knows a group until he has been up and down all its valleys."

In 1862, again with George, Moore did more serious Alpine climbs, joining Leslie Stephen for the first crossing of the Jungfraujoch. In subsequent years, Moore did practically every difficult climb then possible in the Alps. He and his friend Horace Walker hired the best guides, including Christian Almer (see pp.122–23) and Melchior Anderegg (see pp.126–27).

Like Whymper, Moore had a hugely successful summer in 1864. Whymper and his guide, the great Michel Croz, joined Moore and Walker at the start of their season in the wild and little-known Dauphiné Alps. They made the first crossing of the high mountain pass Brèche de la Meije and the first ascent of the Barre des Écrins. That summer, Moore traversed Mont Blanc with Almer, descending via the Mur de la Côte to the

northeast, which gave them a dramatic view of Mont Blanc's Brenva Face. Most thought that this route up the mountain was impossible, but Moore was convinced otherwise.

IRRESISTIBLE MAGNET
In 1865, now climbing with Jakob Anderegg (see p.127), Moore and Walker had further successes. That summer, determined to try the Brenva Face, they travelled to Courmayeur, on the Italian side of Mont Blanc, to meet English climber George Spencer Mathews. They were joined by Walker's father Frank and the Andereggs. Leaving the town on 14 July, the team bivouacked on the moraine of the Brenva Glacier, leaving early the following morning to climb its upper icefall.

NEW FRONTIERS
Moore was a pioneer of climbing in the Caucasus. In 1868, he scaled the 5,642-m (18,510-ft) Mount Elbruz, Europe's highest mountain, which he painted in his journal (above).

Above this, they reached what is now called Col Moore, a depression in the spur they hoped would lead to the top of the Brenva Face. Overcoming a rocky buttress took another two hours and they finally arrived at the crux of the route – a steep ice ridge that barred progress to the upper face. Even with nailed boots and ice axes, this section took an hour to complete, and Moore had to resort to straddling the ridge like a horse ("*à cheval*") to inch his way along. Steep snow above the ridge led to a band of ice cliffs, which Melchior overcame with difficulty. Moore was still waiting to follow, when he heard a yell from above: "'What is it?' said we to Mr Walker. A shouting communication took place between him and Melchior, and then came the answer, 'He says it's all right.' That moment was worth living for." The party's achievement set the standard for the next two decades.

Moore continued to explore the Alps and was among the first mountaineers to spend a winter there. He also went on two expeditions to the Caucasus Mountains, making the first ascents of Kazbek and Mount Elbruz.

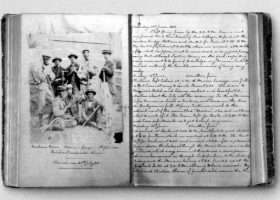

CLIMBING JOURNAL
Moore recorded his climbs in six journals, filling them with photographs, paintings, and detailed notes on each climb. This page includes a photograph of his climbing party in Switzerland in July 1863.

CLINTON DENT

PIONEER ON ROCK PEAKS

ENGLAND   1850–1912

During the Golden Age, interest was focused on climbing the highest Alpine peaks, usually by moderately steep snow and ice slopes. But as the number of these unclimbed giants diminished, mountaineers turned their attention to the next tier. These were often rockier and more difficult challenges. Clinton Dent was one of the climbers in the vanguard of these attempts. His name is most associated with the first ascent of the Grand Dru, the majestic granite spire that dominates the upper portion of the Arve valley above Chamonix.

MOUNTAIN PHOTOGRAPHER
Dent took this image of Mount Ushba in the Caucasus. A contemporary of Dent's, Vittorio Sella (see p.199), was already pioneering the field of mountain photography.

A LIFE'S WORK

- **Starts climbing at 14**, but doesn't climb a snow peak in his first two seasons because he feels that he is not yet ready

- Most of his **biggest climbs are made with the great Swiss guide Alexander Burgener**

- After 18 failed attempts, he eventually makes the **first ascent of the Grand Dru** in 1878

- Believing there are no new challenges left in the Alps, he **helps pioneer climbing in the Caucasus Mountains**, making several first ascents

In an early edition of the *Alpine Journal*, Clinton Dent, with a heavy dose of irony, wrote: "The older members of the [Alpine] Club have left us, the youthful aspirants, but little to do in the Alps. We follow them meekly, either by walking up their mountains by new routes, or by climbing some despised outstanding spur of the peaks they first trod under foot. They have left us but these rock aiguilles. They have picked out the plums and left us the stones."

Dent's article was about his early attempts on the Grand Dru — for a mountaineer one of the most inspiring peaks in the Alps. It was hardly a poor consolation for having missed the Golden Age. His true attitude is revealed in the phrase "walking up their mountains".

Dent, in his decorous, English way, was indicating that the game was changing, and changing fast. Difficulty for its own sake was becoming part of the appeal of mountaineering.

Dent was born into a wealthy family and educated at Eton and Cambridge, becoming an eminent surgeon. His passion for climbing was ignited at a young age and, before he was 18, he had six seasons in Switzerland under his belt, with ascents of the most prized peaks, such as the Matterhorn and the Schreckhorn. He had also made some first ascents, including the Lenzspitze in 1870, and the classic Portiengrat, above Saas Fee, in 1871, a rock climb that was a sign of things to come.

GRAND DRU

SOUTHEAST FACE, 12 SEPTEMBER 1878

— **Daybreak**
From their tent at the head of the Charpoua Glacier, Dent, Hartley, Burgener, and Maurer follow the left bank of the gully leading to the ridge above.

— **Moving onto the face**
The team use a pre-placed ladder to overcome difficult ground and then climb down a chimney before resuming the ascent.

— **Breaking through to the upper peak**
Burgener leads a difficult traverse into an icy gully. "Where in the wide world will you find a sport able to yield pleasure like this?" Dent writes later.

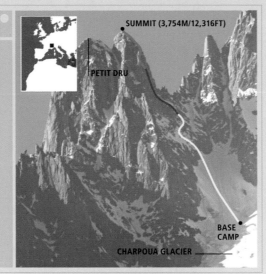

SUMMIT (3,754M/12,316FT)

PETIT DRU

BASE CAMP

CHARPOUA GLACIER

As an 18-year-old, Dent had hired the young Alexander Burgener (see pp.166–67). Both out to make their mark, the pair may have been client and guide, but from a distance their relationship resembles a modern climbing partnership, as they dared each other on: "In those days we were not of an age ready to take good advice," Dent recalled later.

In 1872, they made the first ascent of the Zinal Rothorn from Zermatt, by then the classic, standard route up the mountain. This was a much desired prize for local guides and Burgener's success infuriated the old guard at Zermatt, who questioned whether the route was possible and whether he was making the whole thing up. It wasn't only the older members of the Alpine Club who were hostages to the past.

A LOOSE MORAINE
Dent (second from the right) picks his way through boulders in the company of the guide Melchior Anderegg (right). Though Burgener became his favoured guide, Dent climbed with many of the leading guides of the time.

ICE, SNOW, AND ROCK

Dent's later career spanned several important developments that breathed new life into mountaineering. The first was a willingness to tackle difficult rock climbing. "The snow mountains no longer attract as they did of yore," he wrote. "Different terms are applied to them. People talk of one form of mountaineering as a rock-climb while they stigmatise the other as a snow grind."

This shift in attitude was exemplified by Dent's obsession with climbing the Grand Dru. He returned again and again to this one mountain with Burgener and other guides, finally succeeding on his 19th attempt. Such caution was perfectly understandable, when equipment was so rudimentary. Falling off wasn't an option, as Dent explained: "From the moment the glacier is left, hard climbing begins, and the hands as well as the feet are continuously employed. The difficulties are therefore enormously increased if the rocks be glazed or cold; and in bad weather the crags of the Dru would be as pretty a place for an accident as can well be imagined."

The party reached the summit via the Southeast Face in September 1878, and with a wry sense of bathos, waved what Dent described as "a piece of scarlet flannel like unto a baby's undergarment" on a pole in the hope that there were some in Chamonix watching his victory. Writing about the ascent afterwards, Dent prefigured the mountain's enormous popularity with climbers: "Those who follow us, and I think there will be many, will perhaps be glad of a few hints about this peak. Taken together, it affords the most continuously interesting rock climb with which I am acquainted. There is no wearisome tramp over moraine, no great extent of snow fields to traverse."

OPENING UP THE CAUCASUS

In later life, believing the Alps to have run out of new routes, with "really nothing left worth risking much for", Dent spent much time exploring the Caucasus Mountains, making first ascents of Gestola with fellow English alpinist William Donkin in 1886, and Tsiteli in 1895 with Hermann Woolley. He also assisted in the search for clues as to the fate of Donkin and Harry Fox, who disappeared on Koshtan-Tau in 1888. His concern about the rising number of accidents led him to formulate the international Alpine Distress Signal. Dent was also an expert photographer, an early enthusiast of winter climbing, and a fluent writer who, in 1892, was probably the first man to argue that climbing Mount Everest would be physically possible.

A MAN OF TALENTS
Dent became such a well-known climbing figure (he was president of the Alpine Club from 1886–89) that mountaineers of the time were often unaware of his equally high renown in post-surgical insanity and heart surgery.

THOSE WHO FOLLOW US, AND
I THINK THERE WILL BE MANY,
WILL BE GLAD OF A FEW
HINTS ABOUT THIS PEAK

CLINTON DENT ON THE GRAND DRU

ALEXANDER BURGENER

GREATEST OF THE ROCK-CLIMBING GUIDES

SWITZERLAND   1845–1910

IN THE 1870S, A GROWING INTEREST in climbing rock peaks gave rise to a different type of guide: one who could do more than cut steps in snow and ice. Alexander Burgener came from the Saas Valley, where the lower rock peaks gave him a good grounding in the new style. Apart from many climbs with English mountaineers Albert Frederick Mummery and Clinton Dent, he also worked with some of the European clients who were beginning to rival the British, including Moriz von Kuffner and Paul Güssfeldt.

THE HAUNTED CRAGS
Here, a climbing party with lanterns sets off before dawn. On such climbs, Burgener's eyes searched fearfully for the lights of the spirits he believed haunted the slopes.

Powerful, daring, and tenacious, Burgener was described by Clinton Dent (see pp.164–65) as having "a full share of the rashness of youth". Born in the village of Eisten, Burgener began his career as a guide aged 22, working regularly for Dent over the next decade. "A strong belief in his own powers," Dent wrote later, "and the natural desire of a young man to earn a reputation among amateurs led, in the early days of the alliance, to certain performances on the mountains on which the writer does not wish to dilate at present."

In many ways, Burgener and his younger client grew up together, making the first ascents of peaks such as the Lenzspitze and the Portjengrat, as well as a new route on the Zinal Rothorn from the Trift Glacier. In 1876, they climbed the East Face of the Täschhorn. However, their greatest achievement, and their last such exploit together, was the first ascent of the Grand Dru in 1878, the climax of Dent's protracted and exhausting campaign to reach it.

PERFECT PARTNERS

The following year, Burgener was introduced to the 23-year-old A F Mummery (see pp.168–71). The guide was no longer a youngster, but a square-bearded, stocky veteran whose immature excesses had been tempered by experience. Mummery had the good sense not to bridle at Burgener's scepticism of his ability and submitted to a series of probationary climbs, even though this almost cost him the Matterhorn's Zmutt Ridge. He quickly came to appreciate Burgener's engaging mix of superstition, Catholic piety, and a love for the finer things in life.

Holed up beneath the Zmutt Ridge on a foul day, Mummery reported that his guide's thoughts turned repeatedly to the luxuries of the Monte Rosa Hotel, but once it was clear Mummery meant business, he "settled himself in a sheltered corner, and charmed by the caresses of

Lady Nicotine, told me weird tales of the ghosts and goblins which still haunt the great circle of cliffs towering above the Val Anzasca."

Burgener's partnership with Mummery was long and fruitful. Following their success together on the Zmutt Ridge in 1879, they made the first crossing of the Col du Lion and a strong attempt on the Matterhorn's Furggen Ridge. In Chamonix, boosted by the skills that the guide Benedikt Venetz brought to their group, they achieved the first ascents of several rock peaks, including the Aiguille du Grépon in 1881.

BEYOND THE ALPS

In later years, when Mummery began climbing without a guide, Burgener worked for some of the leading European clients, climbing one of the most beautiful and popular routes in the Mont Blanc range – the Frontier or Kuffner Ridge on Mont Maudit – with the Austrian

THE CHAMOIS HUNTERS
Burgener belonged to a group associated with legend and romance to 19th-century urbanites, for whom the wildness of mountain life held a mythic allure as industrialization gained pace.

A LIFE'S WORK

- His early career is dominated by his association with Clinton Dent, culminating in the **first ascent of the Grand Dru** in 1878

- Despite initial scepticism, he forms a strong and lasting partnership with A F Mummery; in 1879 **they climb the Zmutt Ridge**

- Climbs **important new routes** in the Western Alps at Chamonix, including the Charpoua Face of the Aiguille Verte, as well as rock peaks such as the Grépon

climber Moriz von Kuffner, as well as repeating the Zmutt with Mummery and the Duke of the Abruzzi (see pp.198–99). He began travelling, too, to South America with German climber Paul Güssfeldt in 1882, and to the Caucasus with the Hungarian explorer Maurice de Déchy in 1884, returning there with Dent two years later.

IRRATIONAL FEARS

Burgener lived in fear of the *Geister*, or ghosts, that he believed haunted the mountains, arguing furiously with Mummery on the Furggen Ridge of the Matterhorn after seeing the blue light of will-o'-the-wisps dancing around them as they walked up to the mountain. Soon after witnessing this natural phenomenon, the team saw a lantern shining on the Gorner Glacier, which Burgener identified with complete confidence as a ghost. This was serious. As Mummery knew from Burgener, anyone seeing a ghost in the mountains could expect to die within a day.

It is possible that Burgener's superstition was born from his passion for chamois hunting – an activity he pursued throughout his life – and the long, lonely nights he spent in remote places in search of his quarry. At the age of 63, he shot four of the animals on one trip, tied two of them across his shoulders and walked some four hours back down into the valley.

BURGENER HAS A FULL SHARE OF THE RASHNESS OF YOUTH

CLINTON DENT

This passion for hunting, however, had led to accusations of murder in his youth, and when the body of the priest and mountain guide Johann Joseph Imseng was found in a lake in 1869, suspicion fell on Burgener, who had been fingered by Imseng for illicit hunting. Burgener said that if he was guilty then the mountains would claim his life. This they did decades later, when an avalanche swept him, and his son, to their deaths.

MAN OF THE MOUNTAINS
A rugged individualist, Burgener cared more about the ghosts of his superstitions than what anyone thought of him.

MONT MAUDIT

SOUTHEAST RIDGE

— **4 July 1887**
Also known as the Kuffner or Frontier Ridge, the climb, according to Moriz von Kuffner, was difficult rather than dangerous, along a snow crest and completed during a period of unsettled weather. It is still regarded as one of the finest ridges in the Mont Blanc range.

SUMMIT (4,465M/14,649FT)

ALBERT FREDERICK MUMMERY

FOUNDER OF MODERN ALPINISM

ENGLAND   1855–95

FAMOUS FOR BRILLIANT new climbs, such as the Zmutt Ridge on the Matterhorn, Fred Mummery was also noted for his ideas about the development of alpinism. His climbing career was divided into two main stages: guided, and then, from 1889, mostly unguided. He wasn't the first to climb without guides, but this became important through his advocacy. He also climbed with women, acknowledging their ability despite convention. Mummery disappeared while attempting the 8,126-m (26,660-ft) Nanga Parbat.

Born into a prosperous family, Mummery was a sickly child, suffering from poor vision and a spinal deformity. As a young man, he joined the family firm, later inheriting a portion of the business, which gave him the means to pursue his passion for mountaineering.

Mummery began climbing in 1871 and later wrote, "At the age of fifteen the crags of the Via Mala and the snows of the Théodule roused a passion within me that has grown with years, and has to no small extent moulded my life and thought. It has led me into regions of such fairy beauty that the fabled wonders of Xanadu seems commonplace." Tall and gangling, he had a habit of removing his glasses when he walked, making him seem clumsy. However, in the mountains he was precise and controlled on technical ground, and endured bivouacs without complaint.

At 17, Mummery climbed Monte Rosa, and a year later, the Matterhorn, for which he developed an intense passion, scaling it seven times. "I have been one of the great peak's most reverent worshippers," he wrote, "and whenever the mighty rock appears above the distant horizon, I hail

LOST AXE
This axe, left by the Mummery party on the summit of the Aiguille du Grépon in 1881, was recovered by the French second ascent party in 1885.

its advent with devoutest joy." His devotion was rewarded with the first ascent of the finest way up the peak: the Zmutt Ridge.

FRIENDLY RIVALS
In 1879, he crossed the Tiefenmattenjoch to Zermatt, which gave him a close view of the Zmutt, a view that Edward Whymper (see pp.142–45) had also seen, pronouncing the ascent impossible that way. Mummery thought otherwise, and on arriving in the village discovered that the guide Alexander Burgener (see pp.166–67) was available. Burgener thought it "cursed stupidity" to attempt such a challenge with a young man he barely knew, and who was not yet a member of the Alpine Club, so together they embarked on a series of tough training climbs together.

By the time they were ready, Mummery discovered that a young medical student named William Penhall and his guides had left Zermatt the day before with the same intention. Certain that Penhall would succeed, Mummery settled for an alternative plan. But the weather deteriorated, and as the party walked up the mountain, they met Penhall, who was retreating without his prize. Despite the foul conditions, Mummery persevered, switching back to his original ambition of climbing the Zmutt Ridge. Brushing aside Burgener's concerns about the weather, he wrapped himself in blankets

THE TRUE MOUNTAINEER IS A WANDERER ... WHO LOVES TO BE WHERE NO HUMAN BEING HAS BEEN BEFORE

ALBERT FREDERICK MUMMERY

FINAL PHOTOGRAPHS
This expedition photograph, taken of Mummery's camp near Nanga Parbat in 1895, is from an album compiled by Norman Collie and presented to Mummery's family after his death. English climber Charles Bruce keeps him company while Gurkha Ragobir mends boots.

and slept through the afternoon. Burgener woke him "with a great thump" to clearing skies. They climbed higher to a bivouac and endured a frosty night, leaving as soon as they could see. Reaching Penhall's bivouac, they breakfasted and then, making use of the steps Penhall had left in the snow ridge above, they quickly reached the rocky ridge. But this proved almost too much for them and it took a further nine hours to reach the summit.

Back in the valley, Penhall's guide, Ferdinand Imseng, anxious not to be beaten by his rival Burgener, persuaded his client to turn straight around and go back up. They tackled a different line on the West Face, and two hard new climbs on the Matterhorn were completed on the same day. Penhall and Mummery climbed together a few days later, so there were clearly no hard

THE MUMMERY CRACK
On their repeat climb of the Grépon, Lily Bristow took this famous photograph of Mummery with his knee wedged into the vertical crack that bears his name.

feelings. Yet despite his success, there were some in the Alpine Club who took against Mummery. His application in 1880 was blackballed for reasons that are obscure. Perhaps he was considered unsporting for "taking" Penhall's route, but it is most likely his radical new ideas and obvious ability were problematic.

MASTER OF ROCK
The decision affected Mummery badly and, according to his letters, it hurt his guides too, as they found themselves unemployed because of their association with him, especially Benedikt Venetz, a neighbour of Burgener's who proved a brilliant rock climber. With Venetz as their secret weapon, Mummery and Burgener took on the Grépon, one of the Chamonix Aiguilles, a seemingly impregnable fortress of granite.

Having tried from the Mer de Glace, the team switched sides to the Nantillons Glacier, climbing a steep gully between the Charmoz and the Grépon to a striking flake of rock stuck to the main face. From its top they soon reached the ridge to the north summit, but after descending, Mummery wondered whether the peak's south summit wasn't higher. So they returned, finding the south summit to be a blank and seemingly impossible block. Only

MATTERHORN

ZMUTT RIDGE, 3 SEPTEMBER 1879

4.15am start
Despite bad weather the previous day, Mummery remains at the bivouac with Burgener, Petrus, and Gentinetta, and they leave at 4.15am, roping up for the snow arête.

Along the ridge
A series of rocky teeth slow the party down but competition from Penhall spurs them on and they reach easier ground.

Onto the West Face
At the prominent Zmutt Nose, the party traverse rightwards onto the West Face and then continue upwards, avoiding kicking stones onto Penhall's party.

SUMMIT (4,478M/14,692FT)

WEST FACE

ZMUTT RIDGE

CLIMBING TIMELINE

Makes first ascent of the Grands Charmoz and a strong attempt on the Matterhorn's Furggengrat, but is blackballed by the Alpine Club

Gives up mountaineering and concentrates instead on political economy, developing his ideas about expenditure during a recession

1855–78	1879–81	1882–86

A sickly child, Mummery suffers from a spinal deformity, preventing him from carrying heavy loads, and very poor vision

Begins first, guided phase of his career; hires the great Alexander Burgener and makes first ascent of the Zmutt Ridge of the Matterhorn

Makes further first ascents, including the Charpoua Face of the Aiguille Verte and the Grépon, where the brilliant rock climber Benedikt Venetz leads the way

NANGA PARBAT
This peak in northern Pakistan has earned the nickname "Killer Mountain": it has claimed dozens of lives since Mummery's disastrous expedition in 1895.

Venetz's patient skill saved them, Mummery reported, and when he pulled over the top, "Burgener and I yelled ourselves hoarse." These were years of immense achievement for Mummery. Along with the Zmutt and Grépon climbs, he made the first ascent of the Grands Charmoz, and climbed the lower half of the Furggen Ridge of the Matterhorn, traversing across the East Face to the Hörnli.

With Burgener he also made the first ascent of the Charpoua Face of the Aiguille Verte, above Chamonix. Surprisingly, his failures were often just as impressive as his first ascents. He tried the Hirondelles Ridge of the Grandes Jorasses, not climbed until 1927, and made two attempts on the North Face of the Aiguille du Plan, which fell to a French team in 1924. Mummery could see where the future of mountaineering lay.

A RADICAL APPROACH

On his second attempt at the Plan, in 1893, Mummery climbed with Cecil Slingsby, Norman Collie, and Geoffrey Hastings, a group of similarly ambitious friends. This was not how alpinism was usually done, with no guide to cut steps and look out for his clients. Although frowned on by the Alpine Club, the practice was soon accepted by Europe's best climbers. Mummery and his friends enjoyed great success, making the first guideless ascent of Mont Blanc's Brenva Face and the first ascent of the Dent du Requin. Mummery knew that with artificial

aids many of the great peaks he dreamed of climbing could be scaled more easily. On the Dent du Géant, a pillar of rock on the frontier between France and Italy, Mummery tried twice and built a small cairn at his high point, leaving a card behind with the words: "Absolutely inaccessible by fair means."

Although he loved the Matterhorn, Mummery loved exploration too. He made two trips to the Caucasus, the first in 1888 when he climbed Dych Tau. In 1895, he realized a longstanding ambition to climb in the Himalaya, attempting the gigantic Nanga Parbat. It was only the third climbing expedition to the Himalaya, and the team was out of its depth. While attempting to reach the Rakhiot valley via an unclimbed pass, Mummery and his two Gurkha companions disappeared, most likely swept away by avalanche.

GURKHA SHERPA
When European climbers arrived in Nepal, the Gurkhas were already renowned for their bravery, and were natural choices as porters. They were not experienced climbers, however, and two Gurkhas perished with Mummery on Nanga Parbat.

SUMMER CLIMB
Here, Mummery is photographed with H Topman by their climbing companion Martin Conway (see pp.184–85) on the summit of the Grivola in northwest Italy, which they reached on 10 August 1891. The 3,969-m (13,022-ft) peak in the Graian Alps was first climbed in 1859. The shortage of original new climbs in the Alps drove Mummery to search out new challenges in Asia.

Makes expedition to the Caucasus with Heinrich Zurfluh, and climbs Dych-Tau (5,198m/17,054ft); is belatedly elected to the Alpine Club

Launches expedition to Nanga Parbat with Collie, Hastings, Charles Bruce, and a Gurkha team, two of whom are with him when he disappears trying to reach the Rakhiot Valley

1887–91   1892–94   1895

Marries and takes his new wife to the Alps after a hiatus of five years; they make the first ascent of the Teufelsgrat on the Täschhorn in the Valais

Second major period of Alpine climbing, with Collie, Slingsby, Hastings, and Lily Bristow. First ascent of Dent du Requin, and the first guideless ascent of the Brenva Spur

LILY BRISTOW
ENGLAND   ACTIVE 1883–94

Possibly the most accomplished female climber of her time, Lily Bristow joined A F Mummery for several of his climbs in the Alps, including his second attempt at the Grépon in 1893.

Mummery had great respect for Bristow's abilities and was happy to let her take the lead on some pitches. Although he joked about the Grépon becoming "an easy day for a lady", the mountain was in tough condition the day Mummery climbed it with Bristow, and he ranked this as one of his hardest climbs. He was impressed by Bristow's performance: "Miss Bristow showed the representatives of the Alpine Club the way in which steep rocks should be climbed." Bristow carried a heavy plate camera with her on the Grépon, and captured memorable images of the climb. She accompanied Mummery on other Alpine climbs, too, including the Charmoz, Zinal Rothorn, and the Matterhorn. Possible jealousy on Mrs Mummery's part may have ended their climbing partnership, as they did not climb together in 1894. Bristow stopped climbing altogether after Mummery's death in the Himalaya a year later.

ZSIGMONDY BROTHERS

DARING MOUNTAINEERS OF THE EASTERN ALPS

AUSTRIA   1860–1918; 1861–85

OTTO ZSIGMONDY   EMIL ZSIGMONDY

How MUCH RISK A CLIMBER should tolerate became a burning issue in the late 19th century. The trauma of the Matterhorn accident in 1865 deeply affected British mountaineers, but in Austria and Germany young alpinists were prepared to push the limits. This was particularly true of two Austrian brothers, Otto and Emil Zsigmondy. Their traverse of La Meije, so swiftly followed by Emil's death, crystallized attitudes about risk.

A LIFE'S WORK

- Along with their two younger brothers, Otto and Emil are **introduced to the natural world** from a young age by their father; their mother **encourages them all to explore the outdoors**

- As teenagers they are **already climbing without guides**, despite widespread disapproval from other mountaineers; only Mummery and his friends are doing likewise

- In 1884, they climb the 4,506-m (14,782-ft) Weisshorn, **make a guideless traverse of the Matterhorn** (4,478m/14,692ft), and climb a **new route on the South Face of the Bietschhorn** (3,934m/12,907ft)

- In 1885, the brothers complete the **landmark traverse of La Meije**, but Emil is **killed just days later** on another new route

- American climber and W A B Coolidge (see p.145) **condemns their risk-taking**, saying, "If mountaineering is allowed to degenerate into a form of gambling in which the players **stake their lives**, it would cease to be what it is now … **it could no longer be defended**"

By any measure, the Zsigmondy family was remarkable. Of Hungarian extraction, they lived in Vienna, where father Adolf encouraged his four sons in the natural sciences. Youngest son Richard won the Nobel Prize for Chemistry in 1925, while Karl, a mathematician, produced Zsigmondy's theorem in 1892, which is still a valuable tool in number theory. The boys' mother, Irma Szakmáry, encouraged her sons to enjoy the arts and an outdoor life, and all four at some point pursued a degree of mountaineering.

For Otto and Emil, however, the sport became their passion. Otto followed his father into dentistry and Emil qualified as a doctor, but they formed one of the most dazzling climbing partnerships in the sport's history. Emil was famous for being more pushy, and it was a grim irony that his book *The Dangers of the Alps* was published the year he died in a climbing accident.

CONTRASTING CHARACTERS

The urbane Slovenian climber Julius Kugy regarded Otto as "the purest soul I have ever met in my life." By comparison, Emil was "like a flame shooting towards heaven." Kugy stopped climbing with the brothers because of risky Emil. "Otto was more to my taste, with his prudence and constant warning against excess. Purtscheller was more Emil's hot-headed type." On the other hand, Emil was regarded as the better climber, the man who got things done,

even if, as Clinton Dent (see pp.164–65) observed, he was "too venturesome to be imitated." The Zsigmondy brothers were the first in a succession of mountaineers from the Eastern Alps who pushed the sport forwards, the forebears of Willo Welzenbach (see pp.236–37) and Reinhold Messner (see pp.308–11). Just as A F Mummery (see pp.168–71) formed a nucleus of energetic climbers such as Norman Collie and Cecil Slingsby, the Zsigmondys were part of an Austrian group pushing alpinism into the modern era. Ludwig Purtscheller (see opposite) was arguably the leader of the group, which included the Dolomites climber Karl Schulz, who made the first ascent of the difficult Crozzon di Brenta.

Even though he wasn't quite 24 when he died, Emil packed a staggering amount into his life. As teenagers, he and Otto went into the mountains unaccompanied, climbing Austria's Reisseck in a round trip of 26 hours. Some of their early climbs were guided, but by the late 1870s they were operating independently,

GENDARMES ON GUARD

The Zsigmondys' impressive 1895 traverse of La Meije is seen in all its seriousness in this view of the North Face. The four *gendarmes* pierce the skyline to the left of Grand Pic, the highest point of La Meije.

IF MOUNTAINEERING IS ALLOWED TO DEGENERATE INTO A FORM OF GAMBLING ... IT COULD NO LONGER BE DEFENDED

W A B COOLIDGE ON THE ZSIGMONDY'S RISK-TAKING CLIMBS

climbing many routes in the Zillertal Alps in western Austria. In 1881, they made the difficult ascent of the Ortler from the Hochjoch, which became the subject of Emil's first climbing essay. He proved a lively writer, and a classic account of his climbs, *Im Hochgebirge*, appeared after his death.

In 1882 and 1884 – Emil was doing military service in 1883 – the brothers teamed up with Purtscheller, climbing in the Dolomites and the Valais, where they made a guideless ascent of the Marinelli Couloir on Monte Rosa. In summer 1885, they chose La Meije (3,984m/13,071ft) in the French Dauphiné as their goal. The traverse from the Pic Central to the Grand Pic to its west was a well-known objective, and had been studied and attempted by several leading climbers. Both peaks had been climbed but the narrow ridge between them, barred by four looming *gendarmes* – rock towers – seemed insurmountable.

HIGH-TECH ASCENT

The Austrians were more than willing to use the new technology that was becoming available, using crampons to climb the Pic Central quickly in excellent snow conditions. Having left the village of La Grave just before 2am, they were on the summit by 9.30am, contemplating the dizzying ridge in front of them. The first tower was passed on the north side, thanks to their crampons and good snow.

Passing the second barrier was harder. Snow gave way to ice, and the slope was steeper. At the next gap, they were forced to take the third tower straight on, a vertical climb to its summit. The fourth tower was "a very thin wedge, its west face … a sheer precipice, some 30 or 40 metres [100–130ft] high." Using "an iron hook", the three abseiled off this fourth hurdle into what is now known as the Brèche Zsigmondy. They had anticipated that the climbing would now ease, but the route up the Grand Pic proved daunting. Emil wrote later, "Purtscheller, having left his knapsack and boots with us, had very hard work to overcome this *mauvais pas*." At 4.15pm they were all on the summit. Some British climbers were aghast at the lack of guides and the use of aids, but the *Alpine Journal* was full of praise: "This expedition ranks with the most difficult and dangerous that has ever been made in the Alps." It is now usually climbed from west to east.

Just days after their triumph, the Zsigmondy brothers were back climbing on La Meije, this time with Karl Schulz. Otto suggested the ordinary route, but that wasn't enough for Emil, who chose instead to try a new route on the South Face. While leading a difficult section, Emil fell and his rope snapped. Schulz and Otto retreated, and after four hours saw the body. "The first look told me," Otto wrote later, "that my last hopes were gone."

LUDWIG PURTSCHELLER
AUSTRIA   1849–1900

Purtscheller is best remembered for joining the explorer-academic Hans Meyer on the first ascent of Kilimanjaro.

However, he was also a brilliant climber who made more than 1,700 routes in the Alps, and shared the Zsigmondys' daring approach. Ten years older than the brothers, he was a handsome, athletic physical education instructor, not wealthy, and modest about his achievements. But it was he who established the Eastern Alps tradition of pushing the limits. Ironically for a champion of guideless climbing, he died after his guide's ice axe broke in a fall below Les Drus, dragging Purtscheller into a crevasse. He broke his arm and died of influenza after six months in a Swiss hospital.

EUGEN GUIDO LAMMER

SELF-RELIANT MOUNTAIN IDEALIST

AUSTRIA   1863–1945

Unjustly condemned for his later links to Nazism, Lammer was a leading climber in the 1880s and 90s. He had several notable ascents to his credit, and used the mountains as an arena for philosophical exploration. In many ways, his ideas prefigured environmentalist ideas about damage caused to wild places by infrastructure. He also extolled self-reliance as the mountaineer's most important virtue, an idea co-opted by the Nazis. However, Lammer opposed the banning of Jews from the German and Austrian Alpine Club.

MODERNIZING THE ALPS
In 1898, the Gornergrat Railway above Zermatt opened, transporting tourists 3,089m (10,135ft) up the mountain. Lammer deplored such mechanized conveniences.

In the late 19th century, as the development of the Alps continued and railways reached the most inaccessible places, many feared that engineering ingenuity could soon tame the wildest peaks. A F Mummery (see pp.168–71) had left the beautiful Dent du Géant, a granite spire in the heart of the Mont Blanc range, unclimbed because it could not be done "by fair means" – that is, without pitons and other equipment. Local guides weren't so high-minded, and draped the peak in ropes and fixed equipment to help their clients to the summit.

This mechanization of the Alps provoked strong reactions in those who wanted the mountains to remain unspoiled. One of the leading exponents of this principle, and one of the best German-speaking climbers of the century, was Guido Lammer, a high-school teacher of German and history and an admirer of the German philosopher Friedrich Nietzsche.

MOUNTAIN PHILOSOPHER

With Nietzsche as his mentor, Lammer used the mountains as a means to explore his own identity, writing: "A passionate involvement in the act of mountaineering, and the constant menace of danger disturbing the very depths of our being, are the source of powerful, moral or religious emotions which may be of the greatest spirituality."

With such views he found himself in opposition to the corporate populism of the German and Austrian Alpine Club and had a bitter argument with a senior member, Heinrich Steinitzer, who argued that, with their network of huts, "the alpine clubs have unlocked the majesty and beauty of the high mountains for the masses."

Lammer had reacted against the bourgeois lifestyle he experienced as a high-school teacher in Stockerau, on the outskirts of Vienna, during the dying days of the Habsburg empire. He suffered a morbid fear of conformity, and felt

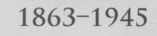

OSCAR SCHUSTER
Lammer made many climbs with Schuster, who pioneered climbing in the Alps and the Caucasus.

that mountains were an almost sacred space where he could meet nature on its own terms. "Such lessons," he wrote, "are worth years of everyday life; they are sweeter for shattered nerves than opium."

In Lammer's view, rockfall and bad weather were welcome parts of the game, not things to be avoided. Infrastructure of whatever kind – fixed ropes, pitons, mountain huts – were anathema. Climbing with a guide was an abdication of self-reliance. However, he also said, "There is not just one but a hundred different kinds of mountaineering."

In this way, sometimes in the company of fellow zealot August Lorria, but more often alone, Lammer made a series of hard new climbs in the Bernese Oberland, Valais, and elsewhere, more than once risking death. In 1887, with Lorria, he attempted the West Face of the Matterhorn, the route taken by William Penhall in 1879 the day Mummery climbed the Zmutt Ridge.

The two men reached a point level with the teeth on the Zmutt, but opted to retreat as the rock became too icy. Descending carefully, they were hit by a small avalanche and swept 150m (500ft) down the mountain.

A LIFE'S WORK

- Born in the village of Roseburg am Kamp, Lammer **works as a high-school teacher** in Stockerau, near Vienna

- Despairing at the mechanization of the Alps, Lammer argues for a return to the simpler **fundamentals of mountaineering**

- With August Lorria in 1885, climbs the **Hinter Fiescherhorn and the Klein Grünhorn** in the Bernese Oberland

- Publishes **polemical memoir** *Jungborn* (1923)

Lammer dislocated his foot, but Lorria had broken a leg and was unconscious. When he came to, he was disoriented and began thrashing around.

Alone, and in an era before organized rescue, Lammer's predilection for self-reliance was now severely tested. Wrapping Lorria in his jacket and putting socks on his hands, Lammer hobbled and crawled down the moraines of the Zmutt Glacier to an inn, where he raised the alarm. Lorria was found next morning, naked, having removed all his clothes in a hypothermic delirium. He was unconscious, but still alive.

SOLO HARD CLIMBER

Lorria stopped climbing after this, but Lammer continued, and in 1898 made the first ascent – solo – of the North Ridge of the Hinterer Brochkogel. Earlier important ascents included, in 1884, a solo climb of the Fusstein-Olperer traverse in the Zillertal, one of the Tyrol's classic climbs. Lammer later climbed with Oscar Eckenstein (see pp.196–97) and the Dolomites pioneer Oscar Schuster.

In 1923, Lammer published his influential book *Jungborn*, which railed against the pollution, as he viewed it, of mountaineering. He saw the year 2000 as the millenarian date

BEYOND GOOD AND EVIL

German philosopher Friedrich Nietzsche's ideal of a strong individual responsible for his own actions has appealed to many solo mountaineers, from Lammer to the inspirational US climber Mark Twight (b.1961), who called one of his routes "Beyond Good and Evil" after Nietzsche's 1886 book. Equally, there were other climbers who viewed their endeavours from a socialist perspective, and saw climbing's teamwork and selfless aspects as an illustration of humans co-operating to achieve seemingly impossible goals.

FRIEDRICH NIETZSCHE (1844–1900), WHOSE ESOTERIC PHILOSOPHY OF THE "SUPERMAN" APPEALED TO INFLUENTIAL GERMAN MOUNTAINEERS IN THE 19TH CENTURY

when the mountains might revert to their earlier simplicity. "Let us hope," said a reviewer in the Alpine Journal, "that his entertaining pamphlet may hasten the advent of this happy day."

The dangers of Lammer's thinking became apparent later in his life, when the Nazis preached a similar message. Ironically, younger generations of climbers revelling in the fight against nature – which the Nazis gladly publicized – were happy to use all the accoutrements Lammer despised, such as pitons and huts. Lammer was equally appalled by the banning of Jews from the German and Austrian

Alpine Club, then a hotbed of anti-Semitism. In protest, he joined the Alpenverein Donauland, which had been set up to accept Jewish members and which itself was banned when the Nazis annexed Austria in 1938. Also ironically for someone who hated infrastructure, a bivouac hut was named after him, as well as a street in Vienna.

19TH-CENTURY CLIMBING ELITE
Lammer, seated on the ground, second from right, poses for a photograph outside the Monte Rosa Hotel in Zermatt around 1886. Oscar Eckenstein is seated on the far left.

PAUL PREUSS

ADVOCATE OF ETHICALLY PURE CLIMBING

AUSTRIA   1886–1913

ALTHOUGH BARELY 27 YEARS OLD when he died, Paul Preuss was to his contemporaries the most exciting European climber to have emerged since Emil Zsigmondy perished on La Meije in 1885. In his short climbing career he made more than 1,200 ascents, a quarter of them alone, including the first traverse of the Aiguille Blanche de Peuterey. His audacity overshadowed his clear-sighted ideas about mountaineering, but in the final years of his life, he became one of the most popular climbing lecturers in Europe.

THE PITON DISPUTE

Many alpinists associate the Austrian and German climbers of this period with artificial climbing and the use of pitons (metal pegs driven into cracks in the rocks with hammers to anchor the climber against a fall or to aid progress). Preuss was a dedicated and persuasive opponent of their use, arguing that they were a form of cheating. The controversy set Preuss on a collision course with his fellow climbers, but his idealism was soon forgotten as pitons appeared all over the Alps.

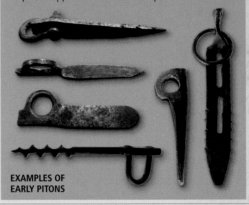

EXAMPLES OF EARLY PITONS

Paul Preuss was born at Altaussee in Styria, his father a Hungarian music teacher of Jewish descent and his mother a former tutor to an Austrian baron. As a child he contracted a polio-like illness that left him temporarily paralysed. When he recovered, he was determined to get fit, and the physical discipline he acquired as a boy stayed with him into adulthood. He trained specifically for climbing, and was able to perform one-arm pull-ups decades before this became a regular exercise for top rock climbers.

MOUNTAIN TRAINING

Preuss's father was an amateur botanist who took him on nature walks in the mountains, and from these he developed his deep love for the Alps. His father died when he was ten but

Preuss continued to make strenuous excursions, sleeping out on the mountains and scrambling up easy peaks alone or with his sister and school friends. He roamed throughout the Eastern Alps – the Wilde Kaiser, the Dachstein, the Dolomites, and the Silvretta – repeating existing climbs, and gathering experience. This patient development explains how he was able to tackle the colossal challenges he took on later without the pitons that were then coming into vogue.

An intelligent and deeply cultured man, Preuss was also sociable and fun-loving. After his death, his friend Günther von Saar wrote of him: "Self-conceit and self-complacency were strangers to him. His solid knowledge, his ready wit, and his overflowing humour made him a charming companion." Other friends recalled his habit of telling the same unfunny joke ten times a day, but they still loved him.

Following his father's interests, after high school Preuss studied plant physiology and received a doctorate from Munich University, where he then worked and studied philosophy.

He announced his arrival on the climbing scene in 1911 with a solo second ascent of the West Face of the Totenkirchl – the Chapel of Death in the Wilde Kaiser – in just two and a half hours.

Later that year, on the incredibly exposed Campanile Basso, an elegant finger of limestone in the Dolomites that has moves of Grade V (see p.351), he didn't even take a rope on his first ascent. The first team afterwards to follow his route perished in the attempt. "It was a pleasure to watch how he conquered a difficult piece of rock," von Saar observed, "how systematically he advanced, metre by metre, trying everything, always retreating as soon as he began to tire or did not feel quite safe, all the time with perfect balance of his slender, well-developed body."

A WELL-ROUNDED ALPINIST

Later in 1911, Preuss climbed the East Face of the Crozzon di Brenta with Paul Relly, another climb done ahead of its time with the bare minimum of equipment. Thanks to Preuss's diaries, we know that in his short climbing

A LIFE'S WORK

- Becomes famous for his **bold ascent** of the East Face of **Campanile Basso** in the Brenta Dolomites, which he scales alone, without pitons; the route is still considered difficult today

- Takes part in every arena of mountaineering, from **winter ascents and solo climbs, to ski ascents, and classic Alpine routes**

- Adheres to a strictly ethical "pure" climbing style that **opposes the use of artificial aids**

- Publishes a polemic against the increasing use of pitons; it sparks off a debate among top alpinists that becomes known as **the Piton Dispute**

IT WAS A PLEASURE TO WATCH HOW HE CONQUERED A DIFFICULT PIECE OF ROCK 99

GÜNTHER VON SAAR ON PAUL PREUSS

career he made 1,200 ascents, a quarter solo, and 150 of them first ascents. He admired the Zsigmondy brothers (see pp.172–73) and shared Guido Lammer's dislike of artificial climbing aids, but not his misanthropy (see pp.174–75).

After doing exposed, steep rock climbs in the Eastern Alps, Preuss became a capable skier and ice climber too, which allowed him to extend his range into the Western Alps. From 1912 13, poor weather thwarted his plans but he managed the Southeast Ridge of the Aiguille Blanche.

CLIMBING WITHOUT AIDS

Preuss's preference for solo ascents was reinforced in 1912 when he witnessed the deaths of the British climber Humphrey Owen Jones, his new wife, and their guide. The party were ascending the Mont Rouge de Peuterey. Preuss was climbing solo on the mountain. The guide pulled on a hold, which came away, and he dragged the newlyweds off the peak with him.

In his final years, Preuss's writings and climbing reputation made him a sought-after speaker; at the time of his death he had 50 speaking engagements booked for the following year. His most famous essay was *Artificial Aids in Climbing*, a response in part to the arrival of pitons. He developed six principles for mountaineers, which stressed self-reliance, caution, and the use of equipment for safety, rather than to aid progress on an ascent.

Preuss's last climb was the North Ridge of the Mandlkogel in the Dachstein Alps, which he attempted solo in October. Aware of his interest in the peak, friends looked for him at the base of the wall after he failed to return home, and found him buried in the first snows of winter.

STICKING TO TRADITION
Eschewing the pitons that were just starting to be used to assist ascents, Preuss was accused of inconsistency since the ice axes and ropes he used were also artificial aids.

BEYOND
THE ALPS

BEYOND THE ALPS

1800

1860

1885

◀ **1826**
German scientist **Phillip Franz von Siebold**, a prolific writer on Japan, describes Mount Fuji for Europeans.

1830
G W Traill, British deputy-commissioner of Kumaon, crosses the 5,000-m (17,100-ft) pass between Nanda Devi and Nanda Kot that still bears his name.

◀ **1852**
The survey of India establishes the height of Everest; despite a local name being known, the peak is renamed after a former British Surveyor-General, Sir George Everest.

▼ **1854**
The Schlagintweit brothers set off on a three-year expedition commissioned by the East India Company; they travel through the Deccan Plateau, then to the Himalaya.

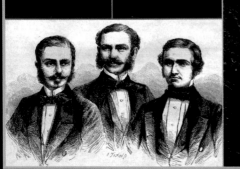

1879
Hungarian **Maurice de Déchy** is the first mountaineer to travel to the Himalaya for the sole purpose of mountaineering.

1857
The **Palliser Expedition** is sent by the British to explore the approaches to the Canadian Rockies.

▶ **1880**
British alpinist **Edward Whymper** (see pp.142–45) climbs Chimborazo in Ecuador.

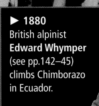

◀ **1866**
British lawyer **Douglas Freshfield** (seated) makes the first of several visits to the Caucasus, the first climbing expedition launched in the region (see pp.186–89).

◀ **1881**
The first stretch of the **Canadian Pacific Railway** opens between eastern Canada and British Columbia.

1882
Irish clergyman **William S Green** makes the first attempt on Mount Cook, New Zealand, with Emil Boss and Ulrich Kaufmann; they turn back close to the summit.

1883
British climber **William Woodman Graham** becomes the first climber to climb successfully in the Himalaya, exploring the Kangchenjunga region.

▼ **1885**
Pundit Hari Ram crosses the Nangpa La pass between Nepal and Tibet; pundits make secret surveys using prayer beads and wheels (see pp.190–91).

1888
A F Mummery (see pp.168–71) ascends Dych-tau in the Caucasus; John Cockin, a UK barrister, also makes a string of ascents that year, including the northern summit of Ushba.

▲ **1889**
Douglas Freshfield returns to the Caucausus to hunt for the missing photographer, William Donkin (see pp.186–89).

◀ **1888**
The Rev William S Green (seated) makes the first purely mountaineering expedition to the Selkirk Range in southeastern British Columbia.

▼ **1889**
German climbers **Hans Meyer** and **Ludwig Purtscheller** make the first ascent of Kilimanjaro, the highest peak in Africa (see p.173).

◀ **PP.178–79** Three mountaineers stand near Haast Bivouac, Mount Cook, New Zealand. Guide Peter Graham (1878–1961) is at the back leaning on an ice axe.

THE IMPROVEMENTS IN TRANSPORT that helped develop mountaineering in the Alps also opened other ranges to exploration. As Alpine tourism soared, those climbers with a passion for the unknown began to look further afield. Douglas Freshfield organized the first climbing expedition to the Caucasus in 1866, dreaming of an "untravell'd world" to explore. Colonialism also offered opportunities.

In 1885, the area around Kilimanjaro became a German protectorate, and in 1887 the geographer Hans Meyer launched his campaign to climb it. These challenges were more familiar in New Zealand, where the end of the Maori wars in 1871 led to a national government. In 1882, there was a spirited near-success on Mount Cook from the Rev William S Green and two climbers from the Oberland.

1890

1900

1910

◄ 1891
English missionary **Walter Weston** begins a long relationship with the Japanese Alps (see pp.210–11) during which he climbs 40 peaks.

1892
British alpinist **Martin Conway** (see pp.184–85) organizes an expedition to the Karakoram Range with Oscar Eckenstein (see pp.196–97).

► 1895
Swiss guide **Matthias Zurbriggen** (left, see pp.208–09) makes the first ascents of Sefton, Tasman, the Silberhorn, and Haidinger in New Zealand.

► 1902
British occultist Aleister Crowley (see p.196) joins Oscar Eckenstein on the first climbing expedition to K2; it is delayed by Eckenstein's brief spell in detention.

1902
The **American Alpine Club** is formed under the leadership of Charles Ernest Fay; the *American Alpine Journal* becomes the pre-eminent record of mountaineering in the world.

1905
Taking inspiration from Walter Weston, the **Japanese Alpine Club** is formed (see pp.210–11).

▲ 1906
Fanny Bullock Workman (see pp.192–93) claims the first ascent of Pinnacle Peak in the Nun Kun Massif, at 6,930m (22,736ft) a female altitude record that stands until 1934.

► 1911
Fanny Bullock Workman leads an important surveying expedition to the Siachen Glacier in the Karakoram.

1911
Scottish physiologist **Alexander Kellas** makes ten first ascents of mountains higher than 6,000m (20,000ft), most notably Sentinel Peak, Chomo Yummo, and Pauhunri in Sikkim.

▼ 1913
British climber **Hudson Stuck** (left) leads the first ascent of Denali, dubbed Mount McKinley in 1897 (see pp.206–07) in honour of William McKinley of Ohio, the presidential nominee.

◄ 1896
Douglas Freshfield publishes his lavish compendium *The Exploration of the Caucasus.*

1897
Matthias Zurbriggen (see pp.208–09) makes the first ascent of Aconcagua, the highest peak in South America, after Edward FitzGerald gives up his attempt.

1907
British mountaineer **Tom Longstaff** becomes the first person to climb a summit higher than 7,000m (23,000ft) in his attempt on Trisul.

▼ 1908
Annie Smith Peck climbs Huascarán in Peru's Cordillera Blanca, later claiming that she, not Fanny Bullock Workman, holds the female altitude record.

1921
British explorer Charles Howard-Bury leads the **first reconnaissance of Everest**; George Mallory leads the team onto East Rongbuk Glacier and the North Col.

► 1897
The **Duke of the Abruzzi** leads his first expedition, climbing Mount St Elias on the Alaskan Yukon border (see pp.198–99).

1899
Douglas Freshfield makes a circumambulation of Kangchenjunga (see pp.186–89).

THE GREATER RANGES

F OR 19TH-CENTURY EXPLORERS AND CLIMBERS, THE GIGANTIC PEAKS OF CENTRAL ASIA, THE HIGHEST ON EARTH, PRESENTED A CHALLENGE OF FAR GREATER MAGNITUDE THAN ANYTHING THEY HAD EXPERIENCED IN THE ALPS. IT WAS ALMOST LIKE VISITING ANOTHER PLANET.

HIMALAYAN PIONEER
In 1907, the English mountaineer Tom Longstaff reached the summit of Trisul in the Indian Himalaya, becoming the first person to ascend higher than 7,000m (23,000ft).

To call the Himalaya a mountain range is like calling *War and Peace* a story – it's accurate but it doesn't convey their scale and complexity. Even in the modern era, when every valley has been mapped from space, the more remote regions still give an impression of what it must have been like for the first intrepid mountaineers who ventured there, and to the other Greater Ranges, in the late 19th century.

TAKING MEASUREMENTS

Although the Himalaya were well documented in antiquity, and Jesuit missionaries travelled through them in the 17th century, it was some time before the true height of their peaks was known. In the 19th century, surveyors working for the East India Company began to measure peaks along the northern frontier and were staggered by the results. The English lieutenant William S Webb, working from measurements begun in 1808, calculated the height of Dhaulagiri at 8,187m (26,862ft).

Much of the early exploration in the region was carried out for political and geographical research purposes, but in 1774, Scotsmen George Bogle and Alexander Hamilton crossed from India to Tibet with the aim of setting up a trade route to China. Britain's victory in the Anglo-Nepalese War of 1814–16 gave the country its first access to a large portion of the Himalaya, and, as the East India Company's

control extended into the mountains, its more adventurous officials began to explore them. In 1830, G W Traill, the deputy-commissioner of Kumaon in northern India, crossed the 5,200-m (17,100-ft) pass between Nanda Devi and Nanda Kot that still bears his name.

> As in the early days of Alpine exploration, the prospect of hidden valleys and unknown vistas in the Himalaya attracted a certain kind of mountaineer. But so little mapping existed that parties often had no idea which peak they were climbing.

SPORT CLIMBING

The first real climbing in the Himalaya was done in 1855 by Bavarian brothers Adolf and Robert Schlagintweit. The men were on a three-year scientific expedition commissioned by the East India Company when they tackled what they presumed was Kamet, in the Garhwal Himalaya, but was later identified as Abi Garmin. They reached 6,778m (22,239ft), which remained an altitude record for some time to come. Adolf was later accused of being a spy for the Chinese and was beheaded by the ruler in Kashgar.

The first climber to travel to the Himalaya for the sole purpose of mountaineering for sport and adventure was the Hungarian Maurice de Déchy in 1879, but he contracted malaria on the approach to Kangchenjunga and withdrew.

In 1883, a young British barrister and experienced alpinist named William Woodman Graham took up the challenge, arriving in Darjeeling with the Swiss guide Josef Imboden. In late March, the men reached Dzongri in the south of the Kangchenjunga range, crossed

the Kang La Pass and climbed an unnamed and thereafter unidentified peak of more than 6,000m (20,000ft). Imboden had to return home because of ill health, so Graham asked the highly experienced Swiss alpinist Emil Boss, who was the landlord at the Bear Inn in Switzerland's Grindelwald, to send a

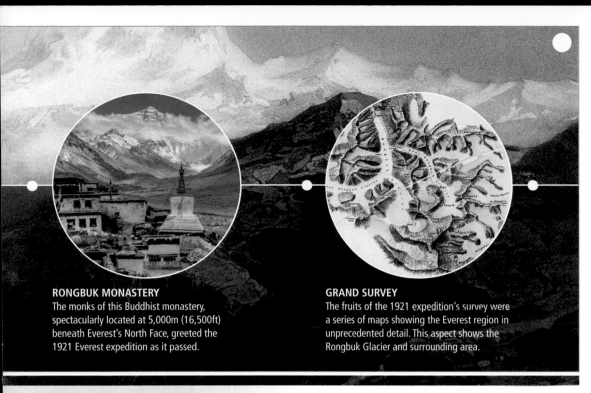

RONGBUK MONASTERY
The monks of this Buddhist monastery, spectacularly located at 5,000m (16,500ft) beneath Everest's North Face, greeted the 1921 Everest expedition as it passed.

GRAND SURVEY
The fruits of the 1921 expedition's survey were a series of maps showing the Everest region in unprecedented detail. This aspect shows the Rongbuk Glacier and surrounding area.

SETTING THE SCENE

- In the early 19th century, Europeans assume that the **Andes** in South America are the **highest mountains on Earth**. As British political hegemony extends into northern India, however, surveys reveal that the **Himalaya are far higher**.

- **Political instability** and the complexity of the terrain in the Greater Ranges **hampers exploration**. The German Schlagintweit brothers are the first to realize that the **Kunlun and the Karakoram are separate mountain ranges**.

- The Survey of India **establishes the height of Everest in 1852** and its field workers do much important exploration. William Henry Johnson, a civilian assistant, climbs higher than 6,700m (22,000ft) in the Himalaya, and also climbs in the Kunlun Mountains.

- Just as Alpine villages such as Chamonix and Zermatt became centres for mountaineering in Europe, so the hill station at **Darjeeling** in India becomes **the focus for Himalayan activity**, thanks to its proximity to Kangchenjunga, good transport links, and the presence of a **large porter workforce**, including Sherpas, to accompany mountaineering expeditions.

replacement for him. Boss decided to join the expedition himself, and took the guide Ulrich Kauffman along, too. In late June, the party travelled to the Garhwal Himalaya and came close to climbing the 7,066-m (23,182-ft) high Dunagiri, but were turned back by bad weather just a few hundred metres from the summit.

FIRST RECONNAISSANCE OF EVEREST
Major Morshead and Gujjar Singh are seen here surveying with a plane table during the British expedition to the Himalaya in 1921. Chief among their aims was to survey a possible route up to the summit.

Graham's party then climbed a peak marked on their rudimentary map as "A21" (6,863m/ 22,516ft) and attempted another called "A22" (6,401m/21,001ft), but were forced to retreat in the face of technical difficulty. What these peaks actually were is a matter for debate.

CONTESTED CLAIMS

Back in Darjeeling, the team regrouped and then set out for Sikkim, spending September exploring the approaches to Kabru before making an attempt on the peak from the east. From a camp at 5,600m (18,400ft), they reached a lower summit and then pressed on for another 100m (300ft), but the final section of steep ice, perhaps no more than 12m (40ft), was too much for them. Graham's claims to have reached this altitude were hotly disputed by the Survey of India – who didn't appreciate his comments on the accuracy of their maps – and other climbers with a vested interest in the region, particularly Martin Conway (see pp.184–85). Conway later changed his stance and supported Graham's claims.

Although the slow pace of travel in the region during this period meant that expeditions were long, it also enabled the European climbers to acclimatize gradually and thus experience few

problems with high altitude. Graham said his party barely suffered: "The air, or want of it, will prove no obstacle to the ascent of the very highest peaks in the world."

The attraction of the Greater Ranges for the first mountaineers was summed up by the British climber Tom Longstaff – one of the giants of early Himalayan exploration who made three expeditions in the 1900s. "We were like Cortez seeing the Pacific for the first time," he wrote, "for no other eyes had seen these peaks from such a height spread as a continuous range.

I was more elated by this enormous vista of the unknown than by any other discovery or ascent that I have accomplished."

MOUNTAIN MEASURER
This huge, 500-kg (0.5-ton) theodolite was one of the instruments hauled through the Himalaya by the Survey of India. In 1852, it was used to measure the height of Everest.

MARTIN CONWAY

EARLY EXPLORER OF THE KARAKORAM

ENGLAND   1856–1937

AT THE END OF THE 19TH CENTURY, as the pattern for modern alpinism was being laid down, those whose passion was mountain exploration moved away from the Alps to the Greater Ranges. Martin Conway was at the forefront of this shift, organizing the first climbing expedition to Asia's Karakoram Range in 1892. He reached a world altitude record there of 6,800m (22,300ft), having climbed to a subsidiary summit of Baltoro Kangri. In 1881, he published *The Zermatt Pocket Book*, the first climbers' guide in any language.

MOUNTAIN WANDERER
This illustration from Conway's book *The Alps from End to End* shows his party ascending the Bionnassay Ridge of Mont Blanc, a climb he undertook in 1894.

In the summer of 1891, Martin Conway, then an art historian in his mid 30s, went climbing in the Graian Alps with A F Mummery (see pp.168–71), by then acknowledged as the greatest alpinist of his generation. Earlier that year, the two men had met at London's Royal Geographical Society to discuss a possible expedition to Kangchenjunga in the Himalaya, but their climbing trip together in the Alps had raised issues about their compatibility. "The more I knew of him," Conway wrote of Mummery, "the more I liked him, and the more evident it became that his attitude toward mountains was fundamentally different from mine."

The difference in the men's philosophies was profound. In Conway's obituary, Claude Wilson wrote: "Conway was a very fast goer in his young days, and a good man on snow and ice, but he avoided rocks when possible." Steeped in the writings of John Ruskin (see pp.86–89), and suffused with the romance of early Alpine exploration, Conway saw the Alpine Club as a kind of mountaineering wing of the Royal Geographical Society. What Mummery was doing looked far too much like sport and Conway dismissed it as gymnastics.

DESTINATION KARAKORAM
Conway was educated at Cambridge University, where he read mathematics and developed an interest in woodcuts – the start of his career in art history. He began climbing in the Alps as an undergraduate and was elected to the Alpine Club in 1877, writing impassioned defences of his view of mountaineering, whose true follower loves "first and foremost to wander far and wide among the mountains, does not willingly sleep two consecutive

nights in the same inn, hates centres, gets tired of a district, always wants to see what is on the other side of any range of hills." This philosophy was realized in his journey from Monte Viso in Italy to the Gross Glockner, Austria's highest mountain – undertaken with two guides and two Gurkha soldiers – which he described in *The Alps from End to End* (1895).

A LIFE'S WORK

- After publishing *The Zermatt Pocket Book*, he teams up with the US scholar W A B Coolidge to produce a **series of climbers' guides**

- His **Karakoram expedition** conducts important surveying work

- Later expeditions include trips to Spitzbergen in Norway and one to the Bolivian Andes, where he makes the **first ascent of Illimani**

CHARLES G BRUCE
A member of Conway's 1892 expedition, Bruce returned to the Himalaya to lead the 1922 Everest expedition (pictured).

By the mid 1890s, Conway was an established art critic and a brilliant networker ambitious to enter politics. He tried first for the Liberal Party, and later succeeded for the Conservatives, ultimately entering the House of Lords. At this point the satirical magazine *Punch* published a cartoon of him called "The Climber".

What set him on this road to the heart of the British establishment was his 1892 Karakoram expedition. This was the idea he had explored with Mummery and Douglas Freshfield (see pp.186–87), first with Kangchenjunga as the goal, and then, when for political reasons that proved impossible, the Karakoram. The model for the expedition was Edward Whymper's trip to the Andes (see pp.142–45) and it set the pattern for the multi-dimensional extravaganzas led by the Duke of the Abruzzi (see pp.198–99) and others. Conway planned for surveying work during the trip, and included in the party an artist, a naturalist, and Alpine guide Matthias Zurbriggen (see pp.208–09), who had been with Whymper in South America.

As his climber, he replaced Mummery with the irascible Oscar Eckenstein (see pp.196–97). It would be hard to imagine two more ill-suited team-mates – Conway, the quintessential late-Victorian English gentleman drawing on his contacts in august institutions, and Eckenstein, the son of a socialist German immigrant.

THE GOLDEN THRONE

Leaving Kashmir in the spring of 1892, the expedition surveyed the Bagrot Valley below Rakaposhi, which Conway had considered as a possible climbing objective. When he saw it, however, he changed his mind. In fact, the more he saw of the Karakoram, the more he seemed to prefer surveying and exploring, which infuriated Eckenstein.

In June, the party moved into the Hunza Valley, explored the northern side of Rakaposhi for a month, and then started up the Hispar Glacier to the Hispar Pass and Snow Lake. They then turned down the Biafo Glacier to its terminus in the Braldu Valley – the longest glacial journey outside of the polar regions.

At the village of Askole, Eckenstein was sacked from the expedition and sent home. The party continued up the Baltoro Glacier to the confluence of glaciers that Conway named Concordia after a similar junction in Switzerland. Conway's leadership of the expedition then became blatantly self-serving. Ignoring the stunning vision of K2 in front of him, he identified a peak he called the Golden Throne, a comparatively insignificant bump, as "the most brilliant of all the mountains we saw."

The truth was that Conway had a realistic chance of climbing the Golden Throne, now called Baltoro Kangri. While he was thwarted in this, the team did reach a subsidiary summit Conway called Pioneer Peak, setting the altitude record in so doing.

Following this expedition, Conway later explored the Arctic island of Spitzbergen, and travelled to the Andes, making a first ascent of Illimani (6,439m/21,126ft).

TAKING A BREAK
Conway is seen here with fellow Alpine Club member George Scriven (second right) and guide Franz Andenmatten (furthest right) resting at the Festi rocks during an ascent of the Dom (Canton of Valais, Switzerland).

THE GAZE OF THE MOUNTAINEER SOON RETURNS TO THE SNOWS. THE PICTURE, SO LONG DREAMT OF ... IS AT LAST BEFORE HIS EYES IN ALL ITS GLORY OF COLOUR AND AERIAL PERSPECTIVE

DOUGLAS FRESHFIELD, *AROUND KANGCHENJUNGA*

CAMPING IN THE CAUCASUS
Once the major peaks in the Alps had all been climbed, European mountaineers started to look further afield. In Britain, attention turned to the Caucasus Mountains, where the climbing was arduous due to their altitude and remoteness. Hermann Woolley accompanied Freshfield there in 1889 and returned in 1893, when he took this image showing the party making camp alongside the Kitlov Glacier.

DOUGLAS FRESHFIELD

DARING EXPLORER WHO OPENED UP THE CAUCASUS

ENGLAND   1845–1934

ONE OF THE GREATEST mountain explorers, Douglas Freshfield travelled and climbed in almost every part of the world, from the Alps and the Pyrenees, to Japan and North America, but he is most famous for his three expeditions to the Caucasus and a landmark circumnavigation of Kangchenjunga in 1899. He achieved his first new Alpine route in 1861, at the height of the Golden Age, climbing with most of the great alpinists of his era, and was still exploring almost 60 years later, making a visit to the US Rockies in 1920.

Freshfield's mother Jane was a "mountain wanderer" and author, and every summer the family would take long holidays in the mountains. In 1854, aged nine, Freshfield was taken to Chamonix and the Bernese Oberland, and "recovered with mulled wine" after a cold crossing of the Gemmi Pass. He completed his first virgin summit on Monte Nero in the Bernina in 1861, and began climbing in earnest two years later, when he climbed Mont Blanc.

According to the *Alpine Journal*, "desperate feats lay outside his sphere", but despite his lack of interest in harder climbing, Freshfield made a large number of first ascents over the next 20 years, mostly in the Eastern Alps, including Piz Cengalo, the Cima di Brenta, and the first traverse of Piz Palu.

Tall and strongly built, Freshfield walked at a ferocious pace and seemed indifferent to heat, which is often more debilitating in the mountains than cold – writer W A B Coolidge (see p.145) called him "a very salamander".

SEARCH FOR UNCLIMBED PEAKS

In 1868, at the age of 23, Freshfield made his first visit to the Caucasus – the mountainous region that forms the traditional dividing line between Europe and Asia – on the first climbing expedition made there by anyone. The Caucasus Mountains were less well known at that time than the Alps had been in the Middle Ages. He teamed up with Adolphus Moore (see pp.162–63), who had climbed Mont Blanc's Brenva Spur in 1865 and was now working for the East India Company, and got access to maps prepared from the latest intelligence smuggled out of Russia.

The rest of the team comprised British climber Charles Comyns Tucker and François Joseph Dévouassoud, a Chamonix guide who would climb with Freshfield on almost all his mountaineering trips until the early 1890s.

After touring the Near East and Syria – and making an attempt on Mount Ararat, for which they weren't acclimatized – the party headed for the Central Caucasus. Having crossed the Krestovoy Pass, they climbed Kasbek, an extinct volcano just over 5,000m (16,000ft),

WILLIAM DONKIN
The unknown fate of photographer William Donkin prompted Freshfield to make a search mission to the Caucasus in 1889.

which was said to be the location where the Greek god of fire, Prometheus, had his liver pecked out each day. It was not a difficult climb, but it was a good start. The group then began a trek along the spine of the Caucasus, travelling west to Elbruz, the highest mountain in Europe. It was like being back in the Alps before the Golden Age, only with a feistier local population.

In the province of Svanetia they caught sight of the twin summits of Ushba, one of the most beautiful mountains in the world: "Tier above tier of precipices rose straight up from the valley, culminating in two tremendous towers, separated by a deep depression. The idea of climbing either of them seemed too insane to be so much as suggested …" Freshfield recalled.

In 1887 and 1889, Freshfield visited the Caucasus Mountains again, on the second trip hunting for clues as to the fate of two British climbers, William Donkin and Harry Fox, who had disappeared without trace with their two Swiss guides during an attempt on Koshtan-Tau, now called Shkhara. He discovered the remains of their final bivouac. Freshfield later published a lavish two-volume account of his travels in the region, *The Exploration of the Caucasus*.

HISTORIC HIMALAYAN TREK

In 1899, when he was 54, Freshfield turned his attention to the Himalaya and decided to make a circumnavigation around Kangchenjunga, the world's third highest mountain, from the north. He assembled a party that included the Italian photographer Vittorio Sella (see p.199) and Edmund Garwood, a British geologist.

HIMALAYAN CAMP
Freshfield (far right) is pictured with his Sherpa headmen. The trials of his epic Himalayan trip were described in *Round Kangchenjunga* (1903).

MOUNT ELBRUZ

EAST SUMMIT, 31 JULY 1868

Setting out in the bitter cold
Freshfield and his party cross into Baksan Valley and camp at 3,600m (11,900ft). They leave at 2.10am in very cold conditions.

Threat of frostbite
Freshfield falls into a crevasse but after "considerable hauling" he is recovered. The appearance of two of their porters encourages the party. "If a porter will go on, I will go on with him," Freshfield says.

Reaching the summit
They reach the summit at 10.40am. "We saw the mountains of the Turkish frontier … the Black Sea and the great peaks between us and Kazbek … The Pennines from Mont Blanc are nothing compared to the east chain seen from Elbruz."

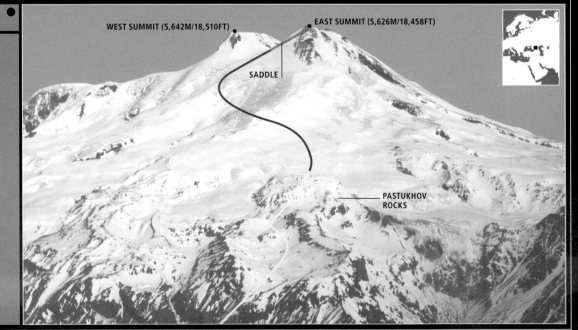

WEST SUMMIT (5,642M/18,510FT)

EAST SUMMIT (5,626M/18,458FT)

SADDLE

PASTUKHOV ROCKS

CLIMBING TIMELINE

Leads first mountaineering expedition to the Caucasus, climbs Kazbek and makes possible first ascent of Elbruz's East Summit

Visits Algeria and climbs in the Atlas Mountains

1845–67	1868	1869–86

After leaving Eton, Freshfield climbs Monte Rosa, and makes a first traverse of Piz Palü and Presanella

As an undergraduate at Oxford, he starts planning an expedition to the Caucasus; climbs new routes in the Bernina and Valais Alps

Spends two seasons exploring the Dauphiné and Maritime Alps

On his second expedition to the Caucasus, he makes a first ascent of Tetnuld

MOUNTAIN MIGRANTS
Among the early migrants to Darjeeling were Sherpas (Freshfield's porters, left), the tribe that had migrated to Nepal from Tibet several centuries before.

The expedition set out from Darjeeling in early September – towards the end of the monsoon – and two weeks later it was camped east of Green Lake by the Zemu Glacier at 4,500m (15,000ft). Sella's photograph of nearby Siniolchu is one of the finest mountain portraits ever taken (see p.200). Freshfield was captivated by the peak, describing it as "the most superb triumph of mountain architecture and the most beautiful snow mountain in the world."

The party's plan was to climb a peak of 6,000m (20,000ft) to get a view of the Nepal Gap on Kangchenjunga's North Ridge as a possible way into the western side of the massif,

but they were thwarted by the monsoon, which ended late. Instead, they crossed the already known Lhonak La and then, trudging through heavy snow, crossed the Jongsong La, a pass of more than 6,000m (20,000ft) into Nepal, in early October, taking three days to descend the Kangchenjunga Glacier to reach Kangbachen. The expedition had a good look at the Northwest Face of Kangchenjunga, which Freshfield judged to be just possible: "The whole face of the mountain might be imagined to have been constructed by the Demon of Kangchenjunga for the express purpose of defence against human assault, so skilfully is each comparatively weak spot raked by the ice and snow batteries," he wrote.

When the party reached Dzongri at the end of the journey, Freshfield had a huge beacon lit, which was answered in Darjeeling by a gun salute ordered by the governor of Bengal.

Although Freshfield didn't get a clear look at the mountain's eastern approaches, and didn't get close to the Southwest Face, which was the eventual line of its first ascent, his account of the climb was influential. It was written "not so much to offer another tale of mountaineering adventure as to provide an account of the scenery and glacial features of the Kangchenjunga Group".

The expedition became a powerful impetus for Himalayan exploration, thanks in part to the stunning photographs taken by Sella, and Garwood's maps, which were a great improvement on anything then available.

In later life, Freshfield received many honours; he was elected president of the Alpine Club (1893–95) and president of the Royal Geographical Society (1914–17).

LIFELONG OUTDOORSMAN
Freshfield enjoyed a long and distinguished career as a climber and explorer. He led expeditions well into old age and also helped establish geography as an academic subject.

THE RISE OF DARJEELING
When the village of Darjeeling came under British control in the early 19th century, it was identified as a good spot for a sanatorium where the sick could escape the heat of the plains; it was also suitable for growing tea. From the 1850s, Darjeeling went from a sleepy backwater to a Raj boomtown, attracting migrants from all over the Himalaya. With Nepal closed until after World War II, and with easy access – including a railway – from the plains, Darjeeling became the obvious centre for mountaineering in Sikkim and for the frontier crossing into Tibet for the Everest expeditions of the 1920s and 30s.

A CAUCASIAN AFFAIR

The Caucasus Mountains were well known to literate Victorians as the place where Jason sought the Golden Fleece, as the home of Gog and Magog in the Old Testament, and as a location in the *Arabian Nights*. For Freshfield, the thought of exploring them was riveting. Yet while they were familiar in cultural terms, knowledge of their topography was negligible. With the Alps already "done" after the Golden Age, climbers saw the Caucasus as a way to recover the excitement of an earlier era. Many of the leading lights of the 1870s and 80s took part. The major achievement was A F Mummery's ascent of Dych-tau in 1888 (see pp.168–71), but English alpinist John Cockin also made a string of important ascents, including the lower, northern summit of Ushba.

A CLIMBING PARTY PREPARE TO BIVOUAC ON THE ROCKS AT KARAOUL IN THE CAUCASUS IN 1890

Makes final journey to the Caucasus to look for Donkin and Fox; travels in Abkhazia	Climbs in Greece, and attempts Olympus but "attempt [is] defeated by brigands"	First climbing expedition to the Rwenzori; he is defeated by "mud-bath and weather"
1887–90	**1891–1905**	**1906–20**
Explores the Kangchenjunga massif, and makes first circuit of Kangchenjunga	Travels to Siberia and Japan and explores the Japanese Alps	Final mountain journey in the Rockies and Selkirks, Canada

MOUNTAIN LIVES

PUNDITS

PLAYED OUT AGAINST A BACKDROP OF THE GREAT GAME – a jostle for supremacy in Central Asia between Britain and Russia – the Pundits were the men in the field who fed intelligence to the British. Natives of the Indian border region recruited for their ability to penetrate deep into Tibet, Nepal, Afghanistan, and the independent tribal sheikdoms, they brought observations and maps that gave insight into the forbidden lands beyond the mountains.

During much of the 19th century, the Karakoram and Himalaya ranges formed a buffer between the two largest imperial powers of the day, Britain and Russia. As Russian expansion into Central Asia crept closer to India, the jewel of the British Empire, the British Raj feared trouble, even invasion. Meanwhile Tibet and Nepal had officially closed their borders to Europeans in 1815, so the demand for intelligence about these mysterious lands intensified – and a rich reward awaited whichever imperial power could gain the upper hand.

For the British, the answer lay in circumventing the travel ban by recruiting Indian agents to pose as pilgrims to the holy sites of the Himalaya. After two years of training, Nain Singh, a schoolteacher from

Sikkim, and his cousin Mani were among the first spies to be sent out in 1865. The codenames for Nain and Mani were "Chief Pundit" and "Second Pundit", after the Hindu word for a man of learning. The name stuck, and all subsequent British spies were dubbed Pundits.

Trained to measure distances by walking a precise 2,000 paces to the mile, the Pundits also used a Buddhist rosary with 100 beads – rather than the usual 108 – for counting. Prayer wheels were used for hiding maps and notes, while miniature sextants were used for surveying. The Pundits contributed a wealth of maps and intelligence that helped the British to protect their interests in India, but some paid a high price – capture meant imprisonment, torture, and even death.

SPYING AND SURVEYING
Among the tricks up the Pundits' sleeves were gauging altitude by timing how long it took to boil water, navigation by the stars, memorizing observations as chanted poems, and eluding suspicious onlookers by whirling a prayer wheel in religious contemplation.

❶ A Pundit map of Nepal and Tibet from 1868. ❷ Indian labourers carry a level and tripod, measuring chains, and a levelling staff for the Great Trigonometric Survey in 1855. ❸ Heavyweight surveying equipment was required for the Survey of India, such as the Great Theodolite, which was carried by 12 men. ❹ Indian surveyors assist with astronomical survey work in 1905. ❺ Pundit observations were vital to mapping the mountainous regions of India.

A ROBUST PHYSIQUE MADE THE INHABITANTS OF SIKKIM – THE MOUNTAINOUS INDIAN STATE THAT BORDERS TIBET TO THE NORTH, NEPAL TO THE WEST, AND BHUTAN TO THE EAST – IDEALLY SUITED TO HIGH-MOUNTAIN EXPLORATION.

PUNDIT PARTICULARS

Potential candidates were drawn from across the border states of India, but were required to have an understanding of the mountains, the ability to read and write, and the physique to withstand the deprivations of prolonged travel and altitude.

❶ A Pundit poses as a holy man on an 1879 expedition. ❷ Kishen Singh, another cousin of Nain, made five journeys between 1869 and 1882. ❸ The Pundit known only as Kinthup explored the Tsangpo River in Tibet between 1880 and 1884. ❹ Sarat Chandra Das was active between 1879 and 1882 and explored the approach to Everest.

NAIN SINGH

INDIA   1830–95

Born in Sikkim at 3,475m (11,400ft), it is little wonder that Nain Singh proved an adept mountain traveller.

Singh travelled 1,930km (1,200 miles) in Nepal and Tibet from 1865 and returned to western Tibet in 1867. His final trip, a two-year journey from Kashmir to Tibet, finished in 1875. Singh received a Gold Medal from the Royal Geographical Society in 1877 for adding "a greater amount of positive knowledge to the map of Asia than any individual of our time".

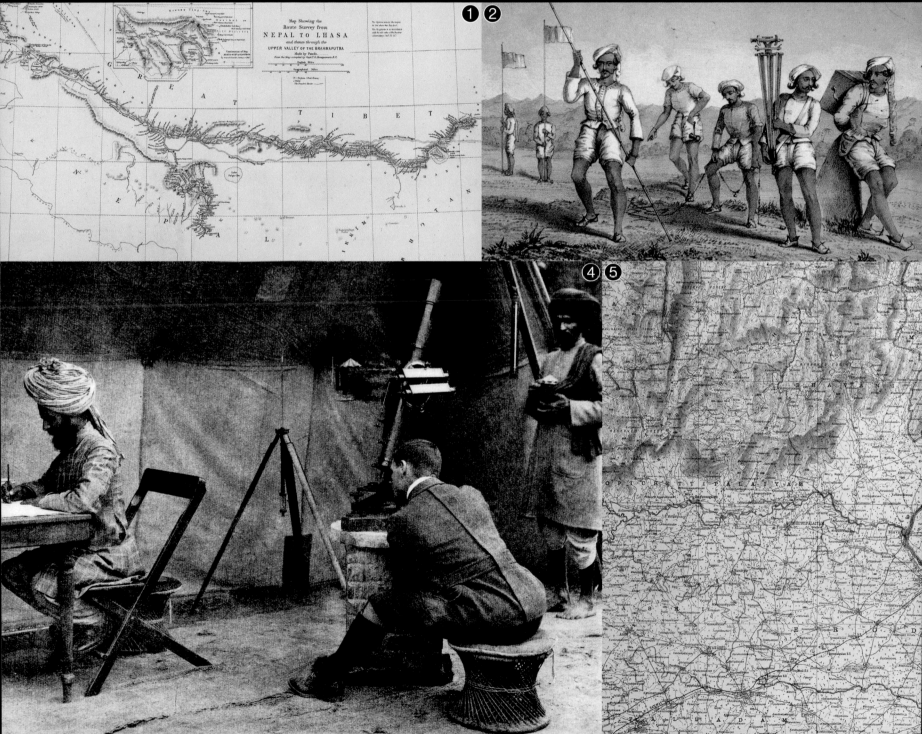

FANNY BULLOCK WORKMAN

UNCOMPROMISING RECORD-CHASER

UNITED STATES   1859–1925

RECORD HOLDER
At the summit of Pinnacle Peak in Kashmir, Fanny claims the first ascent and the world female altitude record. This illustration celebrating her achievement appeared in *Le Petit Journal* on 28 October 1906.

THE HISTORY OF EARLY Himalayan exploration is filled with memorable characters, but few were as redoubtable as Fanny Bullock Workman. In a seven-year period at the turn of the 20th century, the American heiress and her husband made several notable journeys in the western Himalaya, particularly the exploration of the Nun Kun massif in Kashmir, and the Chogo Lungma and Siachen glacier systems in the Karakoram. She also held the female altitude record for almost 30 years, robustly defending her claim against all-comers.

A LIFE'S WORK

- Spends **three years cycling** across southern Asia and India with her husband, before trekking through Ladakh

- The couple make exploratory journeys in the Hispar and Chogo Lungma regions, including a circuit of the Nun Kun massif, and Fanny **sets a new female world altitude record**

- In 1911 and 1912, they undertake **important surveying expeditions** to the Siachen Glacier

Born in Worcester, Massachusetts, Fanny Bullock's father had been that state's Republican governor and a successful lawyer. She was educated by private tutors, and then at a New York finishing school, before living for a while in Dresden and Paris to improve her German and French. In 1881, she married William Hunter Workman, 12 years her senior and a doctor educated at Yale and Harvard.

Small and bustling, Fanny was a marked contrast to her husband, whom friends in the Appalachian Mountain Club described as "quiet, thoughtful and considerate". He introduced her

to the White Mountains in New Hampshire. Suffering from stress, Workman was forced to give up his practice in 1889; however, his retirement would be anything but restful.

THE CYCLING CRAZE

Caught up in the new mania for bicycles, and leaving their only daughter behind in the US, the couple spent the next five years making long cycling journeys in different parts of the world, including the Middle East and North Africa. Fanny soon published the first of her eight books, *Sketches A-Wheel in Fin de Siècle Iberia*,

FORGOTTEN ADVENTURERS

Ten years before the Workmans caused a sensation, a British-Canadian couple, St George and Theresa Littledale, made a series of remarkable journeys across Central Asia. King Edward VII called St George "my greatest traveller", but Theresa, 12 years older than St George, was no less formidable, crossing the Pamirs from north to south in 1888 at the height of the Great Game, a time of rivalry in the region between Britain and Russia when travellers were frequently murdered. The couple also crossed the Chang Tang into Tibet, coming close to the forbidden city of Lhasa. Unlike the Workmans, the Littledales wrote no books and avoided the limelight.

ST GEORGE LITTLEDALE, WHOSE FEATS WERE OVERSHADOWED BY THE WORKMANS

edited, like all her books, by her husband. The couple also climbed in the Alps, making ascents of Mont Blanc and the Matterhorn.

Then it was on to India, starting at the southernmost tip and pedalling north – with Fanny on the front seat of their tandem – on a journey of 22,530km (14,000 miles). Coming at last to the Himalaya, they trekked through Ladakh to the Karakoram Pass and were inspired to organize their first climbing expedition.

No expense was spared. The best equipment was ordered from London, and they sent to Zermatt for a guide, Rudolf Taugwalder. Their objective was Kangchenjunga, the third-highest mountain in the world, but the Workmans did not get far. Fanny showed little patience with local porters, even brandishing a pistol if it would move things along.

SURVEYING THE HIMALAYA

"Almost alone of Victorian travellers," wrote author Dorothy Middleton, "the Workmans had absolutely no sympathy or even common-sense understanding of the local people, into whose poor and remote villages they burst with trains of followers demanding services and supplies."

Though thwarted in their first expedition, the Workmans were sufficiently encouraged to launch another in 1899, the first of seven to the Karakoram. They were accompanied by Matthias Zurbriggen, who had been with Martin Conway (see pp.184–85) in the Karakoram in 1892. They followed Conway's route, in reverse, to the Hispar Pass. But Zurbriggen declared himself unfit, and they returned to Askole. From there they explored the peaks around the Skoro La, making the first ascent of a mountain promptly dubbed Mount Bullock Workman, and of Koser Gunge, almost 6,400m (21,000ft) above the Shigar Valley. "While Zurbriggen and I gasped for breath and the strength to take another step, my wife charged ahead to the summit," Workman recalled.

Descending from what was a new altitude record for women, Fanny ran into porter difficulties again. All their crew had abandoned base camp, taking most of the supplies with them: "We were all cold and hungry and counted ourselves quite fortunate that they had, at least, left a bit of wood behind for a fire."

From 1902 to 1903, the Workmans explored the Chogo Lungma Glacier. Again, there was little new ground

covered, and their surveying work proved unreliable. But their gift for popularizing their travels meant that Fanny in particular was in demand on the lecture circuit in Europe and the US, becoming only the second woman to lecture to the Royal Geographical Society. In 1906, with porters from Italy, they made a circuit of the Nun Kun massif in Kashmir, delving more fully into this large region than previous explorers. With their guide cutting steps, they claimed the first ascent of Pinnacle Peak, third highest in the range at 6,930m (22,736ft), a female altitude record that stood until 1934. The counter-claims of Fanny's US rival, Annie Smith Peck, were swatted aside.

The Workmans' greatest achievements were their expeditions to the Siachen Glacier in 1911 and 1912. They brought with them expert surveyors and the quality of the mapping produced was first class. They made an attempt on Saltoro Kangri (7,742m/25,400ft) and crossed several passes, including the Sia La, from which they explored the head of the Kondus Glacier.

These were their last expeditions together. They settled back in the US and their Siachen book, *Two Summers in the Ice Wilds of Eastern Karakoram,* was published in 1917 – their fifth major work on the Karakoram.

JAMMED IN A CREVASSE
The Workmans' Karakoram expeditions were not without mishap. Here, Matthias Zurbriggen attempts to haul an undaunted Fanny from a crevasse. Later they were abandoned by their porters.

MOUNTAINOUS EGO
At one point on their expedition to map the Siachen Glacier (shown here), Fanny was on the verge of giving up: "'No, I won't come again,' I said as I sat snowed up in my tent for two days … But no sooner had I turned my back to the [glacier] … than my mountain-ego asserted itself, saying … 'Return you must.'"

ALEXANDER KELLAS

UNSUNG GREAT OF EXPLORATORY MOUNTAINEERING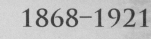

SCOTLAND   1868–1921

A LIFE'S WORK

- Becomes an **authority on the effects of high altitude** on the human body
- Makes several first ascents in the Himalaya and helps **forge a link** between **European** climbers and the native **Sherpas**
- Climbs the **highest summit yet achieved**
- **Joins the first Everest expedition**, but dies of illness en route to the mountain

ALTHOUGH NOT A LEADING technical climber, Kellas made several important contributions to mountain exploration, not least in his work as a scientist. His later research was devoted to understanding the effect of high altitude on the human body. Quietly persistent, Kellas made significant journeys in the Himalaya, doing a number of first ascents there, including Pauhunri, at the time the highest summit yet achieved. He was also instrumental in recognizing and promoting the value of Sherpas in high-altitude ascents.

Known as "Alec", Aberdeen-born Kellas was self-effacing, even shy, and left few detailed accounts of his travels. While studying chemistry at Aberdeen University, he spent a lot of time in the Cairngorms, a mountain range in the eastern Highlands of Scotland, camping out for days at a time. After Aberdeen, he studied in Edinburgh, and then in London. He started teaching chemistry to medical students at a London hospital after receiving his doctorate.

ACCLIMATIZATION STUDIES
Kellas was the first man to make a systematic study of the physiology of acclimatization, and his papers *A Consideration of the Possibility of Ascending the Loftier Himalaya*

and *A Consideration of the Possibility of Ascending Mt Everest* set the context for a long-running argument about whether a human could climb Everest without bottled oxygen. "A man in first-rate training acclimatized to maximum possible altitude could make the ascent of Mount Everest without adventitious aids," Kellas declared, "provided that the physical difficulties above 25,000ft [7,600m] are not prohibitive." Reinhold Messner and Peter Habeler finally settled the question in their ascent of Everest in 1978 (see pp.308–11). However, Kellas's warning about "prohibitive" difficulties has proved justified, and little technical climbing has been done at extreme high altitude.

CHAMPION OF THE SHERPAS
Yet Kellas wasn't just a theorist, he was an active mountaineer, making eight separate climbing expeditions to the Himalaya. In 1911, for example, he made ten first ascents of mountains over 6,100m (20,000ft), most notably Sentinel Peak, Chomo Yummo, and Pauhunri in India's Sikkim, the latter now recalibrated as being

7,128m (23,386ft). During Kellas's lifetime, Pauhunri was measured at 7,065m (23,179ft) and it was assumed that the Englishman Tom Longstaff held the altitude record with his 1907 ascent of Trisul in the Garhwal Himalaya at 7,120m (23,359ft)

Some in the Alpine Club disparaged Kellas, Percy Farrar complaining that he "has never climbed a mountain, but has only walked about on steep snow with a lot of coolies". This unfair assessment was a swipe at another important innovation Kellas had made – as the first man to advocate the use of the Sherpas he found in Darjeeling, rather than Army Gurkhas, while climbing in the Himalaya.

Kellas's introduction to Sherpas came on his first visit to India in 1907, when he was already 39. After visiting Kashmir, he headed for Sikkim and the Zemu Glacier in the Kangchenjunga region. With two Swiss guides, he made three attempts to climb the 6,812-m (22,349-ft)

EVEREST CAMP, 1921
The team poses at their camp at 6,500m (21,300ft). Back row (left to right) G H Bullock, H T Morshead, O Wheeler, G Mallory; front row (left to right) A M Heron, A F Wollaston, C K Howard-Bury, H Raeburn.

FIRST FOOTSTEPS ON EVEREST
The 1921 Everest team cross a ridge in the Kama Valley. The mountain was terra incognita at this time and the team spent four months mapping and exploring its northern and eastern slopes.

Simvu, and also tried to reach the Nepal Gap on the ridge between Kangchenjunga and the Twins, which sits on the Sikkim–Nepal border.

SELECTION FOR EVEREST

Although thwarted in these objectives, Kellas vowed to return, and next time he would "try climbing with Nepalese coolies, who seemed to me more at home under the diminished pressure than my European companions." After two more expeditions accompanied by Sherpas, including his highly successful 1911 expedition, he described the Sherpas as "first-rate climbers" who, with proper training, would prove their worth "for serious climbing of the big peaks like Kangchenjunga and Everest".

Eventually it was Everest itself that came to dominate Kellas's thinking, but with Tibet forbidden, he planned a covert expedition there, actually undertaken by British officer John Noel, who travelled to Tibet in disguise in 1913. He also reverted to the tactics adopted in the pundit era, sending a Sherpa to photograph the eastern approaches to Everest. Kellas and Noel even agreed to mount another clandestine expedition together, a plan thwarted by World War I.

After the war, permission for the first ever reconnaissance expedition to Everest was finally granted, and Kellas was an obvious choice for the team. No other European had a better knowledge of the approaches to the mountain, or understanding of high-altitude physiology. Kellas spent the months leading up to the climb in a frenzy of exploration, returning to Darjeeling just a few days before the expedition set out. Weakened by travel, and suffering from dysentery, he died during the approach through Tibet. British climber Norman Collie later lamented the fact that Kellas, "having looked so many times at Everest from afar … should never set foot on the summit of the monarch of all the mountains on earth."

MOUNTAIN MAN

Kellas made eight expeditions to the Himalaya between 1907 and 1921, and by the time of his death had perhaps spent more time above 6,000m (20,000ft) than anyone on Earth. His studies of high-altitude physiology were his most important legacy, but he also charted the geography of the mountain ranges he visited and documented them extensively in photographs. Kellas was more concerned with being at high altitude than the struggle to get there: as his obituary put it, "he was much more interested in the view from the summit than in the details of the ascent."

TEAM MEMBER C K HOWARD-BURY TOOK THIS IMAGE OF THE 1921 EVEREST EXPEDITION'S SURVEY WORK IN TIBET

OSCAR ECKENSTEIN

INNOVATOR OF CLIMBING GEAR AND TECHNIQUES

ENGLAND   1859–1921

FIERY, BRILLIANT, AND ICONOCLASTIC, Oscar Eckenstein remains a controversial figure even today. He was undoubtedly an original thinker, and an innovator whose contribution towards the development of climbing equipment had a lasting and significant effect on mountaineering. Eckenstein was the first rock climber to write usefully about technique and training, and promoted the sport of "bouldering" a century before it became mainstream. He also led the first serious expedition to K2 in the Karakoram, in 1902.

Eckenstein was born in London to a German father, a Jewish socialist who had fled Bonn following the failed revolution of 1848. He went to University College School and then studied chemistry in London and Bonn, before working as a railway engineer for the International Railway Congress Association, based in Brussels. His job gave him free first-class travel all over Europe, which, in combination with his ragged appearance, led to the assumption that he was an eccentric millionaire.

Tom Longstaff, another Himalayan explorer and a future president of the Alpine Club, described Eckenstein as "a rough diamond", while the wife of Britain's leading alpinist of the day, Geoffrey Winthrop Young, said, "I remember Eckenstein very well at a 1911 party, hammering things in the hall and smoking his

awful pipe tobacco. He had a bushy beard at that time and was regarded as something of a prophet figure." Like many prophets, however, he wasn't always heeded or liked.

SHUNNED BY THE ALPINE CLUB

Eckenstein was direct, argumentative, and quick-tempered – qualities that didn't endear him to the increasingly conservative Alpine Club, which he never joined. Yet Eckenstein was also a tremendous networker, aided in part by his fluent German. He climbed with many of the leading lights of his era across Europe, and his ideas had a big impact on those around him.

Winthrop Young claimed that Eckenstein taught J M Archer Thomson, the great British rock-climbing pioneer, the art of "balance climbing" (in which the feet do most of the work because there are few hand holds available) in North Wales, as well as the value of "bouldering" (a rope-free style of climbing low enough to the ground that a fall is not too serious). He also instructed the Austrian alpinist Paul Preuss (see pp.176–77) in ice-climbing and contributed to Winthrop Young's seminal instructional work, *Mountain Craft*. Eckenstein's alpine career began in 1886 when he completed a number of major first ascents, including the Stecknadelhorn

in the Valais with the guide Matthias Zurbriggen (see pp.208–09) in 1887, and, in 1906, Mont Brouillard in the Mont Blanc range with Austrian alpinist Karl Blodig and Swiss guide Alexander Brocherel.

His antipathy for the Alpine Club deepened during his 1892 Karakoram expedition with Martin Conway (see pp.184–85). He and Conway, who later became president of the club, fell out spectacularly, and Eckenstein was forced to leave the expedition early.

CONWAY'S ENEMY

Ten years later, when he returned to the Karakoram for his attempt on K2, Eckenstein was thrown into prison on suspicion of being a spy. He blamed Conway for it. With Eckenstein were British climbers Aleister Crowley and Guy Knowles, a Swiss doctor, Jules Jacot-Guillarmod, and two Austrians, including Heinrich Pfannl, a judge with a lot of hard alpine rock climbs to his credit. The expedition, conceived by Eckenstein and Crowley, and seemingly paid for by the rest of the team, could only guess at the scale

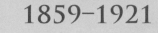

ICE-CLIMBING INNOVATOR
Eckenstein designed and constructed short, light ice axes such as this one, which could be used with one hand.

ALEISTER CROWLEY
ENGLAND   1875–1947

Self-styled occultist, magician, and sexual adventurer, Edward Alexander Crowley was a notorious figure in his day, dubbed the "Wickedest Man in the World" by the media.

Crowley was born into a wealthy, devoutly Christian family. Self-indulgent and self-absorbed but in his youth engagingly iconoclastic, he met Eckenstein, who was 16 years his senior, in 1898. At this first encounter they made "a sort of provisional agreement" to go to the Himalaya together. Crowley had by then been climbing in the Alps for four years, was capable enough, if inconsistent, and regarded Eckenstein as a kind of mentor. He was a trying companion on the 1902 K2 expedition, but showed good judgment, spotting that Heinrich Pfannl was suffering from pulmonary oedema decades before it was diagnosed as a consequence of altitude.

A LIFE'S WORK

- Redesigns the primitive "climbing irons" of the day to **create the modern crampon**

- Is the first to promote the **value of bouldering** in the improvement of rock-climbing training and technique

- **Joins the first serious expedition to K2** in 1902, but, dogged by bad weather, illness, and internal divisions, it fails

of their undertaking, and Eckenstein's choice of route was not a good one. Plagued by atrocious weather and personality clashes, they spent two months on the Baltoro Glacier – breaking the record for the number of days spent at 5,000m (16,400ft) or above. Pfannl reached 6,400m (21,000ft), but suffered a pulmonary oedema and had to be evacuated. The expedition was then abandoned.

Eckenstein's engineering background led him to make major technological contributions to climbing, notably the creation of the modern crampon (see pp.98–99). Tom Longstaff recalled testing the new crampons in 1899, when, "with the assistance of the peculiar Crowley, already notorious and in full Highland kit, Oscar

REMOTE MOUNTAIN
First seen by a European team in 1856, and designated "K2" for the second peak of the Karakoram range, K2 is not visible from any human habitation and has no local name.

gave me a most valuable lesson in their use." He also looked at nail patterns on boots and the nature of knots.

During World War I, Eckenstein served as a Special Constable in London, later marrying and moving to a small town. The Alpine Club's former president, Percy Farrar, was one of the last to see him, in 1921: "I went to see him as he lay dying … His lungs had gone, he could only gasp; but his eye was as clear as ever … wrapped up to the very end in his beloved mountains."

HIDING THE STRAIN
Placid faces conceal the vitriolic personality clashes that dogged the K2 expedition in 1902. Pfannl and Crowley are pictured middle row left and right; Eckenstein is sitting front left.

THE DUKE OF THE ABRUZZI

CELEBRATED MOUNTAINEER AND ADVENTURER

ITALY   1873–1933

THE GRANDSON of King Victor Emmanuel II of Italy, Luigi Amedeo Giuseppe Maria Ferdinando Francesco di Savoia-Aosta, the Duke of the Abruzzi, was a wealthy mountaineer and explorer who used his own resources to mount large, well-equipped expeditions to the Greater Ranges. His exploration of Alaska and the Karakoram was regarded as highly effective, and his teams conducted important surveying work. He was an admiral in the Italian navy during World War I and later settled in Italian Somaliland.

Luigi Amedeo, the Duke of the Abruzzi, was born in Madrid during the brief period that his father, the Duke of Aosta, was King of Spain (following the deposing of Queen Isabella II in the Glorious Revolution). His mother was Maria Vittoria dal Pozzo, his uncle the doomed Umberto I of Italy, and his cousin Victor Emmanuel III. Within days of his birth, his father abdicated, fearful of assassination. The family returned to the Palazzo Cisterna in Turin, his mother's familial home, but she died when the Duke was just three years old. At the age of six he was sent to an Italian naval school.

The di Savoias loved the mountains and several members of the Duke's family became mountaineers, including Umberto's queen,

Margherita di Savoia, an aunt by marriage to Luigi Amedeo, but also a cousin. Margherita lent her name not just to a type of pizza, but also to a mountain hut on one of the summits of Monte Rosa (Switzerland's highest mountain) and, thanks to her nephew, a peak in the Rwenzori Mountains in central Africa.

By his late teens, as well as having travelled the world and been promoted to second-in-command of

A LIFE'S WORK

- Born into Italian nobility, he shares his **family's enthusiasm for mountains**, hunting as a boy in their Gran Paradiso estate

- As a junior officer in the Italian navy, **travels the world**, visiting Italian Somaliland in 1893

- In 1897, leads the **first ascent of Canada's Mount St Elias** in the face of stiff competition

- Seals his reputation as a **leading explorer in the Karakoram** and begins Italy's close association with K2

AFRICAN SUMMIT
The Duke's party made the first ascent of Mount Margherita in Uganda's Ruwenzori range in 1906. Achille Beltrame's engraving of the Duke at the summit appeared in the Italian newspaper *La Domenica del Corriere* in the same year.

MOUNT ST ELIAS

EAST FACE, YUKON TERRITORY, CANADA, JULY 1897

29 July – Route to Camp 21
After more than a month of man-hauling sledges across vast glaciers, Luigi Amedeo and his team arrive at the foot of the slope leading up to the col below the northeast summit.

30 July – Route to Camp 22
They reach the col in six hours. Luigi Amedeo names it Russell Col in honour of Israel Russell, who had come close to reaching the summit seven years earlier.

31 July – Route to summit
Too excited to sleep, the team start preparations for the summit climb at midnight. The going is tough but, at 11.55am, the leading guides step aside to allow Luigi Amedeo to be the first to set foot on the summit.

SUMMIT (5,489M/18,009FT)

RUSSELL COL

CAMP 22

CAMP 21

NEWTON GLACIER

a torpedo boat, the Duke had spent his first season in the Alps, climbing Mont Blanc and the Dent du Géant – a favourite with guided clients, thanks to its dramatic angle and fixed ropes. He also climbed Monte Rosa with Antoine Macquignaz, whom he would hire to join his first expedition to Mount St Elias on the border of Alaska and the Canadian Yukon.

In 1894, he met A F Mummery (see pp.168–71) and Norman Collie in Zermatt, who dissuaded him from attempting the Matterhorn's Zmutt Ridge, which was out of condition. However, they invited him to join them on their next ascent. After climbing the Dent Blanche and Zinal Rothorn with his guide Emile Rey, the Duke returned home, only to be summoned back by Mummery as conditions improved. He coped well with the Zmutt climb, despite the threat of bad weather forcing them to hurry.

The Duke admired Mummery and, when the Englishman perished on Nanga Parbat in the Himalaya in 1895, he resolved to mount an expedition there in honour of his lost friend. However, an outbreak of plague in India thwarted his plans and, when his ship was berthed in Vancouver, he followed the suggestion of a member of the Appalachian Mountain Club, Charles Fay, and decided instead to make an attempt on Mount St Elias.

SCALING MOUNT ST ELIAS

The Duke's approach to his 1897 expedition to Mount St Elias set the pattern for his future campaigns. He was thorough and spared no expense – chartering a boat to ferry supplies, hiring American porters, and buying the best equipment. Along with four of his favourite guides, he took climbing partner Francisco Gonella, doctor and biologist Filippo di Filippi, and the Italian photographer Vittorio Sella, a rising star of mountain photography.

The ascent was an epic trial of endurance – for days on end, they hauled sleds up and down glaciers to reach their objective. Yet they stuck it out, and when good weather came the Italians were in position to try for the summit. As they neared the top, the guides paused so that the Duke could be the first to set foot on the summit. Once there, they slumped to the snow, gasping in the thin air while the Duke pleaded with his climbers to make the planned scientific observations. Even today, Mount St Elias is rarely climbed because of its terrible weather.

In 1900, inspired by the exploits of the Norwegian explorer Fridtjorf Nansen, the Duke led an attempt to reach the North Pole. He didn't succeed (and lost two fingers to the cold in the process), but his team did establish a record for the highest latitude then reached. Later, reading the obituary of the journalist and explorer Henry Morton Stanley, the Duke

learned of Stanley's wish that someone "take the Ruwenzori in hand". In 1906, the Duke duly organized an expedition that explored the whole of the African range. He climbed every major peak, again accompanied by Vittorio Sella.

The Duke's enduring achievement was his expedition to K2 in 1909, during which he made a concerted effort on what has become known as the Abruzzi Spur. He also reached 7,500m (24,600ft) on the nearby peak of Chogolisa – a new altitude record. He took trusted friends from earlier expeditions, including Sella and de Filippi, who wrote a classic account of their exploration.

VITTORIO SELLA
ITALY 1859–1943

Widely regarded as one of the finest mountain photographers in history, Vittorio Sella produced prints of sumptuous elegance and technical precision.

The nephew of Quintino Sella, politician and founder of the Italian Alpine Club, Sella made several first winter ascents in the Alps, including the Matterhorn, before embarking on expeditions around the world. His trips to the Caucasus sealed his reputation, after which he travelled with Luigi Amedeo. Always respectful to his employer, he found his fellow climbers without "a speck of poetry or of interest for the really beautiful things."

Sella adapted saddlebags to protect the glass negatives he carried in the field and, despite his cumbersome equipment, produced photographs that look very modern. He carried on climbing into old age, making a last, thwarted, attempt on the Matterhorn at the age of 76.

EXPERIENCING THE MOUNTAINS

PHOTOGRAPHY

THE IMPACT OF MOUNTAINS on the Western imagination in the early 19th century, along with the stories of early adventurers such as Albert Smith, developed a public appetite for knowing what these places really looked like. Luckily, the development of photography coincided with the birth of mountaineering. The first mountaineering photographs were taken on Mont Blanc in 1861, at the height of the Golden Age. At the start of his career, Edward Whymper was an engraver. By the end of it, he was an accomplished photographer – and humanity's view of the mountains had changed for ever.

"SEE WASHINGTON FIRST." CLIMBING MT. BAKER.

Early photography required heavy equipment. Images were recorded on wet glass plates that had to be chemically coated, then developed immediately in a light-proof tent. But by 1878, dry-plate technology was perfected, allowing for later processing, and in the following decade sheet film replaced glass plates. Nevertheless, photography demanded great physical effort.

Despite the technological challenges, the best mountain photographers from this period achieved exceptional results, as seen in the work of Englishman William Donkin, who encouraged the Italian Vittorio Sella (see p.199), widely regarded as among the greatest photographers of all time. Sella accompanied the Duke of the Abruzzi (see pp.198–99) on his expeditions, photographing remote places such as K2 and Africa's Rwenzori Range.

From the mid 1880s, half-tone printing processes allowed photographs to be published in books, and while Donkin and Sella had been principally interested in landscapes, other pioneers began photographing climbers in

action. One such was Jules Beck of the Swiss Alpine Club, whose 1882 photograph of climbers on the Finsteraarhorn is a rare snapshot of Victorian mountaineering. In Britain, Ashley and George Abraham's rock-climbing photographs were the prototype for the more dramatic work of the later 20th century.

Photography wasn't just for specialists. The invention of roll film in the 1880s led to the development of handheld cameras, enabling tourists without the skills of artists to capture their own fragments of the sublime.

In 1869, the *Alpine Journal* published an article offering advice to climbers on what photographic equipment to take and how to use it. In the Alps, local photographers such as Joseph Tairraz of Chamonix developed new businesses selling postcards to tourists. Smaller cameras, designed for travellers, allowed amateurs such as Lily Bristow (see p.171), who climbed with A F Mummery (see p.168–71), to take more informal snapshots, although these were necessarily of poorer quality.

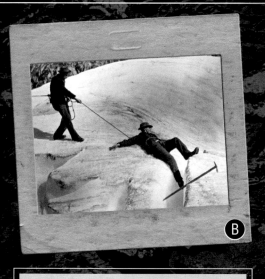

A PUBLICITY POSTCARD
Climbing photographs, such as this 1913 image of a party on Mount Baker in the Cascade Mountains, US, soon became popular souvenirs. In the Alps, Joseph Tairraz established a successful photographic dynasty selling mountain views to tourists.

B CAMERA CRAFT
This 1895 image was taken by Edward Whymper (see pp.142–45) on Mont Blanc. He first worked in his father's engraving studio, and was introduced to climbing through making sketches for a publisher. With the development of photography, Whymper shrewdly switched disciplines.

C LARGE-FORMAT PHOTOGRAPHY
This stunning 1900 shot of Siniolchu in Sikkim, India, is the work of Vittorio Sella, whose beautifully detailed work was shot on huge plates, despite the remoteness of his subjects. US photographer Ansel Adams said his work inspired "religious awe".

A ... GOLDEN WONDER IN A VAST EDIFICE OF STONE AND SPACE

ANSEL ADAMS ON THE YOSEMITE VALLEY

PHOTO BY SANDISON.

D HIGH ART
This 1939 photograph of the Tetons and Snake River, Wyoming, US, was taken by Ansel Adams (1902–84), who is regarded as one of the great US landscape photographers. In 1919, he joined the Sierra Club and worked for four years in Yosemite.

E ARCHITECTURAL APPRECIATION
Bradford Washburn (1910–2007), the doyen of aerial mountain photographers, was a pioneering US mountaineer and map-maker who specialized in Alaska. To many, his images have a deeper understanding of mountain form than those of Ansel Adams, who was not a climber himself.

F EPIC LANDSCAPES
John Noel (see p.222) was a British mountaineer, photographer, and film-maker who captured the beauty of the Himalaya on two Everest expeditions.

G WET-PLATE CAMERA
This heavy camera used sensitized glass plates, with the lens separated from the plate by a bellows. Sella and Donkin began their careers with the wet-plate.

CLIMBING IN THE NEW WORLD

IN THE 16TH CENTURY, RELIGION SPURRED INDIGENOUS PEOPLES TO ASCEND IN THE ANDES. BY THE 19TH CENTURY, THE PEAKS THAT RUN THE LENGTH OF THE AMERICAS FROM TIERRA DEL FUEGO TO ALASKA OFFERED MOUNTAINEERS ENDLESS OPPORTUNITIES FOR EXPLORATION.

CANADIAN-PACIFIC RAILWAY
In 1899, with its new railway up and running, the Canadian-Pacific Railway Company hired Swiss guides to take alpinists into the Rockies, beginning the Canadian climbing boom.

Some time before South America was colonized by Europeans, a 6,739-m (22,109-ft) volcano in Chile's Atacama Desert called Llullaillaco was climbed by the Inca in order to make human sacrifices. This was the highest recorded point reached on the Earth's surface until the German Schlaginweit brothers attempted Abi Garmin in the Himalaya about 350 years later. There are indications that the Inca climbed high on Aconcagua – the highest peak in the Americas – too, but no definite proof.

SOUTH AMERICAN CHALLENGES

During the 18th century, European scientists such as Alexander von Humboldt (see pp.70–71) became interested in the volcanoes of Ecuador because the equator ran through them. Von Humboldt made a serious attempt on Chimborazo, then thought to be the highest mountain on Earth. The summit wasn't reached, though, until Edward Whymper's expedition there in 1880 (see pp.142–45).

ANNIE SMITH PECK
Peck used her mountaineering career to promote her feminism, planting a "Votes for Women" banner on the top of Mount Coropuna in Peru.

In the late 19th century, English alpinist Martin Conway (see pp.184–85) explored Tierra del Fuego, and the Swiss guide Matthias Zurbriggen (see pp.208–09) made the first recorded ascent of Aconcagua in Argentina, but generally there was less impetus in South American exploration than in the Himalaya. One exception was the indomitable Annie Smith Peck, an American writer and lecturer who came to climbing late in life, scaling the Matterhorn in 1895 at the age of 45. Determined to claim the women's altitude record, she made an ascent of Citlaltepetl in Mexico. Then, finding herself in competition with fellow American Fanny Bullock Workman (see pp.192–93), she organized an expedition to Huascarán, the giant of the Cordillera Blanca in Peru, reaching the North Summit in 1908, which she calculated as being about 7,300m (23,950ft). The true altitude, however, was 6,650m (21,817ft), and Workman kept the record.

Before World War I, an Italian missionary in Patagonia called Alberto de Agostini – who was in the mould of earlier climber-priests such as Placidus à Spescha (see pp.106–07) – explored

> With much of the Alps "bagged" by the 1870s, attention turned to more distant ranges. In the Americas, the Andes challenged the hardiest of alpinists while the Canadian Rockies presented an Eden of climbing opportunities.

Tierra del Fuego's Martial Mountains and a peak near Ushuaia, the rocky pyramid of Monte Olivia. He also attempted the beautiful Sarmiento without success, but later persuaded a strong Italian team to try again and make the first ascent, which they did in 1956.

Before World War II, mountaineering in the Andes was dominated by German and Austrian climbers, such as Philip Borchers's team, which made the first ascent of Huascarán's higher South Summit. After the war, some of the best climbers in Europe arrived, including Lionel Terray (see pp.276–77), who made important first ascents, including Chacraraju, perhaps the most impressive peak in the Andes. In the 1950s, Patagonia, at the southernmost tip of South America, became a major centre for hard climbing, a reputation it still has today.

NORTH AMERICAN HEIGHTS

In North America, two men closely associated with exploratory mountaineering in New Zealand also led the way in the Canadian Rockies. Scottish climber James Hector was part of the 1857 Palliser Expedition sent by the British to explore the approaches to the mountains. The Irish priest William S Green, who had attempted Mount Cook, made the first mountaineering expedition to the Selkirk

PATAGONIAN PEAK OF CONTROVERSY
In 1959, Italian Cesare Maestri claimed to
have made the first ascent of the seemingly
unclimbable Cerro Torre (above), but, in the
absence of proof, his record remains disputed.

NORMAN COLLIE
One of the first British alpinists to head for the
Canadian Rockies, Collie made 21 first ascents,
but searched in vain for two mythical giant
mountains supposedly seen by early fur trappers.

SETTING THE SCENE

- In 1879, **Edward Whymper** travels to Ecuador to study the effects of altitude on the human body. He hires his rival from the Matterhorn, **Jean-Antoine Carrel**, as his guide. They **climb several volcanoes, including Chimborazo**.

- Aconcagua is first ascended in 1897 by Matthias Zurbriggen, after earlier attempts by German alpinist Paul Güssfeldt. A party led by Briton **Hudson Stuck climbs the higher South Peak of Denali** in the US in 1913.

- The **American Alpine Club is founded** in 1902, with Charles Fay as president. The **Canadian Alpine Club is formed** in 1906, with Arthur Oliver Wheeler as its first president, supported by the journalist Elizabeth Parker.

- **Americans** H Adams Carter and Bradford Washburn **climb Mount Crillon in Alaska**.

- In 1952, Guido Magnone and Lionel Terray climb **Fitzroy in Patagonia**, beginning the **huge interest in the region** by the world's alpinists.

- **A German team climbs the Moose's Tooth** above Alaska's Ruth Glacier in 1964; in 1977, **Americans** Michael Kennedy and George Lowe **climb the Infinite Spur on Mount Foraker**.

Range in southeastern British Columbia in 1888, climbing Mount Bonney with his cousin Henry Swanzy. In 1890, more climbers arrived: Henry Topham from Britain, and two Swiss, Emil Huber and Carl Sulzer, who made an impressive first ascent of Mount Sir Donald.

Climbers from the American Appalachian Mountain Club, inspired by Charles Fay, led the exploration of the Rockies, taking advantage of the new Canadian–Pacific Railway. The reward for these early pioneers was an enormous area of wilderness full of untouched peaks.

In 1867, the Alaska Purchase brought North America's highest mountains within US borders, giving native climbers peaks on a Himalayan scale. Mount Denali was climbed in 1913, but it was decades before the other major

summits were scaled. From being a curious European import practised by an eccentric few, climbing came of age in Canada in the 1950s. Following US success on Everest in 1963, American alpinists came to the fore in the 1970s. The standard and range of mountaineering has since surged across the continent, transforming the sport in the process.

DISCOVERING THE CANADIAN ROCKIES
Here, climbers traverse Mount Habel – since renamed Mont des Poilus – in the Canadian Rockies. The peak was named after Jean Habel, a German mathematics professor who explored the area in the late 19th century.

CONRAD KAIN

PRINCE OF CANADIAN ALPINE GUIDES

AUSTRIA   1883–1934

FROM THE LATE 1880S, visitors, immigrants, and mountain guides from Europe brought the sport of mountaineering to North America, leaving their mark first on the Canadian Rockies. Of all the guides who emigrated to Canada, Conrad Kain is the most well known. Charming and personable, in a 30-year career he led more than 100 first ascents and new routes, first in the Alps, and then in New Zealand and in Canada, where, from 1909, he set off a wave of first ascents in the highest peaks of the Rockies.

A LIFE'S WORK

- After five outstanding seasons in the Alps, he is invited to become **the first official guide of the Alpine Club of Canada**

- Is credited with more than **60 first ascents and new routes** in the Canadian Rockies and the Interior Ranges of British Columbia

- Makes **five first ascents** in the Bugaboo group, which contains some of North America's **most technical peaks**

- Renowned as a leader, climber, and storyteller, his **personal attributes** are the qualities for which he is most respected

- Guides more than **25 first ascents in New Zealand** and climbs Mount Cook twice

- Organizes a **winter sports festival** in Banff and encourages the promotion of winter sports and tourism in the area

- Travels to **Siberia's Altai Mountains** to help with the collection of mammal specimens for the **Smithsonian Institution**

Born in the Tyrol, Kain's family later moved to Nasswald, southwest of Vienna. He left school at 14 to support his widowed mother and started work as a goatherd and later as a quarryman, but developed an early passion for the mountains under the instruction of a local guide.

Kain's early career was boosted by his interest in botany; he joined expeditions to Spitzbergen in Norway in 1901 and Egypt the following year, and from 1904, when he passed his guide's exam, he started working across the Alps, often for the Viennese climber Erich Pistor. In 1906, he worked in Corsica for the Austrian Albert Gerngross, cementing his passion for travel and making his first ascent – Capu Tafunatu.

TO CANADA
In 1908, Kain stayed in Vienna with Pistor to study English and improve his job prospects. Pistor wrote to the newly formed Alpine Club of Canada suggesting Kain work for them. Offered a job, Kain set sail, and fell in love with the country, eventually settling with his new wife at Wilmer on the Columbia River. Kain's greatest climbs – Mount Robson, Mount Louis, and the Bugaboo Spire – were in Canada,

but he also spent three seasons in New Zealand, where he made more than 25 first ascents in the Southern Alps, and the second traverse of Mount Cook in 1916.

SAGA OF MOUNT ROBSON
Kain's first ascent of Mount Robson in 1913 was complicated by an earlier claim made by George Kinney, who was obsessed with the mountain. In 1907 and again in 1908, Kinney had tried to climb the peak. A year later, aiming to beat an attempt by a rival British team, he rushed to the mountain to try once more, teaming up with Donald "Curlie" Phillips, who didn't even have an ice axe. Returning from their climb, they encountered the British, armed to the teeth with the latest climbing gear, including crampons. But even this crack team were still far short of the summit when they turned back. Doubts grew in the minds of Canadian mountaineers about Kinney's claim to have reached the top, and while never disproved, it would soon be discounted.

ON LOCATION
In 1922, Kain guided photographer Byron Harmon on a trip to shoot film footage of British Columbia's Lake of the Hanging Glacier (left).

In 1911, Kain worked for Arthur Wheeler, director of the Alpine Club of Canada, on a joint scientific expedition with the Smithsonian near Mount Robson, but the mountain wasn't part of their plans. Instead, Kain settled for a solo ascent of Mount Whitehorn. Returning after dark, he had to feel his way across the glacier, testing the ground ahead for crevasses. "My one bit of good fortune was the lightning, which showed me the way," he wrote later. He also sneaked away to climb Resplendent Mountain, this time with a partner, from where he got a clear view of Mount Robson.

DOUBTFUL CLAIM
George Kinney was also part of the 1911 expedition, but when Wheeler saw his and "Curlie" Phillips's route up Mount Robson, his scepticism about their summit claim turned to disbelief. In 1913, Wheeler decided to organize an expedition to climb the mountain for certain. He selected three men for his summit team – W W "Billy" Foster and Albert MacCarthy, and Kain as their guide. Kain cut hundreds of steps for his clients, picking his way through a maze of ice walls near the summit. "Never before on all my climbs have I seen such snow formations," he wrote later.

Finally, Kain found a way through to the summit and turned to the others, saying, "Gentlemen, that's as far as I can take you." At that moment the clouds parted to reveal an incredible view of peaks and glaciers. It was almost 6pm, the temperature was plummeting,

A TOUGH ASCENT
Here, Kain and his companions negotiate the typically poor rock conditions found in the Canadian Rockies.

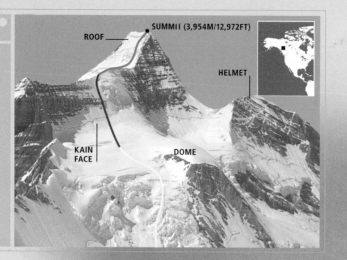

MOUNT ROBSON

KAIN FACE, 31 JULY 1913

— **Up the Robson Glacier**
Rising before dawn at their bivouac, Kain, Foster, and MacCarthy climb the Robson Glacier.

— **The Kain Face**
Kain begins cutting the first of several hundred steps towards the ridge.

— **Up the "Roof"**
Kain leads the way up the ridge, reaching the "Roof", where steep ice cliffs slow their progress.

ROOF

SUMMIT (3,954M/12,972FT)

HELMET

KAIN FACE

DOME

THEY PRAISED MY PERFORMANCE AND SOME ALMOST OVERDID IT. BUT THAT DID NOT AFFECT ME MUCH "

CONRAD KAIN, AFTER A DIFFICULT ASCENT

and searching for an easier descent, Kain led the men down the South Face of the peak. Strung out with cold, they shivered and hallucinated through the night at a bivouac beside the glacier below.

LASTING LEGACY

After his ascents in the Bugaboos – the hardest of his career – Kain climbed less, preferring just to be in the mountains. Out of curiosity as much as need, he tried all kinds of work, including trapping furs and leading bear-hunting expeditions. His last ascents were done with the literary critic I A Richards and his wife, climber Dorothy Pilley, in the Bugaboos. Kain's wife died in 1933, and early in 1934 he contracted lethargic encephalitis, a disease of the immune system, and died aged 50.

After his death, the mountaineering writer J Monroe Thorington said that Kain had "brought glamour and imagination to the sport of mountaineering as few guides have done before him … His approach to mountains was first and foremost an aesthetic one; he saw a peak first as something beautiful – the technical problem was always secondary – and nothing counted beside that vision." Thorington published Kain's diaries and other

writings, as well as reminiscences from friends, as *Where the Clouds Can Go*, a classic work of Canadian climbing.

Several peaks were named after Kain: Mount Conrad in New Zealand's Southern Alps, Mount Kain and Nasswald Peak in the Canadian Rockies, and Mount Conrad, the Conrad Icefield, and Birthday Peak (which Kain climbed on his birthday) in Canada's Purcell Range.

MOUNTAIN PORTRAIT

DENALI

MEANING "THE HIGH ONE" in the local Athabaskan language, North America's highest mountain is officially known as Mount McKinley. Denali is Himalayan in scale, rising higher than 5,500m (18,000ft) from the tundra, and the standard route is 22km (14 miles) long. Denali's high latitude puts it among the world's coldest mountains – due to the lower air density at the poles, Denali corresponds to a Himalayan 7,000-m (23,000-ft) peak.

George Vancouver, while surveying Cook Inlet in 1794, was the first European to record sighting Denali, and in the late 19th century, gold prospectors in Alaska recognized its potential as the highest peak in North America. James Wickersham, later Alaska's representative in the US Congress, was the first to make an attempt to climb it. Frederick Cook claimed to have reached the summit in 1906, a claim that was proved conclusively to be false. In 1910, the Sourdough Expedition, undertaken by four local prospectors inspired by a bet, took about two months to reach the lower North

Peak, but their claim to have reached the South Peak – the true summit – was also discounted. Competition remained fierce and another group came within 60 vertical metres (200ft) of the top in 1912. Hudson Stuck, Harry Karstens, Walter Harper, and Robert Tatum finally climbed Denali via the Muldrow and Harper Glaciers in 1913.

Today, climbers approaching Denali take an air taxi from Talkeetna to Base Camp on the Southeast Fork of the Kahiltna Glacier. At 2,160m (7,100ft), this is 3,000m (1,000ft) lower than Everest Base Camp, but the height gain is 400m (1,300ft) greater.

IN PROFILE

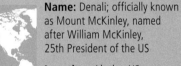

Name: Denali; officially known as Mount McKinley, named after William McKinley, 25th President of the US

Location: Alaska, US

Range: Alaska Range

Height: 6,194m (20,320ft)

Notable features: has two summits – the main South Summit and the lower North Summit (5,934m/19,470ft). Five major glacier systems flow from its flanks, and crevasses are a major danger. High latitude means low temperatures – almost -60°C (-76°F) has been recorded, without wind chill – and less oxygen.

First ascent: Rev Hudson Stuck (leader), Harry Karstens, Walter Harper (first to summit), Robert Tatum, 7 June 1913

First female ascent: Barbara Washburn, 1947

First solo ascent: Naomi Uemura, 1970; he disappeared descending from the first winter solo ascent in 1984

Standard route: West Buttress, first climbed in 1951, expedition led by Brad Washburn

ALASKA

WICKERSHAM WALL

PIONEER RIDGE

NORTH PEAK

HARPER GLACIER

WEST BUTTRESS

SOUTH PEAK

THAYER BASIN

WEST RIB

NORTHEAST FORK

CASSIN RIDGE

NORTHWEST FORK RUTH GLACIER

SOUTH BUTTRESS

EAST FORK KAHILTNA GLACIER

WEST FORK RUTH GLACIER

SCALE

2 MILES
2KM

▲ SUMMIT

N

CLIMBING ROUTES

Denali is a huge mountain of high, glacial basins separated by often-corniced ridges that, while generally not steep, are very long. It is popular. However, of the 1,263 climbers registered with the National Park Service to climb it in 2010, only 670 reached the summit – a success rate of 53 per cent. Snowfall, cold wind, and altitude all conspire to turn climbers back – even on the technically easy routes – and crevasses are a major hazard.

SOUTH FACE
— **SOUTH WEST FACE**
(J Roberts, S McCartney, 1980) Difficult mixed and aid climbing up to A3. The first ascent ended in a protracted rescue as McCartney suffered oedema.

❶ West Rib The upper slopes of the West Rib, which eventually joins the West Ridge, and the upper portion of the West Buttress route (not shown).

— **DENALI DIAMOND**
(B Becker, R Graage, 1983) A hard, technical route first climbed in 17 days and not repeated until 2002.

❷ 8m (25ft) roof Although it's possible to outflank, this large overhang proved the crux during the first ascent of the Denali Diamond.

— **CASSIN RIDGE**
(L Airoldi, L Alippi, G Canali, R Cassin, R Perego, A Zucchi, 1961) Most famous harder route, with 70-degree ice and rock climbing up to 5.7. It was soloed in 15 hours in 1991 by Mugs Stump.

— **SLOVAK DIRECT**
(B Adam, T Krizo, F Korl, 1986) Sometimes called the Czech Route (the climbers were in fact Slovak) this steep ice route has become a modern classic; the most direct line on the South Face.

❸ South Face Holds some of the peak's most difficult and best climbs, including its first route, the popular Cassin Ridge.

SCOTT/HASTON ROUTE
(D Scott, D Haston, 1976) The two Britons were surprised by the cold of Denali, but this was the first major route climbed in alpine style.

❹ Big Bertha Icefall at the heart of the South Face.

— **AMERICAN DIRECT**
(R Laba, D Seidman, G Thompson, D Eberl, 1967) With rock up to 5.7, ice of 65 degrees, and a high risk of avalanche, the first ascent took 28 days.

❺ Japanese Couloir A Japanese team faced huge avalanche risk to climb this variant on the American Direct.

SUMMIT (6,194M/20,320FT)

CASSIN RIDGE

SOUTH EAST RIDGE

① WEST RIB

③ SOUTH FACE

④ BIG BERTHA

②

⑤ JAPANESE COULOUIR

MOUNTAIN FEATURES

Ⓐ **Denali's West Buttress** is descended by a team of climbers below Motorcycle Hill Camp, just above Camp III.

Ⓑ **After landing** on the Kahiltna Glacier near Base Camp, climbers prepare to start hauling loads from an altitude of 2,164m (7,100ft).

Ⓒ **On the superb Cassin Ridge**, first climbed in 1961 by Riccardo Cassin and friends, is one of Denali's harder classic routes.

Ⓐ

Ⓑ

Ⓒ

MATTHIAS ZURBRIGGEN

EXPLORER-GUIDE WHO CLIMBED THE WORLD

SWITZERLAND   1856–1917

IN AN ERA BEFORE THE ADVENT of air travel, Matthias Zurbriggen was an unusually well-travelled guide, enjoying a lifestyle that resembles that of the peripatetic modern mountaineer. He was based in the Alpine village of Macugnaga below the colossal eastern aspect of Monte Rosa, where he was known as the "Lord of the East Face". His most famous climbs were the first ascent of Aconcagua in the Andes and his route on New Zealand's Mount Cook; he also worked on early Himalayan expeditions.

A LIFE'S WORK

- After leaving home, he is employed in an eclectic string of jobs before moving to Macugnaga in the Italian Alps, where he works on the construction of a mountain hut and becomes **one of the leading mountain guides of his generation**

- Leads some of the greatest alpinists of the day, and is one of the few guides who, even at extreme heights, **can defy altitude sickness**

- After a few seasons in the Alps, he is hired for Martin Conway's eight-month **expedition to the Karakoram in 1892**. With the party, he climbs a subsidiary summit of Boltoro Kangri

- On an expedition to New Zealand with British alpinist Edward FitzGerald he makes the **second ascent of Mount Cook solo**, and by a new route – later called the Zurbriggen Ridge

- With FitzGerald, **he also makes first ascents of other New Zealand peaks**: Sefton, Tasman, the Silberhorn, and Haidinger

- Makes the **first ascent of Argentina's Aconcagua** – at 6,962m (22,841ft) the highest point in the Western Hemisphere – again solo, after his client drops out

Matthias Zurbriggen was born in Saas Fee, the son of a shoemaker. When he was two, his family moved across the Italian border to Pestarena, and his father started work in a gold mine. He died there when Matthias was eight and, already working as a goatherd to help make ends meet, the boy learned to fend for himself.

As a young man with a restless spirit, Zurbriggen took to the road, finding work, variously, as an ostler (stableman) and a copper miner, before driving a cart between Sierre and Brig in Switzerland's Valais Canton. He was also employed on construction sites, did military service, and worked in Tunisia for a Swiss gentleman on a shooting holiday, staying on afterwards in Algeria to work as a mason.

FINDING A VOCATION

By the mid 1880s, and turning 30, Zurbriggen was back in Italy, up the valley from Pestarena in the tiny village of Macugnaga, where he began guiding. He was almost instantly good at it, inheriting from the Swiss guide Ferdinand Imseng the title "Lord of the East Face", and taking his first clients up the formidable Marinelli Couloir.

He climbed the Matterhorn several times, guiding the English businessman Edward Fison on it in 1889 and berating his client with characteristic fury when he lay down in the snow and refused to get up again. On another ascent of the Matterhorn, he met Briton Edward FitzGerald, with whom he later travelled

TOUGHING IT OUT
With the rest of the Aconcagua party defeated by altitude sickness and extreme cold, FitzGerald agreed to let Zurbriggen push on alone up the long scree slopes on the peak's northwestern side, from where he reached the summit.

to New Zealand and South America. He also climbed Mont Blanc with Englishman Edward Whymper (see pp.142–45).

ELITE GUIDE

Zurbriggen's most illustrious client was English alpinist Martin Conway (see pp.184–85), who took him on his expedition to the Karakoram in 1892. Conway admired his guide's range of experiences. "Everything that he came to know in after-life was self-taught … He desired to acquire every sort of knowledge and every sort of skill that he could come by. He was also a competent blacksmith, a good carpenter … and a most accomplished craftsman with axe and rope on the mountainside," he wrote.

Zurbriggen had already climbed with the expedition's star mountaineer, Oscar Eckenstein (see pp.196–97), making the first ascent of the Stecknadelhorn with him in 1887. Both men had fiery personalities, but Conway reported that his guide was "extravagant, lusty and overflowing. He was a very hard worker and

unrestrained in his relaxations. He was easy to get on with if taken the right way, and just as easy to quarrel with."

However, Zurbriggen could also be exceptionally charming. His role on Conway's expedition prompted Fanny Bullock Workman (see pp.192–93) to hire him for her first expedition to the Karakoram in 1899, and again in 1902. She left a favourable review in his *Führerbuch* (guide's book): "He is certainly most strongly to be recommended as a lady's guide."

THE ZURBRIGGEN RIDGE

It was with Edward FitzGerald that he made his most famous climbs. In 1894, they travelled to New Zealand, where they made first ascents of Sefton, Tasman, the Silberhorn, and Haidinger.

ON MONT BLANC, 1895
The Alps were Zurbriggen's training ground; on their slopes he became "a consummate technician with ice axe and rope", and forged a career as a highly sought-after guide.

Zurbriggen also made a daring second ascent of Mount Cook, by the route that still bears his name, FitzGerald having lost interest after missing out on the first ascent.

Three years later, Zurbriggen was in South America, again with FitzGerald, who gave up on Aconcagua 600m (2,000ft) from the summit, leaving his guide to make the first ascent alone. An anecdote told about Zurbriggen long after his death by expedition member Philip Gosse, reveals his humour and his mercantile ways. Recovering from the climb over a few drinks, the conquering hero, described as "a good mixer" by Gosse, was surrounded by admirers. Gosse noticed that every so often, Zurbriggen would take one of them aside, reach in his pocket and hand over something, in return for which he got a coin. Zurbriggen later told Gosse he had sold a dozen or so stones as "the actual summits of Aconcagua". Most of them had in fact been gathered by the wayside on the ascent.

In 1900, Zurbriggen travelled to the Tien Shan in Central Asia with Prince Scipione Borghese; they failed in their main objective, the stunning Khan Tengri, but climbed a number of lower peaks. In his autobiography, Zurbriggen revealed that his great ambition was to be the first to climb Everest. Yet in 1907 he gave up guiding and moved to Geneva. His later years were marred by vagrancy and alcoholism and his life ended tragically, by his own hand.

MOUNT COOK

EAST FACE, 14 MARCH 1895

- **Setting off without the client**
  Zurbriggen climbs with Hermitage guide Jack Adamson.

- **Continuing alone**
  At about 2,600m (8,500ft), Adamson turns back, leaving Zurbriggen to climb the 50-degree ice slope alone.

- **Final push to the summit**
  Above the snow and ice face, he overcomes summit rocks to climb the final 350-m (1,150-ft) stretch of the summit ridge.

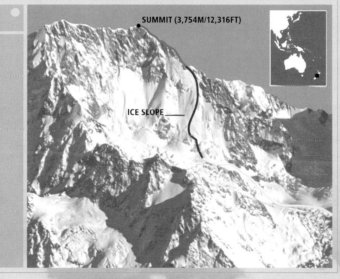

SUMMIT (3,754M/12,316FT)

ICE SLOPE

ALPINISM IN JAPAN

THERE ARE NO GLACIATED PEAKS IN JAPAN, BUT AN ANCIENT CULTURAL INTEREST IN MOUNTAINS AND A TRADITION OF PILGRIMAGE MEANT THAT MOUNTAINEERING WAS ENTHUSIASTICALLY ADOPTED WHEN IT WAS INTRODUCED BY EUROPEANS IN THE EARLY 20TH CENTURY.

HOLY HEIGHTS
A favourite emblem in Japan for its symmetrically perfect cone, Mount Fuji is visited by as many as 2,000 people each day during the climbing season.

The German scientist Phillip Franz von Siebold, a prolific writer on Japan, saw Mount Fuji for the first time in 1826. He was astonished at the number of ordinary Japanese people making pilgrimages to holy mountains, not just out of a sense of piety, but for the sheer joy of it, finding freedom from the cares of their daily lives.

What von Siebold was seeing was a form of spiritualized sport. After Japan opened itself to the world in the mid-19th century, mountains were properly mapped and measured. Visiting European technical experts with an interest in mountaineering began exploring what became known, to the frustration of the Japanese and inaccurately by Westerners, as the Japanese Alps.

EARLY PIONEERS

William Gowland, an English metallurgist who lived in Japan for 16 years from 1872, possibly coined the name. Gowland explored the Hida-Sanmyaku mountains, which became known as the Northern Alps, in north-central Honshu – Japan's main island – and saw how Japanese peaks are craggy, with sharp, shattered edges, holding heavy snow in winter. He also claimed the first European ascent of Yariga-Take (3,180m/10,433ft), the fourth-highest peak in Japan. The English diplomat Ernest Satow was another pioneer; he climbed Mount Tateyama (3,015m/9,892ft) and also contributed to

SUMMIT SHRINE
Here, pilgrims make their way down from the summit of Mount Fuji. At 3,776m (12,389ft), it is the highest peak in Japan, and – as one of the country's three holy mountains – has been a destination for pilgrims since the 7th century.

MAN ON A MISSION
Seen here with porters, Walter Weston came to Japan in 1888. A climber from the age of 17, and having ascended the Matterhorn, Weston transferred his passion to the Japanese Alps.

INTERNATIONAL CLIMBING
By the 1920s, Japanese alpinists had the ambition to mount international expeditions such as this one to Mount Robson in Canada, which included Yuko Maki (see pp.212–13).

SETTING THE SCENE

- The Japanese Alps are a series of ranges located between Tokyo on Honshu's Pacific coast and the Sea of Japan. **They are now divided into three ranges**: Northern, Central, and Southern Alps, with 26 peaks above 3,000m (9,842ft).

- For centuries, the Japanese have a **powerful spiritual connection to mountain landscapes**. In 1828, the ascetic Banryu makes an extreme pilgrimage to the summit of Yariga-Take – a mountain later dubbed "the Matterhorn of Japan".

- British engineers arrive in the mid-19th century to aid **Japan's modernization programme**. Among them is a keen mountaineer named **William Gowland**, who repeats Banryu's ascent of Yariga-Take.

- Japanese students and writers with a **new interest in Romantic literature and natural sciences** start exploring the mountains, forming the nucleus of what will become **the Japanese Alpine Club**.

- William Weston arrives in Japan in 1888, the **catalyst for Japan's emergence as a mountaineering nation**. "Weston Day" is still celebrated among Japanese climbers at a plaque raised in his honour on the path to Yariga-Take.

guidebooks. Along with rugby, which was introduced by Edward Bramwell Clarke, this was Britain's sporting contribution to Japanese culture.

However, climbing in Japan only really gained momentum with the arrival of English clergyman Walter Weston. In 1888, he relocated to Japan for the Church Missionary Society, preaching in churches at Kumamoto and Kobe for six years. A mountaineer from the age of 17, with ascents of the Matterhorn and Breithorn under his belt, Weston transferred his passion to what were already being called the Japanese Alps by Western visitors to the country.

CLIMBING CLERIC
Weston showed real devotion to the cause. Between 1891 and 1894 he climbed more than 40 mountains, including Mount Fuji, which he scaled every year he was in in the country. Like the early Alpine Club stalwarts, Weston carried barometers and collected specimens, and was a great admirer of John Ruskin (see pp.86–89). Weston wrote two books about his experiences: *Mountaineering and Exploration in the Japanese Alps* and *Playground of the Far East*. Although his role in the development of climbing in Japan has sometimes been overstated, the Japanese Alpine Club made him their first honorary member, acknowledging his founding role.

NATURAL HARMONY
A 19th-century pilgrim marks his ascent of Mount Fuji with a studio photograph. In Japan's Shinto religion, the mountain has a spirit.

John Ruskin also had a powerful intellectual impact on Japanese writers, including Kitamura Tokoku, one of the founders of a Japanese Romantic literary movement, whose poem *Horai Kyoku* was influenced by Lord Byron's *Manfred*. Also influential was the work of Shigetaka Shiga, whose piece *On Japanese Landscape* absorbed Ruskin, but reconfigured it for the particular mountains found in Japan.

ALPINISM FOR THE JAPANESE
In 1902, Kinjiro Okano, an employee of the Standard Oil Company in Yokohama, south-central Honshu, saw a book in his American manager's office called *The Japanese Alps*. Flicking through the pages, he was amazed to find pictures of Yariga-Take, the "Japanese Matterhorn", which he had recently climbed with a friend, Usui Kojima. The companions had discovered a small shrine at the summit

of the mountain featuring statues of Buddha, possibly those carried up in 1828 by the monk Banryu who, legend has it, made the first ascent.

Weston had returned to Japan to preach at Yokohama earlier that year, and Okano and Kojima tracked him down. Weston was delighted to meet Japanese climbers and introduced them to European mountaineering gear, later encouraging them to form their own Japanese Alpine Club shortly before he returned to Europe in 1905. The organization was inaugurated in a Tokyo restaurant later that year.

Kojima was a noted collector of Ukiyo-e – stylized Japanese woodblock prints – and the author of 20 books. He also translated Weston's mountaineering books into Japanese. With no first-hand experience of the European Alps, Kojima allowed Weston's favourable assessment of Japan's mountains to grow in his imagination. He was rather embarrassed by the comparison when he saw glaciated peaks for the first time. Nevertheless, Japan's mountains proved a demanding testing-ground for the Japanese climbers who would emerge over the course of the 20th century.

> Mountaineering tapped into a deep-seated cultural desire of the Japanese to visit high places. Soon after Europeans introduced their equipment and techniques, Japanese mountaineers were climbing to the summits of peaks across the country.

ARITSUNE "YUKO" MAKI

GROUNDBREAKING JAPANESE ALPINIST

JAPAN   1894–1989

THE JAPANESE HAVE A SPIRITUAL appreciation for the mountains. Buddhist monks may have climbed Mount Fuji, 3,776m (12,388ft) high, almost a millennium before Mont Blanc was scaled. Yet mountaineering as a sport began as a European import among a handful of enthusiastic novices. Japan's lack of glaciated peaks, however, meant that their climbers had to travel to develop their skills. Yuko Maki was among those pioneers, and his journey would culminate in the Japanese first ascent of the "8,000er", Manaslu.

A LIFE'S WORK

- The **climbing club** Maki helps establish while studying at Keio University becomes one of the most **influential in Japan**

- After graduation, he travels to the US and Europe and makes the **first ascent of the Eiger's Mittellegi Ridge**; he later donates 10,000 Swiss francs for the building of the **Mittellegi Hut**

- Becomes well known in Japan after making the **first winter ascent** of Yari-ga Take (3,180m/10,433ft) in 1922; a later winter attempt on Tateyama **ends in disaster** when one of his team is killed

- In 1925, with the support of the Japanese imperial court, he **makes the first ascent of Mount Alberta** (3,619m/11,874ft) in Canada with the help of three Swiss guides

- Makes winter ascents in Japan and Korea in training for Japan's first Himlayan expedition, but **World War II intervenes**

- Thirty-one years after Mount Alberta, he **leads the third Japanese expedition to Manaslu** in 1956; using oxygen and 20 Sherpas, the attempt is successful

Yuko Maki was born at Sendai in northern Japan and made his own ascent of Mount Fuji aged just ten. In his teens he went on to climb many of the major easy peaks in Japan, from the mountains of Hokkaido to one of the world's most massive volcanoes, Mount Aso, on the southern island of Kyushu. As a law student at Keio University he established a climbing club, which, along with Kyoto and Waseda, would become one of the powerhouses of Japanese mountaineering. He graduated in 1919, and after studying in the US and Britain, travelled to Switzerland, where he stayed for two years.

Maki was not the first Japanese person to visit the Alps, but he created the biggest impression, making the first ascent of the Eiger's Mittellegi Ridge in September 1921 with the Swiss guides Fritz Amatter, Samuel Brawand, and Fritz Steuri. The route had been descended before, roping down the difficult sections, but no one had yet overcome the difficult rock towers on the ridge.

The party's equipment included a 6-m (20-ft) pole with hooks on either end to aid their progress, as Maki described in his 1923 book, *Sanko*. "Steuri, the second man, slotted the lower end into a little crack and putting his whole weight behind it, levered it securely into place. Amatter took a length of rope, fashioned it into a loop, and hung it from the upper hook on the wooden pole. By such means, we thought to limit the force of any possible fall."

Belayed in this way, Amatter hacked out footholds in the rock with his axe, swapping places with Seuri when he got too cold. As last man, Maki wrote, he had to climb with the pole, but with only one free hand he soon had to resort to being pulled up on the rope. He put these Alpine experiences to good use when he returned to Japan, bringing with him Western

climbing equipment. He was soon making significant ascents in the Japanese Alps, including the first winter ascent of Yari-ga Take.

ROYAL ENCOURAGEMENT

Maki's next foreign expedition was the result of a lucky coincidence. By the mid 1920s, he was working as an aide-de-camp to the young Prince Chichibu, an enthusiastic skier. While on a skiing holiday, the prince came across an American Alpine Club guidebook, which had a photograph of Mount Alberta on the cover, a steeply inclined pyramid of limestone, and the last unclimbed giant in the Canadian Rockies. Chichibu showed the photo to Maki and offered his support in raising the necessary finance for an expedition.

Prudently, given that Japanese climbing was still in its infancy, Maki hired the Oberland guide Heinrich Fuhrer and an assistant, Hans Kohler. In July 1925, the six Japanese expedition members – Seiichi Hashimoto, Masanobu Hatano, Tanezo Hayakawa, Yuko Maki, Yukio Mita, and Natagene Okabe – joined them in Jasper. Raging forest fires thwarted their initial progress, but by mid July, Fuhrer had found a way up the mountain's Southeast Face. On 21 July, at 3.30am, a party of nine set out from their high camp on Habel Creek, with Fuhrer in the lead.

The crux came high on the peak, at a short overhanging wall. Hayakawa braced himself against the wall and Kohler climbed onto his

AFTER THE EIGER
Maki is hoisted up after his ascent of the Eiger's Mittellegi Ridge with three Swiss guides in 1921. The triumph was celebrated with fireworks in Grindelwald.

shoulders, wrapping his legs round Hayakawa's neck. Then Kohler was launched to the top of this human pyramid. Pausing to brush aside loose stones, he clambered on top of the obstacle. It was 2pm. The final summit ridge proved awkward, being heavily corniced and with deep gaps that had to be crossed; the team didn't reach the summit until after 7pm. No one repeated their route until 1948. The British Everest climber Frank Smythe (see p.247) was one failure, writing, "I can only say of Alberta that I know of no Alpine peak so difficult by its easiest route, and but one or two Alpine routes to compare with the pitiless limestone slabs with no belays and few resting places."

The following year Maki guided Prince Chichibu to the top of the Matterhorn, and began dreaming of leading the first Japanese expedition to the Himalaya. In this he was thwarted. A Rikyo University team climbed Nanda Kot in 1936, and, before Maki could put his plan into action, Japan invaded China and all thoughts of climbing expeditions were put aside for the next decade.

MANASLU TRIUMPH

After the war, Japan joined the race to climb the "8,000ers", sending a reconnaissance team to Manaslu in 1952, led by Jiro Taguchi and Masataka Takagi, who had been caught in Switzerland at the outbreak of World War II and had spent their time there learning European ice climbing techniques. They formed the nucleus of a full expedition the following year, led by Maki's partner from Alberta, Yukio Mita. When that and a subsequent attempt failed, Maki himself, aged 62, led a third expedition in 1956. With a large team of climbers and 20 Sherpas, this well-financed siege-style expedition succeeded, putting Toshio Imanishi and Gyalzen Norbu, who had climbed Makalu the year before with the French, on the summit.

THIRD TIME LUCKY, 1956
Here, during the third, successful, Japanese attempt, Camp II on Manaslu's Northeast Flank is dwarfed by the East Pinnacle. The team used bamboo poles in their tents and experimented with chemically produced oxygen systems.

RED SUN OVER MANASLU
Toshio Imanishi raises the flag of Japan over the 8,163-m (26,782-ft) summit of Manaslu on 9 May 1956, with Sherpa Gyalzen Norbu behind the camera. Back home in Japan, the triumph produced a wave of enthusiasm for mountaineering.

MOUNTAINEERING INNOVATIONS

MAPPING

NAVIGATION IS CRITICAL FOR SAFELY NEGOTIATING the precipitous terrain of a mountain environment. Paradoxically, the earliest maps of mountain regions could only be compiled with any accuracy by exploring the areas themselves; until then, fanciful, molehill-like representations – applied by the cartographer's pen – had to suffice. Over time, map-maker's tools, including the plane table, theodolite, and measuring chain, charted ever-higher elevations, while cartographic techniques such as spot heights, contours, and shading were developed to depict the valleys and folds of mountainous terrain.

MOUNTAINS INTO MOLEHILLS

The earliest depictions of mountains appeared on Roman manuscripts, and were mostly made without any observation or measurement of the actual terrain. The 12th-century *Tabula Rogeriana*, a map of the known world compiled by Arab geographer Muhammad al-Idrisi for King Roger II of Sicily in 1154, depicts mountain ranges – including the Alps and Atlas Mountains – as multicoloured, snake-like chains standing proud of the surrounding landscape. One of the next developments was to depict uplands as elevated areas, rather than as molehills erupting suddenly from the map surface, while the Strasbourg Ptolemy map of 1513 used shading to depict escarpments and valleys.

Until the 18th-century Enlightenment brought new cartographic techniques, advances were restricted to greater detail on hand-drawn maps, such as Hans Conrad Geiger's 1637 maps of the Swiss cantons. The plane table – a rotating alidade mounted on a portable, horizontal tabletop, upon which topographical

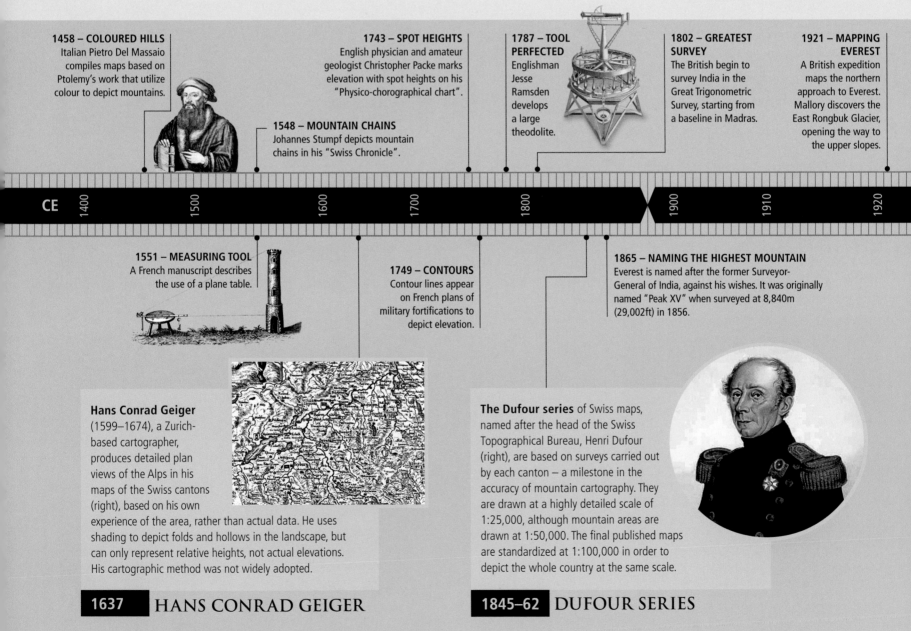

1458 – COLOURED HILLS
Italian Pietro Del Massaio compiles maps based on Ptolemy's work that utilize colour to depict mountains.

1548 – MOUNTAIN CHAINS
Johannes Stumpf depicts mountain chains in his "Swiss Chronicle".

1743 – SPOT HEIGHTS
English physician and amateur geologist Christopher Packe marks elevation with spot heights on his "Physico-chorographical chart".

1787 – TOOL PERFECTED
Englishman Jesse Ramsden develops a large theodolite.

1802 – GREATEST SURVEY
The British begin to survey India in the Great Trigonometric Survey, starting from a baseline in Madras.

1921 – MAPPING EVEREST
A British expedition maps the northern approach to Everest. Mallory discovers the East Rongbuk Glacier, opening the way to the upper slopes.

CE 1400 1500 1600 1700 1800 1900 1910 1920

1551 – MEASURING TOOL
A French manuscript describes the use of a plane table.

1749 – CONTOURS
Contour lines appear on French plans of military fortifications to depict elevation.

1865 – NAMING THE HIGHEST MOUNTAIN
Everest is named after the former Surveyor-General of India, against his wishes. It was originally named "Peak XV" when surveyed at 8,840m (29,002ft) in 1856.

Hans Conrad Geiger
(1599–1674), a Zurich-based cartographer, produces detailed plan views of the Alps in his maps of the Swiss cantons (right), based on his own experience of the area, rather than actual data. He uses shading to depict folds and hollows in the landscape, but can only represent relative heights, not actual elevations. His cartographic method was not widely adopted.

1637 HANS CONRAD GEIGER

The Dufour series of Swiss maps, named after the head of the Swiss Topographical Bureau, Henri Dufour (right), are based on surveys carried out by each canton – a milestone in the accuracy of mountain cartography. They are drawn at a highly detailed scale of 1:25,000, although mountain areas are drawn at 1:50,000. The final published maps are standardized at 1:100,000 in order to depict the whole country at the same scale.

1845–62 DUFOUR SERIES

features could be sighted and marked according to their relative positions – had been in use since the 1500s, while spot heights and contours were introduced in the 18th century. A paradigm shift occurred in 1787 with the perfection of the theodolite, which allowed highly accurate surveying through triangulation.

SURVEYING THE SUMMITS

Serious survey work in mountain regions commenced in the 19th century. The Great Trigonometric Survey began mapping the Indian subcontinent in 1802, systematically laying down a grid of interconnecting triangles that reached the Himalaya in 1847. At the same time, the Dufour series of maps depicted the complex topography of Switzerland at a scale of 1:100,000, mapping the Alps in such detail that the series remained in use until the 1960s.

The theodolite remained the standard surveying tool well into the 20th century, albeit with increasingly accurate instruments. The next sea-change in cartography came with aerial

TABLE-TOP MAPPING

In use since the early 16th century, the plane table was a portable apparatus that enabled surveys to be made in the most inhospitable of environments. Although not as accurate as a theodolite, it could be easily carried over rough terrain and was relatively simple to use. The three telescopic legs could be adjusted separately to set the plane table on the horizontal, before landmarks were sighted through the alidade and marked on a sheet of paper. Useful for initial reconnaissance prior to a theodolite survey, as well as filling in detail on the ground, the advent of aerial photography has made it superfluous.

AS WELL AS IN THE HIMALAYA, PLANE TABLES WERE USED TO MAP ELEVATIONS IN ANTARCTICA

photography in the 1940s and satellite-based remote imaging from the 1950s. Over subsequent decades mapping data was gradually computerized, while digital imaging is now common practice. As 21st-century mountaineers look to their next expedition, satellite images and maps have never been more accessible, with services including Google Maps giving ready access to remote summits at the click of a mouse or the tap of a mobile phone.

1927 – RELIEF SHADING
Swiss cartographer Eduard Imhof begins work on the Swiss school atlas series, setting a new standard in map-making. He uses relief shading and terrain modelling to accurately depict the Alpine terrain.

1940 – AERIAL MAPPING
First used in World War I, aerial photography is used extensively in World War II for military mapping.

1990s – DIGITAL MAPS
Based on data from remote-sensing, such as satellite-based radar, high-quality digital maps are developed.

2011 – HIGH-RESOLUTION
The Indian Cartosat-3 satellite raises standards in remote sensing, with a photographic capture range of 16km (10 miles) and a resolution of up to 30cm (12in).

1930 | 1940 | 1950 | 1960 | 1970 | 1980 | 1990 | 2000

1935 – SURVEYING EVEREST
Eric Shipton leads an expedition with Bill Tilman (see pp.244–47) to survey the Western Ridge of Everest.

1959 – ORBITAL IMAGES
NASA's Explorer 6 satellite captures the first images of Earth from space.

1980s – EVEREST BY AIR
US cartographer Bradford Washburn uses aerial photography to compile a topographical map of Everest.

Everest exploration nears culmination when Bill Tilman explores the southern approaches, adding to the cartographic knowledge of the peak. He reports that a route via the South Col might be feasible. In 1951, Eric Shipton leads an expedition that negotiates the Khumbu Icefall, reaches the Western Cwm and sees a route to the South Col. The Swiss reach the Col in 1952 and in 1953 Edmund Hillary and Tenzing Norgay (see pp.264–67) follow this route to the summit.

1950 A ROUTE TO EVEREST

Google Earth is launched onto an unsuspecting world, surprising computer-users everywhere with the ready availability of digital imagery. Although image resolution varies and is not sufficient to allow the plotting of exact climbing routes, it is the first widely available product to combine satellite imagery with computerized terrain models, enabling mountaineers to plan trips with little more than a computer and internet connection.

2005 GOOGLE EARTH

SLAYING
THE GIANTS

SLAYING THE GIANTS

1900   1920   1930

◄ 1904
Imperial adventurer **Francis Younghusband** enters Tibet leading a British invasion aimed at securing hegemony over the Dalai Lama (see pp.222–23).

▼ 1907
British mountaineer **Tom Longstaff** leads the Alpine Club's 50th anniversary expedition to the Garhwal, which includes future Everest leader **Charles Bruce**; oxygen is tested for the first time.

1913
Clandestine approaches to Everest are made by Sherpas working for Scottish pioneer altitude physiologist **Alexander Kellas** (see pp.194–95).

▲ 1921
The **British Everest reconnaissance expedition** produces detailed new mapping of the Everest region; Alexander Kellas dies there (see pp.220–21).

▼ 1922
Three British climbers, including **George Mallory** and **Howard Somervell** (one of his sketches, below), are caught in an avalanche below Everest's North Col (see pp.224–25).

1931
German **climber Paul Bauer** leads a second failed attempt on Kangchenjunga, still considered an outstanding effort of Himalayan climbing (see pp.234–35).

1931
An expedition led by **Frank Smythe** (see p.247) reaches the summit of Kamet, at 7,756m (25,443ft) the highest summit yet reached.

► 1933
British climber **Eric Shipton** joins Hugh Ruttledge's Everest trip. The expedition reached higher than 8,500m (28,000ft).

1919
British geologist **Noel Odell** gives a paper to the RGS on the "Eastern Approaches to Everest", launching public interest in the mountain (see pp.220–21).

▼ 1924
Edward Norton and **Howard Somervell** reach an altitude of 8,570m (28,100ft) approaching the summit of Everest (see pp.224–25).

▲ 1933
British mountaineers **Colin Kirkus** and **Charles Warren** make the first ascent of Bhagirathi III (above, right) in the Garhwal in lightweight style.

1934
German alpinists **Willy Merkl** and **Willo Welzenbach** perish in their disastrous attempt on Nanga Parbat (see pp.236–37).

► 1924
Three days later, **George Mallory** (right) and **Andrew Irvine** mount a second summit bid and are last seen high on the mountain by Noel Odell (see pp.228–31).

► 1934
British climbers **Eric Shipton** and **Bill Tilman** (back row) solve the riddle of the Rishi Gorge and find a route into Nanda Devi Sanctuary (see pp.244–47).

◄ PP.216–17 Members of the 1953 Mount Everest Expedition use a light metal ladder to cross a large crevasse at the entrance to the Western Cwm

As early himalayan mountaineers soon found, climbing peaks higher than 8,000m (26,247ft) posed challenges they barely comprehended. A F Mummery's idealistic approach on Nanga Parbat ended in disaster in 1895. Attempts on K2 came up a long way short. Would humans even be able to breathe at such altitudes? In 1912, Alexander Kellas arrived in Sikkim. The year

before he'd climbed Pauhunri, the fourth mountain higher than 7,000m (23,000ft) to be climbed. Kellas had in mind an attempt on Kangchenjunga, but was also thinking about how to approach Everest. Having crossed the 7,000-m threshold, there was no reason not to be optimistic. However, another four decades were to pass before anyone reached the summit of one of the elusive "8,000er" peaks.

1935

◢ 1935
Shipton leads a reconnaissance of Everest with Tilman, one of the great exploratory trips in Himalayan history (see pp.244–47).

▼ 1936
Paul Bauer leads a successful German expedition to Siniolchu in preparation for a renewed assault on Nanga Parbat (see pp.234–35).

1936
A joint American and British team organized by **Charles Houston** climb Nanda Devi with a lightweight team (see pp.248–49).

1938
Paul Bauer leads another German attempt on Nanga Parbat (see pp.234–35).

1938
British climbers **Jock Harrison** and **Robin Hodgkin** come close to the summit of Masherbrum in the Karakoram; bad weather stops them, but no lives are lost.

▼ 1938
US mountaineer **Charles Houston** (see pp.248–49) leads the first of two pre-war US attempts on K2, reaching 8,000m (26,247ft).

1939
Influential Swiss climber **André Roch** mounts a successful expedition to Dunagiri.

1939
German-born climber **Fritz Wiessner** comes close to the summit of K2 on a tragic expedition in which team-member Dudley Wolfe and three Sherpas die (see pp.250–51).

1950

▶ 1950
French alpinists **Maurice Herzog** and **Louis Lachenal** reach the summit of Annapurna on their first attempt, the first "8,000er" to be climbed (see pp.256–57).

◀ 1951
British reconnaissance led by Eric Shipton finds a route into **Everest's Western Cwm** (see pp.244–47). Seen here is an alleged Yeti footprint photographed on the journey.

1953
Charles Houston leads his second expedition to K2, but bad weather ends their summit chances (see pp.248–49).

◢ 1953
After 31 years of attempts, Kiwi climber **Edmund Hillary** and Sherpa **Tenzing Norgay** (above) make the first ascent of Everest (see pp.264–67).

1953
Austrian alpinist **Hermann Buhl** makes a bold solo dash to the summit of Nanga Parbat, the first ascent of the mountain (see pp.258–59).

1954
Lino Lacedelli and **Achille Compagnoni** make the first ascent of K2 as members of a well-organized but divided Italian expedition (see pp.270–71).

1955

▼ 1955
British mountaineers **George Band** and **Joe Brown** reach the summit of Kangchenjunga, the world's third highest mountain (see pp.272–73).

▶ 1955
French alpinists **Jean Couzy** (right) and **Lionel Terray** make first ascent of Makalu after a brilliant 1954 reconnaissance (see pp.276–77).

▼ 1958
A strong Italian team led by Riccardo Cassin (see pp.292–93), climbs Gasherbrum IV (Cassin's axe, below).

1963
US mountaineers **Willi Unsoeld** and **Tom Hornbein** climb the West Ridge of Everest in the first traverse of an "8,000er" peak (see pp.278–81).

THE GREATEST SHOW ON EARTH

CLIMBING THE WORLD'S VERY HIGHEST MOUNTAINS BEGAN WITH TENTATIVE ATTEMPTS IN THE LATE 19TH CENTURY. IN THE 1920s, THE ADVENTURE BEGAN IN EARNEST. IT BECAME AN EPIC OF DISCOVERY, ENDURANCE, AND LOSS THAT CAUGHT THE PUBLIC IMAGINATION.

EVEREST RECONNAISSANCE
John Noel travelled to Tibet in disguise in 1913. He photographed the villages around the approaches to Mount Everest, and used these images for his later lecture at the RGS.

On 10 March 1919, less than six months after the end of World War I, a young army officer in the UK's Machine Gun Corps, Captain John Baptist Lucius Noel (see p222), read a paper to the Royal Geographical Society entitled "A Journey to Tashirak in Southern Tibet, and the Eastern Approaches to Everest".

There had already been expeditions to other "8000er" peaks, including K2 and Kangchenjunga, as well as Mummery's attempt on Nanga Parbat (see pp.168–71). But Noel's lecture served as a catalyst for public interest in mounting an expedition to the highest mountain of all – Everest.

Climbing Everest had been much discussed before World War I, and the idea had the backing of Lord Curzon, the Viceroy of India. Plans were laid for an expedition in 1907, the 50th anniversary of the Alpine Club. But politics intervened, and the Secretary of State for India, John Morley, banned the venture on the grounds that it might upset Russian interests in Asia.

The dream, however, didn't die. General Cecil Godfrey Rawling had spent months in Tibet as a surveyor, including a period with Francis Younghusband's force of 1904 (see pp.222–23). He drew up a plan for an initial reconnaissance to determine the route, and then a full expedition to climb the mountain. Rawling's plan, adopted by the RGS, would form the basis of post-war attempts, but Rawling himself died in battle during the war.

A month after the Armistice was signed, the RGS wrote to the Secretary of State for India, asking for permission to mount an expedition, but after three months they had heard nothing.

Noel's lecture was a way to

GIFT OF A BUDDHA
Younghusband was given this figurine in Tibet in 1904. His own intentions towards his hosts were less generous.

EVEREST, 1924
Noel took this picture of porters' dependants registering with their thumbprints prior to George Mallory's 1924 attempt. Mallory ascended into the clouds and vanished.

HIMALAYA GESTURE
Paul Bauer's 1937 expedition to Siniolchu appended a Union Jack to its summit pennant as a courtesy to the host country. The territory was part of British-controlled India at the time.

SETTING THE SCENE

- In 1885, English alpinist Clinton Dent (see pp.164–65) **writes about** the possibility of **climbing Mount Everest**: "I believe most firmly that it is **humanly possible to do so**: and, further, I feel sure that even in our own time, perhaps, the truth of these views will receive material corroboration."

- After World War I, momentum **builds for the first expedition to Everest**. Francis Younghusband is in charge of the British mission to Lhasa, thus securing British access to Everest from the north.

- Two full expeditions and a reconnaissance to Everest in the 1920s fail to climb the mountain and **result in the deaths** of seven porters and Mallory and Irvine.

- Germany and Austria come to the fore and mount their first Himalayan expeditions, first to Kangchenjunga and then to Nanga Parbat, **with disastrous consequences** on the latter.

reinvigorate the issue. In the audience were many of those who would go on to direct the campaign on Everest, including Alexander Kellas (see pp.194–95), Douglas Freshfield (see pp.186–89), and Francis Younghusband.

Permission for Everest was finally granted in early 1921. Choosing the first team to attempt the mountain fell to the Survey of India, which provided the surveyors: Canadian-born E Oliver Wheeler, and Henry Morshead, described by the Everest climber Edward Norton as the hardest man he ever met – "a heartbreaking man to live with." Wheeler was an expert in the new technique of photo-surveying and a mountaineer in his own right, having climbed with Canadian pioneers such as Tom Longstaff and Conrad Kain (see

> **Early attempts at mounting expeditions to Everest were thwarted by the difficulty of gaining access to the peak. Tibet and Nepal were closed to outsiders and only through diplomacy was permission finally secured for a British reconnaissance in 1921.**

pp.204–05). Harold Raeburn was in charge of the climbers. Born in the month Whymper climbed the Matterhorn, Raeburn had been an outstanding climber but was now too old and had become a liability. The other choices were hardly more propitious: Kellas had much experience but was in poor health and died on the expedition. The one bright star was George Mallory (see pp.228–31), young enough to prosper at altitude but old enough to have had experience. Everest would become his obsession – and his grave.

With access to Everest the monopoly of the British, other nations looked to those other "8000ers" to which

they could gain access. Nepal was closed to foreigners, so attention focused first on Kangchenjunga, with Paul Bauer leading two expeditions in 1929 and 1931 (see pp.234–35), while Günther Dhyrenfurth led a team in 1930. Then German and Austrian interest switched to Nanga Parbat, their "mountain of destiny", where the best climbers of the era perished in two disastrous attempts. American climbers chose K2, coming close to success in 1939.

BASE CAMP CONFIDENCE
The large 1922 Everest expedition team poses for a photograph. Their attempt set a new altitude record (exceeded in 1924) but failed to reach the summit after seven porters were swept to their deaths.

FRANCIS YOUNGHUSBAND

THE MAN BEHIND THE FIRST EVEREST EXPEDITION

ENGLAND   1863–1942

PART MYSTIC, PART EMPIRE-BUILDER, Francis Younghusband was the ideal patron for the quixotic project of climbing Everest. Although he became famous as an explorer and soldier, and not as a mountaineer, as president of the Royal Geographical Society (RGS) he provided influence and backing to push the idea of an Everest expedition with the Indian government. He also chaired the Mount Everest Committee, linking senior figures in the RGS and the Alpine Club, not always harmoniously.

JOHN NOEL
ENGLAND   1890–1989

The climber and film-maker John Noel grew up in Switzerland, where he developed a passion for mountains.
After military training at Sandhurst, Noel was commissioned into the East Yorkshire Regiment. While serving in India, he slipped across the border from Sikkim into Tibet, aiming "to seek out the passes that led to Everest and if possible to come to close quarters with the mountain." It was his lecture in 1919 to the RGS on this journey that was the catalyst for renewed attempts for a full expedition to Everest. He joined the 1922 and 1924 teams as photographer and film-maker. Noel was a Catholic and, having had a blessing from the pope, was dubbed by Charles G Bruce "St Noel of the Cameras". He brought lamas from Tibet to London to perform dances while his film of the 1924 Everest expedition was shown.

The polo ground at Chitral in the Hindu Kush still feels like a wild place, but it was doubly so in early 1893, soon after the British extended their influence there. Walking around the dusty field, Charles G Bruce, then a lieutenant in the Gurkhas and fresh from his expedition to the Karakoram with Martin Conway (see pp.184–85), was explaining his idea for climbing Everest to Francis Younghusband.

Younghusband was in Chitral as second-in-command on a mission to place a new ruler on the state's throne. This was proving more peaceful than anticipated and time hung heavily on the 29-year-old soldier, who was obsessed by dreams of travel in Tibet and feared that his glamorous career was stalling. Relief came on odd days off, when he would climb in the Hindu Raj range with Bruce. Their friendship would have dramatic results.

EPIC ADVENTURE

Younghusband was born at the hill station of Murree in what is now Pakistan, but grew up in England, and was commissioned into the British Army in 1882. Determinedly ambitious, at the age of 23 he made a huge journey through China, starting in Beijing and crossing the Gobi Desert before finding a route into India via the Muztagh Pass.

Descending the glacier on the other side of the pass was a challenging piece of climbing, achieved without any specialist equipment. Younghusband and his companions improvised a rope – tying together turbans, pony ropes, and cummerbunds – and lowered the lightest porter down the steep face of the ice. He hacked steps into the ice with an axe as he went, for the others to use. It took six hours for the party to descend the slope and Younghusband recalled that "it seemed utterly impossible that any man could have come down such a place." Two days later, having passed the Baltoro Glacier, he was in the Balti village of Askole.

CO-OPERATION GUARANTEED
This is the passport issued by the Tibetan government for the 1921 Everest party to have assistance given to them by its people.

Crossing the Muztagh Pass made Younghusband famous, and he must have influenced Martin Conway's own ambitions in the Karakoram. His improvised climbing style became almost a calling card among the elite at the Alpine Club. Men like Bruce, who knew the region well and shared Younghusband's imperialist ideals, admired his bravado. Still only 24, Younghusband lectured to the RGS on his eventful journey.

EDGING CLOSER TO THE GOAL

Ten years after Chitral, and with the idea of climbing Everest no nearer realization, Younghusband found himself entering Tibet, leading what was in essence an invasion aimed at securing British hegemony over the Dalai Lama. Commanding with him was the political officer

IMPERIAL TASK FORCE IN TIBET
Younghusband (centre, with his officers) entered Lhasa on 2 August 1904 after massacring Tibetan troops. A month later he signed an agreement that gave the British, and eventually others, access to Tibet.

A LIFE'S WORK

- His **epic crossing of the Muztagh Pass** is widely admired. The British soldier and geographer Kenneth Mason calls him "the father of Karakoram exploration"

- Stationed in Chitral, he meets Charles G Bruce, who explains his **idea of exploring the Everest region** from Tibet

- Leads a military invasion that allows the **British access to Everest**

- As president of the RGS, helps secure permission for the **first Everest expedition**

of Sikkim, who took a photograph of Everest from the fortress town of Kampa Dzong. Younghusband could see the summit, almost 160km (100 miles) away, "poised high in heaven as the spotless pinnacle of the world".

Leaving aside the future impact on Tibetan independence, Younghusband's expedition, supported by his mentor Lord Curzon, Viceroy of India, ultimately gave the British exclusive access to the northern reaches of Everest between World Wars I and II. Withdrawing from Lhasa, two of Younghusband's officers diverted to explore the approach to Everest and believed the North Ridge was feasible. Curzon himself raised the possibility of climbing the mountain, but the Secretary of State for India thwarted plans for an expedition in 1907.

After World War I, and now in his mid 50s, Younghusband became president of the RGS, "determined to make this Everest venture the main feature" of his time in office. He was also by this stage deep into the early type of new age spiritualism that would dominate his later years. His reasons for climbing, articulated in his book

CUTTING-EDGE CARTOGRAPHY
The 1921 expedition included a survey team trained in the latest photo-mapping techniques from Canada. This map was compiled from their data.

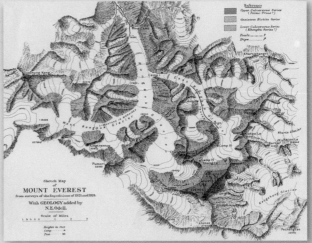

The Epic of Mount Everest, reflect this: "The struggle with Everest is all part and parcel of the perpetual struggle of spirit to establish its supremacy over matter. Man, the spiritual, means to make himself supreme over even the mightiest of what is material."

PASSPORT TO EVEREST

Soon after taking up his role with the RGS, Younghusband led a delegation to the India Office comprising his old friend Bruce, Percy Farrar from the Alpine Club, and Charles Howard-Bury, who led the intricate diplomatic campaign to get permission from Lhasa. When the expedition's passport arrived in late 1920, Younghusband's vision became reality. A few weeks later, he met George Mallory (see pp.228–31) to

persuade him to join the first Everest adventure. "I sometimes think of this expedition," Mallory wrote later from the mountain, "as a fraud from beginning to end, invented by the wild enthusiasm of one man, Younghusband; puffed up by the would-be wisdom of certain pundits in the Alpine Club; and imposed upon the youthful ardour of your humble servant."

SOMERVELL AND NORTON

EVEREST'S EARLY HEROES

ENGLAND   1890–1975; 1884–1954

HOWARD SOMERVELL   EDWARD NORTON

THE ONGOING FASCINATION with the fate of George Mallory has resulted in the other climbers of the early Everest expeditions being overlooked. But, in the absence of concrete proof that Mallory and Irvine reached the summit in 1924, it was Edward Norton who created the new altitude record on the peak. He and partner Howard Somervell faced not only the challenge of the climb, but the struggle to survive at extreme high altitude.

INTO THE THIN AIR
Unable to continue on their summit bid, Somervell took this photograph of Norton as he headed off alone, without oxygen, to his high point of 8,573m (28,126ft). This was an altitude record not equalled until 1952.

On 2 June 1924, Edward Norton, Howard Somervell, and four Sherpas reached Camp V on the North Ridge of Everest – at 7,711m (25,300ft). Although not prone to whining, Norton wrote, "On arrival one crawls into the tent, so completely exhausted that for perhaps three-quarters of an hour one just lies in a sleeping-bag and rests … I know nothing – not even the exertion of steep climbing at these heights – which is so utterly exhausting or which calls for more determination than this hateful duty of high-altitude cooking."

EVEREST PIONEERS

Edward Norton was a 40-year-old decorated artillery officer on his second trip to Everest – he had been a member of the 1922 team, too – and,

with Charles G Bruce incapacitated by malaria, the expedition's leader. Norton's grandfather was Alfred Wills (see pp.118–19), whose ascent of the Wetterhorn marked the start of alpinism's Golden Age, but his own mountaineering experience was slight. Yet ultimately, it was his endurance and ability to bear suffering that counted for more than his technical skill.

Howard Somervell was a burly, prodigiously gifted and compassionate man with a strong Christian faith and a double first in natural sciences from Cambridge University. Born in England's Lake District to a family who owned a shoe-manufacturing business, he joined the Fell and Rock Climbing Club at the age of 18 and by the time he was chosen for the 1922 Everest expedition, he was a capable alpinist.

In the summer season of 1923, Somervell climbed 32 peaks, becoming renowned for his extraordinary stamina. He had served in the Royal Army Medical Corps during World War I, and his experiences at the Somme in 1916, where he spoke to men dying of their injuries outside the tent where he was working, converted him to pacifism. After the 1922

EXPEDITION ARTIST
Somervell was a talented artist and whiled away his free time on expeditions by painting pastels of the scenery. This one depicts the monsoon over Sikkim.

expedition he travelled in India, and was shocked by the poverty he witnessed there. Soon after the 1924 attempt he decided to become a medical missionary, giving up his promising career in London to work in a village in southern India.

CLOSE TO THE SUMMIT

The British party reached Base Camp at the end of April, but in mid May climbing was hampered by snows and Norton feared an early monsoon. The tough conditions demoralized the Sherpas, and as a consequence the team's supply chain had broken down by the end of the month.

So Norton decided to go for broke – he ditched the oxygen equipment and used those Sherpas still prepared to climb high to get tents placed at Camps V and VI. On 3 June, he and Somervell left Camp V with three Sherpas from the previous day who were fit to continue. By 1.30pm, it was clear that at least one of the Sherpas could go no further and with

Somervell experiencing pain from a raw throat, the decision to abort the climbing for the day was made for them. They had reached Camp VI, at 8,168m (26,800ft).

Norton and Somervell left for the summit at 6.40am the next morning. They reached the Yellow Band after an hour's effort but progress was still agonisingly slow. Both were suffering, Somervell with his throat, and Norton from double vision, which required him to remove his snow goggles. Finally, Somervell could move no further; his throat was interfering with his breathing. In fact, the mucous membrane of his oesophagus had become frostbitten, and he would cough it up later on the descent, which possibly saved his life.

Norton went on, leaving Somervell at the top of the Yellow Band, and following its rim into the Great Couloir (now called the Norton Couloir). The route was perilous – across downward-facing tiles of rock that Norton found precarious in his nailed boots and with no rope. "I had perhaps 200 feet more of this nasty going to surmount before I emerged onto the North Face of the final pyramid and, I believe, safety … It was now 1pm and a brief calculation showed that I had no chance of climbing the remaining 800 or 900 feet if I was to return in safety."

Turning around, both men found that, without the prospect of the summit, they were suddenly exhausted. The descent was an ordeal.

That night, back at Camp IV with Mallory and Noel Odell (see pp.228–31), Norton suffered appalling pain from snow blindness caused by the loss of his goggles. Somervell, despite coughing up a chunk of his throat, was strong enough to descend the next day. Three days later Mallory and Irvine left Camp VI for the summit. Norton wrote later to expedition film-maker John Noel: "There is no doubt Mallory knows he is leading a forlorn hope."

FIRST EVEREST DEATHS

Climbing up to the North Col on 7 June 1922 for a third attempt on the summit, three climbers, including Mallory and Somervell, and 14 porters were caught in an avalanche. The party were in four teams, but the last two, with nine men, were nowhere to be seen. They had been swept over an ice cliff and into a crevasse. Two porters were dug out alive, but seven died. The accident had a huge impact on the Tibetans living in the Everest region.

NORTON (LEFT) AND SOMERVELL, WITH SHERPAS. LIFE AS A PORTER WAS HARD AND DANGEROUS.

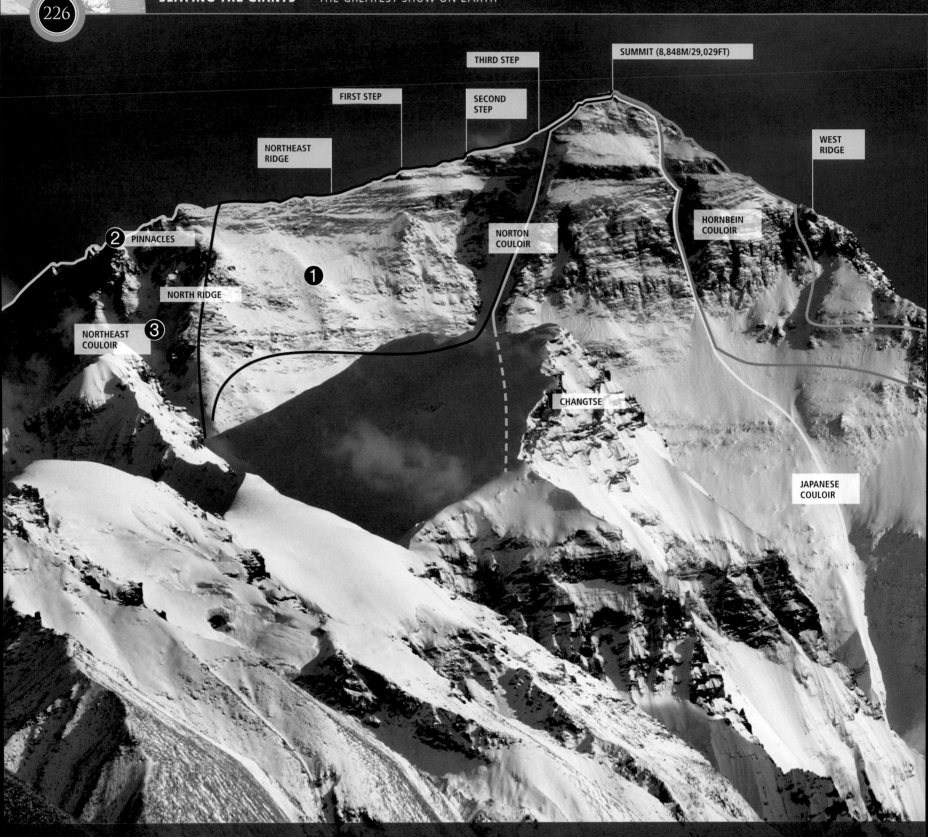

SUMMIT (8,848M/29,029FT)

THIRD STEP

FIRST STEP

SECOND STEP

NORTHEAST RIDGE

WEST RIDGE

HORNBEIN COULOIR

NORTON COULOIR

② PINNACLES

❶

NORTH RIDGE

NORTHEAST COULOIR ③

CHANGTSE

JAPANESE COULOIR

MOUNTAIN FEATURES

(A) **The summit of Everest** can be crowded: 75 people reached the top on 23 May 2008, the most in a single day, after queues on the Hillary Step.

(B) **Descending the Khumbu Icefall** is one of the deadliest parts of Everest. Collapsing seracs are a danger, particularly to Sherpas ferrying loads.

(C) **The East Face** of Everest, photographed in 2009 by Leo Dickinson as part of the first team to fly over Everest in a hot-air balloon.

(A)

(B)

(C)

CLIMBING ROUTES

There are 15 significant routes on Everest, but most climbers reach the summit via just two of them: the South Col/South Ridge route, and the North Col/Northeast Ridge. The peak's three immense faces have their own characteristics. The East Face is snowier and prone to avalanche, the Southwest Face is steep and technically difficult, while the broad sweep of the North Face is capped by a final pyramid.

NORTH FACE

NORTH RIDGE
(F Wang, Gonbu, Y Chu, 1960) Climbed in controversial circumstances by a joint Chinese and Tibetan team, completing the British pre-war route.

❶ **George Mallory's body** was discovered here in 1999.

NORTHEAST RIDGE
(K Furano, S Imoto, P Kami, D Tshering, L Nuru, 1995) The complete Northeast Ridge, through the fearsome Pinnacles, was overcome by a Japanese siege-style expedition. Russell Brice and Harry Taylor climbed the Pinnacles in 1982 but descended before the summit.

❷ **British climbers** Joe Tasker and Peter Boardman disappeared on the Pinnacles in 1982.

MESSNER VARIANT
(R Messner, 1980) Finding snow conditions too awkward, Messner – climbing solo and without oxygen – traversed the North Face and climbed the Norton Couloir to the summit.

WHITE LIMBO
(T Macartney-Snape, G Mortimer, 1984) The Australian pair climbed the length of the Norton Couloir to the summit – the second team after Messner to do a new route without bottled oxygen.

JAPANESE COULOIR
(T Shigehiro, T Ozaki, 1980) This Japanese direct start to the Hornbein Couloir links up with the West Ridge.

❸ **North/Northeast Couloir** Sometimes called the Zhakarov Couloir, it was climbed by a Russian team in 1995.

WEST RIDGE
(W Unsoeld, T Hornbein, 1963) The upper portion of the West Ridge, climbed by the American pair.

WEST RIDGE DIRECT
(J Zaplotnik, A Stremfelj, 1979) Climbed by a Yugoslav team, the direct finish to the West Ridge was the hardest climb made on Everest at the time.

(Dashed line means route hidden from view)

MOUNT EVEREST

IN 1849, BRITISH SURVEYOR JAMES NICOLSON trained a theodolite on a distant mountain known simply as "b" – later designated "XV". With the calculations completed in 1856, the Surveyor-General Andrew Waugh announced that Peak XV was "most probably the highest in the world". Despite having several local names, notably Chomolungma, Waugh ensured that his new discovery would be named after his illustrious predecessor, Sir George Everest.

It would take almost a century before the newly discovered summit of the world was finally reached. By then, Everest had become a metaphor for human aspiration and struggle, its legendary status secured by the daring exploits of men such as George Mallory and Andrew Irvine (see pp.228–31), who perished on the upper slopes of the Northeast Ridge in 1924.

Even after the success of Edmund Hillary and Tenzing Norgay in 1953 (see pp.264–67), the mountain continued to inspire stunning achievements, such as the US ascent of the West Ridge and traverse of

the peak in 1963 (see pp.278–81). In the 1970s, there was exciting progress, with the ascent of the Southwest Face in 1975 by Chris Bonington's British team (see pp.300–01), the first ascent without bottled oxygen by Reinhold Messner and Peter Habeler in 1978 (see pp.308–11), and the direct ascent of the West Ridge by a Yugoslav team, with Andrej Stremfelj and Nejc Zaplotnik summitting first (see pp.332–33). Most impressive of all, perhaps, was Messner's solo ascent in 1980. While it is now possible to climb Everest with a guided group, there is still scope for new adventures.

IN PROFILE

Name: Everest – named in 1865 after Sir George Everest – supplanted the Tibetan *Chomolungma*, commonly mistranslated as "Goddess Mother of the Earth", but possibly a reference to a local, minor goddess Miyolangsangma, said to reside on Everest. A more modern Nepali name also exists: *Sagarmatha*, meaning "Brow of the Sky"

Location: Solukhumbu District, Nepal, and Tingri Country, Tibet Autonomous Region

Range: Mahalangur Himal, Himalaya

Height: 8,848m (29,029ft) China/Nepal; 8,850m (29,035ft) National Geographic Society

First ascent: Edmund Hillary and Tenzing Norgay, 1953

First female ascent: Junko Tabei, 1975

First winter ascent: Leszek Cichy and Krzysztof Wielicki, 1980

First solo ascent: Reinhold Messner, 1980

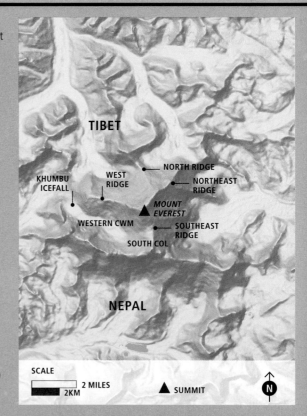

GEORGE MALLORY

THE QUINTESSENTIAL MOUNTAINEER

ENGLAND   1886–1924

IN 1999, ON A SPECIALLY COMMISSIONED expedition, US climber Conrad Anker found the remarkably well-preserved body of George Mallory high on the windswept upper slopes of Everest's North Face. The last sighting of Mallory and his climbing partner Andrew Irvine heading for the summit, at once tantalizing and hopeful, and their mysterious disappearance, captured the public's imagination. Even today, historians still sift the evidence for the proof that these men were in fact the first to conquer Everest.

George Mallory was an attractive figure, a man who articulated better than anyone the romance of climbing Everest. His quiet charisma and athletic ability combined to make him the ultimate mountaineer – someone who is forever climbing towards the next summit. In a 1917 essay about his ascent in 1911 of the Frontier Ridge on Mont Maudit on the Franco-Italian border, he wrote: "One must conquer, achieve, get to the top; one must know the end to be convinced that one can win in the end – to know there's no dream that mustn't be dared ... Is this the summit, crowning the day? How cool and how quiet! We're not exultant; but delighted, joyful; soberly astonished ... Have we vanquished an enemy? None but ourselves."

Born in Cheshire, in northwest England, Mallory's father was the local rector, and as a boy, George's first climbing ground was the roof of his father's church. At 13, he won a

mathematics scholarship to Winchester College, a top public school, where he also excelled as a gymnast. In his final year there he was introduced to climbing by a master, R L G Irving, a member of the Alpine Club. Irving took a small group of pupils to the Alps each season and invited Mallory to join a trip in the summer of 1905, where he developed an aptitude for the sport.

That autumn Mallory entered Cambridge University to study history. His natural grace and charm, and his physical beauty, brought him into the university's inner circles, and he formed close friendships with some of the most celebrated literary and artistic figures of the day. He also became quite a radical figure, interested in socialism, and supporting women's suffrage.

SNOW GOGGLES
The discovery of these in Mallory's pocket, rather than on his face, led to a theory that he died at night, *after* reaching the summit.

NATURAL TALENT

One of Mallory's associates at Cambridge, Charles Sayle, was a founding member of the Climbers' Club, and encouraged him to join a rock-climbing trip to North Wales. Mallory became an enthusiast, adding several new climbs at a standard of approximately "Very Severe" in Britain, or 5.7 in the US – roughly the same grade as the infamous Second Step on Everest's Northeast Ridge, except at sea level. Sayle also introduced Mallory to Geoffrey Winthrop Young, the star of Edwardian alpinism, who became his mentor.

Young invited Mallory to one of his famous climbing meets at Pen-y-Pass Inn at the top of the Lanberis Pass in Snowdonia, Wales, and later proposed him for the Climbers' Club. In the summer of 1909, the pair made significant ascents in the Alps, Young admiring Mallory's natural grace as a climber: "He swung up rock with a long thigh, a lifted knee, and a ripple of irresistible movement". However, he also said that of the climbers he had known from that period, Mallory had the greatest unfulfilled

ONE MUST CONQUER, ACHIEVE, GET TO THE TOP; ONE MUST KNOW THE END "

GEORGE MALLORY, ON CLIMBING MONT MAUDIT

HIGHER AND FASTER
The 1922 Everest expedition pioneered the use of bottled oxygen. Here, Mallory (left) and Norton are pictured wearing their oxygen masks as they, together with Somervell, who took this photograph, set a new altitude record. The record lasted just five days before it was broken by Finch and Bruce on the same expedition.

potential. The list of great climbs never materialized. There was something diffident about Mallory. He drifted into things, uncertain about what course his life should take. At first, he was even unsure whether to go to Everest.

GETTING THE BUG
Before World War I, Mallory had taught at Charterhouse, one of England's historic public schools, and married Ruth Turner, with whom he had three children. He had returned to the school in 1919 and was happy to be home. In the meantime, however, Young was championing him at the Alpine Club for a mooted expedition

to Everest. Young had lost a leg during the war, and while he continued to climb, going to Everest was out of the question. So he turned to his protégé, persuading Mallory that the kudos attached to conquering Everest would help him in whatever future career he chose. Mallory resigned from his teaching job.

Given how little was known about the northern approaches to Everest, the 1921 reconnaissance expedition was a success. It was funded by the Mount Everest Committee, newly formed jointly by the Alpine Club and the Royal Geographical Society, and explored and surveyed from the north and east, crossing important cols, and formulating a way to climb the mountain. Although he failed to locate the foot of the East Rongbuk Glacier, Mallory led a team across the Lhakpa La to reach the head of the glacier, then climbed up to the North Col. The team spent months at altitude, and gained valuable experience and knowledge about the

weather on the mountain. Most important of all, Mallory had found his purpose in life. "This is a thrilling business altogether," he wrote to his wife. "I can't tell you how it possesses me."

OXYGEN: FOR AND AGAINST
In 1922, Mallory returned to Everest as part of a much stronger mountaineering expedition using the experimental oxygen equipment developed by Australian George Finch, a good climber and a brilliant engineer and innovator. The first attempt on 22 May was made without the use of what the Sherpas called "English air". Mallory, Howard Somervell, and Edward Norton (see pp.224–25) reached 8,225m (26,985ft). They were still some way from the summit, but they had reached higher than any human before them. On 27 May, Finch and Geoffrey Bruce, using rudimentary oxygen equipment, went higher, climbing faster too.

It was clear that bottled oxygen could make all the difference, and Finch railed against those who thought it unsporting. A third attempt was mounted as the monsoon arrived, but it ended in tragedy. The team badly misread conditions, not realizing how dangerous fresh snow on the slopes up to the North Col could be. An avalanche swept down, taking with it nine Sherpas and Tibetans. Mallory, too, was dragged down but managed to surface and help in the frantic effort to dig out the porters. Two were rescued, but the others were lost.

LOST ON EVEREST
This is the last image of Mallory (left) and Irvine, taken by Noel Odell at Camp IV on the North Col at 7,070m (23,195ft) three days before they disappeared into the clouds. Only Mallory's body has been found, and he appears to have died in a fall. Recent research has concluded that they probably both died during a storm as they made their way up towards the summit.

DID THEY REACH THE TOP?

The discovery of Mallory's body in 1999 did not solve the riddle of whether he and Irvine reached the summit. Only Irvine carried a camera, and his body has not been found, so there is no conclusive evidence. However, it is almost impossible that the pair would have had enough oxygen to reach the summit. It is also improbable, though not impossible, that they could have climbed the Second Step.

GEORGE MALLORY'S BOOT, RECOVERED FROM THE SLOPES OF MOUNT EVEREST – DID IT SET FOOT ON THE SUMMIT?

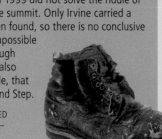

Back home, the Mount Everest Committee paused for thought before deciding to mount another attempt in 1924. Mallory was sent to the US on a lecture tour to raise funds. It was during this trip that he is said to have offered his famous explanation for the purpose of climbing Everest: "Because it's there."

When the time came, Mallory initially refused to join the 1924 expedition because Finch had been forced off the team – it was felt the attempt should be an all-British one. However, the lure of Everest was too strong. Mallory couldn't just step aside.

VANISHING HOPES
The team set out in June 1924, and despite severe setbacks, they managed to place a high camp at 8,170m (26,804ft). Two pushes were made, neither of which made the summit, but Norton and Somervell reached a new record height. For his last climb, Mallory chose Andrew Irvine as his climbing partner. They left Camp VI on 8 June, Mallory having sent down a note with the Sherpas for Noel Odell. "Perfect weather for the job," it concluded.

Odell was at Camp V, and the next day he set out with supplies for Camp VI. He was on superb form, and at about 8,000m (26,247ft), he scrambled up a little outcrop to test himself. Suddenly, the thin mist obscuring the upper part of the mountain cleared and he could see Mallory and Irvine approaching a rock step on the upper ridge. It was 12.50pm and Odell was surprised they weren't higher. He was never sure exactly which rock step they were climbing, but as he watched, the first figure reached its top and the second followed. "Then the whole fascinating vision vanished, enveloped in cloud once more," he said. It was the last time anyone saw Mallory and Irvine alive.

The news of the climbers' deaths was met with great sadness in Britain. Mallory's wife, Ruth, in a poignant letter to Geoffrey Winthrop Young, said: "Whether he got to the top of the mountain or did not, whether or not he lived or died, makes no difference to my admiration for him … Oh Geoffrey, if only it hadn't happened! It might so easily have not."

ANDREW IRVINE
ENGLAND   1902–24

Many have debated why Mallory chose to make his final summit bid with an inexperienced student when Noel Odell, fit and well acclimatized, was close at hand.

We will never know the reason, but, although Irvine had almost no climbing experience, he was a valuable member of the team. A top-class rower whose training had made him physically prepared for the rigours of Everest, he was also good with his hands, able to strip and repair machinery and keep the team's heavy oxygen sets functioning. On the mountain, he was full of the practical efficiency and common sense mountaineering demands. Popular with the other climbers, he worked hard on the mundane chores that make life at extreme altitudes so difficult.

MOUNTAINEERING INNOVATIONS

OXYGEN GEAR

THERE ARE LIMITS TO ACCLIMATIZATION. Even among genetically adapted populations, few permanent settlements exist above 5,200m (17,000ft) – roughly the altitude of Everest Base Camp – where the air contains about half the oxygen as at sea level. The higher you go above this point, the faster your body – and athletic performance – deteriorates. Early Everest climbers became their own experiments on whether it was physically possible to climb so high. Advocates of supplementary oxygen designed systems to use while climbing, but early equipment was cumbersome, heavy, and unreliable.

EXPERIMENTING WITH OXYGEN

The first to use oxygen in mountaineering was the British publisher and mountaineer A L Mumm. In 1907, he took small cartridges prepared by Siebe, Gorman & Co on an expedition to the Garhwal Himalaya, India. The team included Tom Longstaff, a firm opponent of the idea of using oxygen, and the future Everest leader Charles Bruce. Most on the expedition regarded Mumm's trial as a joke.

At the same time, British chemist and technical wizard George Finch was switched on to the possibilities – and potential necessity – of using oxygen by Oxford academic G Dreyer. After conducting research for the recently formed Royal Air Force on hypoxia – the effects of oxygen deprivation – Dreyer told Finch: "I do not think you will get up without [oxygen], but if you succeed, you may not get down again."

Arrangements were made for Finch to experiment inside a decompression chamber carrying a 16kg (35lb) load at a simulated high

1000 BCE – COCA
Traces of coca leaves are found with 15th-century mummies in Peru; archaeology suggests that use of the plant against altitude sickness goes back much further.

1624 –
ANTÓNIO DE ANDRADE
On crossing the Himalaya, de Andrade writes:
"According to the natives, many people die on account of noxious vapours … people in good health are suddenly taken ill and die."

1922 – BOOST TO PERFORMANCE
On the British Mount Everest Expedition, George Finch and Geoffrey Bruce show that using bottled oxygen at altitude improves climbing speed and the ability to sleep.

1933 – SURPLUS KIT
UK doctor Raymond Greene redesigns the system but it is only used on the next Everest attempt for medical purposes.

1923 – OXYGEN CONTROVERSY
George Finch argues in favour of oxygen in the *Alpine Journal*, but others consider it unsporting.

BCE	1000	CE	1500	1600	1900	1910	1920	1930

c.37 BCE –
MOUNTAIN HEADACHES
Chinese civil servant Tookim documents the health impacts of altitude when travelling through Turkestan to Kabul in Afghanistan.

1907 – FIRST OXYGEN
British climber A L Mumm's Alpine Club expedition to Everest carries "pneumatogen" oxygen cartridges – considered a joke by others in the party.

1921 – KELLAS DIES
Pioneer of high-altitude physiology Alexander Kellas dies near Everest, leaving equipment research incomplete.

1924 – IRVINE'S SKILL
Andrew Irvine (see p.231) fulfils the role of oxygen engineer on Everest, improving sets from Siebe Gorman, a diving equipment manufacturer.

Jesuit missionary José de Acosta describes mountain sickness in his natural history of the "Indias" (below). His party becomes sick while crossing a pass at about 4,800m (15,750ft) in the Peruvian Andes:
"The aire is there so subtle and delicate, as it is not proportionable with the breathing of man."
The Incas understood that acclimatization took time. They stationed troops at altitude to keep them physically prepared.

1590 JOSÉ DE ACOSTA

The first oxygen sets comprise a Bergen rucksack frame (right), four steel cylinders, tubes, valves, and two types of mask – the "Economizer" and the "Standard". After George Finch was omitted from the 1924 Everest expedition, Andrew Irvine, seen here testing the apparatus, took over responsibility for maintaining the temperamental equipment. He proved to be skilled at fine-tuning the apparatus and managed to simplify the sets, reducing their overall weight significantly.

1922 BERGEN PACK

altitude. The difference in Finch's performance with and without bottled oxygen persuaded the Mount Everest Committee to put money towards developing an oxygen system.

Scottish chemist Alexander Kellas (see pp.194–95), who had also conducted much work on physiology at altitude, developed two types of oxygen supply. The first was a system of pressurized oxygen stored in heavy steel cylinders. The second method consisted of producing oxygen from a chemical reaction, but could only operate while the climber was resting, so had little practical value.

ADAPTED APPARATUS

The completed apparatus was assembled according to Dreyer's advice by the British government's Air Ministry. It featured four bottles mounted on the frame of a standard, army-issue Bergen rucksack, the necessary tubing, and two kinds of face mask – one with a valve and one that required the user to bite on a tube to stop the flow. Ten sets were built for

HIGH-ALTITUDE PHYSIOLOGY

Although our bodies' response to altitude has only recently been fully understood, hypoxia has been observed for millennia. The Chinese text *Hanshu* describes travellers on "the Great Headache Mountain" in about 37BCE. Although oxygen was discovered in 1775, it was almost another century before French scientist Paul Bert, who built his own decompression chamber, showed the link between atmospheric pressure and hypoxia. Mabel Fitzgerald, a researcher on J S Haldane's expedition to Pikes Peak, Colorado in 1911, did early work on the process of acclimatization.

US MOUNTAINEERS TAKE ALTITUDE TESTS IN A "STRATO-TRAINER", 1952

the 1922 Everest expedition, although most were damaged on the journey to the mountain. Early trials convinced most of the team that the apparatus was worse than useless. The valves feeding the oxygen were too stiff, so Finch –

using a football bladder and a glass T-piece – improvised a robust and usable alternative. This allowed Finch and Geoffrey Bruce, the expedition transport officer with no previous climbing experience, to reach 8,320m (27,300ft).

1947 – HOUSTON TESTS
Charles Houston (see pp.248–49) oversees Operation Everest, in which four subjects are taken in a compression chamber to a simulated altitude of 8,850m (29,035ft) over 34 days.

1953 – SUCCESS ON EVEREST
Improved oxygen sets, including a refined closed-circuit system, are used for the first ascent of Everest.

1961 – SILVER HUT, EVEREST
Physiologist Griffith Pugh researches effects of altitude from a hut on the Mingo Glacier.

1990s – LIGHTER OXYGEN SYSTEMS
Most Everest climbers use oxygen tanks from Russian manufacturer Poisk. One bottle holds 1,280 litres (280 gallons). Most climbers use two on summit day, which lasts 12 to 18 hours.

1940 1950 1960 1970 1980 1990 2000

1938 – "CLOSED" SYSTEM
Rebreathing gear, in which the climber's exhaled breath is recycled, is used on Everest, but it proves unreliable.

1958 – HYPOXIA
Houston pioneers work on pulmonary oedema caused by hypoxia, not pneumonia as previously thought.

1975 – HIGH NIGHT OUT
UK climbers Doug Scott and Dougal Haston bivouac on the South Summit of Everest (see pp.304–05) after their bottled oxygen runs out, the highest night out in history.

1978 – EVEREST WITHOUT OXYGEN
Peter Habeler and Reinhold Messner reach the summit without bottled oxygen (see pp.308–11), finally settling the debate about whether this is possible.

A simplified system is developed by US anaesthetist Tom Hornbein, who discovers the limitations of his Swiss-made mask on Masherbrum in 1960. He designs a mask with a single valve that prevents exhaled air from getting into the rubber bladder into which oxygen flows from the tank. An engineer patient puts his research department at Hornbein's disposal, resulting in the system used on Everest in 1963.

1963 HORNBEIN SYSTEM

The TopOut mask is developed by Everest climber and military engineer Ted Atkins (right) in 2004 to maximize the use of oxygen carried by climbers. The existing "full flow" systems gave a constant stream of oxygen, wasting about 60 per cent of a climber's bottled oxygen while exhaling. Atkins develops a reservoir to hold this excess, reducing wastage. With an ambient air valve, the final part of each breath, which the lungs don't use, is low in oxygen.

2004 TOPOUT MASK

PAUL BAUER

CONTROVERSIAL NAZI-ERA CLIMBER

GERMANY   1896–1990

ONE OF THE LEADING FIGURES of the influential Munich School, Paul Bauer led Germany's first expeditions to an "8,000er" peak – Kangchenjunga in the Himalaya. A capable organizer, as well as an excellent mountaineer, Bauer was among those who felt betrayed and humiliated by Germany's defeat in World War I. His support for the Nazis led to an influential position in the regime, and he oversaw the German Himalaya Foundation, which funded German expeditions before World War II.

A LIFE'S WORK

- Returns from World War I **filled with a burning desire to venture into the mountains** and open up the high peaks of Asia for the glory of the German nation
- First **visits the Alps on a cycling holiday** through the Dolomites to Lake Constance
- **Climbs successfully in the Soviet Caucasus**, which becomes his springboard for the Himalaya
- Makes **two epic expeditions** to the world's third-highest peak: Kangchenjunga. **The first** pushes ten camps up to a spur **1,186m (3,890ft) below the summit**, before being forced to retreat by a five-day storm; **the second** attempts the same spur and **gets a little higher** before being defeated by poor weather, sickness, and fatalities
- Leads **fourth of five** unsuccessful German assaults **on Nanga Parbat** in the 1930s; during the ascent, he finds the bodies of Willy Merkl and Willo Welzenbach, victims of an earlier attempt

When Paul Bauer's book, *Himalayan Quest,* was published in English in 1938, his translator felt that British readers should be offered an explanation for Germany's attitude to mountaineering, which might seem alien to them. "The motive underlying German Himalaya expeditions is to be sought in the events of 1914–1918 and Germany's re-awakened sense of nationalism which was their result," he wrote. "Mountaineering offered a contribution to Germany's reassertion as a nation to be reckoned with."

This was certainly true for Bauer, who was born in Kusel in the Rhineland. As a young man he dreamed of Alpine adventures and burned with patriotism for Germany, returning home from a cycling tour of the Dolomites in 1914 just in time to enlist for World War I. He spent the last weeks of the war in a prisoner of war camp in England and returned to Germany

angry at his defeated homeland, where "love of Fatherland, self-sacrifice and heroism were looked down upon."

JOINING THE ELITE
Bauer studied law in Munich, where his interest in climbing developed and his passion for right-wing politics made him an early admirer of Adolf Hitler. He also joined the Akademischer Alpenverein München (AAVM), the university climbing club whose members were redefining alpinism.

In the early 1920s, Bauer worked as a notary, and in his spare time made several important climbs in the Eastern Alps, including the Kasselerspitze Nordgrat in the Austrian Tyrol. In 1928, he and a few friends went to the Caucasus, where they made a number of first ascents. That same year, the veteran German explorer Willi Rickmers led a Soviet-German expedition to climb Pik Lenin in Central Asia's Pamirs. Bauer now determined that he would go to the Himalaya in 1929.

He put together a team of nine climbers, which included AAVM members Eugen Allwein and Peter

SUMMIT PENNANT
Many of Germany's high-mountain expeditions in the 1930s were funded by the Nazis, although a few climbing clubs were nuclei of resistance. The regime glorified mountaineering for propaganda purposes – to show superior physical strength, will, and self-sacrifice to the death.

Aufschnaiter, and drew up a list of objectives for the British colonial authorities in India. Kangchenjunga was first on the list. With a letter of introduction from Rickmers, Bauer and his team were warmly welcomed before being whisked to Darjeeling, where the newly formed Himalayan Club had arranged Sherpa support.

GERMANY'S HIMALAYAN DREAM
A few days later, in mid-August 1929, the German expedition was camped on the Zemu Glacier, looking out across the vast Northeast Face of Kangchenjunga. Theirs was the first real attempt to get to grips with the third-highest mountain in the world – a vast, complex peak, bristling with ice cliffs and prone to violent storms – and the team did amazingly well. Bauer had chosen a steep route up a spur that led to the peak's North Ridge, and just reaching the foot of the spur was a dangerous and difficult undertaking. They dug an ice cave for Camp X in early October, still only at 6,900m (22,600ft), some 1,500m (4,920ft) short of the summit, before Allwein reconnoitred up to 7,400m (24,280ft). Then a storm hit.

EN ROUTE TO KANGCHENJUNGA
The 1929 team's stated objective was to "test themselves against something difficult, some mountain that will call out everything they've got in them".

IT IS NOW QUITE OBVIOUS TO ME ... WE MUST GO TO THE HIMALAYAS "

PAUL BAUER, WRITING IN 1928

Bauer, Allwein, and two Sherpas remained there for three days before admitting defeat and descending in terrible conditions. The men were lucky to make it off the mountain alive, but Bauer's good judgment as a leader and the hard nature of the climbing won him respect.

In 1931, he returned to Kangchenjunga, and this time the team got higher before being blocked by a dangerous avalanche slope between their high point and the summit. Bauer must have been tempted to press on, but instead he called a halt. Four people had already died – two porters from illness, and then Hermann Schaller and Pasang Sherpa in a fall. But their attempt on this colossal face remains one of the outstanding efforts of Himalayan climbing.

GREAT EXPECTATIONS

After the 1934 Nanga Parbat tragedy almost destroyed German alpinism (see pp.238–39), Bauer was the man who took charge, heading investigations into the culpability of the surviving expedition members and casting judgment on those who had died. He became part of the Nazis' sporting bureaucracy and established the German Himalaya Foundation, becoming the highly political gatekeeper of funding for climbing expeditions.

In 1936, he led a successful first ascent of Sikkim's Siniolchu in preparation for a renewed assault on Nanga Parbat, but his work kept him from joining the 1937 expedition to Germany's "Mountain of Destiny", during which 16 climbers and Sherpas were wiped out in a huge ice avalanche. Bauer flew to India to help dig out the bodies of the seven climbers, who were buried in a communal "heroes' grave".

In 1938, Bauer led another attempt on Nanga Parbat – the fourth German expedition to the peak up to that date. He avoided all unnecessary risks and had the team's supplies airdropped by a plane stationed in the Kashmir Valley. Despite this advantage, the expedition failed. During World War II, Bauer ran a mountain warfare training facility, as well as commanding troops in the Caucasus. He survived the war, but it marked the end of his career as a climber.

WEEK OF HARD STRUGGLE
Bauer took a small team to Sikkim in 1936 to make a lightweight, alpine-style ascent of the 6,887-m (22,595-ft) Siniolchu – thought by some to be the most beautiful snow mountain in the world. Here, Adi Göttner and Karlo Wien are seen working their way up a narrow snow ridge during their successful summit bid. The climb took a week of "hard struggle".

WELZENBACH'S FINAL CLIMB
In the 1930s, Welzenbach began to make difficult and often dangerous climbs with the emphasis on ice. He is seen here taking a breather during the 1934 attempt on Nanga Parbat. After failing to reach the summit, Welzenbach and eight other men died during the descent.

WILLO WELZENBACH

DARING MASTER OF ICE CLIMBING

GERMANY   1900–34

AMONG THE VERY BEST ICE CLIMBERS in the history of mountaineering, Welzenbach was a leading light in Munich's climbing community of the 1920s and 30s, making a host of important first ascents of north faces across the Alps. He pioneered new ice-climbing techniques, and a new system of climbing grades, opening a path to the rapid development of standards throughout the Alps before World War II. Welzenbach's interest in Nanga Parbat, the mountain that became a German obsession, ultimately cost him his life.

A LIFE'S WORK

- At university in Munich he joins a group of climbers who become **the nucleus of German mountaineering** for the next 15 years

- His **first significant climb** is the North Face of the Grosses Wiesbachhorn in Austria, during which his partner improvises the first ice piton

- He climbs hundreds of new routes in both the Western and Eastern Alps and uses his experience to **modify the standard numerical rating system** used to grade the difficulty of climbs, **adding Grade VI**

- **Struck down by a mysterious illness that affects his right arm,** he is confined to a Swiss sanatorium; while he recuperates, he **works on plans for a German expedition to Nanga Parbat** in the Himalaya

- A brilliant rock climber, his diseased right arm requires him to **perfect his footwork, a skill he transfers to ice climbing**

- In 1934, prevented from leading his own expedition to Nanga Parbat, **he joins Willy Merkl's ill-fated German-Austrian team** for their second attempt, but **dies on the retreat** from the summit ridge after a terrible storm

---

For 15 years, Willo Welzenbach was at the heart of a climbing revolution that – according to French climbing impresario Lucien Devies – saw the capital of alpinism shift from London to Munich, "where youth was ambitious and innovations were encouraged."

Welzenbach was born in Munich, but his family relocated to Salzburg during World War I. As a boy, he suffered from osteomyelitis, a poisoning of the bone marrow that left him with weakened arms and excused him from school sports. As a teenager, however, he discovered the Berchtesgaden Alps outside Salzburg and started climbing them.

In 1920, Welzenbach enrolled at the Technical University in Munich, joining the prestigious Akademischer Alpenverein München (AAVM), where a cadre of the best German alpinists helped him perfect his own mountain craft. Within two years he was the best rock climber in the club. He also trained as a civil engineer, working first for the railways, and then as a surveyor of works for Munich city council.

In the early 1920s, single and with a steady job, Welzenbach was in the fortunate position of being able to climb unhindered by Germany's economic woes. By 1924, he had made his first significant new routes – the North Face of the

Grosses Wiesbachhorn, with Fritz Rigele, who almost inadvertently invented the ice piton as they climbed, and in the following year, the North Face Direct of the Dent d'Hérens with Eugen Allwein. In 1926, in the Glockner region, he climbed three more north faces in Austria, culminating with the Grossglockner. Welzenbach was cutting steps as crampons still lacked front points, but shorter axes and his brilliant technique allowed steep ice slopes to be climbed. He was redefining what was possible.

CUT DOWN IN HIS PRIME

Then disaster struck as Welzenbach developed mysterious pains in his arms and underwent surgery and bone grafts on his right arm. Once he recovered, however, he embarked on the most fruitful stage of his climbing career.

By the early 1930s, there were other alpinists venturing onto the great north faces, but Welzenbach showed the way. In the Western Alps he attempted the Grandes Jorasses, and succeeded on the Grands Charmoz with Willy Merkl (see pp.238–39). In the Bernese Oberland, he climbed the north faces of the Lauterbrunnen Breithorn, the Gspaltenhorn, the Gletscherhorn, and the Grosshorn. In 1934, he realized his long-held dream to attempt Nanga Parbat, but the party failed to reach the summit and he was one of nine men who died on the descent.

GRANDS CHARMOZ

NORTH FACE, JUNE/JULY 1931

— **30 June – Lower rocks**
At dawn, Welzenbach and Merkl start climbing the lower rocks. They are strafed by rockfall, and bivouac at the icefield.

— **1 July – Forced back**
At first light, the pair start climbing the icefield and look for a line up the headwall. They end up descending the NW Ridge.

— **9 July – Second attempt**
They traverse in from the ridge to their high point to climb the headwall. Caught in a storm, they endure three bivouacs.

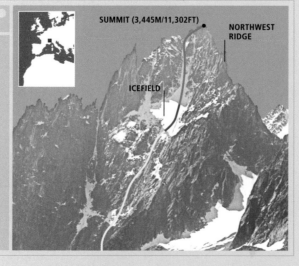

SUMMIT (3,445M/11,302FT)

NORTHWEST RIDGE

ICEFIELD

WILLY MERKL

OBSESSIVE CLIMBER OF NANGA PARBAT

GERMANY   1900–34

IN THE 1930S, Pakistan's Nanga Parbat, the world's ninth-highest peak, became German mountaineering's *Schicksalberg* – mountain of fate. From the moment Willy Merkl first lay eyes on it, from his 1932 expedition's camp in the beautiful Fairy Meadows, he was in awe of this snow-clad behemoth. But Merkl's obsession and his mistakes led to disaster on a subsequent expedition in 1934, in which he and two other top German mountaineers, and six Sherpas, lost their lives in a desperate, drawn-out retreat from a stormy summit plateau.

Born in Thüringen in eastern Germany, Merkl studied mechanical engineering before becoming a railway engineer. He was not as great a mountaineer as his compatriot Willo Welzenbach (see pp.236–37), but he had a formidable rock-climbing record in the Eastern Alps, particularly the Dolomites, and in the Western Alps, where he and Welzenbach met in the summer of 1931 to climb the steep North Face of the Charmoz in the Mont Blanc range.

MAN VERSUS MOUNTAIN

Merkl and Welzenbach's first attempt on the face ended in failure, but a few days later, fearful that Anderl Heckmair (see pp.290–91) would beat them to their prize, they went back. Caught by a storm on the final headwall, they first tried

to climb out of trouble, and then bivouacked on a small ledge just below the summit ridge. There they were stuck for the next 60 hours, freezing cold and soaking wet, lashed by lightning and with thunder cannonading between the jagged granite needles surrounding them. Spindrift avalanches (fine, wind-blown snow) tried to prise them off their ledge and they took it in turns to dig out their bivouac tent.

On the morning of the fifth day they finally escaped and fought their way to the summit and then down to Chamonix. The German press were agog at the story of their valiant struggle for survival and the Nazi Party was alerted to the propaganda value of mountaineering. The courage and determination shown by the German climbers trumped the reverse of the mountaineering coin – prudence and caution. The new mood led to an obsession with claiming the highest Himalayan peak to which Germany had access: Nanga Parbat.

GLORY FOR THE NEW GERMANY

The idea for a German expedition to Nanga Parbat originated with Welzenbach, who had been inspired by A F Mummery's letters (see pp.168–71). However, the brilliant ice climber's plans were thwarted at every turn and he was eventually forced to give up his dream of leading the expedition, nominating instead his friend and climbing partner, Merkl. Although Merkl had mounted a successful expedition to the Caucasus in 1929, his leadership on Nanga Parbat in 1932 was questionable.

For a start, Merkl broke with standard practice by not hiring Sherpas in Darjeeling, relying instead on local, cheaper porters who, while tough, didn't have the Sherpas' expertise. The expedition failed, although the team, which included Fritz Wiessner (see pp.250–51), did make the first ascent of Rakhiot Peak and found a possible route to the summit of Nanga Parbat.

By 1934, the Nazis were in power and the fervour for claiming Nanga Parbat for Germany grew. Merkl and Welzenbach weren't Nazis, but they needed funds and the approval of the state. Paul Bauer (see pp.234–35) was the Nazis' chosen leader of the climbing world, but Merkl went around him, supported by the German Railways' sports association, which was not yet in the hands of the regime.

The German-Austrian team that set out in spring 1934 had strong climbers, and 35 Sherpas this time. Early on, the team suffered a serious setback when one of the best climbers, Alfred Drexel, died of pulmonary oedema. Merkl called everyone back to Base Camp for the funeral and 17 valuable days passed before the climbing resumed. Welzenbach began to realize that Merkl was behaving like a "dictator". In early July, an under-resourced and over-large party of five climbers and 11 Sherpas set out for the top. Two Austrians, Erwin Schneider and

Peter Aschenbrenner, were well in the lead and could have made a push for the summit, but instead chose to wait for their slower comrades and help them set up Camp VIII on the Silver Saddle. That night a hurricane hit the camp and what followed, wrote Merkl's half-brother Karl Herrligkoffer, "for sheer protracted agony has no parallel in mountaineering history." Herrligkoffer would lead the successful expedition to the mountain in 1953, when it was climbed by Hermann Buhl (see pp.258–59).

DAYS OF DEATH AND FEAR

The team remained in Camp VIII on 7 July, to see if conditions would improve, but after a second storm-bound night they realized a retreat to the lower camps was their only option. Merkl told Schneider and Aschenbrenner to lead three of the Sherpas to safety, but just above Camp VII the climbers untied from their charges and raced down the mountain. Merkl, Welzenbach, and Uli Wieland followed more slowly with the other eight Sherpas but got caught out by darkness and suffered a terrible bivouac, during

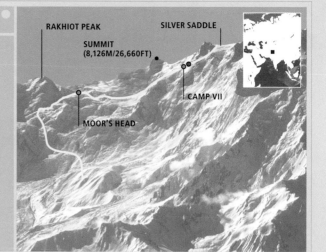

NANGA PARBAT

RAKHIOT FACE, JULY 1934

— **Route across ice wall**
They fail to reach the summit; nine men, including six Sherpas, die on the descent.

○ **11 July – Wieland dies**
As they retreat, Wieland collapses.

○ **12 July – Welzenbach dies**
After making it to Camp VII, Welzenbach dies during the night.

○ **14–16 July – Merkl and Gay Lay die**
Merkl and Sherpa Gay Lay die after collapsing beneath the Moor's Head rock.

RAKHIOT PEAK   SILVER SADDLE
SUMMIT
(8,126M/26,660FT)
CAMP VII
MOOR'S HEAD

which Sherpa Norbu Nima froze to death. Wieland collapsed just above Camp VII. Welzenbach made it, but died there the following night. The next day, 13 July, Merkl collapsed in the snow beneath a rock feature called the Moor's Head, where his body, and that of Sherpa Gay Lay, was discovered four

years later. In all, nine climbers and Sherpas died on the descent of Nanga Parbat and those Sherpas that survived suffered terrible frostbite.

Paul Bauer used the tragedy to further his own ends, investigating Aschenbrenner and Schneider's actions and denouncing Merkl and Welzenbach as "politically unsound".

A TRAGEDY TO OVERCOME
Three Europeans and four porters transport the body of Alfred Drexel – the first casualty of the 1934 Nanga Parbat expedition – to Base Camp. He was buried nearby. "Merkl made us feel we had buried a hero," said team member Fritz Bechtold.

ABALAKOV BROTHERS

SOVIET PIONEERS OF MIXED FORTUNE

SOVIET UNION   1906–86; 1907–48

VITALY ABALAKOV   YEVGENIY ABALAKOV

CLIMBING IN RUSSIA began with visits by the British in the 19th century and the Germans after World War I. Soviet climbers emerged in the 1920s, but standards surged with the arrival of the Abalakovs in the 1930s. Vitaly became known as the great guiding figure in Soviet mountaineering, whose characteristics were philosophically opposed to the sport in the West. His contribution in the Caucasus after World War II was colossal.

Unlike mountaineering in the West, where individual freedom was paramount and hierarchies and formal competition were avoided, Soviet mountaineering developed systems and nomenclature that were entirely the opposite. Vitaly Abalakov was "champion mountaineer" ten times in the USSR – a concept that would have been actively resisted in the West.

Yet climbing was done not for the glory of the individual, but for socialism. Peaks were named after Soviet leaders and notable anniversaries. Yevgeniy Abalakov made the first ascent in 1933 of Pik Stalin (7,495m/24,590ft) – now known as Ismoil Somoni Peak – and

Vitaly made the first ascent of Pik Lenin (7,134m/23,406ft), the two highest summits in what was then the Soviet Union. In 1952, Vitaly also climbed Pik Nineteenth Party Congress. Both brothers were also remarkable for reasons beyond climbing. Yevgeniy was a sculptor and Vitaly an engineer who developed sports equipment. The brothers were Cossacks, born in Yeniseysk in Krasnoyarsk, the heart of Russian Siberia. As teenagers they went scrambling on the Krasnoyarsk Pillars near their home.

PEAK-BAGGERS TO PRISONERS

In 1931, the Abalakovs cut their teeth with an ascent of Dykh-Tau in the Caucasus with Valentina Cheredova, one of the first female Soviet climbers, whom Vitaly was later to marry. The following year, Vitaly climbed the neighbouring Bezengi Wall. These climbs made the brothers' reputations and led to their inclusion on expeditions to remoter ranges, first the Altai, where Vitaly traversed Belukha, and then the Pamirs, where their exploits made them national heroes. Yevgeniy's exploits also included important routes in the Caucasus Mountains, such as the first complete traverse from Dykh-Tau to Koshtan-Tau and the first Soviet traverse of the Bezengi Ridge.

Vitaly's reputation – he was made "Master of Mountaineering" in 1935 – didn't protect him from arrest by the NKVD, the Soviet secret

police, in 1937 for being a German spy – a common charge in the purges of the 1930s. Accused of using Western climbing techniques, Vitaly escaped execution, but remained in prison for 20 months. He spent time in solitary confinement for organizing an exercise programme for fellow prisoners. Yevgeniy was under investigation by the NKVD at the time of his accidental death in 1948.

In spite of persecution, Vitaly developed a camming device years ahead of its time. He also perfected a method of abseiling off ice, the "Abalakov thread", which involves using an ice screw to make connecting holes that can be threaded, supporting the climber's weight.

HERO ONCE MORE

In later years, and despite ill treatment at the hands of the NKVD, Vitaly became a celebrated figure in Soviet sport. He received the Order of Lenin in 1957 after his ascent of Pik Pobeda, and played host to a series of international climbing camps, including a 1962 British team with John Hunt (see p.265) in the Pamirs.

Vitaly protested when the British withdrew due to the deaths of Wilf Noyce and Robin Smith. Hunt speculated that because their row was being filmed for propaganda, Abalakov was uncharacteristically harsh. The distorting veil of propaganda has yet to be lifted from the extraordinary world of Soviet mountaineering.

STALIN'S PURGES

Joseph Stalin initially considered mountaineering to be a suitably Bolshevik activity, and the Soviet elite of the early 1930s included several mountaineers. One of the most accomplished climbers in the Soviet leadership was Sergey Kirov, who was to become an obstacle to Stalin's plans to take absolute control of the Soviet Union. Kirov's assassination might explain mountaineering's fall from grace. Many leading climbers were executed in Stalin's purges, including Vassily Semenowski and Nikolai Gorbunov, who had been Lenin's secretary. Gorbunov had led expeditions to the Pamirs, as had Nikolai Krylenko, who participated in Stalin's "show trials" as a Soviet official before falling from grace. He was shot in prison.

HANGING OUT
Vitaly Abalakov, left, rests alongside fellow mountaineers ahead of a bivouac on the North Wall of Dykh-Tau in the Caucasus. At 5,205m (17,077 ft), the peak is second only to Mount Elbruz in the Caucasus Mountains.

BACK OF AN ENVELOPE

THE SCALE AND PROFILE OF THE EARLY ATTEMPTS ON EVEREST AND OTHER "8,000ERS" FIXED IN THE PUBLIC IMAGINATION THE IDEA THAT BIG EXPEDITIONS WERE ESSENTIAL IN THE HIMALAYA. BUT THERE WAS AN ALTERNATIVE BELIEF – THAT SMALLER, LIGHTER TEAMS WERE PREFERABLE.

CHARLES WARREN
On his first Himalayan expedition, this young English doctor scaled Bhagirathi III, carrying his own equipment and supplies. He was later a key member of three Everest expeditions.

In the 1930s, thanks to the repeated efforts on Mount Everest, most people thought mountaineering expeditions inevitably involved huge trains of pack animals and porters carrying lavish supplies of food and drink for a large team of climbers and their Sherpa servants.

In fact, these well-funded, high-profile expeditions were the exception rather than the norm and came with some awkward side effects, most notably public scrutiny. The Duke of the Abruzzi, an Italian prince (see pp.198–99), had been able to fund his large-scale exploratory journeys himself, but the Everest expeditions relied on outside support and questions were asked: was the money being spent correctly? Why weren't the climbers succeeding? Were such large expeditions even necessary?

BIG VERSUS SMALL

Arguments about the best tactics on big mountains are fiercely contested even today. Yet throughout the 1930s, the tradition of lightweight expeditions – introduced before World War I by British climbers such as Alexander Kellas (see pp.194–95) and Tom Longstaff – continued alongside the higher-profile Everest "shows", and the huge expeditions mounted by Austrian and German teams to Nanga Parbat in Pakistan, which were paid for by the state.

Between the wars there was near-continuous activity in those parts of the Himalaya that were accessible.

English climber James Waller led expeditions to Nun in Kishtwar and Saltoro Kangri in the Karakoram. In 1933, Britons Colin Kirkus and Charles Warren made the first ascent of Bhagirathi III in the Garhwal Himalaya in lightweight style, while in 1938, on another Waller expedition, Jock Harrison and Robin Hodgkin came close to the summit of Masherbrum in the Karakoram, just missing out on what would have been the climb of the decade – and suffering terrible frostbite as a consequence.

In 1937, British ski expert and naturalist Freddie Spencer Chapman climbed Chomolhari, a peak of 7,315m (24,000ft), with the Sherpa Pasang Dawa. Also on the expedition was Charles Crawford, who had no climbing experience at all but made it as high as 6,000m (20,000ft). Chapman had no equipment, borrowing what he needed from the Himalayan Club in Darjeeling. He had no money either: "I have great satisfaction," he wrote in his memoirs, "in the thought that we reached a height of 24,000ft [7,315m] at a cost of under

> For many of today's mountaineers, putting a small team on a big mountain by means of a well executed but simple plan is the ideal. Lavish expeditions and unnecessary luxuries are seen as spoiling the beauty of the climb.

MINIMALIST MOUNTAINEERING
Tilman was part of the small-scale Anglo-American expedition that made the first ascent of Nanda Devi in 1936. The climbers dumped most of their gear on the ascent and Tilman used this old hemp rope to reach the summit.

£20 each, while the Everest expedition, which was being carried out at the same time, was unable to get higher than 23,000ft in spite of the expenditure of several thousand pounds."

KEEPING IT SIMPLE

Saving money was only one part of the appeal of travelling light, though. The great British climber and explorer Eric Shipton (see pp.244–47), who led a lightweight five-man expedition to Everest in 1935, complained that he "loathed the crowds and fuss that were inseparable from a large expedition. I always had the ridiculous feeling that I was taking part in a Cook's tour or a school treat, and I wanted to go away and hide myself … it was all so far removed from the light, free spirit with which we were wont to approach our peaks."

Shipton's climbing partner, H W ("Bill") Tilman (see pp.244–47), argued that "the whole art lies in getting most value for weight", and although he carried his austere approach to the extreme, counting porridge and soup as "luxuries", many of today's climbing elite share his passion for cutting things to the bone – of doing the most with the least. Tilman's famous comment on the early Everest expeditions, that "any worthwhile expedition can be planned on the back of an envelope", captures the simplicity of his approach. While it didn't suit everyone, there was nothing haphazard about it.

LOW-TECH AT HIGH ALTITUDE
In 1937, Freddie Spencer Chapman led a cut-price, six-man British expedition to the Tibetan holy mountain, Chomolhari (above); the party reached the summit from Bhutan.

CROSSING A CREVASSE ON EVEREST
Britain was uniquely placed for Himalayan exploration given its political influence in the region. In the 1930s, it launched four light- and heavyweight expeditions there.

SETTING THE SCENE

- While public attention focuses on attempts on the giants of the Himalaya, a **large number of much smaller expeditions** tackle peaks higher than 7,000m (22,966ft).

- In 1931, a British expedition led by Frank Smythe (see pp.247) reaches the **summit of Kamet**, at 7,756m (25,466ft) **the highest peak yet climbed**.

- After studying and **rejecting the tactics used on Everest**, a **US expedition climbs Minya Konka** in China in 1932; Terris Moore and Richard Burdsall reach the summit.

- A **joint American and British team climbs India's Nanda Devi** in 1936, two years after Tilman and Shipton find a route to the mountain.

- In 1939, a Swiss team makes a successful ascent of Dunagiri, while the **Poles and Japanese enter the Himalayan scene**. The Poles make the first ascent of Nanda Devi East.

SMALL-SCALE TRIUMPH
During the 1930s, the larger expeditions – especially those to Nanga Parbat – often ended in tragedy. Small teams making alpine-style ascents, such Paul Bauer's on Siniolchu (below), had a better record.

TILMAN AND SHIPTON

CELEBRATED MOUNTAIN EXPLORERS

ENGLAND   1898–1977; 1907–77

H W ("BILL") TILMAN   **ERIC SHIPTON**

THE PRE-EMINENT mountain explorers of the 20th century, Tilman and Shipton are remembered not just for what they did but the way they did it. In contrast to the elaborate and very public attempts on Everest in the 1930s, in which they both participated, their own expeditions were conducted with the minimum of expense and personnel, and to great effect. Their journeys were an inspiring mix of bare-bones resilience and wild ambition.

On the face of it, the two men could not have been more different. Although Tilman was older, he was the less experienced mountaineer when the pair first met in Kenya in 1930. Shipton was gregarious and enjoyed the company of women. Tilman was almost pathologically self-reliant, avoiding the company not just of women, but most men too.

However, in terms of mountain exploration, the two men shared the same goals: to travel and climb light, in remote places and in small teams. They found in each other psychological qualities they each lacked, but shared a great sense of fun, even of the absurd. Both became successful writers, whose wry, self-deprecating works have outlasted those of their contemporaries.

Harold William ("Bill") Tilman was the son of a self-made Liverpool sugar merchant. He left his private school to join the army and was on the Western Front a month before his 18th birthday in 1916. Awarded the Military Cross twice, Tilman fought in the Battle of the Somme. After the war, and barely out of his teens, he won a remote parcel of land in Kenya in an ex-serviceman's lottery. He spent the next decade clearing it and establishing a farm.

Eric Shipton was born in Sri Lanka (then Ceylon), the son of a tea planter who died when Shipton was two. His mother took her son and his older sister around the world, something that suited Shipton's nomadic instincts. On a holiday in the Pyrenees, he discovered something he could do well – mountaineering.

By his early 20s, Shipton was an experienced alpinist. Faced with the necessity of finding a job, he took a course in estate management and headed to Kenya with the idea of starting a coffee plantation. In 1929, he climbed the twin peaks of Mount Kenya – Batian and the slightly lower Nelion – writing up the adventure in the *East African Standard*, which prompted Tilman to contact him.

ELUSIVE ROUTE THROUGH THE HIMALAYA
Shipton is seen here surveying in Rishi Gorge en route to Nanda Devi in 1934. Two years later Charles Houston's party reached the summit.

TILMAN ON TOP OF THE WORLD
Surrounded by a ring of high peaks, Nanda Devi, the highest mountain entirely within India, was long considered impossible to reach. But once Tilman and Shipton traced a way through the Rishi Gorge in 1934, it was only a matter of time before an ascent was attempted. In 1936, Tilman, with fellow Englishman Noel Odell, reached Nanda Devi's summit – the highest summit yet climbed by man. Recording their jubilant arrival at the peak, Tilman drily observed, "I believe we so far forgot ourselves as to shake hands on it."

NO ONE GOES SO FAR OR SO FAST AS THE MAN WHO DOES NOT KNOW WHERE HE IS GOING "

BILL TILMAN

AFRICAN SUMMITS

Tilman's interest in climbing had been sparked by a brief visit to the Lake District in the 1920s. Unfazed by an approach from a novice, Shipton suggested they climb Kilimanjaro, concluding, "though having virtually no mountaineering experience, [he] was ideally suited to the game." Later, in 1930, they made the first traverse of Mount Kenya, a landmark in African climbing.

In 1931, Frank Smythe (see opposite) invited Shipton on his expedition to Kamet in India's Garhwal Himalaya – a peak that had been attempted ten times before by many of the legends of early Himalayan climbing. Lavishly supplied, with a Sherpa crew to take care of the chores and a gramophone to pass the evenings, Smythe's approach was rather different from the pattern Shipton would set. Shipton proved popular with his companions and was indefatigable at altitude. The peak, at 7,812m (25,629ft), was the highest climbed at that time.

Back in Kenya, Shipton paired up again with Tilman in 1932 to explore and climb in the Rwenzori Range. That autumn, Shipton was invited to join Hugh Ruttledge's 1933 Everest expedition, the first since Mallory and Irvine's disappearance in 1924 (see pp.228–31). Shipton did well on the Everest trip, but the complexity and politics of the attempt didn't appeal to him. He had his own pony, a camp bed, champagne, and caviar – but he felt the whole approach was wrong and described the experience as "mostly a grim and joyless business". The expedition reached 8,500m (27,887ft), but the final thousand metres seemed as elusive as ever.

AN EXTRAVAGANT SUMMER
The 1935 reconnaissance of the western approaches to Everest was one of the greatest expeditions in Himalayan history, with 26 first ascents of peaks higher than 6,000m (20,000ft).

KARAKORAM

CENTRAL REGION, 1937

— **Route taken by entire party**
Tilman and Shipton, together with surveyors Auden and Spender, cross the Sarpo Laggo Pass and trek to the northern approaches to K2. Crossing the Shaksgam River, they spend three weeks exploring the Aghil Range.

— **Route taken by Tilman**
The party divides, with Shipton and Spender exploring approaches to the Shimshal Pass and the Braldu Glacier. They cross into Hunza and head home. Auden heads south down the Panmah Glacier back to Askole.

— **Route taken by Shipton and Spender**
Travelling with two Sherpas, Sen Tensing and Aila, Tilman crosses the Lukpe La to explore Snow Lake and the mountains to the south before returning to Askole.

Map labels: SHIMSHAL PASS, YARKAND RIVER, SHAKSGAM RIVER, BRALDU GLACIER, SNOW LAKE, HISPAL PASS, BASE CAMP, AGHIL PASS, LUKPE LA, PANMAH GLACIER, SARPO LAGGO PASS, K2, BIAFO GLACIER, ASKOLE, BALTORO GLACIER

CLIMBING TIMELINE

Shipton arrives in Kenya to work as a coffee planter; he and Percy Wyn Harris climb SE Face of Nelion

Tilman and Shipton climb in the Rwenzori, reaching the summits of Speke, Baker, and Stanley

Landmark exploration in the Garhwal, first up the Rishi Gorge, then in the Badrinath region, before returning to Nanda Devi and crossing Sunderhunga Col

1918–28	1929–32	1933–36

Shipton has his first full Alpine season in 1925, guided by Elie Richard

Tilman makes contact with Shipton and the two begin climbing, making the first traverse of Mount Kenya

Shipton joins 1933 Everest expedition and Frank Smythe on summit attempt; Tilman cycles across Africa

Tilman joins Shipton and others for Everest reconnaissance; about 26 peaks in the Everest region are climbed for the first time

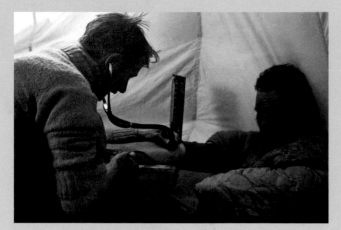

LIGHTWEIGHT TEAM
Dr Charles Warren takes Shipton's blood pressure during the 1938 expedition. Tilman was sceptical about the need for a team doctor, selecting Warren mainly for his climbing skills.

Back in Britain, Shipton issued another invitation to Tilman in 1934. He wanted to detach himself from the "big and cumbersome organisation" of a big expedition, and to wander instead "with a small self-contained party ... forming our plans to suit the circumstances, climbing peaks when the opportunity occurred." The pair would do this in India's Garhwal Himalaya, finding a route into the fabled Nanda Devi Sanctuary with three Sherpas from the 1933 Everest expedition.

A landmark in Himalayan expeditions, their exploration of the Rishi Gorge allowed them to reach Nanda Devi, where they spent weeks surveying. After that, they explored the region west of the Alaknanda River. In 1935, Shipton led a lightweight reconnaissance to Everest, and invited Tilman; the plan was to get a look into the Western Cwm and try out new climbers. One of the porters was a young Tenzing Norgay (see pp.266–67).

Shipton was back on Everest the following year, but an early monsoon stalled the strong team. Tilman, considered a poor acclimatizer, went instead to India, where he made the first ascent of Nanda Devi with a US expedition.

SURVEYING K2 AND EVEREST

Shipton and Tilman were reunited in 1937 in an exploration of the northern approaches to K2, some of the remotest terrain on Earth. In all, they surveyed 4,661 sq km (1,800 sq miles), spending months in the field. "No experience of mine has been fuller, no undertaking more richly rewarded," Shipton wrote.

In 1938, Tilman led a cut-price trip to Everest, which Shipton joined, and which again ended in failure. After World War II, Tilman made extraordinary journeys through Central Asia and Nepal, while Shipton got caught up again in the struggle for Everest, leading a reconnaissance expedition in 1951. His party saw the Western Cwm and the south side of Everest for the first time: here, at last, was a route to the summit. However, he was not chosen to lead the successful 1953 Everest expedition, a bitter disappointment that he bore with dignity.

SNOWSHOES
Tilman wore these snowshoes on his Everest expeditions in the mid-1930s. They made it back to England and were given to the Royal Geographical Society.

EVEREST RECONNAISSANCE
Eric Shipton, Michael Ward, and Bill Murray (pictured, left to right) keep the sun off while bathing in the Arun River during Shipton's 1951 reconnaissance of Everest. Shipton had also invited a young New Zealander, Edmund Hillary, on the expedition.

FRANK SMYTHE
ENGLAND   1900–49

Frank Smythe was the leading British alpinist of the 1920s, making the first ascents of the Sentinelle Route and Route Major on Mont Blanc's Brenva Face with Thomas Graham Brown.

Smythe's climbs were the most important British contribution in the Alps between the wars. In 1930, he was part of an international expedition to Kangchenjunga in Nepal, and the following year he led the first ascent of Kamet, a longstanding objective and the first mountain higher than 7,620m (25,000ft) to be climbed. During the 1933 Everest expedition, he equalled Edward Norton's altitude record of 8,573m (28,126ft); he also took part in the 1936 and 1938 attempts on Everest with Shipton and Tilman. Smythe was a notable photographer, but earned his living as a writer, publishing 27 books. He was also a keen gardener, and wrote about plant collecting in the Himalaya.

Shipton returns to Everest, but Tilman isn't selected because of poor acclimatization

Tilman leads low-budget Everest expedition but poor weather means they make no further progress

Tilman leads four-month exploratory expedition to Langtang, Jugal, and Ganesh regions of Nepal

1937–38	1939–45	1946–53

With surveyors John Auden and Michael Spender, Tilman and Shipton explore Shaksgam region

Shipton and Tilman make attempt on Muztagh Ata and a year later, Bogda Feng

Shipton leads reconnaissance to south side of Everest but is later removed from leadership of 1953 expedition

CHARLES HOUSTON

K2 HERO AND PIONEER OF HIGH-ALTITUDE MEDICINE

UNITED STATES   1913–2009

PHYSICIAN, HIGH-ALTITUDE PHYSIOLOGIST, writer, and climber, Charles Houston led several important expeditions, including two attempts on K2. He narrowly avoided death during his second try. In the interests of his family he quit climbing after that, but continued with his research on altitude sickness, offering alpinists advice in his book *Going Higher: Oxygen, Man, and Mountains*. For his admirers, Houston stood for all that is best about climbing, putting friendship and teamwork above the summit and fame.

Houston was born in New York into a world of considerable privilege, reaching maturity in the aftermath of the Wall Street Crash of 1929, but insulated from that disaster by his father's prospering legal practice. Oscar Houston had something of the thwarted explorer about him, and bankrolled his son's mountain enthusiasms, developed during holidays in France.

At Harvard University, Houston fell in with a group of ambitious young thrusters who would become known as the Harvard Five, and he joined some of them on his first exploratory expedition to Alaska's Mount Crillon in 1933.

His upbringing instilled in Houston an expectation of success, but having encountered the easy, nomadic fulfillment on offer in mountaineering, he was loath to knuckle down to domestic regularity. Family and career came later, but for now his expedition life was fixed in his mind as an expression of friendship and common purpose.

A MISSED OPPORTUNITY

A year after Mount Crillon, Houston's father suggested an expedition to another remote Alaskan peak, Mount Foraker. Oscar was the nominal leader and the party included the middle-aged British mountaineer T Graham Brown. They made the first ascent of the peak and forged a friendship that led Houston to invite four grizzled British veterans on a projected attempt on the formidable Kangchenjunga in 1936.

Bill Tilman (see pp.244–47) had explored the Nanda Devi Sanctuary in 1934, and suggested to the 22-year-old Houston that still-virgin Nanda

Devi was a more realistic goal. Houston was supposed to go for the summit with Everest veteran Noel Odell, but a corroded tin of meat gave him food poisoning and so Tilman replaced him; the pair reached the top of Nanda Devi.

LANDMARK BIDS FOR K2

In 1938, Houston led the first of his two expeditions to K2, reaching the Shoulder of the Abruzzi Spur with Paul Petzoldt by wading through thigh-deep snow. "I felt that all my previous life had reached a climax in these hours of intense struggle," he wrote later.

PETE SCHOENING'S OUTSTANDING ROPE WORK SAVED THE K2 TEAM MEMBERS FROM DISASTER

A LIFE'S WORK

- **Co-leads** an Anglo-American expedition to **Nanda Devi** in northern India, which puts climbers on the summit of the **highest mountain** to be scaled at that time

- Leads two landmark expeditions to K2. After **escaping death** on the second one, he makes no more serious climbs and devotes his life to his family, medicine, and good works, becoming the **director of the US Peace Corps** for India

- Combines his experience as a mountaineer and his skill as a physician to pioneer a **better understanding** of the physical affects of **high altitude** on the human body – his lasting legacy for mountaineers and trekkers

HIGH ON "AMERICA'S" MOUNTAIN
Despite his harrowing experience on K2 in 1953 (right), Houston contemplated going back. In July 1954, the news that a huge Italian team had reached the summit came as a crushing blow.

STORMS AND STRUGGLE ON K2
Here, Houston's 1953 team battle up to the Abruzzi
Spur. The men's response to the events that unfolded
came to exemplify the selflessness of a true climbing
team. Houston called it "the brotherhood of the rope".

During World War II,
Houston trained pilots
how to avoid the effects of hypoxia. After
the war he persuaded the US Navy to allow
further research with a decompression
chamber. Called Operation Everest, it
was ostensibly about achieving air combat
superiority, but had the happy side-effect
of demonstrating that climbers could survive,
for short periods at least, on the roof of the
world. It was the start of a research interest in
high-altitude physiology that would last the
rest of Houston's long life.

In 1953, Houston led another attempt on
K2 with a strong group. By the end of July,
Art Gilkey and Pete Schoening had established
Camp VIII just below the Shoulder and a few
days later the whole team – seven climbers
– moved up to it for a summit attempt. But
their dreams were undone by relentless bad
weather, which trapped them in their tents.

After eight nights at 7,700m (25,300ft),
Gilkey had developed blood clots in his left leg.
The climbers knew that he was dying but they
resolved to get him off the mountain at once.
In the retreat and fall that followed, Gilkey
disappeared and Houston almost died. Lying
unconscious on an exposed ledge, a team
member brought him round, and got him
moving again. He recovered and descended the
mountain to begin a new chapter in his life.

NANDA DEVI

SOUTH RIDGE, AUGUST 1936

— **12 August – Route to Camp III**
The team establish Camp III at
6,400m (21,000ft).

— **24 August – Houston descends**
Noel Odell and Houston bivouac
at 7,150m (23,500ft), then make a
reconnaissance towards the summit.
Houston is taken ill, and is replaced
by Bill Tilman.

— **29 August – Push to the summit**
Odell and Tilman move the bivouac
tent 150m (500ft) higher. They reach
the summit nine hours later, at 6pm.

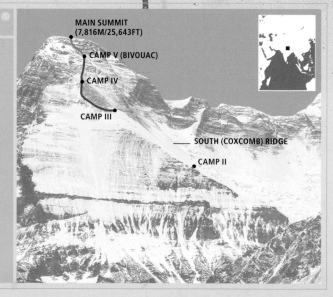

MAIN SUMMIT
(7,816M/25,643FT)

CAMP V (BIVOUAC)

CAMP IV

CAMP III

SOUTH (COXCOMB) RIDGE

CAMP II

FRITZ WIESSNER

A GALVANIZING FIGURE IN US CLIMBING

GERMANY/UNITED STATES   1900–88

A PIVOTAL CLIMBER in both Europe and the US, where he emigrated in 1929, Wiessner brought hard-won lessons from an apprenticeship on the sandstone towers near his native Dresden to the high mountains. A string of important ascents in the US was followed by bitter controversy after his bold but ultimately tragic attempt on K2 in 1939. Wiessner came within 240m (800ft) of the summit, but team member Dudley Wolfe later died, along with three Sherpas who tried to rescue him. Wiessner was blamed.

A LIFE'S WORK

- Learns to climb at the renowned rock-climbing area of Elbsandsteingebirge near Dresden, **famous for its free-climbing ethics and intolerance of pitons**

- Has a profound impact on the different schools of the sport, from **rock climbing to Himalayan mountaineering**

- **Plays a major role in the development of North American mountaineering**. He also makes important ascents there, including Mount Waddington in Canada, and Devils Tower in Wyoming in the US

- **Leads a tragic, but almost successful American expedition to K2**, which sets a new world altitude record by reaching 8,382m (27,500ft) on the Abruzzi Spur

- His reputation slowly recovers after the K2 tragedy, and **his zest for rock climbing and hard alpine climbs remains undiminished**. He reaches the summits of all the peaks over 4,000m (13,000ft) in the Alps

The 1939 attempt on K2 remains, in the words of historian Jim Curran, "a tender scar" in US climbing history. Expedition member Tony Cromwell called Wiessner "a murderer", an American Alpine Club inquiry proved bitterly controversial, and Wiessner, facing a wave of anti-German feeling at the onset of World War II, resigned his membership. The ill-feeling was still apparent when Wiessner was re-elected as an honorary member a quarter of a century later.

The aftermath of the tragedy overshadowed a remarkable climbing career that began before World War I on the Elbsandsteingebirge, an area of vertical sandstone towers outside Dresden, where free-climbing standards were the most exacting in the world. After the war, Wiessner made a number of difficult Alpine climbs, culminating in 1925 with the first ascent of the Southeast Face of the Fleischbank in Austria's Wilder Kaiser – then one of

K2'S FIRST VICTIM
Wealthy US adventurer Dudley Wolfe was inexperienced at high altitude, but insisted on climbing as high as he could on the 1939 attempt on K2. His eagerness to follow Wiessner up the mountain was to cost him his life.

the hardest climbs ever done. A week later, with Emil Solleder (see opposite), he climbed the North Face of the Furchetta in the Dolomites.

MOVING TO AMERICA

Germany's economic woes forced Wiessner to abandon his chemistry studies and open a pharmacy. He moved into the import-export business, which took him to the US in 1929. What was supposed to be a temporary visit became permanent. Wiessner became a US citizen in 1939, and broke his commercial links with Germany. In 1932, he joined the first German expedition to Nanga Parbat, led by Willy Merkl (see pp.238–39). Wiessner had persuaded two Americans to join the team: his friend Rand Herron and journalist Elizabeth Knowlton. Trouble with porters undermined their efforts, but they still reached a height of more than 7,000m (23,000ft).

Wiessner became a galvanizing force in American rock climbing. In 1935, he discovered the Shawangunks, the extensive conglomerate cliffs north of New York that became a crucible for the development of the sport in the US. He was still to be found climbing there well into his 80s. With

Bill House, a young graduate student at Yale University, he also made the first ascent of remote Mount Waddington in Canada – dubbed "Mount Mystery" by *Life* magazine and considered "unclimbable".

In 1937, Wiessner, House, and Lawrence Coveney made the first free ascent of Devils Tower in Wyoming, the strange, fluted natural rock structure sacred to American Indians. Wiessner resorted to placing just one piton on the climb, a precaution he later regretted.

CLOSE TO THE TOP OF K2

Inspired by the images of Vittorio Sella (see p.199), Wiessner sought permission for a US expedition to K2 in 1938. When it arrived, though, business interests kept him in the US, and Charles Houston led the team that reached almost 8,000m (26,247ft) on the Abruzzi Spur.

Wiessner decided to make a fresh attempt in 1939, but with the more experienced climbers recovering from the previous year's effort, he was forced to assemble a weaker party that included a number of wealthy climbers and adventurers who, although inexperienced, could fund the expedition. Among them was the socialite Dudley Wolfe who, like Wiessner's deputy, Tony Cromwell, had only made guided climbs – not the best preparation for K2.

Wiessner was an autocratic leader, and some of the climbers, not used to being told what to do, dropped out. The American Alpine Club sent the young Jack Durrance to Wiessner to bolster the party's talent, but personality clashes between the two men were to weaken morale even further. Initially, the expedition made good progress, thanks to an excellent team of Sherpas and Wiessner's determination. Though inept, Wolfe also proved surprisingly resilient. On 18 July, Wiessner pitched Camp IX on the shoulder of the Abruzzi Spur, at a little over 8,000m (26,247ft). Wolfe waited alone, 200m (700ft) below. Despite spending five nights at Camp VIII or higher, Wiessner remained optimistic and left for the summit with Sherpa Pasang Lama at 9am on 19 July. After nine hours' work, they reached 8,382m (27,500ft), just 240m (800ft) from the top – but still three hours or so away. Wiessner wanted to continue, but Pasang Lama stopped him and the pair turned around, reaching Camp IX at 2.30am.

DISASTER ON THE DESCENT

The expedition had begun to fall apart. At Base Camp, Cromwell sent Durrance a note at Camp II to start clearing the lower camps. One of the Sherpas assumed Wiessner and the others were lost, and the higher camps were stripped too.

But Wiessner had just taken the day off to rest before going back for another try. When this attempt failed and the party descended, they found Wolfe at Camp VIII out of supplies.

The retreat was gruesome. Wolfe fell, and his sleeping bag was lost, so it was decided to leave him at Camp VII. Wiessner hoped to find supplies at the next camp but that too was empty – as were all the camps below. Three of the Sherpas mounted a courageous bid to rescue Wolfe, but they and the American died.

Wiessner never returned to the Himalaya after the K2 expedition, but he remained an active climber right up to his death in 1988. In 1945, he married Muriel Schoonmaker, who would become his climbing and skiing partner for the rest of his life.

EMIL SOLLEDER
GERMANY   1899–1931

Born in Munich into modest circumstances, Solleder was an apprentice engineer before serving in World War I. Afterwards, he worked as a locksmith while planning a career as a mountain guide.

He qualified in 1925, the same year he introduced the "Sixth Grade" into Alpine climbing, with his first ascent of the North Face of the Furchetta in the Dolomites, with Wiessner. His other major climbs include the Northwest Face of the Civetta, also in 1925, and the East Face of Sass Maor. Solleder was also an expert skier and instructor. He was killed in a freak accident while guiding a client on La Meije. The client's abseil anchor failed and, in attempting to grab the rope, Solleder overbalanced and fell 600m (2,000ft). The client was unharmed, landing on a ledge.

A DANGEROUS MOUNTAIN
Perhaps because it is the most difficult of the 8,000-m (26,247-ft) peaks, even by its easiest route, K2 has attracted the most ambitious climbers. By 2008, of the 302 successful climbers, 31 of them had died on the descent.

EXPERIENCING THE MOUNTAINS

FILM-MAKING

With the invention of moving images in the late 19th century, a new dimension was added to the interpretation of mountain experiences. Even photography could only go so far in illustrating the mysteries of mountaineering, but now for the first time the non-climbing public could see for themselves what the sport entailed. The drama of bold young people in stunning surroundings was first exploited in the German *Bergfilme* of the 1920s, starting an ongoing debate about whether mountains were merely a backdrop for human stories, or the stars of the show.

Leni Riefenstahl

At first, it was simply enough to point a movie camera at the mountains and marvel at the result. Elizabeth Le Blond (see pp.156–57), the first mountain film-maker, shot footage in early 1900 of Alpine activities around St Moritz in Switzerland. In 1902, the US climber Frank Ormiston-Smith filmed ascents of Mont Blanc and the Shreckhorn for Charles Urban's production company.

Bergfilme, or mountain films, achieved huge popularity in Germany in the 1920s, where the work of Arnold Fanck packed cinemas. Fanck had suffered asthma and tuberculosis as a boy, so his father moved the family to the Alps. He saw his first movie in 1913 and, after World War I, while working as a carpet salesman, he bought a camera, learned to edit, and made his first film about an ascent of the Jungfrau. Thus began a genre that some film critics regard as a German equivalent to the Spaghetti Western.

In 1920, Fanck set up a production company and began turning out a series of *Bergfilme* that brought the glamour and danger of the Alps to the silver screen. His two big hits of the decade were *The Holy Mountain* (1926) and the *White Hell of Piz Palü* (1929), both starring Leni Riefenstahl, who went on to direct a mountain film of her own – *The Blue Light* (1932) – before tarnishing her talent with powerful documentaries for the Nazis. Riefenstahl had met Fanck through one of his earlier stars, Luis Trenker. Although the *Bergfilme* loosely suited Nazi propaganda, both Fanck and Trenker resented their work being hijacked, and fell out with the regime.

Later film-makers rejected the use of mountains as a mere backdrop to melodrama. French director Marcel Ichac created a kind of vertical *cinéma verité* in his influential *Les Étoiles de Midi* (1959), filmed above Chamonix, a pioneering work of docu-drama.

Although mountain films lost their mass appeal after World War II, the genre continued. Clint Eastwood was taught to rock climb before making *The Eiger Sanction* (1975), while *North Face* (2008) recreated the feel of the *Bergfilme*.

A STARRING LENI RIEFENSTAHL
Notorious for her later Nazi propaganda films, Riefenstahl got her big break as an actress from the pioneering *Bergfilme* director Arnold Fanck.

B STAR OF THE TYROL
Luis Trenker got his break in films from Fanck, too. He made a movie about the Matterhorn tragedy in 1938, *The Mountain Calls.*

C DANGEROUS FILMING
Arnold Fanck's camera crew perch precariously on a pinnacle to film a scene from *Storm over Mont Blanc,* a 1930 mountain melodrama.

D *LES ÉTOILES DE MIDI*
Lionel Terray (see pp.276–77), right, acts under the direction of Marcel Ichac with assistant director Jacques Ertaud. Shot on location, Ichac gave equal billing to the peaks and to Terray and the climbers.

FOR FOUR WEEKS PABST HAD THEM OUT IN THE OPEN ... HALF BURIED IN SNOW "

MARK SORKIN, ASSISTANT DIRECTOR TO G W PABST ON *WHITE HELL OF PIZ PALÜ*

E

D

E *WHITE HELL OF PIZ PALÜ*
Fanck co-directed this film with the great Austrian director G W Pabst. The film became a classic for its authentic feel, but drew a tart review from the *Alpine Journal*, which summed up its plot as "slush".

F ROPE CLIMAX
Clint Eastwood prefigures the main plotline of *Touching the Void* (see p.337) in the spy thriller *The Eiger Sanction* (1975) as he prepares to cut his rope during the film's climax. Leading climbers worked on the film, including Dougal Haston (see p.298) and Hamish MacInnes, as well as climbing photographer John Cleare.

G BOX CAMERA AND REEL, 1900
This heavy box camera was similar to the one Elizabeth Le Blond hauled into the Norwegian mountains.

H *NORTH FACE*
Echoes of the *Bergfilme* were caught in 2008's *Nordwand* (North Face), which dramatized the doomed attempt on the North Face of the Eiger in 1936.

F

G

H

"A mountaineering adventure MORE TENSE, more EDGE-OF-THE-SEAT SUSPENSEFUL, than *Touching the Void*!"
Anthony Quinn, THE INDEPENDENT (UK)

"A GRIPPING CLIFFHANGER!"
Philip French, THE OBSERVER (UK)

★★★★★ THRILLING!"
Nigel Andrews, THE FINANCIAL TIMES

NORTH FACE
A TRUE STORY

THE HIMALAYAN GOLDEN AGE

B EFORE WORLD WAR II, NONE OF THE 14 "8,000ERS" HAD BEEN CLIMBED. AFTER THE WAR, STARTING WITH THE FRENCH SUCCESS ON ANNAPURNA IN 1950, THE MOUNTAINEERING EQUIVALENT OF A GOLD RUSH BEGAN. BY 1964, ALL 14 HAD BEEN CLIMBED. SO WHAT HAD CHANGED?

EVEREST, 1953
Edmund Hillary sits with Kiwi team member George Lowe, talking on the radio. Wireless sets were used for communication between the camps and to listen to weather reports.

For a start, there were far fewer restrictions on freedom of movement in the Himalayan region. China had invaded Tibet in 1950 and subsequently denied access to its mountains for the next 30 years. Nepal, on the other hand, opened its frontiers to visitors for the first time. With eight of the 14 "8,000ers" accessible from Nepal, the number of potential prestige objectives for expeditions more than doubled.

HEADING FOR THE BIGGEST PRIZE
Porters of the British 1953 Everest expedition head for Base Camp. The best equipped and most expensive Himalayan expedition to date, it had to split into two walking groups because of its size.

Climbing equipment had benefited from the rapid technological advances made through the necessity of war. A shortage of manila, for example, led to the development of nylon ropes. For the first time in mountaineering's history, climbers could rely on their ropes not to break. The US quickly took the lead in developing synthetic fibres, which revolutionized outdoor clothing after the war. Vibram soles, developed

in Italy just before the war, replaced nailed leather, improving comfort and efficacy. The oxygen sets developed for pilots were more reliable than those previously used by climbers.

STARS OF THE NORTH FACES
There was also a large cadre of skilled European climbers who had banked a great deal of experience on the steep ice routes of the great

TRAVELLING LIGHT ON BROAD PEAK
In 1957, Hermann Buhl (above) took the lightweight climbing style used in the Alps to the Himalaya – a tactical change that influenced many of the ascents that followed.

TOSHIO IMANISHI ON MANASLU
After three failed attempts on the peak they had long considered a "Japanese mountain", the Japanese returned in 1956 with a 12-man team and put two people on the summit.

SETTING THE SCENE

- At the same moment India and Pakistan achieve independence in 1947, a Swiss team is in the Garhwal on **one of the first Himalayan expeditions** after World War II. When their Sherpa sirdar falls sick, **Tenzing Norgay** is promoted to the position, starting a train of events that leads him to the summit of Everest.

- After India's independence, **Nepal opens its borders to foreigners**, giving permission to mountaineering expeditions. Among the first climbers in the region is Englishman **H W "Bill" Tilman** (see pp.244–47), who explores the Langtang and Ganesh regions, and also Manang, where he makes **an attempt on Annapurna IV**.

- In 1950, Tilman **attempts Everest from the south** and the French **conquer Annapurna**.

- **Access to Tibet ends** following China's invasion in 1950. It will be three decades before it is restored.

north faces of the Alps. French climbing, which had continued during the war, had a surfeit of talent and was controlled and promoted by capable administrators such as Lucien Devies.

The Swiss, too, had some powerful individuals, including André Roch, who before the war had climbed the North Face of the Triolet and made the first ascent of Dunagiri. His was the voice of experience on the trail blazing Swiss expedition to Everest in 1952, when Raymond Lambert and Tenzing Norgay (see pp.266–67) came so close to the summit.

RACE TO THE HIMALAYA

With the immediate privations of the post-war period behind them, the defeated European powers, Germany, Austria, and Italy, with a pool of strong climbers to draw on, viewed mountaineering as a way to restore a little national pride and sporting élan.

The British lacked these countries' technical experience – no Briton climbed the North Face of the Eiger until Chris Bonington and Ian Clough in 1962 (see pp.300–01) – but they possessed deep exploratory experience and the necessary logistical ability. Few large expeditions before the war were led well, whereas the reverse was true in the 1950s. John Hunt and Charles Evans both proved outstanding leaders, although

with very different styles. Competition between nations undoubtedly played a major role. France's success on Annapurna in 1950, achieved without the benefit of a reconnaissance and on their first attempt, galvanized European climbers. The ascent broke a psychological barrier and mountaineers around the world quickly realized that all of the "8,000ers" would soon be climbed. Those who didn't act quickly would have nothing to show. Despite the rush, there was a huge variety in the size and style of expeditions, from the logistical behemoth of the Italians on K2 in 1954 to the four-man Austrian team, functioning without porters or supplementary oxygen, on Broad Peak in 1957.

> After World War II, nations with an alpine tradition, and even those without, set their sights on claiming the 14 highest peaks. Some of the best climbs of the era were below the magic 8,000m, but these sparked less public interest.

RISE OF THE SHERPAS

Perhaps the greatest lightweight effort was by another Austrian team, who climbed Cho Oyu in 1954. Among them were the geologist Herbert Tichy, and Sepp Jöchler, who had

SPIRIT OF ADVENTURE
On climbing Cho Oyu, Herbert Tichy wrote that he felt "as glorious as God and at the same time no more than an insignificant grain of sand".

partnered Hermann Buhl (see pp.258–59) on the North Face of the Eiger in 1952. The powerhouse of the team, however, was Pasang Dawa, the head Sherpa who had forced Fritz Wiessner to turn back on K2 in 1939 (see p.250–51). Pasang led critical portions of the route, as the Sherpa's role grew in importance.

In 1956, another Sherpa, Gyalzen Norbu, became the first man to climb two "8,000ers" when he partnered Japanese climber Toshio Imanishi on the first ascent of Manaslu in Nepal.

Their triumph was the culmination of a sustained effort by members of the Japanese Alpine Club, which mounted a reconnaissance of Annapurna IV and Manaslu in 1952 and then sent three expeditions in consecutive years before finally achieving success.

UNDER THE RADAR

There were also important ascents at lower altitudes, too, notably in the Karakoram. In 1956, British climbers Joe Brown (see pp.272–73) and Ian McNaught-Davis reached the summit of the spectacular Muztagh Tower, just five days ahead of a French team. A strong Italian team led by legendary alpinist Riccardo Cassin (see pp.292–93) climbed Gasherbrum IV in 1958, while in the same year, a British-Pakistani team put Tom Patey and Mike Banks on the summit of Rakaposhi.

HERZOG AND LACHENAL

DIVIDED HIMALAYAN PIONEERS

FRANCE   B.1919; 1921–55

MAURICE HERZOG   LOUIS LACHENAL

ON 3 JUNE 1950, Maurice Herzog and Louis Lachenal became the first men to climb a mountain higher than 8,000m (26,247ft) when they stood on the summit of Annapurna, the tenth-highest peak in the world. Their achievement, and that of their expedition, was all the more remarkable because no attempts had been made before on Annapurna, and the peak had to be located, reconnoitred, and climbed in a single season.

The French Himalaya expedition of 1950, well financed by the *Club Alpin Français*, was a matter of national prestige – a way to restore pride after the ignominies of World War II. Ironically, French mountaineering had emerged from the war in good shape, with many of the leading protagonists able to continue their activities.

The team included the very best French climbers of their generation: Lachenal, Gaston Rébuffat, Lionel Terray, and Jean Couzy (see pp.276–77), all of whom played a pivotal role. Herzog was a business executive and war hero

with political ambitions and – unlike the others, who were mountain guides – was an amateur climber. The others were less keen on Herzog's romantically inspired public relations, and despite the expedition's success, controversy and recrimination undermined Herzog's account.

DIFFERENT ROOTS

At 31, Herzog was the oldest of the six lead climbers. The eldest child of eight, he grew up as another mountaineering fan of Nietzsche (see p.175), describing himself as a taciturn, awkward

young man who spent his summers at the family's chalet near Chamonix. After studying philosophy and business in Paris, he went to work for the tyre firm Kléber-Colombes.

Although a capable amateur climber, Herzog wasn't in the same league as Louis Lachenal. From a young age, Lachenal rebelled against his petit-bourgeois roots – his parents ran a grocery shop in Annecy, southeast France. He would sneak into cinemas without paying and developed an early appreciation of Savoie cider. By his teens, the edgy, driven Lachenal was exploring the mountains around Annecy.

Working as a climbing and skiing instructor, and for a time a member of the *Jeunesse et Montagne* movement established to fill the hours of frustrated young Frenchmen, by the time the war had ended Lachenal was starting to make his mark. In the spring of 1945, he met Lionel Terray, who was fighting in the Companie Stéphane, a mountain-based guerrilla unit.

Lachenal was adamantly pacifist, but despite their differences, that meeting led to one of the most formidable climbing partnerships in mountaineering history. In the summer of 1945, Lachenal and Terray made the fourth ascent of the Walker Spur on the Grandes Jorasses, and two years later made the second ascent of the Eiger's North Face. The pair later compared who had climbed the hardest Alpine routes: Terray counted 157, Lachenal 151. Terray and

ANNAPURNA

NORTH FACE, 3 JUNE 1950

— **31 May – Route to Camp IV**
Having switched to Annapurna's North Face on 23 May, a series of camps is quickly established to Camp IV at 7,150m (23,500ft).

— **2 June – Route to Camp V**
With Ang Tharkay and Sarki in support, Lachenal and Herzog move up to Camp V at 7,500m (24,600ft).

— **3 June – Route to the summit**
Leaving at 6am, they reach the summit at 2pm, but struggle on the descent as the weather worsens and suffer severe frostbite.

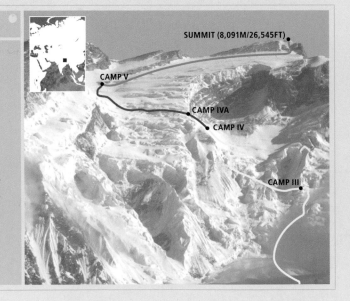

SUMMIT (8,091M/26,545FT)

CAMP V

CAMP IVA

CAMP IV

CAMP III

Lachenal – along with gifted fellow-guide Gaston Rébuffat – would go on to form the nucleus of the Annapurna team.

FOR FRANCE

The expedition sprang from the *Comité de l'Himalaya* of the *Club Alpin Français*, overseen by Lucien Devies. It bothered the fiercely patriotic Devies that the French had yet to achieve anything of note in the Himalaya. It was bad enough that the Germans and Italians had poached the greatest prizes in the French Alps. He raised funds through public subscription and put Herzog in charge. Devies even required the team to swear an oath of allegiance – but such nationalistic pressure did not sit well with the independent-minded climbers.

The expedition didn't leave Paris until 30 March 1950 – late for such a huge undertaking, which had to be completed before the monsoon arrived in early June. But they had the latest gear: modern synthetic materials, down-insulated clothing, and lightweight boots. Their footwear was a factor in the severe frostbite the summiteers were to suffer.

SCRAMBLE FOR THE SUMMIT

The expedition began by exploring the approaches to Dhaulagiri, a higher mountain 34km (21 miles) to the west, but by mid May the climbers had been unable even to reach its foot. They turned their attention to nearby Annapurna, whose approaches they had briefly explored. Despite confusing topography, by 18 May they had reached the foot of the Northwest Buttress – only to discover that the climbing was harder than expected.

While Terray and Herzog persevered with the buttress, Rébuffat, who had been sceptical of their chances, scouted a route on the north face with Lachenal. This proved to be much more viable. The pair sent a note down to Herzog to come quickly with as many Sherpas and supplies as possible. Despite heavy afternoon snow and the threat of avalanches, the party shot up the North Face, and by the evening of 2 June Lachenal and Herzog were poised for their summit bid, which they attained on 3 June. Their descent from the summit and subsequent fight for survival as the weather turned bad

forms the climax of Herzog's classic book *Annapurna*. Despite losing digits to frostbite, Herzog went into politics as minister of sport and later became a member of the International Olympic Committee. Lachenal, bitter at the loss of his toes, became reckless for his own safety. He died after falling into a crevasse while skiing in Chamonix's Vallée Blanche in 1955.

SUMMIT OF ACHIEVEMENT
Herzog (pictured), and Lachenal reached the summit of Annapurna on 3 June 1950. Herzog suffered such severe frostbite on the two-week descent that he required emergency amputations.

"OTHER ANNAPURNAS"

Herzog's account of the Annapurna expedition is a mountaineering classic. Readers responded to his otherworldly state of mind as he neared the summit: "An astonishing happiness welled up in me, but I could not define it." His mental state may have been the consequence of taking maxiton, a drug then popular with racing cyclists. Studies of the expedition suggest it wasn't as harmonious as Herzog attested, but the freshness of his view of Nepal, his phlegmatic acceptance of his injuries, and his final exhortation – "There are other Annapurnas in the lives of men" – made the book hugely popular.

HERZOG'S *ANNAPURNA* **HAS SOLD MORE THAN 11 MILLION COPIES**

ANNAPURNA

The First 8,000 metre Peak (26,493 feet)

MAURICE HERZOG

HERMANN BUHL

UNCOMPROMISING INNOVATOR

AUSTRIA   1924–57

(see pp.238–39)

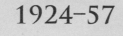

WEEKS AFTER HILLARY AND TENZING climbed Everest, Hermann Buhl reached the summit of Nanga Parbat, the third of the 8,000-m (26,000-ft) peaks to be claimed. His bold solo push, in defiance of orders from base camp, was one of the greatest climbing performances of the 20th century. Buhl's preference for a light and fast approach pointed the way forward, and his passion for the mountains, eloquently captured in his autobiography, inspired the following generation of climbers.

TOE SAVERS
Buhl spent the night in Nanga Parbat's "Death Zone" without his warm clothes, which he had abandoned on the ascent. His boots provided some protection and he lost only two toes to frostbite.

On 30 June 1953, Buhl was at Camp III on the Rakhiot Face of Pakistan's Nanga Parbat, attempting the same route that had killed so many Austrian and German climbers and their Sherpas in the 1930s. The expedition was made in memory to one of the fallen, Willy Merkl (see pp.238–39). Its leader, Karl Herrligkoffer, was Merkl's half-brother and the climbing leader, Peter Aschenbrenner, was a veteran of the 1932 and 1934 attempts.

After a change in the weather, it was decided to abort the expedition. They radioed Buhl twice, ordering him and his three companions to retreat, but they refused. "Mad desire to go on," Buhl wrote in his diary. By noon the next day, the group were up at Camp IV, digging out the tents and preparing the route ahead. By the evening of 2 July, Buhl and his partner, Otto Kempter, had established Camp V, just below 7,000m (22,000ft), under a feature called the Moor's Head.

PUSHING BEYOND THE LIMITS

Buhl was up at 1am to make tea and pack for the summit climb. Kempter found it difficult to rouse himself from sleep, and so Buhl left on his own at 2am, expecting Kempter to catch up. It was a starry night with a sliver of moon to light the ridge above him. By 5am Buhl had reached the start of a long traverse to a col below the summit pyramid. Two hours later he was there, basking in the sun's warmth.

Yet the higher he got, the slower he climbed. He watched Kempter below him give up and turn around. The route seemed never ending. By lunchtime Buhl still had 300m (1,000ft) to go, up the most technical ground he'd yet faced. After a moment's hesitation, he took two pills of Pervitin, an amphetamine, and his pace improved. The climbing got harder, but still he went on,

sometimes crawling on all fours, breaking onto the final summit ridge at 6pm. An hour later he was on the summit, tying a flag to his ice axe.

On the way down, just below the summit, Buhl lost a crampon and was forced to bivouac, standing through the night on a small ledge, gripping a single handhold. By 4am he could see well enough to continue. Plagued by thirst, spitting blood, hallucinating food and a companion, and with his right foot frozen, he took more amphetamines to keep himself moving. He reached Camp V at 6:30pm, 40 hours after leaving the tent.

Buhl believed it was only his iron will that kept him going, but where did such determination come from? Born in Innsbruck, Buhl was placed in an orphanage at the age of four, after his mother died. He was a sickly and sensitive child, and his isolation at this young age left him with a burning ambition to succeed at the thing that most captured his imagination – alpinism.

Starting in the Austrian Alps during World War II, he would use his periods of leave to climb as much and as hard as he could. "The mountains, they are my homeland," he wrote at the start of his first climbing diary. After the war, he trained as a mountain guide and launched himself on the hardest routes of the day, bringing the technical skills he had learned in the

BUHL SETS OFF FOR THE SUMMIT
After Buhl struck out from Camp V during the ascent of Nanga Parbat, his companions anxiously awaited his return. "Our comrade, alone but on behalf of us all, was engaged in the final combat," Herrligkoffer wrote later.

BITTER AFTERMATH
Buhl's solo push to the summit of Nanga Parbat in 1953
saved the honour of the expedition, but instead of
rejoicing with the rest of the team, expedition leader
Herrligkoffer denounced him for defying his orders.

Austrian Alps to longer climbs such as the
Walker Spur on the Grandes Jorasses and the
Eiger's North Face.

His grand, solitary adventures culminated
with Nanga Parbat. His triumph there made
him an international star, but landed him in
fierce legal disputes with the expedition's
leader. Buhl found himself increasingly isolated
from the Austrian climbing community.

Recovering quickly from the frostbite and
toe amputations he suffered on Nanga Parbat,
Buhl did more hard climbs in the Alps, and
then returned to Asia to make the first ascent of
Broad Peak (8,047m/26,401ft), this time with a
small team. Soon afterwards, coming down
from a failed attempt on another Karakoram
giant, Chogolisa, he fell through a cornice
and was lost; his body was never found.

NANGA PARBAT

RAKHIOT ROUTE, JUNE/JULY 1953

— **11 June – Route to Camp III**
Buhl and Frauenberger establish
Camp III. Poor weather and lack of
Sherpas had delayed progress.

— **30 June – Route to Camp V**
Despite demands they return to
Base Camp, Buhl, Ertl, Frauenberger
and Rainer prepare to push on
towards Camp V.

— **3 July – Route to summit**
Buhl and Kempter leave Camp V,
but Kempter drops back. Buhl has
to climb 1,200m (4,000ft) and
cover 6km (4 miles) to reach the
summit at 7pm.

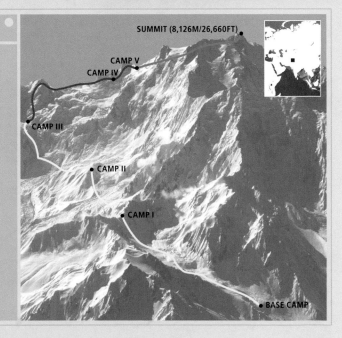

SUMMIT (8,126M/26,660FT)

CAMP V
CAMP IV

CAMP III

CAMP II

CAMP I

BASE CAMP

KURT DIEMBERGER

VETERAN MOUNTAINEER OF "8000ER" FIRST ASCENTS

AUSTRIA   B.1932

ONE OF ONLY TWO MEN to make the first ascent of two "8,000ers", Diemberger was also the last person to see Hermann Buhl alive, during their alpine-style 1957 attempt on Chogolisa. Three weeks earlier, they had climbed Broad Peak. His second 8,000m "trophy" was Dhaulagiri in 1960 as part of a Swiss team. Ebullient, emotional, and often controversial, Diemberger's passion for the mountains sustained him through a career spanning decades – and brought him down from one of the worst tragedies in climbing history.

Diemberger may not have had the wild ambition of Hermann Buhl (see pp.258–59) or the technical brilliance of Walter Bonatti (see pp.296–97), but over the years he proved himself a tough and resilient survivor. His career spanned the immediate post-war period, the "gold rush" to bag the first ascents of the "8000er" peaks, and the resurgence of interest in Himalayan climbing from the 1970s onwards, partly inspired by Reinhold Messner (see pp.308–11).

Born in Carinthia in Austria, Diemberger was introduced to the mountains while crystal hunting with his father. One day in the Hohe

Tauern, when he was 16, he chose instead to climb the summit of the Larmkogl. By his mid 20s he was already an accomplished alpinist, with the Matterhorn's North Face and the first direct ascent of the Königswand in the bag.

TO THE KARAKORAM

Diemberger's growing reputation brought him an invitation to join Buhl, Marcus Schmuck, and Fritz Wintersteller on the first ascent of Broad Peak in 1957. The team used a tactic Buhl termed *Westalpenstil* – climbing without porters or oxygen. The following year, after Buhl's death, Diemberger climbed the Eiger's North

BROAD PEAK

WEST SPUR, 9 JUNE 1957

— **28 May – Safe climbing**
The four climbers establish Camp III.

— **29 May – Initial disappointment**
They reach the expected summit, but the true summit is seen some distance away. They descend to Base Camp.

— **9 June – To the true summit**
Schmuck and Wintersteller reach the summit first. Leaving Buhl behind, exhausted, Diemberger joins them, but he then returns for Buhl and leads him back to the summit at dusk.

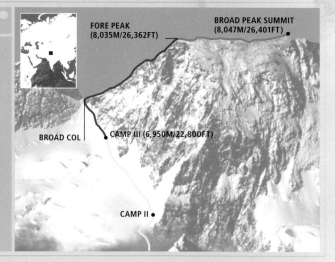

FORE PEAK
(8,035M/26,362FT)

BROAD PEAK SUMMIT
(8,047M/26,401FT)

BROAD COL

CAMP III (6,950M/22,800FT)

CAMP II

Face, the Walker Spur on the Grandes Jorasses, and the Peuterey Ridge on Mont Blanc. He filmed his ascent of the Peuterey Ridge, launching his career as a film-maker.

In 1960, under the leadership of Max Eiseln, Diemberger made the first ascent of Dhaulagiri on a very different type of expedition, which used a skiplane to deliver supplies. The three summit climbers decided to make the ascent without bottled oxygen, although the expedition had it available. Later in the 1960s, when the Himalaya were closed for political reasons, he concentrated on the Hindu Kush, Greenland, and Africa. But his Himalayan career was reinvigorated in the 1970s with ascents of Makalu and Everest. His immense drive and physical strength, as well as a burgeoning film career – he won an Emmy in 1982 – kept him climbing the Himalayan giants well into his 50s.

STORM OF TRAGEDY

While working in a film crew on Nanga Parbat in 1982, Diemberger formed a relationship with British mountaineer Julie Tullis that would dominate the next few years of his life. In 1986, they reached the summit of K2 in what was to be the most tragic season on record. Descending from the summit on 4 August, Tullis fell, pulling Diemberger with her. They finally stopped in soft snow above a dizzying drop. After a

DIEMBERGER THE "DOCTOR"
After climbing Broad Peak in 1957, Diemberger gives Buhl an injection to ward off frostbite damage. Days later, Diemberger looked back along the ridge of Chogolisa to see that a cornice had broken off and Buhl had fallen to his death.

freezing bivouac, Diemberger helped Tullis down to Camp IV, but later that day a vicious storm trapped them – and five others – at 8,000m (26,250ft). When their tent was destroyed, Tullis sheltered with Austrian Willi Bauer and his two compatriots, while Diemberger crammed in with Briton Alan Rouse and the Polish climber Dobroslawa Wolf.

Tullis died after ten days on the mountain. Diemberger was heartbroken, and his account of the tragedy, *The Endless Knot* (1991), is a raw, compelling outpouring of grief and enquiry. "Julie once said that perhaps the best way to die would be to fall asleep, high in the mountains," he wrote. "Is that, then, how it was?"

The storm raged on and Rouse, who had just made the first British ascent of K2, began to deteriorate. Then Diemberger found frostbite on his own hand: "The end of my finger has swollen into a huge blueish blister … I guess that's had it. Not nice, to die off piecemeal, like this."

When the weather eased on 10 August, Diemberger, Wolf, and Bauer snatched their one chance to escape – Rouse was delirious and beyond rescue. Wolf died during the descent above Camp II, the fifth victim of the storm. Only Bauer and Diemberger made it back.

In the years after K2, Diemberger, by then in his late 50s, turned increasingly to research and film work, often in the company of his daughter, the anthropologist Hildegard Diemberger, but always in the high mountains.

RECORD FIRST ASCENT
Diemberger (left) rests on top of Dhaulagiri, his record second first ascent of an "8,000er", alongside Albin Schelbert. The ascent was made without bottled oxygen.

MOUNTAIN LIVES

SHERPAS

THE SHERPAS OF NEPAL have played a crucial role in Himalayan climbing. Traditionally traders, in the early 1900s, many of them migrated to Darjeeling to find work, where they were "discovered" by British climber Alexander Kellas. They proved themselves capable porters, assisting expeditions that would otherwise have got nowhere. Reliable under tough conditions and hard–working, their mountain skills are always in demand.

The word "Sherpa" is used to describe both a people and a job. Sherpas as a people originated in the Tibetan province of Kham, and migrated to various parts of Nepal about 400 years ago, including to the region south of Everest known as Khumbu. Today, there are some 150,000 Sherpas in Nepal and the best known live in the Everest region.

Like Tibetans, they are superbly adapted to altitude. Their historical role as traders and their long exposure to different cultures gave them an advantage in the 1920s and 1930s when large European expeditions arrived and needed reliable support. On Everest before World War II, about half of the porters working on the mountain were Sherpas, the rest being Tibetans. After the war, the Sherpas predominated.

Sherpa as a job description refers to someone who works in the mountains doing the job we traditionally associate with the tribe of Sherpas. Tourists call their porters Sherpas, even though they may come from another tribe, such as the Rais or Limbus.

The best mountaineering Sherpas, those who see Everest as their factory floor, come from villages such as Pangboche and Phortse in Khumbu, or from the nearby valley of Rolwaling. They earn thousands of dollars on a typical climbing trip, and this wealth has transformed their valley. There are now hospitals and schools, and Sherpas can afford to educate their children in Kathmandu. Trekking lodges are another source of revenue. The old tasks of farming and herding are now performed by hired hands.

NAMCHE BAZAR, NEPAL, THE CHIEF SHERPA VILLAGE, IN THE KHUMBU REGION NEAR MOUNT EVEREST. THE VILLAGE IS AT AN ALTITUDE OF 3,440M (11,290FT). IN THE BACKGROUND IS THE 6,011-M (19,721-FT) PEAK KWANGDE.

THE NEW ELITE
Sherpas have developed from being willing helpers to stars in their own right. Experienced Everest climbers now earn thousands of dollars in a season, which is often invested in lodges or education.

❶ Tenzing Norgay (right) was a Tibetan-born Sherpa who was the first to climb Everest in 1953. ❷ Apa Sherpa (left) climbed Everest for the 20th time in 2010; Babu Chiri (right) camped on the summit without bottled oxygen. ❸ Tibetan Buddhism plays a central role in Sherpa life, and a puja ceremony, in which prayers and offerings are made to the mountain gods, is held at Everest Base Camp before each climb.

SHERPAS AT WORK
Sherpas soon adapted to their new high-altitude role, and many became experienced mountaineers in their own right. Those who did well were described as "tigers". Those with outstanding management skills, such as Ang Tharkay, became sirdars, or lead Sherpas.

❶ A Sherpa on the 1953 Everest expedition attaches crampons to his boots in the Khumbu Icefall. ❷ The Sherpa "tigers" who established Camp IV on the 1933 Everest expedition. ❸ A Sherpa steps across a crevasse above Camp II on the 1953 Everest expedition.

MAKING THEIR NAME

Born, brought up, and genetically adapted to life at high altitude, Sherpas accompanied Europeans almost from the start of Himalayan climbing. Kellas wrote that they "seemed to me more at home under the diminished pressure than my European companions".

❶ Leiva, the chief sirdar on the 1933 Everest expedition, poses for a portrait. ❷ Dawa Tenzing was the sirdar on the 1955 Kangchenjunga expedition. ❸ A Sherpa child on the 1953 Everest expedition wears snow goggles made from hair. ❹ A Sherpa looks out of a tent on the 1955 Kangchenjunga expedition.

ANG THARKAY
NEPAL   1908–81

Ang Tharkay was among the best Sherpas to emerge in the 1930s, and was the lead Sherpa of the French expedition to Annapurna in 1950.

Born in the Khumbu village of Khunde, he migrated to Darjeeling for work. His first expedition was Kangchenjunga with the Germans in 1931, but he spent much of the 1930s with Bill Tilman and Eric Shipton (see pp.244–47), who called him "a most lovable person: modest, unselfish and … sincere".

EDMUND HILLARY

FIRST TO CLIMB MOUNT EVEREST

NEW ZEALAND   1919–2008

THIRTY-TWO YEARS AFTER the first expedition to Everest, the highest mountain on Earth, two climbers finally reached the summit. One was a Tibetan-born Sherpa, Tenzing Norgay, the other a laconic beekeeper from New Zealand. "I looked up to my right," Hillary wrote later, "and 40 feet above me was a rounded snow cone. A few blows of the ice axe, a few weary steps, and I was on the top. My first reaction was that of relief." Hillary shot to international fame overnight and received a knighthood for his feat.

The photograph Edmund Hillary took of Tenzing on the summit of Everest is one of the most famous images of the 20th century (see pp.266–67). But there are no photographs of Hillary himself; presuming the Sherpa would have had little experience with cameras, he didn't bother to ask him to return the favour. After Everest, Hillary would become more aware of the commercial value of his achievement, and use it to the advantage of those less fortunate.

LONGING FOR ADVENTURE

Hillary's father, a fomer newspaperman who had served in the Gallipoli Campaign in World War I, was allocated land near Tuakau, south of Auckland, so the young Edmund grew up in the country and was well fed by his father's orchard and market garden. But father and son had a stormy relationship and, while Hillary thrived at primary school, by secondary school his progress had tailed off. Shy, and small for his age, he took refuge in books and dreamed of adventure.

At 14, he had a growth spurt, and learned to box, but he became preoccupied by questions of religion and what the purpose of his life should be. At university, switched on to the appeal of mountains on a school trip, he joined a group of "trampers" for winter treks in the Waitakere Ranges west of Auckland. The physical hardship of ploughing through snow came as a welcome

relief for the serious-minded young man. Hillary dropped out of university to work with his brother Rex and his father, managing the family's 1,600 bee hives. At the outbreak of World War II, still in the throes of his evangelical phase, Hillary didn't immediately join up, but changed his mind in 1944 and served as a navigator on Catalina flying boats, before being badly burned in an accident.

During his military service Hillary did his first notable climb, of Mount Tapuaenuku on New Zealand's South Island. After the war he climbed whenever he could, and was taken under the wing of his first real mentor, Harry Ayers, one of the great New Zealand ice climbers. Together they climbed the South Ridge of Mount Cook, a longstanding and dangerous challenge.

AIMING HIGH

Although the mountains in New Zealand are Alpine in scale, their approaches are often much tougher than in the Alps. This served Hillary well when he joined an expedition to India's Garhwal Himalaya in 1951. He and his friend

George Lowe laid the groundwork for success on Mukut Parbat, although they were muscled aside on the summit climb by the expedition's leader, fellow Kiwi Earl Riddiford.

As the party prepared to return to New Zealand, they received a telegram from British climber Eric Shipton (see pp.244–47), inviting two of them to join his Everest reconnaissance of 1951. Riddiford had the cash to get them to Nepal, so he and Hillary travelled to Khumbu, south of Everest. Anxious about how he would get on with a team of stiff Englishmen, Hillary was relieved to discover that Shipton was very much his kind of mountaineer. Like Ayers, the Everest veteran became a mentor, taking Hillary to Cho Oyu – the world's sixth highest peak – the following year in preparation for Everest.

EVEREST DREAM TEAM

In 1953, Shipton was levered off that year's British Everest expedition and replaced with a military man, Colonel John Hunt. Hillary knew nothing of Hunt and felt aggrieved for his friend. If the expedition was to succeed, Hunt needed the nucleus of climbers Shipton had built up – Tom Bourdillon, Charles Evans, and Alf Gregory – and these men warned that without the New Zealanders Hillary and Lowe, they would quit. Hunt brought the latter into the team, and Shipton wrote to Hillary asking him to transfer his loyalty to the new expedition leader. Once the climb was underway, it soon

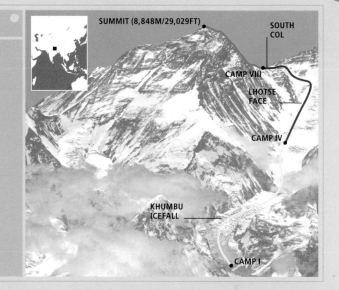

MOUNT EVEREST

SOUTH COL, 1953

— **23 April – Through the icefall**
After steady progress, Camp IV is established under the Southwest Face to start supplying higher camps.

— **21 May – Climbing Lhotse Face**
Progress slows as the team spend 12 days overcoming the Lhotse Face.

— **29 May – Route to the summit**
After Charles Evans and Tom Bourdillon reach the South Summit, Tenzing and Hillary move up to Camp IX, and finish the job.

SUMMIT (8,848M/29,029FT)

SOUTH COL

CAMP VIII

LHOTSE FACE

CAMP IV

KHUMBU ICEFALL

CAMP I

became apparent that Hillary and Tenzing were, in Hunt's words, "unmistakeably outstanding at the time, climbing faster and more strongly than the rest of us." Hillary knew that Hunt would struggle to allow him to climb with Lowe, so he built up a good climbing relationship with Tenzing, who, unusually for a Sherpa, was equally ambitious for the summit.

Hunt chose Evans and Bourdillon to make the first assault on the summit and the pair came within 90 vertical metres (300ft) of it before being forced to retreat by oxygen-tank failures and bad weather. The fate of the expedition then fell to the second summit party: Tenzing and

Hillary. Together they set off, establishing Camp IX at 8,500m (27,900ft) before spending a ferociously cold night in a howling gale trying to sleep. The next day they left the camp at 6.30am and began their push. Poised below the South Summit at 9am, Hillary was unnerved by the loose snow, fearing an avalanche. "Ed, my boy," he told himself, "this is Everest. You've got to push a bit harder." Crossing the final ridge, they came to a steep, icy rock step 12m (40ft) high now called the Hillary Step, but they found a vertical crack and managed to scale it. The last few feet to the summit were relatively easy and by 11.30am, the job was done.

JOHN HUNT
ENGLAND   1910–98

A great-nephew of the explorer Richard Burton, Hunt spent childhood holidays in the Alps and had climbed the Piz Palü by the age of 14.

As a young man, he joined the army and served in the King's Royal Rifle Corps, stationed in India, where he climbed during periods of leave. In World War II he was awarded the Distinguished Service Order. In 1952, when he was approached to lead the British Everest expedition, Hunt was a staff officer at Supreme Headquarters Allied Expeditionary Force in Germany. One of the keys to success in 1953 was the efficient delivery of equipment and supplies to Everest's South Col, something Hunt's leadership ensured. Like Hillary, he was knighted after Everest, and returned to active duty in the army before retiring and becoming the first director of the UK charity The Duke of Edinburgh Award Scheme.

ONWARDS AND UPWARDS
On the 1953 expedition, a series of climbs by co-ordinated teams established ever-higher camps on the icy slopes and hazardous rock ledges of Everest. Here, Hillary and Tenzing are seen approaching the site of Camp IX, from where they launched their summit bid.

TENZING NORGAY

FIRST SHERPA TO SUMMIT EVEREST

NEPAL   1914–86

ONE OF MOUNTAINEERING'S most famous names, Tenzing Norgay's route to climbing was less straightforward than most. His heroic efforts to reach the summit of Everest are a testament to his extraordinary persistence and ambition. Born in Tibet, he migrated first to Khumbu in Nepal and then to Darjeeling in India, escaping a life of poverty and disadvantage to become one of the best known Asians in history. A hero for mountain people everywhere, Tenzing brought the tough and hardy Sherpa race to world prominence.

TOM BOURDILLON AND CHARLES EVANS AT THE SOUTH COL, DEJECTED AFTER THEIR ATTEMPT ON THE SUMMIT

At the head of Tibet's Kama Valley, below the East Face of Everest, lies a small lake tucked out of sight of the mountain. Tenzing Norgay was born here, below a huge cliff shaped like the head of the Buddha, in a yak-herder's tent.

At first he was given the name Namgyal Wangdi, but later his parents asked for a new name from a revered Buddhist lama, who told them a wealthy man had recently died, and their child was his reincarnation. They should call him Tenzing, meaning "supporter of religion", and Norgay, meaning "wealthy". Tenzing was one of 13 children, most of whom

died young. His father cared for a large herd of yaks for a local monastery and the family's life revolved around these extraordinary beasts.

It is possible that when George Mallory (see pp.228–31) explored the eastern side of Everest in 1921, the young Tenzing saw him, but it was the Tibetans living in Darjeeling and working for the British mountaineers who inspired him. They were exciting, adventurous types with smart new boots and strange clothes. Tenzing could see a bigger world beyond his valley.

SEIZING EVERY OPPORTUNITY

In the late 1920s, the family's yak herd was wiped out by disease, and they were reduced to abject poverty. Tenzing's father was forced to offer his teenage son as a servant to a relatively wealthy family in the Sherpa homeland of Khumbu.

While in Khumbu, Tenzing fell in love with Dawa Phuti, the daughter of a wealthy trader. When the Sherpa girl's father arranged a more suitable match, the two lovers eloped to Darjeeling, where

Tenzing scratched a living as a labourer while trying to break into expedition work. His chance came in 1935 when British climber Eric Shipton (see pp.244–47), looking for a couple of extra porters at the last minute for his reconnaissance expedition to Everest, was charmed by his ready smile. Tenzing proved himself indispensable, and he was hired again on British expeditions in 1936 and 1938.

During World War II, with no expeditions arriving in the Himalaya, Tenzing worked as an orderly for the Chitral Scouts in India's Hindu Kush. His wife died, leaving him with two young daughters, so he returned to Darjeeling and married another Sherpa girl, who cared for the children while he worked.

A LIFE'S WORK

- At the age of 19 he is chosen as a porter for Eric Shipton's reconnaissance expedition to Everest. In the years that follow, he **takes part in more Everest expeditions than any other climber**, often serving as head porter

- Forms a close bond with leading Swiss climbers and **reaches a new altitude record on Everest** with Raymond Lambert

- Joins the tenth expedition to **Everest** in 32 years; he and Edmund Hillary, partnered as the second assault party, **reach the summit**

- After Everest, he becomes **Chief Instructor of the Himalayan Mountaineering Institute** in Darjeeling, India

WELL-MATCHED PAIR
Tenzing and Hillary spent just 15 minutes on the summit of Everest before making the slow and tortuous descent. They are pictured here enjoying a celebratory cup of tea at Camp IV.

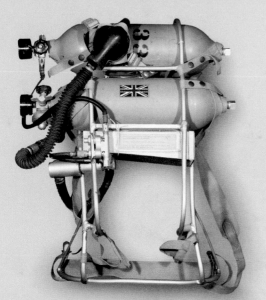

OPEN-CIRCUIT OXYGEN SET
This oxygen set, carried by Tenzing on his back, was state-of-the-art equipment in 1953. He and Hillary also carried a spare cylinder containing five hours worth of air.

In 1947, he went to the Garhwal Himalaya with a Swiss expedition led by the leading alpinist André Roch. He found the Swiss more open than his British employers, and more trusting too, and the relationship brought him his chance on Everest. In 1952, a Swiss team appointed him *sirdar* (or lead Sherpa) on their Everest attempt. Tenzing formed a close bond with climber Raymond Lambert, and together, via the South Col route, the pair reached 8,570m (28,120ft), as high as anyone had climbed before.

TO THE TOP OF THE WORLD

In 1953, the British, aware that Tenzing now had more experience than anyone of climbing high on Everest, selected him for their next expedition. Tenzing was given the dual role of climber and leader of the big team of Sherpas, but by now his natural authority had blossomed into real leadership. As he stood on Everest's summit with Edmund Hillary (see pp.264–65), Tenzing didn't look around at the neighbouring peaks, but into the valleys where he had spent his childhood and youth, thinking of his family.

Tenzing and Hillary's relationship on the mountain was not a close one. Tenzing made no secret of the fact that he preferred the Swiss, and he felt patronized by the expedition's leader, John Hunt (see p.265), when the team returned to Kathmandu after the ascent. But later in life, he became good friends with Hillary.

After his historic climb, Tenzing was hailed as a hero in India and Nepal, and was awarded the George Medal by Britain. India's prime minister, Nehru, asked him to help establish a new climbing school in Darjeeling. He married for a third time and had four more children, but did little serious climbing after Everest.

TENZING ON THE ROOF OF THE WORLD
Edmund Hillary took this iconic shot of his partner raising his flag-draped ice axe on Everest's summit on 29 May 1953. Tenzing, a Buddhist, buried biscuits and chocolate in the snow as an offering to the mountain's gods.

BRACED FOR THE SUMMIT OF EVEREST, 1953
Edmund Hillary and Tenzing Norgay (see pp.264–67), probably the fittest and most determined pair on the 1953 expedition, are pictured here on 28 May on Everest's Southeast Ridge. They are on their way from the South Col to establish Camp IX on the ridge below the South Summit. On 29 May, they reached the summit at 11:30am and the news quickly spread around the world. Later, there was intense public speculation about who had stepped onto the summit first.

COMPAGNONI AND LACEDELLI

CONTROVERSIAL HEROES OF K2'S FIRST ASCENT

ITALY   1914–2009; 1925–2009

ACHILLE COMPAGNONI   LINO LACEDELLI

AFTER 1945, the Italians developed a strong interest in K2. A successful ascent of the world's second-highest mountain would go some way towards restoring national pride after the ignominy of World War II. In 1954, a strong, well-equipped Italian team – using oxygen for the first time on K2 – took their chances and prevailed. Afterwards, however, accusations of foul play among the climbers led to decades of bitter controversy.

ARDITO DESIO
ITALY   1897–2001

The leader of the K2 expedition was not a climber, but a 57-year-old academic with a profoundly hierarchical view of the world.

Nicknamed "The Little Duke" by the K2 climbers, thanks to the communiqués he sent up the mountain to exhort his climbers – and threaten them should they fail – Desio went to the Karakoram in 1929 at the start of a long and productive research career in the Himalaya. In many ways he was the natural leader for the joint scientific and climbing expedition to K2. Riccardo Cassin (see pp.292–93) was the obvious man to lead the climbers, having joined a pre-expedition sortie in 1953 – but he was levered off the team on the grounds of ill health. Desio, a former Alpini himself, preferred men like Compagnoni.

At dusk on 31 July 1954, Lino Lacedelli was standing on the summit of K2, remonstrating with his climbing partner Achille Compagnoni. The pair had just made the first ascent of a peak much more difficult and dangerous than Everest, and after what had been an exhausting ordeal, Compagnoni was close to the limit of his endurance. He told Lacedelli he would prefer to spend the night on the summit and descend the following morning.

Knowing this meant certain death, Lacedelli threatened his companion with his ice axe and warned him he would get a thwack if he didn't start descending immediately. And so the two

men began the slow process of picking their way down in near darkness, frequently stumbling and sliding short distances in the snow, suffering frostbite but surviving. They made it back to their team's top camp at 11pm.

Back in Italy, a crowd of 40,000 people greeted the returning climbers as national heroes. The stain of Italy's wartime humiliation faded a little, and the nation was grateful. The climbers were awarded the Italian order of merit and granted an audience with the Pope. Yet the expedition had not been a happy one. Claims and counter-claims over potentially fatal decisions made near the mountain's summit would overshadow the team's achievement.

CLIMBING ROOTS
Lacedelli was born in a mountain town in the Dolomites and from a young age was obsessed with climbing and mountaineering. One day, escaping his father's attention, he followed a local guide and his client onto the Torre Grande of the Cinque Torri peaks, earning himself a reproach from the guide and some chocolate from the client. His father was furious, but the course of Lacedelli's life had been set. Shortly before World War II, a group of Dolomites

LA DOMENICA DEL CORRIERE

ITALIAN PRIDE
Here, an Italian weekly trumpets the K2 victory for Italy. After World War II, climbing the "8,000ers" became highly nationalistic, and success offered uncontroversial glory to defeated nations.

climbers formed a club called the Scoiattoli – the "squirrels". One of the best climbers there, Luigi "Bibi" Ghedina, saw Lacedelli's potential and took him under his wing. The pair repeated many of the hardest routes in the Dolomites, as well as Walter Bonatti's route on the Grand Capucin in the French Alps (see pp.296–97).

Achille Compagnoni was born in a town at the foot of the Ortler Alps in northern Italy and as a young man he joined the Alpini, Italy's mountain infantry. Skiing and mountain sports were integral to the Alpini, and Compagnoni became a strong ski-tourer and climber. After World War II he trained as a guide and opened a hotel. He did few new climbs – the usual hallmark of a top mountaineer – but made 100 ascents of the Matterhorn and Monte Rosa and was involved in countless mountain rescues. His physical strength was well known, and although he was almost 40 years old when he went to K2, he remained a powerful and ambitious climber.

A LIFE'S WORK

- Lacedelli and Luigi "Bibi" Ghedina make the first repeat of **the technically difficult Bonatti-Ghigo route** on the East Face of the Grand Capucin in a remarkably fast 18 hours

- Lacedelli and Compagnoni head an Italian team in **the first ascent of K2**. They and their compatriots become internationally famous, but personal rivalries and accusations of unsporting tactics during the expedition leave **a legacy of recriminations and litigation**

- **After K2**, Compagnoni climbs less and focuses on his skiing business. Lacedelli continues to climb and works as a guide

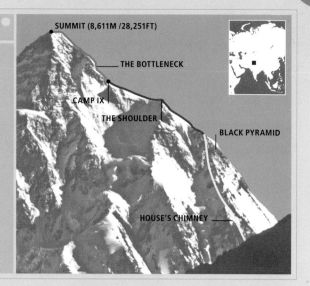

K2

ABRUZZI SPUR, 30 JULY 1954

— **Good early progress**
The Italians use a winch to haul supplies low down and another in House's Chimney, below the Black Pyramid.

— **The weather closes in**
The death of Mario Puchoz weakens the team's resolve. Getting oxygen to Camp IX above the Shoulder is key.

— **Push to the summit**
After climbing down to collect oxygen left by Bonatti and Mahdi, Compagnoni and Lacedelli reach the summit at 6pm.

SUMMIT (8,611M /28,251FT)

THE BOTTLENECK

CAMP IX

THE SHOULDER

BLACK PYRAMID

HOUSE'S CHIMNEY

A BAD START

The Italian K2 expedition had plenty of technical ability, but none of the 12 climbers had been to the Karakoram or Himalaya before. Nor did they have the assistance of experienced Sherpas. In mid June, Mario Puchoz, one of the fittest in the group, developed what was probably pulmonary oedema and died at Camp II. The team vowed to go on. Using a winch to haul supplies up House's Chimney, the key to the lower section of the Abruzzi Spur, camps were advanced up the mountain, but hostile conditions slowed progress. Further disaster was narrowly avoided when Cirillo Floreanini survived a 250-m (820-ft) fall. In mid July, the expedition's leader, Ardito Desio, put Compagnoni in charge of the summit attempt. The site for Camp VIII was dug out at 7,740m (25,393ft) and plans were laid to pitch another tent at about 8,000m (26,200ft), an advance post for the final summit push the next day. But crucial oxygen equipment was below Lacedelli and Compagnoni, at Camp VII, so the team's youngest member, Walter Bonatti, was sent down to collect it.

SUMMIT RIVALRY

As night fell, Bonatti returned with the best of the Pakistani porters, Amir Mahdi, searching desperately for the new Camp IX. A headlamp came on far above him, and Lacedelli shouted down, telling Bonatti to dump the oxygen gear. Lacedelli assumed that Bonatti would then descend, but it was too dark, and he and Madhi were forced to endure a freezing, open bivouac. Mahdi suffered terribly, losing nearly all his toes and fingers to frostbite. In the morning, Compagnoni and Lacedelli retrieved the oxygen bottles and made the ascent to the summit.

The events of that night were disputed for decades, but in 2004, Lacedelli confirmed what Bonatti had always believed: that Compagnoni had moved Camp IX to a site too high for Bonatti and Madhi to reach because he had not wanted Bonatti to join them on the summit. Compagnoni had countered Bonatti's accusations with claims that Bonatti had used up some of their oxygen. The two men remained unreconciled right up to Compagnoni's death.

A BITTER LEGACY
In 2004, Lacedelli published a book in which he repudiated Compagnoni (left) and broadly endorsed Bonatti's claim – that he had been deliberately abandoned in K2's "Death Zone".

BAND AND BROWN

PIONEERS ON WORLD'S THIRD-HIGHEST PEAK

ENGLAND   B.1929; B.1930

GEORGE BAND   **JOE BROWN**

COMING SOON AFTER the first ascent of Everest, George Band and Joe Brown's success on Kangchenjunga in the Nepal Himalaya – the world's third-highest peak – made only a small impact on the public. Yet purely in mountaineering terms, it was an exceptional achievement. Most of the route up Everest had been climbed before Tenzing and Hillary succeeded, whereas the route up Kangchenjunga was almost completely unknown.

A LIFE'S WORK

- Band becomes **one of the leading climbers of his generation** while still a student

- Brown **contributes greatly to the resurgence of British alpinism** after World War II, putting up some of the best and most famous lines in Britain and going to the Alps to climb hard, bold new routes

- At 23, Band becomes **the youngest team member** to be chosen for the first successful expedition to climb Everest

- With funds generated by the success on Everest, Band **attempts Rakaposhi** in the Karakoram

- Band and Brown **complete the first ascent of Kangchenjunga** on a largely unexplored route

- After his success on Kangchenjunga, **Brown cements his position among the greatest British climbers** of the 20th century, climbing new routes into his 80s

- Brown reaches the summit of the unclimbed Muztagh Tower in the Karakoram in 1956, **perhaps the hardest route successfully negotiated at that time in the Himalaya**

Until 1852, Kangchenjunga was thought to be the highest mountain in the world, and it had a ferocious reputation for difficulty and bad weather. Several expeditions had attempted the peak, including a team headed by Aleister Crowley in 1905 (see p.196), and another that included Frank Smythe (see p.247) in 1930. They made some progress up the Southwest or Yalung Face, before turning back. Smythe considered that side of the peak too dangerous.

However, a reconnaissance of the Southwest Face in 1954 led to a re-think, and Charles Evans, the leader of the successful British assault on the peak in May the following year, again chose this route for the attempt on the summit

by a larger team. Evans had been deputy leader on the 1953 Everest expedition, reaching the South Summit just before Hillary and Tenzing's ascent. In his understated way, he believed that climbing should be a collegiate affair, rather than an indulgence for "stars" – an approach that won the respect of his team of eight climbers and a doctor who came predominantly from the north of England.

DESTINED FOR SUCCESS

The background of Joe Brown, a builder, was very different from those of the men climbing in the Himalaya before World War II. Born in Manchester, in northern England, his mother took in other people's washing to support the family after his father died when he was still a baby. He came to climbing not through a mentor in the Alpine Club, but as an extension of his gang's adventurous games in bombed-out corners of the city, and camping trips further afield.

TEAM LEADERSHIP
Expedition leader Charles Evans is seen here just below Camp IV at about 7,000m (23,000ft). Evans's harmonious leadership proved critical to the expedition's success.

From the moment he touched rock, it was clear Brown had an exceptional natural talent, and he went on to re-draw the shape of British climbing. He had no teachers – he simply followed his instincts. In the early 1950s, he formed a legendary partnership with Don Whillans (see pp.298–99) and the pair became members of the Rock and Ice Club, a climbing club formed by a group of forward-thinking climbers from Manchester. The arrival of the Rock and Ice Club was a seminal moment in post-war British alpinism, but more traditional forums for young alpinists, including Oxford and Cambridge universities, were also resurgent. Brown and Whillans's early exploits in the Alps, which included the third ascent of the Dru's West Face in a fast time, helped return British mountaineering to the front rank.

George Band was born in Taiwan, the son of missionaries, but moved to London during World War II. A talented athlete in his youth, he took up climbing at Cambridge University and established himself as a rising talent. Chosen for the 1953 Everest expedition aged just 23, he didn't perform as well as he'd hoped, but on Kangchenjunga he proved a dynamic force.

QUEST FOR THE SACRED SUMMIT

Although the 1955 Kangchenjunga team used fixed camps and Sherpas, along with oxygen and the innovative boots developed for Everest, it was still a lighter expedition, with all the thrill of true exploration. Their objective was to reach the mountain's upper slopes – dubbed the Great Shelf – at 7,000m (24,966ft). This involved getting up the desolate Yalung Glacier. The lower section was technically challenging, particularly for Sherpas with little rock-climbing experience. Luckily, they discovered a small gully and bypassed most of the danger.

The upper section proved more amenable, and Evans and New Zealander Norman Hardie, using a closed-circuit oxygen system, broke through onto the Great Shelf and found a sheltered spot to set up Camp V. Having reached their objective, they decided just to keep going.

Evans now needed to choose who would try for the top first, and who would go in support. He quietly announced it would be Band and Brown on the first attempt, with Hardie and army officer Tony Streather next. He and Neil Mather, together with the best Sherpas, would establish Camp VI and let them get on with it.

Once on the Great Shelf, however, the summit team and their support were trapped in a storm for 60 hours. Taking the chance to

KANGCHENJUNGA

SOUTHWEST FACE, 25 MAY 1955

— **Glacial approach**
Faced with a dangerous approach, the team find a safe line through the lower icefall to the more stable upper icefall.

— **Pushing onto the Great Shelf**
Using closed oxygen sets, Charles Evans and Norman Hardie push over and above the Great Shelf to establish Camp V at more than 7,700m (25,250ft).

— **Band and Brown climb to summit**
With the monsoon approaching, Band and Brown leave Camp VI and follow the Gangway to emerge on the West Ridge.

SUMMIT
(8,586M/28,169FT)

GANGWAY

CAMP VI

CAMP V

GREAT SHELF

CAMP IV

regroup when it was over, they continued and placed Camp VI at almost 8,000m (27,247ft). The way to the summit was still unknown, but Band and Brown used aerial photographs taken by the Indian Air Force. After five hours, they emerged onto the West Ridge with another 120m (400ft) to go. Just before the summit they

faced a tall rock wall split by cracks. Cranking his oxygen up, Brown banged in a peg, wedged himself into a crack and scaled the wall. "George!" he cried, "we're there!" Out of respect for the local people, who consider the summit sacred, the pair left the last few steps to the top untouched.

SUMMIT OF THE GODS
Having emerged from the Gangway on the Southwest Face, George Band pauses on the summit ridge of Kangchenjunga at about 8,500m (27,880ft). The summit itself was left untrodden in deference to the local gods.

THE OTHER SUMMITEERS
Here, New Zealander Norman Hardie peers warily into a crevasse on the British Kangchenjunga expedition of May 1955. The day after George Band and Joe Brown's ascent of the peak (see pp.272–73), Hardie and army officer Tony Streather climbed towards the summit, but, on seeing the vertical crack, looked for an easier way to the top. They walked around the cliff and found a sloping ramp, which enabled them to scramble quickly to the final slope.

COUZY AND TERRAY

FIRST TO CLIMB MAKALU

FRANCE   1923–58; 1921–65

JEAN COUZY   LIONEL TERRAY

WHILE THE FRENCH PUBLIC celebrated the success of Annapurna in 1950, the Comité de l'Himalaya cast around for the next objective. With Britain's interest in Everest declared, the French settled on Makalu in Nepal, the world's fifth-highest peak. They had absorbed the lessons of Annapurna and mounted one of the most successful Himlayan campaigns ever. On Makalu, Terray cemented his reputation as one of history's great mountaineers.

Of the leading members of the 1950 Annapurna team, Maurice Herzog and Louis Lachenal (see pp.256–57) were incapacitated by frostbite injuries, while Gaston Rébuffat, the most famous guide in France, was disillusioned and never returned to the Himalaya. The French public knew Lionel Terray as the man who had forgone the summit of Annapurna to support others, but after Annapurna he stepped to the fore.

Terray was born near Grenoble, his father a doctor, his mother an artist, neither of whom understood their son's passion for mountains. "A man must be completely crazy to wear himself out climbing a mountain, when there isn't even a hundred franc note to be picked up on the summit," his father told him.

THE GOLDEN GENERATION
Terray was one of the generation of French alpinists who came to prominence after World War II. He formed a close friendship with Louis Lachenal, making the second ascent of the Eiger's North Face and the Walker Spur on the Grandes Jorasses with him. Terray followed the success of Annapurna with first ascents of mountains all over the world: Fitzroy in Patagonia, Mount Huntington in Alaska, Jannu in Nepal, and Chacraraju Este in Peru. A guide by profession, Terray wrote a brilliant memoir, *Conquistadors of the Useless*.

Jean Couzy had been anonymous on Annapurna and was barely mentioned by Herzog in his account of the expedition. But he was a force of nature – driven, energetic, and intellectually curious. Born in the Lot and Garonne, he began climbing in the Pyrenees, and when studies took him to Paris, he teamed up with Marcel Schatz to enjoy a prolific Alpine career.

Couzy taught himself Italian so that he could read climbing guidebooks. By profession he was a test pilot. He would borrow an aircraft from his local flying club to make quick visits to the mountains to have a dash at hard routes. When he married, he climbed with his wife.

CLIMBING LEADER
Jean Franco (left), who led the 1955 Makalu expedition, is seen here giving advice to Walter Bonatti. Terray was to join Franco on the first ascent of Makalu II in 1956.

MAKALU BOUND
The Makalu trip was again overseen by the doyen of French climbing, Lucien Devies, and began with a reconnaissance in 1954, during which the team made a string of first ascents.

Without permission, Couzy and Terray secretly climbed Chomolonzo, Makalu's stunningly beautiful neighbour. At 7,804m (25,603ft), the mountain was a major undertaking in its own right. Despite a vicious storm the night before their summit climb, Couzy wasn't deterred. As Terray recalled: "I had no thought but to get down out of it all as quickly as possible. Only Jean's magnetic personality constrained me to follow him like one condemned to the scaffold."

From the summit, they took a crucial photograph of Makalu's northern aspect, allowing the team to judge the route to the summit of Makalu itself. Terray also made the first ascent of Makalu II with Jean Franco, who led the full expedition in 1955, with twice the number of Sherpas. According to Terray, "a veritable 8,000er machine" had been created. "The teams [of climbers] relayed each other like a well-trained corps de ballet, five camps went up in practically no time at all, and a ton and a half of food, kit and oxygen bottles were stockpiled at Camp V. Thanks to these reserves and the almost uninterrupted system of fixed ropes linking it to Camp III, this advanced outpost became a place where one could remain in comfort and safety, secure in the knowledge that one could retreat in any weather."

Camp VI was established at about 7,800m (25,600ft) with the help of three Sherpas, leaving Couzy and Terray to make the first summit attempt. Leaving their tent at 7am, they were on the summit at 11am. Terray was later to recall that they'd reached the summit with such relative ease that their triumph came as something of an anticlimax. So thorough was the Comité's preparation that they put all nine climbers of the 1955 expedition on the summit.

Within ten years, both the heroes of Makalu had died in accidents on far safer peaks: Jean Couzy struck by a single stone climbing near Grenoble; and Lionel Terray in a fall from Le Gerbier in the Vercors, along with his climbing partner Marc Martinetti.

MAKALU

NORTH FACE, MAY 1955

— **2 May – Up to the Makalu La**
Despite indifferent weather, the French quickly reach the bottom of the wall leading to the Makalu La. Using ropes left in place from their 1954 reconnaissance, they reach the col and establish Camp V at 7,400m (24,000ft).

— **15 May – Easy progress**
From Camp VI at about 7,800m (25,600ft), Couzy and Terray set out at 7am. They reach the East Ridge and then the summit in just four hours.

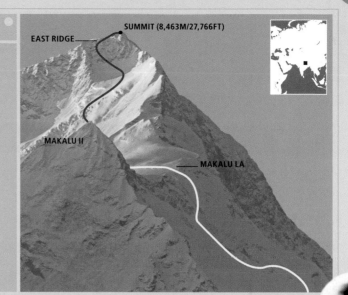

EAST RIDGE

SUMMIT (8,463M/27,766FT)

MAKALU II

MAKALU LA

FILM ACTOR
Such was Terray's fame after Makalu that he appeared in the French mountaineering film *Étoiles de Midi* of 1959. Here he casts his rope across a crevasse.

HORNBEIN AND UNSOELD

THE FIRST TO TRAVERSE EVEREST

UNITED STATES   B.1930; 1926–79

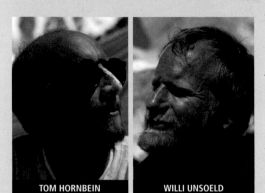

TOM HORNBEIN   WILLI UNSOELD

PRESIDENT JOHN F KENNEDY'S election message in 1960 urged the American people to look for "new frontiers", so Norman Dyhrenfurth's suggestion of a US expedition to Everest fell on fertile soil. Far from being simply an exercise in patriotism, however, the highly successful 1963 American Mount Everest Expedition marked another step forward in the development of Himalayan climbing.

Swiss-born Norman Dyhrenfurth, the son of an explorer, had set his sights on Everest much earlier. He had been on the mountain with the failed Swiss expedition in 1952 and had led the 1955 attempt on Lhotse. In the early 1960s, now living in the US, he started to raise the money needed to put an American on top of Everest. Dyhrenfurth planned to conduct scientific research during the expedition and this attracted the interest of the National Geographic Society, who backed him with a quarter of the funding and lent him their photographer-mountaineer, Barry Bishop, to document the climb.

AMERICANS ON EVEREST

With his funding finally in place, Dyhrenfurth set about assembling the strongest climbing team ever to have left the US. It included "Big Jim" Whittaker, a climber and guide who would become the first American to reach the top of Everest, and 26-year-old Lute Jerstad. Also central to the plans were Willi Unsoeld, who was appointed climbing leader, and Tom Hornbein. Both men had been on the 1960 US expedition that climbed Masherbrum in the Karakoram; Unsoeld had reached the summit. Unsoeld was a philosophical character, a "free-range thinker" and performer who referred to himself in the third person as "the old guide", and liked to say that "life begins at 10,000ft". He had studied divinity and travelled

through India, where Hinduism gave his intellectual life an added perspective. He saw deep spiritual value in the mountains, and wasn't shy about spreading the good news. He had started climbing as a boy scout, and as a young man had made an attempt on Nilkantha, a peak at the head of the Gangotri Glacier, one of the sources of India's River Ganges. He'd also taken part in the 1954 US attempt on Makalu.

Born in St Louis, Missouri, Tom Hornbein had been fascinated by mountain exploration as a boy. Later, he studied geology, climbed new routes in the Front Range of the Rockies, and taught mountain rescue, before going to medical school back in Missouri. He later specialized in anaesthesiology and this expertise made him a logical choice to oversee the Everest team's oxygen equipment. He was serving in the US Navy in 1963, but Dyhrenfurth procured his honourable discharge so he could participate in the expedition. Talking at Hornbein's San Diego home, Dyhrenfurth suggested the team descend Everest via the West Ridge rather than going back down via the ascent route – an added twist to pique the public's interest.

Understandably, Hornbein wasn't keen. Trying to find your way down an unknown route having just struggled to the summit of Everest sounded like a recipe for disaster. But as he thought about Dyhrenfurth's proposal, he realized that by turning it on its head – going

A GRANDIOSE PLAN
Initially, Dyhrenfurth's plan struggled to attract finance – Americans were generally uninterested, feeling that Everest had been "done". In a bid for the hearts and minds of the public, he suggested a "grand slam" of Everest, plus Lhotse and Nuptse, three of Earth's highest peaks. This was soon scaled back to putting the first American on top of Everest itself. Here, Barry Bishop approaches the Geneva Spur on the Lhotse Face.

HEAVYWEIGHT EXPEDITION
Dyhrenfurth's team comprised 20 climbers and scientists, 32 Sherpas, and 909 porters, who carried 25 tonnes of food and equipment.

up the West Ridge rather than down it – a more interesting and attention-grabbing project than simply repeating the 1953 climb was possible.

CONFLICTING GOALS

Dyhrenfurth knew that if all the resources and people were put into the West Ridge and they failed, his powerful sponsors, not to mention the US public, might not be so understanding. Others in the team, particularly Whittaker and Jersted, felt they should just get the mountain climbed. The expedition became philosophically split between those in favour of a West Ridge route and those who preferred the "safer" South Col route established by Hillary and Tenzing in 1953. At times this would lead to friction.

The team started early, leaving Kathmandu in February to allow sufficient time for good acclimatization. On 22 March, they started reconnoitring the Khumbu Icefall, but on the following day an ice cliff collapsed, killing young mountaineer Jake Breitenbach. Morale was massively undermined, and problems with the Sherpas added another layer of tension.

Breitenbach had been one of the "West Ridgers", and as the expedition's problems mounted, and members of the group failed

to acclimatize, opinion turned against the West Ridge route. Hornbein's enthusiasm had been dented by a reconnaissance of the West Ridge, and now even Dyhrenfurth was having second thoughts about it. Many in the team wanted to focus on getting Everest climbed via the South Col. Unsoeld, Hornbein, and Bishop stood on the West Shoulder, looking across at the North Face where all the pre-war expeditions had struggled, and the decision was made to take the Sherpas off the West Ridge.

Bishop, with obligations to the National Geographic, chose to switch routes, and the expedition made rapid progress up the Western Cwm. On 1 May, Whittaker, climbing with Tenzing's nephew, Nawang Gombu, left Camp VI on the Southeast Ridge at 6.15am. The pair were on the summit of the mountain before 1pm, taking the last few steps together. A second summit party, including Jerstad and Bishop, postponed their own push to help the exhausted climbers descend.

WEST RIDGE ATTEMPT

Having got someone onto the summit so early, there was still time for an attempt on the West Ridge. The West Ridgers occupied their Camp IV and Hornbein and Unsoeld reconnoitred the route leftwards, away from the ridge to a couloir of snow now known as the

WHY CLIMB?

The 1963 Everest Expedition was one of the first attempts to make a serious psychological enquiry into what kinds of people climb big mountains, and how they relate to each other. The research required climbers to undergo three days of assessment before the expedition and then fill in cards detailing their mood throughout its 14 weeks. Mountaineers emerged from the study as a self-reliant, detached, and rebellious crowd, not ideally suited to forming long-term stable relationships.

A STEP INTO THE FUTURE
Whittaker's ascent made the front page of the *New York Times*; Unsoeld and Hornbein (right) got a short piece on page 28, but their alpine-style traverse of Everest stunned the climbing world.

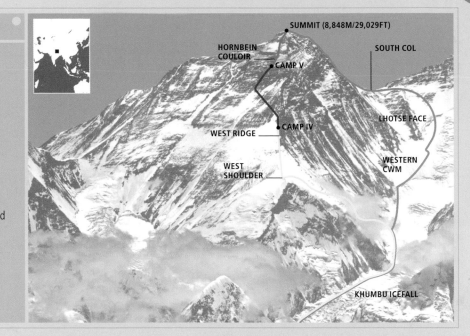

EVEREST

WEST RIDGE, APRIL/MAY 1963

11 April – Route to the West Shoulder
Hornbein and Unsoeld establish Camp III on the West Shoulder, where they spy out the Hornbein Couloir as a possible route to the top.

15–21 May – Up to to Camp V
The "West Ridgers" establish Camp IV at 7,650m (25,100ft), but it is wiped out the next day in a storm. Camp V is established in the Hornbein Couloir where it enters the Yellow Band.

22 May – Climb to the summit
Abandoning their tent at 7am, Hornbein and Unsoeld find slow, awkward climbing in the narrow upper couloir through the Yellow Band before they rejoin the West Ridge to reach the summit at 6.15pm.

22 May – Descent to the South Col
Missing Bishop and Jerstad on the summit by 3 hours, Hornbein and Unsoeld descend the Southeast Ridge, finding their colleagues at 9.30pm. All four men survive a bivouac at 8,000m (26,247ft).

Hornbein couloir. That night, Camp IV was hit by a storm that blew the tents – with climbers and Sherpas inside them – 30m (100ft), narrowly avoiding a long drop down the North Face.

Still, the West Ridgers didn't give up. On 20 May, Camp IV was re-occupied, and the next morning support climbers Barry Corbet and Al Auten left to establish Camp V, followed by the summit pair of Unsoeld and Hornbein, with Dick Emerson and a team of five Sherpas. Camp V was located in the Yellow Band at 8,305m (27,250ft), about 60m (200ft) lower than Camp VI on the Southeast Ridge, where

Bishop and Jerstad now waited for their own bid, which would be via the South Col. A tent fire sparked by a stove delayed Bishop and Jerstad's push and left them without fluids. Things didn't improve once they got going, as ferocious winds battered them for the entire seven-hour climb to the summit. They had hoped to meet Hornbein and Unsoeld at the top and make the descent together, but with their oxygen dwindling, they could not afford to wait and started back alone.

RESISTANCE AND FINAL BREAKTHROUGH

The West Ridge summit pair, Hornbein and Unsoeld, left their tent at 7am, taking just oxygen, a little food, and their radio. The face was steep, at 55 degrees, and covered in loose, granular snow. Progress was awkward, and it took them four hours to do just 122m (400ft). "The rotten rock, the softening snow, the absence of even tolerable piton cracks only added to our desire to go on. Too much labor, too many sleepless nights, and too many dreams had been invested to bring us this far," Hornbein wrote later in his account of the expedition, *Everest: The West Ridge*.

Above the Yellow Band, however, the rock improved, and then gave way to snow. Dumping a spent oxygen bottle gave Hornbein a boost, and they marched up the final ridge, the huge South Face dropping away beneath their feet. They were at the top at 6.15pm, more than 11 hours after setting out from their tent. "The sun's rays sheered horizontally across the summit," Hornbein recalled. "We hugged each other as tears welled up, ran down across our oxygen masks, and turned to ice."

A NIGHT IN THE DEATH ZONE

Hornbein and Unsoeld saw Bishop and Jerstad's footprints leading down from the summit. As they descended, they found their colleagues slumped in the snow above the South Col. As darkness fell, the four climbers chose to spend the night on a rocky outcrop, without tents or sleeping bags, drifting, half-asleep in "a last, lonely outpost of the world".

The next day, elated at having survived the night, they continued to Base Camp. Once there, Unsoeld and Bishop were unable to walk further on their frostbitten feet and were carried down by Sherpas. Whittaker would take the plaudits of the public for reaching the top first, but to climbers, Unsoeld and Hornbein's ascent of the West Ridge was the greater triumph.

PRESIDENTIAL RECEPTION
President John F Kennedy personally welcomed the climbers home in a ceremony at the White House, praising them for "demonstrating that the vigorous life still attracts Americans".

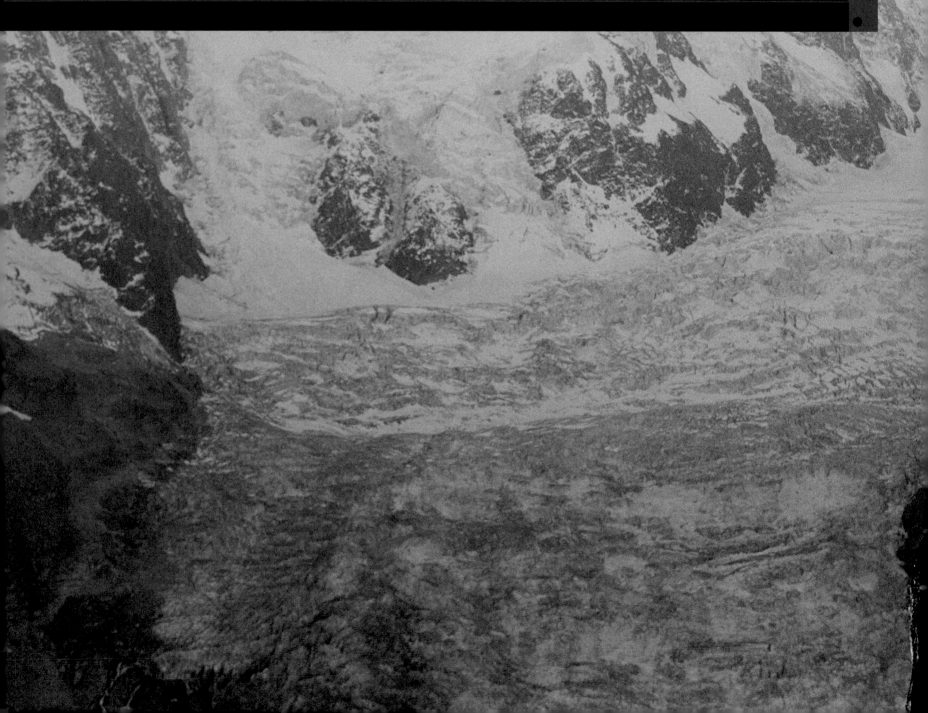

THE AGE OF EXTREMES

THE AGE OF EXTREMES

▲ 1925
German alpinist **Willo Welzenbach** (above) climbs the North Face Direct on the Dent d'Hérens, opening a new phase in alpinism (see pp.236–37).

► 1927
Scottish mountaineer **Thomas Graham Brown** teams up with **Frank Smythe** (right, see p.247) to climb Red Sentinel on the Brenva Face of Mont Blanc. The partnership ends in acrimony.

◄ 1929
Italian alpinist **Emilio Comici** climbs the first Grade VI in the Dolomites with his ascent of the North West Pillar of the Sorella di Mezzo above Cortina d'Ampezzo (see pp.288–89).

► 1931
The **Schmid brothers** win the race to climb the North Face of the Matterhorn, cycling to the mountain from their home in Munich and enduring a bivouac high on the mountain.

1931
With **Willy Merkl** (see pp.238–39), Welzenbach climbs the North Face of the Grands Charmoz. Their ascent and survival of a protracted storm makes headlines around Europe.

1933
Thomas Graham Brown completes his trilogy of routes on the Brenva Face of Mont Blanc, climbing the Pear Buttress.

1928
Brown and **Smythe** put their differences aside to climb Route Major on the Brenva Face, one of the most important ascents ever made in the Alps.

▼ 1938
The deadly struggle to climb the **Eiger's North Face** reaches a climax when Anderl Heckmair leads the way for a joint Austro-German team (see pp.290–91).

1935
After fierce competition, **Martin Meier** and **Rudolf Peters** win the race to establish a route on the North Face of the Grandes Jorasses – the Croz Spur.

1951
Italian alpinists **Walter Bonatti** and Luciano Ghigo climb the East Face of the Grand Capucin in the Mont Blanc Range (see pp.296–97).

1954
Following their fast repeat of the West Face of the Dru, **Joe Brown** and **Don Whillans** climb the difficult West Face of Blatière above Chamonix (see pp.298–99).

1955
Walter Bonatti, following his disappointment on K2, returns to the Alps with a brilliant new route, the Southwest Pillar of the Dru, climbed solo over five days (see pp.296–97).

▲ 1958
Italian alpinist **Riccardo Cassin** (see pp.292–93) leads an expedition to Gasherbrum IV in the Karakoram, where Bonatti and Carlo Mauri reach the summit.

1962
French post-war legend Lionel Terray (see pp.276–77) caps his career with the brilliant first ascent of the difficult Jannu in Nepal.

1963
Americans Tom Frost, John Harlin, Gary Hemming, and Stewart Fulton make the first ascent of the remote **South Face of the Fou** above Chamonix, a big wall reminiscent of climbs in Yosemite.

◄ 1961
British mountaineers **Don Whillans** and **Chris Bonington** (left), and Ian Clough and Jan Dlugosz, make the first ascent of the Central Pillar of Frêney (see pp.300–01).

▼ 1962
Yosemite legend Royal Robbins (below) and Gary Hemming climb the American Direct on the West Face of the Dru, a classic of modern alpinism now largely destroyed by rock-fall.

1966
British climber Dougal Haston (see p.298) joins forces with a German team – Siegi Hupfauer, Jörg Lehne, Günter Strobel, and Roland Votteler – to complete the Eiger Direct.

1967
French guide René Desmaison and Robert Flematti climb the Central Pillar of Frêney in winter, climbing the ice route "The Shroud" – Le Linceul – on the Grandes Jorasses the following year.

◄ PP.282–83 French mountaineer Catherine Destivelle climbs a pinnacle near Chamonix, France, in 1994.

WITH THE EXPLORATION OF THE ALPS complete, and its summits climbed, alpinists were faced with a conundrum. How should mountaineering develop? The answer would prove controversial. In 1925, two Munich climbers, Willo Welzenbach and Eugen Allwein set off up the North Face of the Dent d'Hérens. Climbing steep rock and ice, the two Germans forged a sobering new route on this big face threatened by ice cliffs. The *Alpine Journal* was withering. The German route, it said, came "under the category of foolish variations." Mountaineers should stick to ridges, not climb faces. But the future was with Welzenbach. As French climber Lucien Devies put it, the capital of mountaineering moved from London to Munich, "where youth was ambitious and innovation encouraged."

1970

1980

1990

1984
Patrick Gabarrou and **François Marsigny** climb Divine Providence on the Grand Pilier d'Angle, one of the hardest climbs ever done in the Alps in such a remote location.

▼ 1984
Norbert Joos and **Erhard Loretan** (below, see pp.334–35) climb the East Ridge of Annapurna, 7.5km (4.5 miles) long, most of which is spent at altitude above 7,500m (24,600ft).

1990
Slovenian **Tomo Cesen** claims to have soloed the immense South Face of Lhotse but his account is widely doubted. The face is later completed by a Russian team, using siege tactics.

▲ 1991
French alpinists **Pierre Béghin** (see pp.334) and **Christophe Profit** climb the North West Ridge of K2 in alpine style.

1991
Everest veteran Andrej Stremfelj and the fellow Slovenian legend Marko Prezelj make an alpine-style first ascent of the South Ridge of Kangchenjunga South (see pp.332–33).

1975
Reinhold Messner and **Peter Habeler** bring their alpine-style speed to the Himalaya, climbing a new route on Gasherbrum I and ushering in a new era in Himalayan climbing (see pp.308–11).

▲ 1975
Bonington's expedition overcomes the Southwest Face of Everest. **Doug Scott** (see pp.304–05) and **Dougal Haston** (above) become the first Britons to reach the summit.

▼ 1985
Polish climber **Wojciech Kurtyka** (right, see pp.328–29) completes what some peers judge the climb of the century, the West Face of Gasherbrum IV in the Karakoram.

1986
Messner becomes the first person to climb all of the 14 "8,000ers", closely followed by the Polish legend **Jerzy Kukuczka** (see pp.312–13).

1997
British climbers **Andy Cave** and Brendan Murphy reach the summit of Changabang having climbed the North Face; Murphy is lost in an avalanche.

▼ 2002
German rock climber **Alex Huber** (below) solos the Direttissima on the Cima Grande, a 500-m (1,600-ft) route graded 5.12a, with nothing but rock boots and a chalk bag (see pp.340–41).

1977
Scott and Bonington make the first ascent of "**The Ogre**", one of the most difficult objectives in the Karakoram. Scott breaks both legs on the descent and crawls back to Base Camp.

▲ 1978
Messner and Habeler solve the physiological riddle of Everest by reaching the summit **without bottled oxygen**. Messner goes on to make a solo ascent two years later.

► 1979
A Yugoslav team climb a more direct version of the West Ridge, part of a **new wave of climbing development** in the Himalaya from Eastern European climbers.

1987
Mick Fowler, the British climbing taxman, and partner Victor Saunders climb the difficult and stunningly beautiful Golden Pillar of Spantik in the Karakoram.

THE NORTH FACES

FOR MOUNTAINEERS, THE PHRASE "NORTH FACE" – *NORDWAND* IN GERMAN – HAS A FORBIDDING RESONANCE. IN THE NORTHERN HEMISPHERE, THEY ARE SHADOWY AND COLD, ADDING EXTRA DIFFICULTIES TO A CLIMB, AS WELL AS PSYCHOLOGICAL PRESSURES.

WALL OF FAME
Munich climber Martin "Martl" Maier, seen here peering from a bivouac on the North Wall of the Grandes Jorasses, was one of the central players in the race to claim the Croz Spur.

In his 1954 classic work *Étoiles et Tempêtes*, the great French mountain guide Gaston Rébuffat identified the six most desirable north faces. He was also the first to climb all six. They included the north faces of the Matterhorn, the Eiger, and the Grandes Jorasses, which are substantially more demanding than the other three – the Piz Badile, the Cima Grande, and the Petit Dru.

Rébuffat's list is a great one, but it excludes the classic routes climbed by Willo Welzenbach (see pp.236–37). Welzenbach was one of the pioneers behind the surge of interest in north faces, first with his climb on the Dent d'Hérens and then, in 1932, with a string of hugely serious ventures in the Bernese Oberland – the north faces of the Grosshorn, Lauterbrunnen Breithorn, and Gletscherhorn. The climax was the huge North Face of the Gspaltenhorn, at 1,600m (5,250ft) almost as long as the Eiger.

This last climb was horribly dangerous. He and his companions didn't bother with a rope: "The rock was so friable and devoid of holds, covered with snow, ice and pebbles, running with water and so exceptionally steep

KURZ AND HINTERSTOISSER
Germans Toni Kurz and Andi Hinterstoisser are pictured before their ill-fated attempt on the North Wall of the Eiger in 1936. Both died as they retreated in bad weather.

besides, that methodical belaying would have been impossible. Looking after the rope would have increased the stone-fall hazard and slowed us down."

PRESS HEROES
In 1931, Welzenbach and Willy Merkl (see pp.238–39) had climbed the North Face of the Aiguille des Grands Charmoz, which almost cost them their lives. Trapped by storms for days, they fought their way out of trouble. The press was spellbound, and throughout the 1930s, mountaineering epics became a staple of the popular press.

Welzenbach climbed as a hobby, unconcerned whether the public knew his name. Competition for the more famous routes was inevitable, but for impecunious mountaineers, the attention they brought could be a potential source of income. Newspapers saw an opportunity, and offered prizes to those making first ascents of well-known objectives. The combination was both intoxicating and potentially deadly. On top of this, the rise of political extremism in Europe in the 1930s fed into the race for these great prizes. Attempts on the north

> By the 1930s, advances in climbing techniques and the extension of mountaineering to working-class Germans, Austrians, and Italians saw attention shift to the great north faces of the Alps – the most feared and technically challenging of climbs.

faces were media events, and later came to be viewed as superlative propaganda, particularly in Nazi Germany. It is no surprise that Munich climbers from humble backgrounds, struggling in a time of high unemployment, accepted financial help from anyone who offered it.

NORTH FACE PIONEERS
One prize that escaped Welzenbach was the North Face of the Matterhorn. This fell in 1931 to two young German brothers, Toni and Franz Schmid, who arrived in Zermatt by bicycle. With a hemp rope, a few pitons, and some food, they raced up the initial ice slope before the morning sun caused rockfall. After a bivouac, and some complex route-finding, they reached the summit at 2pm the next day, just as a storm broke. They were trapped for two days in the Solvay bivouac hut before descending to a rapturous welcome.

The battle for the North Face of the Grandes Jorasses was even more intense. Its two great spurs, the Walker and the Croz, were tantalizing almost every leading climber of the day. The great Giusto Gervasutti, a visionary Italian who brought the technical skills of the Eastern Alps to the Mont Blanc range, climbed a long way up the Croz Spur with Piero Zanetti in 1933 before bad weather forced them down.

In 1934, it was the turn of Armand Charlet (see p.125) and Robert Gréloz to attempt the North Face of the Grandes Jorasses, with several

MATTERHORN NORTH FACE
The North Face of the Matterhorn, which rears over Zermatt, fell to the nimble Schmid brothers in 1931, catching the mountaineering world by surprise.

SPURRED BY COMPETITION
Rudolf Peters was in fierce competition with Heckmair for the Croz Spur, but got there first, in June 1935. He teamed up with Maier after his partner Rudolf Harringer was killed.

SETTING THE SCENE

- Willo Welzenbach, a government surveyor in Munich, **applies extreme rock-climbing approaches to ice**, changing attitudes about what is possible for mountaineers. Anderl Heckmair, leader of the first ascent of the Eiger's North Face, calls it **"the evaporation of deep awe** which had been felt for the massive, sheer faces and their difficulties."

- **Demographic changes also have an impact**. Until World War I, mountaineering had been almost exclusively the preserve of the wealthy, professional classes. Working-class Germans, Austrians, and Italians take up climbing during the 1920s and 1930s, **further pushing boundaries**.

- The death toll among this new cadre is high, and traditionalists **fear that alpinism is being taken over by reckless hotheads**. Edward Lisle Strutt, editor of the *Alpine Journal*, dismisses Heckmair's route on the North Face of the Eiger as **"the most imbecile variant"**.

- The drama of the north faces excites press interest, **catching the attention of the Third Reich's propaganda machine** in Germany. Edi Rainer and Willi Angerer, on their way to their fatal encounter with the Eiger, tell journalists: **"We must have the wall, or the wall must have us."**

other teams hot on their heels. The Austrian Rudolf Peters survived savage storms on the face, enduring three bivouacs as he fought to descend alone after his partner was killed in a fall. It was perhaps only fair that in 1935 it was Peters, with Martin Maier, who finally achieved the first ascent of the Croz Spur.

The north face pioneers – Welzenbach, Anderl Heckmair (see pp.290–91), and Riccardo Cassin (see pp.292–93) chief among them – were among the greatest climbers in history. That they achieved so much before the arrival of major technical developments makes the 1930s a second "golden age" of alpinism for many.

FACE OF DEATH
In this scene from the film *North Face* (2008), Kurz and Hinterstoisser begin their doomed ascent of the Eiger's North Wall.

EMILIO COMICI

A MASTER OF TECHNIQUE

ITALY   1901–40

ALTHOUGH HIS FIRST PASSION WAS for caving, Emilio Comici discovered mountain climbing during the mid-1920s and quickly became adept, showing a natural flair that earned him the nickname "Angel of the Dolomites". Bavarian climbers dominated alpinism after World War I, introducing an approach that was bolder than anything seen before. Charismatic and ebullient, Comici brought Italian climbing up to the Germans' standard with his first masterpiece, a new route on Monte Civetta, in 1931.

SOLITARY VICTORY
In 1937, Comici returned to the Cima Grande's North Face (shown here) to make a solo ascent in just three and a half hours. "I knew that climbing a big wall alone is the most dangerous thing that we can do … But living in the moment like that is so sublime, it is worth the risk," he said later.

The Northwest Face of Monte Civetta, at about 1,200m (3,900ft), is the largest face in the Dolomites and was first climbed in 1925 by the German climber Emil Solleder and his partner Gustav Lettenbauer. It is often considered the first climb in the Alps to be graded VI on the UIAA grading system. By adding a new, Italian route of a similar standard, Comici enthused a generation of Italian alpinists. He was promoted by Mussolini's government, of which he was an enthusiastic supporter, and sent on lecture tours throughout Italy.

MAN OF SPORTS

The Comici family lived in Trieste, a sea port in the northeast of Italy. At the age of 18, more interested in athletics than a career, Comici joined the city's new *XXX Ottobre* youth organization to develop his passion for sports. Along with rowing, cycling, football, and gymnastics, he took up caving in the limestone hills outside Trieste and became successful at it. But one day, friends from the *Alpina delle Giulie*, the Trieste section of the Italian Alpine Club, suggested he go climbing with them instead. That day, he said later, "lit a flame that became for me almost my entire life."

Comici trained on cliffs near Trieste in the Val Rosandra, and by 1927 was climbing new routes in the Dolomites, the first of more than 200 major first ascents. In 1929, with Giordano Fabian, he climbed a new route on

the Northwest Pillar of the Sorella di Mezzo above Cortina d'Ampezzo. It was the first Grade VI climbed by an Italian, and it put Comici in the front rank of his nation's climbers. These successes, and his warm personality, made him a popular climbing instructor and, after quitting his job at the docks, he opened Italy's first rock-climbing school.

AN ARTIST OF ALPINISM

In 1932, Comici moved to the mountains, settling in the tiny village of Misurina in the Dolomites, where he opened a new school. The following year Riccardo Cassin (see pp.292–93) invited him to his local cliff of Le Grigne to teach his club the latest climbing techniques. In 50 years, Cassin said, he never saw anyone climb with more grace. He called Comici "*maestro*". While he was at Le Grigne, Comici met the alpinist Mary Varale, with whom he made the first ascent of Yellow Edge on the Cima Piccola di Lavaredo in 1933.

A slender, vertical pillar of limestone with breathtakingly exposed climbing, Yellow Edge illustrated Comici's deeply aesthetic attitude to climbing: "I wish some day to make a route and from the summit let fall a drop of water and this is where my route will have gone." The romance of his philosophy and the elegance of his style prompted the Italian Hans Vinatzer, himself a brilliant mountaineer, to say that "on the wall, Comici is an angel."

Comici's name is most closely associated with the Tre Cime di Lavaredo. These three cliffs, which Comici dubbed his "Indian gods", are the focal point of climbing in the Dolomites, standing as a separate group with no other peaks in the immediate vicinity to lessen their impact. The North Face of the Cima Grande, or Big Peak, is 500m (1,600ft) high and overhangs by five degrees in its lower half. A German, Hans Steger, and his Italian wife, Paula Wiesinger, made an attempt at the start of the 1930s but were forced down. The Veneto climber Raffaele Carlesso tried his luck but also retreated. An aura of impossibility grew around the wall. For Comici, that kind of reputation was irresistible. In 1932, with Renato Zanutti, he reached the previous high point and traversed leftwards in a wildly exposed position, before

their attempt ran out of steam. By 1933, German alpinists were rumoured to be interested in the peak, and there were two more attempts by Italians to forestall them.

On 13 August 1933, Comici was back in the game, climbing with the Italian Giuseppe Dimai and his brother Angelo. The climb was like almost nothing done before in the Alps: technically hard and, to begin with, formidably steep, demanding real nerve from the climbers as they set out on a vertical plane of limestone. The climb took two days, and marked a new technical milestone in the Alps.

Some in the old guard of the mountaineering fraternity criticized Comici's overuse of pitons, however. The *Alpine Journal*'s editor dismissed the achievement, saying, "Needless to say, conquest was only effected by the means employed by steeple-jacks when dealing with factory chimneys." But Comici's vision was widely admired by younger climbers and his ascent made him a star. Later, he became the director of a ski school. He died there while teaching novice rock climbers.

PIONEERING ROCK STAR
On the walls of the Val Rosandra, Comici developed his skills in free climbing and in the "artificial" techniques of using pitons, stirrups, and double ropes.

ANDERL HECKMAIR

GENIUS BEHIND EIGERWAND'S FIRST ASCENT

GERMANY   1906–2005

FROM THE MID-1930S, the Eiger's North Face became the biggest prize in the Alps. Concave in shape, this complex wall lured climbers up before bad weather, rock fall, and technical difficulties combined to defeat them. After six deaths, the Swiss banned all attempts on the face, but nothing could dissuade the new generation of climbers – including Anderl Heckmair – from taking their chances. The face's reputation, Heckmair's genius, and the rise of the Nazis came together in a compelling moment in mountaineering history.

HEINRICH HARRER
AUSTRIA   1912–2006

An Olympic-class skier and experienced climber, Harrer (here between Heckmair and Hitler) was in the Eiger party of 1938.

Harrer was a Nazi Party member, and joined the SS as a sports instructor. But he was more interested in advancing his own prospects than Hitler's – for him the Eiger was a way to reach the Himalaya, which he did in 1939. Interned during World War II, he escaped to Tibet and his extraordinary sojourn there was captured in his bestselling book, *Seven Years In Tibet*. But when the book became a film starring Brad Pitt in 1997, Harrer's Nazi past resurfaced.

In 1938, when Andreas ("Anderl") Heckmair arrived to try the Eiger with fellow German Ludwig Vörg, eight climbers had already died attempting its North Face. Vörg had helped bring the bodies of two of the victims off the mountain before an attempt in 1937 with Matthias Rebitsch. They got higher than Death Bivouac, where the Germans Max Sedlmayer and Karl Mehringer had perished in 1935, before returning safely in bad weather, their prudence and ability undermining the myth that anyone trying the Eiger was certain to meet with disaster. In 1938, Rebitsch went to Nanga Parbat and wrote to Heckmair, suggesting Vörg could join him on the Eiger. A terrific rock climber, Vörg was dubbed the "bivouac king" for his ability to get comfortable under the worst conditions. He was five years younger than Heckmair, who at 32 was in his prime.

Heckmair was born in Munich. His father died during World War I, and his mother was forced to send her two young sons to an orphanage run by nuns, where they endured endless prayers and near-constant hunger. At 14, Heckmair started work as an apprentice at a gardening firm. His brother introduced him to climbing, first on the local Munich crags, but soon after in Austria's Wilder Kaiser, and his natural talent was immediately apparent. By the late 1920s, he was one of the leading lights in the Munich scene, climbing all the big routes in the Kaisergebirge and in the Wetterstein.

READY FOR THE "DEATH WALL"

Heckmair roamed further, cycling to the Dolomites in Italy, and also taking part in failed attempts on the North Face of the Grandes Jorasses. He started guiding to make ends meet, but the big climb he needed always seemed to elude him. At almost 30, he felt his chance was slipping away and the Eiger seemed like his last opportunity. In 1937, he spent six weeks camped under the wall, waiting for good weather. Running out of cash, he returned home to an offer of work guiding a rising star of German cinema, Leni Riefenstahl. He led her up tough rock climbs in the Dolomites, and she introduced him to Adolf Hitler. Heckmair was unimpressed by the Führer.

By 1938, Heckmair had taken a job as a climbing instructor in Hitler's training school for future leaders of the Third Reich. His employers gave him leave and the latest equipment to mount his Eiger attempt.

But Heckmair's expedition had rivals: four Austrians, who arrived as the Germans emerged from their bivouac at the foot of the Difficult Crack at the start of the hard climbing. Heckmair's party chose to retreat, partly because of the weather, but mostly because they were concerned about the numbers on the face. Later that day, though, two of the Austrians retreated, and the Germans raced back up to the foot of the face. Leaving at 2am, by 4:30am Heckmair's team were back at their bivouac and, at 8am, they were across the Hinterstoisser Traverse, dodging the chips of ice sent down by the remaining Austrians, Harrer and Kasparek, who were laboriously cutting steps in the traditional way. By

AFTER THE DESCENT
From left to right, Heinrich Harrer, Fritz Kasparek, Anderl Heckmair, and Ludwig Vörg are jubilant after their successful ascent of the North Face of the Eiger. On their return to Germany, a parade was held for them by Hitler to mark the achievement.

A LIFE'S WORK

- Brought up in an orphanage, he lives on his wits, and has few resources, but **manages most of the hard climbs in the Eastern Alps**

- Attempts what is now known as **the Croz Spur on the Grandes Jorasses**, before switching to the Eiger after missing out on the summit

- Leads a German-Austrian party on a **dramatic four-day ascent of the Eiger's notorious North Face**, marking the climax of the race to vanquish all the great north faces in the Alps

- In later life, **he works as a guide** and ski instructor, making expeditions with a rich patron

11:30am, the teams had caught up at the top of the Second Icefield. The Germans now faced a "ticklish situation". Should they join forces with the slower Austrians or not? Vörg suggested it, and Heckmair agreed.

He led the party into the Ramp, where they bivouacked. This was further than anyone had climbed before. The following day, Heckmair fought his way up steep rock to a traverse line that led to the White Spider. They were forced to bivouac in bad weather in the Exit Cracks, and the next day became a fight for survival. Battered by avalanches, freezing cold, and with hard climbing ahead, Heckmair used cunning and luck to lead the party to the top. The local guides had already given them up for dead, and, in a state of exhaustion, the party dragged themselves down from the summit.

EIGER

NORTH FACE, 21–24 JULY 1938

— **Heckmair and Vörg bivouac**
Harrer's group of four Austrians find Heckmair and Vörg bivouacking below the Difficult Crack. The two Germans retreat, but return when two of the Austrians turn back.

— **Climbing the Ramp**
The next day, Heckmair and Vörg catch Harrer and Kasparek at the top of the Second Icefield. Heckmair takes the lead to the top of the Ramp, where they bivouac.

— **Through a storm to the summit**
After a hard pitch, Heckmair leads the group across the Traverse of the Gods into the White Spider. The four climbers have to fight their way out of a storm to the summit.

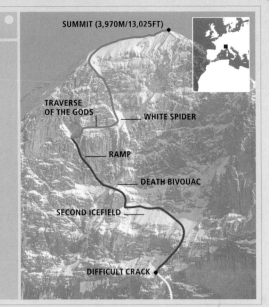

SUMMIT (3,970M/13,025FT)

TRAVERSE OF THE GODS

WHITE SPIDER

RAMP

DEATH BIVOUAC

SECOND ICEFIELD

DIFFICULT CRACK

RICCARDO CASSIN

ITALY   1909–2009

IN THE HISTORY OF MOUNTAINEERING, just a handful of climbers rank alongside Riccardo Cassin. He epitomized the impact working-class men had on the European scene after World War I. Tough and good-humoured, Cassin had a down-to-earth approach to the practicalities of climbing, underpinned by shrewdness and a good eye for the most beautiful routes up the most difficult peaks. "Without a considerable sense of poetry," he wrote, "you cannot confront the discomfort, exhaustion and danger of a climb."

THIRD TIME AROUND
In 1987, when he was 78, Cassin re-climbed the Cassin Route up the Piz Badile to mark the 50th anniversary of his first ascent. Astonishingly, he repeated the feat a week later to provide the media with photographs.

Riccardo Cassin's legacy is a series of new routes completed before and after World War II – climbs that still dominate the sport's consciousness as immutable landmarks. Among these were the first ascents of the North Face of the Piz Badile in Switzerland, the Walker Spur on the Grandes Jorasses in the French Alps, and what is still called the Cassin Ridge on Denali (Mount McKinley) in the US (see pp.206–07).

Born to a peasant family in San Vito al Tagliamento in northeastern Italy, Cassin never knew his father, a migrant worker who died in a mining accident in Canada. Cassin was brought up by strong-minded women who did their best to control an already restless spirit. At 12, he was working in a blacksmith's forge and, at 17, he moved to Lecco near Lake Como, where the pay and prospects were better.

Until then, Cassin had spent his spare time boxing, but when he discovered the Grigna, a region of small peaks and cliffs near Lecco, he was gripped by a passion for climbing and spent his days off developing rock-climbing skills.

THE "LECCO SPIDERS"
Money was tight, so Cassin and his friends pooled their savings to buy ropes and made their own equipment where they could, including pitons made at the steel fabricators where he worked. They relied on trains and bicycles to reach the mountains, keeping in superb shape by pedalling uphill. Later, Cassin founded his own business designing and making climbing gear.

Cassin was gregarious and thrived in the collegiate atmosphere of Italian mountaineering, proving to be a natural leader. He joined a group of climbing friends from Lecco who called themselves the Nuova Italia, later the Ragni di Lecco – "the Lecco spiders". Among his closest companions there was Vittorio Ratti, with whom he climbed the first of his great Alpine climbs, the North Face of the Cima Ovest di Lavaredo in the Dolomites, in 1935.

Two years later, the pair, together with Gino Esposito, turned their attention to the huge granite North Face of the Piz Badile in

A LIFE'S WORK

- Begins climbing in the Grigna in 1928. He later **forms the "Lecco Spiders" and starts climbing in the Dolomites**
- **Takes lessons from Emilio Comici**, (see pp.288–89) and then sets out on his own campaign, with **new routes on the North Faces of the Cima Ovest and the Piz Badile**
- Leads the **landmark first ascent of the Walker Spur on the Grandes Jorasses**, having missed out on the Eigerwand
- **Fights as a partisan** against the Germans in World War II
- **Makes the first ascent** of an elegant spur on Denali, **now known as the Cassin Ridge**

WHAT I START, I FINISH. I NEVER CAME DOWN FROM A MOUNTAIN WITHOUT REACHING THE TOP

RICCARDO CASSIN

Switzerland. On the ascent, the team faced competition from a rival pair from Como. As the two parties climbed, a terrible storm blew up and the men decided to join forces. Although they successfully completed the route, the climbers from Como died on the descent.

In 1938, Ratti was on military service, so Cassin, again with Esposito, and Ugo Tizzoni, set off to try the infamous North Face of the Eiger, only to discover a German–Austrian team led by Anderl Heckmair (see pp.290–91) had just done it. The only challenge left that could rival this was the Walker Spur on the North Face of the Grandes Jorasses peak in the Mont Blanc range, so the team raced back to Italy and headed for Courmayeur, below Mont Blanc.

CLIMBING MASTERPIECES

Cassin had never climbed in the area, and his knowledge of its geography was sketchy, so he asked directions to the Grandes Jorasses from the guardian of a mountain hut. The man failed to recognize him, but he got a shock three days later when Cassin reached the top of the most prized and beautiful route in the French Alps.

Exempted from fighting during World War II because he worked in a munitions factory, Cassin had few chances to climb, but in the 1950s he went on a series of expeditions to the Himalaya, and North and South America. In 1958, he led an Italian team in the first ascent of Gasherbrum IV in Pakistan, an incredible achievement on a formidably difficult peak that has still only been climbed 10 times.

In 1961, now in his 50s, Cassin led a team to the summit of Denali in Alaska, taking a stunning line that remains a coveted challenge. Adorned with honours from the Italian state and the international climbing community, he was still making difficult rock climbs in his 80s.

CLIMBING INNOVATOR
Cassin's early climbing was done with equipment modern climbers would consider primitive, using hemp ropes and hand-made pitons. In 1947, he turned his attention to designing climbing equipment. He is pictured here in the Grigna in 1950, demonstrating the technique for climbing over a roof with rope-steps.

GRANDES JORASSES

SUMMIT
(4,208M/13,806FT)

POINTE
WHYMPER

POINTE
WALKER

GREY TOWER

WALKER SPUR, AUGUST 1938

— **4 August – Start of climb**
Leaving the hut early in the morning, Cassin, Esposito, and Tizzoni climb ice then rocks first left then back right to a difficult 75-m (250-ft) corner.

— **5 August – Tough going**
Difficult climbing above their bivouac forces them right towards a dangerous couloir, so Cassin leads back left into worsening weather to bivouac at Grey Tower.

— **6 August – Route to the summit**
As the climbing eases, bad weather sweeps in, catching the climbers high on the face. The storm passes and they reach the summit at 3pm.

THE UNWRITTEN RULES

BUILDING ON THE HUGE ADVANCES OF THE 1930s, AND TAKING ADVANTAGE OF TECHNOLOGICAL BREAKTHROUGHS MADE DURING WORLD WAR II, CLIMBING DEVELOPED QUICKLY DURING THE 1950s. BUT OLD QUESTIONS ABOUT HOW MUCH TECHNOLOGY WAS PERMISSIBLE RESURFACED.

DEEP BREATH
The long-standing debate about the possibility of climbing Everest without bottled oxygen was finally settled by Messner and Habeler's (above) oxygen-free ascent in 1978.

After the privations of World War II, mountaineering burst into renewed life in the 1950s, re-energized by a string of circumstances. The development of nylon for clothing and equipment, particularly rope, made climbing exponentially safer. The lifting of travel restrictions in the Himalaya inspired a dash for the "8,000ers", beginning with the French ascent of Annapurna in 1950, typically by large-scale expeditions using new technology.

Away from such high ambition, ordinary people saw a surge in income, which meant that trips further afield were no longer the preserve of national mountaineering bodies, but for local climbing clubs and individuals, too. This democratized exploration. Climbing's social base broadened, bringing new energy to the sport and breaking down old psychological barriers about what was possible – or permissible.

ASSISTED ASCENDING

Artificial climbing – using pitons to aid progress up steep ground – was already commonplace in the Eastern Alps, but it was now taken up around the world, particularly on the huge granite walls of Yosemite National Park in California, which became a crucible for the future of the sport worldwide. The use of rivets and expansion bolts in drilled holes allowed climbers to find protection or aid anywhere they chose, rather than where the rock allowed, removing another aspect of uncertainty. After the Americans climbed the West Ridge of Everest in 1963, attention in the Himalaya turned to the great faces. First among them was the vast South Face of Annapurna in 1970, and

then the Southwest Face of Everest. With fixed ropes, Sherpa support, artificial aid, and oxygen, it seemed anything could be climbed.

Some of the tactics used in the Himalaya, such as fixing ropes for supplies and for retreating in bad weather, were imported to the Alps as the drive to push standards grew more competitive. In 1966, while attempting a new direct route on the North Face of the Eiger, US climber John Harlin fell to his death when the fixed rope he was jumaring (climbing using an ascending device) broke. His partner Dougal Haston (see p.298) and a German team completed the climb.

For some, this process culminated in 1970, when the Dolomites climber Cesare Maestri led a team that winched a petrol-powered compressor up the vertical Southeast Face of Cerro Torre (see pp.306–07) in Patagonia to drill holes for bolts up blank sections of rock – a kind of extreme steeplejacking. This provoked a bitter controversy and the feeling that technology had been taken too far.

HAMMER TIME
From the 1970s, big-wall climbers in Yosemite prided themselves on climbing "hammer free", without a peg hammer to get them out of trouble.

> As mountaineering became increasingly enhanced by technology in the second half of the 20th century, the question was, what should – not what could – be attempted. Engaging with climbing ethics was the only way to find an answer.

In a seminal essay entitled *Murder of the Impossible*, Reinhold Messner (see pp.308–11) argued that if any mountaineering challenge could be done, given enough gear, then it was time to change the game. "Today's climber," he said in 1971, "carries his courage in his rucksack." For Messner and his supporters the scale and complexity of large-scale expeditions was antithetical to the fundamental principles of the sport, and threatened to undermine its future.

BACK TO BASICS

Messner concluded his essay with a call for a return to the lighter approach taken in the past. In Yosemite, in the same period, the damage caused by pitons prompted the development of less harmful methods of protecting a climb. Yosemite also became a hotbed for the free-climbing revolution, when aid routes that had first been climbed by pulling up on pitons were done increasingly with just hands and feet and the skill and strength of the climber. The equipment that revolutionized climbing after World War I became a means only to safeguard the climber, not aid their progress.

Messner's philosophy found its fullest expression in the debate over the use of bottled oxygen. After World War II, the view that it was a form of cheating looked foolishly quaint. But research undertaken during the war suggested that bottle-free climbs of high peaks might be possible.

ICE PEG
Swiss skier and climber Walter Prager places
an ice peg on a climb in the White Mountains,
New Hampshire, US, in 1945. Ice-climbing
techniques would change little until the 1970s.

YOSEMITE SOLO
A climber soloing near Yosemite Falls in
California, US. "The Valley" in Yosemite
National Park became an experimental crucible
for climbing's future from the 1950s onwards.

SETTING THE SCENE

- After World War II, with improved access
to the Himalaya and more affordable air
travel, mountaineering becomes **more
internationalist in outlook**. Competition
for objectives becomes more intense and
improvements in equipment allow climbers
to **push the limits of difficulty**.

- In the 1920s and 30s, French alpinism differs
from alpinism in the Eastern Alps. The French
tradition of **climbing fast and avoiding
bivouacs**, exemplified by climbers such as
Armand Charlet (see p.125), fades in the 1950s.
**Fixed ropes make an appearance in the
Alps** as climbers tackle harder routes.

- Emilio Comici's dictum about **a falling drop of
water showing the ideal line** becomes the
obsession, while expansion bolts mean that **any
piece of rock can be climbed**. This leads
activists such as Reinhold Messner and Yvon
Chouinard to **reassess climbing ethics**.

Messner and Peter Habeler's ascent of
Everest in 1978 without bottled oxygen,
and in particular, Messner's solo of
Everest's North Ridge during the monsoon
of 1980, again without bottled oxygen,
recalibrated the limits of the possible.
Messner became a fierce critic of what he
called "infrastructure" in the mountains,
seeing bolts and pitons as an extension of
the railways and mountain huts that had
enraged Guido Lammer (see pp.174–75).

All these ideas would be further
developed in the 1980s. But how did
such changes come to be accepted?
There are no governing bodies in world
mountaineering, and no rule book.
Practitioners set their own rules, limited
only by their consideration for majority
opinion – or lack of it. What is and isn't
considered allowable takes on a quasi-
theological aspect, as climbers debate the
finer points of ethics in journals, and
increasingly, online. Culture has played
a significant role, too. There were
deep ideological differences between
mountaineers from the US and the former
Soviet Union, for example. As climbing
has become more popular, commercial
pressures have also had an impact on
climbing ethics.

STAIRWAY TO HEAVEN?
A climber reaches to clip a point of aid while standing
in étriers (stirrups). Aid climbing reached its zenith in the
1950s and 1960s, before a movement to do such climbs
"free" of aid gathered momentum in the 1970s.

NEW HORIZONS

Bonatti was most fulfilled by technically challenging climbs, what he called "the pursuit of the impossible". A consummate loner, one of the reasons he climbed was to avoid human contact: "My disappointments came from people, not the mountains," he wrote in his memoir.

A LIFE'S WORK

- Bursts onto the scene with an ascent of the **Walker Spur at the age of 19** and then the East Face of the **Grand Capucin at 21**

- Assists in the first successful **Italian ascent of K2** but the **experience leaves him bitter**

- His five-day solo ascent of the Southwest Pillar of the Petit Dru is one of the **greatest mountaineering exploits of all time**

- Makes other **solo firsts, winter ascents, and numerous routes** up Mont Blanc

- Quits climbing for a career in **photojournalism**, travelling the world for *Epoca* magazine

WALTER BONATTI

FOREMOST EXTREME ALPINIST OF THE 1950S

ITALY   B.1930

JUST AS RICCARDO CASSIN was the star of alpinism just before World War II, Bonatti dominated the scene immediately after it. Although his career was much shorter – he abruptly stopped climbing at the age of 35 to pursue a career in photojournalism – his vision and the quality of his ascents mark him out as one of the sport's greatest talents. He was also the quintessential outsider, the victim of untrue allegations about his behaviour on a K2 expedition and the survivor of a terrible tragedy on Mont Blanc.

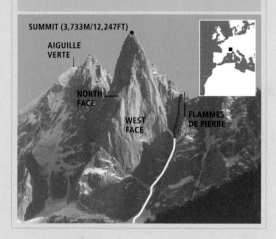

PETIT DRU

BONATTI PILLAR, 22 AUGUST 1955

— **Aborted attempt**
Bonatti makes three attempts via the couloir.

— **17 August – Avoids dangerous couloir**
Abseils down from the Flammes de Pierre.

— **18–22 August – Up the pillar**
Makes slow progress on the pillar. After a fourth bivouac, he makes a series of pendulum swings to bypass a blank section before a final night on the pillar before reaching the summit.

SUMMIT (3,733M/12,247FT)
AIGUILLE VERTE
NORTH FACE
WEST FACE
FLAMMES DE PIERRE

Born in Bergamo, Bonatti was a precocious talent, making his mark at just 19 with a repeat of Riccardo Cassin's masterpiece, the Walker Spur (see pp.292–93) in the Mont Blanc massif, and then at 21, climbing the technically harder East Face of the Grand Capucin.

These achievements won him a place on the Italian expedition to K2 in 1954, but the event turned into a disaster for him when one of the lead climbers, Achille Compagnoni (see pp.270–71), resentful of his ability, not only thwarted his summit ambitions and put his life at risk, but also accused him of stealing oxygen.

Bonatti's obsession with proving his version of events sometimes distorted his view of mountaineering. "Just as if I had been burned by a fiery brand," he wrote in his memoir *The Mountains Of My Life*, "I felt a diabolical incubus had entered my soul."

LONELY AT THE TOP

Bonatti wrote later that he was never sure whether he was born a loner or became one after K2, but his response to Compagnoni's accusations was first to seek legal redress and then to climb his way out of trouble.

In 1955, he climbed solo what became known as the Bonatti Pillar on the Petit Dru, a line that equalled the very best of Cassin's achievements. For five days, he recalled, "it was like living in another world, like entering an unknown dimension, like being in a mystical, visionary state in which the impossible did not exist and anything could happen."

Bonatti had tried the route before, first with his great friend Carlo Mauri in 1953, when they were thwarted by bad weather, and then with a team of four in July 1955, when a terrifying rockfall shook the mountain as they slept on their bivouac ledge. Yet within days of this second reversal, Bonatti was back, this time on his own. The climb was a masterpiece of concentrated, individual effort, requiring all his technical know-how and route-finding sense.

At one point he had to lasso a rock spike and climb up the rope, convinced the rock was going to collapse and send him into the abyss. After five bivouacs he reached the summit. British alpinist Doug Scott (see pp.304–05) later described Bonatti's ascent as "probably the most important single climbing feat ever to take place in mountaineering."

TRAGEDY ON MONT BLANC

Bonatti also added major new routes on Mont Blanc – with Toni Gobbi in 1957 on the Grand Pilier d'Angle, and the Red Pillar of Brouillard in 1959. But his attempt on the mountain's greatest remaining problem – the Central Pillar of Frêney high on the South Face – ended in a desperate retreat down the Frêney Glacier in terrible weather, and the deaths of four men.

Approaching the pillar in July 1961, Bonatti and his companions Andrea Oggioni and Roberto Gallieni met four French climbers, led by Pierre Mazeaud, intent on the same objective. The two groups joined forces and made good progress, but, close to success, a storm trapped them near the summit, dumping huge amounts of snow.

Their retreat, drawn out over many days, was among the most harrowing episodes in climbing history. Bonatti finally staggered into the Gamba Hut with Gallieni close behind to find a rescue party sleeping inside. The only other survivor was Mazeaud, who thanked Bonatti for saving his life. The French government awarded Bonatti the *Légion d'Honneur*, but the Italian press vilified him.

BOWING OUT

Bonatti's career came to a brilliant climax in 1958 when he reached the summit of Gasherbrum IV with Carlo Mauri – a technically difficult peak that is among the finest objectives in the Karakoram. The Italian team, led by Cassin, climbed the Northeast Ridge. Bonatti didn't respond well to being under someone else's control, but their ascent was a landmark in the Karakoram. In 1965, he climbed a new direct solo route in winter on the North Face of the Matterhorn and then promptly retired from mountaineering.

DON WHILLANS

STRAIGHT-TALKING MOUNTAIN LEGEND

ENGLAND   1933–85

AFTER WORLD WAR I, working-class climbers came to the fore in Alpine countries, leading to a surge in standards. For British climbers, however, the cost of foreign travel was still too great and they were limited to exploring their local crags. That changed in the 1950s with the emergence of a new wave of ambitious young British alpinists eager to make their mark. Leading the charge was Don Whillans, a short but implacable figure with a rebellious, down-to-earth determination to change his fortune.

DOUGAL HASTON
SCOTLAND   1940–77

With Whillans, Haston climbed the South Face of Annapurna in 1970, and with Doug Scott (see pp.304–05), climbed the Southwest Face of Everest in 1975.

Haston formed a brilliant but edgy partnership with Robin Smith while a student. Smith died in the Pamirs in 1962, and it was left to Haston to realize their early promise. He came to prominence after making the first ascent of the Direct Route on the Eiger in 1966 and starred on Chris Bonington's expeditions to Annapurna and Everest in the early 1970s. Hard-drinking and self-absorbed, Haston exuded cool. "It's as though he was behind glass," Whillans said of him. "You can see him but you can't touch him."

Whillans was born in Salford in the north of England, the son of a grocer. Escape to the hills beyond the town came first with the Boy Scouts and then under his own steam. Carrying heavy army surplus camping gear, he and his friends would undertake huge walks in the Peak District, building up their stamina and finding freedom in natural surroundings.

At 15, Whillans started work as an apprentice plumber and not long afterwards, became an apprentice climber, too, making his first rock climb on the gritstone crag of Shining Clough. Soon he was making first ascents, his speciality a series of overhanging cracks that are still considered demanding challenges. He might have been an outsider at school, the short boy who learned to fight to escape bullying, but the cliffs were an arena where he could prove himself as head of the pack.

TOP CLIMBING DUO
Meeting fellow northerner Joe Brown (see pp.272–73) while out climbing in 1951 galvanized Whillans and connected him to Brown's group – which later formed the legendary Rock and Ice Club – offering the kind of competition he thrived on. The pair formed one of the great partnerships, climbing some of Britain's most famous routes: Vember on Clogwyn D'ur Arddu, Cemetery Gates on Dinas Cromlech, and Sassenach on Ben Nevis.

Whillans made his first trip to the Alps in 1952, tempering his ambition with some lessons well learned. The following year he was invited to join the Alpine Climbing Group, a group of young climbers who felt that the Alpine Club, still suffering from its pre-war ethos, no longer served their interests. The group was a productive mix of ambitious young alpinists, schooled on hard domestic rock and ice and highly aware of the difficult new routes made by European climbers in the Alps during the 1930s and 40s.

In 1954, Brown and Whillans completed a line they had tried the year before: the West Face of the Aiguille de Blatière, with two of the hardest pitches in the Alps. Then they made the third ascent of the West Face of the Dru – cutting the ascent time to just 25 hours.

A LIFE'S WORK

- With Joe Brown, forms one of the most **famous partnerships** in British climbing history
- His feats on British and Alpine rock earn him **a legendary reputation** for pioneering bold climbs at the highest standards of the day
- Scales the **Central Pillar of Frêney** with Bonington in 1961. **Aborts attempt on the Eigerwand** with Bonington to make a courageous rescue of an injured climber
- After failures on Masherbrum and Gauri Sankar, he secures his place in climbing history with the **first ascent of Annapurna's South Face**
- His career declines and he starts to drink and smoke heavily, before **dying at the age of 52**

LEAVING CAMP FOR THE TOP OF MASHERBRUM
Whillans almost made it to the top of this Karakoram giant; his attempt was followed by a second summit bid, which reached Camp VI before one of its members died.

Chamonix took notice and the illustrious Louis Lachenal (see pp.256–57) visited the British team's campsite; Whillans had arrived.

However, it was Joe Brown who was invited on an expedition to Kangchenjunga the following year. Whillans took the rejection badly. Although he knew he was still too young for a Himalayan climb of that magnitude, he saw it as a slight. Brown himself captured his partner's strengths and weaknesses best: "The spiky side of Don's nature was dormant on the mountain. He was easy-going, and took my advice as readily as I took his on matters of route-finding … climbing with Don was much safer than with anyone else."

ONE THING TO REMEMBER ON THE EIGER, NEVER LOOK UP, OR YOU MAY NEED A PLASTIC SURGEON "

DON WHILLANS

RISE AND FALL OF A LEGEND

Whillans's own debut in the Himalaya came in 1957, with a British expedition to Masherbrum. The ascent was plagued by bad weather, but Whillans got to within 152m (500ft) of the summit before retreating.

In the early 1960s, he enjoyed considerable success in Patagonia, where he made the first ascents of Aiguille Poincenot and the Central Tower of Paine with Chris Bonington (see pp.300–01) and in the Alps, where in 1961, with Bonington, Ian Clough, and Jan Dlugosz he climbed the Central Pillar of Frêney. There were expeditions to the Andes and Gauri Sankar in Nepal, too.

His mountain judgment became legendary. British photographer John Cleare, part of a fractious international team on Everest in 1971, recalled how Whillans kept a clear head and acted effectively when an Indian team member fell and other climbers were panicking: "[He] showed great forethought, much moral courage, and considerable pragmatism in getting all the ill-prepared rescuers back to camp alive."

Yet by the mid-1970s, Whillans was a fading force, overweight and suffering from bouts of vertigo and knee injuries. Bonington hesitated before inviting him to Annapurna in 1970, but after climbing with him in Scotland, he decided Whillans could still make a major contribution and appointed him deputy leader. Success, achieved after sitting out bad weather at Camp VI, added a lustrous gloss to Whillans' career. In later years, heavy drinking and cigarettes destroyed his health, yet the mellower version of the Whillans legend prompted deep affection.

ON THE CENTRAL PILLAR OF FRÊNEY
Just one month after Bonatti's tragic attempt (see pp.296–97), Whillans and his team made the first successful ascent up Mont Blanc's most difficult route.

CHRIS BONINGTON

THE "FACE" OF BRITISH MOUNTAINEERING

ENGLAND   B.1934

FOR MANY IN BRITAIN, Chris Bonington is the quintessential climber, thanks in part to his ability to communicate real mountaineering achievements to the general public. In a series of high-profile, large expeditions, he led a powerful cadre of post-war British mountaineers who took Himalayan climbing to the next level – the huge faces of the 8,000-m (26,246-ft) peaks – on Annapurna and Everest. On the surface an establishment figure, Bonington's career and contribution are more complex than they seem.

A LIFE'S WORK

- Serves as a tank commander in the army before becoming an **instructor at the Army Outward Bound School**
- Makes the **first ascent of Annapurna II** in 1960, followed by an ascent of Nuptse the day after the first ascent by his team-mates Dennis Davis and Tachei Sherpa
- Becomes one of **Britain's leading alpinists** with his first ascent of the Central Pillar of Frêney on Mont Blanc in 1961
- **Writes and edits more than 20 books** and makes a television series for the BBC
- Leads a large British team on the **South Face of Annapurna** in 1970, marking the start of a new era in Himalayan climbing. Team member Ian Clough is killed at the end of the expedition
- Leads a successful **expedition on the Southwest Face of Everest** in 1975, although Mick Burke disappears near the summit
- In 1982, attempts the **unclimbed Northeast Ridge of Everest**. Pete Boardman and Joe Tasker disappear on the summit attempt
- Continues to **travel and climb in his 70s**

In the summer of 1954, aged 20, Bonington was living in a road-mender's hut in North Wales, usually with a conscientious objector and artist called Ginger Cain. He was ecstatically happy. Climbing every day it didn't rain and living a simple life after the discipline of basic training in the RAF and the disappointment of failing to qualify as a pilot, he was waiting to take up a place at the military academy at Sandhurst.

What his girlfriend couldn't understand was why he would give all this up for a commission in the Royal Tank Regiment. "Looking back," Bonington wrote later, "neither can I, but at the time, although I loved the feckless, irresponsible way of life in Wales,

I felt I had to have a steady career, and in fact, actively looked forward to life in the army." In 1950s Britain, climbing couldn't pay the rent; too few people did it and there were no equipment manufacturers to sponsor a professional. Nor was it enough for Bonington to live the life of a vagabond. He needed structure and status, the sense that his life was taking a path that would lead him upwards.

The source of Bonington's ambition was an isolated and rootless childhood in London. His father left when he was a baby, and was largely absent from then on. During World War II he went to a succession of boarding schools where he was seldom happy. He was "an enthusiastic

escaper", running away just for the sake of it. Towards the end of the war he returned to London to live with his mother and attend University College School.

ASCENT OF THE EIGER

Bonington was the classic bourgeois climbing recruit: an ambitious misfit whose adolescence coincided with his introduction to the mountains. At 16, he travelled to Ireland's County Wicklow to stay with his uncle, where he went for long walks in the Wicklow hills and discovered the freedom and easy happiness that being in the mountains offered him.

He later served in the army, first as a tank commander in Germany and then as a mountaineering instructor, and enjoyed great success in the Alps, making the first British ascent of the Southwest Pillar of the Dru in 1958 and then the first ascent of the Central Pillar of Frêney on the south side of Mont Blanc in 1961 with Don Whillans (see pp.298–99), Ian Clough, and Polish alpinist Jan Dlugosz. At that time, this was one of the most difficult climbs in the Alps. He also made the first British ascent of the North Wall of the Eiger in 1962 with Clough.

ANNAPURNA

SOUTH FACE, MAY 1970

- **7 April – Straightforward first section**
  The team progresses swiftly to Camp III on an ice ridge at 6,100m (20,000ft).

- **3 May – To the base of the rock band**
  Hard snow and ice lead to the foot of a 600-m (2,000-ft) rock band.

- **17 May – Push to the summit**
  Don Whillans and Dougal Haston lead the way to the upper section and make a bid for the summit, reaching it on 27 May.

SUMMIT
(8,091M/26,545FT)

CAMP VI

ROCK BAND

CAMP V

CAMP IV

CAMP III

CAMP II

His Himalayan career also started while he was in the army. Invited on the joint British-Indian–Nepalese Services Expedition to Annapurna II in 1960, he reached the summit.

A year later, Bonington left the army and joined Unilever, his last attempt at a conventional career, but resigned after nine months to become a freelance mountaineer, photographer, and adventure journalist.

EXEMPLARY CLIMBING LEADER

In 1963, he made a first ascent of Patagonia's Central Tower of Paine with Whillans and, following a successful career as a photojournalist, led a highly successful ascent of the South Face of Annapurna in 1970. This was the first of the big Himalayan faces to be attempted and only the third ascent of the mountain overall. Balancing military efficiency with good man management, Bonington became one of the more successful leaders of large-scale expeditions, repeating the Annapurna success on the Southwest Face of Everest in 1975 with one of the strongest teams in British mountaineering history on an objective that had attracted huge international attention. He led one more siege-style expedition, to the West Ridge of K2, but when his close friend Nick Estcourt was swept away by an avalanche, the bid was abandoned.

He had great success with lightweight teams too, starting with the first ascent of Changabang in 1974. Three years later, with Doug Scott (see pp.304–05), he made the first ascent of The Ogre in the Karakoram. In 1983, with Jim Fotheringham, he climbed the elegant Southwest Ridge of Shivling in alpine style. In 1985, he realized a long-held ambition by reaching the top of Everest himself.

THE "V02 MAX"

During the 1981 Kongur expedition, physiologist Michael Ward tested team members for their "VO2 max". This is the maximum amount of oxygen in millilitres one can use in one minute per kilogram of body weight. The average for an untrained male is 45. Bonington, then 47, scored in the mid 50s, while Joe Tasker and Pete Boardman scored in the mid 60s. Oddly, Reinhold Messner scored only in the high 40s. The US climber Ed Viesturs scored in the 80s, in line with a Tour de France cyclist.

BONINGTON'S LUNGS BEING PUT THROUGH THEIR PACES TO MEASURE HIS V02 MAX.

ON TOP OF A CHINESE GIANT
In 1980, China re-opened some parts of Tibet to foreign climbers. Bonington (pictured second from left) led the way with an ascent of the remote, unclimbed Kongur Tagh.

YVON CHOUINARD

YOSEMITE VETERAN AND ENVIRONMENTALIST

CANADA   B.1938

THE GRANITE "BIG WALLS" of Yosemite inspired the movement for national parks in the US. At first, climbing them seemed surreally impossible. Before and just after World War II, rock climbing in "the Valley" gathered pace, but controversy raged about which climbing style was acceptable. Yvon Chouinard had a stringent ethical vision, which he took from Yosemite to the mountain walls of South America's Patagonia. His approach to climbing also became the foundation for a broader environmental programme.

In the 1950s, the biggest prize in Yosemite was the Nose of El Capitan. In 1958, a maverick called Warren Harding climbed this mammoth challenge with two companions but the ascent was highly controversial. Harding used 900m (3,000ft) of fixed ropes (the entire height of the face), made about 675 peg placements and drilled 125 bolts. He and his team spent 45 days on the route, spread over 18 months.

Many Yosemite climbers felt Harding's tactics were wrong and that a lighter approach to climbing the park's big walls was appropriate and desirable. Climbing legends Royal Robbins, Tom Frost, Chuck Pratt, and Joe Fitschen made an ascent of Harding's route in one single push

in 1960. This early controversy made Yosemite climbing a focus for ethical debate in which Chouinard – who became a leading light on the scene in the 1960s – played a central role.

The son of a French-Canadian blacksmith who moved from Maine to California in the mid 1940s, Chouinard grew up speaking French. His interest in rock climbing was sparked as a young falconer exploring the bird's eyries. Later, he and his friends would jump freight trains to reach the large boulders at Stoney Point, at the end of California's San Fernando valley, where they learned the basics. They then moved on to Tahquitz Rock, a tall, imposing rock formation, where Chouinard met

Sierra Club members Robbins, Frost, and T M Herbert. As a teenager, he started climbing at Yosemite and settled happily into the beatnik, alternative scene that was emerging there. He and his friends became known as the "Valley Cong" when they hid out from rangers after overstaying their two-week camping limit.

GOING INTO BUSINESS

Chouinard would spend his winters making hard-steel pitons, a technique he'd learned from the Swiss-born blacksmith and Yosemite pioneer John Salathé, who had scaled the Lost Arrow spire in 1947 with his new pegs.

In 1957, he bought a used coal-fired forge, an anvil, tongs, and a hammer, and using old harvester blades, began fabricating his own hard-steel pegs, selling them for $1.50 each. He opened a small shop in his parents' backyard and also sold pegs directly from the boot of his car, working in the winter and spending the rest of the year surfing and climbing. His profits were small, however, and he'd live on as little as 50 cents a day, supplementing his diet with cat food and poached ground squirrels.

With his Yosemite friends he climbed some of the Valley's major new routes, including North American Wall in 1964 with Chuck Pratt, Robbins, and Frost. It was arguably the hardest aid climb in the world at the time. The next year he climbed Muir Wall with Herbert.

A LIFE'S WORK

- **Falls in love with nature** when his family move to California; joins the Sierra Club, a group founded to conserve the US's natural resources

- As a teenager he starts **making hard-steel pitons** to sell to his friends – the only pitons available at this time are made of soft iron, which, once they are placed, have to be left in the rock. The business grows and his company, Chouinard Equipment, becomes the **biggest and most environmentally aware climbing hardware brand** in the US

- Along with **major new routes in Yosemite**, he climbs important mountain routes such as the North Face of Mount Edith Cavell in the Rockies

- On a climbing trip to Scotland he buys a rugby shirt and, when it proves popular with other climbers, he imports more. He calls his **new outdoor clothing company Patagonia**

CLIMBING A YOSEMITE BIG WALL
Chouinard had mixed feelings about Yosemite. "I would rather climb in the high mountains," he said. "I have always abhorred the tremendous heat, the dirt-filled cracks … and worst of all, the multitudes of tourists … during the summer".

FORGING INNOVATIONS

Chouinard's hardened-steel pitons were a big improvement on earlier soft steel pegs, which moulded to cracks and were difficult to remove. His development boosted big-wall exploration and led to a worldwide surge in aid-climbing. Other innovations, developed with Tom Frost, included the Realized Ultimate Reality Piton, for nailing very thin cracks, an ice axe with a curved pick, and other ice gear, including ice screws with a broader diameter. Recognizing the damage done by pegs, they developed metal wedges or "nuts" to use as protection – a far less damaging alternative.

CHOUINARD PUTS HIS BLACKSMITH'S SKILLS TO USE ON ONE OF HIS ENVIRONMENTALLY FRIENDLY CLIMBING PRODUCTS

MOUNTAINS ARE FINITE, AND DESPITE THEIR APPEARANCE ... FRAGILE

YVON CHOUINARD, ON "CLEAN CLIMBING"

This era of big-wall climbing in Yosemite had an immense impact on world mountaineering. Chouinard was among the first to realize how this future might look. In 1963 he wrote, "Yosemite Valley will, in the near future, be the training ground for a new generation of super-alpinists who will venture forth to the high mountains of the world to do the most esthetic and difficult walls on the face of the earth."

ROCK-CLIMBING TESTBED

As Chouinard predicted, in the last 50 years, wildly steep cliffs on mountains from the Karakoram to Antarctica and from Patagonia to the Arctic have been climbed using techniques developed in the Valley. Equally, when free climbing in Yosemite became the vogue in the 1970s, culminating in US rock climber Lynn Hill's free ascent of the Nose in 1993, that ethic was taken into the mountains, too.

Chouinard's ascent in 1961 of South Howser Tower in Canada's Bugaboos with Fred Beckey – a maverick legend in American exploratory climbing – and Dan Doody was an early example. But, as he explained, such routes were "merely the beginning of a totally new school of American climbing."

In 1968, Chouinard travelled to Patagonia, the wild and windswept region on the southern tip of South America, with Briton Chris Jones and fellow Americans Dick Dorworth, Lito Tejada-Flores, and Doug Tompkins to climb a new route on Fitzroy, the peak's third ascent overall. He saw Patagonia as the perfect arena for his new kind of "super-alpinism".

Although Chouinard's other pursuits – surfing, kayaking, and fly-fishing – and his growing business interests in his outdoor clothing brand diverted him from climbing in later years, his passion was always for the Earth's

wild places. He said: "Who are businesses really responsible to? Their customers? Shareholders? Employees? We would argue that it's none of the above. Fundamentally, businesses are responsible to their resource base. Without a healthy environment there are no shareholders, no employees, no customers and no business."

EL CAPITAN

NORTH AMERICAN WALL, 22–31 OCT 1964

— **22 Oct – Pratt and Chouinard join forces with Frost and Robbins**
They take four days to reach Big Sur Ledge.

— **26 Oct – Hard route to the summit**
Frost, and then Pratt and Robbins, solve the "Borderline Traverse" into the Black Dihedral.

SUMMIT (3,169M/10,367FT)

CYCLOPS EYE

BIG SUR LEDGE

DOUG SCOTT

LEADING HIGH-ALTITUDE AND BIG-WALL CLIMBER

ENGLAND   B.1941

THE FIRST ENGLISHMAN to climb Mount Everest, Doug Scott's career spanned a crucial transition in world mountaineering from the siege-style tactics of fixed ropes and camps with Sherpa support, to something more akin to the tactics employed in the Alps, where climbers are self-reliant and fast-moving. Scott's own journey mirrored this process. An enthusiastic aid-climber in the late 1960s, with several Yosemite big walls to his credit, by the end of the 1970s he had become a guru of lightweight Himalayan climbing.

A LIFE'S WORK

- After several Alpine seasons, his first expedition is to **Chad's Tibesti mountains**
- Climbs Koh-e-Bandaka's South Face, his **first success in the Greater Ranges**
- Joins Bonington's second attempt on **Everest's Southwest Face** and **reaches the summit**
- Apart from Everest, **all his climbs are done in lightweight, alpine style**, without the use of supplementary oxygen
- Reaches the **Seven Summits** – the highest peaks on all seven continents
- Sets up **a charity** to help the people of Nepal

GROUNDBREAKING CLIMB
Scott's ascent of Kangchenjunga with Boardman and Tasker – seen here where they joined the West Ridge just below the summit – and Bettembourg was a journey into the unknown, climbing via a new route, and without bottled oxygen.

Born on the fringes of Nottingham in central England, Scott grew up building dens and climbing trees. He discovered rock climbing on a trip to Black Rocks in the Peak District. Barred from trying it for himself, he cycled out with his friends the following weekend with his mother's washing line. "We slithered and slipped, grazing our bare legs, but managed to climb the easier chimneys," he wrote later.

Barrel-chested with strong legs, Scott's passion for hill walking and rugby stood in the way of him becoming a top rock climber. But his apprenticeship on the gritstone crags near his home "inculcated a combative instinct when dealing with problems on rock." After a long training period in Britain and the Alps, Scott's first expedition was to Central Africa and the rarely visited Tibesti mountains in Chad,

setting a pattern of focusing on less well-known objectives. He was a pioneer on Baffin Island in the Canadian Arctic, too, climbing a classic line on Mount Asgard. He also explored the Atlas Mountains in North Africa in the 1960s, and put up new routes in Iceland and Tierra del Fuego in South America.

TRIUMPH ON EVEREST

It is for his 45 Himalayan expeditions that Scott is most famous, though, beginning in 1972 with two attempts on Everest's Southwest Face, the first with a fractious international party led by German impresario Karl Herrligkoffer, the second with Chris Bonington (see pp.300–01) on his first attempt. Scott's stamina and ambition made him relentless at high altitude; he had found his natural milieu – the high Himalaya.

His success on Everest came in 1975 as part of the summit team of a large British expedition. Paul Braithwaite and Nick Estcourt solved the crux section of the route, a technically difficult stretch up a snow-covered ramp. With support from Chris Bonington, Mike Thompson, Mick Burke, and two Sherpas, Scott and Dougal Haston (see p.298) established Camp VI on the upper part of the Southwest Face.

Scott's summit push with his partner Haston was hugely committing. They left the tent at dawn, reaching the couloir leading to the South Summit at 1pm, but soft snow delayed them and they only reached the South Summit at 3pm. Knowing that a bivouac was inevitable, the pair faced a choice: stop at once and then

HEROIC DESCENT

Abseiling from the summit of The Ogre in 1977, Scott slipped on some ice and swung violently into rocks on the other side of a couloir. He broke both his legs at the ankle. He and Bonington – who was also injured – endured a freezing bivouac, and then fought their way off the mountain, ascending on a rope over the West Summit to reach the descent. Trapped by a storm, they spent two days in a snow cave with two team-mates before continuing down. In all, the descent took eight days. The worst part for Scott was having to crawl 5km (3 miles) back to Base Camp. "No one else but you could have made it back," Bonington told him afterwards.

continue the next day, or bag the main summit and bivouac on the way down. "Knowing how wretched I feel after a bivouac, I was keen to avoid this," Scott wrote later. "After a rest and a brew [cup of tea] I led a pitch along the ridge and found the snow was more consolidated."

They were climbing in the post-monsoon season and the famous, almost vertical rock face Hillary Step was smothered in granular snow, demanding the greatest care. By the time the pair reached the summit, darkness was falling. They were forced to bivouac just below the summit at 8,760m (28,740ft). It was a brutal night, but afterwards Scott knew the boundaries of his game had shifted: "If I could survive a night up there without oxygen and a sleeping bag, and avoid frostbite, I could probably survive a night out anywhere there was snow to dig into to escape the biting winds."

After their success, many of the climbers on the Everest expedition recognized that the future lay in smaller, lightweight teams, moving fast and not relying on Sherpa support and well-stocked camps. Scott was already balancing

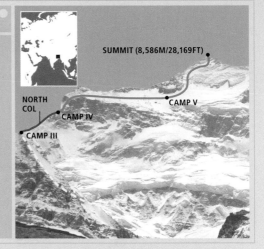

KANGCHENJUNGA

NORTH COL/NORTH RIDGE, MAY 1979

— **Up to the North Col**
Scott, Bettembourg, Tasker, and Boardman climb the steep face to the North Col at 6,890m (22,600ft).

— **Pushing up the North Ridge**
The team dig a snow cave at 7,400m (24,300ft). All four attempt the summit but they turn back to Camp IV in bad weather.

— **Committed climb to the summit**
Tasker, Boardman, and Scott try again, bivouacking at Camp V before pushing on.

(Dashed line means route hidden from view)

SUMMIT (8,586M/28,169FT)

NORTH COL

CAMP IV

CAMP III

CAMP V

between his exploratory instincts and ambition to climb the biggest mountains. Between his Everest trips, he had made the first ascent of Changabang as part of an Indo-British party.

In 1977, he and Bonington reached the summit of The Ogre in the Karakoram – an extremely difficult climb that would not be repeated for another 24 years. It

was a huge achievement, overshadowed somewhat by the accident Scott suffered during the descent, when he broke both his legs (see opposite). Scott had been on brilliant form climbing to the summit, free climbing awkward ground at more than 7,000m (23,000ft). He wrote later, "It was the hardest climbing I've ever done at that altitude, on superb brown weathered granite. An overhang barring the way to the final snow gully was overcome using combined tactics where I stood on Chris's back."

PUSHING THE BOUNDARIES

In the Himalaya, Scott continued to mix smaller, more technical climbs with attempts on the highest peaks. In 1979 he made the first ascent of Kusum Kanguru with Frenchman Georges Bettemboug, and in 1981, the stupendous East Ridge of Shivling with Australians Greg Child and Rick White, and Bettembourg, in a mammoth 13-day effort.

His greatest achievement, however, was the new route he climbed on Kangchenjunga with Joe Tasker and Pete Boardman, the brightest British stars of the generation that followed Scott's. The route tackled Kangchenjunga from the northwest, but climbed steep slopes to the North Col and then up to the North Ridge to the Great Terrace that leads towards the final summit pyramid. Their first attempt ended when a bitter storm caught them high on the Terrace, but on their third try, they reached the summit. On this climb, Scott faced "the closest call I've ever had, the finest line I'd drawn between being here and not being here, and yet it was curiously exhilarating."

Later in his career, Scott was prepared to accept failure as he tested his skills. He went four times to K2, and came within a hair's breadth of climbing a new line on Makalu in alpine style. In the 1980s, he climbed more new routes, on Shisha Pangma and Lobsang Spire in the Karakoram, and became a mentor for a younger generation of leading British alpinists.

SNOW MUSHROOM **2**

CERRO TORRE SUMMIT
(3,128M/10,262FT)

SOUTHEAST
RIDGE

TORRE EGGER

AGUJA
STANDHARDT

EAST FACE

EAST FACE

COL OF
PATIENCE

COL OF
CONQUEST

1 SNOW PATCH

3

MOUNTAIN FEATURES

Ⓐ **Remote west side** Cerro Torre's
West Face, showing the Col of
Conquest. The Italian route from
1974 takes the right-hand ridge.

Ⓑ **El Arca de los Vientos** The first
climbers to follow the bulk of
Maestri's claimed line found no traces
of the Italian's climb with Toni Egger.

Ⓒ **Cerro Fitzroy** The other great
Patagonian peak (3,405m/11,171ft),
it was first climbed in 1952 by Lionel
Terray and Guido Magnone.

Ⓐ

Ⓑ

Ⓒ

There are no easy ways up Cerro Torre, but Maestri's 1970 Compressor Route has proved something approaching popular because of its bolted protection. Most routes are on the East Face, seen here, and South Face, including two impressive lines: the South Face climbed by Silvo Karo and Janez Jeglic in 1988 – at the time, the hardest big wall in the world – and Infinito Sud, a contribution from Italian climber Ermanno Salvaterra.

SOUTHEAST RIDGE
— COMPRESSOR ROUTE
(C Maestri, C Claus, E Alimonta, 1970) Maestri and his team hauled a 180kg (400lb) compressor to drill bolts as they climbed the 700m (2,300ft) Southeast Ridge from the Col of Patience.

EAST FACE
— DEVIL'S DIRETTISSIMA
(S Karo, J Jeglic, 1986) This major new route features climbing up to 7a and A4 (see p.351), and took weeks to complete.

— QUINQUE ANNI AD PARADISUM
(E Salvaterra, A Beltrami, G Rossetti, 2004) Another hard route, climbed in a continuous 8-day push.

❶ Snow patch on Cerro Torre's East Face where Maestri's gear cache was found.

— BRITISH ATTEMPT
(T Proctor, P Burke, 1981) A British route that fell short of the summit, climbing the prominent corner that borders the East Face.

❷ The summit mushroom of snow and rime is a frightening climax to the difficult rock climbs below.

— EL ARCA DE LOS VIENTOS
(E Salvaterra, A Beltrami, G Rossetti, 2005) The only route that climbs Cerro Torre from the north, climbing the East Face to the Col of Conquest.

❸ The glacier below the Col of Conquest where Fava found Maestri in 1959. Egger's body was discovered in 1975, some way down the glacier, but it shed no fresh light on the controversy.

TORRE EGGER
— TITANIC
(M Giarolli, E Orlandi, 1987) A brilliant line almost 1,000m (3,300ft) long up the peak's East Buttress.

AGUJA STANDHARDT
— EXOCET
(J Bridwell, J Smith, G Smith, 1988) A superb climb, 500m (1,650ft) long.

(Dashed line means route hidden from view)

CERRO TORRE

Jutting proudly into the wildest winds on Earth, Cerro Torre is a fantastical peak on the edge of the South Patagonian Icecap, its golden granite walls plastered with rime and sculpted snow or – more rarely – bathed in sunshine. In recent years Cerro Torre and its neighbouring peaks have seen some of the hardest new climbs achieved anywhere, but a storm of controversy still rages about the mountain's earlier exploration – and its future.

Separated from neighbouring peaks by the Col of Conquest to the north and the Col of Hope to the southwest, Cerro Torre may not be the highest mountain in Patagonia, yet its aura of invincibility and strange, ethereal beauty, makes it the most desirable.

Francisco Moreno named the peak during an exploration to fix the Argentina-Chile border in the 1870s. In the early 20th century the Patagonian missionary and mountain explorer Father Alberto de Agostini photographed the region. The first two expeditions to Cerro Torre, in 1958, both failed, despite the presence of Walter Bonatti. Italian ex-patriot Cesarino Fava sent pictures of Cerro Torre to friends back home in Europe, and one of them – the Dolomites legend Cesare Maestri – was bitten. He brought the Austrian guide and ice specialist Toni Egger to South America, and the pair proceeded to make an attempt on the mountain. On 3 February 1959, Fava found the half-frozen Maestri, more dead than alive, on the glacier below the peak. He claimed that he and Egger had reached the summit – but that Egger had died on the descent. Hailed as a hero in Italy, many Patagonian experts now doubt his claim.

IN PROFILE

Name: Cerro Torre

Location: Patagonia, between Argentina and Chile (disputed territory)

Height: 3,128m (10,262ft)

Notable features: Huge granite walls, with no straightforward ascent route. An unstable snow-and-ice "mushroom" caps the summit.

First undisputed ascent: Daniele Chiappa, Mario Conti, Casimiro Ferrari, Pino Negri, 1974

First alpine-style ascent: Dave Carman, John Bragg, Jay Wilson, 1977

First solo ascent: Marco Pedrini, 1985

First winter ascent: Maurizio Giarolli, Paolo Caruso, Andrea Sarchi, Ermanno Salvaterra, 1985

First female ascent: Rosanna Manfrini, 1987

First traverse of the entire massif: Rolando Garibotti, Colin Haley, 2008

CHILE

CERRO FITZROY

AGUJA STANDHARDT

TORRE EGGER

COL OF CONQUEST

CERRO TORRE

COL OF PATIENCE

COL OF HOPE

TORRE GLACIER

SOUTH PATAGONIAN ICECAP

ARGENTINA

SCALE

2 MILES

2KM

▲ SUMMIT

N

REINHOLD MESSNER

HISTORY'S MOST RENOWNED MOUNTAINEER

ITALY   B.1944

THE FIRST MAN TO CLIMB all 14 "8,000ers", and the first to climb Everest without bottled oxygen, many regard Reinhold Messner as the greatest ever high-altitude mountaineer. A handful of climbers might justifiably claim otherwise, but Messner's impact on the sport is unrivalled. Controversial, imperious, and wildly committed to his chosen objectives, his unique style was at the forefront of mountaineering for decades. In the words of Australian climber Greg Child: "Like him or not, all roads lead to Messner."

Philosophically, Messner is the modern-day equivalent of the great Austrian climbers of the late 19th century – men such as Guido Lammer (see pp.174–75), who decried infrastructure in the mountains and preferred solitude to the masses crowding the peaks. In his climbing style, however, he resembled Hermann Buhl (see pp.258–59): wholly committed to the task in front of him. Yet Messner surpassed even Buhl in both ambition and achievement.

GOING HARD, FAST, AND LIGHT
Born one of nine children and raised in the tiny village of Villnöss in the Italian South Tyrol, Messner climbed his first mountain at the age of five, the 3,350-m (11,000-ft) Geisler Peak. By his teens, climbing had become an obsession – one that he shared with his younger brother Günther. Among the hundreds of climbs he did during this period were the first ascent of the Ortler's North Face and the direct route on the South Face of Marmolada.

In 1967, Messner enrolled at Padua University, and he and Günther started climbing the hardest routes of the day in the Alps. He also began climbing on his own, in 1968 making the first solo ascent of the classic Philipp-Flamm route on the Civetta in the Dolomites. By 1969, he had topped this with the first solo of the gloomy North Face of Les Droites in just eight and a half hours, an axe in one hand and a light

ice dagger in the other. The fastest ascent up to this point had taken three days, and several other climbing teams had met with disaster.

IN HIS HERO'S FOOTSTEPS
In 1970, Reinhold, then 26, and Günther, 24, went on their first Himalayan expedition to the ninth-highest peak in the world, Nanga Parbat. The mountain's Rupal Face fascinated Messner, not least because Buhl had deemed it impossible. But expedition leader Karl Herrligkoffer's "siege tactics" did not suit Messner's own lightweight climbing ethics and he quickly fell foul of the German's autocratic style of leadership. Events high on the mountain that summer shadowed Messner for decades afterwards, resulting in legal action and bitter recrimination.

On the morning of 27 June, he set off a little after 2am, leaving his brother and Gerhard Baur in the tent at Camp V. The plan was for the pair to fix ropes in the Merkl Couloir, which Messner was now climbing in the dark on difficult ground, on occasion scratching up ice-covered rocks in his crampons. At times he had to go back down and try another route.

Looking down the Merkl Couloir, he saw Günther racing to join him. Together they went on; when Messner tired, Günther stepped into the lead, and as the afternoon wore on they reached the summit. A bivouac was now inevitable. The route up was too difficult to

A LIFE'S WORK

- Climbs his **first "sixth-grader"**, the Tissi Route on the First Sella Tower, and his **first north face**, the Similaun in the Ötztal Alps **at the age of 18**

- Becomes known as one of Europe's best alpinists through his feats in the **Alps**, where he makes more than **500 climbs**, many of them first ascents, and in record time

- Hoping to **kick-start a full-time climbing career**, he joins a fateful Austrian expedition to **Nanga Parbat**. The death of his brother on the peak, and the subsequent allegations by his team-mates, have repercussions that last for decades

- Achieves an **unmatched record** of climbing firsts on the world's highest peaks, taking his lightweight climbing ethos – travelling very light and using a minimum of external help – to new extremes. Champions **climbing without bottled oxygen**

UP EVEREST WITHOUT OXYGEN
On 8 May 1978, Messner stood with Habeler on the summit of Everest, the first men ever to climb it without bottled oxygen. Previously it was disputed whether this was physiologically possible. With them was Reinhard Karl, the first German to reach the summit (with oxygen).

I WAS NOTHING MORE THAN A SINGLE, NARROW, GASPING LUNG, FLOATING OVER THE MISTS AND SUMMITS "

REINHOLD MESSNER ON HIS ASCENT OF EVEREST, MAY 1978

reverse, so without ropes, they hunted out another way back into the Merkl Couloir and then scratched out a ledge to spend the night in temperatures of −30°C (−22°F).

FROM TRIUMPH TO TRAGEDY

The following morning Messner caught sight of two expedition members, Felix Kuen and Peter Scholz, climbing up their steps from the day before. There was a shouted exchange, with Messner asking them to come in their direction and bring a rope. But the men continued straight up. Messner lost control for a while, a kind of madness enveloping him, but Günther brought him round and together they began to descend the easier Diamir Face. Low down, after night had fallen, they lost contact with each other. By now Messner was half out of his mind with fatigue, and suffering from terrible frostbite. And Günther had simply disappeared.

The brothers' ascent had been the first traverse of an "8,000er" since the Americans on Everest in 1963. Messner returned the following year to look for his brother's body, to no avail. "Nanga Parbat changed my life forever," he said. "But I had to take responsibility and live with the tragedy." He later criticized his fellow climbers for not coming to his aid, but they in turn accused him of abandoning his brother. The discovery of Günther's remains on the Diamir Glacier in 2005 at least offered evidence to support Messner's account of his death.

As a result of his frostbite, Messner had six toes amputated. Without them, he could no longer climb on rock at the highest level, so he specialized in making fast ascents of snow and ice routes, putting his ethical beliefs into practice.

He teamed up with Austrian alpinist Peter Habeler (see opposite), and they climbed some major north faces in record time, including the Eiger in just ten hours in 1974. The following year the pair raced up the 8,068-m (26,470-ft) Gasherbrum I in the Karakoram in just three days, emulating the blistering, bold style of Messner's hero Buhl, and spearheading an interest in lightweight ascents of big peaks.

ACHIEVING THE IMPOSSIBLE

It was also good experience for the ultimate prize in high-altitude mountaineering. Could Everest be climbed without oxygen? There were conflicting opinions on this among high-altitude physiologists, but Fritz Wiessner's experience on K2 (see pp.250–51) showed that it was at least worth trying.

On 6 May 1978, climbing as part of an Austrian Everest expedition, Messner and Habeler set out from Camp II. Habeler had changed his mind back and forth about whether he could face the trials and risk of climbing without oxygen, but by the time they left the South Col, both men were committed. They

ON TOP OF NANGA PARBAT
In 1978, carrying just an ice axe and crampons, and without oxygen, Messner climbed to the summit of "his" mountain via a new route; one of his many "firsts".

MOUNT EVEREST

NORTH RIDGE, AUGUST 1980

18 August – Messner sets off alone
Messner sets off at 5am from Advanced Base Camp; despite falling in a crevasse, he reaches the North Col and heads up the ridge to 7,800m (25,500ft).

19 August – Across to Norton Couloir
Deep snow makes him rethink climbing the ridge; he traverses towards the Norton Couloir instead, across a potential avalanche slope. He bivouacs just 400m (1,300ft) higher.

20 August – Perilous ascent to summit
Moving into the Norton Couloir, the weather turns bad and visibility is reduced to 50m (150ft); he reaches the summit at 3pm: "I was in continual agony," he wrote.

SUMMIT (8,848M/29,029FT)

SECOND STEP

NORTHEAST RIDGE

WEST RIDGE

NORTON COULOIR

NORTH RIDGE

HORNBEIN COULOIR

CLIMBING TIMELINE

Aged 18, he climbs his first "sixth-grade" route, the Tissi Route on the first Sella Tower

First Himalayan expedition to Nanga Parbat; having reached the summit with Günther, his brother is lost, prompting decades of controversy

He and Peter Habeler astonish the climbing world by ascending the North Face of the Eiger in only ten hours

1944–63	1964–69	1970–75	1976–77

At the age of five, he is taken by his father into the Dolomites, his first experience of mountains

Begins climbing with his brother Günther, two years his junior; together they climb the North Face of Sass Rigais

With Günther, he makes the first winter ascent of the North Face of the Furchetta

With Peter Habeler, makes the first pure alpine-style ascent of an "8,000er" – Gasherbrum I

ADVANCED BASE CAMP, EVEREST
In 1978, Messner and Habeler climbed into the Western Cwm with the rest of the team before making a separate bid.

reached the summit on 8 May, breathing only the natural thin air. Messner later described feeling as though he were "nothing more than a single narrow, gasping lung."

The same powerful individualism that had soured relations with the team on Nanga Parbat soon broke apart his relationship with Habeler. It made no difference to Messner because he had set his mind on the next challenge – climbing Everest without oxygen, but also without the logistical and psychological support offered by a big team. He would be completely on his own.

He warmed up with a solo ascent of Nanga Parbat's Diamir Face, which proved to him that he had the supreme will required to climb high without anyone around to help.

"Step by step I tormented myself," he wrote of his 1980 ascent of Everest. When he fell in a crevasse, he simply climbed out and kept going. Choosing the North Ridge in the monsoon season, he camped twice, battling through deep snow, talking to his rucksack for company. At times he crawled on all fours – but he never gave up. For many mountaineers, Messner's

achievement is among the greatest in climbing history. Although he went on to complete all the "8,000ers" before anyone else, it was his pioneering of the ultimate lightweight style on the highest peaks that made him great. Today, he is still adventuring; he also makes films, writes books, and runs a mountain museum.

RETRACING ERNEST SHACKLETON'S FOOTSTEPS
In 2000, Messner, pictured (right) with US alpinist Conrad Anker, together with the British climber Stephen Venables, retraced the 42-km (26-mile) crossing of the island of South Georgia by explorers Ernest Shackleton, Frank Worsley, and Tom Crean. Shackleton's crossing followed an epic 800-km (500-mile) voyage in the *James Caird*, a tiny 8-m (23-ft) open-topped whaler, across the South Atlantic during the Antarctic winter of 1916. Messner called Shackleton's Antarctic expedition "the greatest adventure ever".

PETER HABELER
AUSTRIA   B.1942

If Messner is direct and self-absorbed, Peter Habeler – the man he climbed with in the 1960s and 1970s – is courteous and easy-going.

Messner and Habeler grew up in different countries but only 50km (30 miles) apart, and went climbing together as teenagers; one of their early ascents was the Walker Spur on the Grandes Jorasses. In 1974, they made rapid ascents of the Eiger, in ten hours, and the Matterhorn's North Face in just four. "We were fast and strong, and fitted together well," Habeler recalled. "When I was with Messner I felt he could not fall. He probably felt the same about me. That gives you strength." After their historic ascent of Everest without bottled oxygen in 1978, the climbers parted company, but they have recently restored their friendship. Habeler went on to climb Nanga Parbat and Cho Oyu, but he judges his ascent of Kangchenjunga's North Ridge in 1988 as his best. He shared that summit day with American climber Carlos Buhler and the Basque mountaineer Martin Zabaleta. "On Everest I was a schoolboy. I was naïve. Very naïve. On Kangch, everything fell into place," he said. In 1972, Habeler created a successful guiding and skiing business in his home town, which is still going strong.

With Habeler, he makes the first ascent of Everest without supplementary oxygen	With Hans Kammerlander, climbs the regular route on Lhotse, becoming the first man to climb all 14 "8,000ers"	He and Arved Fuchs reach the South Pole, using parasails to help them along
1978	**1979–80**	**1981–86**	**1987–90**
Becomes the first man to solo an 8,000-m (26,247-ft) peak – Nanga Parbat's Diamir Face	In the high-altitude climb of the century, he climbs Everest solo without oxygen, from the north during the monsoon	Begins period of wild travel, crossing eastern Tibet on foot, from Tarchen Gompa to Lhasa

JERZY KUKUCZKA

GIANT OF HIMALAYAN MOUNTAINEERING

POLAND   1948–89

IN THE 1980S, high-altitude mountaineering was dominated by Polish climbers. Despite the country's economic and political woes, an elite group created new routes and made first winter ascents on the 8,000-m (26,247-ft) peaks in the Himalaya. Pre-eminent in this plethora of talent was Jerzy Kukuczka. In 1979, he made his first ascent of an "8,000er", and just eight years later, had climbed all 14 – all but one by a difficult new route or during the grip of winter.

Poland has a long history of mountaineering, and the Tatra Mountains, on the border with Slovakia, are a proving ground for climbers. From the late 1950s, the Communist regime allowed the elite of Polish mountaineering to visit the Alps, provided they brought glory to the state by climbing something difficult. Jan Długosz was part of the team that made the first ascent of the Central Pillar of Frêney on Mont Blanc in 1961. In 1980, expedition organizer Andrzej Zawada led the first winter ascent of Everest and a few months later set up another trip, inviting a rising star called Jerzy Kukuczka.

THE RHINOCEROS

Kukuczka was a genial but low-key character, burly in frame and dubbed "a psychological rhinoceros" for his thick-skinned endurance of the suffering and risks of high-altitude climbing. For him, mountaineering was an escape from his life as a coal miner in Katowice in southern Poland but he never felt much need to examine his motivation: "I went to mountains and climbed them. That is all," was how he explained it in his autobiography. Like all Polish climbers, Kukuczka struggled to find sufficient time and money to mount and equip climbing trips, especially abroad, which required foreign currency. He raised funds by painting factory chimneys, accessing them with climbing ropes instead of scaffolding.

Kukuczka's high-altitude climbing career started badly. He took a long time to acclimatize and was "brought to his knees" with altitude sickness on Mount Denali (see pp.206–07) and then again in the Hindu Kush, on the 7,000-m (22,700-ft) Kohe Tez. Each time he ground on, putting up with the nausea and headaches and eventually reaching the top. His first "8,000er" was Lhotse in 1979. He carried oxygen but switched it off to see if he could cope without it. Pretty soon, he abandoned his set and pushed on for the top. Then, in 1980, came Everest.

Zawada's second Everest expedition climbed a new route on the South Face. Kukuczka led a section of Grade V (see p.351) above 8,000m (26,247ft) as they fixed rope towards the summit. "To climb this [grade] at that altitude," he wrote, "took so much out of me that at one stage the effort made me simply wet my pants. At times my vision blurred." Kukuczka's reward was to have first try at the top with Andrzej

Czok, and although their oxygen ran out on the South Summit, they pushed on along the final ridge without it, reaching the summit at 4pm.

QUEST FOR THE 14 SUMMITS

Kukuczka's experience on Everest gave him immense confidence in his own reserves, and an appreciation for the politics of a large expedition. In 1981, he went to Makalu with Wojciech Kurtyka (see pp.328–29) and Alex MacIntyre (see pp.330–31), attempting a wildly difficult line on the peak's West Face. When conditions persuaded the others to give up, Kukuczka went up on his own, climbing a new route via the Northwest Ridge to the summit of the world's fifth-highest peak.

Over the next six years, with Reinhold Messner (see pp.308–11) just in front, Kukuczka worked his way through the remaining 11 "8,000ers". In 1983, with Kurtyka, he climbed new routes on Gasherbrum I and II in the same season. He climbed Broad Peak, also in the Karakoram, twice, on the second occasion, in 1984, traversing the mountain with Kurtyka. In 1986, he climbed three more, including the first winter ascent of Kangchenjunga with Krzysztof Wielicki. That summer, with Tadeusz Piotrowski, he climbed a new route on the South Face of K2, overcoming ground even more difficult than he'd faced on Everest. They

A VERY LUCKY ESCAPE
Kukuczka (left) is pictured with Czok on Everest in 1980. During the descent, Kukuczka tripped and, as he pitched towards an abyss, stuck out his hand, catching by chance a fixed rope hidden in the snow.

ANDRZEJ ZAWADA

POLAND   1928–2000

A passionate climber and expedition leader, Andrzej Zawada was a guiding light for the generation of Polish climbers who rewrote the record book for achievement in the Himalaya in the 1980s.

Zawada's inspiration was winter climbing on 8,000-m (26,247-ft) peaks, which he saw as a new arena in which Poles could excel. A natural rebel, he was detained for his dissident activities and banned from travel until 1971, after which his intense energy kept him on the scene for two decades, beginning with expeditions to Pakistan and Afghanistan. In 1979, after years of effort, he obtained permission to try Everest in winter. The expedition encountered grim conditions, and Zawada survived a night in the open high on the peak, supporting lead climbers Leszek Cichy and Krzysztof Wielicki in their successful summit bid.

reached the summit in a state of near-exhaustion and, while descending the Abruzzi Spur, Piotrowski lost both crampons. Kukuczka watched helplessly as his unroped partner lost his grip on his ice axe and fell to his death.

When he finally completed the list, just a year after Messner, many expected Kukuczka to retire from high-altitude mountaineering. But he had one ambition left. He had climbed all the "8,000ers" in a new way, except the first one – Lhotse. The peak's South Face was one of the most coveted climbs of the 1980s and he wasn't going to miss out. He was high on the face in October 1989 when the fixed rope he was climbing broke and he plunged to his death.

NANGA PARBAT

RUPAL FLANK, 13 JULY 1985

— **Route to Camp III**
A long approach and shortage of fixed ropes slows down Kukuczka and his Polish and Mexican companions. Avalanche is a major risk on this section.

— **Pushing on to Camp IV**
Piotr Kalmus is killed in an avalanche. Kukuczka and Zyga Heinrich push the route up to Camp IV and alpine style with Carlos Carsolio and Slawek Lobodzinski.

— **Summit bid in a snow storm**
Difficult ice slows their summit bid. Caught in a snow storm, they dig a snow cave at 8,000m (26,247ft) and endure a bivouac before reaching the top the next day.

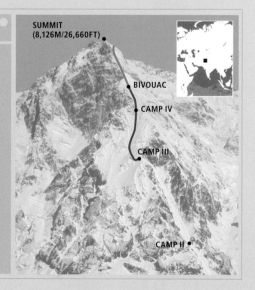

SUMMIT
(8,126M/26,660FT)

BIVOUAC

CAMP IV

CAMP III

CAMP II

WOMEN MOUNTAINEERS

W OMEN WERE A PRESENCE IN MOUNTAINEERING
FROM THE BEGINNING, BUT JUST AS THE SUFFRAGE
MOVEMENT GAVE WOMEN CLIMBERS MOMENTUM
BEFORE WORLD WAR I, SO FEMINISM IN THE 1970s
GALVANIZED THE POLITICALLY AWARE TO STRIKE
OUT ON THEIR OWN.

TRIO OF SMILES
French climbers Micheline Morin and Alice
Damesme and Briton Nea Morin, the *"Cordée
féminine"*, pose without men at the Aigle Hut
after making a traverse of La Meije in 1933.

In the late summer of 1959, a British climber named Eileen Healey trained her husband's new cine camera on two figures setting out for the summit of Cho Oyu in the Himalaya, the world's sixth-highest peak. The climbers were the French swimwear designer and alpinist Claude Kogan and the Belgian Claudine van der Straten, members of the first all-female expedition (supported by male Sherpas) to an 8,000-m (26,247-ft) peak. Sadly, the footage of dazzling snows and deep blue skies captured the

two women unwittingly setting out on their last climb. An avalanche destroyed their tent at Camp IV, killing them and their Sherpa, Ang Norbu. Another Sherpa who attempted to rescue them was also killed. It was a tragic end to an expedition that had been Kogan's own. She had almost succeeded in climbing Cho Oyu five years earlier with the Swiss guide Raymond Lambert. Cold conditions and strong winds had driven them back, but Kogan felt that they hadn't tried hard enough and was left with

what she described as "a boiling, impotent rage". She wanted to show that, far from being weaker in the mountains, women would prove more resilient than men to the trials of high altitude.

DAMNED IF SHE DOES …
Women mountaineers, small in number, have struggled to have their achievements recognized. When climbing with men, they have faced the presumption that they're relying on someone else's superior skill. When climbing alone,

ALL-FEMALE ASCENT OF ANNAPURNA
Until Arlene Blum's all-female expedition to Annapurna in 1978 (above), the peak had been climbed by only eight people – all men. She raised funds for the trip by selling T-shirts with the slogan "A woman's place is on top".

EVEREST FIRST
The first woman to climb Everest, having been selected from a shortlist of 15 by the expedition's media sponsors, Junko Tabei founded the Ladies Climbing Club in Japan.

FEMALE CLIMBING GLAMOUR
Claude Kogan (centre) began climbing during World War II, and became one of the most glamorous climbers of the 1950s, organizing the first all-female expedition to an "8,000er".

SETTING THE SCENE

- In 1926, the **brilliant US climber Miriam Underhill** makes the first ascent of the Diable Ridge on Mont Blanc du Tacul with French guide Armand Charlet (see p.125). She goes on to make **all-female ascents** of the Grépon and the Matterhorn.

- Underhill publishes an essay in the National Geographic in 1934 entitled *Manless Alpine Climbing*, arguing that if women are to take responsibility for a climb, they must do so **without any men** in the party.

- Loulou Boulaz, a secretary from Geneva, becomes the **most successful female climber before the 1980s**, with ascents such as the Croz and Walker Spurs on the Grandes Jorasses, before taking part in the all-female 1959 Cho Oyu expedition.

- German Daisy Voog makes the **first female ascent of the Eiger's North Wall**, in 1964. A Swiss tabloid runs the headline: "Blonde Munich Secretary Daisy Breaks Wall of Death Taboo."

- In 1997, a British female team comprising Kath Pyke, Glenda Huxter, and Louise Thomas added a **highly technical big-wall route** at altitude on Mount Beatrice in Canada.

or with other women, they have faced criticism as attention-seekers. Praise for an achievement is often undermined by the implication that it's only being given because the climber is a woman. In fact, throughout the history of climbing, there have been capable women operating near the limits of the day, usually in the face of this kind of prejudice.

> For decades hampered by social mores that obliged them to wear constraining dress or to take chaperones, women mountaineers have gradually dissolved male prejudice with their most impressive weapon: outstanding climbing skill.

WOMEN NEAR THE LIMITS

Included on Kogan's all-female Cho Oyu team was Loulou Boulaz, a secretary from Geneva who, before the war, had been involved, with Raymond Lambert and others, in the race to climb the North Face of the Grandes Jorasses. She made the second ascent of the Croz Spur in 1935, and attempted the North Face of the Eiger in 1937, a year before it was climbed.

Eileen Healey and another member of Kogan's team, the charismatic Countess Dorothea Gravina, had contrasting views on what the expedition meant. Healey was not overtly political in her climbing. She was simply happy to climb with anyone who enjoyed it as much as she did.

For Gravina, on the other hand, the expedition was overtly political. She wanted to show what women from around the world could achieve by working as a team. It was a political stance shared by US climber Arlene

Blum, who organized another all-women expedition to Annapurna in 1978, the first to succeed on an "8,000er", and the first successful American ascent. Her book about the experience, *Annapurna: A Woman's Place*, is considered a classic. Blum, a ground-breaking environmental scientist, took a defiantly feminist position.

Other US climbers, such as Marty Hoey and Catherine Freer, came to the fore as women who proved themselves in the face of male scepticism. Hoey was the first female guide to work for Rainier Mountaineering, despite the reservations of owner Lou Whittaker. She so impressed, however, that Whittaker later invited her on his expedition to attempt a new route on Everest, where she died in a fall after her harness came undone.

Catherine Freer, in particular, was an inspiration to a new generation of talented US climbers, as well as to British climbers such as Alison Hargreaves (see p.319). In the Himalaya, Freer made the first ascent of Cholatse's North Face in alpine style, climbing with her partner Todd Bibler. She went on expeditions to K2, Dhaulagiri, and Everest but preferred

rock climbing, at which she excelled. She died at 37 on Mount Logan's Hummingbird Ridge.

DEMOLISHING PREJUDICE

While US women were content to climb as equals with men, the Polish climber Wanda Rutkiewicz (see pp.316–17) persevered with all-female expeditions. In 1975 she climbed the world's highest still-virgin peak, Gasherbrum III (7,952m/26,090ft), with the British climber Alison Chadwick, and two men, one being Chadwick's husband Janusz Onyszkiewicz. It was the highest first ascent by a woman. Women continue to reap the benefits of both mixed and all-female expeditions, the latter offering a welcome change of atmosphere and the space to enjoy some truly exceptional climbing.

DOROTHY PILLEY, 1930
With her husband and a guide, leading British climber Pilley made the first ascent of the difficult Dent Blanche North Ridge. Her memoir *Climbing Days* is a classic.

WANDA RUTKIEWICZ

GREATEST EVER FEMALE HIMALAYAN CLIMBER

POLAND   1943–92

TOP WOMEN'S TEAM
The ascent by Rutkiewicz and Alison Chadwick (left) of Gasherbrum III heralded the first wave of Himalayan expeditions to be organized and led by women.

THE PRE-EMINENT HIGH-ALTITUDE female mountaineer of the 20th century, Rutkiewicz was the third woman to climb Everest, the first to climb K2, and the first to reach the summit of eight of the world's fourteen 8,000-m (26,247-ft) peaks. Single-minded, forceful, and determined, she overcame an impoverished childhood and personal tragedies to become a successful climber and film-maker. Keen to raise the profile of female climbers, she led what was intended to be the first all-woman expedition to the Karakoram.

Born Wanda Blaszkiewicz in Plunge in Lithuania, after World War II Wanda's Polish family returned to their homeland, where they lived in a half-ruined house in Wroclaw. From an early age, Wanda was queuing for whatever food was available and taking responsibility for her siblings. "We grew up on goat's milk, which is perhaps why I'm so healthy," she said later.

In 1948, her elder brother and his friends discovered an unexploded bomb in the ruins they were playing in; they told Wanda that because she was a girl she couldn't share in the fun of lighting a fire under it. Outraged, Wanda found her mother to complain about this injustice. Her mother was running to her son when the bomb exploded. The sense of life

being harsh and unpredictable never left her. Years later, her parents separated, then her father was murdered.

FREEDOM IN THE OUTDOORS
A brilliant mathematician, Wanda enrolled at Wroclaw University of Technology at 16 and gained a degree in Science and Engineering. Intellectually curious and a dedicated athlete, she was selected for the 1964 Olympics. At the age of 18, a fellow student invited her rock climbing, and from that moment on she was hooked. "I was totally possessed by climbing from that very first moment. The experience was like some inner explosion. I knew it would somehow mark the rest of my life." Those early

years, she wrote later, were her happiest, sleeping out in caves around a fire and living a life removed from the political system where neighbours spied on each other for the state. At first Wanda climbed with men, but she slowly developed a network of women climbing partners. She made trips to the Alps and Norway with Polish alpinist Halina Krüger-Syrokomska, climbing the East Buttress of the Troll Wall in Norway with her in 1968.

In 1970, Wanda married Wojtek Rutkiewicz, also a mathematician and climber. Almost immediately, she embarked on her first expedition, to the Pamir Mountains in Central Asia, which put a strain on her marriage. "In effect, I was taking myself on honeymoon," she said. "Wojtek felt bitterly hurt." While in the Pamirs, Rutkiewicz climbed Pik Lenin, but she hated the hierarchical and male-dominated expedition system she encountered in the Soviet Union: "I always took anything that might limit my independence as a personal attack."

THE SUMMIT ABOVE ALL
Reaching the summit was always the driving factor in Rutkiewicz's life, to the cost of all else. She was married and divorced twice, and had no children.

A LIFE'S WORK

- In 17 years she **makes 22 expeditions to the Himalaya and Karakoram**

- Leads an international expedition of ten women and seven men to Pakistan's Gasherbrum range, making the **first ascent of Gasherbrum III**

- Makes the **first female ascent of K2** in 1986

- Becomes the **third woman to climb Everest**

- Her 1991 **solo ascent of the South Face of Annapurna** is perhaps her greatest climb

I DON'T MIND THE IDEA OF DYING ON THE MOUNTAINS ... MOST OF MY FRIENDS ARE THERE, WAITING FOR ME

WANDA RUTKIEWICZ

Two years after Pik Lenin, she went to Afghanistan on an expedition to Noshaq in the Hindu Kush and got to know Alison Chadwick, an Englishwoman whose Polish husband was an activist with Solidarity, the Soviet Bloc's first independent trade union. There were other women on the mountain that year, including the feminist and scientist Arlene Blum. All the talk about what might be possible for women climbers made Rutkiewicz consider her future with fresh eyes.

GROUNDBREAKING CLIMB

In 1973, she climbed the North Face of the Eiger with fellow Poles Danuta Wach and Stefania Egierszdorff, spending three days on the wall and suffering frostbite. The all-female party's success was a big story in Poland, and Rutkiewicz enjoyed the attention, talking to journalists and raising her profile. She faced the paradox many women climbers experienced in this period – getting headlines for doing something as a woman, but wanting to be regarded as equal to male mountaineers.

With this in mind, in 1975 Rutkiewicz decided to organize an all-female expedition to Gasherbrum III in the Karakoram range of the Himalaya in Pakistan, then the world's highest unclimbed mountain. However, conservative local sensibilities ensured that the team grew to include seven men with their own leader, who would climb Gasherbrum II. Misunderstandings and arguments about the role of the men in the group ensued, and Rutkiewicz tried to downplay the contribution made by the male members.

Rutkiewicz and Alison Chadwick reached the summit of Gasherbrum III, with Chadwick's husband and another male climber hovering in the background. Two women assigned to climb up in support, Anna Okopinska and Halina Krüger-Syrokomska, switched objectives in disgust, making the first female ascent of Gasherbrum II instead. But despite the

arguments and bad feeling – which were exposed in the expedition film *Boiling Point* – the ascent had proved a huge success.

Rutkiewicz followed this with expeditions to Nanga Parbat in Pakistan, a winter ascent of the North Face of the Matterhorn, and her ascent of Everest in 1978. Then came her long campaign on K2, leading a women's expedition there in 1982, hobbling to base camp on crutches after breaking her femur in the Caucasus Mountains. Team member Halina Krüger-Syrokomska, however, suffered a stroke and died at Camp II.

Rutkiewicz also enjoyed a career as a writer and film-maker, and while she sometimes regretted the immense personal cost that climbing exacts, her love of the mountains never failed. "I never seek death," she said. "But I don't mind the idea of dying on the mountains."

After a second attempt on K2 in 1984 in a four-woman team, Rutkiewicz succeeded in the fateful summer of 1986, when 13 climbers died on the mountain. Her ascent was the first by a woman, but the triumph was seriously marred when her climbing partners Liliane and Maurice Barrard both died on the descent. In addition, Wojciech Wróz, her partner from her previous attempt Dobroslawa Miodowicz-Wolf, and Jurek Kukuczka's partner Tadeusz Piotrowski all lost their lives that summer.

In the last three years of her life, Rutkiewicz enjoyed a string of successes, including an ascent of Shisha Pangma from Tibet, Gasherbrum II with British climber Rhona Lampard in 1989, and a new variation on Gasherbrum I's Northwest Face in 1990 with Pole Ewa Pankiewicz. In 1991, she added Cho Oyu and the South Face of Annapurna, both in Nepal, but doubts about her ascent of the latter left her feeling isolated within the Polish climbing scene. Determined to climb all the "8,000ers", she joined an expedition to the North Face of Kangchenjunga, but disappeared close to the summit.

BRIDGING THE GAP WITH FINGERS AND TOES
In 1992, after solo climbs on the desert spires of
Utah, Destivelle scaled "El Matador" on the Devils
Tower, Wyoming. The accompanying film is one of
nine that document her climbing career since 1985.

A LIFE'S WORK

- **Climbs the Bonatti Pillar** on the Dru solo

- **Opens up a new route** on the West Face of
  the Dru during a multi-day solo ascent

- In 1992, climbs the near-mythical **North Face
  of the Eiger** in 17 hours

- Achieves winter solo ascents of the **North Face
  of the Grandes Jorasses** and the **Bonatti
  Route** on the Matterhorn's North Face

- Is the **first woman to make a solo ascent**
  of the North Face Direct on the Cima Grande

- Restricts her climbing to focus on motherhood
  and **a career as a motivational speaker**

CATHERINE DESTIVELLE

QUEEN OF ROCK AND ICE

FRANCE
B.1960

WOMEN MOUNTAINEERS NEEDED to fight for credibility in the 1970s, but Catherine Destivelle took a different approach. Side-stepping the political debates, she became famous around the world for her rock-climbing skills and, later, her courage in the mountains, making first female solo ascents of the North Face of the Eiger, the Walker Spur on the Grandes Jorasses, and the Bonatti Route on the North Face of the Matterhorn. She has made brilliant use of film and press publicity, becoming a national figure in France.

ALISON HARGREAVES
ENGLAND   1963–95

A contemporary of Destivelle's, Hargreaves made notable Alpine ascents, including the first female winter solo of the Croz Spur on the Grandes Jorasses.

In May 1995, she became the first woman to climb Everest without bottled oxygen or Sherpa support. Two weeks later, after a brief reunion with her husband and children, she left for Pakistan, where, after months of frustration, she reached the summit of K2. Descending into a gathering storm, she and three others were blown off the ridge to their deaths. In the aftermath of the tragedy, the media claimed that Hargreaves had acted irresponsibly in leaving her children behind to attempt something so risky. Destivelle was among those who defended her, pointing out that the same judgments weren't made about male mountaineers with families.

Destivelle was born in Oran, Algeria, to French parents. When she was a young teenager, the family moved to a suburb of Paris. Her father had an interest in climbing and a passion for the outdoors, and Destivelle soon became a regular at the forest of Fontainebleau near Paris, famous for its sandstone boulders and a proving ground for generations of French climbers.

She was also climbing in the mountains, and by the age of 16, had notched up a number of impressive Alpine routes, including the Couzy-Desmaison on the Olan and the Devies-Gervasutti on the Ailefroide, both in the Dauphiné, shortly followed by an ascent of the American Direct on the Dru near Chamonix.

Destivelle took a five-year break from climbing to train for a career in physiotherapy. However, her appearance in French television's version of *Survival of the Fittest* led to climbing films shot in France's Verdon Gorge and in Mali, West Africa, which made her famous.

While Destivelle was making films, the new competition climbing circuit in Europe caught her interest. She entered her first event in 1985, at the age of 25, and did well, which allowed her to become a professional climber. Destivelle was highly successful in competitions, but retired in 1989, characteristically torn between her freewheeling instincts and her desire to excel. "You can't eat, you can't drink," she explained. "I was too old maybe. I like to climb

when I want. And competitions have a lot of pressure. I prefer more adventure. Sport-climbing is a good game but going to the mountains is another story."

CLIMBING SOLO

In the early 1990s, Destivelle returned to the Alps to make a solo ascent of the Bonatti Pillar on the Dru in just four hours. By then she was living with the US alpinist Jeff Lowe. Under his influence, she improved her aid-climbing skills and pioneered a Yosemite-style, big-wall route on the Dru in 11 days, once again attracting media attention.

Destivelle herself acknowledged the route was not a great classic. The film made about it shows her at the foot of the Dru, surrounded by support crew and organizers – hardly the authentic mountain experience she craved. But her winter solo of the 1938 route on the Eiger's North Face in 1992 was a triumph and the accompanying film was arguably her best. Like many who climb the face in winter, Destivelle found

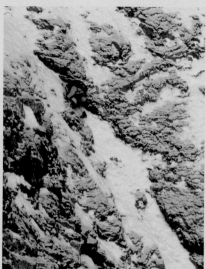

the Exit Cracks to be the hardest section. She was left with only a few metres of rope after the ropes jammed and she had to cut them free. She reached the summit after 17 hours. Of all her hard Alpine climbs, she said, the Eiger was the one she enjoyed most.

In 1993, she added the Walker Spur to her tally, climbing alone but once more using a rope to protect herself. Her three-day repeat of Walter Bonatti's (see pp.296–97) 1965 swansong on the North Face of the Matterhorn completed the trilogy in 1994. Destivelle's Himalayan campaigns met with mixed success; she never liked the strangeness of high altitude. She climbed the Nameless Tower above the Baltoro Glacier and made an attempt on the difficult North Ridge of Latok I, both in the Karakoram range. She also made a first ascent in Antarctica in 1997. In recent years, since becoming a mother, she has climbed less often.

ON THE EIGER
Telephoto lens cameras followed Destivelle's lonely route up the Eiger's North Face in 1992, which she completed in just 17 hours.

HANGING FROM MOSES TOWER

French rock climber Catherine Destivelle (see pp.318–19) dangles by her fingertips from Moses Tower in Utah, US, in 1992. The media could not get enough of her stunning, camera-friendly feats, making her one of the most famous rock climbers in the world. After a solo climb of the Cima Grande's North Face in 1999, Destivelle climbed less to focus on raising a family.

KITTY CALHOUN

FIRST WOMAN TO CLIMB TWO "8000ER" PEAKS

UNITED STATES   B.1960

In the 1970s, women alpinists faced scepticism and even hostility from their male counterparts, but a number of pioneers – such as Pole Wanda Rutkiewicz and Americans Marty Hoey and Catherine Freer – changed attitudes. In the 1980s, a handful of female climbers side-stepped the issue by climbing with men on equal terms. Kitty Calhoun has led successful ascents of Dhaulagiri and Makalu, preferring hard routes with an uncertain outcome, and has a deep scepticism towards the media spotlight.

A LIFE'S WORK

- First climbs on an Outward Bound course in North Carolina; **begins winter climbing** in New Hampshire while at college in Vermont

- Chooses an **itinerant lifestyle, guiding and climbing around the world**; climbs in the Cordillera Blanca in 1984, making classic ascents of Alpamayo and Quitiraju

- **Makes the first American female ascent of Dhaulagiri** via the Northeast Ridge in 1987, and the **first female ascent of Makalu by the difficult West Pillar** in 1990

- Climbs **new routes in the Ak Su Valley of the Pamirs** in Kyrgyzstan in 1995; the following year, makes a second attempt at Thalay Sagar

- From 2000, climbs a number of **hard big-wall routes, often with other women**, including Lurking Fear in Yosemite and Hallucinogen Wall in the Black Canyon, Colorado, with Kim Czismazia and Julie Faure

In 1986, Kitty Calhoun and Andy Selters trekked to the base of Thalay Sagar in the Garhwal Himalaya, a stunning, formidably challenging peak of ice and granite, 6,904m (22,651ft) high. They planned to climb a difficult 1,500-m (5,000-ft) new route on the North Face, bringing custom-made equipment to help them make their alpine-style attempt. Among their kit was a super-lightweight portaledge and half a sleeping bag each that zipped straight into their sleeping mats – whatever it took to save weight.

They made good progress over the course of four days, and had reached 6,700m (22,000ft) when it began to snow. For the next eight days, Selters and Calhoun were pinned down by a major storm, buffeted by spindrift avalanches that threatened to lever them off the mountain. After 12 days of living on their portaledge, and four days without food, they had no choice but to descend when the weather cleared.

STYLE OVER SUBSTANCE
Calhoun was, to put it mildly, disappointed that she had failed to reach the summit of Thalay Sagar by her preferred route. She later admitted: "After months of soul-searching, I understood that if the summit was all-important to me, I would have attempted the standard route instead. I discovered that I could not compromise the style of climbing just to make the summit. To me, the means was more important than the end; the process of climbing more important than the summit."

Many of her climbing partners, hardly lackadaisical themselves, attest to Calhoun's immense drive and determination. When she started out, she was a nomadic rock-hopper, indifferent to creature comforts. She lived out of her car for so long that her friends dubbed it "Camp Subaru" and commented on the mice that were sharing it with her. On the expedition she led to Dhaulagiri in 1987, she forbade the team from employing porters to carry camp chairs to Base Camp, seeing this as an unnecessary luxury. But it is her respect for the fundamental principles of mountaineering that have earned her the respect of her peers.

CLIMBING BEGINNINGS
Born Catherine Howell Calhoun in Greenville, South Carolina, Kitty retains a strong southern accent whose slow drawl belies a flinty determination. Her father was a corporate lawyer and a descendant of John C Calhoun, who served as vice president to successive US presidents John Quincy Adams and Andrew Jackson between 1825 and 1832. At school, she played hockey and tennis, and was skiing from the age of four in the Appalachian Mountains. Climbing came later, as an 18-year-old on an Outward Bound course, and she kept it up when she enrolled at the University of Vermont.

Her first experience of winter climbing was in the White Mountains of New Hampshire. An attempt to hike across the range in winter conditions in a single day ended at midnight, with Calhoun digging a snow hole for her and her hypothermic companion to shelter in. "Four hours later, I woke, shivering. The sun had just risen and the sky was fiery red. I had never seen anything so beautiful," she said.

DOUBLING UP
Calhoun's successful climb to the 8,463-m (27,765-ft) summit of Makalu in 1990 (right), via the challenging West Pillar route, made her the first female mountaineer to have climbed two "8,000er" peaks.

With no career in mind, and a passion for climbing, Calhoun left Vermont in 1982 determined to live on US$3,000 a year and explore her potential. Working as an outdoor instructor for Outward Bound and as a climbing guide for the American Alpine Institute, Calhoun built up her experience with climbs in Peru in 1984. A year later she climbed the Cassin Ridge on Denali, sitting out a five-day storm high on the route before continuing to the summit. In 1986, she made the second ascent of the Bouchard Route on Chacraraju Oeste in Peru with Jeff Lakes, before heading to the Himalaya and her date with Thalay Sagar.

HIGH ACHIEVER

In 1987, with future husband Colin Grissom and John Culberson, she reached the summit of Dhaulagiri via the Northeast Ridge – the first ascent by an American woman. The climb wasn't straightforward. The trio were caught in an avalanche while using fixed ropes left by a Japanese team and swept 150m (500ft) down the mountain. Seven of the eight anchors holding the ropes failed before they finally came to a halt. Despite various sprains and a deep rope burn to Calhoun's elbow, they recovered sufficiently to climb the peak two weeks later.

Three years after climbing Dhaulagiri, Calhoun made the first female ascent of Makalu, the world's fifth-highest mountain. This she did not by the standard route, but by leading an expedition to the West Pillar – a demanding route that had only been climbed twice before. But Calhoun didn't restrict her ambitions to the "8,000ers", preferring to attempt hard new routes on peaks a little lower, such as the 7,145-m (23,442-ft) North Ridge of Latok I

in the Karakoram. In the mid 1990s, Calhoun's "dirtbag" existence evolved into a more settled pattern of life – she went back to college in 1993 and gave birth to a son in 1996. Yet her climbing went from strength to strength. In 1997, with Jay Smith, she climbed a new route on the West Face of Middle Triple Peak (2,693m/8,835ft) in Alaska, and attempted the West Face of Latok III (6,949m/22,799ft) in Pakistan. After a series of impressive big-wall climbs at the start of the decade, her climbing was curtailed by chronic injury, but after surgery in 1996, she was soon back on the cliffs of Yosemite.

OFF THE BEATEN TRACK
During her expedition to the Pamir Mountains of Kyrgyzstan in 1995, Calhoun put up two new wall routes on the Yosemite-like granite big walls of the Ak Su Valley (below). The routes were rated Grade VI (see p.351).

MOUNTAINEERING INNOVATIONS

PROTECTION

THE WIDE VARIETY OF METHODS CLIMBERS USE to attach their rope to a mountain can seem confusing to those unfamiliar with the principles of "protection". Techniques range from the age-old practice of hanging a sling on a rock spike to hi-tech camming devices, and from nuts wedged in cracks to expansion bolts drilled into blank rock. The conflicting ethics behind these and other climbing aids may appear arcane, but underpinning it all is a basic philosophical question: how much are you prepared to change the nature of the challenge to make things safe and convenient?

PROTECTING THE CLIMB

Climbing protection and the controversy surrounding its different forms is almost as old as the sport itself. Before the golden age of alpinism and the formation of the Alpine Club, rock climbing began on the ethereal towers of the Elbsandstein in Saxony, Germany, where standards after World War I reached levels not seen in Britain or the US until the 1950s. At the start of the 20th century, Elbsandstein climbers developed the technique of tying a knot in a rope sling that was then wedged into a crack.

The principle behind this innovation – that knots were wedged rather than hammered like pitons – was to find protection that did not damage the region's fragile sandstone. This method would become the norm in Britain and the US some 60 years later, but in the form of metal wedges, which could be used repeatedly, rather than rope knots, which could not.

In the Alps, the arrival of the piton in the early 20th century caused dismay to the Alpine Club and some European climbers – such as

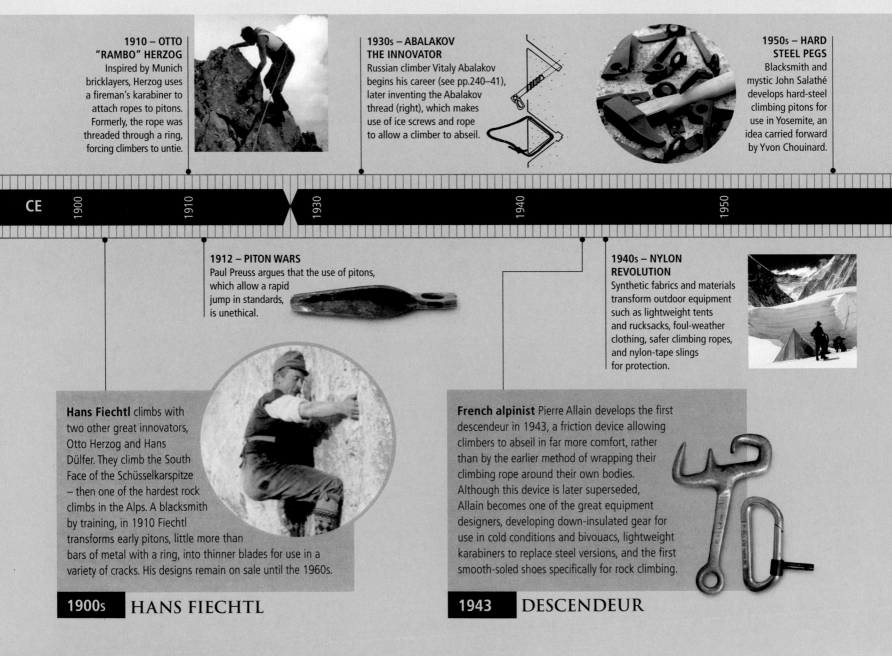

1910 – OTTO "RAMBO" HERZOG Inspired by Munich bricklayers, Herzog uses a fireman's karabiner to attach ropes to pitons. Formerly, the rope was threaded through a ring, forcing climbers to untie.

1930s – ABALAKOV THE INNOVATOR Russian climber Vitaly Abalakov begins his career (see pp.240–41), later inventing the Abalakov thread (right), which makes use of ice screws and rope to allow a climber to abseil.

1950s – HARD STEEL PEGS Blacksmith and mystic John Salathé develops hard-steel climbing pitons for use in Yosemite, an idea carried forward by Yvon Chouinard.

CE   1900   1910   1930   1940   1950

1912 – PITON WARS Paul Preuss argues that the use of pitons, which allow a rapid jump in standards, is unethical.

1940s – NYLON REVOLUTION Synthetic fabrics and materials transform outdoor equipment such as lightweight tents and rucksacks, foul-weather clothing, safer climbing ropes, and nylon-tape slings for protection.

Hans Fiechtl climbs with two other great innovators, Otto Herzog and Hans Dülfer. They climb the South Face of the Schüsselkarspitze – then one of the hardest rock climbs in the Alps. A blacksmith by training, in 1910 Fiechtl transforms early pitons, little more than bars of metal with a ring, into thinner blades for use in a variety of cracks. His designs remain on sale until the 1960s.

French alpinist Pierre Allain develops the first descendeur in 1943, a friction device allowing climbers to abseil in far more comfort, rather than by the earlier method of wrapping their climbing rope around their own bodies. Although this device is later superseded, Allain becomes one of the great equipment designers, developing down-insulated gear for use in cold conditions and bivouacs, lightweight karabiners to replace steel versions, and the first smooth-soled shoes specifically for rock climbing.

1900s   HANS FIECHTL

1943   DESCENDEUR

Austrian purist Paul Preuss (see pp.176–77) who believed the mountains should be left unaltered by the climber's presence. One of Preuss's principles was that a climber should only climb up what he can climb down. Pitons allowed climbers to venture onto steeper ground where that wasn't possible, leading to a rise in standards.

EVOLVING EQUIPMENT

Tyrolean mountain guide and blacksmith Hans Fiechtl developed a standard for piton design in the early 20th century. These pitons were made from soft steel, which meant that they deformed and became stuck fast when hammered into cracks. Alpine climbs eventually became littered with these pegs, which were often impossible to remove. The development of hard steel pegs by John Salathé and Yvon Chouinard in the 1950s (see pp.302–03) meant that pegs could be hammered out and reused. This, however, damaged the rock. To attach these pegs to the rope, so that the rope could run freely behind the climber as he moved up, some kind of link

RACKING UP

As technology improves and the scope of what can be climbed grows, the range of protection available has never been so wide, as demonstrated by this big-wall climber's assortment of gear – or "rack" – clipped to loops on his harness. In his left hand is a pulley, useful for hauling bags behind him. A range of camming devices allows him to make use of different-sized cracks. These can be retrieved and used again on the next rope length.

HIS HANDS TAPED FOR JAMMING, A CLIMBER SORTS GEAR BEFORE THE CLIMB

was required. German climber Otto Herzog, whose nickname was "Rambo", observed builders in his native Munich adapting firemen's karabiners to clip a haul-rope when hoisting bricks up scaffolding. Herzog realized that a

similar device would be perfect for clipping a climbing rope to pegs. In the late 1960s, an alloy version of karabiners, much lighter than steel, was introduced. More recent innovations include wire gates, further reducing weight.

1960s – BELAY PLATES
Fritz Sticht develops a sprung metal disc with a slot for the rope to pass through and around a karabiner. Rope burns from belaying are vastly reduced.

1961 – ACORN NUT
Building on the use of machined nuts or pebbles slotted into cracks instead of pegs, John Brailsford invents the first climbing-specific nut.

1976 – GORE TEX
W L Gore's fabric allows sweat to escape and keeps rain out, boosting performance of protective clothing.

1980s – PLASTIC BOOTS
Insulated plastic boots are warmer and offer better protection from frostbite.

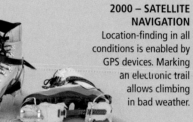

2000 – SATELLITE NAVIGATION
Location-finding in all conditions is enabled by GPS devices. Marking an electronic trail allows climbing in bad weather.

1960   1970   1980   1990   2000

1960 – MODERN PROTECTION
Advances include aluminium karabiners (top) and nuts on wires (bottom).

1970 – FIRST SIT-HARNESS
A rope around the waist was standard practice, but climbers would soon asphyxiate if hanging. Troll develops the first sit-harness to combat this.

1990s – ICE SCREW PROTECTION
Ice pitons were either hammered in or screwed in. The latter were more reliable but harder to place. Improvements in design mean that screws are now much easier to fix in ice.

Although the mathematical principle behind cams (devices inserted into cracks) was patented as far back as 1901, the most likely candidates for the realization of this invention were US alpinists Jeff and Greg Lowe in the 1970s. Another US inventor, Ray Jardine, developed a spring-loaded version with a trigger that could be retracted to close the cams, allowing them to be inserted in a crack, whereupon the released trigger would allow the cams to expand into contact with the rock.

| 1978 | HI-TECH CAMMING |

Improvising equipment with whatever lies to hand is a hallmark of climbers. In the 1970s, finding that the hammocks available for sleeping on big walls were too constricting, climbers in Yosemite began hauling aluminium-framed camp-beds with them. Local climber Mike Graham began selling a specifically designed "portaledge" in the early 1980s. Hanging from a central suspension point for balance, they now include a fly sheet.

| 1980s | PORTALEDGES |

FAST AND LIGHT

I N THE 1980s, HIMALAYAN CLIMBING DEVELOPED ALONG DIFFERENT PATHS. SOME MOUNTAINEERS CONTINUED WITH THE OLD METHODS OF FIXED ROPES AND SUPPLIED CAMPS, BUT A NEW ELITE CHOSE TO FACE NEW CHALLENGES WITH THE MINIMUM OF EQUIPMENT AND SUPPORT.

LIGHTNING-FAST APPROACH
Argentine climber Rolando Garibotti (see pp.342–43) on a big wall in Patagonia, where lightning-fast ascents suit the region's rare and short-lived fair-weather windows.

In the 1890s, A F Mummery (see pp.168–71) attempted the gigantic Nanga Parbat with no prior Himalayan experience, insufficient support and equipment, and little understanding of the physiological limits of high altitude. By the 1950s, Himalayan peaks were being climbed with help from Sherpas, oxygen, and fixed ropes. In the modern era, that's still the case for many expeditions to the region, particularly on famous peaks such as Everest.

BOLD NEW BREED

For a small group of elite alpinists in the 1980s, the romance of Mummery's quixotic attempt on Nanga Parbat became reality. The solo ascent of Everest by Reinhold Messner (see pp.308–11) showed the way, and others, such as Doug Scott (see pp.304–05), were equally energized by this freewheeling style. A new generation of technically brilliant, physically relentless mountaineers began to employ tactics used in the Alps – carrying everything required – on new routes on the highest mountains without bottled oxygen, fixed ropes, or supports.

Practical and even desirable on peaks of about 7,000m (23,000ft), this "alpine style" has been in use throughout the history of Himalayan climbing. German alpinist Hermann Buhl (see

ESSENTIAL SUPPLIES
Food for Mick Fowler's (see pp.338–39) four-man, four-day expedition to Ushba in Russia was kept to the bare minimum.

pp.258–59) climbed Broad Peak in what he called *Westalpinstil* – using pre-placed tents, but neither oxygen nor porters. During the 1980s, however, the technical standards and scale of lightweight Himalayan climbing gathered huge momentum. Aided by technological improvements in clothing and equipment, this period was – for some – the true golden age of Himalayan mountaineering. Many of the most impressive and appealing ascents in the history of the sport came from the realization of a dream – climbing the biggest peaks in the purest style.

By 1982, the spectacular South Face of Annapurna had three routes: the British 1970 route and two neighbouring spurs, climbed in 1981 by Japanese and Polish teams. These had been climbed using fixed ropes and camps. In 1982, Alex MacIntyre (see pp.330–31) and René Ghilinni attempted a new route on this vast face, but in pure alpine style. They did well, but were forced to retreat, and MacIntyre was killed by a rockfall.

In the autumn of 1984, Spanish climbers Nil Bohigas and Enric Lucas took up the challenge of this same route in

> The debate about tactics and ethics continues today. Even on lower peaks commercial, guided expeditions use fixed ropes and porters, in contrast to guided climbing in the Alps. But this approach is popular with clients and employs many local people.

the same style. Well acclimatized, they carried more pitons than their predecessors for a difficult band of rock two-thirds of the way up the face. Rockfall was a constant menace, and the pair climbed through the night to be high on the face before the sun returned. In a six-day push, involving hanging bivouacs and a fierce tussle with the technical difficulties that had thwarted MacIntyre and Ghilinni, they made it to the top. They were shrewdly prepared for the descent down the Polish Spur, using their last piton to make the final abseil back to safety.

STRIPPED BARE

There were no hard-and-fast-rules. Even dedicated adherents of alpine style resorted to occasional use of fixed ropes to speed their progress. Alpine style became more a philosophical ideal – of doing the most with the least – than a reality. It could be incredibly committing, especially on the "8,000er" peaks. Peter Boardman and Joe Tasker, two of the brightest stars during Britain's strongest period of mountaineering, disappeared on a lightweight attempt on the then-unclimbed Northeast Ridge of Everest (see pp.226–27). If bad weather set in, a small team high on a big mountain was in trouble. But equally, climbers were exposed to danger for much less time. In speed was safety – as well as elegant simplicity.

SETTING THE SCENE

- Small-scale expeditions have always prospered in the Himalaya, **particularly on peaks below 7,500m (24,600ft)**. But the biggest peaks, such as Everest, require large support teams and financial support.

- In the 1970s, leading climbers begin to turn their backs on the complexity of these ventures, **preferring to climb in small teams with no support** from Sherpas on the mountain.

- These new shoots blossom in the 1980s, when a **large number of alpine-style ascents** are made of new and existing routes, **pushing back the boundaries of the sport**.

- Just as in the Alps in the 1930s, this change of approach has inherent dangers, and many climbers lose their lives. **But the new direction reinvigorates mountaineering**.

CHASING THE CHALLENGE
One of Britain's leading climbers, Andy Cave has followed the modern British pattern of climbing hard routes on peaks under 7,000m (23,000ft), such as Changabang's North Face.

EVEREST ALPINE-STYLE
In 1988, the four-man team of Stephen Venables, Ed Webster, Paul Teare, and Robert Anderson made judicious use of fixed ropes to climb a new route in lightweight style.

GOING LIGHTWEIGHT
Seen here travelling light in 2008 on one of Denali's massive walls, one of the Japanese climbers known as the Giri Giri Boys (see pp.346–47) epitomizes the pared-back alpine-style approach.

WOJCIECH KURTYKA

VIRTUOSO OF LIGHTWEIGHT CLIMBING

POLAND

B.1947

IF JERZY KUKUCZKA COULD BE described as an indefatigable rhinoceros, then Wojciech ("Voytek") Kurtyka was a climbing virtuoso – technically capable, fast, and fiercely intelligent. Climbing, for Kurtyka, was both a quest and a pilgrimage, and he was unimpressed by those who wanted to classify the sport or chase media attention. His partnership with Alex MacIntyre helped him realize his vision. With Robert Schauer he scaled the West Face of Gasherbrum IV, one of the outstanding climbs of the 20th century.

A LIFE'S WORK

- **Hones his skills in the Tatra Mountains** on the Poland-Slovakia border, and makes several first winter ascents and new routes there

- Starts climbing in the Himalaya, becoming a member of the Polish team who make **the first ever winter expedition** to an "8,000er"

- Is a pioneer of new routes on the highest peaks in the Himalaya in pure alpine style, with no support and the **minimum of equipment**

- **Makes new routes** on Kuh-e Bandaka in the Hindu Kush, on Changabang in India, and on the "8,000er" Dhaulagiri in Nepal

- After the death of his philosophical ally Alex MacIntyre, he forms a super-team with Jerzy Kukuczka, **making rapid, lightweight first ascents** on Gasherbrum I and II

- Makes mountaineering history with a dramatic 10-day ascent of Gasherbrum IV. He and partner Robert Shauer **barely make it back alive**

- With Swiss greats Erhard Loretan and Jean Troillet he **makes non-stop ascents** of Shisha Pangma and Cho Oyu in the Himalaya

- Was still doing **hard rock climbs** in his 50s

Kurtyka's father was Tadeusz Kurtyka, a writer who, under the pseudonym Henryk Worcell, published an influential novel in 1936 based on his days as a waiter in Krakow's Grand Hotel. Tadeusz had been a forced labourer in Germany during World War II, and returned to work a smallholding in the formerly German village of Skrzynka, in western Silesia. This atmosphere of rural and intellectual freedom had a marked influence on his young son. In 1957, however, after falling out with local party bosses, Tadeusz took his family to Wrocław, whose drab streets were a kind of dystopia for the young Voytek.

Kurtyka felt an affinity with climbing from the moment he first laid hands on rock. He graduated in electrical engineering, but regular employment was never going to work out for him and he financed a nomadic lifestyle through entrepreneurial smuggling. He would truck Polish goods to Asia, and sell Asian goods for hard currency on the black market in Poland.

INTO THE HINDU KUSH

Climbing in Afghanistan was the fashion in the mid 1970s. Accessible overland from Eastern Europe, hundreds of Polish climbers cut their teeth at high altitude in the Hindu Kush. Kurtyka already had a strong reputation when he first went there in 1972 on an expedition led by Andrzej Zawada (see p.313). He'd served his apprenticeship in the Tatra Mountains, climbing Poland's hardest route.

Now he applied the alpine style he had used in Poland to the high mountains, climbing the North Face of Akher Chogh. At just over 7,000m (23,000ft), this was a big mountain to be climbed in pure style. If the rest of the world failed to pay his achievement much attention, Kurtyka himself came to realize what might be possible on even higher peaks.

His introduction to the Himalaya confirmed his view that small, lightweight expeditions climbing

NIGHT ON A BARE MOUNTAIN
Kurtyka and compatriot Krzysztof Zurek settle into their bivouac after a dinner of borscht and noodles on Changabang in 1978.

quickly was the way forward. Kurtyka took part in Zawada's winter attempt on Lhotse in 1974, but the ponderous nature of the enterprise didn't suit him. He was much happier with a few like-minded allies, and through the late 1970s and 1980s teamed up with some of the most progressive climbers around: Alex MacIntyre (see pp.330–31), Erhard Loretan (see pp.334–35), and Swiss-Canadian climber Jean Troillet.

With MacIntyre and British climber John Porter, he climbed new routes on the Northeast Face of Kuh-e Bandaka in the Hindu Kush and, in an eight-day push, the South Face of Changabang in the Indian Himalaya. In 1980, Kurtyka and MacIntyre climbed a new route on Dhaulagiri's East Face, retreating in the face of bad weather without reaching the summit. They also went twice to the West Face of Makalu, the Holy Grail for many elite climbers, teaming up with Jerzy Kukuczka (see pp.312–13).

STRONG PARTNERSHIP

After MacIntyre's death, Kurtyka climbed with Kukuczka more often. Kukuczka was a pragmatist, unconcerned about tactics, and prepared to take big risks, while Kurtyka was obsessed with style – "We once joked about climbing naked at night, the ultimate lightweight" – and was more neurotic in the mountains, walking away if things didn't feel right. In 1983, they climbed two new routes in

CHANGABANG ASCENT
This steep granite peak was first climbed in 1974. Four years later, MacIntyre (pictured, left), Kurtyka (right), and Porter (behind the camera) spent eight days climbing its South Face with Krzysztof Zurek.

one season on Gasherbrum I and II, in pure alpine style, and traversed the summits of Broad Peak the following year.

Two years later, with Austrian Robert Schauer, Kurtyka climbed the West Face of Gasherbrum IV, often acknowledged as the greatest single feat of mountaineering in the last century. They didn't even make it to the summit, descending after finishing the face in appalling weather.

Kurtyka was one of the few Poles who carried on as before after the fall of the Iron Curtain. Success was rare. He went repeatedly to the West Face of K2, which was finally climbed by a Russian team using siege tactics. But there was some success, notably on Cho Oyu and Shisha Pangma. In his 50s, he was still climbing routes graded 8a in the Tatras.

GASHERBRUM IV

WEST FACE, JULY 1985

— **13 July – Pure alpine style**
Kurtyka and Schauer climb the initial snow couloir unroped. The face is free of snow after a long spell of good weather.

— **14 July – Technical rock wall**
Above the couloir, the rock has few cracks for pitons and the climbing is exceptionally technical. The possibility of retreat is slim, with insufficient pitons to abseil the wall.

— **18 July – No route to the summit**
Out of food, they reach the top of the difficult section but are trapped by a storm for two days. They descend without reaching the summit.

SUMMIT
(7,925M/26,001 FT)

ALEX MACINTYRE

HIGH-ALTITUDE ALPINE-STYLE PURIST

ENGLAND   1954–82

EMERGING FROM A GROUP of talented climbers at northern England's Leeds University in the early 1970s, Alex MacIntyre personified a growing obsession with style among alpinists. This was a period of resurgence in British mountaineering. His bold ethos, that "the face was the ambition, the style was the obsession", encapsulated a fundamental goal for the new generation. He lived a bohemian existence, and with his good looks and daring lifestyle achieved cult status among alpinists.

ABOVE THE CLOUDS ON CHANGABANG
MacIntyre's team was interested in the psychological side of high-altitude climbing – what Kurtyka called "a state of nakedness", where climbers are self-reliant, even vulnerable, yet confident in their ability.

In the spring of 1980, four friends met in Kathmandu in Nepal en route to Dhaulagiri. Two were Poles, Wojciech Kurtyka (see pp.328–29) and Ludwik Wilczynski, the others were French-Italian guide René Ghilini and a young English alpinist, Alex MacIntyre.

This kind of expedition would have been unheard of just ten years earlier. There had been international expeditions to the peak, but they were mostly made up of "stars" on high-profile ventures that often ended in acrimony. The friends had come together not for the sake of sponsors, but from a shared climbing philosophy.

MacIntyre attended Leeds University to study law, but was captivated by the re-energized British climbing scene that he found there. Unlike today's top alpinists, he wasn't a great rock-climber, but devoted himself to the new ice-climbing techniques. He was irreverent, opinionated, even arrogant in his youth, but never hesitated to undermine his own credentials. His attitude to training was inspired by the Irish climber Terry Mooney, who said: "Climbing at altitude is somewhat akin to going to work with a monster hangover."

CLIMBING LIGHT IN THE ALPS

In truth, however, MacIntyre was no hedonist, and his self-deprecation masked an intense drive and a reluctance to compromise. In 1975, he announced his arrival with the first one-day ascent of the Shroud on the Mont Blanc massif's Grandes Jorasses, with British climbing partners Gordon Smith and Terry King.

The following year, he and Nick Colton completed a new route on the North Face of the Grandes Jorasses in alpine style; it had previously been attempted with fixed ropes in a 17-day siege by Dougal Haston (see p.298), Chris Bonington (see pp.300–01), Mick Burke, and Bev Clark in 1972.

At the time, it was one of the hardest routes in the Alps, and an indication both of MacIntyre's ambition and of where alpinism was heading.

INTERNATIONAL CLASS

In 1977, MacIntyre received an invitation to join an Anglo-Polish group that included Wojciech Kurtyka in the Hindu Kush in Afghanistan. It was the first joint East–West expedition during the Cold War to a country beyond the Iron Curtain. Crossing the Soviet Union by train without the correct papers and using made-up Polish names was the kind of anti-authoritarian lark MacIntyre enjoyed.

Kurtyka showed MacIntyre and his Anglo-American climbing partner John Porter his proposed objective, the North Face of Koh-e-Bandaka, a big, dangerous climb 2,200m (7,200ft) long on a peak almost 7,000m (23,000ft) high that had been tried several times without success. On one part of the route, the rockfall was so bad they had to wait for it to ease up before continuing. After six days they had made a

FAST AND LIGHT IN AFGHANISTAN
Kurtyka, Porter, and MacIntyre organize their food supplies on the night before making their epic, alpine-style ascent of Koh-e-Bandaka, a remote peak in Afghanistan, in 1977.

major new climb. Due to its remote location, their route didn't achieve the recognition it deserved as one of the first big-face climbs completed in alpine style at high altitude.

In 1978, the same team, with Pole Krzysztof Zurek, climbed a hard new technical route on the South Face direct of Changabang in a single eight-day push, cementing their shared ideals.

ALPINE-STYLE IN THE HIMALAYA

Using the same committed approach on Dhaulagiri in 1980, the four friends climbed mostly without tying into a rope. On the second day, the weather deteriorated. "The thunder which had begun the previous evening persisted and the spindrift had become torrential," MacIntyre wrote later. "… Ludwik and I found ourselves stranded on front points in an all-engulfing stream of the stuff, unable to move … The bivouac spot was non-existent." The next evening they made the Northeast Ridge and easy ground to the summit, but chose to retreat next morning because of the continuing storm.

An attempt in 1981 on the West Face of Makalu with Kurtyka failed, but in 1982 MacIntyre climbed a new route on Shisha Pangma with a British expedition. That autumn, little more than ten years after Bonington's large, siege-style expedition overcame Annapurna, MacIntyre set off up a new route on the same south face in pure alpine style with Frenchman René Ghilinni. The two climbers took just three pegs and one ice screw between them, but were stopped by a 30-m (100-ft) step and forced to retreat. On the descent, MacIntyre was hit by a falling stone and fell to his death.

A MODERN CLASSIC
MacIntyre and Colton's line on the Grandes Jorasses (above) is a mostly steep ice route up the left side of the peak's Central Couloir; today, it remains a challenging and very popular climb.

ANDREJ STREMFELJ

PUSHING THE LIMITS OF ALPINE-STYLE CLIMBING

SLOVENIA   B.1956

JUST AS THE POLES were at the forefront of Himalayan climbing in the 1980s, Slovenia came to prominence in the 1990s. As part of Yugoslavia, Slovenians had benefited from socialist organization, and faced fewer travel restrictions than even their Western counterparts. A large cadre of talented climbers emerged in the 1980s and right at their head was Stremfelj, who reached the summit of Everest via the West Ridge Direct in 1979. He went on to make an inspiring, alpine-style ascent of Kangchenjunga.

Slovenians have a passion for mountains. An Alpine country with a deep cultural attachment to the Julian Alps, the limestone peaks that fringe its northern border, its highest summit – the 2,864-m (9,396-ft) Triglav – appears in stylized form on its flag. Andrej Stremfelj was born in Kranj, close to the mountains, in what was then Yugoslavia, and started climbing at the age of 16 with his brother Marko.

CLIMBING CULTURE

Thanks to Marshal Tito's policy of "non-alignment" with either the West or Communism, Yugoslavs were able to travel freely, while climbers enjoyed a well-developed club scene. Competition for places on expeditions was intense, but Stremfelj was selected for Tone Skarja's landmark Yugoslavian expedition to Everest in 1979. "I remember the ascent from Camp V to the top of Everest, as well as the descent down the Hornbein Couloir to Camp IV, as one of my hardest Himalayan ascents," Stremfelj wrote. "A completely unknown West Ridge toward the top, great technical difficulties, heavy rucksacks, bad weather, and complete uncertainty regarding the descent."

Stremfelj's partners on summit day were Nejc Zaplotnik and his brother Marko, who was forced to turn back because of a defective oxygen system. Stremfelj's own oxygen valve also failed, and Zaplotnik gave him his spare.

When that proved defective too, Stremfelj spat on the hissing valve, and as his saliva froze, sealed it. Climbing without ropes, braced against the strong wind blowing across the ridge, there was no room for error. Having climbed a new route together on Gasherbrum I two years earlier – Stremfelj's first "8,000er", aged just 20 – the two trusted each other implicitly.

Higher up, they moved out above the Southwest Face to tackle a section of rock they dubbed the Grey Step, 100m (330ft) long and often vertical. Here, Zaplotnik tackled the hardest climbing yet attempted on Everest, climbing barehanded and risking frostbite, to emerge on easy ground with an open path to the summit.

Growing up under the Slovenian system meant large, siege-style expeditions. Despite this, in 1983 Stremfelj made lightweight ascents in the Pamirs of the Bezzubkin Pillar on the North Face of Peak Communism. Along with several other climbs, the experience served to stoke his enthusiasm for alpine-style climbing.

ELATED ON KANGCHENJUNGA SOUTH

Stremfelj had already climbed Everest and other "8,000ers" by new routes, but his alpine-style ascent in 1991 with Marko Prezelj of Kangchenjunga South – by its difficult Southwest Ridge – was the highlight of his long career.

Throughout the 1980s, Stremfelj put up a series of new routes on 8,000m peaks, including the East Face of Dhaulagiri in 1985 and the South Face of Shisha Pangma in 1989. He was well aware of the cost in lives, however, which was particularly high among Slovenian climbers. Many of the stars of Stremfelj's generation — all with major Himalayan ascents under their belts — lost their lives in the mountains: Slavko Sveticic, Janez Jeglic, Vanya Furlan, and Tomaz Humar, as well as Nejc Zaplotnik and Stremfelj's partner on Shisha Pangma, Pavel Kozjek.

IN SEARCH OF PERFECTION

Stremfelj eloquently described the psychological aspect of high-altitude climbing, asserting that it is this as much as training that extends the limits of the possible. "The best ascents are a cause for radical changes, above all in mentality, which is from my point of view the basis for progress in alpinism." He proved the point with his elegant alpine-style climb up the Southwest Ridge of Kangchenjunga to its 8,476-m (27,808-ft) South Summit in 1991, a route regarded as one of the greatest Himalayan climbs of any era.

That climb had been made with Marko Prezelj, nine years Stremfelj's junior and a rising star of the new generation. Soon after leaving base camp they were climbing mostly without ropes up ground that Stremfelj compared to the Supercouloir on Mont Blanc du Tacul in the Alps — extremely steep ice on an "8,000er" peak. On the third day they were forced onto the Southwest Face to escape strong winds, climbing back onto the ridge above via a couloir. As the ridge neared the summit, the climbing got harder again — they stashed their sleeping bags and stove in a dash for the top, but then agreed that returning the way they had

MENLUNGTSE HOLIDAY
Stremfelj said that after Kangchenjunga he was too exhausted to tackle anything similar for a while, but he and Prezelj (above) still managed the first ascent of the main summit of Menlungtse, in Nepal's Rolwaling Himal, in 1992.

come would be impossible. Instead, they retreated down an existing route, then crossed unknown terrain to return to base camp.

Stremfelj later said, "After the Kangchenjunga ascent, neither Marko nor I were capable of doing anything similar. We had an opportunity to go to the west face of K2 two years later, but we had no real zeal." Instead, the following year they made the first ascent of Menlungtse, which Stremfelj described as "one of the most beautiful Himalayan ascents, executed in pure alpine style."

He also includes the 1999 first ascent of the North Face of Gyachung Kang in that bracket. "It is not easy to find a face that has not been climbed yet, a 'hidden' or forgotten peak that offers a good alpine ascent." Stremfelj has continued to climb new routes at a high standard, well into his 50s. Married with three children, he climbed Everest with his wife Marija in 1990, becoming the first married couple to do so.

KANGCHENJUNGA

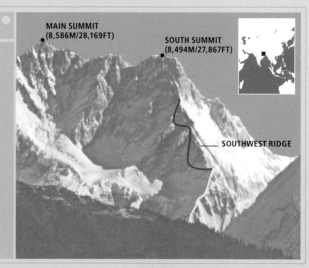

MAIN SUMMIT
(8,586M/28,169FT)

SOUTH SUMMIT
(8,494M/27,867FT)

SOUTHWEST RIDGE

SOUTHWEST RIDGE, APRIL 1991

— **Hard free and aid climbing**
  Stremfelj and Prezelj reach the first bivouac at 6,200m (20,300ft). Climbing is easier on the second day.

— **Route to third bivouac**
  Difficult ground forces them left but they find a couloir back to the ridge and a third bivouac at 7,600m (25,000ft).

— **Hard climbing to the south summit**
  Hard climbing slows them down. Next day they reach the South Summit and descend along the Polish route.

ERHARD LORETAN

MASTER OF THE SINGLE-PUSH ASCENT

SWITZERLAND   1959–2011

THE THIRD PERSON TO COMPLETE the list of 14 "8,000er" peaks, Loretan was renowned for his fast and lightweight style, often climbing with his compatriot Jean Troillet. Their 41-hour ascent of the North Face of Everest and two-day ascent of K2 were revolutionary. His Alpine record was impressive – in the winter of 1989, he climbed 13 Bernese Oberland north faces in 13 days. Modest, committed, with a low profile, guiding work funded his expeditions. He died in a fall on his 52nd birthday, leading a client on a route in the Alps.

PIERRE BÉGHIN
FRANCE   1951–96

Like others of his generation, Béghin was obsessed with climbing difficult new routes in the lightest style possible.

He had many failures, but when he succeeded, his exploits were among the grandest imaginable. He climbed several "8,000ers" alone, including Kangchenjunga and Makalu, and also made several attempts on the North Face of Everest. Yet he is best known for an incredible ascent, with Frenchman Christophe Profit, of the Northwest Ridge of K2 in alpine style. Parts of their route had been climbed before, but the purity of their ascent won many admirers.

Erhard Loretan began climbing in 1970 at the age of 11, reaching the summit of the Dent de Broc, the mountain that overlooks his village in Fribourg. "From that day I knew I would be a guide," he said later. While neither of his parents climbed, his cousin Fritz was already guiding, and was the custodian of one of the Swiss Alpine Club's mountain huts around Kandersteg in the Bernese Alps. Loretan spent five summers there, gaining experience and adding new routes.

By the end of this apprenticeship, he was leading friends and did his first north face at 13. He became part of a gang of aspiring climbers calling themselves the "Dzozets" – a nickname for people from that corner of Fribourg. In the late 1970s, they worked through the classics of the Chamonix range. Member Pierre Morand said of their climbs together: "When the rest of us had given our all, it was then that Erhard truly began to climb … he would keep his cool and find the right route."

BUILT FOR SPEED

Thinking that a climbing trip to the Himalaya would be too difficult to organize, the Dzozets opted for Peru, climbing five mountains, three of them first ascents. Loretan returned home to earn his guide's diploma, and received an invitation from Swiss climber Norbert Joos to climb the Diamir Face of Nanga Parbat.

It was a traditional, fixed-rope trip and its success was a little too inevitable for Loretan: "I learned a lot but I didn't like the fixed-rope style. It was good to know how it works but it was boring. It's better and usually safer not to do it." At the age of 24, he went to the Karakoram with Swiss climbers Marcel Rüedi and Claude Sonnenwyl and in 17 days they climbed three "8,000ers" – Gasherbrum I and II, and Broad Peak – dispatching each peak in a two-day burst. Loretan's partner for ten years, Jean Troillet, summed up their approach: "The rules are simple: no oxygen, not even at base camp, no high-altitude porters, no intermediate camps, no fixed ropes except perhaps down low, to cross a bergschrund or something like that.

We take a very light pack for speed. Nothing extra. We climb night and day without stopping, without sleeping. We eat and drink very little. We go for it. It's all in the head."

Such tactics rely on a deep understanding of the mountains. Loretan could wait for the right conditions, then move fast. "I was lucky to be in good shape … to have excellent circulation, so I took advantage of it. If we broke medical taboos, then that just proves medicine is made from theories. I'm a practical man."

In 1984, he went to Nepal for the first time, climbing Manaslu's Northeast Ridge on skis and then traversing the Annapurna massif, up the East Ridge. Most regard this as his greatest achievement. He and Norbert Joos took six days to reach the summit. "It was obvious we couldn't return the same way so we decided to descend the normal route. And that was the beginning of the adventure," Expecting to encounter fixed ropes from more conventional teams trying the mountain, they instead found a tortuous descent through huge seracs with only the 50m (160ft) of rope and two ice screws they carried with them.

In 1986, Loretan and Troillet went to Everest. After waiting for clear weather, they ploughed a rapid furrow up the North Face to the summit then slid all the way down, in just 41 hours. Everest has been done quicker but only in good conditions and on easier routes.

A LIFE'S WORK

- With the "Dzozets" he makes **a first ascent** of the central pillar of Les Droites' North Face

- Conquers his first "8,000er", Nanga Parbat, at the age of 23 and goes on to **complete all 14 summits** by the age of 36

- Specializes in climbing difficult routes at extreme altitudes **in pure alpine style**: very fast, with a minimum of equipment and food, and without the use of supplementary oxygen or porters

- Notches up an **exceptional record of hard climbs** in the Alps, the Andes, and the Himalaya

WE EAT AND DRINK VERY LITTLE. WE GO FOR IT. IT'S ALL IN THE HEAD "

JEAN TROILLET, ON CLIMBING WITH LORETAN

SCALING AN ICE WALL IN CHAMONIX
When not in the Himalaya, Loretan continued to climb hard in the Alps, linking routes together in huge "enchainments". In this way, he and André Georges climbed 13 north faces between the Eiger and the Doldenhorn in the Bernese Oberland in just 13 days.

EXPERIENCING THE MOUNTAINS

CLIMBING BESTSELLERS

Mountaineering stories sold modestly before World War II, and were largely confined to a specialist audience. During the 1950s, that changed. Stories of success on the Himalayan giants or grim struggles on shadowy north faces suddenly appealed to a much wider audience. Maurice Herzog's inspirational *Annapurna* sold millions, and the metaphor of "climbing a mountain" became rooted in popular culture.

In Britain, adventure stories in the mid-20th century were dominated by wartime accounts of bravery, such as Paul Brickhill's *Reach for the Sky*. In Europe, wartime tales were more problematic, but the mountains offered a morally benign context in which to set stories of courage and hardship. Herzog's classic story about the first ascent of an 8,000-m (26,246-ft) peak (see pp.256–57) transcended the obscure details of mountaineering to become an optimistic metaphor for postwar France. The *Paris Match* issue featuring the Annapurna expedition was the highest-selling edition in the magazine's history, and Herzog's book remained at No. 1 in the bestseller lists for a year.

Although not as widely read as *Annapurna*, a number of the most admired mountaineering books were published in the 1950s, such as *The White Spider* by Heinrich Harrer (see p.290), *Nanga Parbat Pilgrimage* by Hermann Buhl (see pp.258–59), *Conquistadors of the Useless* by Lionel Terray (see pp.276–77), and *K2: The Savage Mountain* by Charles Houston (see pp.248–49).

Buhl's and Terray's work inspired new generations of young climbers, and remained influential into the 1970s. A renewed interest in adventure non-fiction in the 1990s brought mountaineering back into the public eye. Unlike in the 1950s, however, the mood was more equivocal. Jon Krakauer's *Into Thin Air* told the story of the 1996 Everest tragedy, when a number of paying clients and their guides were caught out in bad weather, and eight died. The commercialization of the Himalaya fitted a pattern of consumerism that undermined once-heroic deeds. In France, biographies of 1950s heroes – including Gaston Rébuffat – revealed a darker aspect to the Annapurna myth. Other bestsellers included Joe Simpson's *Touching the Void*, which fed a growing interest in survival stories in an era of diminishing risk. Aron Ralston's story of how he cut off his own arm to escape death in 2003 has been equally successful.

ANNAPURNA... WAS A TREASURE ON WHICH WE SHOULD LIVE THE REST OF OUR DAYS

MAURICE HERZOG

Ⓐ ENDURING APPEAL
The modest, quixotic style of Eric Shipton (see pp.244–47) was outsold by Frank Smythe's romanticism in the 1930s, but Shipton's books have a lasting appeal to climbers.

Ⓑ NORTH FACE THRILLER
Heinrich Harrer's *The White Spider* followed the success of his first book *Seven Years in Tibet*. A later edition included additional chapters co-authored with Kurt Maix.

Ⓒ MOUNT EVEREST MEMOIR
Edmund Hillary's account of the first ascent of Everest (see pp.264–65) was the first of his autobiographies.

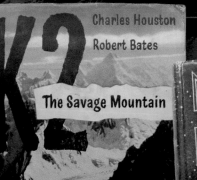

D OVERCOMING THE ODDS
Houston's account of the US 1953 K2 expedition portrays a group in dire trouble working selflessly: "We entered the mountains as strangers, but we left as brothers."

E INSPIRING READ
More than any book published in the 1950s, Buhl's work inspired new generations of climbers to emulate the author's commitment and adventurous spirit.

F EVEREST UNWRAPPED
A dedicated climber, Jon Krakauer wrote critically about his time on Everest in *Into Thin Air*. Russian guide Anatoli Boukreev wrote *The Climb* in response to Krakauer's account.

G SURVIVAL ON FILM
Ralston's book *Between a Rock and a Hard Place*, an account of his ordeal trapped in a canyon in Utah during which he was forced to cut off his own arm, was made into the film *127 Hours* by British director Danny Boyle.

H RESURGING INTEREST
The BAFTA-winning film *Touching the Void* was based on Joe Simpson's book of the same name, which was part of a resurgence in adventure non-fiction in the 1990s.

JAMES FRANCO

127 HOURS

EVERY SECOND COUNTS

MICK FOWLER

LEGENDARY EXPLORATORY MOUNTAINEER

ENGLAND   B.1956

WHILE MEDIA ATTENTION has focused on the climbers collecting the highest mountains, Mick Fowler has made harder routes on lower peaks his speciality. As an amateur with a full-time job, he docs not have the time to acclimatize for an "8,000er", and prefers the more technically challenging climbing found on lower-altitude peaks. With a small cadre of friends, Fowler has accomplished a sequence of outstanding, difficult, and beautiful new routes in the Himalaya, with occasional forays to the Andes and Alaska.

In the loud hyperbole of the professional era, Mick Fowler is something of a throwback, an enthusiastic amateur who fits his climbing around family and career and is comically self-deprecating about his world-class achievements. Climbs are not desperate and terrifying, he says, they are "somewhat interesting" and "not unfrightening". This attitude is a tradition in British mountaineering, originating with Leslie Stephen (see pp.134–35) and A F Mummery (pp.168–71), and continuing through to Fowler.

Fowler's success has been built on exploratory zeal, superb organization, a very high level of technical skill, and the ability to relax in situations of extreme danger. Victor Saunders, one of the small group of friends he has climbed with over four decades, described Fowler's abilities: "Without doubt he's the finest mixed climber I've ever climbed with. But his great strength is being able to laugh when he's frightened … He is emotionally very stable … and this has been a great benefit on the psychologically demanding climbing he excels at."

Fowler's mother died when he was a child, and his father George dedicated himself to giving his son a supportive childhood. One friend described George as "Mick's secret weapon". He performed

WE ENJOYED OURSELVES AND LIVED TO CLIMB ANOTHER DAY. THESE ARE IMPORTANT THINGS

MICK FOWLER, ON A FAILED ASCENT

SPANTIK

GOLDEN PILLAR, AUGUST 1987

- **6 August – Climb to base of headwall**
  Saunders and Fowler climb initial tower and then snow arête.

- **7 August – Up the "1,000-ft slabs"**
  Technical difficulty increases as they gain height.

- **10 August – Route to summit**
  Steep, technical ground, as well as a hanging bivouac, lead to the rim of the face. The summit is reached just before bad weather.

SUMMIT (7,027M/23,054FT)

DESCENT SPUR

"1,000-FT SLABS"

the role of conditions assessor, support team, boatman, and, in the early days, teacher. He took Fowler walking in Scotland and the Alps, giving him a foundation that he came to appreciate as his mountaineering career took off.

A DOUBLE LIFE

By the mid-1970s, Fowler was rock climbing on sandstone cliffs outside London. Aged 20, he moved to South Yorkshire, a more useful base for a climber than London, but found the full-time climbing life wasn't to his taste.

Instead, he got a job with the Inland Revenue in London, and drove up to Scotland on many weekends – a 2,000-km (1,300-mile) round trip – with a group of dedicated climbers. Other eccentricities included his passion for climbing the chalk cliffs of England's south coast using ice-climbing gear, since the rock was soft enough to pierce with the pick of an ice axe. He also explored the huge cliffs of north Devon and Cornwall, some of them wildly loose, and made a speciality of finding and climbing obscure sea stacks off the coast of Scotland.

His exploratory instincts reached their zenith in the Greater Ranges. However, limited to 30 days' leave from work, and never having been further than the Alps, he was uncertain

how to proceed. "My girlfriend's father had a calendar on his wall with a picture of a mountain called Taulliraju," Fowler recalled, so he went to Peru to climb it.

His ascent of Taulliraju's South Face with partner Chris Watts was the first in a series of technical climbs made in pure alpine style, with little equipment or support. A French alpinist had predicted that the route would require expansion bolts, but Fowler politely dismissed such tactics: "You can't beat an ascent that starts at the bottom and ends at the top and doesn't rely on any artificial aid of any kind. Placing a bolt is the antithesis of that," he insisted.

In 1987, with Victor Saunders, he went to Pakistan to attempt a line on Spantik known as the Golden Pillar. The route met his basic criteria for what a great climb should look like: "The Walker Spur [on the Grandes Jorasses] is my benchmark. It's exactly the kind of route I like." Higher than 7,000m (23,000ft), Spantik was on the limit of what Fowler could achieve in the time available to him. The climbing was hard – thin ice plastered on steep rock and bands of loose shale – and protection was limited. On one bivouac they hung from the same piece of protection, their tent suspended from ice screws that would go only halfway in.

On the sixth day, however, they reached the summit ridge and the great masterpiece was complete, the climb Fowler himself has said is his favourite.

With the confidence earned on Spantik, Fowler has spent the last 25 years repeating the formula, tackling intimidating challenges in alpine style with one partner. His most recent successes were the first ascents of two peaks in Tibet, and the North Face of Sulamar in China.

TECHNICAL CLIMBERS

In 2000, Fowler and Andy Cave (left) made the first alpine-style ascent of the 1,800-m (6,000-ft) North Buttress of Mount Kennedy in Canada. The climb started and ended in good weather, but at one point heavy snowfall trapped them on a spur for two days, "with nasty avalanches roaring past on either side".

HIGH-SPEED ASCENT
In 2009, the Hubers took just four days to free climb the Eternal Flame – a route up the Nameless Tower of Trango in the Karakoram. The vertical face is among the world's hardest climbs due to a combination of technical difficulty and altitude.

THOMAS AND ALEX HUBER

WORLD-CLASS FREE-CLIMBING BROTHERS

GERMANY   B.1966; B.1968

THOMAS HUBER   ALEX HUBER

IN THE 1980S, rock-climbing standards surged as a new generation adopted rigorous training techniques and new ethics. As in the past, this rise in technical proficiency was carried into the mountains. Free climbers expert at climbing big walls moved onto the steepest faces on some of the highest mountains. Brothers Thomas and Alex Huber were at the forefront of this new wave, raising technical standards in the Himalaya and beyond.

EXTREME ATHLETE
Here, Thomas Huber races up a local rock face in a training session. The brothers climb rapidly and fearlessly, but their daredevil feats require intensive practice and split-second judgment.

Thomas and Alex Huber are the latest in a succession of German climbers to make this transition. They have climbed multi-pitch routes in the Alps that are almost at the very limit of rock-climbing standards, including Bellavista and Pan Aroma on the Cima Ovest in Italy, both graded 8c in the new sport-climbing system (see p.351), in which the hardest climbs receive ratings of 9a or more.

At sea level, Alex has gone even harder, with Open Air at Austria's Schleierwasserfall, now graded 9a+, and one of the hardest rock climbs in the world. They have also performed at high altitude, making the first free ascent of the classic Eternal Flame on the Nameless Tower above the Baltoro Glacier in the Karakoram. The brothers were also on the first ascent of Tsering Monsong on Latok II in the Karakoram in 1997, but Thomas has since focused more on mountaineering achievements, winning the prestigious Piolet d'Or award for his ascent with Swiss climber Iwan Wolf of Shivling's North Pillar direct. More recently the brothers have been making technically demanding climbs in Antarctica, with Swiss alpinist Stephan Siegrist.

ADRENALINE ADDICTION

The Hubers were born in Upper Bavaria to parents who were passionate about climbing and hiking in the mountains. Thomas, as the elder son, was introduced to climbing first, which frustrated Alex enormously. However, when Alex was 11, he persuaded his father to allow him to join his brother on an ascent of the Allalinhorn, a 4,000-m (13,100-ft) peak in the Valais. From then on, the brothers climbed together, but they remained competitive.

From the start of their careers, they mixed the hardest rock climbing with trips to bigger cliffs in the Wilder Kaiser, working their way through the greats of the past, such as the Wiessner-Rossi route on the Fleischbank.

Not content to repeat the routes of others, they started adding their own, beginning with the South Face of Wagendrischelhorn, one of the three high peaks in Austria's Reiteralm. Although they were steeped in mountaineering, in the mid 1980s the Hubers couldn't help being influenced by the free-climbing boom then taking place in Germany, and both men applied themselves to the new sport with ferocious zeal.

They worked their way up the scale of technical difficulty on the fashionable crags of the day, such as Buoux in Provence, France, and as soon as Thomas got his driving licence, the pair sped off to the Dolomites, ascending the hardest routes there, such as Weg durch den Fisch on the South Face of the Marmolada.

In the late 1980s, they still saw long routes in the mountains as their primary focus but, while studying physics at university in Munich, Alex began to spend more time at Schleierwasserfall, one of the world's best sport-climbing cliffs.

Having tested the limits of his technical ability, Alex has focused on bigger projects. In the last 15 years, he and Thomas have made a series of landmark ascents, particularly on El Capitan in Yosemite Valley, USA, with routes such as El Niño and Free Rider. They still climb together, but both have been open about their rivalry: "In the past," Thomas said in an interview, "it was the case that Alexander was usually the number one, and I was number two. Alexander was more determined to make it to the top, but … when we were climbing alpine routes together, we were absolutely matched."

A LIFE'S WORK

- Pursue an intensive training regime, **rising to the highest rock-climbing standards**

- Their free ascent of El Capitan's Salathé Wall begins a **long association with Yosemite**

- Alex climbs **new sport routes in the Alps** and with Thomas and others, climbs the West Face of Latok II in the Karakoram in 1997

- Alex **solo climbs the Direttissima** on the Cima Grande, a **500-m (1,640-ft) route** graded 5.12a

- Team up to **free climb** Eternal Flame, on the **Nameless Tower of Trango**

ROLANDO GARIBOTTI

ACCOMPLISHED CLIMBER OF PATAGONIAN PEAKS

ITALY   B.1971

THE HIGH GRANITE SPIRE of Patagonia's Cerro Torre, with its wind-whipped topping of rime, is among the most inspiring climbing challenges in the world. The history of its first ascent, however, is fraught with controversy. Claimed by Cesare Maestri in 1959, many no longer believe the Italian's story is plausible. Rolando Garibotti, chief among Maestri's critics, has a prolific climbing record in Patagonia, including a traverse of the Torre Group in 2008, and has spearheaded major conservation projects there.

Born in Bari, in southern Italy, Garibotti grew up in Bariloche, a major skiing centre in Argentine Patagonia. Having spent his formative climbing years there, he has a deep attachment to the region, working and campaigning to protect its environment.

Garibotti has also climbed around the world, from the sandstone desert cliffs of Jordan's Wadi Rum to the South Face of Marmolada in Italy's Dolomites. He has made lightning-fast climbs in California's Yosemite and in 2001, with Steve House (see pp.344–45), made a 25-hour ascent of the Infinite Spur on Alaska's Mount Foraker, a route that took 11 days when first climbed by two of America's finest alpinists in the 1970s.

Today, Garibotti works as a mountain guide in the US, at Boulder, Colorado, but has continued his deep involvement with the mountains close to his childhood home.

CERRO TORRE CONTROVERSY
In more than a dozen seasons, Garibotti has made many first ascents and early repeats of existing routes in Patagonia. In 2006, with Italian climbers Alessandro Beltrami and Ermanno Salvaterra, he claimed the first ascent of El Arca de los Vientos, on the Northwest Face of Cerro Torre. There was no question that the three had completed their route, but the idea that it was a first ascent was controversial.

A LIFE'S WORK

- **Begins climbing aged 15** with his first Patagonian technical spire: Aguja Guillaumet
- Makes the **first completed ascent** of Via del Tehuelche on the **North Face of Fitzroy** in 1996, climbing in alpine style with Doug Byerly over two days
- In 2006, with fellow Italians Ermanno Salvaterra and Alessandro Beltrami, makes the **first authenticated ascent of the Arca de los Vientos** route on Cerro Torre
- He and American Colin Haley become the first to make a **traverse** of the notorious **Torre Group**
- Leads a **project to restore footpaths** in Patagonia's Los Glaciares National Park

SNOW MUSHROOM
Ermanno Salvaterra reaches the great rime mushroom on Cerro Torre's North Face. He and Garibotti teamed up twice to attempt the traverse before Garibotti's success in 2008.

Cesare Maestri had claimed a similar line for the first ascent of the peak in 1959, maintaining that his partner, Toni Egger, had died as they returned from the summit. There was no other evidence of their ascent beyond Maestri's word – usually enough for mountaineers – but when others travelled to Cerro Torre and looked at the climb, they began to doubt the claim's veracity.

Although Maestri always insisted he had reached the summit, in 1970 he returned for a second go, this time with a petrol-powered compressor and a drill, which his team used to place expansion bolts up the peak's 350-m (1,150-ft) headwall on the Southeast Face. Even then, he didn't climb Cerro Torre's summit ice. Today, many climbers regard the 1974 ascent of Cerro Torre by another Italian team as the first.

Very few climbers have as deep a connection to the story as Garibotti, who has researched and written authoritatively on Maestri and Cerro Torre. His 2006 climb, during which no trace of an earlier attempt was found, only added weight to the view that Maestri's claim could not be substantiated.

TORRE GROUP

TRAVERSE, JANUARY 2008

— **21 January – Aguja Standhardt**
Garibotti and Colin Haley climb via the route Exocet.

— **22 January – Torre Egger**
Slow progress on the North Ridge after carbon monoxide poisoning from stove.

— **24 January – Cerro Torre**
Overcoming ice-filled cracks takes a day. Haley tunnels through the soft summit snow mushroom to the top.

(Dashed line means route hidden from view)

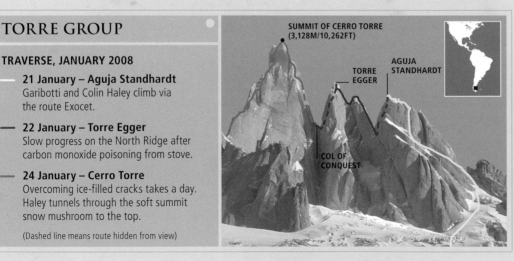

SUMMIT OF CERRO TORRE
(3,128M/10,262FT)

TORRE EGGER

AGUJA STANDHARDT

COL OF CONQUEST

Garibotti has climbed most of the major peaks in Patagonia, including his favourite ascent, a route known as Tehuelche on the North Face of Fitzroy, but he is now best known for an astonishing traverse of the formidable Cerro Torre group, made in 2008 with the brilliant young US climber Colin Haley.

CONNECTING FOUR PEAKS

Originally conceived by Salvaterra, the Torre Traverse was a prize some of the world's best alpinists, including Thomas Huber (see pp.340–41), had tried to win. Garibotti's own obsessive attempts spanned several years. Patagonia's savage weather, which can keep climbers stuck in base camp for weeks on end, thwarted him and a variety of partners. With

American Hans Johnstone, he managed to climb from north to south – linking the peaks Aguja Standhardt, Punta Herron, and Torre Egger – but the snow mushroom on top of Cerro Torre was too huge to overcome and they retreated. After a long wait, he returned with Haley to complete the traverse. Haley burrowed a long tunnel through the overhanging rime to reach the summit on their third day.

Garibotti is a fierce defender of a pure climbing ethic, particularly in Patagonia, where attempts to add more bolts to Cerro Torre for a climb sponsored by a soft-drink manufacturer have led to fresh controversy. "I have had some of the greatest experiences of my life in this Park," he says, "so it seems only fair that I devote a little time and effort to give back."

DARING TRAVERSE
Haley jumars up heavily iced-up rock pitch on Cerro Torre's North Face in 2008, during his and Garibotti's one-push, alpine-style ascent. The traverse is a mix of snow, ice, and rock, and requires finely tuned alpine skills.

AT THE TOP … ALL THE ADRENALIN AND DRIVE THAT HAVE CARRIED ME … VANISH, LEAVING ME NAKED AND VULNERABLE

ROLANDO GARIBOTTI ON COMPLETING THE TORRE TRAVERSE, 2008

STEVE HOUSE

CLIMBER OF THE HIGHEST PEAKS IN THE BEST STYLE

UNITED STATES   B.1970

ONE OF THE LEADING MOUNTAINEERS of the last few decades, House's reputation was cemented when he climbed a major new route on the Rupal Face of Nanga Parbat in 2005 with Vince Anderson. It was, he said, the culmination of "years of a physical and psychological journey." The route was more than 4,000m (13,000ft) long, and technically demanding: the pair climbed in alpine style, without support, in an eight-day round-trip. Their ascent is widely regarded as a benchmark in modern high-altitude mountaineering.

STEELY DETERMINATION
Spurred on by his early failure on Nanga Parbat as a 20-year-old aspiring alpinist, House acquired a single-minded determination that has seen him make solo first ascents on Denali and in the Himalaya.

In his book *The Naked Mountain*, Reinhold Messner (see pp.308–11) compared the Rupal Face of Nanga Parbat to the East Face of Monte Rosa, with an Eigerwand stacked on it, and then topped off by the North Face of the Matterhorn. Vast, difficult, and committing, Messner himself had completed a route on the left side of the face with his brother Günther in 1970. In 1985, along with two Polish friends and the Mexican Carlos Carsolio, Jerzy Kukuczka (see pp.312–13) climbed the Southeast Pillar to the right. The Central Spur, right up the middle of the Rupal Face, would require something exceptional. It truly was a challenge for the 21st century.

EAST EUROPEAN GRIT
House's relationship with Nanga Parbat dates back to his early days as a mountaineer. Before studying ecology at the progressive US college

Evergreen State, he spent a year in Slovenia, which in recent decades has been among the strongest mountaineering nations of all. Resources were tight, but that bred resilience and optimism. Some East European determination seems to have entered House's soul. He retains a strong affection for his adopted home, and has climbed several times with the Slovenian star Marko Prezelj.

In 1990, after his first year at Evergreen, House joined some of his Slovenian climbing friends on an expedition to Nanga Parbat's Schell Route on the left of the Rupal Face, which finished up on the mountain's Southwest Ridge. Two of the team made it to the summit, but House found himself struggling with the scale of the mountain. "I have been shown how much I did not know," he wrote in his diary. "Becoming an alpinist, an alpinist who can reach these summits, including Nanga Parbat. That is what I want to become."

Many young climbers have felt that ambition, but House spent the next 14 years in relentless preparation for his return. Such an exclusive passion for climbing wasn't

obvious from his background. House's father was an accountant and his mother a schoolteacher. There is something professorial about his attitude – he is both diffident and intellectually secure. And at 1.77m (5ft 10in) in height and weighing less than 76kg (167lb), he looks compact rather than athletic. His gaze, however, can turn dark and fierce, revealing the intensity typical of someone pushing the frontiers at high altitude.

CAREER CLIMBER
After graduating, House moved to Washington, working as a climbing and skiing guide in the Cascade Mountains. Over the next decade he established himself as one of the leading US alpinists, with 30 Alaskan trips under his belt. After Nanga Parbat he had promised himself: "I have to find a way to surround myself with good climbers. Good partners will make me a better climber." House submerged himself in America's elite climbing scene, getting to know Alex Lowe,

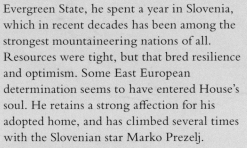

THE HIMALAYA IN ALPINE STYLE
Vince Anderson (left) and House took just eight days to climb the new route up the Central Pillar of the Rupal Face on Nanga Parbat in 2005, a feat that won them that year's Piolet d'Or.

Barry Blanchard, and Mark Twight, all stars of the previous generation. Twight in particular shared his disdain for what he termed "business climbing". Patiently, House acquired a deep reservoir of experience. In 1995, with Eli Helmuth, he climbed Denali's 1,340-m (4,400-ft) Father and Sons Wall in 33 hours. Five years later, with Scott Backes, he raced up Denali's 2,740-m (9,000-ft) Slovak Direct in 60 hours. In 2001, he and Rolando Garibotti (see pp.342–43) completed Foraker's Infinite Spur in 25 hours – eight days faster than any of the previous four ascents.

His list of new routes is just as impressive as these fast, repeat ascents. Perhaps his best known is M16 on Howse Peak's East Face, in the Waputik Range of the Canadian Rockies. Climbed in the winter of 1999 with Blanchard and Backes, House described it as "the best adventure route of them all. Finishing this route almost took more than we had to give."

HIMALAYAN EXPLOITS

Apart from Nanga Parbat, House has climbed several difficult and committing new Himalayan routes in alpine style. His 2004 solo ascent of K7 in the Karakoram is a route of almost 2,500-m (8,200-ft) with rock climbing up to 5.10 on the US system (see p.351), and ice as steep as 80 degrees. He has made some fast ascents of easier routes as well, sprinting up and down the 8,201-m (26,906-ft) Cho Oyu in a day.

Like Messner, House articulates the ethics of mountaineering with ruthless intensity and no willingness to compromise: "Climbing is a form of expression that has no practical purpose – it's

ALEXANDER ODINTSOV
RUSSIA   B.1957

Born in St Petersburg, Alexander Odintsov and Steve House have deep philosophical differences.

At the 2004 Piolet d'Or award ceremony, House stormed out when Odintsov's team won the prize for their ascent of the North Face of Jannu in Nepal, a difficult climb on a peak 7,710m (25,295ft) in height. The 10-man team had used thousands of metres of fixed ropes and spent 50 days pushing the climb in desperate conditions. But, Odintsov argued, the communitarian approach is better: "Imagine a team with Huber and House and so on. It would be an excellent team, but each one of them is not ready to give up something of their own personality."

for one's own personal satisfaction. So to climb in a manner that is not what I call moral is to diminish your own experience. We already know we can climb any route with enough technology. So what's the point?"

Since Nanga Parbat, he has made a series of technically difficult climbs in the Canadian Rockies, including routes on the Emperor Face of Mount Robson with rising star Colin Haley in 2007, and in 2008 a new route on the North Face of Mount Alberta. Then followed two attempts on Makalu's West Face with Anderson and Prezelj. In 2010, he took a fall in the Canadian Rockies that fractured his pelvis and several vertebrae and ribs, and collapsed his right lung – injuries that put him out of climbing for the rest of the year.

NANGA PARBAT

RUPAL (EAST) FLANK, SEPTEMBER 2005

— **1 September – Starting out**
Leaving at 4am, House and Vince Anderson start up the route pioneered the year before with Bruce Miller.

— **4 September – Progress up the face**
With more snow than in 2004, the team moves right and up onto the pillar in the centre of the face.

— **6 September – Route to summit**
Easier climbing and a fifth bivouac at 7,400m (24,300ft) lead to the summit slopes but hard days take their toll.

(Dashed line means route hidden from view)

SUMMIT (8,126M/26,660FT)

THE GIRI-GIRI BOYS

ELITE JAPANESE MOUNTAINEERING TEAM

JAPAN

MOUNTAINS HAVE OCCUPIED a central place in Japanese culture for millennia, and while mountaineering was initially learned from the West, in recent years a cadre of talented young Japanese climbers has come to the fore. They call themselves the Giri-Giri Boys as a twist on a popular Japanese girl band. Matching their European and US counterparts for difficulty, style, and imagination, their activities are still unmistakably Japanese.

A LIFE'S WORK

- College students Ichimura and Yokoyama climb the **Shi-Shi route** on Mount Huntington, the start of their **infatuation with Alaska**

- Yamada, Ichimura, and Sato climb **three new technical routes** in Alaska's Ruth Gorge

- The Boys spend **two weeks** climbing Crossing Korube on Japan's **Mount Tsurugi**

- They complete a **monumental link-up** of hard routes on Alaska's Denali, but their success is marred by the **disappearance of two members of the group** on the Cassin Ridge

- Climb a **new line on Kalanka** in the Garhwal Himalaya

- Make an **alpine-style** third ascent of the British Route on the **Golden Pillar of Spantik** in Pakistan's Karakoram

- Ascend one of the **great unclimbed walls** in North America: the South Face of Mount Logan, Canada's highest peak

- Make an unsuccessful attempt on the North Ridge of Latok I, one of the much-tried **"last great problems"** in the Karakoram

Completing a form before taking a flight into the Alaska Range in 2008, a group of five Japanese climbers were asked for the name of their expedition. Without thinking about it too much, Tatsuro "Tats" Yamada suggested the "Giri-Giri Boys", a play on the name of 1990s pop group the Giri-Giri Girls. Giri-Giri means "hardly at all", and by extension, "by the skin of your teeth", which seemed appropriate for the group's approach to climbing. The name stuck.

TRIUMPH OVERSHADOWED

That season in Alaska, Fumitaka "Itchy" Ichimura, Yusuke Sato, and Katsutaka "Jumbo" Yokoyama climbed an *enchaînement* linking two routes on the South Face of Denali – the Isis Face and the Slovak Direct. The scale and imagination of their enterprise, which was of Himalayan proportions, caught other climbers off guard. Steve House (see pp.344–45) had considered Alaska to be "climbed out" in terms of new challenges. "When Jumbo told me of their intent to link up the Isis Face to the Slovak Direct," he wrote in *Alpinist* magazine, "I was forced to slap my forehead and utter a Homeresque 'Doh!' In a flash I realized that it wasn't the terrain that wasn't big enough. It was my imagination that had been too small."

Yokoyama lost his sunglasses near the top of the 2,190-m (7,200-ft) Isis Face, and had to make the difficult 1,200-m (4,000-ft) descent

of the Ramp Route to the start of the 2,700-m (9,000-ft) Slovak Direct without them, his eyes squinting against the dazzling light during the hard ice climbing. Days later, high on the Slovak Direct, he was snowblind, so he offered to jumar (ascend by rope) with their gear as the third man and so speed up the ascent. It was grunt work, but it showed his commitment when his partners were thinking retreat might be inevitable.

The other two members of the Giri-Giri Boys, Yamada and Yuto Inoue, had set themselves the task of linking West Kahiltna Peak, East Kahiltna Peak, and the Cassin Ridge. But when Yokoyama and the others descended after their epic climb, there was no sign of them,

just their empty tent at Base Camp. Later, a flight around the South Face revealed footsteps crossing their chosen objectives to 5,800m (19,000ft) on the Cassin Ridge – and then nothing. Sato described the loss of his friends as "an unanswered question".

INSPIRED BY THE SAMURAI

The Giri-Giri Boys thrived in Alaska, which they could reach on limited budgets while still making high-calibre climbs. One of Yokoyama's new routes, on the Southwest Face of Mount Huntington, he called Shi-Shi, a reference to a 19th-century samurai notion from

KALANKA

BUSHIDO ROUTE, NORTH FACE, SEPT 2008

— **15 September – Climb to the Central Spur**
Ichimura, Sato, and Amano leave Advance Base Camp. Next day they reach the Central Spur.

— **18 September – Difficult central section**
They climb most of the steep central section and bivouac. The following day a storm stops them.

— **22 September – The weather relents**
After more than two days' bad weather, the skies clear and in a 13-hour round trip, the team make it to the summit and return.

SUMMIT
(6,931M/22,740FT)

CENTRAL SPUR

the late Edo period meaning "men of high purpose". Interviewed for *Alpinist*, Yokoyama said, "To live with purity you must be able to imagine your own corpse and feel no qualms about it." In spite of the samurai allusions, Yokoyama is regarded as one of the nicest and least intense of the current top alpinists.

Nicknamed "Jumbo" for – by Japanese standards – his large frame, his Alaskan record has been matched in recent years by major achievements in the Karakoram. In 2009, with Kazuaki Amano and Ichimura, he attempted a new line on the Golden Pillar of Spantik, but had to settle for a repeat of the British 1987 route. In

2010, with Ichimura and Sato, he made a strong attempt on the North Ridge of Latok I, another longstanding problem.

TRAPPED BY A STORM

Yusuke Sato was twice nominated for a Piolet d'Or in 2008, for his Alaskan ascents and also for a new route on the North Face of Kalanka in India's Garhwal Himalaya, a peak of almost 7,000m (23,000ft). For their ascent of Kalanka, Sato and his partners Amano and Ichimura left their Advanced Base Camp on the Bagini Glacier at 5,100m (16,700ft), and climbing left of the face's Central Spur, bivouacked 1,000m (3,300ft) higher. The next day they made a huge traverse right into the centre of the face to reach the spur and after another bivouac started up this steeper, more technical section.

They bivouacked at 6,500m (21,300ft) and again a short distance above, where they were trapped for three days by a storm. Even so, they continued to the summit. The round-trip took ten days, and the team survived on just five days' worth of food. They named their new route Bushido ("the way of the warrior").

Although such long, committing climbs are not unknown in the Himalaya, the Giri-Giri Boys have, more surprisingly, found similarly

draining projects in Japan. Poor rock, changeable weather, huge dumps of snow, and highly vegetated approaches add to the complexity of mountaineering there.

HOME CHALLENGE

Sato has identified his hardest route as Crossing Kurobe, a line on Mount Tsurugi in the Northern Alps of Japan. The route was named after the river the team had to cross in order to reach the mountain. Although only 2,999m (9,839ft) high, the route, which was climbed over New Year in 2007, took 14 days from start to finish. Two of the team were caught in an avalanche at 1,000m (3,300ft). "I lost 5kg [11lbs] on that route," Sato said later. "We did it before our Denali link-up as training for Denali. What we climbed on Denali was technically harder, but this was mentally harder. It was a big mountain range, remote. Really deep snow and no helicopter rescue, no escape."

Sato lives with his family in Yamanashi – the prefecture where Mount Fuji and several mountainous national parks are located – and works as an engineer. "We all work full time and plough all our money back in to climbing, we're not rich men," he says of the Giri-Giri Boys, "So our life is literally at the edge."

ALASKAN LEGEND
Yusuke Sato cuts a lonely figure as he traverses a vast ice wall on Alaska's Denali in 2008.

PACHINKO

Taking its name from a popular Japanese version of pinball that originated in the 1970s, Pachinko refers to the imaginative conceptualization of climbing challenges in a world where thinking up difficult things to do is half the battle. In the original game, movement seems erratic, but in the climbing version, it's a way of removing oneself from the limits of the past. "Because we live in a rational world," Katsutaka Yokoyama says, "the value of climbing increases with its irrationality. Pachinko – climbing up, coming back down, then repeating the process – has no rationale ... The more you think about how to enjoy the mountain fully, the more possibilities you'll discover."

MOUNTAIN LIVES

PROFESSIONAL CLIMBERS

The earliest professional climbers were guides – men with local knowledge who led amateurs up their chosen objectives – while the entertainer Albert Smith made money by appealing to a public excited by the sensational. In the mid-20th century, a new type of climber was emerging, earning a living selling stories about their adventures, increasingly sponsored by equipment manufacturers.

Edward Whymper (see pp.142–45) had much in common with modern professional climbers, making trips to the Alps and South America to gather material for lectures, while Paul Preuss (see pp.176–77) was also a popular lecturer. Early Everest climbers were restricted in their commercial activities – the Mount Everest Committee tightly controlled any intellectual property from the exploration of Everest. Money from books and lectures was used to finance future attempts.

By the 1930s, mountain explorers such as Frank Smythe (see p.247) made money from their books, but it wasn't until after World War II that the first fully professional climbers emerged. Some, like Lionel Terray

(see pp.276–77), used their public profile to boost their guiding activities. Nevertheless, many post-war expeditions were financed by national organizations, which continued to control the income they generated. This was often for the good of climbing: the Mount Everest Foundation still sponsors British expeditions with the money earned from lectures given by the successful 1953 team.

With the demise of national expeditions, climbers are free to profit from their activities. Outdoor clothing and equipment brands – small businesses until the last few decades – now sponsor climbers. These commercial relationships present new challenges to young mountaineers trying to make their mark.

THE VETERANS
The next generation of professionals has drawn an audience from the growing number of participants in mountain sports, such as climbing and trekking, inspired in part by lectures and books of Messner's generation. A few have carved out a career in exploratory climbing.

❶ Italian Simone Moro is known for daring ascents in the Greater Ranges, often climbing alpine-style, without oxygen, in winter. ❷ Bavarian Stefan Glowacz is famous for technical big-wall climbs in Patagonia, Greenland, and Canada. ❸ Slovenian Tomaz Humar shot to fame with a hard new route on the East Face of Dhaulagiri. He died on Langtang Lirung in 2009. ❹ With seven Everest ascents, Ed Viesturs was the first American to climb all 14 "8,000ers".

THE NEW PROFESSIONALS
With commercial interests firmly ensconced in the mountains, today's professionals have a range of potential revenue streams to fund their ambitions. Sponsorship from outdoor brands is increasingly prevalent, raising questions over the ethics – and risks – of climbing partly for promotional purposes.

❶ Austrian David Lama has attracted both sponsors and critics for his high-profile climbs. ❷ Basque climber Edurne Pasaban is widely credited as the first woman to climb all 14 "8,000ers". ❸ Briton Kenton Cool was a leading exploratory mountaineer in his youth and is now best known as an Everest guide, with eight ascents by 2010 and a ski descent of Manaslu.

DON WHILLANS (LEFT), PICTURED HERE WITH DOUGAL HASTON (SEE PP.298–99) ON EVEREST'S SOUTHWEST FACE, DEVELOPED AND TESTED CLIMBING GEAR – A BOX TENT AND A SIT-HARNESS – ALONGSIDE HIS MOUNTAINEERING ACTIVITIES.

THE LEGENDS

Pioneering professionals began to carve out a niche as full-time climbers without having to work as guides in the 1970s. Lectures, film projects, and writing allowed them to concentrate on climbing, although not without some resentment from other talented alpinists who lacked their marketing skills.

❶ Reinhold Messner (see pp.308–11) applied the same determination he showed on the first oxygen-free ascent of Everest to building up a "brand". ❷ Chris Bonington (see pp.300–01) sought public recognition without compromising his mountaineering integrity. ❸ Kurt Diemberger (see pp.260–61) launched a film career with his epic ascent of the Peuterey Ridge.

UELI STECK

SWITZERLAND   B.1976

One of the best-known stars of international alpinism, Ueli Steck is famous for his lightning-fast ascents.

He climbed the North Face of the Eiger in 2008 in 2hr, 47mins, and 33secs, and the North Face of the Matterhorn in under two hours in 2009. In 2011, he climbed the South Face of the "8,000er" Shisha Pangma in 10hr, 30mins. Sponsored by Audi, like other top mountaineers he is a regular speaker on the corporate lecture circuit.

MOUNTAIN DIRECTORY

This directory contains only those peaks and ranges mentioned in the book. *Italic* text indicates a peak or range with its own entry. ▲ Indicates an **"8,000er"** (one of the 14 peaks higher than 8,000m/26,247ft).

Abi Gamin (7,355m/24,131ft); *Himalaya.*
Aconcagua (6,962m/22,841ft); *Andes,* Argentina.
Ahornspitze (2,976m/9,764ft); *Zillertal Alps.*
Aiguille Blanche de Peuterey (4,112m/13,490ft); *Mont Blanc massif.*
Aiguille d'Argentière (3,901m/12,799ft); *Mont Blanc massif.*
Aiguille de Bionnassay (4,052m/13,294ft); *Mont Blanc massif.*
Aiguille de Blatière (3,522m/11,555ft); *Mont Blanc massif.*
Aiguille de Triolet (3,870m/12,697ft); *Mont Blanc massif.*
Aiguille du Dru *Mont Blanc massif*; has two peaks: Grand Dru (3,754m/12,316ft) and Petit Dru (3,733m/12,247ft).
Aiguille du Midi (3,842m/12,605ft); *Mont Blanc massif.*
Aiguille du Plan (3,673m/12,050ft); *Mont Blanc massif.*
Aiguille Poincenot (3,002m/9,849ft); *Fitzroy* range.
Aiguille Vert (4,122m/13,523ft); *Mont Blanc massif.*
Ailefroide (3,954m/12,972ft); *Dauphiné Alps.*
Akher Chogh (7,025m/23,048ft); *Hindu Kush.*
Alaska Range Range in Alaska, US; contains *Denali.*
Aletschhorn (4,195m/13,763ft); *Bernese Alps.*
Alps A major range in Europe crossing parts of Austria, France, Germany, Italy, Leichtenstein, Slovenia, and Switzerland; contains *Mont Blanc.*
Andes World's longest range, running for 7,000km (4,300 miles) along the west coast of South America; stretches across parts of Argentina, Bolivia, Chile, Colombia, Ecuador, Peru, and Venezuela.
Ankogel (3,246m/10,649ft); *Hohe Tauern.*
▲ **Annapurna I** (8,091m/26,545ft); *Himalaya.*
Appalachian Mountains Range in the US and Canada; runs for 2,400km (1,500 miles).
Arwa Tower (6,352m/20,840ft); *Himalaya.*
Baintha Brakk (7,285m/23,901ft); *Karakoram.*
Balkan Mountains Range on the border of Bulgaria and Serbia.
Balmhorn (3,698m/12,133ft); *Bernese Alps.*
Baltoro Kangri (7,312m/23,990ft); *Karakoram.*
Barre des Écrins (4,102m/13,458ft); *Dauphiné Alps.*
Batian (5,199m/17,057ft); highest peak of *Mount Kenya.*
Beaupré (2,778m/9,114ft); *Victoria Cross Ranges.*
Ben Nevis (1,344m/4,409ft); *Scottish Highlands.*
Bernese Alps Sub-range of the *Alps*; Switzerland.
Bernina Alps Sub-range of the *Alps*; Italy/Switzerland.
Bhagirathi III (6,457m/21,184ft); *Himalaya.*
Bietschhorn (3,934m/12,907ft); *Bernese Alps.*
Birthday Peak (2,924m/9,595ft); *Purcell Mountains.*

Blue Mountains Range in New South Wales, Australia.
Bogda Feng (5,445m/17,864ft); *Tian Shan.*
Bregaglia Alps Sub-range of the *Alps*; Italy/Switzerland.
Breithorn (4,164m/13,661ft); *Pennine Alps.*
▲ **Broad Peak** (8,047m/26,401ft); *Gasherbrum* massif in the *Karakoram.*
Brocken (1,141m/3,743ft); *Harz Mountains.*
Bugaboo Spire (3,204m/10,512ft); *Purcell Mountains.*
Cairngorms Range in the *Scottish Highlands.*
Canadian Rockies Canadian section of the *Rocky Mountains.*
Capo Tafunato (2,335m/7,660ft); Corsica.
Cascade Mountains Range in North America.
Caucasus Mountains Range in Eurasia, stretching across the borders of Armenia, Azerbaijan, Georgia, Iran, and Turkey.
Central Tower of Paine (2,460m/8,100ft); *Cordillera del Paine.*
Cerro Kishtwar (6,200m/20,341ft); *Himalaya.*
Cerro Torre (3,128m/10,262ft); *Fitzroy* range.
Chacraraju Este (6,001m/19,688ft); *Cordillera Blanca.*
Changabang (6,864m/22,520ft); *Himalaya.*
Chimborazo (6,310m/20,702ft); *Andes,* Ecuador.
▲ **Cho Oyu** (8,201m/26,906ft); *Himalaya.*
Chogolisa (7,665m/25,148ft); *Karakoram.*
Chomo Yummo (6,829m/22,405ft); *Himalaya.*
Chomolhari (7,314m/23,996ft); *Himalaya.*
Chomolonzo (7,804m/25,604ft); *Himalaya.*
Chomolungma Tibetan name for *Mount Everest* ("Saint Mother").
Cima di Brenta (3,155m/10,352ft); *Dolomites.*
Cima Grande (2,999m/9,839ft); *Dolomites.*
Cima Ovest (2,973m/9,754ft); *Dolomites.*
Cima Piccola (2,857m/9,373ft); *Dolomites.*
Cima Tosam (3,173m/10,410ft); *Dolomites.*
Cinque Torri (2,361m/7,746ft); *Dolomites.*
Citlaltépetl (5,636m/18,491ft); Mexico.
Columbia Mountains Range stretching across British Columbia, Canada and the states of Idaho, Montana, and Washington, US.
Cordillera Blanca Sub-range of the *Andes,* Peru.
Cordillera del Paine Mountain group in Patagonia, Chile; part of the *Andes.*
Cordillera Real Sub-range of the *Andes,* Bolivia.
Cotopaxi (5,896m/19,344ft); *Andes,* Ecuador.
Cottian Alps Sub-range of the *Alps*; France/Italy.
Crozzon di Brenta (3,135m/10,285ft); *Southern Limestone Alps.*
Dauphiné Alps Sub-range of the *Alps,* France.
Denali (Mount McKinley) Highest mountain in North America (6,194m/20,320ft); *Alaska Range.*
Dent Blanche (4,357m/14,295ft); *Pennine Alps.*
Dent d'Hérens (4,171m/13,684ft); *Pennine Alps.*
Dent de Broc (1,829m/6,001ft); *Bernese Alps.*
Dent du Géant (4,013m/13,166ft); *Mont Blanc massif.*
Devils Tower (386m/1,267ft); Wyoming, US.
▲ **Dhaulagiri** (8,167m/26,795ft); *Himalaya.*
Diablerets (3,210m/10,531ft); *Bernese Alps.*
Doldenhorn (3,643 m/11,952ft); *Bernese Alps.*
Dolomites Sub-range of the *Alps,* Italy.

Dôme du Gôuter (4,304m/14,121ft); *Mont Blanc massif.*
Dunagiri (7,066m/23,182ft); *Himalaya.*
Dych Tau (5,205m/17,077ft); *Caucasus Mountains.*
Dzongri (4,100m/13,451ft); *Himalaya.*
Eiger (3,970m/13,025ft); *Bernese Alps.*
Elbruz (5,642m/18,510ft); *Caucasus Mountains.*
Elbsandsteingebirge Range in Germany/Czech Republic.
El Capitan (3,169m/10,367ft); Yosemite National Park, California, US.
Emei Shan (7,066m/23,182ft); *Himalaya.*
Fernerkogel (3,298m/10,820ft); *Stubai Alps.*
Fineilspitze (3,514m/11,529ft); *Ötztal Alps.*
Finsteraarhorn (4,274m/14,022ft); *Bernese Alps.*
Fitzroy (3,405m/11,171ft); *Andes,* Patagonia.
French Prealps Range in southeast France.
Front Range Sub-range of the *Rocky Mountains.*
Furchetta (3,025m/9,925ft); *Dolomites.*
Garhwal Himalaya Sub-range of the *Himalaya*; India.
▲ **Gasherbrum I** (8,068m/26,470ft); *Karakoram.*
▲ **Gasherbrum II** (8,035m/26,362ft); *Karakoram.*
Gasherbrum IV (7,925m/26,001ft); *Karakoram.*
Gauri Sankar (7,134m/23,406ft); *Himalaya.*
Gestola (4,860m/15,945ft); *Caucasus Mountains.*
Glarus Alps Sub-range of the *Alps*; Switzerland.
Gletscherhorn (3,983m/13,068ft); *Bernese Alps.*
Graian Alps Sub-range of the *Alps*; France/Italy/Switzerland.
Grand Capucin (3,838m/12,592ft); *Mont Blanc massif.*
Grand Cornier (3,962m/12,999ft); *Pennine Alps.*
Grandes Jorasses (4,208m/13,806ft); *Mont Blanc massif.*
Grands Charmoz (3,445m/11,302ft); *Mont Blanc massif.*
Greater Ranges The high mountain ranges of Asia, including the *Himalaya, Karakoram, Hindu Kush, Hindu Raj, Pamir Mountains, Tien Shan, Kunlun Shan,* and *Nyanchen Tangla.*
Grépon (3,482m/11,424ft); *Mont Blanc massif.*
Grimsel Alps Sub-range of the *Alps*; Switzerland.
Gross Fiescherhorn (4,049m/13,284ft); *Bernese Alps.*
Gross Mörchner (3,287m/10,785ft); *Zillertal Alps.*
Gross Wiesbachhorn (3,564m/11,693ft); *Hohe Tauern.*
Grosshorn (3,754m/12,316ft); *Bernese Alps.*
Gspaltenhorn (3,436m/11,273ft); *Bernese Alps.*
Habicht (3,277m/10,751ft); *Stubai Alps.*
Haidinger (3,070m/10,070ft); *Southern Alps.*
Harz Mountains Highest range in Germany.
Himalaya Major range in Asia, separating the Indian subcontinent from the Tibetan Plateau; straddles parts of Afghanistan, Bhutan, India, Nepal, and Tibet; contains some of the world's highest peaks, including *Mount Everest.*
Hindu Kush Range stretching across central Afghanistan and northern Pakistan; forms part of the *Greater Ranges.*
Hindu Raj Range in northern Pakistan between the *Hindu Kush* and *Karakoram.*

Hinterer Brochkogel (3,635m/11,926ft); *Ötztal Alps.*
Hinter Fiescherhorn (4,025m/13,205ft); *Bernese Alps.*
Hohe Tauern Sub-range of the *Alps*; Italy/Austria.
Howse Peak (3,295m/10,810ft); *Canadian Rockies.*
Huascarán (6,768m/22,205ft); *Cordillera Blanca.*
Hugihorn (3,646m/11,965ft); *Grimsel Alps.*
Jannu (7,710m/25,295ft); *Himalaya.*
Japanese Alps Series of mountain ranges on the main island of Japan.
Jongson Peak (7,462m/24,482ft); *Himalaya.*
Jugal A section of the *Himalaya.*
Jungfrau (4,158m/13,642ft); *Bernese Alps.*
Jura Mountains Range in France/Switzerland.
▲ **K2** (8,611m/28,251ft); *Karakoram.*
Kabru (7,412 m/24,318ft); *Himalaya.*
Kaisergebirge Sub-range of the *Alps,* Austria.
Kalanka (6,931m/22,740ft); *Garhwal Himalaya.*
Kamet (7,756m/25,446ft); *Himalaya.*
▲ **Kangchenjunga (Sewalungma)** (8,586m/28,169ft); *Himalaya.*
Karakoram Range in Asia stretching across parts of China, India, and Pakistan; forms part of the *Greater Ranges* and contains *K2.*
Kazbek (5,033m/16,512ft); *Caucasus Mountains.*
Khan Tengri (7,010m/22,999ft); *Tian Shan.*
Kilimanjaro (5,895m/19,341ft); Tanzania.
Klein Grünhorn (3,913m/12,838ft); *Bernese Alps.*
Koh-e-Bandaka (6,812m/22,349ft); *Hindu Kush.*
Koh-e-Tez (6,995m/22,944ft); *Hindu Kush.*
Koser Gunge (6,401m/21,000ft); *Karakoram.*
Koshtan-Tau (5,144m/16,877ft); *Caucasus Mountains.*
Kumaon Himalaya Sub-range of the *Himalaya*; India.
Kunlun Shan Range in Western China between the Tibetan Plateau and the Takla Makan Desert; part of the *Greater Ranges.*
Kusum Kanguru (6,367m/20,889ft); *Himalaya.*
La Meije (3,984m/13,071ft); Les Écrins massif.
Latok I (7,145m/23,442ft); *Karakoram.*
Lauterbrunnen Breithorn (3,780m/12,402ft); *Bernese Alps.*
▲ **Lhotse** (8,501m/27,890ft); *Himalaya.*
Le Gerbier (1,551m/5,089ft); *Massif Central.*
Le Grigne (2,410m/7,907ft); *Alps,* Italy.
Lenzpitze (4,294m/14,088ft); *Pennine Alps.*
Lepontine Alps Sub-range of the *Alps*; Italy/Switzerland.
Les Droites (4,000m/13,123ft); *Mont Blanc massif.*
Llullaillaco (6,739m/22,110ft); *Andes,* Argentina/Chile.
Lobsang Spire (5,707m/18,724ft); *Karakoram.*
Lost Arrow Spire (2,112m/6,930ft); Yosemite National Park, California, US.
Lyskamm (4,527m/14,852ft); *Pennine Alps.*
Lyngen Alps Range in Norway.
▲ **Makalu** (8,463m/27,766ft); *Himalaya.*
▲ **Manaslu (Kutang)** (8,163m/26,781ft); *Himalaya.*
Mandlkogel (2,439m/8,002ft); *Northern Limestone Alps.*
Martial Mountains Range in Tierra del Fuego, Argentina; part of the *Andes.*
Masherbrum (K1) (7,821m/25,659 ft); *Karakoram.*

Massif Central Mountainous region in southwest France.

Matterhorn (Monte Cervino) (4,478m/14,692ft); *Pennine Alps.*

Mieminger Range Part of the *Southern Limestone Alps.*

Minya Konka (Mount Gongga) (7,556m/24,790ft); Daxue Shan range, China.

Mönch (4,107m/13,474ft); *Bernese Alps.*

Mont Aiguille (Mons Inascensibilis) (2,085m/6,841ft); *French Prealps.*

Mont Blanc (4,808m/15,771ft); *Alps,* France/Italy.

Mont Blanc massif Range in the western *Alps;* France/Italy/Switzerland.

Mont Buet (3,096m/10,157ft); Giffre massif, France.

Mont Cenis (2,083m/6,834ft); *Cottian/Graian Alps.*

Mont Maudit (4,465m/14,649ft); *Mont Blanc massif.*

Mont Pelvoux, (3,946m/12,946ft); Massif des Écrins, *Dauphiné Alps.*

Mont Rouge de Peuterey (2,941m/9,649ft); *Mont Blanc massif.*

Mont Ventoux (1,912m/6,273ft); France.

Monte Civetta (3,220m/10,564ft); *Dolomites.*

Monte Moro (2,985m/9,793 ft); *Pennine Alps.*

Monte Olivia (1,326m/4,350ft); Tierra del Fuego, Argentina; part of the *Andes.*

Monte Pelmo (3,168m/10,393ft); *Dolomites.*

Monte Rosa (Dufourspitze) (4,634m/15,203ft); *Pennine Alps.*

Monte Sarmiento (2,246m/7,369ft); Tierra del Fuego, Chile; part of the *Andes.*

Monte Viso (3,841m/12,602ft); *Cottian Alps.*

Moose's Tooth (3,150m/10,335ft); *Alaska Range.*

Mount Alberta (3,619m/11,873ft); *Canadian Rockies.*

Mount Ararat Comprises two peaks: Greater Ararat (5,137m/16,854ft) and Lesser Ararat (3,896m/12,782ft); Turkey.

Mount Aso (1,592m/5,223ft); Japan.

Mount Athos (Holy Mountain) (2,033m/6,669ft); Greece.

Mount Baker (4,844m/15,892ft); *Rwenzori Range.*

Mount Bonney (3,100m/10,171ft); *Selkirk Range.*

Mount Cook (Aoraki) (3,754m/12,316ft); *Southern Alps.*

Mount Crillon (3,879m/12,726 ft); *Saint Elias Range.*

Mount Edith Cavell (3,363m/11,033ft); *Canadian Rockies.*

Mount Elbruz (5,642m/18,510ft); *Caucasus Mountains.*

▲ **Mount Everest** (8,848m/29,029ft); *Himalaya.*

Mount Foraker (5,304m/17,400 ft); *Alaska Range.*

Mount Fuji (3,776m/12,389ft); Japan.

Mount Habel (3,087m/10,128ft); *Canadian Rockies.*

Mount Hemus (636m/2,087ft); *Balkan Mountains.*

Mount Huntington (3,730m/12,240ft); *Alaska Range.*

Mount Kailash (6,638m/21,778ft); *Himalaya.*

Mount Kain (2,880m/9,449ft); *Canadian Rockies.*

Mount Kennedy (4,300m/14,000ft); *Saint Elias Mountains.*

Mount Kenya (5,199m/17,057ft); Kenya.

Mount Kongur (7,649m/25,095ft); *Kunlun Shan.*

Mount Koya The collective name for the eight mountain peaks of Koya-san, Japan.

Mount Louis (2,682m/8,799ft); *Canadian Rockies.*

Mount of Olives (818m/2,683ft); Jerusalem.

Mount Olympus (2,917m/9,570ft); Greece.

Mount Omine (1,719m/5,640ft); Japan.

Mount Robson (3,954m/12,972ft); *Canadian Rockies.*

Mount Sealy (2,627m/8,619ft); *Southern Alps.*

Mount Sinai (Jebel Musa) (2,285m/7,497ft); Egypt.

Mount Saint Elias (5,489m/18,009ft); *Saint Elias Range.*

Mount Tapuaenuku (2,885m/9,465ft); South Island, New Zealand.

Mount Tasman (3,497m/11,473ft); *Southern Alps.*

Mount Teide (Pico del Teide) (3,718m/12,198ft); Spain.

Mount Tsurugi (2,999m/9,839ft); Hida Mountains, Japan.

Mount Tyndall (4,275m/14,025ft); Sierra Nevada range, US.

Mount Vesuvius (1,281m/4,203ft); Italy.

Mount Waddington (4,019m/13,186ft); Coast Mountains, *Pacific Coast Ranges.*

Mount Whitehorn (2,621m/8,599ft); Canada.

Mukut Parbat (7,242m/23,760ft); *Himalaya.*

Muztagh Ata (7,546m/24,757ft); *Karakoram.*

Muztagh Tower (7,273m/23,862ft); *Karakoram.*

Nadelhorn (Stechnadelhorn) (4,327m/14,196ft); *Pennine Alps.*

Nameless Tower One of the *Trango Towers* group in the *Karakoram.*

Nanda Devi (7,816m/25,643ft); *Garhwal Himalaya.*

Nanda Kot (6,861m/22,510ft); *Kumaun Himalaya.*

▲ **Nanga Parbat** (8,126m/26,660ft); *Himalaya.*

Nasswald Peak (3,042m/9,980ft); Canada.

Nesthorn (3,822m/12,539ft); *Bernese Alps.*

Niederhorn (1,950m/6,398ft); *Bernese Alps.*

Northern Limestone Alps Sub-range of the *Alps;* Austria/Germany.

Noshaq (7,492m/24,580ft); *Hindu Kush.*

Nun Kun massif (7,135m/23,409ft); *Himalaya.*

Nyanchen Tangla (7,152m/23,465m); *Himalaya.*

Oberalpstock (3,328m/10,919ft); *Glarus Alps.*

Ogre, The See *Baintha Brakk.*

Ol Doinyo Lengai (2,960m/9,711ft); Tanzania.

Oldenhorn (3,132m/10,276ft); *Bernese Alps.*

Ortler Alps Sub-range of the *Alps;* Italy/Switzerland.

Ötztal Alps Sub-range of the *Alps;* Austria/Italy.

Pacific Coast Ranges Range running along the west coast of North America.

Pamir Mountains Range in Central Asia formed by the junction of the *Himalaya, Tian Shan, Karakoram, Junlun,* and *Hindu Kush;* stretches across parts of Afghanistan, China, Kyrgyzstan, Pakistan, and Tajikistan.

Pauhunri (7,065m/23,179ft); *Himalaya.*

Pennine Alps Sub-range of the *Alps;* Italy/Switzerland.

Pic Canigou (2,784m/9,134ft); *Pyrenees.*

Pic d'Arzinol (2,998m/9,836ft); *Pennine Alps.*

Pic Tyndall (4,241m/13,914ft); *Pennine Alps.*

Pichincha volcano (3,896m/12,782ft); Ecuador.

Pik Lenin (7,134m/23,406ft); *Pamir Mountains.*

Pinnacle Peak (6,930m/22,736ft); *Nun Kun massif.*

Pioneer Peak (1,950m/6,398ft); Chugach Mountains, Alaska, US.

Piz Aul (3,121m/10,240ft); *Lepontine Alps*

Piz Cengalo (3,369m/11,053ft); *Bregaglia Alps.*

Piz Palü (3,901m/12,799ft); *Bernina Alps.*

Piz Terri (3,149m/10,331ft); *Lepontine Alps.*

Piz Urlaun (3,359m/11,020ft); *Glarus Alps.*

Pollux (4,092m/13,425ft); *Pennine Alps.*

Portiengrat (3,654m/11,988ft); *Pennine Alps.*

Purcell Mountains Range in western Canada, part of the *Columbia Mountains.*

Putuo Shan (286m/939ft); island mountain southeast of Shanghai, China.

Pyrenees Range straddling the border of France and Spain; separates the Iberian Peninsula from the rest of mainland Europe.

Rakaposhi (7,788m/25,551ft); *Karakoram.*

Resplendent Mountain (3,408m/11,181ft); *Canadian Rockies.*

Rheinwaldhorn (Piz Valrhein) (3,402m/11,161ft); *Lepontine Alps.*

Rimpfischhorn (4,199m/13,776ft); *Pennine Alps.*

Rochemelon (3,538m/11,608ft); *Graian Alps.*

Rocky Mountains A major North American mountain range stretching from British Columbia in western Canada to New Mexico in the southwestern US.

Rwenzori Range A mountain range in central Africa, located between Uganda and the Democratic Republic of Congo.

Saint Elias Range Sub-range of the *Pacific Coast Ranges,* Canada; contains *Mount Saint Elias.*

Saltoro Kangri (7,742m/25,400ft); *Karakoram.*

Schrammacher (3,411m/11,191ft); *Zillertal Alps.*

Scottish Highlands Mountainous region in Scotland.

Selkirk Range Mountain range running from British Columbia, Canada, to eastern Washington State, US.

Sentinel Peak (883m/2,897ft); Tucson Mountains, Arizona, US.

Sgurr Alasdair (993m/3,258ft); Cuillin Range, Isle of Skye, Scotland.

Shawangunks Ridge of peaks in New York State, US.

▲ **Shisha Pangma** (8,012m/26,286ft); *Karakoram.*

Shivling (6,543m/21,467ft); *Garwhal Himalaya.*

Shreckhorn (4,078m/13,379ft); *Bernese Alps.*

Sierra Nevada Range in the states of California and Nevada, US.

Siguniang (6,250m/20,505ft); Qionglai Mountains, China.

Silberhorn (3,695m/12,123ft); *Bernese Alps.*

Silberhorn (3,303m/10,837ft); *Southern Alps.*

Silvretta Alps Sub-range of the *Alps;* Austria/Switzerland.

Siniolchu (6,888m/22,598ft); *Himalaya.*

Southern Alps Range in South Island, New Zealand; contains *Mount Cook (Aoraki).*

South Howser Tower (3,292m/10,801ft); *Purcell Mountains.*

Spantik (7,027m/23,054ft); *Karakoram.*

Speke (4,890m/16,043ft); *Rwenzori Range.*

Stanley (5,109m/16,762ft); *Rwenzori Range.*

Strahlkogel (3,295m/10,810ft); Austria.

Stubai Alps Sub-range of the *Alps;* Austria.

Sulamar (5,380m/17,651ft); Xuelian massif, China.

Sustenhorn (3,503m/11,493ft); *Urner Alps.*

Täschhorn (4,491m/14,734ft); *Pennine Alps.*

Tatra Mountains Range on the border between Poland and Slovakia.

Taulliraju (5,830m/19,127ft); *Cordillera Blanca.*

Tetons Series of peaks in the *Rocky Mountains.*

Tian Shan Range in Central Asia stretching across parts of China, India, Kazakhstan, Kyrgyzstan, Pakistan, and Uzbekistan.

Tibesti Mountains Range of inactive volcanoes, located mainly in Chad.

Tirich Mir (7,708m/25,289ft); *Hindu Kush.*

Titlis (3,238m/10,623ft); *Urner Alps.*

Tödi (3,614m/11,857ft); *Glarus Alps.*

Torre Egger (2,685m/8,809ft); Patagonia, Argentina/Chile; part of the *Andes.*

Totenkirchl (2,190m/7,185ft); *Northern Limestone Alps.*

Trango Towers (6,286m/20,623ft); *Karakoram.*

Tre Cime di Lavaredo (2,999m/9,839ft); *Dolomites.*

Trisul (7,120m/23,360ft); *Himalaya.*

Troll Wall (1,700m/5,577ft); Norway.

Ushba (4,710m/15,453ft); *Caucasus Mountains.*

Victoria Cross Ranges Sub-range of the *Canadian Rockies.*

Wagendrischelhorn (2,251m/7,385ft); *Northern Limestone Alps*

Weisshorn (4,506m/14,782ft); *Pennine Alps.*

Wetterhorn (3,692m/12,113ft); *Bernese Alps.*

Wetterstein Range in the *Northern Limestone Alps;* Germany/Austria.

White Mountains Mountain range in New Hampshire, US.

Wildstrubel (3,243m/10,640ft); *Bernese Alps.*

Wutai Shan (3,058m/10,033ft); China.

Zillertal Alps Sub-range of the *Alps;* Austria/Italy.

Zinal Rothorn (4,221m/13,848ft); *Pennine Alps.*

GRADING SYSTEMS

In this book we have most often used the UIAA (*Union Internationale des Associations d'Alpinisme*) system of Roman numerals to categorize alpine rock, which grades climbs from I (easy) to XII (extremely difficult), with the symbols + or – being used for further clarification. However, there are other systems in common use, notably the Yosemite Decimal System in the US and the French numerical system. The UIAA grade VI+, for example, is roughly equivalent to 5.10b in the US scale and 6a in the French.

Mountain routes are also graded. The most common system is French, which begins with *Facile* and rises to *Extrêmement Difficile*, which is subdivided from ED1 up to ED4. Ice and aid climbing have their own systems, too, with ice rising from WI1 to WI7 and aid rising from A1 to A6.

Due to the various systems in use, a challenging peak could carry a long explanatory grade, such as: ED2, 6b+, A2, WI3, 1800m. This covers all climbing styles and gives an overall impression of a route's difficulty. Ultimately, however, the conditions on the ground and a climber's own skills must also be taken into consideration.

INDEX

ACKNOWLEDGMENTS

The Alpine Club would like to thank the following members for checking facts, unearthing rare images, and providing the invaluable benefit of their experience: Jerry Lovatt, John Cleare, Anna Lawford, Hywel Lloyd, Glyn Hughes, Andy Cave, Peter Mallalieu, John Porter, and Tadeusz Hudowski.

The Royal Geographical Society (with IBG) would like to thank Alasdair Mcleod, Eugene Rae, Jamie Owen, Joy Wheeler, and Julie Cole.

Dorling Kindersley would like to thank Ed Douglas for his outstanding contribution, everyone mentioned above, and the following people for their help in the preparation of this book: Nicky Munro, Ed Wilson, Satu Fox, and Simone Caplin for editorial assistance; Michael Duffy for design assistance; Phil Gamble for the mountain icon artworks; and Ed Merritt and Simon Mumford for cartography.

Tall Tree Ltd would like to thank: Debra Wolter for proofreading and Chris Bernstein for the index.

The publisher would like to thank the following for their kind permission to reproduce their photographs:

Key:
a-above; b-below/bottom; c-centre; f-far; l-left; r-right; t-top.

ACPL - Alpine Club Photo Library, London - ACPL; DAV - Archiv des Deutschen Alpenvereins, München; DT - Dreamstime.com; RGS - © Royal Geographical Society.

1 from Owen Glynne Jones, *Rock-Climbing in the English Lake District*, 1911. **2-3 Giri Giri Boys/Yusuke Sato. 4-5 RGS. 6 ACPL**: (tr). **Corbis**: Burnstein Collection (tl); Robert Harding World Imagery / Sybil Sassoon (tc). **RGS**: (bl, bc, br). **7 DAV**: (bc). **ACPL**: (tl, tc, tr). **Corbis**: Hulton-Deutsch Collection (bl). Huberbuam.de: Hinterbrandner (br). **8-9 Alamy Images**: MARKA (b/6). **DAV**: (b/8). **ACPL**: (t/1, t/4, t/6, t/7, t/8, t/9, t/11, t/12). **Corbis**: Bettmann (t/2); Michael Nicholson (t/3); Sygma / Catherine Destivelle (b/10). © **Archiv Kurt Diemberger**: (b/9). © **Rolando Garibotti**: (b/12). **Getty Images**: Hulton Archive / Evening Standard (b/11); Photographer's Choice / Jochen Schlenker (c). **Bogdan Jankowski**: (b/4). **Jerzy Kukuczka**

Archives: (b/2). **Józef Nyka**: Ewa Abgarowicz (b/3). **John Porter**: (b/7). **RGS**: (t/10, b/1, b/5). **10-11 Getty Images**: Archive Photos. **12 Corbis**: Wolfgang Kaehler (clb); Araldo de Luca (ca/339BCE); Gianni Dagli Orti (cra). **Getty Images**: The Image Bank / David Sanger (ca/399). **Till Niermann** (cb). **V. Berger** (br). **13 ACPL**: (bc). **Corbis**: Craig Lovell (tc); James Sparshatt (cr). **Getty Images**: Hulton Archive / Imagno (cb); The Image Bank / Travelpix Ltd (cl); National Geographic (bl). **14-15 DT**: Irina Efremova (t). **14 DT**: **Jorisvo** (tr). **Getty Images**: The Bridgeman Art Library (bl). **15 Corbis**: Tom Nebbia (tl); James Sparshatt (b). **RGS**: (tc). **16 Corbis**: Wolfgang Deuter. **17 The Bridgeman Art Library**: South Tyrol Museum of Archaeology, Bolzano / Wolfgang Neeb (br). **18 Corbis**: Sygma / Vienna Report Agency (t, bl). **19 Getty Images**: Patrick Landmann (bc). **South Tyrol Museum Of Archaeology - www.iceman.it**: (r). 20 **Corbis**: Bettmann (tl); Chris Hellier (tr); Hoberman Collection (c). **20-21 Corbis**: Stapleton Collection (b). **22-23 DT**: Kantor (t). **Getty Images**: Discovery Channel Images / Jeff Foott (b). **22 Corbis**: JAI / Nigel Pavitt (tr). **23 ACPL**: George Band (tc). **DT**: Alexei Fateev (tl). **Getty Images**: De Agostini Picture Library / Gianni Dagli Orti (crb). **24 Alamy Images**: The Art Archive (tr). **25 Corbis**: Robert Harding World Imagery / Sybil Sassoon (b); Lebrecht Music & Arts (tr). **27 Alamy Images**: Ulrich Doering (t). **Corbis**: Paul Souders (br). **DT**: Vince Gayman (bc). **Getty Images**: Stone / Pete Turner (bl). 28 **Alamy Images**: JTB Photo Communications, Inc. (tl); Mary Evans Picture Library (b). **29 Corbis**: Michael Freeman. **30-31 Corbis**: Reuters / Toru Hanai. **32 Getty Images**: Aurora / Whit Richardson (bl); National Geographic / Peter V. Bianchi (tr); Stone / David Hiser (crb). **33 Corbis**: Richard A. Cooke (cra); National Geographic Society / W. Langdon Kihn (tl, bl); Dewitt Jones (tr); National Geographic Society / Scott S. Warren (cla, ca); George H.H. Huey (br). **34-35 Corbis**: RelaXimages (t). **34 Corbis**: Reuters / Ferran Paredes (tr). **DT**: (c). **35 Corbis**: Bettmann (tl); Homer Sykes (tc); Reuters / Goran Tomasevic (b). **36 Corbis**: The Art Archive (tl). **37 Alamy Images**: The Art Archive (c). **Corbis**: Burnstein

Collection (b). **DT**: Robert Paul Van Beets (t). **38 Getty Images**: De Agostini Picture Library. **39 Corbis**: Robert van der Hilst (b). **Dorling Kindersley**: Courtesy of the Musée de Saint-Malo, France (tr). **40 ACPL**: (cla, cr). Map by Stumpf, 1548 (bc). **41 ACPL**: (tr). **Getty Images**: Gallo Images / Travel Ink (b). **42 akg-images**: André Held (bl). **DAV**: (clb). **DT**: Arnphoto (cl). **The Kobal Collection**: Dor Film / Lunaris Film (br). **Mountain Camera / John Cleare**: (cr). **43 Alamy Images**: Photos 12 (br). **ACPL**: Swiss Foundation (tr). **DT**: Pancaketom (cl). **RGS**: (bl). **44 Corbis**: Academy of Natural Sciences of Philadelphia (bl); Heritage Images (tl). **45 DT**: Yurchyk. **46 Corbis**: Michael Nicholson (tl). John Evelyn, Sylva, 1669 (cr). **47 Alamy Images**: Cristina Lichti (l). **Getty Images**: Archive Photos / Kean Collection (crb). **Library Of Congress, Washington, D.C.**: (tc). **48-49 ACPL. 50 ACPL**: (crb). **Corbis**: (clb); Bettmann (cla/1600). **Getty Images**: The Bridgeman Art Library (ca/1761, ca/1741); Robert Harding World Imagery / Duncan Maxwell (cra/1785). **51 The Bridgeman Art Library**: Staatliche Kunstsammlungen, Dresden (cla). **ACPL**: (tr, ca). **Corbis**: The Print Collector (bl). **Dorling Kindersley**: Judith Miller / Branksome Antiques (bc). **Getty Images**: The Image Bank / Joseph Van Os (clb); Time & Life Pictures / Mansell (tc). **Image courtesy History of Science Collections, University of Oklahoma Libraries; copyright the Board of Regents of the University of Oklahoma**: (tl). **52-53 Getty Images**: The Image Bank / Luis Castaneda Inc. (t). **52 Dorling Kindersley**: Judith Miller / Law Fine Art Ltd. (bl). **Getty Images**: Hulton Archive (tr). **53 ACPL**: (b). **Dorling Kindersley**: Courtesy of the Natural History Museum, London / Colin Keates (tl). **RGS**: (tc). **54 ACPL**: (bc). **H. Zell** (cr). **55 ACPL. 56 Alamy Images**: North Wind Picture Archives (tl). Corbis: (tr). **57 DT**: Matthew Hart (b). **Image courtesy History of Science Collections, University of Oklahoma Libraries; copyright the Board of Regents of the University of Oklahoma**: (cr). **58 ACPL**: (cl/1780s, cl/1840s, cr/1881, bl, crb, br). **RGS**: (cr/1933). **59 Alamy Images**: Aurora Photos (bl). **Corbis**: Aurora Photos / Keith Ladzinski (tr). **DT**: Titelio (crb). **Getty Images**: Hulton Archive (cl/1940). **Mountain Camera**

/ John Cleare: (cl/1974, clb). **60 ACPL**: (tl); Martin Hartley (bc). **61 ACPL. 62 ACPL**: (tl, crb). **63 Alamy Images**: The Art Archive (b). **Dorling Kindersley**: Judith Miller / Branksome Antiques (tl). **64** from F.J. Hugi, *Naturhistorische Alpenreise*, 1830. **65** F.V. Lang, *Botanischer Garten der Höheren Lehranstalt Solothurn*, 1840 (bl); Martin Disteli, *Risikoreiches Bergsteigen und Eisklettern auf einer Expedition mit F. J. Hugi*, 1830 (r). **66 ACPL**: (tl). **67 Corbis**: Bettmann (cr). **Mountain Camera / John Cleare**: (b). **69 Corbis**: Aurora Photos / Mario Colonel (br). **Ed Douglas**: (bl). **Getty Images**: Aurora / Mario Colonel (bc). **Mountain Camera / John Cleare:** (t). **70 DT**: Le-thuy Do (cr). Friedrich Georg Weitsch, *Alexander von Humboldt*, 1806 (tl). **71 akg-images**: (b). **RGS**: (tr). **72 Dorling Kindersley**: Judith Miller / Branksome Antiques (cr). **Image courtesy History of Science Collections, University of Oklahoma Libraries; copyright the Board of Regents of the University of Oklahoma**: (cla). **73 ACPL**: (tc, tr, cra). **Corbis**: Bettmann (bc). **74 Corbis**: George Steinmetz (bl). **National Geographic Stock**: (cra, crb). **75 Corbis**: Charles & Josette Lenars (tl). **Getty Images**: National Geographic (tc). **National Geographic Stock**: (tr, cra, clb, bl, br). **Tijs Michels** (cla). **Jason Quinn** (ca). **76-77 DT**: Peter Wey (t). **76 Corbis**: Massimo Listri (bl); Gustavo Tomsich (tr). **77 ACPL**: (tc). **Corbis**: The Gallery Collection (b). **78-79 akg-images**: (b). **79 akg-images**: (tl). **ACPL**: (cra). **80-81 ACPL**: (tc). **81 ACPL**: (br). **82 The Bridgeman Art Library**: Abbot Hall Art Gallery, Kendal (r). **Getty Images**: Time & Life Pictures / Mansell (cla). **83 The Art Archive**: Eileen Tweedy (br). **The Bridgeman Art Library**: Fitzwilliam Museum, University of Cambridge (tr). **84 DT**: Timothy Nichols (tr/Frame). **Getty Images**: The Bridgeman Art Library (tr). **85 Alamy Images**: Lebrecht Music and Arts Photo Library (bl). **Dorling Kindersley**: York Archaeological Trust for Excavation and Research Ltd. / Geoff Dann (c/Quill). **DT**: (cr/Ink). **Getty Images**: The Bridgeman Art Library (tr, bc); Photographer's Choice / Guy Edwardes (tl); Matt Cardy (c). **Library Of Congress, Washington, D.C.**: (cra, cr). **86 Alamy Images**: Prisma Bildagentur AG. **ACPL**: (bl). **87 Corbis**: Hulton-Deutsch Collection (tc). **Dorling Kindersley**: Courtesy of

Images: Time & Life Pictures / Grey Villet (cra). **The Mountaineers Books** (www.mountaineersbooks.org): Used with permission from the family of Charles Houston (br). **249 Harish Kapadia. The Mountaineers Books** (www.mountaineersbooks.org): Used with permission from the family of Charles Houston (t). **250 DAV**: (cla). **Jennifer Jordan**: Courtesy of the Susan Cercone and George Sheldon Family (bc). **251 DAV**: (tr). **Getty Images**: The Image Bank / Art Wolfe (b). **252 Corbis**: Rykoff Collection (tr). **Getty Images**: Hulton Archive (br). **253 akg-images**: (tc). **Alamy Images**: Moviestore Collection Ltd (cra); Photos 12 (tl). **Dorling Kindersley**: Alamy / Eye Candy Images (br); Courtesy of the Science Museum, London / Dave King (crb). **Getty Images**: Hulton Archive (cl). **The Kobal Collection**: Dor Film / Lunaris Film (bl). **254-255 RGS**: (t). **254 RGS**: (tr, b). **255 DAV**: (tl). **The Japanese Alpine Club**: (tc). **256 Getty Images**: Gamma-Keystone (cla/Lachenal); Time Life Pictures / Halley Erskine (cla/Herzog). **Mountain Camera / John Cleare**: (bc). **257 Mountain Camera / John Cleare**: (b). **258 Alamy Images**: MARKA (cla). **DAV**: (bl). **259 Alamy Images**: MARKA (t). **Corbis**: Galen Rowell (br). **260 © Archiv Kurt Diemberger**: (cla). **Mountain Camera / John Cleare**: (bc). **261 © Archiv Kurt Diemberger**: (l, tr). **262 Getty Images**: Gallo Images / Herman du Plessis (bl). **RGS**: (tc, tr, crb). **263 Corbis**: Aurora Photos / Stefan Chow (cra); Nomad Expeditions (ca). **RGS**: (tl, tc, tr, cla, bl, br). **264 RGS**: (cla). **264-265 RGS**: (bc). **265 Mountain Camera / John Cleare**: (tr). **RGS**: (crb). **266 Getty Images**: Hulton Archive / Baron (cla). **RGS**: (cra, br). **267 RGS**: (tl, r). **268-269 RGS**: Alfred Gregory. **270 Corbis**: Bettmann (cla/Compagnoni, tr). **Arch. Lino Lacedelli**: (cla/Lacedelli). **271 Arch. Lino Lacedelli**: (l). **Mountain Camera / John Cleare**: (tr). **272 RGS**: (cla/Band and Brown, bl). **273 Mountain Camera / John Cleare**: (tl). **RGS**: (b). **274-275 RGS**: Charles Evans. **276 Alamy Images**: MARKA (br). **DAV**: (cla/Terray). **ACPL**: (cla/Couzy). **277 Getty Images**: Gamma-Keystone (b). **Mountain Camera / John Cleare**: (tr). **278 Getty Images**: National Geographic / Barry C. Bishop (cla/Hornbein, cla/Unsoeld). **279 National Geographic Stock**. **280 Getty Images**: National Geographic /

Barry C. Bishop (r). **National Geographic Stock**: (tl). **281 Getty Images**: National Geographic / George F. Mobley (br). **Mountain Camera / John Cleare**: (tr). **282-283 Corbis**: Sygma / Catherine Destivelle. **284 Alamy Images**: Aurora Photos (cr); Nature Picture Library (tc). **DAV**: (tl). **© Archives of Fondazione Riccardo Cassin**: (crb). **ACPL**: (cl) Photo Leblanc, Dauphiné-Libéré, Chamonix (tr). **Corbis**: Keystone (bc). **285 Alamy Images**: StockShot (ca). **Photo courtesy Amael Beghin**: (tr). **ACPL**: Doug Scott (tl). **Leo Dickinson**: (clb). **DT**: (bc). **Huberbuam.de. Bogdan Jankowski**: (cb). **286-287 DT**: Yasushi Tanikado (t). **286 DAV**: (tr, bl). **287 Alamy Images**: Moviestore Collection Ltd (b). **DAV**: (tc). **DT**: (tl). **289 Corbis**: Sygma / Erik Decamp (b). **290 DAV**: (cla). **ACPL**: (tr). **291 Getty Images**: Gamma-Keystone (b). **Mountain Camera / John Cleare**: (tr). **292 DAV**: (cla). **© Archives of Fondazione Riccardo Cassin**: (tr). **293 © Archives of Fondazione Riccardo Cassin**: (r). **Mountain Camera / John Cleare**: (bc). **294-295 DT**: Karen Graham (t). **294 ACPL**: (bc); Luke Hughes (tr). **295 Alamy Images**: Aurora Photos (b). **Corbis**: Galen Rowell (tc). **Getty Images**: Time & Life Pictures / Jerry Cooke (tl). **296 DAV**. **297 Getty Images**: The Image Bank / David Sharrock (cra); Keystone (cla). **298 ACPL**: (cla, cr). **Getty Images**: Keystone / Frank Barratt (tr). **299 Chris Bonington Picture Library**. **300 DT**: Steve Estvanik (bc). **Getty Images**: Hulton Archive / Evening Standard (cla). **301 Corbis**: Hulton-Deutsch Collection (b). **Getty Images**: Hulton Archive / Evening Standard (cra). **302 Alamy Images**: Aurora Photos (cla, bc). **303 Alamy Images**: Aurora Photos (t). **Corbis**: Momatiuk - Eastcott (br). **304 Mountain Camera / John Cleare**: (cla). **305 ACPL**: Doug Scott (bl). **Corbis**: Galen Rowell (tr). **306 Alamy Images**: Danita Delimont (bl); Oyvind Martinsen (bc). **Corbis**: Francesc Muntada (br). **Getty Images**: Hedgehog House / Colin Monteath (t). **308 DAV**: (cla). **309 Leo Dickinson**. **310 DT**: Dmitry Pichugin (cb). **Reinhold Messner**: (cla). **311 ACPL**: Stephen Venables (clb). **Leo Dickinson**: (t, cr). **312 Jerzy Kukuczka Archives**: (cla, bc). **312-313 Jerzy Kukuczka Archives**: (c). **313 Bogdan Jankowski**: (tr). **Mountain Camera / John Cleare**: (br). **314-315 DT**: (t). **314 Arlene Blum**: (b). **ACPL**: (tr). **315

ACPL**: (br). **Getty Images**: Gamma-Keystone (tc); Hulton Archive / Keystone (tl). **316 DAV**: (bc). **Józef Nyka**: Ewa Abgarowicz (cla); Janusz Onyszkiewicz (tr). **317 Corbis**: Galen Rowell. **318 Corbis**: Sygma / Catherine Desitvelle. **319 Corbis**: Sygma / John Van Hasselt (tr); Sygma / Catherine Destivelle (cla, bc). **320-321 Corbis**: Sygma / Catherine Destivelle. **322 Kitty Calhoun**: (bc). **Getty Images**: Allsport / Mike Powell (cla). **323 Kitty Calhoun**. **324 Alamy Images**: Aurora Photos (cr). **DAV**: (cl, bl). **ACPL**: (br). **DT**: (cb). **RGS**: (crb). **325 Corbis**: Aaron Black (br); Paul A. Souders (tr). **DT**: (cra/Boots, crb); Martin Kawalski (c); Paulo Resende (bc). **Courtesy of Garmin (Europe) Ltd**: (cra/GPS). **The Nuts Museum/Photo Stéphane Pennequin**: (cla, clb). **326-327 Giri Giri Boys/Yusuke Sato**: (t). **326 ACPL**: Mike Fowler (bc). **© Rolando Garibotti**: (tr). **327 ACPL**: Mick Fowler (tl); Stephen Venables (tc). **Giri Giri Boys/Yusuke Sato**: (b). **328 Bogdan Jankowski**: (cla). **John Porter**: (bl). **329 Corbis**: Science Faction / Ed Darack (br). **John Porter**: (t). **330 John Porter**: (cla, bl). **331 Getty Images**: The Image Bank / Werner Van Steen (tr). **John Porter**: (b). **332 © Piolets d'Or**: (cla). **333 Mountain Camera / John Cleare**: (br). **Andrej Štremfelj**: (l, tr). **334 Alamy Images**: StockShot (cla). **Photo courtesy Amael Beghin**: (tr). **335 Alamy Images**: StockShot. **336 ACPL**: (tr). **Hedgehog House Photo Library**: (tc, cr). **337 Alamy Images**: Photos 12 (br). **ACPL**: (tl, tc). **Corbis**: Frank Trapper (bl). **Getty Images**: National Geographic / Gordon Wiltsie (tr). **338 Pat Littlejohn**: (cla). **338-339 Andy Cave**: (b). **339 ACPL**: Mick Fowler (cra). **340 Huberbuam.de**: Hinterbrandner. **341 Huberbuam.de**: (cla); **Huberbuam.de (tr)**. **342 © Rolando Garibotti**: (cla, cr). **Getty Images**: Hedgehog House / Colin Monteath (bc). **343 © Rolando Garibotti**. **344 Alamy Images**: Aurora Photos (cla). **Steve House**: (bl). **345 Alamy Images**: F1online digitale Bildagentur GmbH (br). **Steve House**: (l). **Alexander Odintsov**: Photo Anna Piunova / www.mountain.ru (tr). **346 Giri Giri Boys/Yusuke Sato**: (cla, br). **347 Giri Giri Boys/Yusuke Sato**. **348 Getty Images**: AFP / Pierre-Philippe Marcou (tc); Hulton Archive / James Finlay (tr); AFP / Yves Boucau (crb). **Mountain Camera / John Cleare**: (bl). **349 Kenton Cool**: (br). **Corbis**:

Sygma (cr/Humar). **Getty Images**: Vittorio Znino Celotto (cl/Moro). **Mountain Camera / John Cleare**: (tl). **Courtesy of Edurene Pasaban**: (bl). **Courtesy of Archiv Ueli Steck GmbH**: (tr). **Ed Viesturs**: Photo: Jake Norton (cr/Viesturs).

All other images © Dorling Kindersley For further information see: www.dkimages.com

BISHKEK ○
Gora Manas
4482m

KYRGYZSTAN

Almaty
(Alma Ata)

Urumq

TOSHKENT
(TASHKENT)

UZBEKISTAN

Ozero Issyk-Kul'

Hantengri Feng
6995m

Tomür Feng
7443m ▲

Tien Shan

Gora Ak-Tash
4718m ▲

Kokshaal-Tau

Bedel Pass
4741m

Qatorkühi Zarafshon

TAJIKISTAN

DUSHANBE ○

Alai Range

▲ Gora Sugut
4697m

Turugart Pass
3752m

Turugart Shankou
3752m

Tarim Pendi

C

H

▲ Pik Lenin
7134m

▲ Qullai Revolyutsiya
6974m

Kongur Shan
7649m ▲

Sarikol Range

▲ Muztagh Ata
7546m

AFGHANISTAN

Nicholas Range

Hindu Kush

Kilik Pass
4827m

Baroghil Pass
3777m

Karakoram Highway

Kunjirap Daban
4890m

Kunl

Altu

▲ Tirich Mir
7708m

Kashmünd
Ghar

Dastegil Sar
7885m ▲

Rakaposhi
7788m ▲

Karakoram Range

K2
8611m ▲

Broad Peak 8051m
Gasherbrum II 8035m

Gasherbrum I
8080m

Muztag
7282m ▲

un

Sha

Mu
697

Lawarai Pass
3118m

▲ Nanga Parbat
8126m

Aksai Chin

Karakoram Pass
5568m

Khyber Pass
1080m

Peshāwar ○

Srīnagar ○

Nun Kun massif
7135m

ISLĀMĀBĀD ◉

Rāwalpindi

Potwar
Plateau

PAKISTAN

Mangla Reservoir

Demchok/Dêmqog

Qin

Jammu ◎

Gujrānwāla ■

▲ Nganglong Kangri
6596m

Lahore ■

Faisalābād ◉

Gangdisê Shan

H

Ludhiāna ■

Shimla ◎

I

M

Chandīgarh ◎

Badarināth
7140m ▲

Sivalik

A

Punjab
Plains

▲ Nanda Devi
7816m

Api ▲
7132m

L

Thar Desert

Delhi
NEW DELHI ■

R

A

NEPAL

Langoi Kang
6392m

Dhaulagiri
8167m ▲

Māchhāpuchhre

I

N

D

I

A

Jaipur ◉

Annapurna ▲ 6993m
8091m

Manaslu
8156m ▲

Shisha Pangma
8013m ▲

Cho Oyu
8201m ▲

ange

KATHMANDU ◎

Lhotse
8501m

Mount Everest
8848m

Makalu
8481m

Kāngchenju
85

Kānpur ■

Lucknow ■